A Literal Reading
of Spenser's Book of Holinesse

A Literal Reading of Spenser's Book of Holinesse

William E Heise

Jackson Graham, LLC
Chicago Ridge, IL

A Literal Reading of Spenser's Book of Holinesse
By William E. Heise

Copyright © 2013 by Jackson Graham, LLC.
www.jackson-graham.com

All rights reserved. No part of this book be reproduced or transmitted in any form or by any means, electronic or mechanical, including photocopying, recording, or by any information retrieval system, without written permission from the author, except for the inclusion of brief quotations in a review.

Publisher's Cataloging-in-Publication
(Provided by Quality Books, Inc.)

Heise, William Earnshaw, 1962-
   A literal reading of Spenser's Book of holinesse / William E. Heise.
   p. cm.
   Includes bibliographical references and index.
   LCCN 2012905744
   ISBN 978-0-9819476-0-0
   ISBN 9-78-0-9819476-4-8 (pbk.)

   1. Spenser, Edmund, 1552?-1599--Criticism and interpretation. 2. Spenser, Edmund, 1552?-1599. Faerie queene.--Book 1. 3. Spenser, Edmund, 1552?-1599--Characters--Redcrosse. 4. Spenser, Edmund, 1552?-1599--Characters--Una. 5. Literature--Philosophy.
I. Title. II. Title: Book of holinesse.

PR2358.H385 2012   821'.3
                      QBI12-600166

To Joan Larsen Klein,
without whose extraordinary act of faith
this work would not have been possible.

Table of Contents

Introduction ... 1

    The Birth of Modern Philosophy 2 • The Birth of the Modern Aesthetic 3 • The Fate of Allegory in the Modern World 5 • The Treatment of Allegory in Hamilton's Two Texts 8 • A New Reading of the Book of Holinesse 11

Reading Allegory from New Margins ... 13

    Augustine's Engagement with Skepticism 13 • Aristotle's Invention of the Problem of Fiction 14 • Plato Fights Back 17 • Plato as a Guide to Truth in a Divided World 20 • Augustine's Discovery of the Substantiality of Consciousness 21 • The Reformation's Reliance on Augustine 24 • Spenser's Reformation Allegory 26 • The Restoration of Allegorical Levels 27

The *Letter to Raleigh* ... 30

    Raleigh's Understandable Question 30 • Spenser's Baffling Answer 30 • The Reception of the *Letter* in Modern Criticism 31 • Variant Meaning in Spenser's Historical Poets 34 • The Role of Aeneas in Augustine 37 • Tasso's Disseverance of Politics from the Good 40 • The Introduction of Redcrosse 43 • Una's Convenient Magical Armor 45

The Passive Man of Action ... 48

    The Presence of Inequality in *The Faerie Queene* 48 • Aesthetic Assumptions about Inequality 49 • Drifting Without Purpose in the Wandering Wood 52 • Logical Confusion at the Entrance of Errour's Cave 53 • Redcrosse's Encounter with Errour 56 • Similes of Patience and Immediate Action 58 • The Lessons of Redcrosse's Encounter with Errour 61 • Comparing Spenser's Treatment of Redcrosse's Battle with His Sources 63 • The Meeting with Archimago 67 • Archimago Returns to His Study 70 • Augustine's Allegory of Silence and Speech 71 • Spenser's Allegory of Silence and Speech 74 • Waking Up Redcrosse 77

The Triumph of Divisive Science Over Moral Goodness   82

   Fixing the Location of Relative Stars 82 • Frege's Puzzle 85 • Modern Philosophers Weigh In On Frege's Puzzle 88 • Spenser's Complex Solution to Frege's Puzzle 91 • The Representation of Elizabeth 93 • Absolute Being's Encounter with Inequality 95 • Action and Potential 96

Action After Division   100

   The Misformed Thought of Archimago 100 • Archimago and Redcrosse on Ends 102 • Justice and Native Virtue in Redcrosse's Defeat of Sansfoy 105 • Friend of Duessa 108 • Fradubio 111

Una in the Extremity of Time   117

   Una in the Wilderness 118 • Una's Animal Protector 119 • The House of Corceca 121 • Una Meets Archimago Again 124 • The Simile of the Mariner 126 • Una's Meeting with Sansloy 128 • Action after a Breach in the Text 131 • Una Among the Satyrs 133 • Una's Rescue by Satyrane 135 • Una's Confrontation of a Paradox in Reality 136

Redcrosse Within the World of Time   140

   The Permanent Imbalance of Values Within the World of Time 140 • Boundaries in the House of Pride 143 • The Triumph of Pride 145 • The Unritualized Battle with Sansjoy 148 • The Ritualized Battle with Sansjoy 151 • Duessa's Journey into the Realm of Night 154 • Science and Necessity Near Avernus' Hole 158 • Resting (Again!) with Fidessa 160 • Redcrosse's Defeat by Orgoglio 162

A Paradox in Una's Imagination   165

   Una's Causal Dwarf 165 • Una's Reaction to the Captivity of Redcrosse 168 • A Theory of Romance 169 • Una Confronts a Paradox in Her Imagination 171 • Absolute Metaphysics and Relative Reason 175 • Another Detour to the Proem 176

Arthur   178

   The Appearance of Arthur 178 • Opening Up Una's Closed Mind 180 • The Rescue of Redcrosse 184 • Una's Expression of Gratitude 188 • Ignaro 188 • The Enlargement of Una 190 • The Golden Chain 192 • The Tale of Arthur and Gloriana 194

The Failure of Will in the House of Despair   199

   Another Distraction 199 • Meeting Despair 200 • A Discourse on Justice 201 • Despair on the Ends of Experience 203 • The Balance of Argument Shifts In Favor of Despair 204 • Una Finally Speaks Up 206

Redcrosse in the Extremity of Heaven   209

   To Blame the Woman... 210 • ...Or Not 211 • The House of Holinesse 212 • First Guides to the House of Holinesse 213 • Cælia 214 •

Alciati's *Emblemata* 216 • Fiction in the House of Holinesse 218 • Fidelia and Speranza 219 • The Correction of Redcrosse 220 • Redcrosse's Disdain For Life 223 • Compassion and Torment as Cures for What Ails Redcrosse 224 • Una's Role in the House of Holinesse 225 • The Appearance of Charissa 227 • Mercie 231

Reorienting Redcrosse 233

Spenser's Introduction of Contemplation 234 • Contemplation Snubs the Man of Action 235 • More Correction of Errant Redcrosse 236 • The Naming Scene 238 • Rereading the Naming Scene 239 • Freudian Dream Work 241 • The Purge of Figural Meaning in the Naming Scene 242 • Changelings and Kings in Spenser's World of "Faery Theft" 244 • Contemplation Mistakes George's New Purpose for Pride 245 • George Returns to Una 246

Science Outside the Walls of Eden 248

Una Gets Her Way at Last 248 • The Return to Una's Native Soil 248 • Invoking Clio 249 • The Description of the Dragon 250 • Day One: The Fight Begins 253 • Spenser's Reworking of Du Bartas 255 • The Amplification of Simile 256 • The Poet's Comparison of George to Hercules 258 • George's Judgment and His Actions 260 • George's Baptism 262 • Day Two of the Dragon Fight 264 • The Tree of Life 267 • Victory on Day Three of the Dragon Fight 269 • After the Fall 270

Loose Ends in the Restored Kingdom 272

The Restless Ship of Poetry 272 • The Caution of the Distant People of Eden 272 • Walking Through the Brazen Gates of Eden 273 • The Uncertain Location of Eden 275 • Paradoxes in the Rascal Kingdom 276 • George's Interaction with the King of Eden 277 • The King of Eden's Vow 279 • The Appearance of Una 280 • Aristotle on Goodwill, Friendship, and Love 282 • The King of Eden's Interrupted Speech 284 • The King's Response to New Information 286 • Una's Resolution 288 • The Marriage of Heaven and Earth 289 • The Narrator's Final Words 290

Conclusion 291

Spenser's Correction of Modern Aesthetic Assumptions 291 • A Note on Frank Kermode 293 • Redcrosse in Later Books 294 • Redcrosse in Book II 296 • Redcrosse in Book V 297 • Last Words 298

Works Cited 301
Index 311

Introduction

This book has its genesis in a question I had in reading the following passage in Robert Kellogg's summary of the adventure of Redcrosse in *The Spenser Encyclopedia*:

> Redcrosse's quest, considered as a whole, is most immediately understood as an allegory of the making of a Protestant saint, both the fall into sin once separated from Christian truth, and the gradual restoration, through the intervention of grace and the loving guidance of holy church, to spiritual health, wholeness, and conformity to the image of Christ.[1]

The question that I sought to answer was this: if, as Kellogg says, the Redcrosse Knight is so whole and perfect at the end of Book I, why should there *be* a Book II?

This is not a new question, and Spenser provides a clear answer to it. When the Palmer meets the Redcrosse Knight, who has just finished his adventure, he congratulates Redcrosse that he "a Saint with Saints your seat haue wonne" (II.i.32.5).[2] The Palmer suggests that he and his charge Guyon will now follow a similar adventure: "But wretched we, where ye haue left your marke, / Must now anew begin, like race to ronne" (II.i.32.6-7). Redcrosse contradicts the Palmer's assessment of the similarity of their situations, telling the Palmer that he can expect to "report thrise happie

---

[1] "Red Cross Knight" in A. C. Hamilton, *The Spenser Encyclopedia* (Toronto: University of Toronto Press, 1990), 588.

[2] Edmund Spenser, *The Faerie Queene*, ed. A. C. Hamilton, Hiroshi Yamashita, and Toshiyuki Suzuki, 2nd ed. (Harlow: Pearson Education, 2001). Unless otherwise indicated, all quotations in this work are derived from this edition.

newes" (II.i.33.8) after his adventure with Guyon has been completed; for the Palmer "can wish [his] thought" (II.i.33.7), whereas Redcrosse has merely been the instrument of God, "Who made my hand the organ of his might" (II.i.33.3). In other words, Redcrosse is not whole and perfect at the end of Book I—that honor belongs to God—and this is why Guyon appears after Redcrosse's adventure is over to be *consciously* led through a similar but not identical set of experiences with the rational Palmer as his guide but without the guarantees of success given to Redcrosse in advance of any action on his part by his possession of God's goodwill.

This answer is not hidden beneath layers of allegory: it is available for any careful reader to grasp. That gives rise to the question of why so many modern critics of *The Faerie Queene* have missed this obvious fact. The answer appears to have to do with the expectations brought to the text by the modern reader. Rather than taking Spenser at his word, modern readers insist on translating allegory out of the aesthetic in which the poem was written into more precise scientific aesthetic terms. It is my contention that this act of translation masks the truth of what is going on is Spenser's masterpiece.

The Birth of Modern Philosophy

René Descartes is often considered the father of modern philosophy.[3] He began his thought with the already accepted premise that ancient and medieval claims to knowledge had been built up over centuries without ever fixing the basis of epistemological problems in a firm ontology. That all changed with Descartes, who was the first to invent a coordinate geometry in which every point in the universe could be resolved into a point on a grid.[4] The development of the coordinate grid sped the way for Isaac Newton's invention of the theory of gravity, as well as paving the way for the invention of an infinitesimal calculus by both Newton and Leibnitz.[5] Those developments represented major advances over the work of ancient mathematicians, and they started off what became known as the Battle of

---

3 See Roger Scruton, *From Descartes to Wittgenstein: A Short History of Modern Philosophy* (London: Routledge & Kegan Paul, 1981).

4 See René Descartes, "Geometry," in *Discourse on Method, Optics, Geometry, and Meteorology* (Indianapolis, IN: Hackett, 2001).

5 This had the effect of making Newton a god for Enlightenment thinkers everywhere. His status brought the battle between ancients and moderns to a head. These developments decisively changed the human relationship to the world "far more drastically than it had been changed by the doctrines of Luther and Calvin," as Peter Gay notes in his *The Enlightenment, an Interpretation: The Science of Freedom* (New York: W.W. Norton, 1977), 126.

the Books between ancient and modern philosophers.[6]

Before Descartes, the universe could be scientifically explained through pagan gods and demons, who were not just mythical creatures. They acted as scientific agents of change in the universe.[7] After Descartes, such beings were not considered beings at all, but fables; and men began to look askance at the scholastic scholars who mistook them for facts in their philosophy.[8]

Descartes coordinated his geometrical discoveries with a new philosophy[9] that is credited with breaking with both ancient and medieval scholastic philosophies. The basis of Descartes' philosophy was his embrace of a recently revived skepticism[10] that allowed him to discard the "example and custom" that had built up over time, which he thought darkened "our natural intelligence, and incapacitate[d] us in great measure from listening to reason."[11] Once a man or woman could listen to their natural reason without the distraction of man-made habits, they could see for the first time the coordination between human epistemology and natural ontology that had eluded ancient and medieval philosophers.

The invention of a scientific approach to experience gave birth to the Enlightenment. The Reformation that it replaced had brought with it the benefit of clearing out the cobwebs of centuries of tradition built up over time without any basis in the historical facts of the Bible. That housecleaning was a good thing, as the Church had grown complacent in its power; but it also led to the wholesale social destruction of the Thirty Years War. The triumph of science in the Enlightenment brought even more order to a troubled world.

The Birth of the Modern Aesthetic

In the Enlightenment, literature was reformed to bring it in line with

---

6 For the battle of ancients and moderns, see Richard Foster Jones, *Ancients and Moderns: A Study of the Background of the Battle of the Books* (St. Louis, MO: Washington University Press, 1936).

7 For the impact of daimonic thought on the development of allegory, see the chapter "The Daemonic Agent" in Angus John Stewart Fletcher, *Allegory: The Theory of a Symbolic Mode* (Ithaca, NY: Cornell University Press, 1964), 25-69.

8 For this process, see Frank Edward Manuel, *The Eighteenth Century Confronts the Gods* (New York, NY: Atheneum, 1967).

9 *Meditations on First Philosophy: With Selections from the Objections and Replies*, ed. Michael Moriarty (Oxford: Oxford University Press, 2008).

10 Richard H. Popkin, *The History of Scepticism: From Savonarola to Bayle*, Rev. and expanded ed. (Oxford: Oxford University Press, 2003).

11 *Discourse on Method of Rightly Conducting the Reason and Seeking Truth in the Sciences*, in *The Rationalists* (Garden City, N.Y.: Doubleday & Company, 1974), 45.

the discoveries of modern philosophy. At first, the works of Nicolas Boileau-Despréaux in France and Alexander Pope in England provided models for bringing mankind in line with natural philosophy, rather than theology, through the imitation of classical models. In his *Essay on Man*[12] Pope declares his Cartesian belief that "the science of mankind is, like all other sciences, reduced to a *few clear points*."[13] He wished to consider man "without wandering from the precision, or breaking the chain of reason,"[14] because (again following Descartes) he has capped his knowledge of divinity at the level of human reason:

> Say first, of God above, or Man below,
> What can we reason, but from what we know?[15]

This turns speculation away from the scholastic emphasis on the metaphysics of God to an emphasis on a reason that is under the control of man.[16]

Although Voltaire praised Pope to the skies, not everyone agreed with Pope's rational approach to experience that places the species of man at the midpoint of a "Vast chain of being, which from God began" and descended through "Nature's aethereal, human, angel, man, / Beast, bird, fish, insect!"[17] Alexander Baumgarten realized that Pope's solution to the problem of man put the principles of rational nature, not man, at the center of the universe. Rational nature's cap of the power of reason did not go far enough in considering the full extent of man in the universe. Rather than traveling back to theology, Baumgarten went back to Longinus, whose treatise *On the Sublime* made the case that sublimity lies beyond ordinary reason but could be reached through a deeper human capacity to feel powerful emotions.[18] His invention of the science of aesthetics[19] made clear the principles that many felt the French Enlightenment had overlooked,

---

12 *An Essay on Man in Four Epistles* in Alexander Pope *The Major Works,* ed. Pat Rogers, Oxford World's Classics (New York: Oxford University Press, 2006).

13 Ibid., "The Design," p. 270. This reflects Pope's reading of Descartes, who reduced the complexity of human life to a few clear principles.

14 Ibid., "The Design," p. 271.

15 Ibid., Epistle I.I.17.

16 This process of transforming philosophical speculation from the metaphysics of God to human reason is detailed in Ernst Cassirer, *The Philosophy of the Enlightenment* (Princeton, NJ: Princeton University Press, 1951).

17 Pope and Rodger, *Essay on Man,* Epistle I.VIII.237-238.

18 Longinus, *On the Sublime,* in *Poetics* (Cambridge, MA: Harvard University Press, 1995).

19 Alexander Gottlieb Baumgarten, *Aesthetica* (Hildesheim: G. Olms, 1961).

Introduction 5

and when his aesthetic work was taken up by Herder and Goethe, the Romantic aesthetic was born. In that aesthetic, mankind could realize in their own minds the deeper beauty of nature directly without the interference by any intermediary Cartesian logical processes. Even the Enlightenment thinker Immanuel Kant, whose favorite poet was Alexander Pope, created his third critique in order to show how mankind could connect himself to the deeper sublime through a deeper reason.[20]

The Fate of Allegory in the Modern World

Allegory was one of the primary causes of this new aesthetic process, as Goethe made it equivalent to a lesser capacity of reason to bind thoughts to nature rather than the more immediate process that bound them to man. Reason survived by being co-opted by the deeper symbol. This process is at work in Angus Fletcher, who begins his work on allegory with the traditional definition of allegory as the trope of saying one thing while meaning another.[21] That definition ultimately derives from the etymology of the Greek word ἀλληγορία ("speaking otherwise"), but Fletcher decides that the 2,000 year old definition "destroys the normal expectation that we have about language that our words 'mean what they say.'"[22]

> When we predicate quality *x* of person Y, Y really is what our predication says he is (or we assume so); but allegory would turn Y into something other (*allos*) than what the open and direct statement tells the reader.[23]

If he were to let that definition stand, it would mean the destruction of language: "Pushed to an extreme, this ironic usage would subvert language itself, turning everything into an Orwellian newspeak."[24]

In order to save language from falling into Orwellian newspeak, Fletcher turns what he supposes is only bit of confusion on the part of the ancients over meaning of allegory into a more precise modern scientific and therefore whole meaning. This translation of allegory from the simple trope of saying one thing while meaning another to "a mode" that represents "a fundamental process of encoding our speech"[25] expands the simple definition

---

20 The birth of modern aesthetics is covered in great detail in John H. Zammito, *The Genesis of Kant's Critique of Judgment* (Chicago: University of Chicago Press, 1992).
21 Fletcher, *Allegory*, 2.
22 Ibid.
23 Ibid.
24 Ibid.
25 Ibid., 2-3.

of allegory while allowing Fletcher to cover "a quite extraordinary variety of literary kinds."[26] As he does this, he maintians the historical emphasis on the priority of the figural over the literal, the kernel over the chaff, the inner over the outer, the invisible over the visible, the ideal over the real, and the divine over the worldly that through time had turned allegory into more of a test of religious conviction than the simple trope could ever account for. Through such translation of ancient and shallower views of allegory to Kant's deeper rational processes, Fletcher believed that he had ended inquiry into the nature of allegory through an expansion of the meaning of the simple trope into a more comprehensive scientific view.

The problem with this view of a permanent valuing of one sort of meaning over another meaning was pointed out by Jacques Derrida, who denied the easy granting of free access to symbol to a higher truth in his *On Grammatology*.[27] Derrida posited a universe of discourse based in the notion of λόγος that he said "everywhere and always, had controlled the concept of writing."[28] He denied the ontology of λόγος, which he correctly saw as an epistemologically-constructed and so fictional object. On the basis of its lack of ontology, Derrida denied the usefulness of the λόγος as a permantent stopping point for language. His view was that the reference of words was best described as an endless chain of horizontal reference, as words are described in terms of other words that never achieves any permanent stability.

Derrida's work serves as a useful warning about treating merely *rhetorical* constructions as though they pointed to a permanent, metaphysically-sound, and immovable reality based in what he had identified as a completely illusory sphere of λόγος. The critic's role in Derrida's deconstruction is not to enter into a passionate discussion with the poet's rhetorical constructions—a situation that had bound previous generations of critics to a specific rhetorical ways of looking at the world—but to stand back from works of literature and to criticize them from an appropriate aesthetic distance, dispassionately deconstructing what passionate cultures had constructed in the heat of the cultural moment.

This new way of looking at the literary world was soon dubbed postmodernism in response to the previous generation's Modernism[29]; and

---

26 Ibid., 3.

27 Jacques Derrida, *Of Grammatology*, trans. Gayatri Chakravorty Spivak, Corrected ed. (Baltimore: Johns Hopkins University Press, 1997).

28 Ibid., 3.

29 In this work, I distinguish modernism from Modernism. Descartes introduces small

postmodernism quicky undermined the systematic values on which Modernism had built its aesthetic by picking up on aspects of literature that the Moderns had overlooked. For instance, Cicero defines allegory as the trope of extending a metaphor through time,[30] and he gives the following concrete example of allegory in action:

> I shall not allow myself, like the Argive fleet
> of old, to run a second time on the same rock.

If one thinks about it, this definition has no place in Fletcher's whole definition of allegory as the mode of encoding speech. This indicated to postmodern critics that Fletcher was being selective in his definition of allegory after all *and that he was blind to that fact!* If this was true, then perhaps Fletcher's continuing prioritization of one form of meaning over another was a deconstructable proposition, as well.

Paul de Man had no reservations about falling into Orwellian newspeak if that is where his investigation into language took him. In his influential view, Cicero's claims about the temporal extension of allegory through time dragged reference out of Fletcher's view of stable reference in another world back into this world, where language continued to thwart efforts to stabilize reference in any particular place. In de Man's view, "Allegory...is quite the opposite of what it pretends to be: the recovery of pure visibility of the truth, undisguised by the local and accidental."[31] This move did nothing to set up a new definition of allegory as much as it made it possible for critics to continue to propose new definitions for allegory without coming to any exact definition of what they were talking about.

---

capital modernism to the world. Within that larger modernism, Modernism is a distinct subset of the broader modernism that had its greatest success in the period that spanned 1890-1980. For an introduction to Modernism, see Michael H. Levenson, *The Cambridge Companion to Modernism* (New York, NY: Cambridge University Press, 1999), as well as Malcolm Bradbury and James Walter McFarlane, *Modernism, 1890-1930: A Guide to European Literature*, Reprinted with a new preface (New York, NY: Penguin Books, 1991). For a brief introduction to literature of postmodernism, see Steven Connor, *The Cambridge Companion to Postmodernism* (New York, NY: Cambridge University Press, 2004), as well as Johannes Willem Bertens, *The Idea of the Postmodern: A History* (New York, NY: Routledge, 1995). For some of the most important (though by no means all) essays in the history of postmodern, see Joseph P. Natoli and Linda Hutcheon, *A Postmodern Reader* (Albany: State University of New York Press, 1993).

30 Marcus Tullius Cicero, *De Oratore*, ed. Edward William Sutton and Harris Rackham, 2 vols., Loeb Classics (Cambridge, MA: Harvard University Press, 1942), I.66.

31 Paul de Man, "Pascal's Allegory of Persuasion," in *Allegory and Representation*, ed. Stephen Greenblatt (Baltimore: Johns Hopkins University Press, 1981), 1.

Postmodernism left Maureen Quilligan free in her exploration of allegory, *The Language of Allegory*,[32] to redefine the *trope* of allegory as a *genre*. In Quilligan's view, the "vertical conceptualization of allegory and its emphasis upon distinct 'levels' is absolutely wrong as a matter of practical fact. All reading proceeds linearly."[33] As a result, the genre of allegory is not defined by its reliance on otherworldly Platonic ideals but is "hung up on 'words, words.'"[34] Like de Man's estimation of allegory, her "absolute" distinctions surrounding allegory says that allegorists run up against problems with achieving stability for language, tumbling back into words that refer only to other words.[35] But rather that accounting for ancient, medieval, or early modern knowledge of any difficulty with allegory, Quilligan continues to treat allegorists as ignorant of what she views as a *modern* discovery. This leads her to state the problem with medieval and Renaissance writers of allegory in general: they were unaware of the impossibility of the task they had set for themselves. This in turn leads her to separate the act of writing allegory from the actor, concluding in a passage that deals with the role of Edmund Spenser's *Faerie Queene* that the genre of allegory plays a role that Spenser himself was unaware of: "the habit of cosmically extended verbal echoing and wordplay is not Spenser's, but allegory's."[36]

The Treatment of Allegory in Hamilton's Two Texts

The reader can witness the tension between these conflicting modern definitions of allegory in A. C. Hamilton's two critical editions of *The Faerie Queene*. The first edition of *The Faerie Queene*, which was published in 1977, features introductory essays on each of Spenser's books which are intended to aid students in the difficult task of reading an obscure poem. That is what critics are supposed to do, but during his introductory essays Hamilton makes assumptions about Spenser's meaning in the absence of any certainty on the critic's part. For instance, in the introduction to Book III, he makes the following observation about the immensely difficult Garden of Adonis episode, whose meaning eludes critics to this day:

---

32 Maureen Quilligan, *The Language of Allegory: Defining the Genre* (Ithaca, NY: Cornell University Press, 1979).

33 Ibid., 28. This is contradicted, of course, by Spenser's *Letter to Raleigh* (in Spenser, *Faerie Queene (2001)*, 715-18.), where he notes the differences between his own practices as a "Poet historical," who writes works that the reader can return to again and again, and that of "a Historiographer" who must write lines that are meant to be read serially. I will deal with this question more fully in my chapter on "The Letter to Raleigh."

34 Quilligan, *Language of Allegory*, 13.

35 Ibid., 33-51 and passim.

36 Ibid., 41.

> Generally, critics have been content to try to identify some philosophical source or sources for the Garden. If one grants that the episode may be read as a philosophical statement rather than as part of a poem, and that the language is logically consistent, what are its sources?[37]

Hamilton asks a question—and it is a good one; what are the sources of the Garden of Adonis?—but he makes the mistake of providing a speculative answer to the philosophical question he has raised.

Hamilton appears to have realized that he had overstepped the bounds of responsible criticism in such comments; and by the time he published his 2nd edition of the poem in 2001, he had stepped back from engaging in speculation in order to retake his position as critical arbiter between various reader responses to a poem that was thought to be unknowable in itself but was now being explored by New Historicists through the extension of reference to other knowable references.[38]

Although Hamilton's revision of his work on *The Faerie Queene* was undertaken under the pressure of a postmodern skepticism about the ends of literature in a stable, autotelic λόγος, these corrections were in line with his earlier work of criticism. In his *The Structure of Allegory in the Faerie Queene*,[39] Hamilton had noticed that the writer has something on his mind, but the reader does not have full access to the authorial mind. He likened the process of reading to the process of Redcrosse's being able to get out of the Wandering Wood. If, in Hamilton's mind, the reader could not get to a stable meaning and so close the gap between reader and writer, the reader would be stuck in the wandering wood of error just as Redcrosse was.

Hamilton was corrected in his desire to close every gap by the arrival of postmodern skepticism, but in 1960 he attempted to close the gap by

---

37 Edmund Spenser, *The Faerie Queene*, ed. A. C. Hamilton, 1st ed., Longman Annotated English Poets (New York: Longman, 1977), 302.

38 This was largely due to the work of Stephen Greenblatt, whose *Renaissance Self-Fashioning: From More to Shakespeare* (Chicago: University of Chicago Press, 1980) set an entirely new and welcome tone for criticism after it had exhausted the possibilities of an autotelic New Criticism. In the 2nd edition of *The Faerie Queene*, Hamilton writes of how the new field of scholars managed to wrest control of the poem from speculation:

> Instead of examining how Spenser fashions the virtues in his poem, the New Historical critics consider how the poem was fashioned by its culture and also how its readers are fashioned by their culture. (4)

39 A. C. Hamilton, *The Structure of Allegory in the Faerie Queene* (Oxford: Clarendon Press, 1961). In the introductory notes to the 2001 edition of *The Faerie Queene*, he says he regards his work of 1960 as a "work of a historical critic partly rehabilitated by myth and archetypal criticism" (3).

pointing critics away from the allegorical meaning of the poem to a meaning of the poem that could be found at the literal level:

> Such [allegorical] interpretation must leave the literal level to flee ever farther from the poem towards the 'something' which the poem is an allegory of. For there is the rest of the continued allegory to be fitted into the Procrustean background. The reader is left to wander in a wilderness where Spenser may have been, but without his imaginative powers to return.[40]

Hamilton felt that "By destroying the literal meaning [modern critical methods] destroys the reader's response."[41] His solution in 1960 was to fuse the various allegorical levels of Spenser's work into a single literal image, and then to read the whole poem through the "literal level in its depth"[42] for the meaning of the whole image, as well as the whole poem.

Although Hamilton's system failed to make sense of all the evidence that could be had in *The Faerie Queene*, his mistake was not focusing on the literal level at the expense of the allegorical level. It was focusing on Enlightenment aesthetics as being enough to makes sense of a poem written in a pre-Enlightenment age. The modern reading of allegory may be explained by the Enlightenment's displacement of the effect of metaphysics of God into humanly realizable terms. As good as that sounds to the modern ear, there are several problems with that configuration of thought. The first is that it holds in its definition of the problem the fact modern readers are better readers than pre-Enlightenment readers.

As a result, no pre-Enlightenment reader could have known what modern critics know in the present day. This means that no one is obliged to look at Spenser's poetry to see if he was not in fact a naïve poet but was in fact engaged with the skepticism that occupies such a large place in the philosophical universe after Derrida. This assumption appears to be in line with the withdrawal of the medieval foundation of truth in an unknowable heaven to a modern, relative, and measurable science. But because modern critics rarely look for evidence of skepticism in Spenser's work, but simply assume its absence, they continue to rely on their definition of the problem to explain away something that they think is either extremely unlikely or downright impossible. But the use of definition rather than evidence undermines the claim of modern criticism to superiority over other artists,

---

40 Ibid., 9.
41 Ibid., 8.
42 Ibid., 12.

periods, and other cultures on the basis that the modern critic is looking at all of the evidence and not just the evidence that they think is most likely to pay off.

A New Reading of the Book of Holinesse

The problem of modern criticism's reliance on definition rather than evidence lies at the heart of my exploration of Spenser's Book of Holinesse. I believe that I can prove that Spenser was reacting to skepticism in his construction of his narrative of Book I of *The Faerie Queene*. That fact radically changes my reading of the poem, but it does more than that. It shows the extent to which the aporias that appear in modern criticism are maintained by the *de facto* valuing of modern critical values over other ways of looking at the world. This was the same thing that caused the postmoderns to react to Modernism's maintenance of what postmoderns saw as a completely arbitrary authority over the text. It was also the very thing that had caused Hamilton to re-edit *The Faerie Queene,* removing the authoritative stance towards a poem about which he was no longer as sure as he had been early in his career.

While I believe that Hamilton's 2nd edition represents a vast improvement over his 1st edition, I believe that the aesthetic position he takes as impartial arbiter is at odds with Spenser's meaning in the poem itself. Spenser wants us to take a specifically Christian position in our lives. He warns the reader that if they do not that there will be serious consequences to their actions. Having said that, I want to be quite clear. In ridding myself of assumptions of the *de facto* superiority of modern ways of looking at the world over Spenser's ways of looking at the world, I hope to demonstrate that Spenser was a poet whose meaning is far clearer and more coherent than many critics who have worked under the banner of modernism have given him credit for being. I do not think that it is necessary or even desirable to force readers to follow Spenser into his Christian vision just because Spenser is the author of the poem.

In this book, I plan on building on Hamilton's early insight that it is on the literal level that images should be resolved. My chief difference with Hamilton is that I will not rely on Enlightenment aesthetic distinctions that are not based in nature after all but in the work of Descartes. Instead, I will go back to Spenser's pre-Enlightenment text with an eye to figuring out how Spenser dealt with scientific problems without Descartes' perfect vision of the universe to guide him.

In my reading of *The Faerie Queene,* Spenser is not as naïve as he is usually held to be in modern criticism. Instead of requiring translation out of literary naïveté into a modern scientific idiom in order to make sense of Spenser's allegorical masterpiece, my position is that Descartes overlooked some important sources in his solutions that Spenser had taken into account. As a result, my reading of Spenser's allegory will be reconfigured along lines that make a very different set of assumptions about art than we do in the modern world.

With that end in mind, my book will follow a close, line-by-line reading of Spenser's text, punctuated by brief excursions into the worlds of ancient, medieval, and modern philosophy.[43] To supplement this line-by-line reading, I have also included a detailed index as an aid to the reader's memory so that they will be able to see connections between far-flung episodes that may not be apparent on their first horizontal reading through the text.[44] In this way, I believe I can get a much better sense of what *Spenser* thought he was doing in *The Faerie Queene*, and not what modern scientific and aesthetic methods tell us he *ought* to be doing but is not.

---

43 The major exception to this orderly progression will be my compression of the separate journeys of Una and Redcrosse into one place after Redcrosse's abandonment of Una (cantos ii-vi). This is largely due to the poet's the poet's attempting to generate suspense over the fate of Una, who the reader has seen left in the hands of the rapist Sansloy at the end of canto iii. I feel that the reader is better served by having both fragmented journeys in one place so that they are in a position to understand the significant differences in their approach to their separation.

44 For instance, see the entries on "blind" and "blindness." Blindness is associated with Cupid's (as opposed to God's) love and also with Corceca's eyes. This would give an uncareful reader a reason to associate blindness with moral evil. But the thoroughly moral Contemplation also sports blind eyes. And both Redcrosse and Una are also associated with blindness at some point in their adventures. Rather than merely assuming our modern possession of Spenser's meaning is correct and overlooking such contrary evidence as meaningless poetic ornament, I believe Spenser is giving his readers clues to his meaning that is accessible if we sort that meaning through the lens of reason. The problem with doing this is that the whole reading of the poem is radically different than that which the moderns have assumed it to be on the basis of their translation into post-Enlightenment terms.

Reading Allegory from New Margins

Augustine's Engagement with Skepticism

Skepticism was brought to the fore of the Renaissance by the discovery of the work of Sextus Empiricus.[1] The fact that the legacy of Sextus Empiricus played such a large role in the later thought of René Descartes has eclipsed the fact that by the time Spenser was born skepticism had already weakened the Church's authority enough that Germany and England had dropped their national affiliation with the universal Church in favor of a more accessible form of belief made available to man directly through the Bible without the interference of the sclerotic traditions wielded by what the Reformers thought of as increasingly corrupt popes and Church hierocrats. The chief opponent of skepticism in the Reformation was Augustine of Hippo.

However popular he was in the pre-modern era, the reputation of Au-

---

1 According to Popkin's chapter on "The Revival of Skepticism" in his *History of Skepticism*, 17-43, the first reference by any European to Sextus' work was in a letter from Francesco Filelfo to Giovanni Aurispa in 1441 (19). Sextus played an enormous role in the Reformation, as his work provided powerful tools to reformers skeptical of the Church's positive arguments that they had direct access to the mind of God that others lacked.

The first printed edition of Sextus' works had to wait until Henri Estienne's edition of the *Hypotyposes* (17). Sextus' works became "central in the intellectual battles of the late sixteenth century" (17-18), and "by the end of the seventeenth century, was regarded as the father of modern philosophy" (18) after his position was taken as the starting point for René Descartes' own philosophy, which many regard as the first truly modern philosophy.

For the work Sextus Empiricus, see Sextus, *Sextus Empiricus, with an English Translation*, trans. Robert Gregg Bury, 4 vols., Loeb Classical Library (Cambridge, MA: Harvard University Press, 1961).

gustine suffered in the Enlightenment, where he was thought of as a man who supported the elevation of superstition over a more perfect reason.[2] This sidelining of Augustine in favor of more rationally exact thinkers like Plato and Aristotle has meant that thinkers have tended to advert to classical reason when looking for the sources of philosophical knowledge and not to a backward-looking theology in ages in which science was making great progress and religious thinkers had tended to become reactionary and conservative in their defense of faith.[3]

But there are good reasons to take Augustine's engagement with skepticism seriously in the pre-Enlightenment era, not only because his thought was at the root of the Reformation that dominated the era in which Spenser was working, but also because of his insight into the thought of Plato and Aristotle, who in Augustine's mind were not as whole and perfect as they were thought to be in the Enlightenment.

Aristotle's Invention of the Problem of Fiction

Plato had given his readers the Allegory of the Cave in *The Republic*[4] as a demonstration of the relationship of individual men to the form of their being. In the allegory, Socrates describes men as living in a cave staring at shadows on a wall, which they mistake for reality. The philosopher describes his work as turning men around to face the source of shadows, the true sun. But Aristotle had challenged his mentor and teacher on this point, famously claiming that the Theory of Forms was nothing more than a "poetic metaphor" that was not possible realize in nature:

> But further all other things cannot come from the Forms in any of the usual senses of 'from'. And to say that they are patterns and the other things share them is to use empty words and poetical metaphors.[5]

---

2 Voltaire, for instance, for years signed his letters with the motto *ecrasez l'infame* ("kill the monster") by which he meant the infamy of Christian superstition.

3 For examples of conservatism, see the chapter "The Counterattack Begins" in Popkin, *History of Scepticism*, 99-111.

4 Plato, *Republic*, 514a–520a. Unless otherwise indicated, all references to the works of Plato will be to *The Collected Dialogues of Plato, Including the Letters*, ed. Huntington Cairns and Edith Hamilton, Bollingen Series 71 (Princeton, NJ: Princeton University Press, 1993).

5 Aristotle, *Metaphysics*, I.9 991a20-22. Unless otherwise indicated, all references to the works of Aristotle will be to *The Complete Works of Aristotle: The Revised Oxford Translation*, ed. Jonathan Barnes, Bollingen Series (Princeton, NJ: Princeton University Press, 1984).

I call this the Problem of Fiction.

During their lifetimes, and for hundreds of years after, the two philosophers were seen as differing over the location of Forms in the universe. Plato dealt with the Problem of Fiction by relying on a perpetual separation of general Forms as true instances of Being from false instances of Forms in the world of individual Becoming. As such, Plato placed his emphasis on the predicate manness of Socrates in the proposition "Socrates is a man." For Plato it was there that the humanity of mankind resided and not in the individual subject of Socrates.

Aristotle dealt with the Problem of Fiction by attempting to *eliminate* the unbridgeable gulf between Being and Becoming in Plato's Theory of Forms by shifting the Forms out of a separate world that could only be realized through metaphor into the domain of nature, where they could be seen in fact. Universals—Aristotle's name for his natural Forms—inhered *within things themselves*. They could be mentally abstracted from our experience by a process described in his *De Anima*, where the mind was divided into two parts, a passive intellect, which processes the whole of one's experience, and an active intellect, which processes the raw data of experience into a rational framework provided, not by the mind itself, but by nature. This meant that universals could be abstracted from human experience by reason in an *epistemological sense only* without necessitating the destruction of the ontological world of Becoming by an interfering metaphor.

Aristotle's invention of logic and of his ethics followed from this system of psychology. The goal of the human being, according to Aristotelian ethics, is to rise above our animal nature, which he conceived of a being governed by the passive intellect's response to undifferentiated data of experience, to grasp the rational perspective governed by the active intellect in which things are sorted according to reason. Aristotle says the human being is the only animal in the universe that has the ability to use reason to negotiate his way through the universe, and this becomes the "specific difference" in his logic between human beings and the genus of animals. This fixes the human being's role at the center of the universe as the rational animal; and our obligation as human beings is to rise above our individual selves, governed by our animal desires, to our collective rational sense, where we become men.

Aristotle's *Nichomachean Ethics* begins with the notion that "Every art and every inquiry, and similarly every action is thought to aim at some good; and for this reason the good has rightly been declared to be that which all things aim."⁶ He notes, however, that a "certain difference is found among ends."⁷ According to Aristotle, some activities are pursued for aims that fall outside of their action: the medical arts pursue health; shipbuilders build ships.⁸ But there are other things that man pursues "for its own sake (everything else being desired for the sake of this)."⁹ He discovers the ultimate end of human thought in politics, "for it is this that ordains which of the sciences should be studied in the state."¹⁰

This leads to a dramatic difference between self-sufficiency in the modern world and in the world of Aristotle. Aristotle thought that the ultimate goal of human life was found in the building of a collective human state; and so he, like Plato, built his self-sufficiency on a predicate analysis of the proposition that "Socrates is a man." "A social instinct is implanted in all men by nature,"¹¹ he writes; and "The proof that the state is a creation of nature and prior to the individual is that the individual, when isolated, is not self-sufficing; and therefore he is like a part in relation to the whole."¹²

While this Aristotelian process was the basis of Alexander Pope's rational system of man, it is obviously quite different than the self-sufficiency that is required of mankind in the modern age, where existentialist philosophers believe that the individual subject Socrates is an end unto himself. The existentialist attempts to separate the individual self from society, nature, God, and even themselves. This leaves the individual standing alone as autonomous creators of themselves and their environment without the need for any intermediary reason or belief that could stand between themselves and the unique human ability to create one's own "authentic" self. As such, the existentialist take on human existence is precisely the opposite of that taken by Aristotle, who places mankind as an intermediate traveler between extremes and not, as the existentialist would have it, as an individual and autonomous being at war with a world outside himself.

The "natural" state of man in Aristotle is the product of a political education in which mankind perfects his imperfect individuality: "For man, when perfected, is the best of animals, but, when separated from law and justice, he is the worst of all."¹³ In another famous passage, Aristotle denies

---

6 ———, *Nichomachean Ethics*, 1.1.1094a1-3.
7 Ibid., 1.1.1094a3.
8 Ibid., 1.1094a7-8.
9 Ibid., 1.2.1094a18-19.
10 Ibid., 1.2.1094a27-1094b1.
11 ———, *Politics*, I.2.2135a30.
12 Ibid., I.2.2135a25-26.
13 Ibid., I.2.2135a31-32.

the existentialists' case in favor of a more cooperative society: "But he who is unable to live in society, or who has no need because he is sufficient for himself, must be either a beast or a god."[14]

Plato Fights Back

Aristotle's scientific ideas, which played such a large role in the Middle Ages and Renaissance, were not as successful in the ancient world, because Plato dismissed the logic of his student Aristotle with an extremely clever argument put forth in his *Parmenides*. Determining that Aristotle's work depends on the directionality of time, Plato reverses time in the *Parmenides*, giving his reader an impossible-to-realize-world in which Aristotle is pictured as the youngest member in a debate overseen by a much older Parmenides.[15] Between the two was Socrates, who Plato positioned as having not yet having figured out his exact position on the Theory of Forms.

In the second part of the dialog, a young Aristotle debates his elders over the principles that lay at the center of his logic, as Parmenides engages the younger Aristotle on age and the precedence of things in time.[16] Parmenides maintains that the One is above time, from which he draws the conclusion that the One grows older and younger at the same time:

> So the conclusion of all these arguments is that the one both is, and is becoming, older and younger than itself and than the others, and also neither is, nor is becoming, either older or younger than itself or than the others.[17]

Old Parmenides' argument is specifically designed to undermine the principle of identity on which the younger Aristotle's solution relies. Young

---

14 Ibid., I.2.2135a28-29.

15 I recognize that this is a controversial notion, as there is considerable disagreement about whether we are to understand the character of Aristoteles, who Plato places in his dialog, as Plato's historical contemporary. Gilbert Ryle had argued for the identity of Aristotles and Aristotle in his "Plato's *Parmenides*," *Mind* 48(1939), but the argument does not appear to be widely accepted in a world in which there is so much disagreement about even how we should interpret what appears to be an all-important distinction between truth and falsehood in the dialog. I assert my belief that a major part of Plato's dialog is his deliberate attempt highlight the importance of making such distinctions between truth and falsehood, while attempting to obscure Aristotle's clear picture of universals, which are not as a good guide to making such distinctions as Aristotle thinks they are. I recognize that my argument cannot be proven beyond the shadow of a doubt, but neither can anyone else's; and the elusiveness of a clear scientific distinction may be the deeper point of Plato's dialog.

16 Plato, *Parmenides*, 151e7ff.

17 Ibid., 155c5-8.

Aristotle is ultimately forced to admit that his desire to found universals in the natural world governed by time is undermined by the existence of a Platonic fiction that can reverse the principles of life and death, bringing both Socrates and Parmenides back to life *in mind* for the sake of argument. In this manner, the *Parmenides* undermines Aristotle's reliance on ontologically-based logic as the ultimate ground of metaphysics, asserting the precedence of his "higher" knowledge obtained through a fiction.

Plato extends his vision in the *Timaeus*, a dialog in which Timaeus lays out his vision of the cosmos, which he maintains he is capable of doing because he "has scaled the heights of all philosophy."[18] But before he grounds his picture of the cosmos in "nature,"[19] he must ask the leave of Socrates, who was in the habit of eviscerating his opponents for even small lapses in logical judgment, not to laugh.

Socrates does agree not to laugh at Timaeus' universe and says he expects to hear "a perfect and splendid feast of reason."[20] What he gets instead is a comical vision of the cosmos that sports elements that cannot be true on their face but must be passed through a metaphor before they can be held to be true. For instance, Timaeus' cosmos is pictured as having a body and a soul; and as a result of Timaeus' argument that nothing is created or destroyed in his cosmos, he inserts a low comical description of the universe eating its own waste products.[21] The fact that Socrates does not outwardly laugh does not mean that Socrates does not think that Timaeus' demigod world-creator is not a comical character, nor that Plato's dialog is intended to be taken seriously. Instead, the absurdity of some of Timaeus' descriptions of the universe should cause the reader to question the ultimate judgment of Timaeus as to the ends of things.

Timaeus himself seems to be acutely aware that his expressed intent in bridging the gulf between fiction and natural reality through a mythical cosmology is a departure from strict demonstrative science. Instead of ignoring his departures from science, Timaeus shifts from a one-to-one correspondence between his fiction and reality to one of probability:

> Now it is all-important that the beginning of everything should be according to nature. And in speaking of the copy and the original we may assume that words are akin to the matter which they describe; when

---

18 Plato, *Timaeus*, 20a4.
19 Ibid., 29b1.
20 Ibid., 27b.
21 Ibid., 33c.

they relate to the lasting and permanent and intelligible, they ought to be lasting and unalterable, and, as far as their nature allows, irrefutable and invincible—nothing less. But when they express only the copy or likeness and not the eternal things themselves, they need only be likely and analogous to the former words. As being is to becoming, so truth is to belief. If then, Socrates, amidst the many opinions about the gods and the generation of the universe, we are not able to give notions which are altogether and in every respect exact and consistent with one another, do not be surprised. Enough if we adduce probabilities as likely as any others, for we must remember that I who am the speaker and you who are the judges are only mortal men, and we ought to accept the tale which is probable and inquire no farther.[22]

This reliance on statistical probability puts limits on a human being's ability to inquire too deeply into what are still necessary fictions in the human epistemological reconstruction of the cosmos.[23] But at the same time, it shifts the ground of inquiry into metaphysics from overly-serious tragedy, such as Homer depicted in *The Iliad*, to the redemptive comedy of *The Odyssey*, in which mankind in the person of Odysseus fights and ultimately wins a contest with more powerful gods, not through a process of *imitating* the gods, but through competing devices of deceit, which function as a leveler in a contest in which the two parties have unequal power.

Classical philosophers tended to believe that philosophy had to do with the ends of argument and not intermediate and relative scientific processes; and as a result of such arguments the works of Aristotle were relegated to the basement of Neleus of Scepsis before being widely distributed years later.[24] In the intervening years, the Stoics had undertaken the development

---

22 Ibid., 29b1-29d3.

23 Compare my interpretation of Plato's work with the work of Hans-Georg Gadamer, who is attempting to look beneath the myth and artificial fabrication to the ultimate ground of Being in Plato in his "Idea and Reality in Plato's *Timeaus*," in *Dialogue and Dialectic: Eight Hermeneutical Studies on Plato* (New Haven, CT: Yale University Press, 1980). Gadamer takes the *Timaeus* to be a serious work of philosophy that is presented to the reader without any sense of irony. The ironic perspective only comes into the interpretive framework when the modern reader's engages with Plato's non-ironic text. Thus, Gadamer does not deal with the intermediate fiction except as a barrier to an ontological truth that he, on account of his not having made the shift out of one-to-one correspondence to probability, finds ultimately elusive. Plato's point is a more severe one in which fiction plays a central and necessary role in the metaphysical description of objects.

24 This story was first related by Strabo in his *Geography*, ed. Horace Leonard Jones, 8 vols. (Cambridge, MA: Loeb Classical Library, 1930), xii.1.54. In his Luciano Canfora, *The Vanished Library*, Hellenistic Culture and Society 7 (Berkeley: University of California Press, 1989), Luciano Canfora gives extensive background for this story, providing details on the life of Neleus (26-30), as well as of Strabo, who arrived in Rome at age 20 in 44

of logic.²⁵ It was more than 200 years after Aristotle retook the center stage of philosophy before Plotinus folded Aristotle into his mix of neoplatonism as the relative component on the ladder leading up to a Platonic whole that nevertheless resided in mystery.²⁶ But in its day Plato's solution caused as many problems as it solved, for it delivered a universe that could be understood only with the interference of a fiction that stood between our minds and the direct appreciation of the truth of things as they are in themselves.

Plato as a Guide to Truth in a Divided World

Plato's victory over Aristotle in the ancient philosophical contest meant that there was to be a necessary fiction between our mind's construction of reality and reality itself that could not be overcome by any means. Socrates proposal in his *Ion* to use Homer as the touchstone of true philosophical belief was okay when there was only one philosophical school, but it ran into trouble when philosophy split into competing sects.

When Aristotle was discovered by the more scientifically-inclined Romans, the world of Roman philosophy had already been divided between Stoics, Epicureans, and Academic skeptics. The Stoics had placed the truth of the universe (and so of man) in the logocentric realm. Our obligation as human beings, the Stoics thought, was to transcend our limited individual lives to reconnect with our generic humanity, which they conceived of as residing, not within individual men, but in the general λόγος of humanity. The Epicureans, on the other hand, had placed their confidence in the goddess, Venus, who, according to Lucretius,²⁷ was not an abstract and cold

---

BC and heard the story from Tyrannion, whose student he was, about how Tyrannion had acquired the texts, that had passed to Apellicon of Teos after Neleus' death. When Sulla invaded Athens, he had carted off Apellicon's library. By paying court to Sulla the library had passed directly into Tyrannion's hands (173). Despite the firsthand example of Strabo, there are reasons to believe that this story in false. In his Aristotle, *The Politics*, ed. Carnes Lord (Chicago: University of Chicago Press, 1984), Carnes Lord notes that not all the available facts can be reconciled with this story.

25 See the chapter on "The Megarians and the Stoics" in W. C. Kneale and Martha Kneale, *The Development of Logic* (New York, NY: Clarendon Press, 1984), 113-176.

26 For the importance of Plotinus' neoplatonism in much of modern aesthetic philosophy, see M. H. Abrams "The Great Circle: Pagan and Christian Neoplatonism" in his *Natural Supernaturalism: Tradition and Revolution in Romantic Literature* (New York: W. W. Norton, 1973), 146-154. Abrams specifically points out that the Romantic way of looking at the world involves inserting a break in one's being, a traveling out of oneself, and returning with a fuller understanding of one's place in an expanded universe. Such a journey, he argues, "has in the main been a long series of footnotes to Plotinus" (146).

27 Titus Lucretius Carus, *Lucretius, De Rerum Natura*, ed. Ettore Paratore and W. H. D. Rouse, 2nd edition. ed., The Loeb Classical Library (Cambridge, MA: Harvard Univer-

instance of the principle of λόγος. She operated through the pleasure principle within the individual man. In this way, both classical schools relied on reason's claim to be able "to transcend the limitations of mere subjectivity to grasp the objective world."[28] Problems with the choices made available by the rational sciences led to a third school of Academic skeptics, who doubted reason's ability to grasp the objective world on which one's salvation depended with anything more than a statistical probability.

Seneca notes the irony of relying on Homer as the touchstone of philosophical belief in the more complicated philosophical environment of Rome:

> For at one moment they make [Homer] a Stoic, giving nothing but virtue his approval, steering clear of pleasure, not even an offer of immortality inducing him to stoop to the dishonourable; at another they make him an Epicurean, praising the way of life of a society passing its days at peace and ease, in an atmosphere of dinner-parties and music-making; at another he becomes a Peripatetic, with a threefold classification of things good; at another an Academic, stating that nothing is certain. It is obvious that none of these philosophies is to be found in Homer for the very reason that they all are, the doctrines being mutually incompatible.[29]

If everyone could twist Homer into whatever philosophy they wished, then there was a methodological problem built into the nature of metaphysical philosophy that one could not solve for using reason alone. Seneca's insight into the lack of complete rational consistency when it comes to basing metaphysics on the *fiction* of Homer alone led him to follow the Stoic's path to a more certain knowledge based, not in the mere lives of lowly individuals, but in the other world of λόγος. But his decision relied on his authority as a famous philosopher and not on his having plumbed the depths of truth to its ends.

Augustine's Discovery of the Substantiality of Consciousness

It was to answer the skeptical charges that resulted from classical philosophy's inability to fix an object with anything more than statistical prob-

---

sity Press, 1982).
28 Charles Norris Cochrane, *Christianity and Classical Culture: A Study of Thought and Action from Augustus to Augustine* (Oxford: The Clarendon Press, 1940), 402.
29 "Letter LXXXVIII" in Lucius Annaeus Seneca, *Letters from a Stoic: Epistulae Morales Ad Lucilium*, trans. Robin Campbell (Harmondsworth: Penguin, 1969), 152.

ability that Augustine came to the rescue.[30] He strongly objected to the far-reaching characterization of the powers of reason in the first place: "To [them], Augustine replies with a challenge that reason itself present the credentials by which it presumes to operate."[31] He thought that it could not do so, and thus it failed in its chief claim on human attention. But, unlike the Romantics, who discarded limited allegory based in reason in favor of a more successful symbol after discovering the limitations of Descartes' reason in metaphysical inquiry, Augustine was not done with reason. Rather than looking outward from the self for the truth in the sphere of the λόγος, as the Stoics had done; or to immediate pleasure available to the individual, as the Epicureans had done; or doubting the power of reason at all, as the Academic skeptics had done; Augustine sought the axioms on which classical philosophy had been built. He found them in the being, knowledge, and will of the individual.[32] He found that these were not demonstrable by reason, but were instead the premises upon which all other rational knowledge is built.

This led him to assert what Charles Norris Cochrane calls "the substantiality of consciousness":

> Augustine then proceeds to assert the 'substantiality' of the consciousness of selfhood. By this he means that it is not rendered in the slightest degree more intelligible by being translated into terms other than itself, especially into terms of physiology; to do this is merely to add one mystery to another.[33]

He then proceeded from the premise of a substantial consciousness to an absolute distinction between a Creator, who has the power to create being, knowledge, and will, and human beings as creatures who received being, knowledge, and will as the gift of God. Augustine opens up his treatise *De trinitate* by drawing a firm line between the absolute Creator and the fallible and limited faculties of his creatures:

---

30 My argument in this section is largely derived from the chapter "Nostra Philosophia: The Discovery of Personality" in Cochrane, *Christianity and Classical Culture*, 399-455. This best book I have ever found on the subject of the sometimes complex relationship between the failings of the classical outlook and the rise of a new and in many ways better paradigm for dealing with the problems that arise in the attempt to integrate philosophy into the life we live.

31 Ibid., 402-403.

32 Augustine, *Confessions*, trans. Henry Chadwick, Oxford World's Classics (Oxford: Oxford University Press, 1998), XIII.xi.12. Cited in Cochrane, *Christianity and Classical Culture*, 403.

33 *Christianity and Classical Culture*, 404.

[They] are indeed so much the further from the truth, that nothing can be found answering to their conceptions, either in the body, or in the made or created spirit, or in the Creator Himself. For he who thinks, for instance, that God is white or red, is in error; and yet these things are found in the body. Again, he who thinks of God as now forgetting and now remembering, or anything of the same kind, is none the less in error; and yet these things are found in the mind.[34]

The assumption of the "substantiality of consciousness" was a radical break with the classical tradition. It located being in the individual subject, not in an abstract and general predicate λόγος that Socrates had given up his life for. The Socratic configuration of knowledge had restricted access to collective knowledge of the λόγος to a few philosopher kings, who would be allowed into the inner circle of the knowing only after years of study in which they were supposed to gain access to the metaphysical mystery at the heart of life itself. The substantiality of consciousness argument had the advantage of a personal immediacy that did not, as epicurean solutions tended to do, drive people away from collective action towards whatever selfish pleasure they could take from this short life. Thirdly, the substantiality of consciousness allowed Augustine to *expand* the power of reason beyond the skepticism into which it had fallen, not in the hands of careless would-be philosophers, but in the hands of the most penetrating classical thinkers of the day.

Furthermore, Augustine's reorganization of classical philosophy had the radical result of placing in the hands of every unique individual the power to organize their rational experience on the basis of a prior faith in God. In that process, reason was demoted from a tool of Platonic metaphysics to a tool of Aristotelian relative science. As a tool of the *sciences*, reason still had a limited place dealing with middles, not absolute ends. Augustine borrows from Plato as he does this, as he says that we can never look directly at the world as God had created it. Instead, we are required to look at the universe for the *vestigia* of God's *a priori* creation of it, as we recreate imperfectly God's perfect prior creation in our own minds. Thus, the human mental process of realizing the λόγος in human life is cobbled together after the fact (*a posteriori*) from our unique individual experience of a world that is given to us *a priori* by God. Memory plays an important role in mankind's *a posteriori* education into the *a priori* world of God's creation.

---

[34] Augustine, "On the Holy Trinity," in *A Select Library of the Nicene and Post-Nicene Fathers of the Christian Church*, ed. Philip Schaff (New York: The Christian Literature Co., 1886), I.1.1

The Reformation's Reliance on Augustine

By the middle of the 14th century, Petrarch and Boccaccio had begun rifling the monasteries of Europe for texts that had been neglected by Church scholars, who were primarily interested in using classical texts to bolster their position as leaders both in this world and the next. The humanism that emerged from subsequent revival of learning showed how much of the classical world the medieval world had left out of its scholastic picture. The revival of learning permanently soiled the Church's reputation as an impartial community where leading intellectuals came together for a free exchange of ideas with an eye on truth, changing its reputation to one of self-protective community that circled the wagons around its gains rather than letting inhospitable ideas be heard. This had disastrous results for Church unity, as the Catholic Church had founded its claim to worldly power on a document that was show to be a forgery by the humanist Lorenzo Valla,[35] and it was less than 200 years after the death of Petrarch and Boccaccio that the Church's grip on universal power was eclipsed by a lowly northern priest, Martin Luther.

Luther had used the discovery of humanists to question the Biblical foundation of the practice of granting indulgences. His solution was to revolt against the intermediate practices that had been built up over time by the Church and get back to the more immediate practice of having individuals read the Bible for themselves without the need for corrupt intermediary priests and the corrupt traditions that supported them. But at the same time that he was getting people back to reading the Bible, he was discarding scholastic reason as an intermediary force that stood between the mind of man and the direct appreciation of nature in and of itself.

Luther thought that Catholic art had for centuries raised images in the minds of men that took them away from the substance of an individual's ontological life, leading them instead to wander in epistemologically created fantasies. This led him to proscribe the practice of allegory in no uncertain terms: "Allegories are empty speculations, and as it were the scum of holy scriptures."[36] He believed that "The interpreter must as much as

---

35 This was the *Donation of Constantine*. For Valla's commentary on the *Donation*, see Lorenzo Valla and Christopher Bush Coleman, *The Treatise of Lorenzo Valla on the Donation of Constantine* (New Haven: Yale University Press, 1922). So powerful was the influence of humanism within Italy that the volatile Valla became Nicholas V's papal secretary.

36 Cited in Brian Cummings, "Protestant Allegory," in *The Cambridge Companion to Allegory*, ed. Rita Copeland and Peter T. Struck (New York, NY: Cambridge University Press, 2010), 177.

possible avoid allegory, so that he may not wander into idle dreams."[37] In the place of allegory, which he thought distracted from the individual's direct engagement with scripture, Luther wanted interpreters to rely on "The literal sense of scripture alone."[38]

Luther's skepticism over the intermediate reason of the scholastics was taken up by John Calvin, whose *Institutes of the Christian Religion*[39] severed the easy relationship between mankind's will and God's. Following Augustine's notion that there is always an act of faith required of believers that reason alone cannot bridge, Calvin maintained that the individual does not establish one's relationship to God by an act of reason or of will at all, because grace is completely out of the hands of the individual. Speaking of the Pelagian doctrine that argues that we achieve salvation through our own works, Calvin argues that there is no "movement" in a freely willed decision to accept or reject Christ:

> The apostle's doctrine is not that the grace of a good will is offered to us if we will accept of it, but that God himself is pleased so to work in us as to guide, turn, and govern our heart by His Spirit, and reign in it as his own possession.[40]

In other words, *God* chooses his elect friends. When He does so, *He* changes their hearts and imparts *His* "good will" to them.

This allows Calvin to do away with intermediate hierarchies of Church and state for a more immediate experience of God, who can be directly accessed in the privacy of one's mind through the medium of God's word, which is taken of faith. But that move on Calvin's part comes with a price:

> That intermediate movement which the sophists imagine, a movement which every one is free to obey or reject, is obviously excluded by the doctrine of effectual perseverance.[41]

Rhetorical flourishes are discarded in a Calvinistic universe for a sterner view of reality that has the advantage of *severing* one's easy access to metaphysical reality that Catholics were pursuing in Counter-Reformation works. Election in a Calvinistic universe is *solely* a matter of God's will, and

---

37 Ibid.
38 Ibid.
39 John Calvin, *Institutes of the Christian Religion*, trans. Henry Beveridge (Peabody, MA: Hendrickson Publishers, Inc., 1989).
40 Ibid., II.3.10.
41 Ibid.

Calvin writes, "the Lord both corrects, or rather destroys our depraved will, and also substitutes a good will from himself"[42] by giving the elect a new heart without any interference from a priestly caste.

In Calvin's works, this leads to the separation of the will of man into various distinct areas of operations, as we can clearly when he takes up the question of the operation of man, Satan, and God in the story of Job:

> How can we attribute the same work to God, to Satan, and to man, without either excusing Satan by the interference of God, or making God the author of the crime? This is easily done if we look first to the end, and then to the mode of acting. The Lord designs to exercise the patience of his servant by adversity; Satan's plan is to drive him to despair; while the Chaldeans are bent on making unlawful gain by plunder. Such diversity of purpose makes a wide distinction in the act.[43]

In separating "ends" from "modes of acting" in a "wide distinction in the act," Calvin ends up discussing the various states of the will and asserts: "Thus simply to will is the part of man, to will ill the part of corrupt nature, to will well the part of grace."[44] This "wide distinction" in the actions of individuals opens a gap between the order of nature and the order grace that Hamilton in his 1960 work had prematurely attempted to close into a single image centered in a Leibnizian willing monad.

Spenser's Reformation Allegory

The excursion out of will by Reformation scholars is precisely why I propose to read Spenser's *Faerie Queene* as the product of a pre-Enlightenment environment that had not yet attempted to eliminate the complicating role of Christian religion for a more perfect secular reason. The reintegration of Augustine back into Spenser's poetic universe must change the reader's perspective on exactly what Spenser is doing in the opening book of his poetic masterpiece, as his poetic work is reintroducing in fiction exactly those intermediate things that the moderns of both Modern and postmodern stripes, as well as Augustine and his Reformation followers, hoped to eliminate from their ontological reading of reality. In his allegorical work, Spenser is *building up* those intermediate factors that stand between the mind of the reader and his or her realization of them in their ontology. As he does so, the forms of allegory multiply. The translation of Spenser's

---

42 Ibid., II.iii.7.
43 Ibid., II.iv.2.
44 Ibid., II.iii.5.

allegorical universe into modern scientific terms destroys in its definition Spenser's true position, which is to open up the universe to things that cannot be treated in ontological terms but that can only be realized through the medium of human imagination.

The Restoration of Allegorical Levels

This expansion of allegory means that the various levels of allegory, which cause so many headaches to modern scientific thinkers, become important in our assessment of Spenser's work. These allegorical levels are treated separately by Carol Kaske in her work *Spenser and Biblical Poetics*:

> The symbolic modes are most conveniently organized under the four exegetical senses. They are defined in the mnemonic jingle "Littera gesta docet, quid credas allegoria, / Moralis quid agas, quo tendas anagogia" (The letter teaches the events, the allegory [figura, or typology] what you should believe, the moral [sense, or tropology] what you should do, the anagogy where you should be headed).[45]

Kaske goes on to note the fragmentation of unified literal events into discrete things that can be treated separately:

> The four senses are useful chiefly as pigeonholes for the different kinds of subject matter, the different semantic fields, that an allegorical image or story can simultaneously contain, though all four of them are seldom found simultaneously in any single passage either in the Bible or in secular literature.[46]

The moderns tend to want to read any individual image within an allegorical poem as self-contained—this is my objection to Hamilton's 1960 reading of the poem—but I would note that whenever the reader gets away from the literal level of experience they start to see a dissipation of unified meaning into various characters. This is the case, for instance, with the literal and historical character of Elizabeth, who becomes divided in Spenser's allegorical universe into the characters of Gloriana, Belphoebe, Amoret, Britomart, the goddesses Diana and Venus, and others. Moreover, the allegorical levels are not equally balanced, as Kaske's note on the anagogical sense implies:

---

45 Carol V. Kaske, *Spenser and Biblical Poetics* (Ithaca NY: Cornell University Press, 1999), 15.
46 Ibid.

In Spenser as elsewhere, the anagogical sense is rare; in the FQ, only the last two stanzas of the Mutabilitie Cantos and the "New Jerusalem" which Red Cross glimpses from the Mount of Contemplation are pure anagogy, where you should be headed (FQ I.x.55-57; VII.viii.1-2).[47]

If not all images feature all levels of spiritual existence, and if ontology is fragmented within allegory into discrete parts, then it is fair to ask about the presence of various levels in any individual image. No one, for instance, would argue that Archimago and Duessa are consciously and willingly playing out the role preordained for them by God; but as we shall see, both are *unconsciously* and *unwillingly* playing their roles in God's sacred pageant often against their immediate short term interests, though this view is only apparent to the reader who stands outside the fictional universe of Faery.

This brings the reader to one last and extremely important question about *The Faerie Queene*. Are the characters of Redcrosse and Una, who participate in God's sacred pageant in ways that Archimago and Duessa do not, fully aware of *their* participation in God's sacred pageant; or are they, too, characters who hold only partial answers to metaphysical questions that Luther and Calvin had restricted to God the Creator alone on the basis of Augustine's authority?

The evidence for the latter reading, though overlooked in modern criticism, is striking. One of the most important indications of the limitations of Redcrosse's mindset can be found when, *after his own adventure has been completed*, he says to the next adventurer,

> More then *goodwill* to me attribute nought:
> For all I did, I did but as I ought. (II.i.33.4-5 italics mine)

This is more than a statement of humility (though it is that); it is a statement of fact. Yet it is not a statement of the whole of Redcrosse's adventure, as the poet has emphasized an unrelenting and continual catalog of his *mistakes* in doing things that he ought *not* be doing at every step along the way up to the end of his journey.

The easiest way for a reader to miss Redcrosse's silence on his full responsibility for his own behavior even after he has completed his adventure is to ignore some of the evidence the poet has given them in favor of their own predisposition towards the evidence. The reader is helped in this if he takes the modern definition of the poem as being unmotivated and the

---

47 Ibid. I would add that the presence of Una represents a third anagogic moment in *The Faerie Queene*.

poet as naïve. But questions about Spenser's knowledge about his situation had already appeared in his day; and the poet's answer to such questions is not what the modern critic supposes them to be, as we shall see in the next chapter.

The *Letter to Raleigh*

Raleigh's Understandable Question

The practice of writing allegory was already waning in Spenser's day. In its place literature was tending towards a more integrated sense of image, character, and narrative that was being practiced in the theater by William Shakespeare and was being carefully aligned to classical models by Ben Jonson. This made it difficult for some to read Spenser's archaic masterpiece for either pleasure or instruction without coming across the difficulty of having so many elaborate iconographic images standing between themselves and the clarity of the poem. One of the readers who did not get the message was Sir Walter Raleigh, who "commanded"[1] Spenser to write a letter explaining the meaning of his "darke conceit"[2] in clearer terms. Spenser returned a letter explaining his "*whole intention* in the course of this worke, which for that it giueth great light to the Reader, for the better vnderstanding."[3] His explanation of his whole intention has baffled critics ever since. In this chapter, I offer my explanation as to why that is.

Spenser's Baffling Answer

In his *Letter to Raleigh*, Spenser states his intention boldly: "I labour to pourtraict in Arthure, before he was king, the image of a braue knight, perfected in the twelue morall vertues, as Aristotle hath deuised."[4] This citation of Plato's rival has caused some concern in the critical community that

---

1 Spenser, *Faerie Queene (2001)*, 714.
2 Ibid., 714.
3 Ibid. 714-715.
4 Ibid., 715.

tends to identify their role as accounting for the whole of a work of literature, not just the logical aspects. That desire accords with broader Platonic solutions. This leads modern literary critics to distrust any direct impact of Aristotle on Spenser's poetry. For instance, A. Leigh DeNeef writes in *The Spenser Encyclopedia* that

> Most criticism…assumes that it refers to the twelve moral virtues, and much energy has been devoted to counting that number in the *Nichomachean Ethics*. Yet it is not clear exactly what the clause refers to.[5]

This reflects the modern way of dealing with Spenser's overt declaration of meaning. Critics take the poet to mean what he says. Then they look for sources outside his work. Not finding any source that meets the critic's conditions in a satisfactory way in this case, they tend to dismiss Spenser's pointing to Aristotle's relative and partial science, and they turn to more satisfactory (to the moden critic) Platonic sources that accord with their expectation that Spenser means what he says when he says that he wishes to disclose a picture of his whole meaning of his poem in the *Letter*.

But these are assumptions made by the critic. For all the reader knows, Spenser may not be telling the whole truth in the *Letter*. Moreover, he may *mean* to divide relative science from absolute metaphysics along the lines that Aristotle had laid out in his lifetime, and he may be falling on the side of relative science rather than whole metaphysics. When looked at in this way, the *Letter to Raleigh* and the poem it comments on looks very different.

The Reception of the *Letter* in Modern Criticism

The *Letter* begins with a recognition of "how doubtfully all Allegories may be construed."[6] The poet then declares his "general intention and meaning" of tying his "darke conceit" to a "historicall fiction" "without expressing of any particular purposes or by-accidents therein occasioned."[7] This shift from the particular accidents of allegory to a more general and plain sense available outside the poem in the realm of history mimics the modern critics' own sense of obligation to tie poetry back to a definite meaning that lies outside the work of fiction. Thus, modern critics generally take the poet to mean what he says here in the *Letter*'s accession to the

---

5 DeNeef, A. Leigh, "Raleigh, letter to" in Hamilton, *The Spenser Encyclopedia*, 582b.
6 Spenser, *Faerie Queene (2001)*, 714.
7 Ibid., 714-715.

priority of the realm of history over the realm of fiction.

The problem with this popular line of attack is that as soon as the modern critic starts looking for a definite historical context on which to place his or her understanding of the sense of the poem, he or she finds him or herself frustrated by his or her ability to fix the general meaning of the poem within the *Letter*. This leads to some comical misunderstandings. For instance, DeNeef, who has begun his exploration of Spenser's poem on modern premises, continues in this vein:

> If the Letter has important implications for Spenser's general plans and generic methods, it also raises particular questions about the poem's narrative and characters. These questions are especially important for modern criticism which, as a rule, takes one of these to be the function of the other.[8]

DeNeef then goes on to catalog, not the smooth reconciliation of his modern threads of narrative and characterization into one neat package, but instead goes on to point out several problems with his approach to the poem. These are laid out on philosophical lines. "Narrative is taken to be the logical or 'realized' extension of character,"[9] he says.

> But Spenser says his poem is 'coloured' with an historical fiction. To color, in this sense, is to embellish rhetorically or figuratively, and the coloring of narrative would thus be a function of the 'continued Allegory.'[10]

That is a problem, because this is not what modern criticism tells us to expect from allegory, which has stood in modern criticism as a trope that *leaves* accidental "color" behind for more stable general essences.[11]

---

8 Hamilton, *The Spenser Encyclopedia*, 583a.
9 Ibid.
10 Ibid.
11 The question in modern criticism is not whether this is what is actually happening in allegory, but whether what the modern critic thinks is happening is successful or not. See Fletcher, *Allegory* for a work that represents allegory as successful in its quest for a metaphysical foundation that is lacking in the modern world. Paul de Man, on the other hand, declares in his article "Pascal's Allegory of Persuasion" that the "difficulty of allegory is rather that this clarity of representation does not stand in the service of something that can be represented" (1). He makes the limits of the mind the subject of his inquiry into allegory "that aesthetically more successful works of art, because of this very success, were unable to perceive" (1). I repeat my contention that this decision is made on the basis of the *a priori* premises that the modern critic arrives at the critical table with and is not based in anything the critic finds in the poem itself.

Rather than questioning his modern perceptions of allegory, DeNeef continues to read the allegorical poem for a literal and historical sense through the substituted *Letter*. But even as he does so, he notes that some characteristics of the allegory are left behind, as the reader travels back to the supposedly solid foundation of history:

> One consequence of taking narrative in this metaphorical sense is that, rather than looking for a sequential cause-and-effect logic to the progress of incidents, we would see each incident as an autonomous 'accident' of 'aspect' of the particular virtue a knight's actions express.... The narrative, in short, is more like a set of grammatical inflections or declensions than the modern novelistic notion of a syntactically complete sentence.[12]

"This notion of narrative inflection is valid," says DeNeef, "only so long as the 'continued Allegory' of the 'historical fiction' is underemphasized."[13]

In sticking with his modern reading of allegory, DeNeef has run across one of the cruces of modern criticism, the problem of reference:

> It has been argued that the Letter denies any literal story or narrative in The Faerie Queene....Yet if the narrative is dismissed as illusory, private virtue becomes closed off from any social or even temporal extension.[14]

This is the same problem of reference that Hamilton had with the poem in 1960. The problem of reference as stated here makes every allegorical narrative *generically* a problem for modern critics, since allegory proposes *in its definition* things that cannot be reconciled in the mind of the reader without causing problems with locating the exact foundation of one's knowledge in the real world.

DeNeef then goes on to raise the same objections to character. "Strictly read, the Letter implies that characters are personifications or representations."[15]

> Character is thus figurative, and we cannot speak of intentions, feelings, or motivations: a given character is merely the trajectory of some

---

12 Hamilton, *The Spenser Encyclopedia*, 583a-b.

13 Ibid., 583b.

14 Ibid. This is the same problem identified by Hamilton in his *Structure of Allegory in The Faerie Queene*, where he identified it with the problem of how to get Redcrosse out of the Wandering Wood on his own power.

15 Ibid.

unknown *x* mapped by an algebraic formula of relationships onto a functional grid.[16]

"To enact the operation of a virtue, some character or personality must be portrayed as acting in time"[17] says DeNeef, who then offers a modern solution to the problem of character: "Character, like narrative, is both a shadow and substance, to be read *through* and read *in*."[18]

Once again careful readers find themselves translated out of Spenser's culturally-determined world to the world of modern criticism. Coordinate grids were only invented after Spenser's death by the founder of modern philosophy, René Descartes. It seems reasonable to question whether the use of a later algebraic grid in which nothing is left out of the reader's experience of the universe is really appropriate to reading *The Faerie Queene*, which was written in an age in which serious philosophers still believed in non-spatial demons that could interfere with mankind's perception of the universe. Such Cartesian precision is laid upon Spenser's poem *after the fact* by a modern critic who is operating on different principles than Spenser was operating with *and* who feels the need to translate Spenser's Renaissance and Reformation perceptions into modern scientific terms.

Variant Meaning in Spenser's Historical Poets

The reader can get a clearer picture of Spenser's meaning if they give him credit for understanding the interference caused by the Problem of Fiction in the direct perception of the historical world. His awareness of this problem is apparent if we look closely at Spenser's attempt to tie his poem to a catalog of "antique Poets historicall" with the poet's determination to "fashion a gentleman or noble person in vertuous and gentle discipline."[19] Spenser begins his effort with

> Homere, who in the Persons of Agamemnon and Vlysses hath ensampled a good gouernour and a vertuous man, the one in his Ilias, the other in his Odysseis....[20]

When the reader looks into Homer, Agamemnon is indeed put forward as a model of good kingship, but his presentation in Homer is not as a whole

---

16 Ibid.
17 Ibid.
18 Ibid.
19 Spenser, *Faerie Queene (2001)*, 714.
20 Ibid., 715.

man. Instead, Agamemnon is presented in *The Odyssey* after he has been betrayed by his wife, Clytemnestra, and murdered by her lover, Aegisthus. He he had gone home trusting too much in his wife's love, and this leads to the loss of his life. Odysseus meets him in his underworld journey in Book XI, where Agamemnon tells him that he (Odysseus) will not be murdered by his own wife, the "circumspect Penelope."[21] It is her very *circumspection* that holds the key to maintaining her integrity in a household filled with badly-behaving suitors. And Agamemnon tells Odysseus, who has offended Poseidon by announcing his name after his defeat of the cyclops after concealing it under the guise of "No Man" while he was in the cave, to be likewise circumspect, urging him not to tell even his wife the whole of his adventures:

> ...do not be too easy even with your wife,
> Nor give her an entire account of all you are sure of.
> Tell her part of it, but let the rest be hidden in silence.[22]

This process of hiding one's meaning through deception becomes the key to human survival in a Homeric universe of hostile gods.

Homer has his hero telling his tale of his journey to the underworld in the House of Alcinous, a location where it is notoriously impossible to make a perfect differentiation between truth and falsehood. This lack of facticity in *The Odyssey* brings up the question of where exactly the basis of Spenser's "vertuous man" lies. If Spenser intends us to read his "vertuous" poetic model Homer as *hiding* a part of his tale, this should lead the careful reader to question the precise manner in which such "Poets historicall" can be imitated, if they, too, are attempting to hide their meaning behind a mask. This in turn brings up the legitimate question of how the reader can know when or if they have reached the foundation of a person's being if there is no clear way for the reader to see into the the mind of others.[23] It is not enough to assume away the poet's asking such questions in order to maintain a grip on the facts as modern critics see them. Spenser can just as easily be seen to be pointing the reader *towards* problems with Odysseus as a model of imitation as he can be seen as pointing his reader

---

21 Homer, *The Odyssey of Homer*, trans. Richmond Alexander Lattimore (New York: Harper Perennial, 1999), XI.445.

22 Ibid., XI.441-443.

23 Such questions are common in modern criticism. For an example, see Dorrit Cohn, *Transparent Minds: Narrative Modes for Presenting Consciousness in Fiction* (Princeton, NJ: Princeton University Press, 1978).

away from such problems.

The question of Spenser's orientation towards the character of Odysseus is further complicated by Spenser's recognition of Virgil, "whose like intention was to doe in the person of Aeneas."[24] Virgil can be seen to be continuing Homer's "intention" only as long as the reader does not read too deeply into the tradition, for Virgil does not have his main character follow the Homeric hero's practice of deceiving others as the honorable way of mankind in a universe of hostile gods. Instead, Odysseus is pictured as character of dread[25] in Virgil's cosmos, a malicious and invidious man[26] who is a forger of lies[27] that offended the more rigid sense of Roman honor. Rather than having Aeneas follow Odysseus in deceit, Virgil laments the destruction of Troy and has his hero travel west to found a new Troy in the wake of the destruction of the old. In doing so, Virgil wanted to *redeem* government from the depredations of deceivers in the wake of a century of disastrous civil wars and put in the place of Sulla and Julius Caesar an honest Augustus, while at the same time redeeming the connection between nature and man's humanity that Homer's Odysseus had severed.

Virgil's failure to achieve his end can be measured by the effectiveness of Ovid's *Metamorphoses*, which features the transformation of supposedly stable individual beings by hostile gods. In his 15th and final book, Ovid relates the Roman appropriation of the philosophy of a peaceful epicurean Pythagoras, who, like Ovid himself, lived in exile from his natural home:

> [He] had fled Samos and its tyrannical rulers
> And lived in voluntary exile. Though his gods
> Were far away, he visited their region of the sky
> In his mind, and things that nature denied
> To human vision he took in with his inner eye.[28]

With his sharper insight into such things that did not appear directly in

---

24 Spenser, *Faerie Queene (2001)*, 715.

25 Virgil, *Virgil*, trans. H. Rushton Fairclough, Rev. ed., 2 vols., The Loeb Classical Library (Cambridge, MA: Harvard University Press, 1986), II.261: *dirus Ulixes* translated as "dread Ulysses."

26 Ibid., II.90: *invidiua...pellacis Ulixes* translated as "the malice of subtle Ulysses."

27 Ibid., IX.602: *fandi factor Ulixes* translated as "fable-forging Ulysses."

28 All line numbers are to Ovid, *Metamorphoses*. Translated by Frank Justus Miller. Edited by G. P. Goold. 2nd ed. 2 vols, Loeb Classical Library. (Cambridge, MA: Harvard University Press, 1984), XV.60-64. As the Loeb edition gives a prose translation of Ovid's complec work, English translations will be drawn from Ovid, *Metamorphoses*, trans. Stanley Lombardo (Indianapolis: Hackett Pub. Co., 2010), p. 413.

nature, Pythagoras had related the existence of a golden age in which men had once lived in peace but which has been destroyed by the intrusion of mankind's unbalanced greed into a once equitable universe.[29] As a result, the poet writes

> there is nothing in the whole world
> That is static. Everything flows, is a vagrant form.
> Time itself glides on in constant motion,
> Just like a river. A river cannot stand still,
> Nor can a wispy hour. As a wave is pushed by a wave,
> Pushed on as it comes and pushing on the one before,
> So moments of time run on and follow
> And are always new. What was before is left behind
> And what wasn't becomes, renewed every moment.[30]

From this observation, the reader can see that Virgil's static position on being was not the only position available for an ancient poet to choose from. What is more, Ovid's position on the dynamic nature of time gelled better with the position taken by Augustine on the inadequacy of the Virgilian position, which tended to want to stop time in fiction.

The Role of Aeneas in Augustine

Augustine was drawn into the problems of the status of fiction because of the way that the postions of both poets led each in their own way to skepticism. In his *Confessions*, Augustine had famously dismissed classical philosophy's substitution of the hero Aeneas, who never existed in reality, for his own substantial consciousness that was based in his immediate existence and on the irrefutable fact of Christ's miraculous death and resurrection. Augustine speaks in his *Confessions* of his youthful distaste for learning the lessons of mathematics[31] as well as the lessons taught to him by the grammarians.[32] He tells of his youthful delight in the lessons of Virgil, who taught the delightful but "vain spectacle of the wooden horse full armed

---

29 In my reading of the *Metamorphoses*, Ovid pictures himself as a pacific philosopher who has been wrongfully exiles, while the Roman Empire and its leader, Augustus, are pictured as takers of things (like the philosophy of peaceful Pythagoras) that do not properly belong to them. From the margins of empire, Ovid writes his mocking commentary on the impermanence of stable things, including the fiction of Aeneas.

30 Ovid, *Metamorphoses*, XV.176-184, p. 422.

31 In Augustine, *Confessions*, I.xviii (22), he says that "it was hateful to me to recite 'one plus one is two' and 'two plus two is for.'"

32 Ibid., I.xiii(20).

with soldiers and of the burning of Troy and the very ghost of Creusa."[33]

Later in his life, he reversed his previous evaluation of things, expressing gratitude to his mother and to God, who forced him to learn how to read and write even though it was against his will. As a result, he dismisses the "vain spectacle" of Virgil's poetry:

> This was better than the poetry I was later forced to learn about the wanderings of some legendary fellow named Aeneas (forgetful of my own wanderings) and to weep over the death of a Dido who took her own life from love.[34]

Augustine goes on to express his shame in having wept over Dido, while abandoning his dedication to God:

> I wept over Dido who 'died in pursuing her ultimate end with a sword.'[35] I abandoned you to pursue the lowest things of your creation. I was dust going to dust. Had I been forbidden to read this story, I would have been sad that I could not read what made me sad. Such madness is considered a higher and more fruitful literary education than being taught to read and write.[36]

Augustine does more than make a distinction based on a change of heart; he is reversing the architecture of a classical education, where entry into school was contingent on the acceptance of a mystery that he as a Christian could not believe in. He does so by rending the veil that hung in front of the schools that symbolized entry into a sort of mystery cult:

> It is true, veils hang at the entrances to the schools of literature; but they do not signify the prestige of elite teaching so much as the covering up of error.[37]

Augustine expects resistance from those within the schools, and he demands that "there be no abuse of me from people who sell or buy a literary education,"[38] for in his mind the superiority of reading and writing was as clear to him as the difference between what is real and what is put forward as fiction.

---

33 Ibid., I.xviii (22).
34 Ibid., I.xiii (20).
35 *Aeneid* 6.457.
36 Augustine, *Confessions*, I.xiii (21).
37 Ibid., I.xiii (22).
38 Ibid.

In this, he was following the Roman practice that had caused Virgil to rewrite Homer in an attempt to reconnect lying Odysseus back to some ground in factual experience. In this endeavor, Augustine not only believes that this is possible, he believes that Virgil has failed *and that the educated leaders whose expertise as readers allows them to stand in a position as barriers to entry to the schools know it*:

> If I put the question to [an audience] whether the poet's story is true that Aeneas once came to Carthage, the uneducated will reply that they do not know, while the educated will say it is false.[39]

This leaves educators in charge of the veils of mystery, the knowledge of which turns out to have no fundamental connection to underlying reality. This is revealed only after the knowing have been allowed into the schools.

The same is not true of the facts taught by grammarians:

> But if I ask with what letters Aeneas' name is spelled, all who have learnt to read will reply correctly in accordance with the agreement and convention by which human beings have determined the value of these signs.[40]

As a good Christian who knew that Christ had rent the veil of the Temple of Jerusalem,[41] Augustine was comfortable with rendering so weak a veil as those that hung in pagan temples and schools, and thus he reverses the characteristic judgment made by those who stand within those schools:

> Similarly, if I ask which would cause the greater inconvenience to someone's life, to forget how to read and write or to forget these fabulous poems, who does not see what answer he would give, unless he has totally lost his senses?[42]

In raising grammar, which had given him control of his circumstances, over a content that had the power to eclipse his devotion to God, Augustine changes the orientation towards pagan literature from one of providing entry into the mystery of things to an invitation to an error that drew one *away* from the deeper truths, not only of philosophy, but of one's own experience. Homeric fiction in such a universe is founded on an attempt

---

39 Ibid.
40 Ibid.
41 Matthew 27:51; Mark 15:38; Luke 23:45.
42 Augustine, *Confessions*, I.xiii (22).

to escape the animal violence of the gods,[43] but it comes at the expense of a separation from nature itself. A poet like Virgil, who attempted to redeem the connection between human community and nature in his *Aeneid*, did so by continuing to write fiction that features hostile gods that work against men and women. Augustine was able to redeem philosophy from the Problem of Fiction by founding his work on the one-time-only "fact" of Christ's death and resurrection and reconnecting the world back to its creator, not on the basis of a pagan fiction, but on the basis of one's faith in God's prior creation that is revealed to mankind in their real substantial consciousness.

Tasso's Disseverance of Politics from the Good

Spenser was not merely distinguishing a Christian message based in Augustine from the messages of the pagans. He was also distinguishing his message from his Catholic counterparts in Italy, as he points out in the *Letter to Raleigh* the continuing disseverance of the whole into parts—not a return to wholeness—as he progresses towards the modern age:

> ...after him Ariosto comprised them both in his Orlando: and lately Tasso disseuered them againe, and formed both parts in two persons, namely that part which they in Philosophy call Ethice, or vertues of a priuate man, coloured in his Rinaldo: The other named Politice in his Godfredo.[44]

The reference to Tasso has its genesis in a letter appended to his *Jerusalem Delivered* entitled "The Allegory of the Poem."[45] That letter served as a model for Spenser's own *Letter to Raleigh*. In it, Tasso, discussing himself in the third person as "the poet," is discussing the problem of the one and the many in terms of his poem. In the poem, the individual is considered as a solitary man:

> It was no accident that the poet portrayed the descent as solitary, for that journey also signifies his contemplation of the punishments and the rewards that the souls of the wicked and the just will receive in the other world. Besides, the speculative intellect, which operates as a solitary faculty, is fittingly portrayed by the action of a solitary man.[46]

---

43 I remind my readers that these are the two aspects that are excuded from the construction of intermdiate human society by Aristotle.

44 Spenser, *Faerie Queene (2001)*, 715.

45 Torquato Tasso, *Jerusalem Delivered (Gerusalemme Liberata)*, trans. Anthony M. Esolen (Baltimore: Johns Hopkins University Press, 2000), 415-419.

46 Ibid., 416.

Individuals in Tasso are primarily concerned with their relationship with God, who created them without intermediary reason. But at the same time, he does not dismiss intermediary reason as a detour from human authenticity, as the existentialists do. Instead, he separates reason from personal good and builds on it a collective sense of men working together:

> But political action, which proceeds from and accompanies other faculties of the soul along with the intellect—for they all are as citizens united in one republic—can hardly be figured forth unless by an action in which many people work together.[47]

By this move, collective action is separated from individual obligation. Collective action falls under the province of reason, which can build communities of like-minded people, while individual speculation is based on an extra-rational faith.

Having made that case in the abstract, Tasso personalizes it by separating Godfrey of Bouillon from Rinaldo. Godfrey is the individual leader of the Christian armies and of the intellect on the allegorical level:

> Godfrey, captain of the assembled troops, stands in the place of the intellect, in particular that intellect that judges not the necessary but the mutable—things that could fall out in any number of ways. By the will of God and of the princes he is chosen Captain of this enterprise, for the intellect is from God, constituted by nature Lord over the other powers of the soul and over the body, commanding the former with a civil and the latter with a kingly power.[48]

Rinaldo, by contrast, is the bravest of the Christian warriors who carry out the conquest in Godfrey's name: his is the literal body that carries out the thought conceived of by the intellect:

> Rinaldo, Tancred, and the other princes stand for the other powers of the soul, and the lesser soldiers signify the body. And because, by the imperfection of human nature and the deceit of our Enemy, man does not attain to that happiness without many difficulties and impediments internal and external, these difficulties are figured forth in the composition too.[49]

Tasso's division of the soul in his allegory of his poem into its constituent

---

47 Ibid.
48 Ibid.
49 Ibid.

parts brings up the question of where the principle of action resides: in the individualized mind or in that part of the soul that acts upon the direction given to it by the general intellect?

Not everyone believes that Spenser picked up on the subtleties of Tasso's division here. Douglas Bush, in his *Mythology and the Renaissance Tradition in English Poetry*, dismisses Spenser as ignorant of conflicts brought out by Tasso:

> Indeed he was not of a nature to be conscious, as Tasso was, of disturbing conflicts. He remains, among other things, the wistful panegyrist of an imagined chivalry, the bold satirist of ugly actuality, cosmic philosopher and pastoral dreamer, didactic moralist and voluptuous pagan, puritan preacher and Catholic worshipper, eager lover and mystical Neo-Platonist.[50]

Angus Fletcher dismisses Bush's passive picture of Spenser:

> In the light of the theory of ambivalence, however, this account appears inconsistent; Bush's own list of attributes presents a Spenser full of conflict, while all the violence in Spenser contradicts the denial of a similarity (in this respect) between Spenser and Tasso. How can a man write much about endless fighting, tyranny, and deceit, and not "be conscious ... of disturbing conflict"? Bush does a disservice to Spenser by sentimentalizing him—Spenser is hardly "wistful."[51]

But Fletcher goes on to make an equally mystifying statement that indicates his belief that *The Faerie Queene* lacks dramatic excitement:

> It would have been fairer to attempt to explain the striking lack of dramatic excitement in *The Faerie Queene*. The excitement of reading Spenser, is so to speak ours, not Spenser's. We bring it to the work; the work does not, like a mimetic work, present us with a series of events capable in their autonomy of exciting our attention and sympathy. [52]

In other words, only the modern reader brings a sense of autonomy, of dramatic excitement, and sympathy to the poem that the poet, working in an alien tradition of allegory, never intended for his poem to hold.[53]

---

50 Douglas Bush, *Mythology and the Renaissance Tradition in English Poetry* (Minneapolis: The University of Minneapolis Press, 1932), 88.

51 Fletcher, *Allegory*, 273.

52 Ibid.

53 This would place autonomy, dramatic interest, mimesis, and sympathy as the by-products of symbol in the modern division of things. That may have been okay at the height

However, there is another way to read Spenser's citation of Tasso in the *Letter to Raleigh*. This is that Spenser has picked up on in Tasso's division of collective political action from individual good. If allowed to stand, Tasso's division would lead to the possibility that one could rule with the power of intellect but without the power to effect one's will in the world of collective action. But what is worse, and potentially disastrous, is that it leaves open the possibility that one could rule as a ruthless Machiavellian warrior without having any disposition towards one's subjects' good. This would lead to a parade of ruthless rulers who take power from weak men who are unwilling to be as ruthless as they are. It is to avoid this consequence that modern critics move away from Tasso's disseverance of the political from the ethical back to the idea of unity in the λόγος that they suppose to have been implied by the presence of allegory itself.

This appears not to be the case in Spenser's *Letter*. Instead of refraining from the progressive division of science back to an original Homeric unity that turns out to have no basis in ontological reality, Spenser pushes through the progressive division of the scientific world into discrete parts in the Book of Holinesse. This is easier to see if the reader considers the characters of Una and Redcrosse, not through the distorting lens of the translation of the poem into modern terms, but as they are presented.

The Introduction of Redcrosse

Despite the "command" of Raleigh to translate his "darke conceit" into clearer terms, Spenser tells more than one story in the *Letter to Raleigh* that no reader has been able to locate within the poem itself. The longest is his story of a feast held in the castle of Gloriana, the Queen of Faery. It is there that he introduces the character who we know for ten cantos as Redcrosse:

> In the beginning of the feast, there presented him selfe a tall clownishe younge man, who falling before the Queen of Faries desired a boone (as the manner then was) which during that feast she might not refuse: which was that hee might haue the atchieument of any aduenture, which during that feaste should happen, that being graunted, he rested him on the floore, vnfitte through his rusticity for a better place.[54]

William Nelson bluntly asserts that a Renaissance reader would have known that Spenser was using a comic model:

---

of Modernism, but again the passage of time has given us the postmoderns, who have made symbol as problematic as allegory was seen to be as guide to metaphysical experience.

54 Spenser, *Faerie Queene (2001)*, 717.

No Renaissance humanist could have thought the legendary life of St. George a respectable literary model. By the sixteenth century accretions of impossible adventure and buffoonery of village St George plays must have rendered the story ridiculous."[55]

Spenser forestalls the reader's asking questions about the ridiculous intrusion of a "clownishe younge man" into the ordered world of court by moving the narrative forward. Una appears at the court complaining that "her father and mother an ancient King and Queene, had bene by an huge dragon many years shut vp in a brasen Castle, who thence suffred them not to yssew."[56] She asks Gloriana, the Faerie Queene, "to assygne her some one of her knights to take on that exployt."[57] It is at this point that the "clownishe younge man" speaks up:

> Presently that clownish person vpstarting, desired that aduenture: whereat the Queene much wondering, and the Lady much gainesaying, yet he earnestly importuned his desire.[58]

There are good reasons for believing that the Knight of Holinesse has a pure heart, because there is a long historical tradition, extending back to Chretien de Troyes[59] and Wolfram Von Eschenbach,[60] that provide a model for a clownish man with a pure heart who intercedes in the affairs of the court and saves what the more educated courtly knights could not *precisely on the basis of his clownish simplicity*.

But a reading of the *Letter* in which the comical element is eliminated in favor of a more serious reading on the basis of an *a priori* desire to find a serious Spenser portraying a serious Redcrosse is not entirely based in a critical engagement with the text itself. In fact, the poet is offering a Derridean choice between the *extinction* of Redcrosse's "clownishe" aspect for a more serious aspect and the mere *suppression* of Redcrosse's "clownishe" aspect that continues to affect his behavior from the margins. How the reader decides this matter makes an enormous difference in how they read

---

55 William Nelson, *The Poetry of Edmund Spenser: A Study* (New York, NY: Columbia University Press, 1963), 150.

56 This, of course, brings up the issue of how Una got out of Eden if the Dragon had *completely* shut down the possibility of issuing forth.

57 Spenser, *Faerie Queene (2001)*, 717.

58 Ibid.

59 Chrétien de Troyes, *Perceval : The Story of the Grail*, trans. Burton Raffel (New Haven: Yale University Press, 1999).

60 Wolfram Von Eschenbach, *Parzival*, trans. A. T. Hatto, Penguin Classics (New York, NY: Penguin Books, 1980).

the poem.

Una's Convenient Magical Armor

Spenser provides clues about his intention in the *Letter*, as the reader is treated to a scene in which Una first gainsays the request of the "clownishe younge man" as being unworthy of being her companion on such an important journey. Una accepts him as her hero only *after* she offers him a piece of armor which she conveniently has brought with her to court:

> In the end the Lady told him that vnlesse that armour which she brought, would serue him (that is the armour of a Christian man specified by Saint Paul v. Ephes.) that he could not succeed in that enterprise, which being forthwith put upon him with dewe furnitures thereunto, he seemed the goodliest man in al that company, and was well liked of the Lady.[61]

This represents a switch in the mind of Una that can be placed in a simple philosophical context. Una rejects George as an individual—as an individual he is too "clownishe"—but she accepts him only after he takes from her the external armor *that others had worn before him*. This changes her perception of him from individual George to the more general Redcrosse, who, like the man in "Socrates is a man" in both Plato's dialectic and Aristotle's logic, stands a predicate attached to a more ontologically real subject. This mimics the *Letter*'s focus on general intent to the exclusion of individual accidents. But this switch is problematic, for it means that Una, who stands as the principle of unity in the poem, deals with Redcrosse as a typological abstraction and that her perception of him has no bearing on his actual individuality *as George*, which is merely suppressed, not extinguished, with the change in her perception of him from "clownishe younge man" to her hero.

The modern insistence on the ontology of the historical *Letter* is odd, if one thinks about it. Una just happens to carry around with her the armor of the book of *Ephesians*, and she can pull it out at will. The question 'Where did she get it?' may be answered by the Modern critic, who would allow Spenser his "suspension of disbelief" in service of a higher good: she got it by being the daughter of the King and Queen of prelapsarian Eden. The postmodern critic might question such fictional constructs as having been produced by the poet and might pontificate on the impossibility of Una having access to the glorious armor spoken of in Paul's letter in the

---

61 Spenser, *Faerie Queene (2001)*, 717.

"real world." They would then speak of the impossibility of reaching unity through the use of words, and some of them might even go so far as to question the existence of Una herself before deconstructing the whole affair.

A more important question for the reader is "Where can I get one?" since, if such armor ever existed, it has long since disappeared as a product of the Fall that has permanently severed the relationship between mankind and nature. The fact of the Fall means that the question could *only* be answered by switching from an ontological meaning for the Ephesian armor to an epistemological meaning. With such a switch, all the tricky difficulties with locating the existence of Una's armor in reality disappear, just they disappeared in Ovid's imitation of Pythagoras' speech in his exile from the universe of nature to an purely intellectual—read epistemological—reconstruction of nature in his own mind. This is the reason that Spenser can portray Una and her armor *only* in his work of fiction. Fiction opens up the world to answering questions that cannot be addressed in a world confined by the rules of ontological reality. This move has the same basis that made Plato's *Parmenides* possible, where the philosopher opened up a fictional universe to make distinctions that would be thought impossible in the strict ontological world of Aristotlelian science.

Driving the ontology out of Spenser's fiction comes with a price. Una's magical Ephesian armor, whose existence is guaranteed by Spenser's move out of reality into fiction, guarantees Redcrosse's success in advance of any action he takes in the poem; since the failure of Redcrosse in his ends would mean the failure of the God who granted him sainthood before the beginning of his quest and even before Una's imposition of the name of Redcrosse. This takes the wind out of the narrative if one believes, as Kellogg seems to believe, that Redcrosse is on a circular journey, falling away from his holiness and then returning to it.

Redcrosse's status as saved is defined by God, but both Augustine and Calvin had denied the will access to knowledge of its own salvation. It is clear at the beginning of the poem that Redcrosse does not know this about himself. Only after his adventure is over does he recognize that he has been given his "goodwill" by God in advance of any action he takes. Redcrosse, therefore, does not travel out of his holiness and back to it, as Kellogg alleges. He is on a linear journey of discovery from not knowing his place in the universe to knowledge of it. His adventure focuses on his *failure* to integrate himself into the rational court of educated men that Gloriana surrounds herself with. By portraying Redcrosse's journey in epistemological terms, the reader can experience the consequences of traveling down the road of sin of pride without actually experiencing the realities of the *ontological experience* of sinning, which could be quite severe if not for the poet's assurance that George is saved from the beginning. The reader cannot have the same assurances of his own salvation, and therefore must act differently than the hero of the Book of Holinesse does. In service to this ideal, Spenser deliberately blocks his readers from following his hero, not only vertically back to God, but also horizontally in his beastly characteristic of his warlike assumptions of power, which Spenser associates with the sin of pride.

This move has its source in a passage we have seen before in Aristotle's *Politics*, which I repeat in its entirety because of its importance in understanding Spenser's motivations:

> For man, when perfected, is the best of animals, but, when separated from law and justice, he is the worst of all; since armed injustice is the more dangerous, and he is equipped at birth with arms, meant to be used by intelligence and virtue, which he may use for the worst ends. Wherefore, if he have not virtue, he is the most unholy and the most savage of animals, and the most full of lust and gluttony. But justice is the bond of men in states, for the administration of justice, which is the determination of what is just, is the principle of order in political society.[62]

The result of the poet's distancing his readers from his hero on Aristotelian grounds is that he portrays his hero along the lines of an uneducated man who takes his heroic status for granted, wandering in the wilderness outside of court and civilization, while remaining ignorant to the very end of his adventure of the fact that his success comes, not from his own will, but from God's *a priori* grant of grace. Augustine's take on Aeneas, not Virgil's, provides the model for the reader, who is not supposed to imitate the "clownishe younge man" Redcrosse, a character who takes his salvation for granted and who makes all sorts of mistakes that would damn a reader who could not be sure of his or her having such grace in their own ontologically real lives. Instead, the reader, like Augustine had himself, is supposed to look for another way than direct imitation of the fictional hero in their own substantially real, individual, and ontological existences.

---

62 Aristotle, *Politics*, 1253a31-39.

The Passive Man of Action

The Presence of Inequality in *The Faerie Queene*

That something is not right with Redcrosse is apparent in the opening stanza, when he is introduced as a gentle knight "pricking on the plaine, / Ycladd in mightie armes and siluer shielde" (I.i.1.1-2). The reader soon learns that the "old dints of deepe wounds" and "markes of many a bloudy fielde" that the reader can plainly see on the surface of Redcrosse's armor do not have their origin in any action of his, because "armes till that time did he neuer wield" (I.i.3.3-5). This means that the "markes" that he is wearing on his surface bear no relation to any action he has taken in the past.

In this observation, Spenser is asking his readers to consider the disjunction between the poet's external expression of Redcrosse's character and his interior virtue. On the one hand, the reader may be assured by the poet's insistence that "Right faithfull true he was in deede and word" (I.i.2.7) and that his interior virtue is guaranteed on the outside by the poet's citation of his "deare remembrance of his dying Lord, / For whose sweete sake that glorious badge he wore" (I.i.2.2-3). This can makes sense in an Augustinian universe. Christ's appearance in the world was viewed as the first and only intrusion of vertical truth into the horizontal world of time. After that time, the baton of holiness has passed from one human being to another through faith in that miraculous event. Spenser can be seen to close the gap of reference by tying his exterior portrayal of Redcrosse to an interior faith in Christ. In such a reading, the reader is tempted to view Redcrosse as whole and perfect at the beginning of his adventure.

On the other hand, the same stanza introduces imbalances in Redcrosse's external demeanor in relation to his faith. The poet tells his readers that "his cheere did seem too solemne sad" (I.i.2.8) and that "nothing did he dread, but euer was ydrad" (I.i.2.9). While this may be true, the truth of his being "ydrad" comes from his God-given armor, not from his will.[1] The dissimilarity between his internal mind and his external action seems a small thing at the beginning of the poem; but over time, these small details will grow into major obstacles to Redcrosse's completion of his adventure.

Aesthetic Assumptions about Inequality

This increase in tension is one of the major differences between modern aesthetic assumptions and Spenser's Reformation assumptions about art. Modern aesthetic assumptions are based in the perception that the world has fallen into a state of disrepair and that it is within the power of the human will that has dedicated itself to a higher art to restore balance back to nature. One of the best examples of this sort of cyclical aesthetic thought may be seen in Jean-Jacques Rousseau's "A Discourse on the Arts and Sciences,"[2] an essay in which Rousseau' borrows the descent of man from a golden age to an age of corruption from Ovid's *Metamorphoses* and makes it the basis for his feeling that it is *only* the selfishness of mankind that is responsible for the fall of mankind from a state of nature. Rousseau feels that it is within the power of mankind to throw off their selfish desires for a more collective action and thereby restore mankind to a state of nature

---

1 The reader will be better able to judge this fact after they have been given more evidence of Redcrosse's dread. In canto vii, for instance, the poet introduces Orgoglio by having Redcrosse being awakened by a "dreadfull sownd" (I.vii.7.4) after he has taken his armor off. The thread of dread is repeated in the poet's description of Orgoglio, whom the poet refers to as

> An hideous Geaunt horrible and hye,
> That with his tallnesse seemd to threat the skye,
> The ground eke groned vnder him for dreed. (I.vii.8.4-6)

Orgoglio advances "towardes him with dreadfull fury" (I.vii.11.3), but after Redcrosse has been defeated by the brute force of Orgoglio, Duessa turns his purposeless anger to a greater purpose:

> ...for to make her dreaded more of men,
> And peoples harts with awfull terrour tye.... (I.vii.16.6-7)

The use of dread in Redcrosse's encounter with Orgoglio indicates the misplaced nature of his pride in Redcrosse's own will rather than placing his faith in the armor of God. Here in canto i, he is thinking of the dread he is able to generate in others, but he ignores the possibility of his own internally generated dread, possibly on account of his never having been in a battle.

2 Jean-Jacques Rousseau. "A Discourse on the Arts and Sciences," in *The Social Contract and the Discourses*, ed. G. D. H. Cole (New York, NY: J. M. Dent, 1993).

by an act of will.

This is surely one of the reasons that Hamilton steps back from engagement with any particular critical position in his 2001 edition of the poem, remaining balanced in his superior position as arbiter of many competing reader responses. Hamilton maintains critical distance because it allows him to maintain the freedom to choose between competing ways of looking at the world in a literary environment in which the choices one makes with one's will is an important determiner of the outcome of one's life.

The problem with modern assumptions about the resolution to the problem of ontology and epistemology in the human will is that Descartes could not avoid the breaking of the unity of philosophy into two parts that cannot be resolved through the rational means that gave birth to them.[3]

The position of Enlightenment philosophy is the 1st person perspective by which Descartes resolved everything into a willing mind. He posed a monadic irreducible mind that had its own prior private language much in the same way that Augustine had proposed a pre-linguistic language of the heart. The problem with Descartes' configuration of his private language was given by Wittgenstein in his *Philosophical Inventions*, where he proposed his famous argument about a "beetle in a box."[4] That argument turns on the fact that one can have a beetle in box, but what one is thinking about in their private language may not be the same thing that another human being is thinking when they think about beetles in their private language box. The only way to resolve the meaning of private language is to speak one's meaning in a public sphere.

Roger Scruton calls this public perspective the 3rd person perspective. While it solves many of of the problems of the 1st person perspective, the problem with the 3rd person perspective is that the solid foundation of language is undermined by the differences between the meaning that the speaker intends his words to have and the meanings that the reader brings to the task of unpacking the meaning put forward in the public space.[5]

These two perspectives on language both follow from Descartes' proposal of the Mind-Body problem at the beginning of modern philosophy. But Spenser was operating in an environment in which Augustine was still

---

3 For this section, I am relying on Roger Scruton's *From Descartes to Wittgenstein: A Short History of Modern Philosophy*, in which Scruton divides philosophy into two distinct camps based in the same set of beliefs.

4 Ludwig Wittgenstein. *Philosophical Investigations*, trans. G. E. M. Anscombe, 3rd ed. (Upper Salle River, NJ: Prentice Hall, 1958), §293.

5 This leads to the problem of reader response theory.

an important thinker, and he inserted a break within the complete universe that Descartes was attempting to paper over in his definition of the problem that nevertheless resulted in a division between mind and body. Augustine was far more pessimistic about the possibility that mankind could ever resolve its human nature with nature itself, as mankind was been permanently sundered from nature by the Fall and has no ability to restore itself or Eden without the grace of God. This caused him to propose a breach within nature that could not be overcome by the means of reason.

This has a major effect on the reader's disposition towards philosophy, as well as art. The role of art in Spenser's day was not to make imperfect things whole, as it is in the modern world. For Spenser, imperfect things will always exist. The role of art in Spenser's poem is to magnify our imperfect human beings towards an as-yet-unrealized future perfection. This is different from the modern stance on the poem, where critics maintain their own perfection in regards to a weaker-because-not-yet-modern reader. Hamilton's 1977 edition of the poem was flawed on account of the editor's offering of readings based on his critical assumption that he knew what Spenser was doing in his poem. By 2001, Hamilton had stepped back from such assumptions about the mind of the poet, but he stayed true to his own critical assumptions. This led him to step back from the poem to a safe critical distance from which he could maintain a metaphysical perspective that he thought was missing from his earlier work.

Hamilton's move away from judgment about unequal things to a secure metaphysical state in which all things are put back in balance appears to be a mistake. In Spenser's Augustinian universe, the metaphysical perspective is unavailable, not only to the poet and his contemporaries but to modern readers, as well. The situation of reading described by Spenser is more like that described as the problem of Schrödinger's cat in modern quantum physics. Erwin Schrödinger had posited a cat in a box, but he disguised the state of being of that cat from public view. This is equivalent to a state of private language: the state of being of the cat is hidden from the public in the same way that private language obtains its meaning only in the sphere of public interaction between more than one individual person. However, when one opens up the box in the public sphere of language, people will see the cat as dead or alive, but never both. The change of state from private to public language brings with it changes in the object itself.

Critics like Hamilton who attempt to wrest metaphysical authority from such a mystery *before the box is opened* can be accused of prematurely closing off what would otherwise be an endless debate. This is as true of his

1977 edition as it is of his 2001 edition, because his changes are motivated by his attempt to rescue the aesthetic position that posits a position of metaphysical wholeness as the proper perspective for the critic to operate from. This causes Hamilton in both editions to overlook the fact that Spenser is pointing out the impossibility of achieving any metaphysical position in his poem. The inequalities sported by the poem are not to be dealt with by finding a secure position in which one can see all sides of the issue. Instead, one must read carefully to find out which positions are securely founded in the God created, *a priori* order of being and which are built up by the efforts of deceivers. This is not something that Redcrosse and Una are necessarily comfortable with at the beginning of the poem.

Drifting Without Purpose in the Wandering Wood

Although Redcrosse is accompanied by Una and her dwarf, at the first sign of bad weather all three walk into a forest "with pleasure forward led" (I.i.8.1). This emphasis on epicurean pleasure is striking, and reminds the careful reader of Augustine's rejection of pleasure as an end of human experience. Nevertheless, there were important Renaissance thinkers like Lorenzo Valla who had advocated for an epicurean approach to human experience.[6] This opens up the reader to competing ideas within the Renaissance from which the reader must choose. Making a choice between unequal ways of looking at the world is one of the points that Spenser is attempting to make in the episode of the Wandering Wood.

After they have entered the wood, Redcrosse and Una are "Ioying to heare the birdes sweete harmony" (I.i.8.2), but this comes as they have entered a protected enclave which has been "shrouded from the tempest dred" (I.i.8.3). In such an enclave, the birds "Seemd in their song to scorne the cruell sky" (I.i.8.4). This is natural behavior for birds; it is raining outside, and the birds have sought shelter in a protected wood. But their bird song scorns the larger natural environment, taking their protection for granted in the woods that shelters them from what would have to be considered a hostile nature. The question becomes whether mankind should follow them in singing songs that ignore the larger environment of hostile nature, or whether they should turn away from such frivolities. Whatever the reader decides, Redcrosse and Una seem unaware of any attendant danger as they go about "Ioying."

The trees, too, are "yclad with sommers pride" (I.i.7.4), and they

---

6 Lorenzo Valla, *On Pleasure = De Voluptate*, ed. Maristella De Panizza Lorch, trans. A. Kent Hieatt (New York, NY: Abaris Books, 1977).

Did spred so broad, that heauens light did hide,
Not perceable with power of any starre (I.i.7.5-6)

The reader may see similarities between the situation of the birds in the protected wood and the situation of the poet. Both sing songs; and the poet, who has consciously built into his poem some birds who have fled into a protected wood, has them praising the trees in a catalog form that is derived from epic poetry. But the catalog of trees ends with a warning: the Maple is "seeldom inward sound" (I.i.9.9).

Once again, the question that Spenser's text is posing is whether the outward environment is reflected in the characters or whether is it distinguished from them. Hamilton's critical posture of stepping back and allowing many points of view to play out will do no good for the characters *within* the allegory, who must decide between two incompatible alternatives. Redcrosse and Una certainly do not seem to be aware that anything is amiss in their world, and they wander on "led with delight and thus beguile the way" / Vntill the blustring storme is ouerblowne" (I.i.10.1-2). Their delight in nature gets the pair off their purpose ("way"); and when they attempt to recover their path, they find that they are lost and "wander too and fro in waies vnknowne" (I.i.10.5).

At this moment, Spenser chooses to remind us that they are "Furthest from end then, when they neerest weene" (I.i.10.6). This so frustrates them that it "makes them doubt, their wits be not their owne" (I.i.10.7) as

So many pathes, so many turnings seene,
That which of them to take, in diuerse doubt they been. (I.i.10.9)

Spenser hopes to emphasize the necessity of finding and then holding on to a purpose. Like the maple which they take so much delight in, Redcrosse and Una are perhaps not as "inward sound" as they ought to be. However, although they have lost their way, the hollow man resolves to move forward anyway, and this leads him through a "labyrinth" (I.i.11.4) to "a hollowe caue" (I.i.11.6), where he encounters the first of many abstract personifications: Errour.

Logical Confusion at the Entrance of Errour's Cave

At the entrance to the Cave of Errour, Spenser urges his readers to make a choice from a series of incompatible alternatives, each of which is held by a character within the poem. Una's dwarf urges Redcrosse to "Fly fly," as "this is no place for liuing men" (I.i.13.8-9). However, adventure is exactly what Redcrosse has been looking for, and

> The Champion stout
> Eftsoones dismounted from his courser braue,
> And to the Dwarfe a while his needlesse spere he gaue. (I.i.11.7-9)

Una is more is cautious, and she urges Redcrosse to exercise caution himself:

> Be well aware, quoth then that Ladie milde,
> Least suddaine mischiefe ye too rash prouoke:
> The danger hid, the place vnknowne and wilde,
> Breedes dreadfull doubts: Oft fire is without smoke,
> And perill without show: therefore your stroke
> Sir knight with-hold, till further triall made. (I.i.12.1-6).

Redcrosse then dismisses Una's argument, telling her

> Ah Ladie (sayd he) shame were to reuoke
> The forward footing for an hidden shade:
> Vertue giues her selfe light, through darkenesse for to wade.
> (I.i.12.7-9).

This exchange seem to place the conflict in a dialectical framework: either Redcrosse should act impulsively and charge in without knowing what he is going to confront, or he should remain passive until he has enough information to make a decision. In the dialectical picture, Una seems to have the better case. Redcrosse had not yet acted when Una's dwarf warned him to fly, and he is so reckless that he gives away his "needlesse spere" before rushing headlong into meet whatever awaits him in the cave. In this reading of the dialectical situation, Redcrosse is clearly making a mistake when he lunges forward into the Cave of Errour.

Despite his affectation of critical distance that he believes excludes him from taking sides, Hamilton definitely sides with Una through both editions in the conflict of views that are presented to the reader. Like Una, who urges restraint before action, Hamilton plans to wait until he has enough information before making a decision to act. After all, when he had found that he had been constructing meaning on the basis of his own *a priori* assumptions rather than engaging the *a posteriori* evidence before him, he stepped back to a more secure metaphysical place in order to preserve his critical objectivity.

The problem with the posture of Una and Hamilton is precisely one of their passivity. Within the poem, the question immediately arises of when there will be enough information to act. In Hamilton's case, he is not obligated to act at all: he is a reader. This is because of an inherent asymmetry between reading and acting. Reading is associated with perpetual openness; and readers can turn a work over in their minds forever, finding new and as-yet-un-thought-of meanings. As a critic, Hamilton cannot be blamed for his hesitation to act in the face of newly emerging evidence.

But the same cannot be said of Una. If she waits until she has *all* information before acting, she will *never* act, because there will always be more information and more perspectives that she has not yet conceived. Una presumably shares with the reader the desire to achieve maximum freedom for her beleaguered parents. But she realizes that her passive position[7] is not enough to free her parents, and therefore she must escape perfect Eden, surrounded by brazen walls, to travel to Gloriana's court in search of a man of action to accomplish her goals for her.[8] The poet seems to be asking what her perfect metaphysical position is worth if Una needs others to *act* on her metaphysical knowledge? This, in turn, brings up the question of whether her metaphysical position is as perfect as she thinks it is.

Redcrosse differs from Una in being an actor, and he decides not to stand passive waiting for more information before acting. He plunges in. But being an actor has a different set of obligations from those that underlie Una and the critic who stands outside the necessity of choosing between meanings. Action *takes away* possibilities, as actors make choices in favor of this or that action from a host of conceivable choices; and this means that actors must concern themselves with making not just any choice but *the correct choice* in assessing their environment, because the choices they make in the world of action are irrevocable.

---

7 Whether this is because she is a woman or whether she has lived her life outside the world of time and action in a metaphysically protected realm of Eden, she already realizes that she needs the help of others to accomplish her goal.

8 This brings up the interesting question of how Una escapes from Eden if the Dragon is so powerful a force that her parents are afraid to "yssew" forth. Is this a flaw in Spenser's design of his poetic universe? Is this on account of a weakness on the part of the Dragon? Does it have to with the timidity of Una's parents? In my opinion, we cannot rule out any of these cases until we have received more evidence; but I differ from Hamilton's perpetual skepticism about making any decision about the meaning of the poem, because I believe that the reader will eventually have enough information to decide between these incompatible alternatives.

Redcrosse's Encounter with Errour

When Redcrosse plunges into the Cave of Errour without his "needlesse spere," Errour grabs Redcrosse by the throat and threatens to strangle him. Una, thinking her knight is about to be killed (not for the last time), panics:

> His Lady sad to see his sore constraint,
> Cride out, Now now Sir knight, shew what ye bee,
> Add faith vnto your force, and be not faint:
> Strangle her, els she sure will strangle thee. (I.i.19.1-4)

Maureen Quilligan notes that, although Una asks him to "Add faith vnto your force," Redcrosse continues to focus on using his force alone:

> That when he heard, in great perplexitie,
> His gall did grate for griefe and high disdaine,
> And knitting all his force got one hand free,
> Wherewith he grypt her gorge with so great paine,
> That soone to loose her wicked bands did her constraine. (I.i.19.5-9).

On this basis, Quilligan denies that Redcrosse "had the faith then."[9] According to the modern critic, it is only after he meets Fidelia in canto x that she is able to teach him the true meaning of adding faith unto force. The desired end of knowledge is the understanding that "to add faith unto the understanding given by faith is to realize that the force is not one's own."[10]

Quilligan goes on to note the balance between the light of Redcrosse's armor and its resemblance to darkness:

> The Redcrosse Knight's naïveté about language is in fact a large part of the problem. For instance, at the threshold of Errour's cave he readily repeats the proverb, "Virtue gives her self light, darkness for to wade," taking it primarily in the etymological sense of *virtus*, or manly strength. Spenser undercuts this notion by showing that the knight confronts Errour before her den, it is his armor that gives some illumination, but it is only a "little glooming light," which is, in fact, "much like the shade."[11]

Quilligan's reading is in line with her postmodern assumptions about what

---

9 Quilligan, *Language of Allegory*, 118.
10 Ibid., 119.
11 Ibid., 36.

the passage is supposed to tell us.

Quilligan's reading is a vast improvement over previous readings of the passage, but not all of the evidence provided by the poet is taken into account in her reading. For instance, Una's urging Redcrosse to "shew what ye be" is ambiguous. Una herself presumes that the showing in "shew what ye be" will be of the exterior armor that represents his "true" self. But in the *Letter to Raleigh* she had translated her sense of reference from the individual George to a more unified but figural Redcrosse in order to retain her perception of him as a perfect person. This switch is masked from uncareful readers by the fact that Una is descended from the King and Queene of the unified Kingdom of Eden; but she and Eden can only be seen in Spenser's fictional construction of Faery, which can picture an unfallen universe that is not possible to encounter in ontological reality.

Redcrosse, on the other hand, remains as God created him, a creature with a limited and imperfect reason; but he has access to his own individual and ontologically real self without a translation into the alien terms of "poetic metaphor" that give him on his exterior a status of perfection that he does not deserve if the reader could look to the inside of the character's heart. This is a thing that Una ignored when he was first presented to her until he could be seen to fit into her entirely fictional armor.

Redcrosse ignores Una's advice to add faith unto his force, because he is not interested in proving himself to Una, who has satisfied herself of his worthiness at the beginning of the adventure by granting him the external armor of faith that others have worn before him. That exchange changed Una's perception of individual George to figural Redcrosse, but George does not disappear in that exchange. This is why Redcrosse continues to operate on the assumption that he has been chosen for the power of his natural body, and this is why he responds to the call of Una to "shew what ye be," not with the supplement of an exteriorly granted *a priori* faith, but with his more immediate and not inconsiderable manly force.

The modern critic, operating under dialectical constraints, may be tempted to decide which character has grasped onto the correct reading of experience here, but in fact neither does. Both characters within the poem assume that Redcrosse is on an equal footing with Errour in the fight that ensues. Redcrosse goes into the fight blind to the monster he will be facing, and he finds her more than he was prepared to handle. Una pleas with Redcrosse to "Strangle her, else she sure will strangle thee" (I.i.19.4). But to the reader who stands outside the text it is apparent (or should be apparent) that Una's Ephesian armor is enough to guarantee victory in every battle Redcrosse engages in without any effort on Redcrosse's part, because if he is not given victory over Errour, the blame must be placed at the feet of God Himself.

That brings the reader to the question of why Redcrosse goes into battle with Errour in the first place *unless he does not know the power that has been bestowed on him with his arms.* It also calls into question why Una is so worried about his ultimate victory, unless she does not know the power conferred on the recipient of her sacred arms. The power of God to fix a permanent bias towards good in the universe by His metaphysical ability to create an ontological reality is beyond the ability of human reason to recreate directly in their epistemology. Thus, the human Spenser can only portray the sacred ontology of God in an epistemologically deconstructable fiction. Humans, using their imperfect minds, may be tempted to reach the end of their inquiry into the ends of fiction in an ontological reality, but Spenser seems to be holding off on any such judgment until such a time as he has reached the end of his narrative and all the available information has been gathered.

Similes of Patience and Immediate Action

As he narrates the event, Spenser points to the mind of his protagonist:

> Thus ill bestedd, and fearefull more of shame,
> Then of the certaine perill he stood in,
> Halfe furious vnto his foe he came,
> *Resolv'd in minde* all suddenly to win,
> Or soone to lose, before he once would lin. (I.i.24.1-5 italics mine).

As he points to the mind of Redcrosse, Spenser could be echoing the first of Horace's *Satires*. In that work, Horace addresses the great patron of pagan poetry in Augustan Rome, Maecenas:

> How comes it, Maecenas, that no man living is content with the lot which either his choice has given him, or chance has thrown in his way, but each has praise for those who follow other paths?[12]

Horace goes on to point out the position taken by men of all ages that the

---

12 Horace, *Satires, Epistles, and Ars Poetica, with an English Translation*, trans. H. R. Fairclough, Rev. ed., Loeb Classical Library (Cambridge: Harvard University Press, 1961), 1.1.

grass is always greener on the other side of the fence. In particular, he points to the soldiers' and merchants' envy of each other's condition:

> "O happy traders!" cries the soldier, as he feels the weight of years, his frame now shattered with hard service. On the other hand, when southern gales toss the ship, the trader cries: "A soldier's life is better. Do you ask why? There is the battle clash, and in a moment of time comes speedy death or joyous victory."[13]

The soldier thinks the trader is happy, because he is not broken down by years of fighting; but the trader looks at the soldier as winning his battles all at once without having to wait out long periods of delay before he finds out whether his ventures have succeeded or not. In his division of experience, Horace is pointing out the folly of the specialist's role in the general universe. No one is perfectly happy in Horace's universe, and each specialist looks at others as having something that is lacking in their own lives.

As we have seen, Spenser is following Augustine, a man who does not believe that the individual human being can imitate the wholeness of God's created ontology. In echoing Horace's vision of the warrior who wishes to win all at once or die in the immediate attempt, the poet is pointing to the fact that his warrior protagonist could use a little more of the merchant's patience, which, though not enough to complete him, is nevertheless desirable. It is on this point that the poet Spenser distinguishes himself from Redcrosse, as he interposes a series of epic similes, drawn from a lifetime of continuing education. These amplifications lengthen the distance between the direct imitation of Redcrosse's action and the completion of his battle.

The first epic amplification comes when Errour sees Redcrosse and starts to flee. Redcrosse stops her

> As Lyon fierce vpon the flying pray,
> And with his trenchand blade her boldly kept
> From turning backe, and forced her to stay…. (I.i.17.2-4)

After Redcrosse has forced fleeing Errour to stay so he can fight her, Spenser chimes with another epic simile in which he compares the "sore" (I.i.22.1) that is visited on Redcrosse to the swelling of the river Nilus beyond its banks (I.i.21). This simile seems at first to be directed at Errour, but it can also be profitably be read as a comment on Redcrosse, who has over-swelled his own banks before settling back into an equitable position once again.

---

13 Ibid.

The simile calls into question the wisdom of Redcrosse in this situation by pointing out that none of this would have happened if Redcrosse had had an education and not been instead a "clownishe" rube who rushes into battle "with timely pride" (I.i.21.2) before thinking.

It is precisely his lack of education that gets Redcrosse into trouble in his worldly quest. What gets him out of trouble is his armor, which is not his own. The reader is given a picture of a Redcrosse who travels blind through the world, relying on instincts that are likened to the "loathly frogs and toades, which eyes did lacke" (I.i.20.7) that Errour vomits forth, and not on an education that would have told him to weigh the consequences of such a fruitless engagement with that "monster vile" in *advance* of his impulsive action. Redcrosse's instincts will prove to be wrong more than once before his adventure is over.

It is important to note that is only when Errour sees "His forces faile" and that he "can no lenger fight" (I.i.22.3) that she attacks him. Before that, she has engages in a defensive posture, much like a squid who sprays black ink in order to conceal her escape. She disgorges "books and papers" (I.i.20.6), as well as "Such vgly monstrous shapes elswhere may no man reed" (I.i.21.9). It is only after she has vomited out the things that made her fearsome, that his protagonist lops off the head of Errour. But the children of Errour survive, though they are so insignificant that though they "him encombred sore" they "could not hurt at all" (I.i.22.9). At this point Spenser chimes in with a third epic simile in which Redcrosse is compared with a "gentle Shepheard" (I.i.23.1) who bats away the gnats that encumber him "with his clownish hands" (I.i.23.8) and not to the heroes that populate more serious epics. Furthermore, it is the childen of Errour, not he, who drink every last drop of Errour's blood, meaning that even in death, her body continues to give sustenance to further error.

Spenser's point seems to be that the whole encounter does not matter. Redcrosse's has always had the power to defeat her simply by "virtue" of his gleaming armor without taking any action whatsoever, but he is interested in trying his own power. It is significant that in the end Redcrosse's force yields no results, as Errour is devoured by her own children; and Redcrosse's victory over Errour turns out to be no victory at all *in rational terms*.

But there is more to this episode. The "vgly monstrous shapes [that] elswhere may no man reed" may be profitably read as representing the forces of Spenser's own imagination. This is no accident. Spenser seems to want to distinguish Faery, which exists only in the reader's mind (epistemology), from the very real and undeconstructable work of God's ontological creation. This is the classic distinction of art as a human experience that imitates the prior work of nature but is not equivalent to it. That idea was replaced by Baumgarten's modern aesthetics. Unlike the modern equivalence between art and reality, Spenser's deconstructable art is not to be confused with the end of literary experience. Faery is a temporary stopping place where readers can amplify their experience outside of time before returning to the world better for having visited it. This is the function of Spenser's typological allegory: it is a temporary detour from literal reality that nevertheless holds the key to ontological reality for careful readers. But to make an end out of allegory is to miss the point of Spenser's work.

This is the problem suffered by (of all people) Una. After witnessing Redcrosse's encounter with Errour "from farre" (I.i.27.1), she takes no notice of the fact that Errour could not hurt him on account of his holy armor, nor of the fact that she deconstructs without any help from her hero. Instead, she reverses her previous warning about not going in to the Cave of Errour in the first place and congratulates her champion on his victory over his foe:

> Faire knight, borne vnder happie starre,
> Who see your vanquisht foes before you lye:
> Well worthy be you of that Armory,
> Wherein ye haue great glory wonne this day,
> And prooud your strength on a strong enimie.... (I.i.27.3-7)

The fact is that she has no more learned the lesson of the episode than Redcrosse has, which is that not every fight is worth having. Had he made "triall" of his experience in advance of his impulsive action, he would have seen that error is a permanent feature of the imaginative landscape and that the best thing is to ignore her (especially since Errour is running away from him in the first place) and stick to a deeper purpose.

The Lessons of Redcrosse's Encounter with Errour

The educated reader can read the symbolic universe in which Redcrosse is an actor in a moral landscape. Thus, they can presumably see when he is making a mistake. But whether Redcrosse has access to the relative terms on which Spenser draws his moral landscape for his readers is not as clear. The reader must account for Redcrosse's poor choices and not ignore them based on their desire to save him as a perfect knight that they might have thought they were encountering when they first met him. As it is, both characters within the fiction are beguiled with delight, the birds' song, and the epic catalog of hollow trees as they wander as aimlessly out of the Wandering Wood as happy as they were when they entered on account of a storm.

By contrast, the poet Spenser has learned the lessons that Una and Redcrosse have not. He has recognized his own limits and has sought to supplement them with his vast learning.[14] Nevertheless, he does not tip his hand to his reader every time. This is surely one the reasons that he begins his simile in which he likens him to a "Lyon" with the misappellation of his knight as an "Elfe" (I.i.17.1). Spenser is not lying to the reader. He is pointing to Redcrosse's errant perception of himself and his situation rather than the poet's status as holder of a metaphysical truth. This is designed to give the reader a warning to sort the actual truth from their perception of the truth and not to trust even the poet's creation implicitly. Only a careful reader will learn to mistrust Redcrosse's perception of himself; the poor reader will continue to rely on his *a priori* armor that will guarantee his success in every adventure but will not pay enough attention to the flood of weakness that they will encounter in the journey of the errant Redcrosse.

After the end of his excursion into the Cave of Errour, he turns "backward" (I.i.28.2)—and here we must note the contrast with the "forward footing" that Redcrosse feels it would be "shame to reuoke" before he embarked on his mission that in the end has accomplished nothing—and follows the path that "beaten was most plaine" (I.i.28.3) "unto the end" (I.i.28.5). This leads them both "out of the wood" (I.i.28.6). Redcrosse seems to be learning to follow the path of those who have gone before him and not to get distracted by "any byway bend" (I.i.28.4). But Spenser is very careful to limit the education of the "clownishe" Redcrosse by carefully noting that his backward journey that paradoxically moves him "forward on his way" is accomplished "with God to frend" (I.i.28.7). God's friendship is enough to guarantee Redcrosse's ends, but He guides mankind's steps both backward and forward. The *teleological* purpose of human life is up to individual human beings to discover. This sense of teleological direction is given *a posteriori* to our God-given *a priori* faith and must be learned. Thus far, the reader has seen Redcrosse walking though the world in a random fashion, being granted victory not through any effort of will on his part but through an *a priori* grant of faith of which he remains unconscious.

---

14 For the vast catalog of Spenser's learning, see James Nohrnberg, *The Analogy of the Faerie Queene* (Princeton, NJ: Princeton University Press, 1976).

Comparing Spenser's Treatment of Redcrosse's Battle with His Sources

The ultimate source for battle with Errour is the final battle between Aeneas and Turnus in the *Aeneid*,[15] in which Aeneas triumphs over his rival. The original story is as follows: Aeneas has his foe at his mercy. It appears for a short moment to be willing to spare Turnus' life, but then he sees that Turnus is wearing the belt of his fallen comrade Pallas. This so enrages Aeneas that he kills Turnus with the words "Tis Pallas, Pallas who with this stroke sacrifices thee, and takes atonement of thy guilty blood!"[16] This final act of violence could have been seen even by a Renaissance poet as justified in Virgil's pagan universe by the poet's sense of outrage at the toll taken by war on the bonds of friendship.

This sets the tone for Ariosto's rewriting of the culminating rage of Aeneas in the final episode of his *Orlando Furioso*, in which the pagan Rodomonte appears at the wedding of Bradamante and Ruggiero and accuses Ruggiero of having undergone a "change of faith" when he converted from Islam to Christianity.[17] As a good Christian poet, the Renaissance poet Ariosto expands Virgil's purely political contest into battle with a religious context; and he changes the rage of Aeneas with which Virgil ends his poem to a Christian calm that is disturbed by an irreligious foe. At the end of Ariosto's battle, Rodomonte has been stabbed, and Ruggiero has overcome him. Ruggiero then offers the traditional Crusader solution to the clash of cultures: he offers to let Rodomonte live as long as he agreed to live in a hierarchically-ordered world in which pagan values are forever subordinated to Christian values. On account of the shame of being asked to live a subordinated life, Rodomonte chooses to continue to struggle:

> The thought of death the pagan less affrights
> Than of betraying the least sign of fear.[18]

Ariosto then distinguishes the two combatants in a simile in which he ascribes skill to his Christian hero and rage to Ruggiero's pagan foe:

> A mastiff under a ferocious hound
> Whose fangs are fast embedded in its throat
> In vain will writhe and struggle on the ground,

---

15 *Aeneid* in Virgil, *Virgil*, XII.919-953.
16 Ibid., XII.948-949.
17 Lodovico Ariosto, *Orlando Furioso (the Frenzy of Orlando): A Romantic Epic*, trans. Barbara Reynolds, The Penguin Classics (New York, NY: Penguin, 1975), XLVI.106.2.
18 Ariosto, *Orlando Furioso*, XLVI.137.5-6.

> Its eyes ablaze, and-flecked with spume its coat;
> It knows that in its enemy is found
> A greater strength, a greater skill, though not
> More rage; so now the pagan must despair
> Of throwing off his conqueror, Ruggier.[19]

But Rodomonte is not ready to give in so easily. Being an ill-behaved pagan, Rodomonte's rage is accompanied with a furtive deceptiveness that is intended to hide his true motivations from his calm and wholly truthful foe:

> [Rodomonte] too had drawn his dagger in the fray
> And now attempts to use it furtively.[20]

Such deception does not work on the newly converted Ruggiero, who only wants to live his life in a world ordered according to godly righteousness and not according to Machiavellian principles of pagan rule based on rage and force:

> Ruggiero sees the danger straight away:
> Stabbed in the back he knows that he will be
> If here and now he does not end the strife
> By cutting short the evil pagan's life.[21]

This forces the issue from one in which Christian and pagan could live their lives in an orderly, hierarchical peace in a world of relative values to one in which Ruggiero is forced by external events to make an absolutely black and white decision of life or death that excludes pagan participation in an ordered society. Like Redcrosse after him, Ruggiero "manages to pull his right arm free,"[22] and he then takes appropriate action:

> Raising his arm as high as would suffice,
> He plunged his dagger in that awesome brow,
> Retrieving it not once, but more than twice.
> To Acheron's sad shores, that spirit now,
> Freed from its body, colder far than ice,
> Fled cursing from the world, to disavow
> The right which all his life he had defied

---

19 Ibid., XLVI.138.
20 Ibid., XLVI.139.3-4.
21 Ibid., XLVI.139.4-8.
22 Ibid., XLVI.139.2.

> With insolence and arrogance and pride.[23]

With the dispatch of his enemy by a calm Ruggiero, who is driven to extreme measures by the rage of the enemy other and not by any internal motivation on his part, Ariosto's poem ends.

Like Ariosto, who feels the need to make significant changes to Virgil's ending, Spenser seems not to be satisfied with Ariosto's resolution of the rage of Aeneas in a Christian calm disturbed by only an external other. While it is true that Spenser is translating the heroic struggle of Ruggiero to get one hand free and so to kill his enemy, he also folds into Redcrosse's action some less than flattering actions from Ariosto's portrayal of Rodomonte. Of particular note is Spenser's returning the rage of Aeneas to the center of his protagonist, which Ariosto had excised from his picture of his hero. As such, Spenser translates Ariosto's

> The thought of death the pagan less affrights
> Than of betraying the least sign of fear.[24]

into

> Thus ill bestedd, and fearefull more of shame,
> Then of the certaine perill he stood in,
> Halfe furious vnto his foe he came,
> Resolv'd in minde all suddenly to win,
> Or soone to lose, before he once would lin. (I.i.24.1-5).

This places the burden squarely on the mind of Redcrosse to behave in an appropriate manner that has very little to do with the rage or calm of the other. The reader can see that the "Halfe furious" Redcrosse is not behaving entirely appropriately.

At the same time as he is copying Ariosto's work, Spenser removes the passage from the end of Ariosto's poem, where it serves as an appropriate ending to a long struggle between Christianity and pagan religion, placing it instead as the first episode at the beginning of his own poem. In doing so, Spenser undermines the importance of the metaphysical struggle between Redcrosse and Errour. Errour is fleeing, not the individual Redcrosse, but his holy armor. It is only Redcrosse's desire to engage Errour's individual nature that causes him to stop her in her tracks and make her fight him. Once he has engaged her, he finds himself engaged in an equal fight only

---

23 Ibid., XLVI.140.
24 Ibid., XLVI.137.5-6.

because *Redcrosse* is ignoring the power of his arms, not only to strike fear into his enemies, but to win every battle he engages in.

While the result of his battle may be seen as Redcrosse having struck a blow for justice, truth, and right, Redcrosse does not in fact kill the error of Errour. What is more, and unlike Ariosto's Christian hero, Redcrosse's defeat of Errour comes only after she has disgorged those "books and papers" (I.i.20.6) that are the source of her power to defeat mankind. These "vgly monstrous shapes elswhere may no man reed" (I.i.21.9) are the accidental products of Spenser's fiction. As such, they reflect no underlying substantial reality. But that does not mean that such errors can be ignored. It does mean that if Redcrosse is going to fight Errour that means fighting the power of her ideas, which are perpetuated as an emergent property of human artifice without foundation in God's ontological creation, and not to focus on her external body only. Spenser's Redcrosse reads Errour too literally, and therefore he misses what is important (her ideas, which survive his fight with her) for a meaningless encounter with the body of a mother who is a product of Spenserian fiction and who, even if she had ontological reality that she so clearly lacks, has already bred enough children that she can easily be replaced with her ideas untouched by Spenser's Christian hero.

In his picture of Redcrosse's battle with Errour, Spenser is attempting to deal with the problem posed by the Virgilian tradition of having his poem end on a discordant note of rage. Ariosto's solution is to justify his hero's subjugation of his enemy by laying of blame squarely on his enemy. This is not Spenser's solution to the problem of power, nor is it Augustine's. Ariosto loosens the bonds of deep affection, not only for God but for friends, in favor of a concern for the individual alone. This loosening of attachments that make social cooperation possible makes it easy to drop strong societal attachments for weak ones without any necessity of thinking about the consequences of one's own actions. In such a universe, only the consequences of others' actions matter. These actions are interpreted unsubtly in purely black and white terms. This is why the Protestant Spenser exchanges the Catholic Ariosto's last minute metaphysical resolution, which in Augustine and Calvin stands outside the boundaries of human control, for a rational solution that relies on a merely relative location of truth in his translation of Ariosto's work. In that sense, the poet Spenser shares the relative point of view that modern critics have reserved exclusively to themselves.

This relative scientific perspective on experience is not shared by the poet's protagonists, both of whom share an errant metaphysical perspective on their experience. Una, of course, comes from Eden, a place in which words mean what they say, and she does not have to worry about deceit there. But Una does not possess the power to correct the tragedy that has befallen her kingdom; and so she moves of her stable kingdom, crossing a dividing boundary out of timeless Eden into the world of time, where she finds a human being born in time who can activate what she an only conceive of in her mind. That man is Redcrosse, who has been given armor that guarantees his victory in every battle he ever undertakes, and therefore he does not worry about education, as Spenser has, but is instead concerned to win his battles all at once.

This is one of the reasons why Una translates Redcrosse's individual experience to having been born under a "happie starre" that makes him

> Well worthy...of that Armory
> Wherein ye haue great glory wonne this day
> And proou'd your strength on a strong enimie.... (I.i.27.5-7)

In her translation of Redcrosse's individual experience to the stars, Una is lessening the power of the individual actor to achieve victory over his enemies in the relative world of reason, translating away that lasting but limited power for a metaphysical guarantee that can only be had in the same fiction that created her. Thus, Una speaks the truth to Redcrosse, which is that the origin of his power over Errour resides elsewhere than in his own individuality, but she does appear to understand its origins in God, instead offering the reader a "happie starre." To Redcrosse her words sound like congratulations, and they move out of the Wandering Wood with "God to frend" (I.i.28.7). But the fact is that Redcrosse wants more than victory, he wants credit for his victories; and it is this that Spenser denies him *even if Redcrosse and Una do not know it* at this point in their adventure.

The Meeting with Archimago

The poet contrasts Redcrosse's guaranteed *a priori* goodness that acts without education with an *a posteriori* education that acts without any sense of goodness when he meets Archimago, a Protean magician who has all the power that education bring but without any of the God-given orientation to good that has been given to Redcrosse.

That Redcrosse has not learned enough of the lessons that could be had in the Cave of Errour can be seen when he leaves the Wandering Wood and continues to seek "new aduenture" (I.i.28.8) in a completely random manner that displays a lack of direction in his quest. He has to travel for a long time "before he heard of ought" (I.i.28.9). This must surely frustrate Una, who has a purpose of her own for the knight on the plains surrounding of the brazen-walled castle where her parents are trapped and where there is a Dragon who awaits defeat by Redcrosse's righteous and guaranteed-by-God-to-succeed sword. But she does not speak up, possibly because she is extremely passive and meek, possibly because she thinks more highly of Redcrosse than she should, or possibly because she knows that he is not yet ready to face such a terrible foe as the Dragon, having just witnessed his dismal performance with Errour. Because Una does not speak up and because Spenser remains silent, the reader must hold each of these options in their memory until such a time as they are given enough information on which to sort out Una's reaction.

In the meantime, Redcrosse finally "chaunst" to meet an "aged Sire" (I.i.29.1-2). There is nothing remarkable about him, and at first there is no reason for the reader or for Redcrosse to distrust him, as he is dressed as a holy man

> in long blacke weedes yclad,
> His feete all bare, his beard all hoarie gray,
> And by his belt his booke he hanging had;
> Sober he seemde, and very sagely sad,
> And to the ground his eyes were lowly bent,
> Simple in shew, and voyde of malice bad,
> And all the way he prayed, as he went,
> And often knockt his brest, as one that did repent. (I.i.29.2-9)

Now the reader may be keyed into the possibility that the holy man is not what he seems by the word "seemed," but this is only an invitation to make further "triall" of him before rushing off a second time into error.

But even if the reader has learned this lesson, Redcrosse has not. He remains only interested in adventure. The old man says he does not himself "mell" with "warre and worldly trouble" (I.i.30.8-9), but he knows where adventurous knights can find some:

> But if of daunger which hereby doth dwell,
> And homebredd euil ye desire to heare,
> Of a straunge man I can you tidings tell,
> That wasteth all this countrie farre and neare. (I.i.31.1-4)

Once again, such danger is exactly what Redcrosse is looking for, and he adds, unprompted by anything the holy man has said to him, "For to all knighthood it is foule disgrace, / That such a cursed creature liues so long a space" (I.i.31.8-9). There is nothing wrong with this, but it does reinforce the reader's notion that the locus of Redcrosse's concern is in upholding his as-yet-unearned knighthood rather than his already guaranteed holiness.

The old man may tip his moral hand to the careful reader here, as he directs Redcrosse outside the normal sphere of humanity to a "wastfull wildernesse" (I.i.32.1) to which "no liuing wight / May euer passe, but thorough great distresse" (I.i.32.2-3). The reader may recall the dwarf's words when Redcrosse leapt into the Cave of Errour: "this is no place for liuing men" (I.i.13.9), but this does not trouble the Knight of Holinesse at all. The question the reader must once again ask is should it?

Once again, it is up to Una to sound a note of caution. She reminds him that night is drawing near and that perhaps he should rest before undertaking a fight so late in the day:

> And well I wote, that of your later fight
> Ye all forwearied be: for what so strong,
> But wanting rest will also want of might? (I.i.32.5-7)

For all the force that he can muster, Redcrosse is not fundamentally in charge of his own mind, but is "well content" (I.i.33.8) only after the male hermit tells him that Una has rightly advised him.

Here, the reader will do well to remember the difference between Redcrosse's search for immediate experience and the poet's mediation of experience through poetry. The careful, Renaissance-educated reader might inspect the poet's signs and know the truth, which is that there is no truth in this hermit at all on the basis of his reading of other works. When Spenser's readers follow Redcrosse to "little lowly Hermitage" (I.i.34.1) where the arch-deceiver purports to dwell, they find that it is "Downe in a dale" (I.i.34.2) by the side of a forest (not in the center), "Far from resort of people, that did pas / In trauell to and froe" (I.i.34.3-4), and "a little wyde" (I.i.34.5). This is a holy chapel is that is off center. The question becomes whether any of the information that is made available to the careful reader, mostly by the positioning of things in relative space in the reader's mind, is available to the character of Redcrosse within the narrative itself. The careful reader will have to acknowledge that Redcrosse does not necessarily have access to all the moral information that the reader has available to them from their position outside the text.

But Spenser does not just leave subtle hints as these as to the status of moral virtue of the old man. As soon as the old man starts to tell them of saints and popes and says his *Ave Maria* (I.i.35-8-9), the reader is supposed to know without a doubt that he is evil. That neither Redcrosse nor Una respond to *this* requires some explanation. The reader can leave the "clown-ishe" Redcrosse out of it, since he has not the benefit of an education and is just there as "muscle" to effect Una's will. He will have to learn humility before the end of the book before he can meet the Palmer in Book II and tell him that is was only the "goodwill" that was provided him by God, and not any power that he has of his own, that enabled him to complete his quest. But Una is Spenser's representation of the One True Church. Having been raised in Protestant England, the poet must feel that the saying of the *Ave* is a division of the One True Church in favor of a partisan (and moreover false) position. She *must* react to this, and yet she does not within the text that we have been given. Can Spenser mean that Una is in some way unaware of Archimago's betrayal of the truth? If so, how can she not know? And if she is aware of his betrayal of the truth, why doesn't she speak up? Since Spenser does not say, the careful reader must once again put this question away in their memories to be answered when more information about Una's reaction becomes available.

Archimago Returns to His Study

As he puts them to sleep, the image maker and arch-deceiver Archimago stays awake and

> to his studie goes, and there amiddes
> His magick bookes and artes of sundry kindes,
> He seekes out mighty charmes, to trouble sleepy minds (I.i.36.7-9)

These lines have to do, not with only the physical sleepiness of Redcrosse and Una, but with the moral blindness of both. In opposition to the relative shallowness of his heroes' moral and intellectual depths, Archimago has access to some very deep and very dark forces indeed:

> He bad awake blacke *Plutoes* griesly Dame,
> And cursed heuen, and spake reprochfull shame
> Of highest God, the Lord of life and light;
> A bold bad man, that dar'd to call by name
> Great *Gorgon*, Prince of darknes and dead night,
> At which *Cocytus* quakes, and *Styx* is put to flight. (I.i.37.4-9)

He summons a spright and sends him through "double gates" to the underworld House of Morpheus, the God of Sleep.

It is important to note that the underworld is outside of the world and so of the diurnal turning of day into night and then back again: in the realm of Morpheus, "dawning day doth neuer peepe" (I.i.39.5). This reflects the unity of Morpheus' thought, and leads to an important point about Spenser's poem. Speech in Spenser is not subject to such a unified logocentrism. Words require a speaker, but they also require someone to listen to them. Morpheus remains "Wrapt in eternall silence farre from enemyes" (I.i.41.9) in unified silence. And even when Archimago's messenger attempts to rouse him from his eternal sleep, he finds "his wast wordes returnd to him in vaine" (I.i.42.2). How Archimago's messenger wakes up the god of Slumber and gets him to converse with him requires some explanation, so I will digress into the one of the sources of Spenser's episode in Augustine's thought on allegory and language for a moment.

Augustine's Allegory of Silence and Speech

Augustine only mentions allegory only briefly in *De trinitate*, as he quotes St. Paul:

> I know that wisdom is an incorporeal substance, and that it is the light by which those things are seen that are not seen by carnal eyes; and yet a man so great and so spiritual [as Paul] says, "We see now through a glass, in an enigma, but then face to face." If we ask what and of what sort is this "glass," this assuredly occurs to our minds, that in a glass nothing is discerned but an image."[25]

He then acknowledges that there are many form of allegory:

> And hence some Latin translators, through unwillingness to employ a Greek word, where the apostle says, "Which things are an allegory," have rendered it by a circumlocution—Which things signify one thing by another. But there are several species of this kind of trope that is called allegory, and one of them is that which is called enigma.[26]

Augustine gives his readers an elementary lesson in the logic of definition before proceeding:

> Now the definition of the generic term must necessarily embrace also all its species; and hence, as every horse is an animal, but not every

---

25 Augustine, "On the Holy Trinity," XV.8.
26 Ibid., XV.9.

animal is a horse, so every enigma is an allegory, but every allegory is not an enigma.[27]

Augustine will focus on clarifying the logic of enigma, bringing it out of the darkness of ignorance into the light of reason insofar as this is possible before abandoning the effort in the face of a breach in logic that can only be overcome through faith.

Of course, unlike his pagan forbearers, Augustine does not abandon the individual in his equation for the realm of λόγος, as he feels the pagans had done. It is in the individual that he finds the "substantiality of consciousness" on which he will hang the salvation of mankind. Instead, he redirects his sense inwards to its true source. This movement does not depend on logic, but on the various levels of human memory:

> But let us now speak of those things of which we think as known, and have in our knowledge even if we do not think of them; whether they belong to the contemplative knowledge, which, as I have argued, is properly to be called wisdom, or to the active which is properly to be called knowledge. For both together belong to one mind, and are the image of God.[28]

Augustine's reliance on various levels of thought by which a man can both know and not know a thing at the same time is ultimately derived from Aristotle's *Posterior Analytics*, in which the philosopher makes a similar case:

> But nothing, I think, prevents one from in a sense understanding and in a sense being ignorant of what one is learning; for what is absurd is not that you would know in some sense what you are learning, but that you should know it in this sense, i.e. in the way and sense in which you are learning it.[29]

In Augustine it is within the heart of man for man to find what he could not find without. In this inward turn, Augustine emphasizes the division between the wisdom of the heart and the knowledge of the body:

> Some thoughts, then, are speeches of the heart, wherein the Lord also shows that there is a mouth, when He says, "Not that which entereth into the mouth defileth a man; but that which proceedeth out of the mouth, that defileth a man." In one sentence He has comprised two

---

27 Ibid., XV.10.
28 Ibid., XV.17.
29 Aristotle, *Posterior Analytics*, 71b6-8.

diverse mouths of the man, one of the body, one of the heart.[30]

He then distinguishes the knowledge of the heart by acknowledging that it is expressed not in any individual language. The wisdom of the heart is prior to our expression of it through any individual language:

> For the thought that is formed by the thing which we know, is the word which we speak in the heart: which word is neither Greek nor Latin, nor of any other tongue. But when it is needful to convey this to the knowledge of those to whom we speak, then some sign is assumed whereby to signify it. And generally a sound, sometimes a nod, is exhibited, the former to the ears, the latter to the eyes, that the word which we bear in our mind may become known also by bodily signs to the bodily senses.[31]

According to Augustine, the "real" word is not the word spoken in Latin or Greek, but the word that touches our heart beyond language:

> Accordingly, the word that sounds outwardly is the sign of the word that gives light inwardly; which latter has the greater claim to be called a word. For that which is uttered with the mouth of the flesh, is the articulate sound of a word; and is itself also called a word, on account of that to make which outwardly apparent it is itself assumed.[32]

He continues:

> We must go on, then, to that word of man, to the word of the rational animal, to the word of that image of God, that is not born of God, but made by God; which is neither utterable in sound nor capable of being thought under the likeness of sound such as must needs be with the word of any tongue; but which precedes all the signs by which it is signified, and is begotten from the knowledge that continues in the mind, when that same knowledge is spoken inwardly according as it really is.[33]

Having laid out the difference between Aristotelian language and the higher and prior theory of the language of the heart, he returns to Paul's enigma:

> When, therefore, this image shall have been renewed to perfection by

---

30 Augustine, "On the Holy Trinity," XV.18.
31 Ibid., XV.19. This is the difference between private and public language in modern philosophy.
32 Ibid., XV.20.
33 Ibid.

this transformation, then we shall be like God, because we shall see Him, not through a glass, but "as He is;" which the Apostle Paul expresses by "face to face." But now, who can explain how great is the unlikeness also, in this glass, in this enigma, in this likeness such as it is? Yet I will touch upon some points, as I can, by which to indicate it.[34]

Having said that the whole of our divided thought is an image of God, Augustine is careful to point out that when we treat the lower faculty of thought, knowledge, it is not to be called an image of God:

But when we treat of the lower of the two distinctly and separately, then it is not to be called an image of God, although even then, too, some likeness of that Trinity may be found in it; as we showed in the thirteenth book. We speak now, therefore, of the entire knowledge of man altogether, in which whatever is known to us is known; that, at any rate, which is true; otherwise it would not be known.[35]

Augustine puts an emphasis on learning things mankind already knows by bringing them forth to what Freud calls ego consciousness from their unconscious minds.

In terms derived from Aristotle and passed through Augustine, Redcrosse has the *potential* for action within him, but he has not yet *actuated* his potential. That process of actualizing his potential will involve Redcrosse in the ability to vocalize his thoughts in the *a posteriori* language taught by his also incomplete education and not simply rely on his *a priori* ability to gain victory in any contest he chooses to enter. Even with his formidable courage and his armor by which the reader knows he will succeed, thus far Redcrosse has not realized any of this on a conscious level. Archimago, by contrast, has realized just how much can be accomplished by mastering the limited power of speech.

Spenser's Allegory of Silence and Speech

When Archimago's sprite attempts to rouse the slumbering Morpheus, he does so using the multi-tier architecture of mind that Spenser had derived from Aristotle through Augustine. Eventually, Archimago's sprite manages to rouse the slumbering god by invoking Hecate (I.i.43.1-3), according to Hamilton's note the goddess of bad witchcraft. Aroused by fear, Morpheus awakes and speaks, asking why he has come (I.i.43.5). After he is told, he complies with the sprites request and delivers him an "ydle dream"

---

34 Ibid., XV.xx
35 Ibid., XV.17.

(I.i.46.1).

Armed with his "ydle dream," the sprite flies back through the "Yuorie dore" (I.i.44.6), the gate that signifies false dreams in Virgil's *Aeneid*, where we read

> Two gates of Sleep there are, whereof the one is said to be of horn, and thereby an easy outlet is given to true shades; the other gleaming with the sheen of polished ivory, but false are the dreams sent by the spirits to the world above. There then with these words Anchises attends both his son and the Sibyl, and dismisses them by the ivory gate.[36]

Like Spenser and Ariosto, Virgil was working in an environment in which he had choices in his use of language, and he takes great care in his usage in this passage. Virgil relies on a mimesis between nature and language in his poetics, and therefore he has the gate of true dreams drawing on the identity of nature and language. Thus he gives a transparent noun (*cornea*) when he writes of the gate of true dreams. The gate of false dreams, however, is not actually named in the passage; the name of ivory is referred to only obliquely in poetic usage as *altera candenti perfecta nitens elephanto*. In noting the detachment of the substantive noun *cornea*—the thing in its natural state—from the attributes of the perfection of polished ivory—given to the reader without any reference to the nominative or accusative case—the classical poet seems to be pointing to his own role as an artist in his artificial creation by noting that he takes raw nature (*cornea*) and perfects it (*candenti perfecta nitens elephanto*) through the addition of his artifice, which ties the natural object back obliquely to its animal source (*elephanto*). In this way, Virgil's language of perfection still maintains an intimate connection to the state of *a priori* nature that underlies his *a posteriori* work of art.

Such an easy relationship as we find in Virgil becomes complicated in Spenser's imitation of Virgil by the fact that Spenser is following Plato, who complicated Aristotle's smooth transition between language and nature by posing the interference of a "poetic metaphor" that always comes between the natural object as it is in its ontology and human language's expression

---

36 Virgil, *Aeneid*, VI.893-898:

Sunt geminae Somni portae; quarum altera fertur
cornea, qua veris facilis datur exitus umbris,
altera candenti perfecta nitens elephanto,
sed falsa ad caelum mittunt insomnia Manes,
his ubi turn natum Anchises unaque Sibyllam
prosequitur dictis portaque emittit eburna.

of the natural object in language. Within the pagan world, skeptics like Carneades and Sextus Empiricus appeared who did not believe that there *was* any necessary connection between words and things. Such skepticism was one of the reasons that Plato's loose connection to Homer was allowed to substitute for the divine for so long in the pagan world. But in the Christian universe, pagan skepticism represented a powerful call for philosophical action. In Augustine's view, Homer's follower Virgil was another in a series of inimitable lies told by pagans who had no clue how to close the hermeneutic circle around meaning without the aid of a falsehood. Augustine had reacted by denying the schools of Stoicism and Epicureanism access to truth through reason alone. Instead, Augustine believed that "truth" was the province of a single and inimitable event in human history, the death and resurrection of Jesus Christ.

These considerations make it extremely unlikely that Spenser, living in a Reformation universe that had not yet thrown over Augustine for a glimpse of pure reason brought about through the devices of the Enlightenment, could have imitated Virgil without giving some consideration to the objections raised by Augustine to Virgil's easy philosophical models. Spenser does not simply use the past as a model for passive imitation. Doing so would translate the reader out of his own "substantial consciousness" to follow a fictional and so inimitable creation as though it were a fact. Instead, Spenser changes the philosophical terms of Virgil's engagement with language in relation to ontology. Such access as Virgil grants to nature through reason can only be accessed in a Christian universe through a leap of faith in God and not through reason alone. From the distance provided by faith, human beings could peer at God's prior creation through His *vestigia*, which he left us as signs available to our human minds but which must be approached through an *a posteriori* scientific reason.

This translation out of direct imitation for a mediated view of nature is exactly what the reader finds when they look into Spenser's imitation of the philosophical terms of Virgil's passage. Spenser initially describes and into the hands, not of God the Virgilian gates as follows:

> Whose double gates he findeth locked fast,
> The one faire fram'd of burnisht Yuory,
> The other all with siluer ouercast. (I.i.40.1-3)

Unlike Virgil's naming conventions, which guide him through his poetry back to underlying nature, Spenser's "Yuory" gate, Virgil's gate of "false dreams," is named directly, while his gate of "true dreams" is named only through its *a posteriori* attributes (it is "with siluer ouercast"). Thus, in Spenser's poem *neither gate* by which pagan dreams travel back from the underworld are given in terms that would have rendered them true in the logical terms in which Virgil was working. This is no accident.

Waking Up Redcrosse

Spenser's Morpheus sleeps so deeply precisely because he is in the midst of the pleasant white noise caused by falling water, rain on a rooftop, and a "murmuring winde," all of which are likened to the sound of "swarming Bees" (I.i.41.1-5). Once the sprite wakes up Morpheus with the aid of Hecate, Morpheus complies with the sprite's request, not because the sprite is asking, but because his request is based in Archimago's "intent" (I.i.43.8). *Archimago's intention* drives the action forward, while throughout the episode in which the sprite's actions of waking up the God of Sleep are being reported, Redcrosse remains in a passive sleep. He wakess up only after Archimago's proxy for underworld action returns to him and chooses out a "few wordes most horrible" (I.i.37.1). Spenser likens these horrible words to "little flyes" (I.i.38.2), which like the "cloud of combrous gnattes" (I.i.23.5) that molested him at the end of the previous episode after he had killed Errour, cannot actually harm Redcrosse.

Unlike Morpheus, Redcrosse is supposed to be a man of action, and he cannot afford to sleep through a world in which characters like Archimago are intent on working evil through their active natures. But, though Spenser has directed his readers to the role of Archimago's intent in driving the action of the poem forward, Archimago's intent is not an issue when it comes to *Redcrosse's* action. This is not for want of trying. Archimago attempts to gain control of Redcrosse's mind though a process of doubling, creating a copy of the Redcrosse Knight's consort Una out of another of his sprites. She is spectacularly beautiful and so lifelike that she could tempt the weaker sense of any man (I.i.45.4-5). Archimago and his two sprites approach the sleeping Redcrosse, and the first sprite lays his dream on Redcrosse's head and begins "with false shewes [to] abuse his fantasy" (I.i.46.4).

Having his mind abused with such "false shewes" of "loues and lustfull play" (I.i.47.4), Redcrosse's "manly hart did melt away, / Bathed in wanton blis and wicked ioy" (I.i.47.5-6), as Archimago had hoped it would. But Spenser seems to be a reasonable man who knows that people have sex dreams, and he is okay with that state of affairs.[37] Fantasies are just that: they can be disturbing to prudish dreamers, but the goal in Spenser is always to sort our inexorable fantasy life into piles of truth and falsehood and to align our minds, as far as it is possible, with the path laid out for us, not by a superficial reading of nature, but by the alignment of the mind with the deeper, preverbal and ontological purpose given to us by God that lies beneath the names given by man to natural things.

This is not to say that Redcrosse is not disturbed by his sex dream. In fact, he is so disturbed that he, like Morpheus before him, wakes up. And when he wakes up, he is greeted by an ontological likeness of Una. Archimago wants Redcrosse to betray his inner purpose by having him kiss her outstretched lips. But instead, the man whose end had been determined by God before he even started out on his adventure is

> All cleane dismayd to see so vncouth sight,
> And halfe enraged at her shamelesse guise,
> He thought haue slaine her in his fierce despight.... (I.i.50.1-3)

That he does not kill her is testament to his powers of introspection that spring from the other "halfe" of his divided mind. He forgoes his "hasty heat," and he attempts to make "triall" of her "to proue his sense, and tempt her feigned truth" (I.i.50.4-6). In doing so, he "gan himself aduise" (I.i.50.5).

The False Una responds to Redcrosse's hesitation by pressing forward. She professes her love for Redcrosse, which she says operates through hidden causes:

> Ah Sir, my liege Lord and my loue,
> Shall I accuse the hidden cruell fate,
> And mightie causes wrought in heauen aboue,

---

[37] I point this out because in my reading of an important chapter on Guyon in Stephen Greenblatt's work ("To Fashion a Gentleman: Spenser and the Destruction of the Bower of Bliss" in his *Renaissance Self-Fashioning*, 157-192), Greenblatt accuses Spenser of a prudishness that could be overcome by loosening the artificial strictures of his morality and founding it on something more natural. While I'm as sexually liberal as the next guy, Greenblatt seems to believe that it is *only* Spenser's innate hesitation to engage with the free love of the 1960s, which unleashed the body as a primary mode of expression, that causes him to have missed the presented opportunity of joining epistemology and ontology together in his own mind. That has been the goal of reason since the Enlightenment, but I would argue that the case is more serious, and that Spenser believes in Augustine's radical *denial* of reason's power to access metaphysical realms through the bodily sense.

Or the blind God, that doth me thus amate,
For hoped loue to winne me certaine hate? (I.i.51.1-5)

The invocation of "mighty causes wrought in heauen aboue" and of "cruel fate" seems to put the matter out of her hands and into the hands, not of God, Who presumably sees all, but into the hands of the "blind God" Cupid (I.i.51.4). And yet on account of her giving herself to another, the False Una confesses that she has lost control of her own individual mind.

After she introduces the subject of her love, she confesses that in falling in love she has given up her fate to another:

Yet thus perforce he bids me do, or die.
Die is my dew: yet rew my wretched state
You, whom my hard auenging destinie
Hath made iudge of my life or death indifferently. (I.i.51.6-9)

This answers the question of where she has placed herself in regards to her fate. Her destiny is in Redcrosse's hands, but the key word here is "indifferently." In surrendering her will to the will of Redcrosse, the False Una is surrendering too much. She becomes indifferent to her own fate, because she has surrendered her heart to a "blind god." This, according to Spenser, is not the way to gain control over one's individual fate.[38] Individuals must take control of their own destiny, but they must keep to a path guided by a deeper power than individual will. If the will is set free, it will travel to and fro in the wasteland of the world without any sense of direction.

Of course, the reader is invited to remember (using their memory, which Spenser is also training) that the False Una is not the real Una and that God's deeper purpose is not nature's blind purpose that is indifferent to the choices that we as individuals make. Thus (not unpredictably) the False Una lies as she tells him the origin of her love:

Your owne deare sake forst me at first to leaue
My Fathers kingdom. There she stopt with teares;
Her swollen hart her speach seemd to bereaue,
And then againe begonne, My weaker yeares
Captiu'd to fortune and frayle worldly feares,
Fly to your faith for succour and sure ayde:
Let me not dye in languor and long teares. (I.i.52.1-7)

---

38 I note this in Spenser, because according to Socrates this is exactly how human beings gain control over their minds, as we exchange our individual lives for more permanent concerns given to us by our participation in the sphere of λόγος.

Her explanation of the origins of her experience of love is designed to flatter Redcrosse into thinking that he is more important than he actually is: it was for *his* faith (not hers) that she left the brazen castle and flew to him for succor and sure aid. But this is, too, is false, as the careful reader, who has access to his memory of what they have been told in the *Letter to Raleigh*, will remember. There the poet explicitly tells the reader that Una had *gainsaid* his choice when he first asked to be chosen for her adventure. The real Una's love came only *after* he put on the armor and "dewe furniture" prepared for general use. The False Una's speech is filled with words that come, not from anything truly grounded in reality, but from her "swollen hart."[39]

She continues:

> Loue of your selfe, she said, and deare constraint
> Lets me not sleepe, but wast the wearie night
> In secret anguish and vnpittied plaint,
> Whiles you in carelesse sleepe are drowned quight. (I.i.53.1-4)

Redcrosse does not respond to her protestation of love for him. Instead, he responds with the pity born of an untroubled mind:

> Her doubtfull words made that redoubted knight
> Suspect her truth: *yet since no vntruth he knew,*
> Her fawning loue with foule disdainefull spight
> He would not shend, but said, Deare dame I rew,
> That for my sake such griefe vnto you grew. (I.i.53.5-9 italics mine)

Redcrosse reacts with a profession of pity that for his sake she should have given up her *a priori* state of self-sufficiency for an "vnknowne" grief that "vnto you grew" after the fact (I.i.53.9). The naïve Knight of Holinesse simply does not recognize that he can have caused her pain, since, in his own intent "no vntruth he knew." Secure within his own *a priori* being, Redcrosse is a character who is completely untroubled by thoughts of others. It is for this reason that Archimago fails to push him off his pedestal, and in canto ii he returns to his books again, seeking another way to break Redcrosse.

But Redcrosse is not out of harm's way. He thinks of himself only as an individual atom in a universe of individually acting monads. Thus, he responds to the False Una's assurance that she loves him for himself alone with assurances that are not directed to the pain he has caused to another

---

[39] The reader is invited to remember the swelling of the Nile here.

individual, but to himself alone. But at the same time that Redcrosse tells the False Una to "Assure your self, it fell not all to ground" (I.i.54.1), the reader should start to get worried about the fate of Redcrosse. Being false, she and her profession of love for him *should* have fallen to the ground. Granted, he assures the False Una that he holds her so dear "as life is to my hart, / I deeme your loue, and hold me to you bound" (I.i.54.2-3), but he has already shown himself very reckless with his life.

The lesson that Spenser is interested in the reader taking away from all this is that one must be cautious about keeping things in balance in a moral universe in which evil forces are in play. In Spenser's work, things held in equal balance are held so because mankind does not give enough attention to God's grace, which has the power to permanently switch things in mankind's favor. In the Cave of Errour, Redcrosse gives too much power to his own will and not enough to the armor that would have made the whole adventure unnecessary. In Archimago's lair, Redcrosse ignores the necessity of learning to scout his environment for clues to truth and falsehood. Instead, he finds comfort in the hermit's promise of further adventure.

This renders him a passive actor, although the reader might have thought based on their reading of Aristotle that he was supposed to stand as the active man in respect to Una's potential and passive being. Redcrosse's passivity allows the active Archimago to impart direction to the slumbering god Morpheus with the power of Hecate, the goddess of bad witchcraft, while Redcrosse continues to sleep passively. As a result, there is no positively acting man on the side of good at this point in the poem.

The Triumph of Divisive Science Over Moral Goodness

Fixing the Location of Relative Stars

In many ways Redcrosse's passivity saves him from overreacting to the False Una's profession of love for him. But it is the positive action that he takes in response to her of love for him that defines him. Rather than making "triall" of her truth, he flies from her. That this is not the correct course of action can be seen from a detailed explanation of the first stanzas of canto ii, which opens with a reference to the northern star:

> By this the Northerne wagoner had set
> His seuenfold teme behind the stedfast starre,
> That was in Ocean waues yet neuer wet,
> But firme is fixt, and sendeth light from farre
> To al, that in the wide deepe wandring arre.... (I.ii.1.1-5)

The "Northerne wagoner" refers to the constellation Boötes that in Homer[1] gives direction to the wandering Odysseus. The constellation was named after a plowman who drove a team of oxen tethered to the steady northern star and who therefore drove in circles around it. As with his echoes of epic simile, the poet is not simply engaging in a bit of colorful poetic amplification here. His naming of this constellation has important implications for Redcrosse, because Contemplation will later point out that he was raised in the household of a plowman, who named him George.

At this moment in his poem, Spenser is posing the question to his readers of whether Redcrosse should follow the northern star or not? The answer to the reader's dilemma is wrapped up in the question of where

---

[1] Homer, *The Odyssey*, V.272.

The Triumph Of Divisive Science Over Moral Goodness   83

Redcrosse's home lies: is it in the stars or in ourselves? This should cause the reader to inspect the "fixt" star more carefully.

Following the star would put him in line with Odysseus, who followed it back home in the *Odyssey*. That would make him a carrier of false meaning. At the same time, the star points Redcrosse back to his literal name of George, given to him by his adopted plowmen parents, and away from his newly adopted name of Redcrosse, given to him by Una. The reader is invited to remember that during the *Letter to Raleigh*, when Una first saw him as a "clownishe younge man," she had thought him unworthy of being given such a great adventure as he was asking for. It was only after he had shown himself capable of wielding the arms worn by others that Una changed her perspective towards George, elevating him beyond his humble plowman origins by naming him by his figural status as Redcrosse.

The ability of allegory to divide things into different levels makes the "fixt" star less fixed in the reader's mind. The constellation would give direction to Redcrosse's random wanderings, as it had to Odysseus' adventure; but it is also "farre" away from his location in space. This would fix the identity of Redcrosse to a distant star that is extrinsic to himself and not to his literal self. This is how Una herself interprets his victory over Errour when she congratulates him on having been born under a "happy starre." Redcrosse is happy to be known by this elevated figural name, and he is complicit in fleeing his literal name George for the protection of Una's sacred figural name.

The question becomes what, if any, are the costs of George's fleeing his literal name? The careful reader will remember that Odysseus disguises his true nature beneath a series of lies as a way of surviving in a hostile world. This leads to the question of whether following the northern star is to be interpreted as an imitation of Odysseus' behavior of lying to himself and to others (including his own beloved spouse) as a way of maintaining his humanity in the face of a hostile nature filled with hostile gods. If this were the case, it would introduce an element of necessary deciet into Spenser's Christian universe. It is not Spenser's plan to leave such a paradox in his poem unresolved, and this is why he rewriting not only the pagan epic poetry not only of Homer and Virgil but also the Christian poetry of Ariosto and Tasso to bring it into alignment with Augustine's philosophy.

The careful reader who waits until the end of the book before deciding where the truth lies in the allegorical universe of divided consciousnesses will be given a definite answer to the dilemma they are faced with here. One of the last things Redcrosse learns from Contemplation is that he is human and that he will be remembered not by his figural name of Redcrosse but by his literal name as Saint George. His sainthood will be granted to him only after he has returned to the world and defeated the Dragon from his position as a man who has a substantial consciousness grounded in his literal and individual human being.

This means that the figural name of Redcrosse, which he was so happy to obtain and which is the creation of Una, herself a creation of Spenserian fiction, is a detour from the direct path to George's preordained victory over the Dragon. This brings up the question of whether Spenser means for his readers to dismiss the pure unspotted Una as a guide for life in favor of a man who is just about to leave her and take up with a woman who is dressed as the Whore of Babylon. The reader's revulsion at the moral implications of that prospect should not cause him or her to refrain from asking questions about how much Una is to blame for her own complicity in guiding Redcrosse away from his destiny by translating him his literal self into the figural name of Redcrosse by which he is able to hide from himself his own human limitations. At this point in the narrative, the answer to the reader's dilemma is far from clear.

The action of characters guides the ends of our reader response to texts, though not our ability to ask difficult questions of the texts in the intermediate period when we still do not have all the answers that arise in the meantime. Whatever the modern reader or the contemporary Reformation reader thinks he should be doing, Redcrosse fails to follow the "fixt" star; so the interpreted meaning of the star is in the end a moot point. Instead, the poet points out that Redcrosse waits until "*Hesperus* in highest skie / Had spent his lampe" (I.ii.6.6-7) before "hastily" dressing and fleeing the hermitage of Archimago with "*her* Dwarfe" (I.ii.7.8 italics mine) no less and leaving Una on her own with less than she came to the relationship with.[2]

This makes him into a bad person whether we are modern or Reformation readers, as he abandons Una, the principle of unity in the poem, taking something that does not belong to him (her dwarf) in the process, as he heads back into the wilderness to seek more unmotivated random adventures in which he can prove his worthiness for having been chosen by God and Una for this adventure, an adventure he shows himself paradoxically not worthy of by his actions here. The careful reader must inspect the star that Redcrosse follows for clues to its meaning before deciding arbitrarily.

---

2 This is another instance of inequality in Spenser's work.

Frege's Puzzle

The star that Redcrosse follows plays a key role in what some would say is the foundational work in the modern philosophy of language, Friedrich Ludwig Gottlob Frege's "On Sense and Meaning."[3] The thorny problem that emerges from Frege's work is known to this day as Frege's Puzzle, and no single solution to it has definitively emerged in the modern day.

Frege's Puzzle is built around references to two stars in the night sky: the morning star (Phosphorus) and evening star (Hesperus), each of which had separate names despite referring to the same underlying planet, Venus.[4] Frege began his groundbreaking essay with the same question that had troubled Plato in his *Parmenides*, the question of equality and identity: "Equality," he says, "gives rise to challenging questions which are not altogether easy to answer."[5] He knows that the identity of certain names, like those of the morning and evening stars are not identical, but he also recognizes that they refer to the same ontologically-existing object. This raises an important question in Frege's mind: "Is it a relation?" he asks. And if so, is it "A relation between objects, or between names or signs of objects?"[6]

He continues:

> In my *Begriffsschrift* I assumed the latter. The reasons which seem to favour this are the following: $a = a$ and $a = b$ are obviously statements of differing cognitive value; $a = a$ holds *a priori* and, according to Kant, is to be labelled analytic, while statements of the form $a = b$ often contain very valuable extensions of our knowledge and cannot always be established *a priori*.[7]

In other words, "Hesperus = Hesperus" is an *a priori* statement, complete unto itself,[8] while statements like "Hesperus = Phosphorus" are "very valu-

---

3 Frege, "On Sense and Meaning." in *Translations from the Philosophical Writings of Gottlob Frege*, ed. Peter Geach and Max Black (Totowa, NJ: Rowman & Littlefield, 1980).

4 Frege does not refer to the stars by their given names, but refers to them only generally. The importance of the stars is that both stars refer to the same underlying object in their logical division of what would otherwise be thought of as an integral ontological image. In spite of Frege's generic reliance on generic names, it is common to refer to the paradox through the proper names of the stars. For the sake of making comparison with Spenser easier for the modern reader, I will follow the modern practice of referring to each proper name in this book.

5 Frege, "On Sense and Meaning," 56.

6 Ibid.

7 Ibid.

8 I note that while he says this, he refers to the authority of Kant to prop up his

able extensions of our knowledge" that can be approached through accessible *a posteriori* methods of inquiry.

Unlike Plato and Augustine, but like the post-Enlightenment Kant, Frege resolves questions of identity and difference without acknowledging any break in reason's ability to explain itself to itself through its own means. He uses reason to explain the "discovery that the rising sun is not new every morning, but always the same," which he feels "was one of the most fertile astronomical discoveries."[9] He then notes that "if we were to regard equality as a relation between that which the names 'a' and 'b' designate, it would seem that a = b could not differ from a = a (i.e. provided a = b is true)."[10]

> A relation would thereby be expressed of a thing to itself, and indeed one in which each thing stands to itself but to no other thing. What is intended to be said by a = b seems to be that the signs or names 'a' and 'b' designate the same thing, so that those signs themselves would be under discussion; a relation between them would be asserted. But this relation would hold between the names or signs only in so far as they named or designated something. It would be mediated by the connexion of each of the two signs with the same designated thing.[11]

In other words, the claims of reference in "a=b" depends on the existence of the underlying ontology of the planet Venus that lies beneath the reference to the two stars to complete a reference to the outside world.

But Frege points out the absurdity of such a claim:

> But this is arbitrary. Nobody can be forbidden to use any arbitrarily producible event or object as a sign for something. In that case the sentence a = b would no longer refer to the subject matter, but only to its mode of designation; we would express no proper knowledge by its means. But in many cases this is just what we want to do. If the sign 'a' is distinguished from the sign 'b' only as object (here, by means of

---

reference to something that he takes to be *a priori* and complete unto itself. The sense of self-reference seems to imply that someone, in this case Kant, had reached the ground of knowledge, but that also means that if someone were ever to dismantle Kant's thought on *a priori* statements, one would have dismantled Frege's solution to the origins of proper names, as well as all that follows after it.

9 Frege, "On Sense and Meaning," 56. When Homer refers to Hesper in *The Iliad* at 22.317-320, he describes it being reflected in the spear point of Achilles' armor as it shakes with anger at Hektor's having slain Patroklos. Homer did not know that his reference at 23.226-228 to the "dawn star [that] passes across the earth, harbinger / of light" referred to the same planet. But the fact was discovered by the time Ptolemy wrote his *Almagest*.

10 Ibid., 56.

11 Ibid., 56-57.

The Triumph Of Divisive Science Over Moral Goodness   87

its shape), not as sign (i.e. not by the manner in which it designates something), the cognitive value of a = a becomes essentially equal to that of a = b, provided a = b is true. A difference can arise only if the difference between the signs corresponds to a difference in the mode of presentation of that which is designated.[12]

Simply put, Frege wishes to point out that we can in fact refer to things through their "mode of presentation" without reference to any underlying ontology.

Having differentiated the ontology of the planet Venus from the "mode of presentation" of the planet Venus (the "signs" that we use to designate the planet), Frege switches his reference from a historically conditioned event—the ancient discovery that Hesperus and Phosphorus refer to the same planet—to a product of pure reason, the intellectual form of a "perfect" shape, in this case a triangle:

Let a, b, c be the lines connecting the vertices of a triangle with the midpoints of the opposite sides. The point of intersection of a and b is then the same as the point of intersection of b and c. So we have different designations for the same point, and these names ('point of intersection of a and b,' 'point of intersection of b and c') likewise indicate the mode of presentation; and hence the statement contains actual knowledge.[13]

He then draws this process of differentiation that he has located in the human imposition of names on the objects of pure reason back to their ground in "nature":

It is *natural*, now, to think of there being connected with a sign (name, combination of words, letter), besides that to which the sign refers, which may be called the reference of the sign, also what I should like to call the sense of the sign, wherein the mode of presentation is contained. In our example, accordingly, the reference of the expressions 'the point of intersection of a and b' and 'the point of intersection of b and c' would be the same, but not their senses.[14]

We may sum up Frege's Puzzle as follows: he discerns that there is a difference between an *a priori* identity proposition (a=a) and an *a posteriori* sense (a=b), and he believes the true knowledge comes from the extension of knowledge in the relational proposition, a = b. He notes the difference as

---

12 Ibid., 57.
13 Ibid.
14 Ibid. Italics mine.

one between an *a priori* sense and an *a posteriori* reference: "The reference of 'evening star' [Hesperus] would be the same as that of 'morning star' [Phosphorus], but not the sense."[15] "Reference" in Frege is associated with the *a priori* similarity given to things by their ontological existence, while the difference of "sense" is given to things by the *a posteriori* imposition of names.[16] It is on the basis of his dissevering sense from reference that Frege solves the puzzle of distinguishing Hesperus from Phosphorus, while keeping both referring to the underlying star of Venus.

Modern Philosophers Weigh In On Frege's Puzzle

Frege's thought has had an enormous impact on modern philosophy, as he played a large role in the division of modern philosophy into two camps: a camp known as analytical philosophy, where logic could play its role within a closed and perfect system, and a grammatical camp, where perfect logic broke down due to the interference of various irrational factors. Frege's advancements in his perfect system of logic was given a huge boost by Bertrand Russell and Alfred North Whitehead, who popularized Frege's work in their *Principia Mathematica*.[17] The *Principia* was supposed to catalog all the ways that the ontological world could be modeled by translating our imperfect grammatical speech into a series of perfect logical propositions.

This was not a sustainable proposition in the modern day any more than it had been in Augustine's day, and within a generation of the publication of the *Principia Mathematica*, Kurt Gödel published a work in which he discovered what Augustine had realized 1,400 years before: that there were systematic inconsistencies proposed in every rational philosophical system that reason could not solve for on its own.[18] This could have raised the Augustinian problem of the difference between what we recreate in our minds (epistemology) of a prior world as it is (ontology) all over again. But perhaps because Gödel was living in a post-Cartesian scientific age, and because he used formal logic to make his case, and because science was expanding our knowledge of the universe by leaps and bounds, Augustin-

---

15 Ibid.

16 See the chapter on "Intentions and Impositions" in Kretzmann, Kenny, and Pinborg, *The Cambridge History of Later Medieval Philosophy: From the Rediscovery of Aristotle to the Disintegration of Scholasticism, 1100-1600*, 479-495.

17 Bertrand Russell and Alfred North Whitehead, *Principia Mathematica* (Cambridge: Cambridge University Press, 1910).

18 Kurt Gödel, *On Formally Undecidable Propositions of Principia Mathematica and Related Systems* (New York: Basic Books, 1962).

ian superstition was driven even farther back to the edges of the intellectual universe.

In this way, grammar, which had been used as a sop for what spilled out of Frege's "perfect" logic became subject to logic itself, as Ferdinand Saussure placed language into a system in which "linguistic signs" are composed of "signifier" and the "signified."[19] Words floated free, as each word was defined by its context within a semantic field without reference to any stabilizing λόγος. In this way, Frege's division of philosophy into two logical camps at the beginning of the scientific 20th century, one logically "perfect" and one "whole," led aesthetes like Jacques Derrida to come down on the side of complete "wholeness" at the expense of limited logical "perfection." But at the same time, Derrida followed the *logic* of Saussure's irrational grammar and came to the conclusion that it was impossible to use logic to refer to stable reference in vertical, because mythical, λόγος. This led to skepticism about the ultimate ontological stability of mythical worlds, which were built upon nothing more than "words, words."[20]

Derrida's skeptical solution is not the only solution to the problem of Frege's Puzzle. Saul Kripke used the problem of Hesperus and Phosphorus to raise the problem of the meaning of names in his landmark book, *Naming and Necessity*.[21] Using the "Leibnitzian principle of the indiscernibility of identicals"[22] as the basis for his argument, he was able to show that name of the planet Venus was a "rigid descriptor," not something that one could arbitrarily substitute in order to make Russell's notion of a perfect logic hold together. In Kripke's work, the statement "Hesperus = Hesperus" is considered an indivisible statement of identity (a=a). But the statement "Hesperus = Phosphorus" joins two possibly separate things in a single statement (a=b). In this way, Kripke distinguishes necessary things we discover empirically from *a priori* statements while still following Frege's lead in his treatment of knowledge through the extension of terms rather than

---

19 Ferdinand de Saussure, *Course in General Linguistics* (New York, NY: Philosophical Library, 1959).

20 Quilligan, *Language of Allegory*, 13.

21 Saul A. Kripke, *Naming and Necessity* (Cambridge, MA: Blackwell Publishing, 1980). Kripke is especially interesting to a Spenserian scholar because his theory of names deals with many of the same issues that Spenser is dealing with in his abstract allegory, including Hesperus and Phosphorus, the process of "initial baptism," and the principle of adoption of the queen in relation to her status as queen. All of these issues will be dealt with in the chapter on "Reorienting Redcrosse" in which Contemplation tells Redcrosse the origin of his name given to him by his adopted parents and of his birth that binds him to the queen.

22 Ibid., 3.

going back to a unified ontology.

Although Kripke extends his logic through division of once unified things, much in the same way that Archimago has separated a unified Una from the "clownishe" Redcrosse in order to make it clear to Redcrosse that he alone is not adequate to the task before him, there are problems with Kripke's method if approached from perspective of ontological description. For instance, in his groundbreaking article "Can There Be Vague Objects?" Gareth Evans was able to show that strict rational order cannot escape being pushed into paradox even if strict Leibnitzian principles are followed.[23] But it is interesting that Evans undermined the consistency of nature in order to maintain a perfect Leibnitzian consistency of mind. This process indicates the priority of mind over matter in much the same way that Wittgenstein had undermined any notion that what our minds cannot put into logical terms "thereof one must be silent."[24]

Pieter Seuren[25] reviews Kripke's work on names and determines that Frege had it right but that Frege's intension is "a cognitive search procedure that may or may not yield a result in the shape of an actual reference object."[26] This would seem to indicate that some objects have no reference except in the mind—a thing that we have seen in Spenser's Cave of Errour. But he is soon dismissing the notion of any logical intermediary between the mind and the described object (which I find so important in evaluating Spenser's work) even as he is talking about the source of artificiality in Kripke's judgment:

> Kripke's notion of proper names shows with painful clarity the neglect of cognition in logically oriented accounts of natural language comprehension. We conclude that the whole problem of rigid descriptors is to be dismissed as contrived. Kripke's rigid descriptors do not occur in natural language. They are artifacts of those philosophies that feel

---

23 Gareth Evans, "Can There Be Vague Objects?," *Analysis* 38, no. 4 (1978). This strikes me as an indication of the emergence of Gödel's formally undecidable principles within Leibnitz's thought.

24 Wittgenstein, *Tractatus Logico-Philosophicus*, §7. Although this seems to make sense, it leads to the problems with how we account for the discovery of new objects in the world like the telephone, the lightbulb, the automobile, the radio, the television, the transistor, the computer, the rocketship, or any of the other discoveries that are the province of modern life.

25 Pieter A. M. Seuren, *Western Linguistics: An Historical Introduction* (Oxford, UK: Blackwell Publishers, 1998).

26 Ibid., 379.

awkward in the presence of minds.[27]

For Seuren, it is *only* that lack of cognitive values that prevents Kripke's thought from being whole, and not an inexorable disseverance between the being of things as they are (ontology) and human recreation of things as they are in a limited imagination (epistemology).

Reality begins to break down under the pressure of the modern Cartesian system that insists in its premises on a perfect coincidence between ontology and epistemology for the same reason that the Aristotelian system had begun to break down under the pressure of Plato's attack on reason as the end of inquiry into nature. Aristotle had raised the Problem of Fiction in regards to Plato's Theory of Forms and proposed to fix it in his theory of universals. However, according to Plato, Aristotle had proposed a nature whose presence in one's mind was necessary to fulfill mankind's purpose as a rational thinker but whose existence was subject to the charge that it, too, was a fiction. Plato made room for human imagination in his configuration of the universe, whereas Aristotle insisted on a firm belief in something that could not be addressed without the possibly falsifying intrusion of fiction.

Spenser's Complex Solution to Frege's Puzzle

Spenser seems to follow Frege when, instead of pursuing identity with Una, the principle of truth and beauty in the poem, he declares that his hero is restless and waits until dawn when "Hesperus in highest skie / Had spent his lampe" (I.ii.6.6-7) before "hastily" dressing and fleeing the hermitage of Archimago with Una's dwarf. This introduces the division of reference that Frege is attempting to deal with in his "On Sense and Meaning," but the exact reference of the passage proves difficult for modern readers to make sense of. Some readers will attempt to diminish its importance as a modern invention of which the Reformation poet Spenser had no inkling. And even if Spenser knew of Frege's Puzzle, recognizing that fact does not answer the question of which of two incompatible principles (a=a or a=b) Spenser grabs a hold of. For those who want answers to the question of what exactly is going on here, the best way to read this passage is to divide the passage up into the perspectives of Redcrosse, the reader, and the poet.

Redcrosse is pursuing the only quest he has ever had in his mind: he wants to prove his worthiness to serve in the court of Gloriana through his as-yet-untested action. To do so, he follows the unified sun of being rather than the shadows of becoming, just as Plato had urged in the Allegory of

---

27 Ibid., 381.

the Cave. If this were all, this would make him into a good person. The two-tiered problem of identity of the planet Venus (a=a) and its expression through signs of Hesperus and Phosphorus (a=b) that preoccupies modern philosophers in Frege's solution to his Puzzle in the division of sense from reference would be for naught.

But Redcrosse waits until the morning star Phosphorus appears. That star was known in Spenser's day as Lucifer.[28] That fact, combined with the fact that he abandons Una as he does so, might lead the reader to consider Redcrosse a bad man because he abandons Una, the principle of unity in the poem, as he does so.

Spenser's readers have a different perspective on events. They are being urged to *delay* their judgment of Redcrosse and Una until the end of the poem, when they will have all the evidence available to them that the poet has available to him at this moment but which he is doling out over time. One of those bits of evidence is the fact that the poet will explicitly liken Una to the morning star when she reveals her beauty to him for the first time in the restored Kingdom of Eden at I.xii.21.5.

The problem of putting such positions into philosophical terms is that each of these readings comes with a separate philosophical viewpoint, and they are fundamentally incompatible with one another. Rather than allowing the reader to make an immediate decision on the basis of a modern understanding of the problem of sense and reference,[29] or of Plato's Allegory of the Cave that posits the true sun as the thing that gives meaning to the shadows of human experience,[30] or of deconstruction that places the stability of the λόγος in doubt,[31] Spenser has deliberately thwarted the purpose

---

28 Phosphorus appears in Juan Luis Vives' 1522 AD commentary on Augustine's *City of God*, XXI.8 as Lucifer. Vives notes that it was Pythagoras or Parmenides who had discovered the likeness of unlike things in their reference to the planet Venus. The passage in Augustine plays an important role in Spenser's poem, as it deals with a break in the nature of Venus when it grew larger than it had ever appeared before or since. Augustine disagrees with the assessment of what was going on by the quintessential Roman scientist Varro. The subject of Augustine's engagement with Varro will be treated more fully in the subsequent chapter "Redcrosse in the Extremity of Heaven."

29 This would make Redcrosse into a bad man by having him follow Lucifer. This reading makes sense of Redcrosse's abandonment of Una but ignores the evidence that he could be following the true sun of Plato.

30 This reading would have Redcrosse following the true sun of Plato and the problem of sense and reference in relation to the planet Venus would simply vanish, as well as the problem of Redcrosse's abandonment of Una.

31 Deconstruction requires a differentiation of objects in construction before they can be deconstructed. It appears to me that Spenser is making it impossible for his reader

of his all too human readers, who will be pushing towards a resolution of his poem before they have obtained all the evidence that the poet has at his fingertips.[32] The mark of the *poor reader* is his confidence that he has enough evidence to make a decision about what is going on at this point in the poem.

Spenser is forcing his readers to decide between incompatible positions, and the choice they make matters. Moreover, forcing his reader to choose will limit the whole perspective that has been so important to aesthetic criticism in the modern day; but as the reader has already discovered, Spenser is not a modern man. The poet who wrote *The Faerie Queene* never had the sense that he or his readers are whole, nor does he have the moderns' *a priori* sense that reason could ever be an adequate substitute for the metaphysics of God's creation, joining ontology with epistemology in a sure identification (a=a), as Descartes had done for the modern age.

The Representation of Elizabeth

The reader can trace the differences in Spenser's Reformation approach to experience and the modern way of dealing with the same experience if they look at the reasons that he divides his poem into various allegorical levels. At the beginning of his poem, Spenser raises himself out of the literal level of his thoughts, which he says are "too humble and too vile" (I.proem.4.6), possibly on account of coming only from his own individual self, to the level of "true glorious type" (I.proem.4.7). In his new typological orientation, he shifts his perspective away from himself (a=a) to another (a=b), in this case to thoughts of a "Goddesse heauenly bright" (I.proem.4.1), who is also a "*Mirrour* of grace and Maiestie diuine" (I.proem.4.2 italics mine) and who is like the sun "whose light / Like *Phoebus* lampe throughout the world doth shine" (I.proem.4.3-4).

In raising Elizabeth from the literal to the typological level, Spenser is not just shifting levels on which the poet operates; he is changing the terms of reference for his readers. On the literal level, Elizabeth is an ontologically existing individual who has a substantial consciousness that has been created by God; but within his poem Spenser has used the power of fiction

---

to make any firm construction at this point in his poem as a way of making deconstruction impossible.

32 The differentiation of Hesperus and Lucifer is an illusion, as both refer to the planet Venus. This will become apparent to those people like Socrates who are wise enough to look at things from the perspective of the light of the sun and to ask questions of the universe they occupy. Redcrosse, in my opinion, is not that sort of man.

to divide her into diverse representations such as Belphoebe, Britomart, the goddesses Venus and Diana, and even Una herself. This means that the critic can identify each of these fictional characters with Elizabeth in a Kripke-esque 1:1 identification of cause and effect without a problem. But the opposite is not true: the reader cannot allow any of the representatives of Elizabeth to substitute for the whole Elizabeth. Each of these is only a partial representation of what exists in reality only in Elizabeth.

In shifting away from representing the whole and literal existence of Elizabeth in reality for partial, typological representatives of his queen in his fiction, the poet is attempting to take the whole scope of Elizabeth's role in English and world history, as well as her role in metaphysics of rule, into account. On the typological level, Elizabeth becomes a member of a long line of Anglo Saxon kings that will continue beyond her individual life, a generalized character of chastity in women (Belphoebe), of woman in action (Britomart), the goddess of love (Venus), the goddess of the hunt (Diana), and a creature of unity (Una). As a result, Elizabeth represents within his created poetry more than her literal self can hold, but this comes at the expense of a firm sense of her ontological reality in his fiction.

This break in Kripkean symmetry between cause and effect has the effect of introducing a level of inequality of reference into the poem that the reader must account for. Modern man tends to divide the world in his premises into two parts (e.g. mind and body, or epistemology and ontology) and then either to declare that they are about to reach (or have reached) the end of inquiry in which their divided subject is made whole (as the Moderns had done), or they retreat to skepticism about ever reaching the end of inquiry into their subject (as the postmoderns had done). In neither case do they consider whether their initial premises that place emphasis on ends are solidly grounded in reality and not in their own mind's construction of its subject.

Spenser deals with absolutes in a different way. In an environment in which Augustine, Luther, and Calvin had denied access of the limited human mind to the metaphysical ontology of things as they were created by God (a=a), he sides with Aristotle, who attempted to thread his way through the Scylla and Charybdis of reason by maintaining a temperate balance between extremes. This is why Spenser abandons his identification of himself or his poetry with a 1:1 correspondence with the work of God, which he feels would make an illicit closure of the hermeneutic gulf of reference through the processes of reason. Instead, he attempts to rewrite the absolute aesthetic works not only of the pagans Homer and Virgil but also the Catholic Christians Ariosto and Tasso on the ground of a relative scientific aesthetic.

Absolute Being's Encounter with Inequality

Within Spenser's poem, both Una and Redcrosse represent absolute tendencies that are only possible either because they are products of fiction (in the case of Una) or because (as in the case of Redcrosse) they are ignorant of the true seat of their being, which is not within themselves but with God's unseen hand that guides them from afar.

It is only after

> the rosy-fingred Morning faire,
> Weary of aged *Tithones* saffron bed,
> Had spred her purple robe through deawy aire,
> And the high hils *Titan* discouered (I.ii.7.2-4)

that Una wakes to find the knight on whom she had pinned all her hopes gone. The critic can find biblical sources for identifying Una with the morning star, including Revelation 22:16, which says ""I, Jesus, have sent My angel to testify to you these things for the churches. I am the root and the descendant of David, the bright morning star." The passage from Revelation *can* be seen in Frege's terms as one of identity (a=a).

The modern solution is generally to ignore the difference that arises when Una is left by her beloved and to place blame elsewhere than within her own unified personality. This leaves her identical with Heaven, and the modern reader is urged to look to Redcrosse or Archimago to account for Una's sadness. But this reading suffers from some serious flaws. Una, the principle of unity in Spenser's poem, believes that Redcrosse is identical to Jesus (a=a) on the basis of his ability to wear the armor of God. But that armor, however powerful it may be in causing the balance to tip in favor of God in every battle that Redcrosse will ever engage in, is external to the individual man. Una's identification of Redcrosse and Jesus masks from her the tendencies of the uneducated "clownishe younge man" that will ultimately result in the singularly awful behavior that Redcrosse engages in with Fidessa, figured by the poet in his allegory as the Whore of Babylon, after he has left Una. This breach opened up in Una's personality when her beloved leaves her cannot be ignored by placing all blame elsewhere in order to retain her as the principle of indivisible unity. If the careful reader does not take the bait of looking elsewhere, they will see that Una, the principle of unity, is shown to have an incomplete character here and so is a partial vision of the whole truth in Spenser's allegorical universe.

Una's mistake is to believe that the rules of identity that she grew up with in Eden apply here on earth, which is subject to diurnal changes between day and night. Thus she ignores the possibility of difference between Redcrosse and Christ that arise in the brave new world of time. She assumes that God is enough because in Eden God *is* enough. But her return to sacred principles is not sufficient in the world of time; and she, like Redcrosse, knows it on a certain level! This is why she runs out of Eden to Gloriana's court seeking a man of action to fulfill her sacred potential. Like Redcrosse, she knows "no vntruth," and this is why she falls in love with him when she finds him able to wear her impossible-to-realize-in-ontological-reality Ephesian armor.

But the world of time is governed by that "most dreaded impe of highest *Ioue*, / Faire *Venus* sonne" (I.proem.3.1-2) who links two hearts together "with [his] cruell dart" (I.proem.3.2). Cupid has shot someone, but the fact that he has "cunningly...that glorious fire...kindled in his hart" (I.proem.3-4) does not mean that Una's assumption that he has kindled a fire in Redcrosse's heart *for her* is justified. Una merely assumes so based on her *a priori* assumption that this is the case long before she discloses her love for him in words, which at this point she has not done.

The problem with words is they can be misunderstood, as they, too, operate within the temporal world where they can and often do have more than one meaning. Una, being from Eden and operating the Edenic principles of identity, has no experience with deception. She takes her intention as binding on others without making further "triall" of her assumptions through the medium of speech. She continues to assume after she has passed into the world of time that nature is not brutal and that creatures within it are not out to do her harm. Yet the reader can see that this is exactly what causes her to flee after she is left alone with Archimago by Redcrosse without even the dwarf she came to court with. She will spend subsequent cantos seeking to restore natural balance, not between herself and herself (a=a), something that is already has available to her simply because she exists (even if her existence is granted to her only in fiction), but between her and her love (a=b).

Action and Potential

The division of Una from Redcrosse is a deliberate act on Spenser's part. It reflects the shift in classical philosophy brought about by Christianity, whose founding father Augustine took the position that metaphysical solutions were ultimately unavailable to the limited but rational mind of mankind. The Enlightenment thought this position anti-rational and that it disqualified Augustine access to complete knowledge of the whole of mankind. But in part of the medieval world, Augustine's position allowed mankind to bring Plato's separate world of being back into contact with the world of becoming by locating the soul in the substantial consciousness of the individual rather than in a distant and potentially fictional λόγος. The result was the difference between a two dimensional world of ontologically oriented classicism, which offers stark choices between incompatible philosophies (e.g. Stoicism and Epicureanism), and a three-dimensional world of Christianity, which denies access to metaphysical reality but leaves mankind in charge of the world of limited reason, a domain that made *good choice* important in a world of *free choice*.

Aristotle more than Plato was the philosopher of the relative and limited reason. Against Plato's assertion of a break in continuity between base matter and the Forms that man participated in that made them whole but were nevertheless unrealizable except in mind, Aristotle defines the relation between the potential of mankind and its realization in action through the excercise of free will in explicitly rational terms. This made Aristotle's thought accessible in ways that Plato's more complete thought was not.

Aristotle begins with a discussion of potential:

> ...all potentialities are either innate, like the senses, or come by practice, like the power of playing the flute, or by learning, like artistic power, those which come by practice or by rational formula we must acquire by previous exercise....[33]

This passage holds the possibility of practicing to make oneself a more perfect human being than one's natural gifts alone would allow for, but it also comes with a warning about the potential for failure. The same thing that holds true of oak trees holds true of men. A fully grown oak tree produces thousands of acorns, which hold the *potential* to become an oak tree within themselves, but not all acorns become oak trees in the world of action.

In Aristotle, the first step in actuating one's potential is to get in contact with the source of potential in oneself. These sources were held by Aristotle to be completely within the power of reason, which he held to be the specific difference that differentiated man from the genus of other

---

33 Aristotle, *Metaphysics*, IX.5.1047b31-36.

animals.³⁴ In Aristotle's world, things that exist in potential are "infinite," but they are also "void."³⁵ One of the consequences of Aristotle's infinite void is that though human potential may exist in the human mind, it cannot be accessed as it is.³⁶ The unrealizable nature of potential outside the mind means that things that can be separated in epistemology cannot be separated in ontological reality:

> The infinite does not exist in potential in the sense that it will ever actually have separate existence; separateness is only in knowledge."³⁷

The only way to activate one's potential is to impart a direction to one's life in time. This imparting of direction changes human beings from creatures in touch with the infinite foundation of themselves in their as-yet-unrealized *a priori* creation to creatures who make good or bad choices based in their limited *a posteriori* minds' encounter with external nature. Aristotle recognizes the switch from absolute to relative and limited ends in the *Metaphysics*: "Since of the actions which have a limit none in an end but all are relative to the end...."³⁸ Though this trade-off comes with a diminution of the metaphysical role of classical philosophy, it comes with certain benefits. Rather than relying on our natural human potential alone to rise above other creatures, we can use the power of education to rise above other men within our society. This was one of the sources of the power of a human art to rise above a hostile nature.

---

34 The modern aesthetic has dispensed with reason as the specific difference of mankind for a more complete unreason, but they have kept the notion that there is no need for anything external to the mind of man to realize mankind's potential in the world of action. All the modern man need to do to be in touch with his whole nature is to disconnect from the desires of his limited material being and switch to the still accessible foundations of our infinite being. This switch to the infinite has been the province of artists and critics, and it betrays the same sort of idealism that were held by academics in Augustine's day. Their exclusionary practices caused him to break with them.

35 The exact phrase is "infinite and void." Ibid., IX.6.1048b10.

36 In this way, it is like Schrödinger's cat: an inaccessible part of the mind that cannot be accessed in ontological reality without destroying its original form.

37 Ibid., IX.6.1048b14-15. This is one of the chief differences between the ancient thought of Aristotle and the modern thought of a philosopher like Nietzsche. Nietzsche believes that we can marginalize ourselves from normal habits of thought and so get in touch with something more fundamentally real that is lost on the masses. This quest for difference has been at the heart of the argument between the Moderns, who believe in weighing difference in the spatial organization of art, and the postmoderns, who tend to organize artistic difference on temporal lines. Aristotle does not believe that location in the reality of space or time has any bearing on human ability to activate what exists in potential.

38 Ibid., IX.6.1048b18-19.

The Triumph Of Divisive Science Over Moral Goodness

Reading Aristotle's *Politics* the reader can see just how poorly Spenser frames Redcrosse's realization of his potential *in the world of action*:

> For man, when perfected, is the best of animals, but, when separated from law and justice, he is the worst of all; since armed injustice is the more dangerous, and he is equipped at birth with arms, meant to be used by intelligence and virtue, which he may use for the worst ends. Wherefore, if he have not virtue, he is the most unholy and the most savage of animals, and the most full of lust and gluttony. But justice is the bond of men in states, for the administration of justice, which is the determination of what is just, is the principle of order in political society.[39]

The reader may consider Redcrosse as a virtuous man who is innocent of the consequences of his behavior; but the issue in Spenser's Augustinian poem is not his *a priori* virtue but the *location* of his virtue in the *a posteriori* world of time, which Redcrosse mistakenly ascribes to himself rather than to God. As a consequence, Spenser portrays his hero, despite his salvation by God in an inaccessible Heaven, in the *world of action* as the "most unholy and the most savage of animals" who uses his arms "for the worst ends" and not in the service of "intelligence and virtue" from which good government springs.

God's reasoning in choosing such an unlikely hero is inaccessible to the reader, to the poet, and it goes without saying to Redcrosse himself. The "clownishe younge man" Redcrosse has brought no reason to his actions and he has shown no interest in pursuing education. He is still relying on his own force and will when he leaves Una. He has not yet realized that his power is not his own but comes from God's "goodwill," as he will declare in Book II after his adventure is over. Before he can get to that realization, he will have to exchange his *a priori* confidence that his own will is enough to accomplish his goals for the realization that others—Una, Arthur, and God to name but three key figures—are required in order to impart direction to his will. And this is why the science of speech wins out over holy silence in Archimago's hermitage. But the consequence of this is that Archimago is able to divide Redcrosse from Una. She holds to her inner purpose, but she remains too confident in her silence in the world of time. This allows Archimago to divide his foe Redcrosse from her, sending him into the wilderness without her.

---

39 Aristotle, *Politics* 1253a31-39.

Action After Division

The Misformed Thought of Archimago

Unlike Redcrosse, Archimago has no innate moral virtue; but he has an enormous amount of rational intelligence, as the arch-deceiver has taken a great deal of care to educate himself. He has become a master of "Legions of Sprights" (I.i.38.2) charges that are also "well instructed" (I.i.47.1). This leaves them able to travel through the gates of ivory and silver, which he, as a substantial individual, finds "locked fast" (I.i.40.1).[1] But when his initial plan fails to bring Redcrosse's potential into action, he believes that there is something wrong with his artificially created sprite, who he has in some way "misformed" (I.i.55.9). He begins to vent his anger at his "messengers of hell" (I.ii.2.1) for having "his skillful might / Deluded so" (I.ii.2.5-6), until he realizes "his threatening was but vaine" (I.ii.2.8). He then returns to search "his baleful books againe" (I.ii.2.9).

The careful reader is in a position to see that his miscreation is not a matter of *form* at all. Instead, it is a matter of his *a priori* belief in the ontology of his creations. We recall his creation of False Una by means of "charmes and hidden artes" (I.i.45.1), as he gives the ungendered sprite a female form:

---

1 This, like the brazen walls of Eden is another case of porous borders. My reading is that the sprites, being immaterial, can travel where the substantial Archimago cannot. This would make Archimago a real force in the universe, as opposed to the purely imaginary sprites, who share with Errour their artificial creation. Given my discussion of the fact that both the names and unnamed gates refer to Virgil's gate of ivory, I presume that Archimago's education is only in false dreams, while the gate of true dreams remains locked to Archimago and his sprites.

> And fram'd of liquid ayre her tender partes
> So liuely, and so like in all mens sight,
> That weaker sence it could haue rauisht quight:
> The maker selfe for all his wondrous witt,
> Was nigh beguiled with so goodly sight. (I.i.45.3-7)

Beneath the hylomorphic forms of "liquid ayre" there remains the question of the substance of the sprite itself. Spenser is asking his readers to consider whether the *substance* of the sprite, which Morpheus has called up from "deepe darknes dreadd" (I.i.38.1), exists anymore than the form that the subtle magician lays on top of it. The careful reader can see this in the poet's expression of his own disbelief in "those accursed messengers of hell" (I.ii.2.1), which he expressly terms, along with "that faire-forged Spright," as a "feigning dreame" (I.ii.2.2), as they come to tell their master of "Their bootelesse paines, and ill succeeding night" (I.ii.2.4).² For all the labor expended in Archimago's effort to shift the attitude of Morpheus from neutrality to the side of evil and so to shift the ontology of the universe in his favor, none of this makes any difference on account of Redcrosse knowing in his mind "no vntruthe," and this is why it makes no difference.

This observation about the negative content of Redcrosse's mind does not make Redcrosse into a *positive* role model. Spenser's hero cannot reconcile the picture of Una, who– he had thought to be "the chastest flowre, that ay did spring / On earthly braunch" (I.i.48.4-5), with the creature he now sees as a "gentle Dame so light" (I.i.55.2). He goes back to sleep despite his doubts about what he has seen; and it is only after Archimago has returned to his books and fashions another "seeming body of subtile aire" (I.ii.3.3) in the form of a young squire that he rouses Redcrosse from his slumber and points him to the False Una, who has knit herself in "*Venus* shameful chain" (I.ii.4.8). This showing of Una's love for *another* (a=b) rouses Redcrosse, who had remained passive throughout the False Una's profession of his love for *him* (a=a), to action; and he threatens to slay them both "in his furious ire" (I.ii.5.8) that had blinded the "eye of reason" (I.ii.5.7).

In one of the great moments of Spenserian irony, Redcrosse "hardly was restreined of that aged sire" (I.ii.5.9), as Archimago comes to her rescue, not because of any pity on his part, but because he is a man of "weaker sense" who had presumably has fallen in love with the creation of own false imagination. Thus, Archimago does the work of God by saving Redcrosse from a mortal sin, all the while thinking he has failed because he is thinking

---

2 I perceive a pun on Boötes in Spenser's citation of their "bootelesse paines."

in ontological terms about his own creation. Rather than rooting for Redcrosse and delighting in the defeat of Archimago, Spenser is pointing his readers to the severe limitations of both when it comes to the Aristotelian notion of combining intelligence with virtue that is necessary to rule the public state. At this point in his adventure, Redcrosse's naïve "clownishe" innocence is not adequate to the task of dealing with the "other" in the world. This is why, in spite of himself, Archimago's divisive science triumphs over Redcrosse's unitary innocence born of his "clownishe" naiveté.

We can see the limits of Redcrosse's innocence when confronted by the (completely unfounded) possibility that Una might be "so light." Rather than making "triall" of her, he immediately abandons her, adding insult to injury by taking her dwarf with him as he goes.[3]

Archimago and Redcrosse on Ends

Though he relies on "diuelish arts" (I.ii.9.4) that attempt to imitate God's creation directly, Archimago is on the right track as far as his utilization of his intellect in pursuing his ends. The "clownishe" Redcrosse, unbeknownst to himself at this point in the poem, relies on Una's magical and altogether fictional armor to win his battles for him. As such, he is alienated from the source of his power, which lies outside of himself. Archimago is a master of worldly science; and rather than Redcrosse's end, which is to *shorten* the distance between himself and his end by wrapping up his battles immediately, Archimago's end is to permanently separate Una from Redcrosse, thus *lengthening* the distance between Una and Redcrosse. Thus, Archimago is satisfied when sees the two

> diuided into double parts,
> And *Vna* wandring in woods and forrests,
> Th'end of his drift…. (I.ii.9.2-4)

In the modern world, readers are likely to dismiss this division of Redcrosse and Una into "double parts" as an unmitigated evil, but Archimago also performs a great service to Redcrosse when he divides him from Una,

---

3 This is more than he brought with him, and thus introduces another instance of inequality into Spenser's poem. The fact that Una's dwarf goes with him speaks to the fundamental inequality of gender roles in Book I, but also of Una's weak standing as a figure of mere potential in a world that requires actors to activate their potential in the world of time. The inequality of gender roles is not a permanent feature of Spenser's universe, as we can see by considering the role of Britomart in Book III or the dedication of the poem to Elizabeth.

the creature of unitary virtue. Una has brought her unitary sense of values with her from Eden into the world of time; but her sense of how to evaluate people and ideas in the world of time has already failed her. This is because she does not have any sense that anyone could be deceiving her by saying one thing while meaning another. It is up to Archimago to introduce the "other" into her unitary value system. Despite the reader's reservations about Archimago's intentions in dividing the pair, it is a good thing. Archimago's problem is not just that he has a misplaced sense of value. It is that he is motivated by wrath rather than goodness. Wrath is a vice that does not escape Redcrosse early on in the book (he will be cured of wrath only after he meets Charissa in the House of Holinesse (I.x.33.5)). Being subject to wrath, Archimago "hated [Una] as the hissing snake" (I.ii.9.8).[4]

Archimago uses his "mightie science" that is motivated by wrath to build a False Redcrosse to fool Una, as he had built a False Una to fool Redcrosse:

> He then deuisde himselfe how to disguise;
> For by his mighty science he could take
> As many formes and shapes in seeming wise,
> As euer *Proteus* to himselfe could make:
> Sometime a fowle, sometime a fish in lake,
> Now like a foxe, now like a dragon fell,
> That of himselfe he ofte for feare would quake,
> And oft would flie away. O who can tell
> The hidden power of herbes, and might of Magick spell? (I.ii.10)

This magical science, which we in the modern world have such a hard time accepting,[5] would have seemed possible for a man to believe in in Spenser's day. The question is whether Spenser believes that his own ability to work his magic is confined within his fiction, or whether he believes that his magic will survive the deconstruction of his fiction, as the ontologically real

---

4 The reader will later learn that Charissa hates Cupid with equal vitriol.

5 The use of magic played a role in the construction of the universe until the birth of purely mechanical explanation of phenomena in modern science. The most notable person in the construction of a purely mechanical universe in which God played no role in everyday operations was Isaac Newton, whom the Enlightenment thought of as taking the place of God. For an explanation of how the Enlightenment thought to transfer all religious thought to nature and of the attempt to replace God with "Newtons of the Mind," see Gay, *The Enlightenment, An Interpretation: The Science of Freedom*, 126-166. Interestingly, the Enlightenment made of their hero more of a mechanist than he actually was. For a brief explication of Newton's embarrassing foray into the history of religion, see the chapter "The Euhemerists and Isaac Newton" in Manuel, *The Eighteenth Century Confronts the Gods*, 83-125.

reader will. That question is subject to the individual reader's estimation of various options available to the poet. In a universe in which human beings must rely on their perception of things and not on an metaphysically secure knowledge of things as they are, the proper role of the reader is to make "triall" of their experience and confront it head on through a still fallible reason, dividing the rational content still available to the *a posteriori* mind into smaller and smaller pieces and leaving alone the *a priori* things created by God as unapproachable mysteries.

This strategy of taking fallible reason to its end before surrendering to its inevitable downfall was employed by Augustine in his consideration of enigmatic allegory. The strategy allows Augustine to maintain his skeptical position as a rational *and* moral man among deceptive objects in a hostile nature that classical philosophers took to be the ends of their inquiry into the universe. This is the same moral lesson that Spenser draws for Redcrosse: he should not simply "flie away" from his experience as both Una and her dwarf urge him to do on the verge of his entry into the Cave of Errour. Flying from his fears will forever be at odds with his end, which is to *confront* the Dragon and so achieve *worldly* glory. The proper response in Spenser's day was to stay and make "triall" of Archimago's magic, which would have been shown to wield its power on account of Redcrosse's belief *in its effects* but not on any ontological reality that it possesses.

By the end of Book I, Redcrosse will have learned that he must do more than to rely on his *a priori* sense of animal being. That animal state of being is guaranteed by God, his Creator, in the pre-linguistic state of ontology before the imposition of human names on things. At this point in the poem, Redcrosse is being driven instead by his own "will," which itself is being driven by "gealous feare" and a "griefe" that causes his to flee his own thoughts:

> But he the knight, whose semblaunt he did beare,
> The true *Saint George* was wandred far away,
> Still flying from his thoughts and gealous feare;
> *Will was his guide*, and griefe led him astray. (I.ii.12.1-4 italics mine)

In that same passage in which he is fleeing Una, the principle of unity in the poem, Spenser refers to him as the "true *Saint George*," indicating that the poet feels that even now, *before he has met and defeated the Dragon*, that God has chosen him as one of his saints. That decision was made before the poem had begun, before Una had given him the armor of Ephesians, before he had put it on, and before Una had switched her view of the individual George into the figural state of Redcrosse. The condition of the sainthood of George is thus prior to his being and is unalterable by any decision on the part of Redcrosse's will or of Una's perception of him.

The journey that defines the narrative is therefore not one of falling away from and returning to God's *a priori* creation of saints. Instead, Spenser is redefining mankind away from his own image of himself as perfect and whole being, introducing his readers to an imperfect George who must act on imperfect information presented to him within the world of time. Within that world, the meaning of things can be taken in more than one sense. Seen from this perspective, Redcrosse is still a "clownishe younge man" who still *hopes* to be granted admission to Gloriana's court, which "of all earthly things he most did craue" (I.i.3.5).

That means that *in spite of his already guaranteed salvation* Redcrosse is judged by the superbly-educated courtiers who administer the government of society in Gloriana's court to be a "clownishe younge man" whose preference for the use of his arms in search of instant victory is thought to reflect "the worst ends" of mankind. Redcrosse's reliance only on his animal genus without the specific difference of reason disqualifies him from membership at court, whose governance of society requires a reason that sets up society, not in accordance with nature, but against it. The human community is created as a supplemental and *a posteriori*ly-created thing that stands between men and their encounter with a brutal nature that has created men as animals with the brutal instincts and which must be carefully protected from onslaughts by clowns like Redcrosse who would use his animal powers to *increase* violence without the calming effects of human reason.

Spenser's readers should be beginning to realize that Redcrosse is not all that they thought he was when he started on his adventure. His having no "vntruthe" in his mind is not a virtue but a flaw, though neither he nor Archimago recognize the fact that his trusting nature gives Archimago no power to defeat Redcrosse as long as God has chosen him as His friend.

Justice and Native Virtue in Redcrosse's Defeat of Sansfoy

Having had his will divided from the source of his armor, if not from God himself, Redcrosse meets the opposite of his God-given *a priori* grace in the character of Sansfoy, who "cared not for God or man a point" (I.ii.12.9). As we have seen in the Cave of Errour, after Augustine not everything in the world has an ontologically real opposite; some things (like evil) are merely privative of good. This is the case with Sansfoy, whose name reveals only his lack of faith. Rather than checking his diverse sense impressions against a deeper truth grounded in his God-given potential and acting out of that deeper grounding, Redcrosse acts once again just as he had acted in Cave of Errour, endeavoring to win or lose his battle all at once. Sansfoy, like Redcrosse, is "prickt with pride" (I.ii.14.6), and he, too, is impatient.

The two great opposites meet in a poetically-constructed epic simile:

> As when two rams stird with ambitious *pride*,
> Fight for the rule of the rich fleeced flocke,
> Their horned fronts so fierce on either side
> Do meete…. (I.ii.16.1-4 italics mine)

However, the clash of these two proud rams is inconclusive, as they both are so powerful and hit each other so hard that they both forget why they have come to fight:

> that with the terror of the shocke
> Astonied both, stand sencelesse as a blocke,
> Forgetfull of the hanging victory. (I.ii.16.4-6)

As the following stanza explains, the strength of each combatant is equal:

> Each others equall puissaunce enuies,
> And through their iron sides with cruell spies
> Does seeke to perce: repining courage yields
> No foote to foe. (I.ii.17.4-7)

Spenser reinforces the notion that both Redcrosse and Sansfoy are filled with pride with a double entendre, substituting fier, the French word for pride, for fire:

> The flashing fier flies
> As from a forge out of their burning shields,
> And streames of purple bloud new dies the verdant fields. (I.ii.17.7-9)

What changes things out of equal balance, of course, is the Saracen's exclamation, "Curse on that Crosse" (I.ii.18.1). He believes that the power of Redcrosse to stand up to his blows can be attributed, not to the inexorable foreordained will of God, but to some exterior magical "charme" which has "forwarned" Redcrosse's victory (I.ii.18.4).

Spenser offers his careful readers another and stronger explanation, and unlike the magical armor of Una, this aspect is imitable in the hearts of readers after the fiction has been closed and they are back living their ontological lives. It is the native virtue of God that has been planted within Redcrosse's heart:

> Who thereat wondrous wroth, the sleeping spark
> Of natiue vertue gan eftsoones reuiue,
> And at his haughtie helmet making mark,
> So hugely stroke, that it the steele did riue,
> And cleft his head. (I.ii.19.1-5)

In drawing on the tradition of native virtue here, Spenser is drawing on a division of will that goes far beyond John Calvin. In the 12th century Gilbert of Poitiers, had posited a "native virtue" on which he had built an *a posteriori* education based on Boethius' liberal arts.[6] In Gilbert's 12th century work, the connection between the human mind and God came through access to "native virtue." Spenser was a bit more wary of such easy access through Philosophy and her liberal arts curriculum than Gilbert had been, since between the 12th and the 16th centuries thinkers had begun to question the exact role that Philosophy, who was a creature wrought by imperfect nature, played in the mind's ascent to God. In the 13th century in particular, Jean de Meun had weighed Reason in the balance and found her wanting.[7] Thereafter, Philosophy had dominion over the liberal arts, which were granted access to the external, scientific world. But there was something more needed to gain access to the whole of life. Spenser does not seem to have accepted Calvin's absolute break between science and faith, preferring to approach faith through a=b means through the medium of a deconstructable fiction.

As a result of Sansfoy's curse on God cross, Redcrosse kills him instantly with his sword, and Sansfoy

> tumbling downe aliue,
> With bloudy mouth his mother earth did kis,

---

6 Etienne Gilson, *History of Christian Philosophy in the Middle Ages* (New York, NY: Random House, 1955), 140-144.

7 For a more prevalent but contrary opinion on the *Roman de la Rose,* in which Reason is offered to the Lover and it is the Lover's fault that he does not respond as he should, see D. W. Robertson, Jr., *A Preface to Chaucer*, John V. Fleming, *Reason and the Lover*, (Princeton, N.J.: Princeton University Press, 1984), and the introduction by Charles Dahlberg to Guillaume de Lorris and Meun Jean de, *The Romance of the Rose*, trans. Charles Dahlberg (Princeton, NJ: Princeton University Press, 1971).

> Greeting his graue: his grudging ghost did striue
> With the fraile flesh; at last it flitted is,
> Whither the soules do fly of men, that liue amis. (I.ii.19.5-9)

The question for the reader is not whether Redcrosse, a clownish country bumkin, has native virtue. He clearly does. The question is what, if anything, he can build on top of his native virtue. It appears at this point that he can build very little, as he is still focused on fighting his battle with a mind to winning all at once. In this case he wins, but it to God that he owes his victory. Redcrosse's flaws are more serious than not recognizing God's part in his victory. Once he has defeated his enemy he sends Una's stolen dwarf to pick up his fallen enemy's shield, indicating a willingness to take up, not just the arms of the just man of Ephesians, but the arms of *anyone* he defeats in battle as "signe of the conqueroure" (I.ii.20.7) This indifference to the great moral difference between the two armors must be considered a flaw in Spenser's universe.

Friend of Duessa

Redcrosse now turns his attention to Sansfoy's traveling companion, Duessa. Seeing "her champion fall / Like the old ruines of a broken towre" (I.ii.20.1-2), she does not stay for a funeral—this is in itself an act of infamy—but attempts to flee the scene. As with Errour, Redcrosse should have let a fleeing enemy flee, but the man whose "natiue virtue" has defeated Sansfoy, runs after her, overtakes her, "and bad [her] to stay" (I.ii.20.8).

Redcrosse attempts to reassure her, telling her "For present cause was none of dread her to dismay" (I.ii.20.9) and

> Deare dame, your suddein ouerthrow
> Much rueth me; but now put feare apart.... (I.ii.21.7-8)

This is true, as far as it goes; she indeed has nothing to fear from him. But the poet's configuration of the situation completely leaves out the question of whether he has anything to fear from *her*. Spenser clearly indicates to the reader his disapproval of his urging her to stay, indicated by his word "bad." But if the reader has not caught this subtle hint, Spenser clobbers his readers with an unmistakable description of her moral character, as

> A goodly Lady clad in scarlot red,
> Purfled with gold and pearle of rich assay,
> And like a *Persian* mitre on her hed
> Shee wore, with crownes and owches garnished,

The which her lauish louers to her gaue;
Her wanton palfrey all was ouerspred
With tinsell trappings, wouen like a waue,
Whose bridle rung with golden bels and bosses braue. (I.ii.13.2-9)

Redcrosse's reaction is not provided by his having looked at the evidence which confronts him, but by the faulty hierarchy of knowledge drawn from his playing at chivalry. His "stout heroicke heart" is "much emmoue[d]" (I.ii.21.6) by her "ritch weedes and seeming glorious show" (I.ii.21.5), which for no obvious reason (because there is no reason) Redcrosse translates into "her humblesse low" (I.ii.21.4).

She, having been caught fleeing, changes her countenance towards him, and she flatters him, appealing to his "mighty will" (I.i.21.4), thereby playing into his belief that his will is the source of his power. For his part, Redcrosse believes her representation of herself as a "virgin widow" (I.ii.24.8), despite the fact that his readers have been previously told that her "crownes and owches" are gifts which "her lauish *louers* to her gaue" (I.ii.13.5-6 italics emphasizing the plural are mine).

Moreover, she audibly betrays her lingering attachment to Sansfoy at several points. She speaks of the "vnhappy howre" that has made her "thrall to your commandement" (I.ii.22.2-3), of "fortune false" which has "betraide me to your power" (I.ii.22.5), and of her former lover as lying "with foule dishonour dead" (I.ii.25.5). These are not the sort of things that one says when one is happy to have been rescued from the hands of evil-doers, and they must make the careful reader wonder once again at the mind of the Redcrosse Knight that does not pick up on these really obvious signs. And that is not all. She openly proclaims herself to be "Borne the sole daughter of an Emperour, / He that the wide West vnder his rule has" (I.ii.22.7-8). Una also has a holy emperor as a father, but the father she claims clearly maintains a secular throne, as he is the Emperor of Rome who has "set his throne, where *Tiberis* doth pas" (I.ii.22.9). Redcrosse's subsequent acceptance of her bespeaks his turning away from Una's kingdom of God to the city of man that Augustine had distinguished in his *City of God*.

The difference between Una and Duessa can be seen in how well each covers themselves in Redcrosse's presence. Una hides her body beneath a wimple that reveals nothing but her face, whereas Duessa openly exposes her body to the world. But for all her bodily openness, Duessa hides her identity, giving her name as Fidessa (I.ii.26.2). Spenser clearly indicates that it is the lower appetite of the knight that knows "no vntruthe" that attracts him to her, as he stares at her open face:

> He in great passion al this while did dwell,
> More busying his quicke eies, her face to view,
> Then his dull eares, to heare what shee did tell.... (I.ii.26.5-7)

Redcrosse seems blithely unaware that he is in any danger as he does this. And for all the reader knows, he may not *be* in any danger. They have been assured by the narrator that his heart is blessed with grace, and his holy armor will secure him victory in any battle he engages in. But by not listening to his experience with the ear of a poet, whom the reader has seen making comparisons to moral examples, Redcrosse is substituting the immediate experience available to his superficial eyes for the deeper experience of bringing one's memory to bear on everything he encounters.

The reader sees once again that Redcrosse is not offered as a model of good behavior when he gives his assurance to Fidessa that she has found a new friend:

> Henceforth in safe assuraunce may ye rest,
> Hauing both found a new friend you to aid,
> And lost an old foe, that did you molest. (I.ii.27.1-3)

On the surface, perhaps, his repetition of an old proverb—"Better new friend then an old foe is said" (I.ii.27.4)—seems adequate. But proverbs are not enough to negotiate the world of contradictory desires, for Redcrosse has constructed the situation he is describing. Fidessa has given him no indication that she feels she has lost an old foe; in fact she has said things that give the reader contradictory indications. This should lead the careful reader to suspect that *Redcrosse* has exchanged an older and truer friend for a new foe when he exchanges Una for Fidessa.

At last they come to a shady grove where "two goodly trees" (I.ii.28.3) spread their leaves. This resembles the sun-shaded wood where Redcrosse, Una, and her dwarf had found the Cave of Errour; and once again Spenser shifts to epic simile once again to tell his readers that normal men should fear this spot:

> The fearefull Shepheard often there aghast
> Vnder them neuer sat, ne wont there sound
> His mery oaten pipe, but shund th'vnlucky ground. (I.ii.28.7-9)

Spenser's point seems to be that it is not by ducking into a cooling spot at the first sign of heat or rain that a man can secure himself against danger. Such places are not in fact safe. They merely hide the ever present dangers from those uncareful enough not to guard themselves against dangers which lie hidden within. Even rude poets know enough to avoid such places.

Spenser describes the pair of lovers as they engage in "Faire seemely pleasaunce" that "each to the other makes" (I.ii.30.1). He describes the intercourse of Redcrosse and Fidessa in terms of "goodly purposes" (I.ii.30.2). Yet he follows this immediately with a qualification that makes it apparent that the poet does not believe that their "goodly purposes" are good at all:

> And in his falsed fancy he her takes
> To be the fairest wight, that liued yit. (I.i.30.3-4)

Redcrosse is not content to remain silent about his affection for Fidessa, and thus he speaks:

> Which to expresse, he bends his gentle wit,
> And thinking of those braunches greene to frame
> A girlond for her dainty forehead fit,
> He pluckt a bough. (I.ii.30.5-8)

In traveling from the *silent* domain of God's pre-linguistic creation of his undeniably true heart to his *expression* of his passion for Fidessa, Spenser clearly feels that Redcrosse has exchanged his true heart for a false one in his faulty *expression* of his desire for her. This is an indication that when it is up to Redcrosse's *will* to choose, he chooses to crown Fidessa as his beloved and *not* Una, who will later be crowned *by others* in a parallel ceremony as "maiden Queene" (I.xii.8.9).

Fradubio

When Redcrosse carelessly plucks a bough to crown the woman he now sees as "the fairest wight, that liued yit" (I.ii.30.4), he instantly hears a voice saying the familiar words that the dwarf had spoken on the verge of Redcrosse's reckless entry into the Cave of Errour: "fly, ah fly far hence away" (I.ii.31.4). This voice frightens him enough to kill his "dreadfull passion" (I.ii.32.1), which presumably stops the copulation of the pair. At the same time it wakens, not his God-given sense, but his sense of his "manhood" (I.ii.32.2). But once again, rather than heeding the advice he has just been given and actually flying, Redcrosse looks around for the source of the voice, which he finds to have come from Fradubio, a man who has been turned into a tree by the magic of Duessa.

After his initial fright was "ouerpast" (I.ii.32.2), instead of fleeing, he begins to doubt his sense (I.ii.32.4), wondering whether he is hearing a

> voyce of damned Ghost from Limbo lake,
> Or guilefull spright wandring in empty aire
> Both which fraile men do oftentimes mistake. (I.ii.32.5-6).

I (and I suspect you) would doubt my senses were I ever to encounter such a thing as a former-man-turned-into-a-talking-tree. The question is whether or not Spenser intends his Reformation readers to question such a ridiculous thing as he is presenting them with here. The modern solution is to believe that Spenser does not expect them to have any questions. But that is a poor bet, as the poet has been cagey in his assertion that Redcrosse is not a man but an elf *in spite of the fact that he knows better*. The modern assertion appears to be an importation into the Reformation of Coleridge's supsension of disbelief as a necessary first step for the production of realistic fiction. But Spenser is not interested in producing realistic fiction. The existence of Fradubio is part of the imaginative fiction which the poet Spenser has access to. The poet *wants* to highlight his own magic here, as well as the magic of Duessa. Within the confines of his ultimately deconstructing fiction, Redcrosse should still be checking his senses against larger-than-individual values drawn from the larger world that surrounds him, even if he has not got access to their ultimate metaphysical ground.

Redcrosse would be right to question "these speaches rare" (I.ii.32.8), because "fraile men do oftentimes mistake" them (I.ii.32.7); and who could be more morally frail than the Redcrosse Knight? But the problem is not resolved by Redcrosse's questioning of the reality of events here. The poet is posing a question of reference *after* he has checked his senses and found them to have an observable source. Throughout this episode, Redcrosse never connects the fact that there are deep and specific parallels between the discrete experience of Fradubio and his own, despite the fact that Fradubio seems to be explicitly warning him that Redcrosse has also taken up with "*this* wretched Lady" (I.ii.31.6 italics mine), the very same Duessa whom the reader learns Fradubio has learned all too late to recognize. And Fradubio is not subtle in his accusation that through the operations of "this wretched Lady, my deare loue, / O too deare loue, loue bought with death too deare" (I.ii.31.6-7).

Unfortunately, Fradubio is unaware of the fact that Duessa has given

Redcrosse the name of Fidessa, nor that Redcrosse is not the sharpest knife in the knight drawer. The careful reader can put this into a philosophical context. Redcrosse mistakes the individual sense of Fradubio's words for a general sense. Individual reference is the name of the game in Spenser's world, and on account of the generally named Redcrosse's not yet having learned this, nor of his membership in the "fraile" class of humanity, he has not learned to recognize the fraud that continues to be played on him and which he is being warned of directly. Instead, he deflects reference away from where it properly belongs: on himself as an individual.

Fradubio denies that he is a ghost or a guileful sprite but a man. Redcrosse then asks the man-tree to explain "by whose mischieuous arts / Art thou misshaped thus, *as now I see*" (I.ii.34.2-3 italics mine).[8] Redcrosse's focus is still on the visible surface, and in response Fradubio responds plainly:

> The author then (said he) of all my smarts,
> Is one *Duessa* a false sorceresse,
> That many errant knights hath brought to wretchednesse. (I.ii.34.7-9)

But in spite of this superficial exchange, Redcrosse does not connect the dots that lie beneath the surface; and Fradubio continues to believe that Redcrosse knows what he is talking about without making "triall" of his words to ensure that they have been taken as he means them.[9]

Fradubio then recounts his own experience as a young knight:

> In prime of youthly yeares, when corage hott
> The fire of loue and *ioy of cheualree*
> First kindled in my brest.... (I.ii.35.1-3 italics mine)

Fradubio had been riding along accompanied by the woman he loved, Frælissa, who has also been turned into a tree.[10] He tells their story:

---

8 Maybe I'm being picky, but Fradubio could just as easily categorize himself as a tree, and this would lead to the same assertion of what Redcrosse "sees." Spenser's point is that sight can be guided by others, but true "sight" in Spenser's universe comes from the deployment of human reason, not sight alone, which can peer beneath things to see how they were made by God. Such reason is conspicuously absent from the mind of Redcrosse.

9 This is not the last time this will happen to Redcrosse. See his diverse discourse with Arthur on the subject of love in canto ix.

10 Frælissa remains silent, as Redcrosse has not broken off any of her bark in an act of violence.

> Me chaunced of a knight encountred bee,
> That had a like faire Lady by his syde,
> Like a faire Lady, but did fowle *Duessa* hyde. (I.ii.35.7-9)

He and the knight fought over whose dame should get precedence in beauty, and Fradubio won the contest. But Fradubio's victory only compounds his problem, for he is left with two dames, both beautiful. After the doubling of his love, which has its parallel in the doubling of True Una with a false one, he needs a new form of judgment to decide how to choose between two loves of equal beauty:

> The wicked witch now seeing all this while
> The doubtfull ballaunce equally to sway.... (I.ii.38.1-2)

Not having been taught any more than Redcrosse has been to rely on a "native virtue" that is deeper than his superficial will, Fradubio had been deceived by Duessa's magic:

> What not by right, she cast to win by guile,
> And by her hellish *science* raisd streight way
> A foggy mist, that ouercast the day,
> And a dull blast, that breathing on her face,
> Dimmed her former beauties shining ray,
> And with foule vgly forme did her disgrace. (I.ii.38.3-8 italics mine)

After Duessa has used her magic to deform her rival's beauty, the scales are no longer in balance: "Then was she faire alone, when none was faire in place." (I.ii.38.9).

Fradubio has chosen poorly, as has Redcrosse, for as soon as Duessa transforms Frælissa, Fradubio announces that she has revealed the true character of his former love:

> Then cride she out, Fye, fye, deformed wight,
> Whose borrowed beautie now appeareth plaine
> To haue before bewitched all mens sight. (I.ii.39.1-3)

It is probable that Fradubio's exclamation that she had deceived "*all* mens sight" because he had deceived his own sight is inaccurate—the reader will later meet Arthur, who founds his thought on reason and not sight alone and so is able to save the helpless Redcrosse—but Fradubio had believed *his* eyes (just as Redcrosse had paid more attention to his own eyes than listening with his ears when he sat down here), and "Thens forth I tooke

Duessa for my Dame" (I.ii.40.1). This clearly is a warning for Redcrosse, who is young and full of unfocused chivalric energy and who has a record of making poor choices.

A mental battle ensues in the mind of Fradubio:

> I gan refraine, in minde to slip away,
> Soone as appeard safe opportunitie. (I.ii.41.6-7)

However, Duessa perceives his "thought," and she takes measures to suppress his senses with "wicked herbes and oyntments" (I.i.42.3).

How long "Are you in this misformed house to dwell?" (I.ii.43.2), asks Redcrosse, echoing Archimago's feeling that it is only a lack of form that has betrayed him and not something deeper that is simply missing in Redcrosse's construction of his universe, like the fact that Fradubio is not in a house at all but through an act of pagan metamorphosis has been rendered into a man-plant who sits in nature *outside* of human shelter.

Fradubio answers

> We may not chaunge (quoth he) this euill plight,
> Till we be bathed in a liuing well;
> That is the terme prescribed by the spell. (I.ii.43.3-5)

The reader might believe that Redcrosse has compassion for Fradubio on the basis of his next question:

> O how, sayd he, mote I that well out find,
> That may restore you to your wonted well? (I.ii.43.6-7)

But his subsequent action betray his *lack* of compassion for the plight of Fradubio, and by extension for his own plight. Redcrosse is filled with dread at the prospect that someone could be transformed out of their humanity through magic, much less the prospect of detouring himself from his course—which the reader is reminded is completely random and has no course—and he thrusts the branches, which he himself had broken off, back into the ground "That from the blood he might be innocent" (I.ii.44.7). Of course, according to Augustine no *man* is innocent within the the extra-Edenic world of time, but Redcrosse still thinks that he is not a man at all, but an "Elfin knight" (I.i.17.1). He travels in the world, therefore, without thinking that the Fall has affected him. When in canto xi he is restored by the very "liuing well" of which Fradubio speaks, the reader is given no indication that he remembers Fradubio at that point.[11]

Once again, Spenser explains that Redcrosse is "*too* simple and *too* trew" (I.ii.45.7 italics mine). This weakness caused him to flee the chaste maid Una without making "triall" of her and causes him to return to Fidessa, whose willingness to show him her body makes her available to his superficial eyes without any more educational effort on his part. Fidessa feigns fear (I.ii.45.1) in opposition to the real fear that is apparent in Redcrosse's "trembling cheare" (I.ii.45.6), and he "oft her kist" (I.ii.45.8) before setting her "on her steede, and forward forth did bear" (I.ii.45.9). This joins the forward motion of the errant knight with an errant intention, and leaves the fearless Fidessa in charge of the direction they will take.

The intrusion of Fradubio in the narrative intercedes between the moment when Redcrosse is about to crown Fidessa and the moment in which he actually consecrates his relationship with her through physical intercourse. Had he been able to sort his experience correctly, he would not be about to make what is after all a *terrible* decision. But the fact is that this may not matter to Redcrosse, who has been given his salvation by God above in advance of any action he takes. God will act as a powerful "frend" and will get him out of any scrapes he gets into.

But the poet's verdict on Redcrosse's *will* thus far is not positive. He has just introduced the Knight of Holinesse to a man who has warned him of the direct parallels between the particular woman with whom he (Redcrosse) has taken up as his companion (Duessa) and Fradubio's own experience with her. It seems to the careful reader that Redcrosse has not heard a word that Fradubio has said. In response to his meeting with Fradubio, Redcrosse should begin having a battle within his own mind (psychomachia) for control of such contrary opinions as he holds.

Sadly, he does not.

---

11 See my discussion of that episode in the chapter "Science Outside the Walls of Eden" for my explanation of why he forgets Fradubio at that point in his adventure.

Una in the Extremity of Time

Although the cyclical reading of Redcrosse's falling away from sainthood and returning to it can be applied to Redcrosse's adventure, this configuration is much harder to apply to the character of Una, who is described by Douglas Brooks-Davies in his article on "Una" in *The Spenser Encyclopedia*, as the "principle of indivisibility, Truth in its philosophical and religious aspects."[1] Una as Truth is never separated from herself; so, although she like Redcrosse wanders in the wilderness and meets a series of characters that react to her essential unity in various ways, the fact that she is never separated from herself leaves her without an arc in the narrative that unfolds after she is separated from her beloved knight. Such a reading renders Una a passive recipient of the active Redcrosse's adoration. She is merely waiting for him to return to her unified self, and at the end of her journey she is the same as she was before.[2]

One can read Una's journey in the wilderness differently. She had brought her prelasparian unified perspective with her into the world of time. She expects her whole perspective to be adequate to the tasks set before her in the world of action within the alien (to Una) universe of time. However, during her separation from Redcrosse, she finds that her perspective is *not* adequate to the tasks set before her. Rather than resting content within herself (a=a) and waiting for others to act for her, Una must learn

---

1 Brooks-Davies, Douglas, "Una" in Hamilton, *The Spenser Encyclopedia*, 705.
2 We can put this into a logical context, of course. Una's identity places her into an a=a relation with herself. She is waiting for Redcrosse, who has gone off in search of a still unsatisfied extension of himself in the world of time (a=b), to return to her. Such a passive position does not do justice to the dangerous position that the careless Redcrosse has left her in.

to divide her whole perspective into its constituent parts through the divisions of science that are appropriate in the world of time. When she does so, her mind will grow to consciously take into account things that she was not conscious of at the beginning of her adventure. And though the reader must feel sorry for her division from her beloved, her adventures during her separation from Redcrosse will give her a sense of control over her environment that she lacked before she she was separated from him. This changes her from a passive object of adoration to an active character who will take control when Redcrosse has been rendered helpless in the Dungeon of Orgoglio and again when the weak Redcrosse it about to plunge a knife into in own heart at the bidding of Despair.

Una in the Wilderness

Una's separation from her beloved begins when the poet says that "she through guilefull handeling" (I.iii.2.4) is "from her knight diuorced in despayre" (I.iii.2.8). The poet laments "her dew loues [being] deriu'd to that vile witches share" (I.iii.2.9) and speaks of Una's unworthiness in neither "word nor deede" (I.iii.2.7) to merit the ills have been visited upon her. This would seem to implicate Archimago and Duessa as the villains of the piece, but in an Augustinian universe they represent only the *temptation* to evil. It is within Redcrosse's power to act or not to act on such temptations, and Spenser is counting on his careful readers to notice the role that this active knight plays in Una's betrayal.

Unlike his unfeeling and selfish hero, Spenser exhibits compassion for Una's plight, writing

> Nought is there vnder heau'ns wide hollownesse,
> That moues more deare compassion of mind,
> Then beautie brought t'vnworthie wretchednesse
> Through enuies snares or fortunes freakes vnkind. (I.iii.1.1-4)

The poet then attempts to locate the reasons he has feelings for her:

> I, whether lately through her brightnes blind,
> Or through alleageance and fast fealty,
> Which I do owe vnto all womankynd,
> Feele my heart perst with so great agony,
> When such I see, that all for pitty I could dy. (I.iii.1.5-9)

Spenser has a hard time locating the source with rational precision, wavering between her external "brightnesse blind" and an internal "alleageance and fast fealtie, / Which I do owe vnto all woman kind." But no matter where such compassion is located, whether externally or internally, the end result is the same. The poet will not abandon her, as Redcrosse had.

In spite of the poet's having more compassion for her than his hero has shown her and even placing blame on Redcrosse's passive shoulders, he has not forgotten the role of Archimago in her narrative. Unlike passive but good Redcrosse, Archimago is an active character who relies on a well-educated intellect that is devoid of good will. Being left with his prey, the arch-deceiver has further plans for Una, which the poet speaks of in terms of means, not ends:

> Yet rests not so, but other meanes doth make,
> How he may worke vnto her further smarts:
> For her he hated as the hissing snake,
> And in her many troubles did most pleasure take. (I.ii.9.6-9)

In the presence of such a character, the passive Una is right to flee.

After she has fled from the immediate threat of Archimago, who for all his enumerated powers seems to have no power to stop her flight, she dismounts from her "vnhastie beast" (I.iii.4.2) and "layd her stole aside" (I.iii.4.6). The "vnhastie" in her "vnhastie beast" might indicate that she has no sense of urgency in her wandering but that she, like Redcrosse, is content to wander through the world at random. And the poet gives his readers real cause for worry when she lays her stole aside, for it was exactly when Redcrosse had laid his armor aside that he had fallen prey to Fidessa. In this case, Una's removal of her covering reveals her indescribable beauty to the world:

> Her angel's face
> As the great eye of heauen shyned bright,
> And made a sunshine in the shady place;
> Did neuer mortall eye behold such heauenly grace. (I.iii.4.6-9)

Her beauty is what saves her after a hungry lion leaps "out of the thickest wood" (I.iii.5.1).

Una's Animal Protector

The "Lyon" who attacks her thinks "To haue attonce deuour'd her tender corse" (I.iii.5.6 italics mine to tie him to Redcrosse, who also acts at once); but as he approaches his "pray," the less likely he is to eat her. His sight, which Redcrosse had used to view Fidessa, grows "amazd" (I.iii.5.9); and, unlike Redcrosse but like the poet, the lion is overwhelmed by compassion for her. He forgets "his furious forse" (I.iii.5.9) as he approaches the holy lady, and he pauses to kiss "her wearie feet" and lick "her lilly hands" (I.iii.6.1-2). Seeing the furious beast in a state of "yeelded pryde and proud submission" (I.iii.6.6), Una' heart, too, "gan melt in great compassion" (I.iii.6.8). The lion is so moved by the sight of her that he stays to protect her.

Just in case anyone has missed the obvious point of contrast between Redcrosse' callous indifference to her and the lion's compassion, the poet puts the question of the similarity between things in the mind of Una, who pointedly asks:

> The Lyon Lord of euerie beast in field,
> Quoth she, his princely puissance doth abate,
> And mightie proud to humble weake does yield,
> Forgetfull of the hungry rage, which late
> Him prickt, in pittie of my sad estate:
> But he my Lyon, and my noble Lord,
> How does he find in cruell hart to hate
> Her that him lou'd, and euer most adord,
> As the God of my life? why hath he me abhord? (I.iii.7)

Her response may be paraphrased thus: What's wrong with that man if even a beast of the field can see the goodness in me and he cannot?

The answer is that Una had removed her stole, and this allowed the beast to see her in her perfect prelapsarian beauty. Had she done this in front of Redcrosse, she might have held onto her knight; for this is exactly how Fidessa seduced Redcrosse. But as an innocent virgin, it would be inappropriate for Una to engage in such behavior in front of the human Redcrosse before they are married. The problem becomes how she can express her inner beauty while maintaining the integrity of her virginal body.

At this point, Una has no answer to that question. She is merely a woman who needs a protector, and she has found one in a lion, who

> Still when she slept, he kept both watch and ward,
> And when she wakt, he wayted diligent,
> With humble seruice to her will prepard:
> From her faire eyes he tooke commandement,
> And euer by her lookes conceiued her intent. (I.iii.9.5-9)

The poet indicates that eyes can be trusted if they look beneath the surface to conceive "intent." Redcrosse, on the other hand, looks at Fidessa with "his quicke eies, her face to view," but does not listen with "his dull eares, to heare what shee did tell" (I.ii.26.6-7) and so conceives his love only superficially. Presumably, he does the same with Una.

The reversal of normal hierarchy here can be seen through the reader's use of his or her memory, which takes individual incidents in the poem and joins them together for comparison with each other. In this case, the careful reader will recall that Spenser had compared Redcrosse to a "Lyon" in the first epic simile in the Cave of Errour, where Redcrosse had "forced" Errour to stay (I.i.17.4), while in the episode in which Una is separated from her violent love the "Lyon" forgets "his furious forse" (I.iii.5.9) when her beauty is revealed to him. Redcrosse chases Errour on account of his desire for glory, not out of any necessity, and he plays no role in her destruction. The lion, on the other hand, has "yeelded pride" (I.iii.6.6), and this involves his abandoning his "natural" family—his pride—for an "unnatural" but deeper affection born of his social role as the king of animals. By contrast, the "clownishe" Redcrosse who puts on the armor of others does not yet recognize that he, too, has such inborn nobility, as he has yet to learn of his connection to the royal house through an education he has not yet received. Only after he realizes this will he be able to exchange his "natural" pride for an "unnatural" social standing as king among men.

The House of Corceca

Una's flaws as a character proceed, not from herself, but from the fact that she is traveling in the foreign land of time far from the land of her "heuenly berth" (I.iii.28.9). She, like Redcrosse, must learn to parse words' ambiguous meanings, because words in the world of time do not always mean what Una thinks they do. This introduces a division into her unified prelapsarian mind, in which a always equals a, and requires her to understand that in the foreign realm of time, words may mean other things (a=b) and so may be misunderstood by naïve creatures.

The next step in her education after she has been separated from her one true love comes after she finds some footsteps in "the trodden grass" (I.iii.10.4) in which "the tract of peoples footing was" (I.iii.10.5). She and the lion follow these footsteps (*vestigia*) to the door of Corceca's House, who in the head note to the canto is described as "blind Deuotion." Spenser literally pictures her as a blind woman who sits in the dark praying. There is, of course, nothing wrong with the activity of being devoted to God in itself; however the consequences of her remaining blind and focusing on God alone is that she neglects to look after the moral well-being of her own family.

On account of this neglect, her daughter Abessa has taken up with a character named Kirkrapine, whose name means "the rape of the churches." He is the source of the wealth of Corceca's House, and his wealth comes through outright thievery:

> He was to weete a stout and sturdie thiefe,
> Wont to robbe Churches of their ornaments,
> And poore mens boxes of their due reliefe,
> Which giuen was to them for good intents. (I.iii.17.1-4)

The careful reader notes the perversion of true "intents" to false ones in his actions. He is robbing "holy Saints of their rich vestiments" (I.iii.17.5), leaving them naked before God, something that Una had done in the previous episode when she "laid her stole aside" (I.iii.4.6). Kirkrapine also uses Corceca's daughter, Abessa, in "whoredome" (I.iii.18.5), as he "fed her fatt with feast of offerings" (I.iii.18.6), and gave her "gold and rings" (I.iii.18.8). When the lion tears down the door of the house, he tears Kirkrapine's heart out and rips his body "in thousand peeces small" (I.iii.20 3).

The next morning,

> when broad day the world discouered has,
> Vp *Vna* rose, vp rose the Lyon eke,
> And on their former iourney forward pas,
> In waies vnknowne, her wandring knight to seeke.... (I.iii.21.1-4)

As they travel "forward" in "ways unknown," the poet compares her with Odysseus, who "for his loue refused deitye" (I.iii.21.6). While Una is contrasted with Corceca—Una is a creature of light while Corceca is a creature who lives in perpetual darkness—*both* characters are given to blind devotion. This is a problem that the poet tries to solve by distinguishing Una from Redcrosse on the one hand and from Corceca on the other. Unlike Redcrosse, who keeps fleeing when he should be staying and forcing fleeing things to stay when he should not, Una is correct to seek a knight "that from her still did flye" (I.iii.21.8). She needs Redcrosse to kill the Dragon that it seems has forced the King and Queen of Eden to live behind brazen walls.

When they see Kirkrapine slain, both mother and daughter run after

Una "like two amazed deare / Halfe mad through malice, and reuenging will" (I.iii.22.7-8) and who catching her

> loudly bray,
> With hollow houling, and lamenting cry,
> Shamefully at her rayling all the way,
> And her accusing of dishonesty,
> That was the flowre of faith and chastity. (I.iii.23.1-5)

This braying behavior indicates that they are acting on principles derived from their "natural" animal instincts and not on the more respectable cultivated behavior raised over nature by "unnatural" but rational social structures. But that is not all; the women *act*, attempting to put a curse on Una:

> And still amidst her rayling, she did pray,
> That plagues, and mischiefs, and long misery
> Might fall on her, and follow all the way,
> And that in endlesse error she might euer stray. (I.iii.23.6-9)

It is notable that the lion, who has been changed from a hostile enemy to a helpful friend that watches over and protects Una, has no power to quell the rage that affects the minds of these two women. His power is only physical and requires physical proximity to its object to have any effect.

When Corceca and Abessa's strategy of following Una does not work (on account of their not catching up to her at once), their anger cools; and the pair return to Corceca's House. Along the way they meet Archimago, to whom Corceca tells her story:

> Therewith she gan her passion to renew,
> And cry, and curse, and raile, and rend her heare,
> Saying, that harlott she too lately knew,
> That causd her shed so many a bitter teare,
> And so forth told the story of her feare. (I.iii.25.1-5)

Archimago has roused Corceca into a whirlwind of passion once again, seeming to bemoan "her haplesse chaunce" (I.iii.25.6). The language which Spenser uses to describe Archimago here is important. Although Archimago laments the lack of fortune of Corceca and Abessa, he himself is always described as having purpose and will. He is able to overcome "haplesse chaunce" through education, and after he has been "taught" the whereabouts of Una, "he forward gan aduaunce" (I.iii.25.8), *and he finds her!* This bespeaks the control that an *a posteriori* education can impart to otherwise *a priori* chance. But because it is in his interest to foment rebellion, he speaks words that are at odds with what he thinks before passing away from the two of them forever.

Una Meets Archimago Again

In fact, Una is pursued by everyone in Spenser's poem *except* Redcrosse, and "Ere long he [Archimago] came, where Una traueiled slow" (I.iii.26.1). The reader is urged to pay attention to some gaps in Archimago's presentation of himself to her in their meeting. Archimago is wearing the feigned armor of Redcrosse; but on account of his knowledge that eyes can see through imperfect superficial disguises, he covers his head up with Redcrosse's helmet. Una, who exchanges her perception of him from concentration on his inner heart to his superficial armor when she exchanges her rejection of literal George for her acceptance of typological Redcrosse, greets him with a salutation that seems to distinguish her once again from Corceca's sitting blind in the dark:

> And weeping said, Ah my long lacked Lord,
> Where haue ye bene thus long out of my *sight*?
> Much feared I to haue bene quite abhord,
> Or ought haue done, that ye displeasen might,
> That should as death vnto my deare hart *light*:
> For since mine eye your ioyous *sight* did mis.... (I.iii.27.1-6 italics mine)

She concludes her speech with a warning that without him,

> My chearefull day is turnd to chearelesse night,
> And eke my night of death the shadow is;
> But welcome now my light, and shining lampe of blis. (I.iii.27.7-9)

Una clearly should see that he is not in fact her "light," but on account of her unified experience of fixing the identity of objects (a=a) based on their superficial appearance without looking beneath appearance to an underlying ontology, (as the reader may think they have just seen the educated Archimago do) she does not even consider that he may be anything other than who he says he is (a=b).

This is highlighted when Archimago replies to Una with a lie:

> My dearest Dame,

> Far be it from your thought, and fro my wil,
> To thinke that knighthood I so much should shame,
> As you to leaue, that haue me loued stil.... (I.iii.28.1-4)

Now Una knows that if he is in fact Redcrosse he *has* abandoned her, and perhaps it might be a good idea for her to ask why he did abandon her. Una overlooks that fact on account of her having found her beloved. All that matters to her in the end is her end, and she still accepts things at face value without looking any deeper into them. This leads to another bit of Spenserian irony, as it is *Archimago* who tells the principle of truth the truth of her story here. She *does* love him, he says, and it is shameful that he has left her. This puts the reader in the uncomfortable position of agreeing that Archimago knows more than Una expresses, not only about her situation but about Redcrosse's bad behavior.

There is a lot at stake in the world if Una does not look any deeper than the surface of her experience. As part of his truth-telling, Archimago tells Una that

> The earth shall sooner leaue her kindly skill
> To bring forth fruit, and make eternall derth,
> Then I leaue you.... (I.iii.28.6-8)

Within the world of time, true love between two willing partners is the principle of government, not a unified individual will acting alone. If Archimago can keep Una's true love separate from the object of its affection, the plentiful earth will suffer dearth. This is why Una *must* be educated out of her *a priori* metaphysical position of closing things with their identity too soon (a=a) into a process where she can recognize that fact that things in the world of time may not be what they appear to be (a=b) and to act on *that* knowledge.

At this point, Archimago's lie is effective, but once again its effectiveness once again is not based in any intention of the part of Archimago. His lie works because Una's mind has been overwhelmed with love for her long-sought knight:

> His louely words her seemd due recompence
> Of all her passed paines: one louing howre
> For many yeares of sorrow can dispence. (I.iii.30.1-3)

And once again, Spenser lays some blame at the feet of Una here, not for loving, but for forgetting what she previously knew:

> She has forgott, how many a wofull stowre
> For him she late endur'd; she speakes no more
> Of past: true is, that true loue hath no powre
> To looken backe; his eies be fixt before.
> Before her stands her knight, for whom she toyld so sore.
> (I.iii.30.5-9)

The inadequacy of true love to cope with the whole situation of the past, present, and future of her love introduces the problem of love as a guide to experience. This, and the inadequacy of Una's unified and *unifying* mind, which is all too willing to accept things on superficial terms as they are presented to her without looking beneath the surface to make "triall" of them, introduces the problem of Una's education. Love alone is not enough to guarantee her any success in her endeavor if she cannot distinguish a true love from a false love. Education requires something more than even the "principle of indivisibility," which rests content with the mere identification of things (a=a), can provide.

Spenser's argument here is fairly straightforward. Only after she had been translated out of the timeless world of Eden was Una given love, a thing that operates by joining two separate individuals together in a linked band.[3] This requires a change in Una's position of seeking identity with herself (a=a) and turning herself outward to seek another (a=b). In her actions, Una has already made the switch, but in her mind she is still operating on the principles of identity that she learned in Eden. Once again, this disjunction between action and the mind's operation on its object in one individual human being may be explained by invoking the divisive philosophical thought of Aristotle. Una, like Redcrosse, is "too simple and too trew" (I.ii.45.7). Her silent acquiescence to appearances without making "triall" of them is a mistake that Spenser will attempt correct before the book is over. But at this point in the poem, Una is unaware of any of the implications of her errant way of looking at things. She operates, therefore, on *partial* information of her situation in spite of being the principle of unified "truth."

The Simile of the Mariner

In stanza 31 Spenser poses a simile for Una's present state:

> Much like, as when the beaten marinere,

---

[3] My reading of Una's "gainsaying" of the individual George implies that she was not in love with him when she first met him.

> That long hath wandred in the *Ocean* wide,
> Ofte soust in swelling *Tethys* saltish teare,
> And long time hauing and his tawney hide
> With blustring breath of Heauen, that none can bide,
> And scorching flames of fierce *Orions* hound,
> Soone as the port from far he has espide,
> His chearefull whistle merrily doth sound.... (I.iii.31.1-8)

This is a continuation of the poet's invocation of Homer's *Odyssey*, a poem in which Odysseus manages to tell a series of lies on his way to his home. Spenser can stand "far" back from the action, which he has invented for the instruction of his readers. He knows that none of the action he is portraying in the Realm of Faery is real. He continues his perspective on his story from the stable shore given to him as the poet who has already worked out the final stanzas of Book I in his head:

> Then the glad marchant, that does vew from ground
> His ship far come from watrie wildernesse,
> He hurles out vowes, and *Neptune* oft doth blesse. (I.iii.32.1-3)

The poet can afford to indulge in "delays, suspense, [and] retardation"[4] as he is the sole creator of his entirely fictional universe.

Such an ironic stance has been offered as the only viable strategy for negotiating historical texts by Hayden White,[5] but within the fictional ontology of Spenser's *Faerie Queene*, Una cannot afford to be so placidly distant from her own actions. She is mistaken in her belief that "her knight she [had] found" (I.iii.32.1), and so the "joy" she expresses at seeing him is not the same as the rearrival of the "faithful mariner" to the truly stable shore. The careful reader knows that Redcrosse has *not* been faithful to her, having fled her, ducked into the shade at the first opportunity, taken off his armor, and betrayed the woman who loves him with someone who is willing to show his superficial eye more skin. This means that there is an enormous

---

4 The quoted phrase is not from a work on Spenser but from Bernard Fenik, *Studies in the Odyssey*, Hermes: Zeitschrift Für Klassische Philologie. Einzelschriften (Wiesbaden: F. Steiner, 1974), 104. In his work, Fenik claims that Odysseus' "secrecy about himself is used to build scene after scene of irony, suspense and poignant emotion" (55). Spenser is modeling his own work on the imitation of one of his model poets, and he, too, builds in delays to build suspense and poignant emotion through the process of standing "far" and looking at his action from a distance.

5 See the use of irony in the section "The Theory of Tropes" in Hayden V. White, *Metahistory: The Historical Imagination in Nineteenth-Century Europe* (Baltimore: Johns Hopkins University Press, 1973), 31-38.

difference between being a character *within* Spenser's fiction and being a critical observer of the action. Taking an ironic perspective will do nothing to fix Una's misapprehension of her situation.

As if to make this clear, at the end of stanza Spenser returns to the characters of Una and Archimago (who Una believes to be Redcrosse):

> So forth they past, and all the way they spent
> Discoursing of her dreadfull late distresse,
> In which he askt her, what the Lyon ment:
> Who told her all that fell in iourney as she went. (I.iii.32.6-9)

Although she is the image of unity in the poem, she, too, takes pleasure in "Discoursing of her dreadfull late distresse" with another (a=b), even though she is wrong to add the adjective "late" to her troubles, as the man she has linked up with is not who she believes him to be, and therefore her troubles are not as far behind her as she thinks.

Una's Meeting with Sansloy

Una finally encounters her error when she meets another knight, Sansloy, who is also described as "pricking towards them" (I.iii.33.2). When Sansloy sees the shield of Redcrosse (carried by the False Redcrosse), he is also fooled and

> He burnt in fire, and gan eftsoones prepare
> Himselfe to batteill with his couched speare. (I.iii.34.3-4)

The problem for Archimago, who is merely *playing* at being Redcrosse, is that he has no problem with Sansloy. As a result of being confronted with the possibility of actual violence on account of his disguise, Archimago's cowardice is exposed:

> Loth was that other, and did faint through feare,
> To taste th'vntryed dint of deadly steele. (I.iii.34.5-6)

The fearlessness of the true Redcrosse, who also has limited experience with "deadly steele," is clearly preferable to the cowardice of False Redcrosse, who would run away if he had the choice. It is worth noting, then, that Una has some power over others to compel them to her will. Just like the lion that came springing out of the wood and was tamed at the sight of Una,

> his Lady did so well [Archimago] cheare,

> That hope of new good hap he gan to feele;
> So bent his speare, and spurd his horse with yron heele.
> (I.iii.34.7-9)

This is an important moment, for even Archimago, the archetype of the evil artificer, can be made to feel "hope of new good hap" by the mere presence of Una. It is, therefore, not out of the question that Una *could* control her circumstances if she knew her own power over events. Sadly, however, she has not been educated enough at this point in the poem that she has such conscious control over her circumstances.

Sansloy vows to take revenge for his brother's death, and sadly, perhaps, Archimago's newfound hope is unfounded. Sansloy's charge knocks the weak man off his horse and wounds him. He begins to unlace Archimago's helmet in order to slay him, but his hand is stayed by Una who begs "Mercy" from unmerciful Sansloy (I.iii.37.5). It is not Una's plea for mercy that saves Archimago. It is the fact that Sansloy recognizes Archimago's white hair, and he realizes that the man he has been fighting is not Redcrosse at all.

This state of affairs confounds Sansloy, because Archimago has never taken the field to fight anyone before:

> His hastie hand he doth amased hold,
> And halfe shamed, wondred at the sight:
> For the old man well knew he, though vntold,
> In charmes and magicke to haue wondrous might,
> Ne euer wont in field, ne in round lists to fight. (I.iii.38.5-9)

This, I repeat, is the power that Una might wield in the world if she could learn to speak in the languages of the world rather than remaining silent in her unified knowledge. But Una is as amazed as Sansloy is, for she too has been fooled by Archimago's false appearance.

Sansloy asks a question about where blame should be placed for his attack on his friend (I.iii.39.4), but the cowardly Archimago does not answer him. Instead, he flees the scene. But Sansloy stays and

> to the virgin comes, who all this while
> Amased stands, her selfe so mockt to see
> By him, who has the guerdon of his guile,
> For so misfeigning her true knight to bee:
> Yet is she now in more perplexitie,
> Left in the hand of that same Paynim bold,

From whom her booteth not at all to flie. (I.iii.40.1-7)

The poet puts her in real danger here, as Sansloy "her cleanly garment catching hold, / Her from her Palfrey pluckt, her visage to behold" (I.iii.40.8-9). Her virtue is in real danger here. She has managed to fall out of favor with Redcrosse because she had covered her face, as a virgin should; and Sansloy is about to tear away her veil, revealing her beauty to the world out of the same sense of lust which has made Redcrosse abandon pure Una for the physically looser Fidessa.

The reason he does not is that the lion, who already has seen her without her veil, attempts to comes to her rescue. Unfortunately, the lion is not strong enough, and the educated Sansloy, who "feates of armes did wisely vnderstand" (I.iii.42.5), stabs Una's animal protector through the heart. As the lion dies, the narrator asks

> Who now is left to keepe the forlorne maid
> From raging spoile of lawlesse victors will?
> Her faithfull gard remou'd, her hope dismaid,
> Her selfe a yeelded pray to saue or spill. (I.iii.43.1-4)

The obvious answer, perhaps, is that Redcrosse should be there to protect her, but he is not. Una could remember that Redcrosse had abandoned her, as the careful reader remembers; but she is in love, and she has no power to look backwards. Thus, her love allows her to ignore any faults in Redcrosse, not through her own will, but because of her attraction to another (a=b) who stands outside her will.

This is not Spenser's intention for the reader, who will be given a more solid education that will allow them to look backward *and* forward at events in the poem,[6] as well as the ability to look at the inner working of characters

---

[6] This is one of the other major differences between readers and the characters within the poem. The characters within the poem live but once, but readers can revive the characters in Spenser's poem again and again, as they read and reread their adventures looking for more hints given to them by the careful poet. It would do no good to have the characters within the poem elevate themselves out of the poem to the status afforded to the reader, as this would elevate them to the status of gods who hover over the text but who do not fully participate in the text. This is exactly what Una and Redcrosse are doing each in their own ways as they travel through the wilderness. Una has been granted a deconstructable existence by the poem and will fade away and be revived only at the reader's bidding. Redcrosse has the substantial consciousness of the individual that Una lacks, but he believes (falsely) that the bestowal of the armor of Ephesians and Una's granting him of a typological name eliminates (as opposed to the mere suppression of) his literal self and thus any need for purposeful individual action on his part.

from a distance not available to characters within his poem. The reader's structure comes in the form of a=b knowledge, rather than from a superficial identity (a=a) that is only available in a deconstructing fiction. This gives readers a sense of control that is not available to Una, whose continuing reliance on her prelapsarian sense of identity means that she is about to become "dismaid," that is deflowered against her will, by a man who has science but who knows no law. It is law that Gloriana's court stands for against a hostile nature that would dismantle the very fragile social bonds if it were not for Gloriana's cohering presence in the world of time.

As it is, however, Una has not pursued an education. Instead, she has relied on the protection of others as she travels from adventure to adventure at random. Relying on external protection, rather than strengthening her intentional mind, she falls into a situation in which the reader cannot at first be sure that she has not been raped:

> He now Lord of the field, his pride to fill,
> With foule reproches, and disdainefull spight
> *Her vildly entertaines*, and will or nill,
> Beares her away vpon his courser light:
> Her prayers nought preuaile, his rage is more of might. (I.iii.43.5-9 italics mine)

The reader has to wait for two cantos before they find out whether their worst fears for the daughter of Eden are or are not founded in reality.

Action after a Breach in the Text

I won't make my reader wait so long: Una has not been raped. After he carries her off, Sansloy's thought is to have "defilde, /And made [her] the vassall of his pleasures vilde" (I.vi.3.4-5). The reason he hesitates is not because she is exercising her power over him, as she had done with Archimago. It is because he thinks that this conquest will be greater if he can get her to consent to his "will" (I.vi.3.9). Therefore,

> With fawning wordes he courted her a while,
> And looking louely, and oft sighing sore,
> Her constant hart did tempt with diuerse guile. (I.vi.4.1-3)

But she remains constant, resisting his "wordes, and lookes, and sighes" (I.vi.4.4) "As rocke of Diamond stedfast euermore" (I.vi.4.5). However, his strategy failing, his lust overwhelms him, and he snatches the veil from her face:

> Yet for to feed his fyrie lustfull eye,
> He snatcht the vele, that hong her face before. (I.vi.4.6-7)

We are told that her beauty began to shine, "as brightest skye" (I.vi.4.8), and this fuels "his beastly hart t'efforce her chastity" (I.vi.4.9), which he cannot convince her to give up willingly. This means that it is not the native virtue available to everyone by their mere existence that will automatically respond to Una's beauty as the lion had. It now appears that the lion's contact with his native virtue could come from his social position as king of the animals. Sansloy, who is not in a similarly elevated social position, reacts to her appearance with lust.

Una shrieks and cries her complaint to the skies. And the sky responds: the "molten starres doe drop like weeping eyes" (I.vi.6.5),

> And *Phoebus* flying so most shamefull sight,
> His blushing face in foggy cloud implyes,
> And hides for shame. (I.vi.6.6-8)

This response, in which the sun hides his face for shame rather than rescuing her, is surely not the response that Una had hoped for. But in response to the disappointing response of the sun and stars, Spenser repeats the question he had asked at I.iii.43 before the break in the text: "What witt of mortall wight / Can now deuise to quitt a thrall from such a plight?" (I.vi.6.8-9).

Spenser answers his own question in the next stanza:

> Eternall prouidence exceeding thought,
> Where none appeares can make her selfe a way:
> A wondrous way it for this Lady wrought,
> From Lyons clawes to pluck the griped pray. (I.vi.7.1-4)

At first blush, the answer to the question is that if Una cannot make "her selfe a way" nobody but God in his Heaven can rescue her. But this *ex machina* solution to her immediate problem leaves us with the longer term problem of her remaining in perpetual state of passivity in a world that requires men and women to activate their potential. Thus far, her only solution to her problems is evoke the pity that some have for her (the lion and the poet, for instance) but which others (Redcrosse and Sansloy) do not. It turns out that in Spenser's pre-Romantic universe, pity without the guiding hand of God—God's hand is available within Spenser's fiction but is not available without—is not necessarily enough to keep people safe in a world of determined rapists.

Una Among the Satyrs

Una has already been shown that she needs others to enact her will in the world of time; and her prayers are answered by God through instruments of His will. How He does this shows the careful reader that Una's cries to the distant sun and the stars are misplaced. His rescue of her is not through His direct intervention. Instead, her rescue comes from the appearance of satyrs, completely fictional creatures who despite their handicap of not having any lasting existence outside of Spenser's deconstructing fiction have the advantage of functioning on the ground of the literal earth. They are alerted to Una by her expression of her plight in screams:

> Her shrill outcryes and shriekes so loud did bray,
> That all the woodes and forestes did resownd;
> A troupe of *Faunes* and *Satyres* far away
> Within the wood were dauncing in a rownd,
> Whiles old *Syluanus* slept in shady arber sownd. (I.vi.7.5-9)

After her horrified expression, the woods echo with the sounds of her cries, and these woodland creatures break their circle and run to her.[7] Sansloy, who knows no law but appears still to have a sense of taste determined by his own cultural ideal of beauty, is so startled by their rude appearance that he mounts his steed and runs away (I.vi.9.9).

The satyrs, too, stand "amazed" at the "uncouth sight" (I.vi.9.6) of Una, who the reader, like Sansloy, may have been thinking is universally beautiful. This speaks to the relative nature of culture in God's created universe; but they soon overcome their cultural tastes by taking pity on her, which speaks to the satyrs' contact with something deeper than their relative culture. They break their closed and relative circle to encounter something deeper than they knew before:

> And gin to pittie her vnhappie state,
> All stand astonied at her beautie bright,
> In their rude eyes vnworthie of so wofull plight. (I.vi.9.7-9)

---

7 This is important for the Christian poet Edmund Spenser, for it betokens the power that is lacking in the pagan universe of cyclical return back to its own initial premises. This had led Augustine to break the circle of arguments that rest only on the agreement of those who hold to pagan premises. He offered a radical configuration of the universe that relied on substantial consciousness and that had the benefit of breaking the *petitio principii* of reason by introducing the priority of relative Aristotelian reason over pagan metaphysics.

Una is afraid of them, as well; but sensing this,

> The saluage nation feele her secret smart,
> And read her sorrow in her count'nance sad;
> Their frowning forheads with rough hornes yclad,
> And rusticke horror all a side doe lay.... (I.vi.11.3-6)

This interpersonal interaction, though not contained in language, bespeaks a deeper sympathy than selfish Redcrosse has been able to muster in response to his having seen Una in a potentially compromising position. In response to her look of pity, the satyrs change their look, as the lion had changed his look, when seeing her naked face:

> And gently grenning, shew a semblance glad
> To comfort her, and feare to put away,
> Their backward bent knees teach her humbly to obey. (I.vi.11.7-9)

Una has it in her power to compel events, however, she still does not consciously understand that power. She remains subject to the whims of others, the outcome of her unwilled efforts being guided by the power of God and twisted by the backward-kneed satyrs.

And yet, Una is slowly changing. Having initially been described as heaven born, she now yields herself to the "extremitie of time" (I.vi.13.2), as she comes to accept the fact that, although they are misguided, they mean her no harm. Thus, the woods echo with the sound of their merry pipes:

> And all the way their merry pipes they sound,
> That all the woods with doubled Eccho ring,
> And with their horned feet do weare the ground,
> Leaping like wanton kids in pleasant Spring. (I.vi.14.1-4)

The echo in the woods introduces a doubling of perspective once more, as *Syluanus* wonders from afar what makes them so glad (I.vi.15.1).

This is another important moment. Spenser introduces into the unified perspective of Una the same perspective of time that he had introduced into the experience of Redcrosse; and here, too, this produces doubling. In the modern world, we are used to finding art on the side of unity and evil on the side of divisiveness. Therefore, we are liable to overlook the role that doubling plays in Spenser's Augustinian universe. Spenser believes that it not enough to have the principle of God's unified good will impressed upon you from the outside. One must choose it of one's own free will. And this means that even characters like unified Una must gain active control over their rational minds as instruments of their will, rather than remaining passive instruments of God's foreordained will. The doubling of her perspective is a necessary step on the way to Una's having sufficient perspective on her experience to make correct judgments about her situation.

The beginning of Una's education comes from her being rescued from Sansloy, a man who has no respect for law at all, by woodland idolaters, who, though they do not realize the true nature of the prize that has fallen into their lap, mean her no harm. This represents an advance in law, though it is not the last advance that she will experience, as she has not yet gotten to the end of her adventure yet.

She remains at this point "the luckelesse lucky maid" (I.vi.19.1) who is at least momentarily "content to please their feeble eyes" (I.vi.19.2), a passive act of being observed by others. But when she actively attempts "teach them truth, which worshipt her in vaine" (I.vi.19.6), her "gentle wit" (I.vi.19.5) is insufficient to the task of turning them away from their idolatry of her exterior image (I.vi.19.7). When she *insists* that they restrain themselves from worshipping her image, they turn from worshiping her to worshiping "her Asse" (I.vi.19.9). Clearly, although her prospects are improving, Una's wit is still insufficient to the task set before it of reforming the opinion of men.

Una's Rescue by Satyrane

On finding herself worshiped by satyrs who, like Errour before them, are composite creatures created by pagan myth (and so fictionally-constructed), Una's quest has stalled in its forward progress. As the principle of unified truth she does not stop believing in them, as would be the appropriate response of the reader who stands outside the text. Instead, she turns from questing for her true love to teaching the truth to these idolaters.

Only after she realizes the limits of her power to control events does Una thinks about escaping:

> But her deare heart with anguish did torment,
> And all her witt in secret counsels spent,
> How to escape. (I.vi.32.4-6)

But even when she is left alone, she does not run away in quest of the perfect freedom desired by the existentialists. Instead, she discloses her "intent" to Satyrane, the master of beasts, and *he* effects her escape:

> At last in priuy wise
> To *Satyrane* she shewed her intent;
> Who glad to gain such fauour, gan deuise,
> How with that pensiue Maid he best might thence arise. (I.vi.32.6-9)

Satyrane helps her on account of her "wisedome heauenly rare / Whose like in womens wit he neuer knew" (I.vi.31.1-2).

Now the reader is only told that Satyrane begins to admire her when he compares her courteous deeds with other women (I.vi.31.3-4), but he blames her troubles *only* on fortune. While we may agree that Una is "hurtlesse, and so trew" (I.vi.31.7) and that Satyrane learns of her the "discipline of faith and veritie" (I.vi.31.9), it is not at all clear that she does not still bear some of the blame for her predicament. When she turns her self inward, she reflects the virtues of her inner life in silence; but when she needs to communicate her inner virtues, the perpetually silent Una still needs the cooperation of others to effect her will. Since she merely assumes that others understand her without making "triall" of her belief that this is so, she has been learning the lesson that in the "extremitie of time" her silent reliance on her *a priori* being is not enough to ensure the recognition of her true nature.

Una's Confrontation of a Paradox in Reality

After effecting her escape, Satyrane and Una meet a pilgrim, who tells them that he has seen Redcrosse "both liuing and eke ded" (I.vi.36.9). It is interesting that Una, who has been presented with a paradox of a living-dead knight, instantly assumes that Redcrosse is dead after being told that "the *Redcrosse* knight was slain with Paynim knife" (I.vi.38.9), because if that were true it would mean the defeat of God himself. This indicates a breach between her empirical and as-yet-unverified experience and her faith. This drives her to express her puzzlement in a paradox of her own, asking Satyrane "how might that bee, / And he the stoutest knight, that euer wonne?" (I.vi.39.1-2).

To resolve the paradox, Satyrane and Una race off to confront Sansloy, who they find resting by a fountain. To Una's relief, he denies killing Redcrosse, but the two knights fall to fighting. At first, as with Redcrosse and Sansfoy, the two knights are evenly matched; but the balance of the fight is soon turned in Sansloy's favor. Having fled the battlefield, his desire for

Una had faded; but with the return of the object of his desire back into physical proximity, Sansloy renews his quest to have "his lewd lusts, and late attempted sin" (I.vi.46.3) fulfilled. This speaks to Spenser's belief in the temporality of desire, which ebbs and flows rather than having any sort of metaphysical permanence. As such, one's desire can be mastered if one has the will to do so.

Sansloy does not have such a will. He attempts catch her, "newly offred to his eie" (I.vi.46.5), but Satyrane stops Sansloy's pursuing the end of his desire with a speech that is intended to give him priority of precedence in the battle for ownership of Una's heart:

> O foolish faeries sonne, what fury mad
> Hath thee incenst, to hast thy dolefull fate?
> Were it not better, I that Lady had,
> Then that thou hadst repented it too late?
> Most sencelesse man he, that himselfe doth hate,
> To loue another. (I.vi.47.1-6)

Satyrane means to be heard as one man talking to another, and if we place these words in a dialectical framework in which one way is better than another, then Satyrane would win the battle for Una's heart. But there is a problem with this resolution. The reader has been learning to take into account the whole of reference in the Spenser's allegorical universe, and Spenser's readers are not constrained to choose between Satyrane and Sansloy as the only possible recipients of Una's affection, and neither is Una.

Since the beginning of her adventure without Redcrosse, Una has learned that not all creatures in God's creation wish her well, as well as the lesson that not every creature she meets can protect her. The lion, the king of beasts that displayed more nobility than her "clownishe younge man" had, was defeated by a man who is negatively defined as having no respect for law. The satyr half-beasts worship her as a passive object and will change into idolaters as soon as she actively asserts herself. Nature, which the satyrs worship, sports a sun that does not guide them to the "truth," as it had in Plato's Allegory of the Cave. Instead, the sun turns away from her peril, in shame to be sure, but it means that creatures far away in the heavens are also helpless to save her.

Throughout her separation from her love, Una is being driven to the realization that she herself is not enough to ensure her own physical salvation in the "extremitie of time." Instead of relying on her confidence in her unspoken identity with herself (a=a), she comes to the realization that she must join herself with another (a=b) in order to activate what exists within her only in potential. This is, after all, why she escapes from the brazen walls of Eden and travels to Gloriana's court, where she meets and falls in love with the "clownishe younge man." The link of love between Una and Redcrosse breaks Una's passivity as she waits for the outcome of a battle between two equally-matched opponents. As a result, as the two evenly matched opponents continue to fight, "the royall Mayd / Fled farre away, of that proud Paynim sore afraid" (I.vi.47.8-9).

The presence of love introduces a permanent imbalance into Spenser's universe that no fight for control between two evenly-matched opponents will ever be able to resolve. Just as good is permanently better than evil in Spenser's universe, the love that ties us to others operates by processes that are out of the individual's control. As such, the processes of love trump mankind's individual identity. Control of love rests with Cupid, whose blind love does not lead clearly to the establishment of an equitable justice. In this sense, it is unlike the priority of good over evil, which is implanted in the mind of man by God at his creation and so is available to anyone who would turn their mind inward to look for the good in their heart.

At the beginning of the poem, Cupid's darts are described not only as "cunning" (I.proem.3.3) but also as "cruell" (I.proem.3.2); and they bind Una to Redcrosse in ways she does not fully comprehend. Nevertheless, the presence of Cupid as governor in the "extremitie of time" does not force Una into withdrawing from the "extremitie of time" back to the Kingdom of Eden; for if she were to do that, she would be forever sundered from her beloved, who, being a creature born in time, can activate what lies within her only as potential.

Instead of choosing between two equally matched enemies who fight for hierarchical precedence by engaging in battle of physical violence for control of her physical *body*, Una takes control of her own being and leaves the equal battle to go looking for the other (a=b) who completes her being in the world of time. Una's access to something more permanent than her physical being is at the same time less substantial than what human beings can see before them with their eyes alone. It is here, Spenser is telling the careful reader, that human beings should direct the attention of their substantial consciousness and not to superficial things (like the Whore of Babylon) that they can "view" with their eyes alone.

Thus, all the sound and fury of the equal battle for possession of her body signifies nothing in the light of God's higher purpose that pushes all the chips in the middle of the table in every hand and never fails to win, even if He operates through the unlikely means of blind Cupid's cruel and unbalanced darts (a=b) and not directly through Una's sense of identity with herself (a=a).

Redcrosse Within the World of Time

The Permanent Imbalance of Values Within the World of Time

Una assumes that the balanced perspective of Eden will suffice in the brave new world she has only recently entered; and for this reason, she does not make "triall" of her love to make sure that he loves her back. She merely assumes that he does. As a result, she spends the rest of the book wondering at the behavior of Redcrosse, who never seems to act as she expects him to. But at the same time, during her separation from her knight-protector, she is being educated in some of the harsh realities of the world of time. There are satyrs who will not take direction from her, but turn towards her ass when she makes demands on them. And there are determined men like Sansloy who would satisfy his bodily desire with her body. After she has been separated from Redcrosse, she learns some hard lessons about her vulnerability and the necessity for caution in the world of time. Realizing that loves are not equal in time, and that some loves are no loves at all but are pursued with the intention of fulfilling another's desire, passive Una flies back to her love for protection.

Spenser is harsh in his judgment of Redcrosse during the two canto breach in Una's adventure that occurs between her capture by Sansloy and the poet's eventual release of suspense of the possibility that Una has been raped. Canto iv opens with the poet's indication of the force that drives the Knight of Holinesse:

> Young knight, what euer that dost armes professe,
> And through long labours huntest after fame.... (I.iv.1.1-2)

It is fame, not the love for Una, Eden, or Heaven that drives Redcrosse forward. And lest there be any confusion that Spenser regards Redcrosse's quest for fame as another in a series of incredibly poor choices, the poet highlights *the source* of the poor choices that Redcrosse has made in the poem thus far in the lines that follow:

> Beware of fraud, beware of ficklenesse,
> In choice, and change of thy deare loued Dame,
> Least thou of her beleeue too lightly blame,
> And rash misweening doe thy hart remoue:
> For vnto knight there is no greater shame,
> Then lightnesse and inconstancie in loue. (I.iv.1.3-8)

These are general attacks, and so could be mistaken by the naïve reader as excepting Redcrosse from inclusion in the set of denoted objects; so the poet concludes his case with a specific example: "That doth this Redcrosse knights ensample plainly proue" (I.iv.1.9).

Spenser then proceeds to elaborate his harsh judgment of Redcrosse in the following canto:

> Who after that he had faire *Vna* lorne,
> Through light misdeeming of her loialtie,
> And false *Duessa* in her sted had borne,
> Called *Fidess*', and so supposed to be. (I.iv.2.1-4)

The poet's specificity in his example makes it clears that Redcrosse is guilty of "ficklenesse / In choice." This has led him to be defrauded by a false love, while removing his heart from a true love, on account of his inability to see beneath the surface of appearance to the heart of either. This leads the poet to embody in Redcrosse the greatest shame a knight can suffer: "lightnesse and inconstancie in loue." Even so, these are negative condemnations of Redcrosse's behavior. When it comes to making positive choices between Fidessa and Una, the poet puts the question to the reader of how they are to know which of the women to choose when the book is closed and they are back in the world of being without the poet's crutch of being able to make up saints, houses of holiness, Unas, and Fidessas.

The answer within *The Faerie Queene* is to make "triall" of one's situation. But again, there are two significant differences between Spenser's approach to the problem of making "triall" and the modern approach to the same problem. In the modern world, we put an emphasis on opening our eyes and looking around us rather than remaining metaphorically blind to our circumstances. In Spenser's world of Faery, one is supposed to already have one's eyes open, but even open eyes can deceive one's mind. Therefore one must *listen* for the echoes of one's experience beyond oneself, as Una did when she was facing the prospect of being raped. Her reward was not rescue by the sun or stars that stand vertically above her, but a visit from the satyrs who come running at her expression of distress as her cry echoes in the woods that surround her on the horizontal plane.

The difference between Redcrosse and Una is that unlike Una, Redcrosse is *not* learning to read the universe by making "triall" of his experience and changing course based on his experience, which is not always in accord with his expectations. *And that fact does not matter*, because he has been assured of victory at the end of every battle he enters before he enters them. But Redcrosse's conviction that there is nothing wrong with his mind because his *end* is guaranteed leads to the poet's condemnation of him. What Redcrosse does between his beginning and his end makes a huge difference in the moral judgment of his actions by the poet, because his behavior in the middle space that opens up between beginning and end is nothing less than atrocious.

The other significant difference between the modern and Spenser's approach to experience is in the lack of balance in the universe the reader confronts when he or she is listening to echoes in Spenser's poem. In the modern world, we tend to assume that nature was originally balanced, and that it was the intrusion of men into it that threw the universe into disarray.[1] But Spenser is working in a universe in which man is good by his having access to a "native virtue" potentially implanted in his (epistemological) mind by God but whose connection with (ontological) nature still needs to be activated in man's mind through virtuous action. Nature is thought to be constructed along different lines, with some things (like mankind) having been created permanently good, while other things (like Errour) being

---

1 It is my contention that this state of affairs is due to the influence of the Enlightenment on modern thought. Descartes subscribed to the original unity hypothesis, and this is why he was able to balance ontology with epistemology so perfectly. Even Ovid subscribed to this view of the original unity of nature, and this is why, when Rousseau was looking for a counter to Cartesian rationalism, he did not go back to the permanent severing of humankind from natural unity proposed by Augustine. Instead, he went back to Ovid's *Metamorphoses*, which holds out hope that the best of us can recover from the Fall if we raise our consciousness above our material state to a state of enlightenment. This leads to an elite core of knowers leading the blind masses. This, of course, leaves open the question of how the knowers know that they are not deluded, and this is the problem that Spenser, following Augustine, is attempting to answer in his poem by denying the Ovidian unity of nature that has been sundered by any action on the part of mankind.

permanently evil on account of their lacking any ontology.[2] The obligation of the individual is to orient oneself to the imbalance of nature by embracing what is good in oneself (given to us by God) through an active posture towards one's external experience, while avoiding the evils that that are always present in the universe but which flee when one approaches them.

This is the basis of Spenser's poor assessment of Redcrosse. He never bothers to make "triall" of the woman he knows as Fidessa, but takes her on account of her display of her body to him. The folly of that superficial posture towards his experience can be seen in his subsequent conversation with Fradubio, where he is listening to someone dictate the folly of his actions to him in advance of his making the same mistakes that got Fradubio turned into a tree; but on account of his uneducated "clownishe" mind, Redcrosse does not connect the dots between the experience of Fradubio and his own. The fact that the reader knows that God will rescue Redcrosse before the end does nothing to stop the reader's perception that there is something wrong with Redcrosse and that it would be a mistake to follow his example. That reaction is a wise one, as Redcrosse gives up the active posture that he had displayed in his battle with Errour and blindly (and so passively) follows Duessa, who "is wearie of the toilesom way" (I.iv.3.8), into the House of Pride.

Boundaries in the House of Pride

The House of Pride is covered gold foil and is guarded by Maluenu, another of those phantom characters who *seems* to separate the wheat from the chaff. But just like the genius who guards the gate of the Bower of Bliss, Maluenu allows entrance to everyone.[3] Maluenu represents the power of the mind to erect and maintain false distinctions that do not hold any real power based in nature. In Book II, Guyon will destroy the Bower of Bliss and its falsifying genius, but in Book I Redcrosse does not destroy the false distinctions erected by Maluenu. Rather, he endures them passively from beginning to end without challenging them in any way.

---

2 Other things, like Una and Errour, have no ontological existence whatsoever, being the product of fiction, but this does not exclude them from moral judgment.

3 This is the same thing that happens when we look into the two gates of dreams derived from Virgil in canto i. The pagan source of Malvenu points to a meaning of division of wheat from chaff, but by allowing everyone entrance into the House of Lucifera the process of separation is subverted in Spenser's Christian poem. It is up to the careful (and presumably Christian) reader to understand the difference between pagan and Christian experience and to choose to ignore pagan inquiries into *a priori* things that *only* Christians (in Spenser's mind) have learned have no true validity.

Lucifera's palace is compared favorably with the wealth of "*Persia* selfe, the nourse of pompous pride" (I.iv.7.6). Redcrosse gets a glimpse of the princess who rules the place, not in the living flesh that her many followers wish to see, but in a tableaux set upon a "cloth of State" (I.iv.8.1). The tableaux portrays her as a woman who disdains the earth (I.iv.10.2), who instead looks "to heauen" (I.iv.10.2), and who sits on high "for lowly she did hate" (I.iv.10.3). Many of the major turning points, not just of Book I but of the whole of *The Faerie Queene* are prefigured here. Lucifera is pictured as having conquered "A dreadfull Dragon with an hideous trayne" (I.iv.10.5), something that Redcrosse has been tasked to do but has not yet accomplished. The fact that her position is illegitimately founded is pointed out in stanza 12, where we read

> Yet rightfull kingdome she had none at all,
> Ne heritage of natiue soueraintie,
> But did vsurpe with wrong and tyrannie
> Vpon the scepter, which she now did hold:
> Ne ruld her Realme with lawes, but pollicie,
> And strong aduizement of six wisards old,
> That with their counsels bad her kingdome did vphold. (I.iv.12.3-9)

There is more than a hint of Mutabilitie here, a woman who also lacks any rightful claim to power when she storms the heavens ruled by Jove, the ruler who orders the kingdom of heaven.

The reasons she is an unfit ruler is that she not only looks upwards beyond her state but that she also looks at herself:

> And in her hand she held a mirrhour bright,
> Wherein her face she often vewed fayne,
> And in her selfe-lou'd semblance tooke delight. (I.iv.10.6-8)

As a ruler of a kingdom, her orientation should be looking horizontally outward towards her people (a=b), not inwardly towards herself (a=a).

The question naturally occurs of what Redcrosse makes of this experience. An uncareful reader might think that Redcrosse rejects the palace and its princess on account of the following passage:

> Yet the stout Faerie mongst the middest crowd
> Thought all their glorie vaine in knightly vew,
> And that great Princesse too exceeding prowd,

That to strange knight no better countenance allowd. (I.iv.15.6-9)

Taken on its own, the passage means that Redcrosse is *immune* to the charms of wealth. But if the reader is able to drag along with them their now-heavy memories, they should connect this moment with other experiences they have had with Redcrosse. They will remember that he has had his "stout heroicke heart" moved by the "ritch weedes and seeming glorious show" (I.ii.21.5) of the Whore of Babylon. His translation of such things into "her humblesse low" (I.ii.21.4) must make the reader question his judgment of what he is looking at when he is presented with heaps of wealth and beautiful ladies in the House of Pride. The reader's intuition of Redcrosse's outright rejection her superficial appearance actually hides the fact that something more subtle is going on here.

One key to the careful reader's recognition of what is going on is the poet's referral to Redcrosse as a "stout Faerie" (I.iv.15.6). The poet is withholding his own knowledge that Redcrosse is a human being. Once again, Spenser is not lying to the reader. He is pointing to Redcrosse's own perspective of himself. The reader will later learn that he is wrong about himself at this point in the poem. Even if linear readers of *The Faerie Queene* have not yet gotten to the end of the poem when Contemplation has revealed the mankindness of Redcrosse to him, the poet expects his readers to use their own stout memories after they have learned the truth to revisit this passage and change it from an absolute truth to relative and incomplete truth once they have better information.

The same thing holds true of the reader's interpretation of the meaning of "No better countenance" at I.iv.15.9. At first this seems to hold the meaning "Harrumph to wealth and worldly show," but on reflection in fuller knowledge of the reader's experience with Redcrosse it may mean "What? Is that all?" The key here is not for the reader to fall back on his or her potentially faulty *a priori* assumptions about what is going on in the passage, but to make "triall" of events in light of the *a posteriori* evidence that is being gradually revealed to the reader's mind.

The Triumph of Pride

Lucifera's counselors are seeking to do no more than "entertayne" (I.iv.15.1) the latest knight to show up on her doorstep. Merely by Redcrosse's having shown up they believe they "haue increast their crew" (I.iv.15.2). Thus they think no more about him, turning themselves to Duessa, who "in that court whylome her well they knew" (I.iv.15.5); and

> each one himself did payne
> All kindnesse and faire courtesie to shew . (I.iv.15.3-4)

Redcrosse's rejection of Lucifera calls her to action in an even more ostentatious display of entertainment, as she "Suddein vpriseth from her stately place" (I.iv.16.1) and climbs into her chariot,

> And stroue to match, in roiall rich array,
> Great *Iunoes* golden chaire, the which they say
> The Gods stand gazing on, when she does ride
> To *Ioues* high hous through heauens bras-paued way.... (I.iv.17.4-7)

This is another preview of the rise of Mutabilitie's journey through the spheres of Jove's heaven. Lucifera, like Mutabilitie, also strives to compete for power with the gods in an illegitimate manner.

The subsequent Triumph of Pride has Idleness leading Lucifera's six counselors on parade through the streets.[4] Once again, Redcrosse does not seem to be affected by them, and the reason for this is not hard to find. Anyone can tell that Redcrosse is not an example of *idleness*. Idleness "greatly shunned manly exercise" (I.iv.20.2), while the reader has been told that Redcrosse is arduous in his desire to prove himself in battle. If the reader takes Redcrosse's response to the *leader* of the Triumph of Pride as indicating his response to the whole spectacle, his response would argue against his being indicted by the charge of pride. He is indifferent to Idleness, and this causes him to sit back and view the triumph from an ironic perspective of entertainment but not as instructive or corrective his own failings.

But Redcrosse's whole perspective on the triumph's leader is undermined when we look at the parade of characters who Idleness leads. When the careful reader reads of Gluttony that

> In greene vine leaues he was right fitly clad;
> For other clothes he could not weare for heat (I.iv.22.1-2)

---

4 The motives of triumph are immediately derived from Petrarch's *The Triumphs of Petrarch* (Chicago, Il: Chicago University Press, 1962). Such triumphs had a long history in Renaissance poetry, but we should not overlook another source of their derivation from those things that are *excluded* from the Garden of Delights in Guillaume de Lorris' section of the *Roman de la Rose* in Guillaume de Lorris and Jean de Meun, *Le Roman de la Rose*, ed. Ernest Langlois, 5 vols. (Paris: Firmin-Didot, 1914).

the careful reader surely should take into account the fact that Redcrosse's armor is a burden to him and that he has taken it off at critical moments, including the episode when he, too, had bent

> his gentle wit,
> And thinking of those braunches greene to frame
> A girlond for her dainty forehead fit,
> He pluckt a bough. (I.ii.30.5-8)

It was at this moment that Fradubio appeared to him as the unrecognized reflection of his own behavior.

When the reader reads of Lecherie, who "ioyd weake wemens hearts to tempt, and proue / If from their loyall loues he might then moue" (I.iv.26.4-5), Spenser does not mean that his readers should overlook Redcrosse's own fickleness in his choice of love, as he changed his love from the fully loyal and fully clad Una for the first woman who shows him her body.

When Envy comes into view, the reader is told that "Accursed vsurie was all his trade" (I.iv.27.8), and he follows up this line with another: "And right and wrong ylike in equall ballaunce waide" (I.iv.27.9). This is important, for Spenser has made it clear that Redcrosse is wearing the armor that will tip the balance of every battle he engages in his favor if only he will give up his willful attempt to be a hero like the fictional Aeneas and instead embrace his substantial consciousness.

At this point in his journey, Redcrosse still believes that he has nothing to learn from the triumph passing before him, and therefore he continues to treat all details indifferently and so equally. Redcrosse unconsciously participates in the Triumph of Pride precisely because he is passively indifferent to the educative value of the pageant. The poet seems to be saying that the man who looks at the allegorical features of the pageant of sin and weighs them equally as an entertaining spectacle, and not according the instructive value given to each by their unequal weight, is participating in a sin which has scattered "Dead sculls and bones of men, whose life had gone astray" (I.iv.36.9). Art has lessons to teach those who are looking for wisdom. Rather than sitting indifferently enjoying the spectacle, as Redcrosse does here, the poet is asking his readers to weigh their own minds against the often differing values that they are confronted with in Spenser's art.

From this perspective, it may be instructive to take a second look at Spenser's warning that it

> May seeme the wayne was very euill led,
> When such an one had guiding of the way,
> That knew not, whether right he went, or else *astray*. (I.iv.19.7-9 italics mine)

This seems a warning directed at Redcrosse, who leads a directionless (as opposed to a purposeful) life, who seeks only an external warrior's glory, and who has lost his direction so much that he has taken up with false faith as his companion on account of her willingness to freely show off her bosom when it suits *her* ends. Redcrosse has been put in the position of not knowing whether he is traveling "right" or "astray." But rather than taking into account the choices in front of him, he is happy with himself and exempts himself from choosing, preferring to view all equally from a safe ironic distance.

The Unritualized Battle with Sansjoy

Sansjoy has seen Una's dwarf holding the armor and shield of Sansfoy, and Spenser hides from his readers the fact that Redcrosse is not meditating on what he has just seen by having Sansjoy challenge him to a fight. He is pictured as "burning all with rage" (I.iv.39.4) as he snatches "that same enuious gage / Of victors glory" (I.iv.39.5-6) from him. The reader is surely not meant to forget that there is an element of pride in the "Elfin" (I.iv.39.7) knight who would pick up such a token of war in the first place.

This moment gives the careful reader another insight into the mind of Redcrosse. He has never been interested in Una or her mission. He has always been intent on proving himself as a worthy warrior; and after Lucifera has passed by with her entertaining Triumph of Pride, he turns immediately back to war without reflecting on the triumph's instructive value, engaging in exactly the practice of war that Spenser has just been warning the reader about when Wrath had passed by:

> Full many mischiefes follow cruell *Wrath*;
> Abhorred bloodshed, and tumultuous strife,
> Vnmanly murder, and vnthrifty scath,
> Bitter despight, with rancours rusty knife,
> And fretting griefe the enemy of life. (I.iv.35.1-5)

As a warrior, Redcrosse is triumphant on account of his armor, but that does not mean that his dealings with things *as a man* are spotless. Redcrosse is a man who descends to the lowest form of animal behavior on a dime, and once again he launches into a furious battle over possession of the arms he has won by conquest. The arms of Sansfoy matter to the Redcrosse Knight because of their power to externalize for others to see his battlefield prowess, but they do not matter at all in his spiritual quest.

As happened when Archimago interceded to stop the destructive behavior of Redcrosse, it falls to Lucifera to intercede here:

> that great Queene vpon eternall paine
> Of high displeasure, that ensewen might,
> Commaunded them their fury to refraine,
> And if that either to that shield had right,
> In equall lists they should the morrow next it fight. (I.iv.40.5-9)

In spite of his having the power to turn battles in his favor by virtue of his Ephesian armor, Redcrosse submits to Lucifera's demands, because he sees submission as a way to gain a footing on the Ladder of Ambition, a thing he has always craved but which he does not yet possess.

The problem with Lucifera's resolution of the irruption of violence into her ordered universe is not that her quelling of violence is wrong and that Redcrosse should be allowed to wreak his destructive animal violence within the social world. It is that ambition must be tied to a deeper moral framework than animal violence. Lucifera, who "rightfull kingdome she had none at all" (I.iv.12.3), has usurped power without latching herself onto the moral framework on which true power depends. Spenser is saying that Redcrosse has not yet reached the foundation on which he should build his kingdom, believing that *animal violence* is the way to respectability. The correct choice here is the building up of an intermediate temperance that *distances* him from his immediate desires but brings him closer to the reason by which man imitates God, albeit through a glass darkly. As it is, Redcrosse will not learn the way of Patience until he meets her in the House of Holinesse at I.x.23.

It is telling that, after Lucifera has interfered with the furious fight which threatens to disrupt her order, it is not the rude and uneducated Redcrosse who makes an apology for his enraged fight: it is the pagan who apologizes for his error:

> Ah dearest Dame, (quoth then the Paynim bold,)
> Pardon the error of enraged wight,
> Whom great griefe made forget the raines to hold
> Of reasons rule.... (I.iv.41.1-4)

This brings up the questions of what "reasons rule" should be and why a pagan knows what the Knight of Holinesse does not. Surely reason is a matter of correctly weighing things of unequal measure. Redcrosse submits to rule by the equal balance of Lucifera, telling himself that "He neuer meant with words, but swords to plead his right" (I.iv.42.9). In turning away from words *towards* swords, he is reversing the progressive role of history, predicted in *Isaiah* 2:4, of a future in which swords are put away as mankind beats them into plowshares.

Subsequent to Sansjoy's apology, both parties pass the night "in ioy and iollity, / Feasting and courting both in bowre and hall" (I.iv.43.5-6). Even an uncareful reader has to wonder about the judgment of Redcrosse, for the steward of the party was "excessiue *Gluttony*, / That of his plenty poured forth to all" (I.iv.43.7-8); and both are called to sleep when "the Chamberlain *Slowth* did to rest them call" (I.iv.43.9). Apparently, the irony of these events never occurs to Redcrosse.

There is more. During the course of his argument with Redcrosse, Sansjoy brings up the fact that his opponent has been won over by Fidessa, who reaps the spoils of war "Sowen in bloodie field" (I.iv.42.5). After all have gone to sleep, Duessa rises and defends herself, saying to Sansjoy in effect that she has never given herself to Redcrosse the way she gave herself to him: "For that I would not yeeld, that to *Sansfoy* I gaue"(I.iv.47.9). She could be lying, of course. After all, she lies when she positions herself as a "silly maid" (I.iv.47.7) carried off by a powerful man who holds her "in darksom caue" (I.iv.47.8) and not, as the reader suspects, as a powerful woman leading a weak Redcrosse around at and for her pleasure. It is not only Spenser's unwillingness to delve into the secrets of sexual pleasure that disguises the truth of the matter from the reader. The reader must be complicit if Redcrosse is to be forgiven his obvious signs of weakness.

That said, even from her position of power Duessa misunderstands Redcrosse's ability to overcome obstacles. She believes that they are operating in a universe in which power is equally balanced between good and evil. Thus, Duessa portrays Redcrosse as a man whose virtues make him "vnworthie" (I.iv.47.4) to possess Sansjoy's "worthie shield" (I.iv.47.5). She is right in a sense, for Redcrosse should never have been fighting for the shield of Sansfoy at all, because, like Errour, Sansjoy is defined by his negative attributes and not by anything positive. Nevertheless, after a brief discussion in which she and Sansjoy both agree that Sansjoy has right on his side, the pagan asks Duessa

> Why dame (quoth he) what oddes can euer bee,
> Where both do fight alike, to win or yield? (I.vi .50.3-4)

Duessa understands at some level that is beyond her comprehension that Redcrosse has some power to tip the balance in his favor. Duessa places that power in some secret external magic held in his shield and arms:

> Yea but (quoth she) he beares a charmed shield,
> And eke enchaunted armes, that none can perce,
> Ne none can wound the man, that does them wield. (I.vi 50.5-7)

After this conversation, Duessa, who has led Redcrosse through the open gate of Maluenu into the House of Pride through her seemingly open posture, allows herself to assist Sansjoy with "secrete aid" (I.vi .51.8).

The Ritualized Battle with Sansjoy

We can measure the distance between Spenser and his hero when the poet opens canto v with the announcement that Redcrosse's resting in silence with his intent is not enough:

> The noble hart, that harbours vertuous thought,
> And is with child of glorious great intent,
> Can neuer rest, vntill it forth haue brought
> Th'eternall brood of glorie excellent. (I.v.1.1-4)

Redcrosse has shown himself weak when it comes to *expression* of his inner intention in regard to Una. Rather than stay and make "triall" of her, he runs away. And Redcrosse is not thinking of Una here. Rather, he has fallen in love with Duessa and has been led by her to the House of Pride, where he watchers the Triumph of Pride without the least bit of self-reflection as to its instructive value for himself. After the triumph has passed, he immediately gets involved in a violent battle with Sansjoy without concern for the destruction wrought on the fragile social order by his actions. His future victory in violent battle is the "noble thought" that he, who prefers swords to words, seeks to express here:

> Such restlesse passion did all night torment
> The flaming corage of that Faery knight,
> Deuizing, how that doughtie turnament
> With greatest honour he atchieuen might. (I.v.1.5-8)

This brings the reader to the core of the problem with Redcrosse. He possesses an *a priori* inner glory, and this glory has been given external expression in the armor of Ephesians that Una happens to be carrying around with her in Spenser's Faery fiction. When Redcrosse leaves Una, who the careful reader knows has been struggling (and slowly succeeding) to express herself in the "extremitie of time" (I.vi 11.2), he is no longer attempting to coordinate his inner heart with its external expression of his goodness given to him within the Spenserian fiction, not by his own will, but by Una's granting him his arms. He ignores the role of his armor in his guaranteed victory over his enemies, as he continues to seek the worldly "honour" that will come *only* to his own human will (and so not to God or Una) if he defeats Sansjoy. Spenser make this explicit. After meditating all night, the sun rises and Redcrosse thinks "with that Pagan proud he combat *will* that day" (I.v.2.9 italics mine). In the battle that follows Spenser makes sure that we understand that the *contest* is governed by the "the *sacred* lawes of armes" (I.v.4.9 italics mine) and that Redcrosse "all for praise and honour he did fight" (I.v.7.6).

Both stanza 8 and 9, the stanzas in which the even battle occurs, open with the same line: "So th'one for wrong, the other striues for right" (I.v.8.1; I.v.9.1) This configuration, which keeps both sides equal in the fight that follows, is the result of "clownishe" Redcrosse having submitted himself to Lucifera, a creature who erases the balance towards good in the world by rendering morally unequal beings equivalent. In this, Spenser seems to be telling his readers that there is more to fighting for right than launching oneself furiously at one's enemy. One must draw on the deeper purpose given by one's mind's relationship with God's *a priori* ontological creation. It is not surprising that Sansjoy has no such sense, but that fact that Redcrosse has no interest in and perhaps no knowledge whatsoever of this deeper level of existence at this point in the poet's narration must be a cause for concern to the reader.

At the end of stanza 8, the poet pictures a wise soothsayer, who interprets what he has seen as a "hideous horrour" (I.v.8.6):

> The wise Southsayer seeing so sad sight,
> Th'amazed vulgar tells of warres and mortall fight. (I.v.8.8-9)

But the widsom of the soothsayer in making a negative judgment is not enough to decide the outcome of the equal battle; and neither is the reaction of the uneducated "amazed vulgar" crowd. Their reaction to the horror of bloodshed causes paralysis in them, and "victory they dare not wish to either side" (I.v.9.9). If theirs were the only reaction possible, then the battle would be prolonged forever, because no one wants anyone to *win*.

That is not what happens. Within the battle, the language suddenly emphasizes doubling, as the "raging yre" of Sansjoy is suddenly "redoubled" (I.v.10.4) after the pagan chances to "cast his eye, / His suddein eye, flaming with wrathfull fyre" (I.v.10.1-2) on Sansfoy's shield, which the reader will remember Redcrosse had taken as the spoil of war. This shifts the balance of the fight in Sansfoy's favor so much that Duessa (who Redcrosse still knows as Fidessa) breaks her silence "and lowd to him gan call / The false *Duessa*, Thine the shield, and I, and all" (I.v.11.8-9).

What follows is not what we should expect, if Richard A. Levin is right about Redcrosse and Una being involved in a romance in which each loves the other.[5] Redcrosse has received a terrible blow on account of Sansjoy's redoubled effort, and he is reduced to a "swowning dreame" (I.v.12.2); but the sound of Duessa's voice—the disloyal voice to whom the reader knows Redcrosse has professed his love in opposition to loyal Una—revives him. He is "mou'd with wrath, and shame, and Ladies sake" (I.v.12.5) to take revenge on his foe "all attonce" (I.v.12.6). The presence of wrath clouds his mind to the fact that Duessa has declared her definite preference for Sansjoy, and she has used her proper name as she has done so. Redcrosse is not listening to the whole of his experience, but he acts on his partial information about his circumstances.

Nevertheless, the revival of his wrath turns the balance in Redcrosse's favor once again. He attempts to kill Sansjoy, but he avoids death by stooping (I.v.12.8), and before Redcrosse is able to land another blow, "a darkesome clowd" (I.v.13.6) falls on the scene. This obscures his enemy, who "no where doth appeare, / But vanisht is" (I.v.13.7-8).

In the stanza that follows, Duessa completely flips her previous position, which Redcrosse had not understood in the first place, as she turns back to lying once again: "The conquest yours, I yours, the shield, and glory yours" (I.v.14.9).[6] Redcrosse remains completely unaware of her changed behavior towards him (since he is not listening very hard), and when she flatters him as "prowest knight" (I.v.14.2), Redcrosse does not object. As she does so, she makes it plain that he chose *her* of all the women in the world (including Una) to love (I.v.14.3).

---

5 Richard A. Levin, "The Legende of the Redcrosse Night and Una: Or, of the Love of a Good Woman," *Studies in English Literature: 1500-1900* 31, no. 1 (1991).

6 Once again, I would point out that it does not really matter if she is lying or telling the truth if Redcrosse is not paying attention to the larger world outside himself.

Like "Th'amazed vulgar" (I.v.8.9), the "clownishe" Redcrosse "standes amazed" (I.v.15.5) that his enemy could have faded away; but the vanishing of Sansjoy does not quell his furious desire, and he and "his thirstie blade" continue to search for the "faithlesse enemy" "To bath in blood" (I.v.15.2-3).

Redcrosse's warrior instinct is more powerful than his moral instinct, and when trumpets sound their triumph and heralds run to him with the shield that was "cause of enmitie" (I.v.15.9), he immediately turns away from his deeper moral duty to serve God to offer his service to his

> soueraine Queene,
> And falling her before on lowly knee,
> To her makes present of his seruice *seene*. (I.v.16.1-3 italics mine)

This statement reveals the limitations of Redcrosse's vision once again. He has the ability to see what is in front of him, but lacks the penetration to peer beneath the surface to look deeper into the truth of matters. Thus he prostrates himself before false and falsifying Lucifera, and not before God, when he wishes to make his loyalty "seene."

After his temporary fury subsides, the adoration by the Queen of Pride and the applause of the crowd captures Redcrosse's attention:

> So marcheth home, and by her takes the knight,
> Whom all the people followe with great glee,
> Shouting, and clapping all their hands on hight,
> That all the aire it fils, and flyes to heauen bright. (I.v.16.6-9)

This is not as it should be.

Duessa's Journey into the Realm of Night

Spenser portrays Redcrosse as a foolish man with no insight into himself or the world around him when he returns to his subject with a poetic simile of the Nile:

> As when a wearie traueiler that strayes
> By muddy shore of broad seuen-mouthed *Nile*,
> Vnweeting of the perillous wandring wayes,
> Doth meet a cruell craftie Crocodile,
> Which in false griefe hyding his harmefull guile,
> Doth weepe full sore, and sheddeth tender teares:
> The foolish man, that pitties all this while

His mournefull plight, is swallowd vp vnwares,
Forgetfull of his owne, that mindes anothers cares. (I.v.18)

Redcrosse is the "foolish man" whose "mournefull plight" is "swallowd vp vnwares" by his forgetting of "his owne" and minding "anothers cares." Duessa, on the other hand, is a "cruell craftie Crocodile" who has the power to look deeper into the structures of the universe and so change the *scientific* powers of the universe in her favor. This is because, although Duessa is imperfect in her reconstruction of the universe, she plays an *active* role in the universe, as opposed to Redcrosse's passive stance towards the same events. This allows her at this point in the poem to travel down to the underworld to meet with Night, the "most auncient Grandmother of all" (I.v.22.2), who we are told is older than Jove himself. As a consequence, the reader is given a look at a world of which "clownishe" Redcrosse, bathing in the applause of others and dedicating himself to the service of Lucifera in exchange for a place on the Ladder of Ambition, is completely unaware.

Night is older than Jove himself. This means that she has seen the secrets of the world both made, as it is today, and "vnmade" (I.v.22.6), as it was before its creation. Thus, she understands the equality of the nature of things, which may be deconstructed as well as constructed. But, unlike Derrida's deconstruction, which is predicated on an Enlightenment assumption that human nature used to be equal with natural law *and could be again*, Spenser's Augustinian universe hold no such hope for mankind. Instead, mankind has been permanently cut off from Eden by the Fall. Man must learn to imitate things that pre-exist the mere *a posteriori* imposition of deconstructable names and found his thought on a deeper faith that connects us back to God's *a priori* creation. But because of the Fall, the ontology of God can be only statistically approximated in the human mind[7] but can never be brought back to an identity due to the limits of human rationality. Nevertheless God's prior creation is true and cannot be deconstructed by a mere human being, who has access only to his or her limited reason, which deals only with the imposition of names that human beings place on top of the ontology of God.

Though she precedes the reign of Jove, Night is not indifferent to her part in the diurnal alternation of day and night. Like Errour before Redcrosse's armor, Night shies away from "*Duessa* sunny bright" (I.v.21.1) and attempts to retire back "to her caue" (I.v.21.6), but she is stopped after "the

---

[7] This, as I noted earlier, is due to the New Academy's embrace of the principles of Arcesilaus and Carneades, which Augustine took up in his own thought.

witches speech she gan to heare" (I.v.21.7).

Duessa rebukes her for her moral indifference to the fate of her sons:

> O what of Gods then boots it to be borne,
> If old *Aveugles* sonnes so euill heare?
> Or who shall not great *Nightes* children scorne,
> When two of three her Nephews are so fowle forlorne? (I.v.23.6-9)

This rouses Night from her moral indifference, changing her position into one in which she stands as a partisan of evil:

> Her feeling speeches some compassion mou'd
> In hart, and chaunge in that great mothers face:
> Yet pittie in her hart was neuer prou'd
> Till then: for euermore she hated, neuer lou'd. (I.v.24.6-9)

But "compassion" in her "hart" is not enough. Though she is moved to hate, Night still feels helplessness in light of the triumph of Joue. She begins her response to Duessa's call to action by expressing her agreement with her:

> Deare daughter rightly may I rew
> The fall of famous children borne of mee,
> And good successes, which their foes ensew. (I.v.25.1-3)

She does not like the state of affairs under Joue that has caused her famous children to fall, but she cannot see any way out of the predicament, neither for herself, nor for her children:

> But who can turne the streame of destinee,
> Or breake the chayne of strong necessitee,
> Which fast is tyde to *Ioues* eternall seat. (I.v.25.4-6)[8]

Thus, she is resigned to her fate in the universe as a principle of evil:

---

[8] This is a reference to Homer's *Iliad* 8.19-27, where Joue sets himself up as the link between heaven and earth by his dangling a cord from his seat on Mt. Olympus. In Plato's *Ion*, Socrates uses this as a metaphor for correct interpretation that the rhapsode Ion himself cannot understand in spite of his actually performing the works of Homer in a rhapsode contest. Ion becomes an empty vessel that is filled with the divine gifts of Homer, but he has no will of his own. It appears obvious that Augustine and Edmund Spenser disagree with Socrates on the basis of Aristotle's charge that the whole thing was subject to deconstruction as a mere "poetic metaphor." Both attempt to correct for Socrates' imperfect reconstruction of the universes by founding their vision of the universe on what they think is a truer faith.

> The sonnes of Day he fauoureth, I see,
> And by my ruines thinkes to make them great:
> To make one great by others losse, is bad excheat. (I.v.25.7-9)

Despite her recognition that Duessa is offering to make her a principle of evil, that is not enough to recover her former position in the universe before Jove overthrew his father. In overthrowing Saturn, Jove ushered in a time of division in which one thing must be subordinated to another on the basis of a merely political position. Thus, the reign of Jove excludes the whole position that is the function of humanity to uphold in the world. In its place comes Jove's insistence on taking sides with the worst *part* of the human inheritance. Such "bad excheat" is what Night is still resigned to after her change from a neutral stance in which she remains indifferent to the evil being perpetuated in the world to a position on the side of evil.

Night resolves the implied problem of free will and necessity by taking control of the partial legacy that is left to her in the world after the overthrow of Saturn by Jove, as she vows to avenge on Redcrosse the pains that she and Duessa have suffered in action:

> Yet shall they not escape so freely all;
> For some shall pay the price of others guilt:
> And he the man that made *Sansfoy* to fall,
> Shall with his owne bloud price that he hath spilt. (I.v.26.1-4)

This notion of someone else paying the price for one's sins furthers, rather than deconstructs, the imbalance that she had just been complaining about in Jove's actions in dividing the world from a unified good. This brings up the question of whether Redcrosse, who has been bathing in applause, bears any responsibility for the change in the great mother's face. Should he, too, have turned away from applause, as Duessa had, and started to learn a magic that would have allowed him to change the face of the universe for good, as Duessa has changed the world for evil? The answer is no, but that answer requires some explanation.

Both Night and Duessa are severely limited in their appreciation of the sources of moral truth in the universe they operate in. Augustine had argued a thousand years before that evil was privative: it had no ontology of its own; and Spenser agrees with Augustine on this. Duessa, on the other hand, believes in an absolute Manichean division between good and evil in which both are *ontologically* real. In her ability to convince Night to take sides in such a Manichean universe, she wins the battle. But insofar as she is wrong, on account of her being unaware of the privative nature of evil, she loses the war. All Redcrosse has to do to win every battle and every war is show up, and God will supply the victory to him. The weakness of George's human will in not understanding this relationship with God has no effect of the outcome of the battles he engages in. Likewise, his ability to win battles has no effect on the progress of his will towards knowledge.

Science and Necessity Near Avernus' Hole

In such an Augustinian universe, the chain of necessity can be broken by looking past appearances, which may be true or false, to the preverbal truth of God's ontologically-created universe. The means to do this are available to *learned* men and women in Spenser's world through education. Unfortunately, the "clownishe" Redcrosse has not yet learned the true source of his power, and has no apparent interest in learning about anything other than what is immediately available to him, being content to win or lose "all atonce." Duessa, on the other hand, is able to succeed in her designs by creating artificial barriers to the action of good men when it suits her in her equally balanced universe through her (still imperfect) science. This lengthens the time between the beginning and the end of Redcrosse's actions, thereby frustrating his desires. That is not wholly a bad thing, despite that result having no part in Duessa's intentions.

Spenser emphasizes the "chayne of strong necessitee" when Night agrees to travel back up to the world and then descends again through the "yawning gulfe of deepe *Auernus* hole" (I.v.31.3) where we are told "there creature neuer past, / That backe returned without heauenly grace" (I.v.31.6-7). Perhaps this is why Night recognizes in Duessa a "true-seeming grace" (I.v.27.4), but *in the very next sentence* Spenser breaks the chains of necessity for the furies:

> But dreadfull *Furies*, which their chaines haue brast,
> And damned sprights sent forth to make ill men aghast. (I.v.31.8-9)

The double meaning of "brast" as "braced" as well as "burst" seems to indicate that the divisions erected by the chains of necessity are only apparent, not real. They have been placed on the universe by Jove's reign, and not by God. Duessa's reign over Night is made possible by the fact that Redcrosse has not bothered to access the source of his own very differently founded power in God's *a priori* choice of him as the vessel for His action in the world. If he had, nothing Duessa could do could ever be successful. But instead, "clownishe" Redcrosse relies on his socially destructive animal wrath to win battles which he thinks of as equal. This leaves Duessa in charge of the unattended world of rational science.

Night gathers up Sansjoy and brings him back through "Auernus hole" to Æsculapius, who has been thrust out of his heaven by Jove on account of his "wondrous science" (I.v.40.1), which is so powerful that it could "could the dead reuiue, / And fates expired could renew againe" (I.v.40.2-3). In order to prevent the possibility of endless life, Jove "vnto hell did thrust him down alive" (I.v.40.5). From his position out of Jove's heaven

> he did alwaies striue
> Himselfe with salues to health for to restore,
> And slake the heauenly fire, that raged euermore. (I.v.40.7-9)

The thrusting of Æsculapius and his "wonderous science" out of Jove's heaven allows him to retain a univocal puropse (τέλος) that is lacking in the Jove's also partial grasp of universe. Duessa's grasp of that partial point gives her power over passive Redcrosse, but not over God.

When Night arrives and asks her for his help in curing her wounded nephew, Æsculapius declines for fear of providing a new cause for redoubling the wrath of Jove:

> Can Night defray
> The wrath of thundring *Ioue*, that rules both night and day?
> (I.v.42.8-9)

Night makes another very clever argument in response to Æsculapius objections. Since heaven's king has excluded him from "hope of heauen," what harm can come from operating under "the power of euerlasting Night?" (I.v.43.1-5). Her answer does not answer all the questions that Æsculapius has raised. If Jove rules both night and day, how can Night provide shelter for his redoubled blows unless Jove has no actual power over all of the universe? In the absence of any knowledge of the ultimate construction of the universe on the part of Night or Æsculapius, "Her words preuaild" (I.v.44.1).

Æsculapius then goes to work:

> the learned leach
> His cunning hand gan to his wounds to lay,
> And all things else, the which his art did teach. (I.v.44.1-3)

In acting, Æsculapius has made a willful decision to exclude himself from participation in the Jovian order, which exists by the passivity of its participants in accepting Jove as their leader.

"Having seene" that her work has been achieved, Duessa "from thence arose away" (I.v.44.4), returning from her foray in the timeless world of eternal Night and the domain of "wondrous science" (I.v.40.1) back to the world of time:

> And backe returning tooke her wonted way,
> To runne her timely race, whilst *Phoebus* pure
> In westerne waues his wearie wagon did recure. (I.v.44.7-9)

Resting (Again!) with Fidessa

At this point, the reader is treated to a canto in which they find out that Una has not been raped and in which she does submit to being passively worshipped by satyrs. But she has at least glimpsed the possibility that her own passivity is part of her problem when she attempts to teach the satyrs their error in worshipping her. Rather than listen to the unified voice of Eden, they turn to worshipping her ass. From this experience, she is gradually learning that not all choices in the world of time are equal and that she has been linked to Redcrosse in love for a reason. She sets out to find the other who completes her.

When Duessa comes back, she finds that Una's dwarf has led him away, and she races after him. Unlike Una, who seems to be learning the lesson of the necessity of action but who is still wandering through the wilderness in a random fashion, Duessa heads right to Redcrosse, who she finds easily on account of her learned and rational approach to experience. She finds him having taken off his armor (again!) and lying under a shady tree, feeding

> vpon the cooling shade, and bayes
> His sweatie forehead in the breathing wynd,
> Which through the trembling leaues full gently playes
> Wherein the cherefull birds of sundry kynd
> Do chaunt sweet musick, to delight his mynd. (I.vii.3.1-5)

This description is quite close to Spenser's description of Gluttony, of whom the reader has recently read,

> In greene vine leaues he was right fitly clad;
> For other clothes he could not weare for heat.... (I.iv.22.1-2)

Spenser does not want his readers to ignore the similarities here. Rather, the reader should be wondering once again whether Redcrosse was paying attention to the presentation of unequal sins during the Triumph of Pride.

Fidessa reproaches him for his "carelesnes vnkynd" (I.vii.3.7). Following her rebuke, with *his* "Vnkindnesse past," they begin "of solace treat, / And bathe in pleasaunce of the ioyous shade (I.vii 4.1-2). It is necessary for the reader to locate exactly who forgives Redcrosse for his unkindness, because the poet seems to express his disapproval of his behavior here:

> Yet goodly court he made still to his Dame,
> Pourd out in loosnesse on the grassy grownd,
> Both carelesse of his health, and of his fame. (I.vii.7.1-3)

This is an important moment, less in the poem itself (although it is that, too) than for what it tells us about the self-imposed limits of modern critical methods for dealing with Reformation poetry. The reader may recall DeNeef's remark that "Narrative is taken to be the logical or 'realized' extension of character."[9] The reader notes the equivalence of logic and reality; but sexual ecstasy exposes a breach in Redcrosse's bodily integrity, as he pours himself out "in loosnesse on the grassy grownd." This is no small thing, because, at the same time that the poet posits a breach in Redcrosse's bodily integrity, he exposes a breach in the modern "rule" that character and narrative function interdependently, each a "function of the other."[10]

DeNeef's rule may be subject to a breach in its integrity in the same way that Augustine had taken on pagan authors' belief in pure reason and Derrida's repetition of skepticism that comes from his following Plato without the acknowledgement of the breach that caused Plato to make room for a necessary fiction in his construction of his metaphysical universe, specifically his *Parmenides* and *Timaeus*. By following Augustine, Spenser causes the reader to shift away from complete bodily integrity of limited individuals to a more nebulous imaginative fiction that makes a more whole picture of the world at the expense of individuals that are divided into parts that are not equal to the whole of the greater prior world. Through this experience of division, the Christian poet makes plain in a distributed allegory what pagan authors thought that they could make plain through the exercise of direct reason. Spenser's resolution comes at the expense of the integrated individual monad that has played such a large role in the modern world's

---

9 Hamilton, *The Spenser Encyclopedia*, 583a.
10 Ibid.

resolution of the problems that attend the problematical relationship of the connection of the microscopic individual to the macrocosmic world.

Fortunately for Redcrosse, he does not consummate his relationship with Duessa, as his seed is spilled "on the grassy grownd"; but his act of onanism nevertheless indicates his willingness to be careless with his body. As soon as the absolute division between his literal body and the body of someone else has been breached, Redcrosse once again encounters the external consequences of his action in distributive allegory, as he immediately hears

> a dreadfull sownd,
> Which through the wood loud bellowing, did rebownd,
> That all the earth for terrour seemd to shake,
> And trees did tremble. (I.vii.7.4-7)

As usual, Redcrosse is more than a little bit surprised to hear his behavior reflected back at him, but of course he does not see it this way. Instead, he believes that he is encountering a purely external danger:

> Th'Elfe therewith astownd,
> Vpstarted lightly from his looser make,
> And his vnready weapons gan in hand to take. (I.vii.7.7-9)

He gathers his "looser make"—that is, his body rather than his mind—together again and prepares to take up his arms against the other. That this reflects Redcrosse's lack of self-knowledge is indicated by the poet's reaction to the "Elfe," who he portrays as reacting with the same astonishment that the "Th'amazed vulgar" who had witnessed Redcrosse's fight for fame and honor had reacted to his appearance before them. But Redcrosse does not react as the soothsayer reacts, who can see beneath the surface of things (I.v.8.8-9) and who had found Redcrosse's quest for individual fame "sad." In fact, up to this point in the narrative Redcrosse has *never* listened to his experience with a mind to apply the lessons of outward nature to himself. And once again, he misses the true significance of events that surround him in the poet-created Faery. He believes still that he *is* a creature of Faery, an Elf who never fell as Adam did.

Redcrosse's Defeat by Orgoglio

This time, he meets the consequences of his own sin in the external representation of the giant Orgoglio. Orgoglio is a creature whose mother

Redcrosse Within The World Of Time 163

was the earth and whose father is blustering Aeolus (I.vii.9.1-2), and thus his head is filled with wind. He has no goodwill from God. Nevertheless, the only way we can account for his easy defeat of Redcrosse is by noting that Orgoglio catches Redcrosse without the armor on that guarantees his victory in every battle he engages in. The reader is told that he catches him "ere he could his armour on him dight, / Or gett his shield" (I.vii.8.1-2). Redcrosse's lack of insight into the fact of his armor's power bespeaks his inability to learn from his experiences and frame his goodwill in terms other than his quest for fame, which he had put at risk yet again when he took his armor off. The poet Spenser believes that his readers should make "triall" of Redcrosse before yielding him a power that he does not deserve. In doing so, the poet directs his reader, not to his name, but to his actions.

During the battle, the clumsy Redcrosse gets his foot stuck in an oak tree—no small feat—but despite this fact, he is saved from being "pouldred all, as thin as flower" (I.vii.12.4), not due to his strength nor to his courage—neither of these are in doubt—but because of a share of "heuenly grace, that him did blesse" (I.vii.12.3). This does not save him completely, though, from Orgoglio. After he gets his victim disentangled from the pesky oak tree,

> Him to his castle brought with hastie forse,
> And in a Dongeon deepe him threw without remorse. (I.vii.15.8-9)

That Orgoglio does not kill him has to do with the unlikely intercession of Duessa, who does God's work of keeping Redcrosse alive, asking that he be spared in order that he may be kept as an "eternall bondslaue" (I.vii.14.8).

Redcrosse himself is shown to be completely helpless in his dealings with the events that he has encountered, and neither the goodwill of God nor his own force can save him from his fate. But all along the way there are people who could have helped him if he could only learn to listen more deeply to the projections of his inner behavior into the outward world made possible in the fictional universe of allegory. Una's dwarf had warned him to fly from the Cave of Errour. Una, too, had urged caution before entering. After he meets with the arch-magician Archimago, he is so frightened by the false reality he is shown that he runs away rather than making "triall" of the reality that confronts him. After he is on his own, he makes more serious mistakes, including making and professing love to Fidessa and submitting himself to Queen Lucifera.

As he builds up a base of experience in the world of becoming in time, the consequences of his sins, which were not all that serious in the Cave of Errour at the beginning of his adventures, are growing more dire, as Redcrosse fails to learn from his experience and place them in a constructed and rational framework through the application of his uniquely human reason combined with his human memory. Instead of his holiness being a model for others to follow, Redcrosse is becoming a model of how much God lets a man get away with if He has given him the gift of grace. The reader knows from the beginning of the Spenser's depiction of Faery in his fictional poem that Redcrosse will succeed, because should he fail, God will fail (and we all know that in Spenser's universe that is not possible). But imitating Redcrosse without such the benefit of God's *a priori* grace, which Augustine and Calvin had denied to all men outside of fiction, is extremely dangerous.

As a result, the ontologically existing reader, who survives the deconstruction of purely fictional Faery, is not invited to imitate the Knight of Holinesse and his authorially-constructed grace. They must find another way to negotiate their way through this world.

A Paradox in Una's Imagination

Una's Causal Dwarf

Not every character in Spenser's universe is as dead to the reflections of things that echo around them as Redcrosse is. Consider Una's lowly dwarf, who plays a critical role in moving the pair forward. It is he who does the heavy lifting of Una's "needments" (I.i.6.3-4). The perception of both Una and Redcrosse is that he "lasie seemd in being euer last" (I.i.6.2). This is a perception born of their exclusive and exclusionary social priorities, but it is a judgment that overlooks the hard work that he does in lightening Una's load.[1]

Spenser does not make the same mistake. The poet portrays the dwarf as a man who brings more rational insight into the world than either of his social superiors. Unlike his masters, who travel through the wilderness in a completely random fashion without interpreting the various things they see, Una's dwarf brings a measure of reason to the things he sees and prioritizes them accordingly. This gives him moral priority in interpretation that his lazy masters lack.

This is evident when he is stolen by Redcrosse and taken to the House of Pride. Redcrosse seems not to notice the huge numbers of "caytiue wretched thralls, that wayled night and day" (I.v.45.9) locked in a dungeon. It is as "ruefull sight, as could be seene with eie" (I.v.46.1), but Redcrosse's eyes are feeble (I.iv.9.6), a fact that we learned when he was dazzled by the prospect of his "glory and aduancement vayne" (I.iv.9.4). All of these bodies piled high are seen again in the Triumph of Pride, when Lucifera rides by:

---

1 One might suppose the Una, being the principle of unity in the poem, would not need anything external to her; but this appears not to be the case.

> And vnderneath their feet, all scattered lay
> Dead sculs and bones of men, whose life had gone astray. (I.iv.36.8-9)

This is supposed to lead the reader to ask what is wrong with Redcrosse that he had not seen any of this as he is being entertained by the steward Gluttony.

The answer is that things available to the sight still require interpretation through rational processes that can look deeper into events and things than a merely superficial thinker like Redcrosse can. This is not the case with Una's stolen dwarf, who looks deeper into the catalog of kings and princes—all Redcrosse's *social* superiors—who had wasted their days in "ydle pompe, or wanton play" (I.v.51.7). The dwarf looks deeper for the "hidden cause of their captiuitie" (I.v.46.3). As a result, the dwarf sees what is going on with his eyes, which deliver an immediate experience of the *a priori* world to his passive intellect; but it is only after he has processed what he has seen through his active intellect (governed by his *a posteriori* reason) that the dwarf is able to make an "ensample of their mournefull sight / Vnto his maister" (I.v.52.2-3). Unlike Redcrosse, who is intent on winning his furious fights all at once or not at all, the dwarf realizes the moral danger that Redcrosse is in. As a result, Una's stolen dwarf sneaks Redcrosse out the back way "by a priuy Posterne" (I.iv.52.7) in order to avoid the "enuious eyes" of others (I.iv.52.8), serving his new master's reputation by not allowing others to see where he has been spending his time.

Spenser's point is that when Una and Redcrosse see the dwarf only as "lasie," they are treating him only in terms of his social position alone. Social position is an accident of birth. As such, it is a condition of being human. But in Spenser's universe, one can improve oneself if one learns to use one's reason to process events that pass before one's mind. This takes practice and cannot be acquired "at once," as Redcrosse is attempting to do in his quest to find a place on the social ladder of Gloriana's court. The dwarf is a man who has acquired more of this precious gift *a posteriori* reason than either of his lazy masters have. Their treatment of him as merely lazy bespeaks their own pride of place as well as their moral ignorance of the uses to which they could put him if they were not such snobs.[2]

In spite of this, reason is not the end of experience in *The Faerie Queene*. It is merely a desirable step along the way to a deeper truth founded in

---

[2] I remind the reader that Una betrays such snobbery in her gainsaying of George until he is able to fit into her magical armor in *The Letter to Raleigh*.

God's *a priori* creation (ontology) that may nevertheless be reproducible only in a statistical manner by the *a posteriori* reason of the human mind (epistemology). In spite of the statistical nature of the mind's reproduction of the *a priori* world, *a posteriori* constructions give one real power. This is why the evil Duessa is able to use her limited powers of reason to lead Redcrosse where she will, ultimately stopping his forward progress (his τέλος) by having him lie with her (although this comes after he has already taken off his armor as he seeks relief from the heat of the day). It is the action of God that thwarts his will and spills his seed on the ground, avoiding what could have been a disaster for his ultimate marriage to Una in canto xii. Like Duessa, the dwarf is able to use his reason to give himself a τέλος within the world, and this allows him to to locate Una, who is randomly wandering in the wilderness looking for Redcrosse without a clue how to find him. The dwarf, however, "had not trauailed long" (I.vii.20.1) before he finds her, meaning that if she had the use of reason that he has, she might have been able to find Redcrosse on her own, because he is not far away. As it is, it is *her dwarf* who leads her back to Redcrosse.

This is an example of the trope of "the world overturned."[3] It is an important trope in a book that is dedicated to the adventures of a "clownishe younge man" who shows up at Gloriana's court hoping for social promotion and who will not only be given an adventure but will eventually succeed in doing what better-mannered and better-educated knights cannot. The division of God-granted and *a priori* holiness from social promotion based on an *a posteriori* education in reason is one of the enduring challenges to modern readers who may be prone ignore the central role of reason in the Elizabethan social hierarchy on account of modern aesthetic predilections set by Baumgarten, Herder, and Goethe, who fly away from limited reason on the basis of their perception that art is dedicated to the whole and that

---

3 This was a longstanding trope that extended through the Middle Ages. See the section on 'The World Upsidedown' in the larger chapter on 'Topics' in Ernst Robert Curtius, *European Literature and the Latin Middle Ages*, trans. Willard R. Trask, vol. 36, Bollingen Series (Princeton, NJ: Princeton University Press, 1953), 94-98. According to this trope, the last shall be first, not only in Heaven but on earth. Spenser uses this trope in his formation of a theory of merit-based social promotion that rewards bourgeois men who sport superior knowledge with advancement on the social ladder. Such a system of leavening the social hierarchy with the new yeast of men who rise on the basis of merit overturns a rigid hierarchy of social promotion based on birth alone. Such a system must have been required in the Elizabethan monarchical state. Spenser himself was not to the manor born. He came from a cloth-making family and was educated at the Merchant Taylors' School, rising to prominence on the basis of his own merit. The same thing was true of his poetic forbearer, Geoffrey Chaucer, as well as Spenser's contemporaries Ben Jonson and William Shakespeare.

reason fails to achieve it. In *The Faerie Queene*, social promotion at court is achieved through a constructive reason, not through a holiness that relies on socially destructive animal violence to achieve its ends.

Una's Reaction to the Captivity of Redcrosse

It is inconceivable that Spenser wants his readers to excuse, forgive, or forget Redcrosse's participation in the wanton behavior that he has so clearly been engaging in. But on account of his inferior social position, when Una's dwarf sees Redcrosse acting in such a reprehensible manner towards his mistress, he does not act to interfere with his social superior. Instead, he waits until Redcrosse's seed has been spilled on the ground and "all was past" (I.vii.19.4) before gathering up Redcrosse's

> forlorne weed,
> His mightie Armour, missing most at need;
> His siluer shield, now idle maisterlesse;
> His poynant speare, that many made to bleed.... (I.vii.19.4-7)

As we have seen, he finds her in short order, because she is not far away (I.vii.20.1).

It is significant that the dwarf tells Una the "whole discourse" (I.vii.26.1), including "The wanton loues of false Fidessa fayre" (I.vii.26.3). In speaking to Una, her dwarf is trying to reflect his realization of exactly how far Redcrosse has strayed away from his mistress' true love of him. But Spenser cleverly hides his intention from uncareful readers through a series of indirections.

The first indirection comes after she sees her dwarf appearing with the armor she had given Redcrosse. Una reacts to "the signes, that deadly tydings spake" (I.vii.20.6) by fainting dead away. In fainting, she has reacted only to outward signs, and not to the inner meaning that those signs betoken. The dwarf's state is, too, described in terms of a mock death. He "Would faine haue dyde" and his heart is described as being dead within (I.vii.21.2). But the reader must be careful to read that sign for what it actually betokens and not for what the reader wants it to hold. The fact of the matter is neither Una nor the dwarf is *actually* dead. The dwarf's *outward* appearance of death springs from his sympathy for his mistress' plight: "Yet outwardly some little comfort shewes" (I.vii.21.3).

After this mock death, the dwarf's heart is revived, and he applies himself to reviving Una, who is also not dead but only appears to be so:

                             he does begin
            To rubb her temples, and to chaufe her chin,
            And euery tender part does tosse and turne:
            So hardly he the flitted life does win,
            Vnto her natiue prison to retourne. (I.vii.21.4-8).

Only then does he "her grieued ghost...lament and mourne" (I.vii.21.9).

A Theory of Romance

This episode reflects one of the key moments in the genre of romance. Northrop Frye[4] has described the process of *scheintod* (seeming death) as being a late phenomenon of a once powerful impulse in literature to have a hero *actually* travel to the underworld and return with knowledge that is only available to heroes.[5] Frye believes that the age of heroes is past and that modern men can only look back through the folds of time for an archetypal form that makes sense of the whole of information in the fictional universe that does not make sense in the merely scientific modern world.

This impulse to test the metaphysical boundaries of the universe had, according to Frye, atrophied in romance literature, but could still be recreated by the insightful critic. But in order for Frye to be able to place works like Spenser's into his perfect system, he must translate the terms on which it was written into modern terms. Those modern terms are the archetypal patterns of literature that Frye supposes lie beneath all works of fiction: the heroic journey to the other world and the return of the hero again with new knowledge. In Frye's reading, Spenser's poem is merely a naïve example of a once powerful notion that we in the modern world can appreciate through modern techniques of reading beneath the surface that come from modern and superior insights into the true foundations of literature that previous generations of superficial scholars were ignorant of.

While I will admit that Frye has noticed the prevalence of *scheintod* in the literature of romance, I do not follow him in his belief that Spenser and other poets are working with an attenuated form of a once powerful literary

---

   4 Northrop Frye, *The Secular Scripture: A Study of the Structure of Romance*, Charles Eliot Norton Lectures 1974-1975 (Cambridge, MA: Harvard University Press, 1976), see especially the chapter on "The Bottomless Dream: Themes of Descent," 97-126 but also passim.
   5 As happens in Homer's *Odyssey* 11, a book where I have noted that Odysseus meets Agamemnon, who tells him not to tell the whole truth. The story itself appears in a series of tales told in the House of Alcinous, where telling the truth from falsehood in the language of Odysseus is so notoriously difficult that is often impossible to say with certainty whether his thought is founded in reality or in his own imagination.

motif, a motif whose power it is the office of the critic to restore to its full effect. Instead, I believe the atrophy that Frye locates in romance is a function of pagan doubts about the possibility of otherworldly journeys outside of fiction.[6] These doubts, which existed within classical philosophy, were interpreted in the excluded Christian world as the belief that pagans had no doubts about the fact that Odysseus and Virgil's Aeneas actually had traveled to the underworld.[7] In response to the overreliance on Homer to make their claim to superior metaphysical knowledge, those claims to knowledge were shown to have a false bottom by Augustine. Pagan academics did not survive the blow to their prestige despite their (perhaps justified) claims to superior metaphysical knowledge.[8] The power wielded by Augustine in the late classical world was to shift the ground altogether away from metaphysical claims to knowledge achieved by the direct application of reason to the ontological problems of nature towards an *a posteriori* reconstruction of the scientific universe in epistemology in the absence of firm *a priori* knowledge of ontological things as they are in themselves. After that shift, pagan knowledge of metaphysics was seen by Christians to be false (at best) and (at worst) a demonic detour from a truth that was unrealizable through rational means.

---

6 Ovid is the poet of doubt in the Roman world. Lucian puts Ovid's doubts into his *True History* in his *Chattering Courtesans and Other Sardonic Sketches*, trans. Keith C. Sidwell (New York: Penguin Books, 2004), 309-346. Both authors believe in pagan religious practices, but both express their doubts about the essential veracity of pagan religious practices when they are passed through a fiction. When these same works are read in a world in which Christians believed that they had found a "true" event that bridged the unbridgeable pagan gap, the Christians exchanged pagan *doubts* about the interference of fiction for a wholesale doubts about these fictional works having any relationship to fact whatsoever.

7 While this is a caricature of the truth of the matter, it is highly likely that there were pagans who believed that their knowledge of metaphysical matters was vastly superior to that of Christians, who on account of their refusal to participate in the "noble lie" of civilization were being thrown to the lions. Augustine points to the uncivilized nature of a civilization that could persecute non-believers in so callous and so politically-calculated manner in order to stabilize the right of the majority to hold power.

In the Reformation era in which Spenser was writing, the hold of Augustine's Church on the minds of men was overthrown by men like Martin Luther and John Calvin, who once again took posture of holding up truth to power. That Reformation policy was doomed to fail for the same reasons that it failed in the pagan era: there is no policy that can ever secure the truth against change in the changing world of time. Spenser knew this, which is why he exchanges a logocentric version of truth (a=a) for a less secure but more flexible a=b version of the truth.

8 In the best pagan thinkers, metaphysical knowledge was threaded through the academic skepticism of Arcesilaus and Carneades, which substituted absolute appreciation for the ends of pagan thought for one of statistical probability about the ends of thought.

Una Confronts a Paradox in Her Imagination

So yes, Spenser gives us an Una who faints three times (I.vii.24.3); but it in *this* life, not the next, that she learns, as another of Spenser's contemporaries says, that there is more in heaven and particularly on earth than she dreams of in her philosophy. It is also in this life that Redcrosse must learn to train his eyes, which he has been using in pursuit of the decadent goal of spying the nakedness of Fidessa. Northrop Frye's translation of Spenser's romance out of the scientific world and back into the metaphysical world can likewise be seen as a falsification of the truth by an eager pagan who is willing to grant to modern reason more power than Augustine or Spenser thought it merited.

Likewise, when Una sets her eyes on her dwarf, she, too, misinterprets what she sees. But, unlike the "clownishe" rube Redcrosse, she has been raised in a royal household and has been taught how to behave. She waits for "Tempestuous fortune" to spend "all her spight" (I.vii.25.1), and only then does she hear

> with patience all vnto the end,
> And stroue to maister sorrowfull assay.... (I.vii.27.1-2)

Only after she has heard the "whole discourse" does she realize that there are more possibilities than she had first imagined. This is a function of time in narrative. She tells her dwarf that

> Thy sad tongue cannot tell more heauy plight,
> Then that I feele, and harbour in mine hart. (I.vii.25.3-4)

Una's is interested in aligning her imagining mind with the scientific information that the dwarf can provide, and she declares that "Who hath endur'd the whole, can beare ech part" (I.vii.25.5). She then lays out all the possibilities she can imagine:

> If death it be, it is not the first wound,
> That launched hath my brest with bleeding smart.
> Begin, and end the bitter balefull stound;
> If lesse, then that I feare, more fauour I haue found. (I.vii.25.6-9)

If it is only his death that the dwarf is coming to report, then that is bad, for he can never be recovered in this time-bound life. But this is not the first time that Redcrosse has wounded her, and she will resign herself to his loss, which will be hard to bear at first but will dissipate over time, as emotions do when they are no longer immediately present. But if he is coming to report that Redcrosse is alive, then she fears more at the same time that she find more favor, because it leaves open the possibility that she will see him again. But this resolution leads to more questions: where is Redcrosse is in space? And why has he left her? Una's desire to get to the end of these questions appears admirable; but she is hampered by her lack of knowledge, not only of the whereabouts of Redcrosse, but also of the contents of his mind, which she simply assumes has been affected by love in the same way that hers has been.

While Una realizes somewhere in her mind that her fate is now bound with Redcrosse, she does not yet have the ability to sort out these facts on a logical level. She is merely cranking up tension in her mind, as conflicts "greater grew, the more she did contend" (I.vii.27.3) with them. The careful reader knows that the way to handle paradoxes in logic is to solve them, not to let them linger; but a still-too-passive Una is waiting for someone else to order her paradoxes that she confronts in her imagination for her. She should take a more active role in the life of her mind, but she does not. And this may be because she is right to believe that her obligation is to stand apart from the everyday give and take of events in the world and to be a beacon of good behavior for men and women in the world to follow. But she is hampered by her automatic assumption of superior position (which she nevertheless deserves), because not all paradoxes have equal outcomes in the world of time, a fact that her birth in Eden hides from her. It matters very much where Redcrosse is in space and time, whether he is living or dead, and why he left her.

All Una cares about when she confronts the paradox in her imagination is getting beyond it. Thus, she asks her dwarf to "*begin*" so that he can "*end* that bitter balefull stound."[9] This sets her question in an absolute metaphysical framework that deals only with the endpoints of experience with little care for the intermediate scientific and relative experiences that come between the beginning and the end.

As such, she is at cross-purposes with her dwarf, who answers her from the standpoint, not just of the immediate empirical experience of having been with Redcrosse and having seen his awful behavior with Fidessa, but from his experience of placing his immediate experience in an interpretive framework of rational and scientific cause. He begins to tell her "the

---

9 A stound is an archaic term for a short time.

whole discourse" (I.vii.26.1) by which he means a point-to-point analysis of events that fall *between* the beginning and the end, thus *lengthening* the "short time" between her asking and his answer, and so increasing the tension in her mind even more:

> The subtill traines of *Archimago* old;
> The wanton loues of false *Fidessa* fayre,
> Bought with the bloud of vanquisht Paynim bold:
> The wretched payre transform'd to treen mould;
> The house of *Pryde*, and perils round about;
> The combat, which he with *Sansioy* did hould;
> The lucklesse conflict with the Gyant stout,
> Wherein captiu'd, of life or death he stood in doubt. (I.vii.26.2-9)[10]

Neither position is in fact representative of the "whole discourse," as being "whole" requires both an absolute metaphysical perspective (which Una brings) *and* a relative scientific perspective (which her dwarf brings). Thus, Una does not get the final positive answer to the question of the status of Redcrosse that she was hoping for, but she is somewhat relieved of the stress that affects her when she learns that Redcrosse is not definitely dead. That is on balance a good thing in spite of the fact that the news was delivered to her in a way that thwarted her desire to close off the question in a stound, because it leaves open the possibility that she will be able to see him again, which a pronouncement of his death would have closed off forever.

Middles matter in Spenser's work. This is why it is so important that characters within the imaginative drama deploy their reason, as Una's causal dwarf does, and not to jump to amenable conclusions that ignore the intermediate steps along the way, as Una does in her quest to get to the end of the story, or as Redcrosse does when he attempts to jump to the conclusion of every battle at once.

After the dwarf ends his story, Una is not satisfied despite having learned that her beloved is not dead. Rather, she falls into a confusion brought about by her having fallen in love, and the fire of love burns her more:

> And loue fresh coles vnto her fire did lay:
> For greater loue, the greater is the losse.

---

10 The dwarf is kind enough to leave out the fact that Redcrosse had gone so far that he had his penis exposed and had spilled his seed on the open ground after his coitus with Fidessa was interrupted by arrival of Orgoglio. That does not mean that Una's dwarf did not witness it.

> Was neuer Ladie loued dearer day,
> Then she did loue the knight of the *Redcrosse*;
> For whose deare sake so many troubles her did tosse. (I.vii.27.5-9)

Love, not reason, is the *a priori* binding force of the world of time. Logic serves as an *a posteriori* binding force in the world, but by itself logic can never assuage the power of love. The purpose of logic is to give one purpose (τέλος) in a world governed by love, as the reader has seen in Una's leaving the equal fight between Satyrane and Sansloy for precedence in her heart, which is not obliged return either of their loves to them, to seek her true love. Una does not deploy her reason as she does this, and the reader can nevertheless see that she is right to do so. But the reader has the sense that she is not in control of herself in the world of time, since she does not deploy her *a posteriori* reason in it, relying instead on the kindness of strangers.

This leaves it an open question as to how much of the dwarf's version of his "whole discourse" Una, the principle of metaphysical unity in the poem, actually hears of his intermediate discourse, as Una does not react at all to the dwarf's pronouncement that her love has partaken of "The wanton loues of false *Fidessa* faire" (I.vii.26.3) or to any of the other troublesome behaviors he has related to her between the beginning and the end of his "whole discourse."

The answer to that question is not to assume that she hears everything because she comes from Eden and has a perfect intelligence. In fact, her ability as a *listener* to the echoes of her experience in the a=b world of time has been shown to be slowly developing, but it is not yet complete. As such, it would be unfair for the reader to assume that she has not heard anything. Such an answer would duplicate her error in rushing too soon toward the end of the "stound" without listening to the middle parts of the dwarf's "whole discourse." Una has learned patience enough to wait for the tempestuousness of fortune to expend all her spite before listening to the dwarf's "whole discourse." All we can be sure about is that the dwarf has spoken and that Una has listened in the public space. Spenser will give the reader a definite answer to the question of how much Una has heard in the Cave of Despair, but the reader will have to hold this question in their memories until the narrative unfolds its answer *in time*.[11]

---

[11] This deference of meaning sounds enough like Derrida's différance that I think it is important to note that there is a difference between the two.

Absolute Metaphysics and Relative Reason

Just how tricky Spenser is being with his deployment of logic can be seen in Una's declaration of love for Redcrosse in stanza 27. At first—in line 7—Spenser seems to be making of Redcrosse the subject of his declaration, as he says "Was neuer Ladie loued dearer day." But line 8 corrects the reader's impression of what is going on here. It is *Una* who is the subject of the sentence, not Redcrosse, a fact that can only come by waiting for the temporal process of reading to be completed, at which time the full meaning of the sentence is revealed. In the full sentence, Redcrosse, who has (or had) existence is treated the poet's logic as a predicate of the love of a woman who has substantial existence *only* in the poet's imagination. That bespeaks a self-referentiality on Una's part that hides the fact that the poet is referring to him, not by his individual and literal name of George, but as "the knight of the *Redcrosse*" (I.vii.27.8). It is Una's belief that she has named him legitimately in her naming of his substantial consciousness as Redcrosse. It is the poet's belief that she has named him illegitimately in a genitive construction that hangs off the name to which his literal substantial conscious is attached. If the reader is not careful to make such logical distinctions, this will cause considerable confusion of reference in their reading.

The reader, who presumably knows Augustine and who is oriented towards their own substantial consciousness in the literal world and not toward the detours of the universal, figural, but ultimately fantastic world of fiction, should know that the individual and literal George should be the subject of that sentence. Within the fiction of Faery, the normal hierarchies of the experience of knowing are reversed, as Plato has argued they could be in his *Parmenides*. But, as Augustine warned his readers in his *Confessions*, the reader should not permanently substitute a fiction for reality, but should instead substitute their own real but limited substantial consciousness for the product of a more perfect metaphysical fiction. That is the only way to truly complete oneself. Una has not yet learned that fact on account of having been engendered only in the poet's (also imperfect) imagination.

That much may be clear, but the problem for the careful reader at this point in the narrative is that Redcrosse has abandoned the pure woman Una for the corrupt woman Duessa. They will not (or at least should not) likewise abandon perfect Una for an imperfect Redcrosse simply on account of his having a substantial consciousness. But Spenser does mean to point out just how imperfect Una's *reason* is, even as he weighs in on her side over Redcrosse's. Una's reason is born in a world in which mankind no longer has access to except in fiction. The poet wishes to educate Una in the reason of the world of time in order[12] to get both she and Redcrosse away from the logic of identity that is getting them nowhere because it relies of a τέλος provided to each of them by God, not their own will. Education of the will means education in how to correctly divide good things (like Una) from bad things (like Errour, the superficial sight of Redcrosse, or his penchant for engaging in furious and socially destructive animal warfare). This is the key to reading the poet's allegory. It is in this world that the poet hopes to build a society that can stand against the forces of nature and the false pagan gods that stand as *detours* from the human community that is embodied in Gloriana's court. That way is through reason, not around it.

Another Detour to the Proem

When the reader reasserts a negotiated middle logic born of reason, they find that it is difficult to put limits on things. For instance, in the proem to Book I, Spenser asks for the help of Venus in tempering the cruelty of Cupid as the poet tells his story:

> And thou most dreaded impe of highest *Ioue*,
> Faire *Venus* sonne, that with thy cruell dart
> At that good knight so cunningly didst roue,
> That glorious fire it kindled in his hart
> Lay now thy deadly Heben bow *apart*,
> And with thy mother milde come to mine ayde. (I.proem.3.1-6)[13]

If the impishness of Cupid must be tamed, then the question for the reader is how much damage Cupid has already done here. Despite the *assumption* of modern critics that Redcrosse returns his love to her, it is at least possible that Cupid has behaved so "cunningly" that he has aroused Una's heart for Redcrosse but has aroused Redcrosse's heart for another.[14] In this case it would be for *Gloriana's heart* that Cupid's "cruell dart" had kindled

---

12 The oddity of perfect Una being lectured to by an imperfect poet is not lost on me, but this appears to be the case.

13 Italics mine in line 5 to emphasis on division in the correction of Cupid.

14 This seems to me to be an eminently possible reading. In the *Roman de la Rose*, Cupid shoots the Lover with his darts but this is not the end of the Lover's love. In order to win her, the Lover must engage in deception, not the truth of Reason, who comes down from her tower and urges him to flee his horizontal and deceptive sexual quest for the plain and straightforward vertical truths with which she is familiar. The problem with Reason's reasoning is that without the deceptive practices that lead to sex, Reason's vertically-oriented generic species cannot be continued; and thus at the end of the poem the Lover explicitly declares that he has accomplished everything without the help of Reason.

a "glorious fire" (I.proem.3.4) in Redcrosse's heart. That would mean that it was not for the *a priori* grant of Ephesian armor nor for Una herself, but for Gloriana, that he continues to proceed through his adventures. As such, Redcrosse remains true to his initial impulse "To winne him worship, and her grace to haue, / Which of all earthly thinges he most did craue" (I.i.3.4-5). By contrast, he drops Una at the first sign of difficulty with her.

Rather than dragging people through the mud of an unredeemed and unhappy love, as so often happens in Ovid's one-sided *Metamorphoses*, Spenser seems to be using the power of reason to put balance into unequal nature by focusing people's attention, not on their own selves, but on a negotiation between the external world and one's fallible self. That process is one in which all human beings have the potential to activate the seed of their humanity, but not all do. All of this takes place after one has been born into the world, and it continues until death through the process of a never-ending education.

Here, in the middle of his narrative, the poet's point is to have his reader wait until they have reached the end of the narrative, when they will have stored up all the available facts in their memories before making a firm decision on the love of one for the other. This makes one of the central questions of Book I whether Una has heard the dwarf's "whole discourse," or whether her focus on beginnings and ends of her experience obscure her perception of the way the world actually is. And at this precise moment, when such a question has been put to the reader but before they have been given enough information to come to a firm answer, Arthur, Gloriana's consort, shows up in the yawning breach between the beginning and the end.

Arthur

The Appearance of Arthur

Arthur shows up "by good hap" (I.vii.29.1), though the careful reader is no doubt supposed to believe that though he shows up by chance the poet, who is creating this fiction out of his imagination, has a deeper purpose in positioning Arthur in his fictional universe. It is the obligation of the reader to look for that purpose, and not take the poet's words at their face value.

In this case, the key to seeing deeper into the poet's reasons for having Arthur can be seen by considering the differing origin of Redcrosse's and Arthur's arms. Unlike Redcrosse's arms, which were made for the general man and later given to a specific individual, Arthur's arms were made for him specifically by another specific individual, Merlin (I.vii.36.4-6). Arthur's shield and spear are made from indivisible material, and this material is described in terms drawn from the science of alchemy, which has the power to transmute things into other things:

> Men into stones therewith he could transmew,
> And stones to dust, and dust to nought at all. (I.vii.35.6-7)

Like the philosopher's stone, Arthur's alchemical arms unite the power of the sun, which rules the day, and the moon, which rules the night (I.vii.34). The combined power of sun and moon has the power to overcome the misguided magical art of Archimago and Duessa, which can *only* bring forth false dreams from the province of Night, because Arthur's shield is built on the deeper substance which God Himself had created before names were imposed on top of them. This is important in Spenser's universe, because the diurnal progress of life in time are subject to rational and scientific inquiry. This means that the poet has found something deeper within the scientific world to hang his hat on than the science of Archimago, which divides things from one another as Tasso divided his Rinaldo from his Godfrey without the power of a purely imaginary λόγος to put them back together again. Spenser feels that by latching onto the science of alchemy that he has grasped onto the scientific principle that can be mastered by men in this life, rather hoping, as Redcrosse must, that God has his back.[1] In this case, Spenser presumably believes that He does; but that is not something that one can imitate in one's own life after the work of fiction has been put down and the reader is returned to their ontological life with nothing but their rational substantial consciousness to rely upon.

The poet likens the central stone in Arthur's arms to the evening star, Hesperus, at I.vii.30.4:

> And in the midst thereof one pretious stone
> Of wondrous worth, and eke of wondrous mights,
> Shapt like a Ladies head, exceeding shone,
> Like *Hesperus* emongst the lesser lights,
> And stroue for to amaze the weaker sights. (I.vii.30.1-5)

Readers with stout memories will remember that Redcrosse, not knowing the source of his arms' power (and not really caring), waited until Lucifer appeared in the sky before taking Una's dwarf, leaving the helpless Una

---

1 Alchemy had a long history in the literature of allegory, appearing in the *Roman de la Rose*, line 16084 as a true art (*Alkimie est art veritable*). That work makes hay of the claims of Reason's works. Spenser is trying to save from the assault launched by Jean de Meun against Reason's claims to superiority over love in that medieval classic. Jean ends his Ovidian poem only after he has reassured his readers that he has not remembered Reason at all (*de Raison ne me souvint*, 21760). This move places the flexibility of art above narrow-minded reason and was one of the reasons that the *Roman de la Rose* was the most popular secular work of fiction in the late Middle Ages.

Spenser seems disturbed by Jean's resolution to his poem in which mankind is completely separated from reason by the intrusion of sexual love in the universe. Not only Spenser, but many in the medieval and modern world, have seen Jean as justifying the rape of the Rose in an antifeminist poem by getting the object of his desire to open her bud with the aid of an Ovidian False Seeming. Spenser seems to be attempting to reintegrate reason back into the process of sexual love. He does this by accepting Jean's claims about the insufficiency of reason's direct approach to the sexual experience through identity propositions (a=a). Instead, he ascribes Jean's arguments about alchemy of an indirect form of *art* that extends outward into the world of others (a=b) as a form of *reason* that Jean's Reason knew not of.

alone with Archimago (who suffers himself from weaker sight) in canto ii. This was a disastrous course of action if the reader thinks of the primary obligation of human beings is to open themselves to others (a=b) and not to to remain closed in a posture that only reflects oneself back at oneself (a=a).

Opening Up Una's Closed Mind

The difference between Arthur and Redcrosse in the poem comes across even more fully when Arthur speaks to Una. She has been lamenting her fate and cannot see any comfort in expressing herself to another:

> What worlds delight, or ioy of liuing speach
> Can hart, so plungd in sea of sorrowes deepe,
> And heaped with so huge misfortunes, reach?
> The carefull cold beginneth for to creepe,
> And in my heart his yron arrow steepe,
> Soone as I thinke vpon my bitter bale:
> Such helplesse harmes yts better hidden keepe,
> Then rip vp griefe, where it may not auaile,
> My last left comfort is, my woes to weepe and waile. (I.vii.39)

In other words, Una insists on seeing the whole; but though Una persists in arguing that "great griefe will not be tould, /And can more easily be thought, then said" (I.vii.41.1-2), she is expressing the difference between thought and speech. In her division, she sides with silence.

Arthur disagrees, telling her that "Mishaps are maistred by aduice discrete" (I.vii.40.7). The key is to examine (make "triall" of) all the parts that make up the whole and not to simply rely our assumption that they are what we thought they were when in our own wholly unified minds. This turns over Stoic assumptions about what the world is telling us when it tells us to forgo our limited but ontologically real individual substantial consciousness for a more stable place in a *fictional* λόγος. But Arthur's resolution leaves the problem with Stoic social justice in doubt. This is one of reasons that the Romans embraced such Stoic principles in the first place. Ricardo Salles writes of the Stoic journey of the soul out of itself to a more stable λογός in the following passage:

> Appropriation or familiarization (οἰκείωσις), understood in its 'social' dimension—i.e. the appropriation or familiarization which in the first stage of life is concerned with the 'egoist' interests of the living being with himself, but later can be developed towards the familiarization with the other members of the species in a sort of 'altruistic move'—is a proper picture of how god or the universal reason expects us to love

our fellow human beings.[2]

From the pagan point of view, Augustine's flipping of the quest for the ends of experience (which he defines out of the realm of philosophy altogether to an inaccessible God) for available middles threatens the notion of cooperation between individuals for the collective good if we believe, as the Romans surely did, that the λόγος is required for cooperative social action. The problem was that the embrace of Christianity did not completely solve the pagan resolution of the problem. In Rome, the embrace of allegory had meant that the emperors needed to maintain the fiction that they should be worshipped as gods and not, as at least one emperor suspected himself to be, as men.[3] In the Roman world, the attachment to the doctrine of λόγος was the motivation for suppressing Christians, who would not accede to the worship of gods they knew to be false.

Out of this rupture came the Christian impetus to reconfigure the social world on premises that did not require the interference of fiction to support a superstructure of belief in a personal and perfect God that operated on the limited being and mind of his creatures. The role of reason is not to be pushed aside in Augustine, as Herder and Goethe had attempted to do in the rational age of Descartes. Instead, reason was placed in the position of being a necessary part of the recreation of God's prior ontology in the imperfect mind of the substantial individual. The Christian effort requires that one bind oneself to others (a=b), because the limited reason of human beings could not identify with any certainty the thing as it was in itself (a=a). If anyone (such as Redcrosse or Una) were to do so, they would be falling into error even though they are the constructions of Spenser's deconstructable fiction. An a=a construction will fail when the reader puts down Spenser's work of Faery; but a=b constructions will survive the deconstruction of Spenser's Faery, as least in the mind of the careful reader.

This is why Arthur advises Una to express herself instead of keeping things to herself in the mistaken belief that "Such helplesse harmes yts better hidden keepe." There is no access to things as they are in (a=a) the world of time *or* in the socially-constructed world that Arthur occupies.[4]

---

2 Ricardo Salles, *God and Cosmos in Stoicism* (New York: Oxford University Press, 2009), 198.

3 I take this to be the motive behind the emperor Vespasian's ironic declaration on his deathbed "I suppose I'm becoming a god now" quoted in Cochrane, *Christianity and Classical Culture*, 142.

4 That is not to say that Una does not have access to such thing, as she is the product of a Spenserian fiction; but it is to say that Arthur cannot help her if she does not speak. In the

He makes his case in a neatly compact argument in stanza 41:

> Right so; (quoth he) but he, that neuer would,
> Could neuer: will to might giues greatest aid. (I.vii.41.3-4)

In this sentence, Arthur says she is right, but he adds that people who just think without acting on their thought suffer from a weakness. By not acting on their inner thought in the world of time, they have made the choice to give their "will" over to others who are not so reticent. These are the mighty in the world of politics or deceitful creatures like Archimago and Duessa. Arthur is advising Una to express her "will to might," because this gives "greatest aid," even to her who has no desire to master others.

Arthur's problem is that Una is not necessarily looking to express her might herself. That is why she left Eden and came to Gloriana's court seeking a champion to fight for her. But Arthur's point is a larger one. Redcrosse has abandoned her because she did not express her love for him, not through her body, as Fidessa did, but at all. Had she expressed her love to him, Redcrosse might never have left her. Arthur might also have pointed to expression as a way of his gaining control over Una's heart, but he does not, because he is not interested in control over others in that way.

On account of her blindness to her own weaknesses within the world of time, as well as Arthur's appeal to a might that she is uninterested in obtaining, Una answers him:

> But griefe (quoth she) does greater grow displaid,
> If then it find not helpe, and breeds despaire. (I.vii.41.5-6)

But Arthur has an answer for her: "Despaire breedes not (quoth he) where faith is staid" (I.vii.41.7).[5] Una answers him that no faith is "so fast" that

---

world of time into which she has traveled and in which she has been linked to another (a=b), her anxiety will only increase without end until she speaks. This would not be the case if she were a completely autonomous existential individual. This is a reflection of the Christian doctrine of confession, after which Augustine named his autobiography.

5 This is an interesting moment. Arthur seems to rule out the question of Una's despairing on account of his (correct) assessment that her faith is "staid," but Spenser explicitly says she has been "diuorced from her knight in despayre" (I.iii.2.8). If Una despairs, someone must be mistaken, and my bet is on Arthur. In spite of his misappraisal of the motives of Una, Arthur manages to turn her away from silence towards expression through his argument. We notice this when Redcrosse, immediately upon being rescued by Arthur, flies to the Cave of Despair and succumbs to his arguments in a way that Una does not. Spenser's point is that words are not always taken as they are meant, but that fact in itself does not absolutely stop them from being effective. We shall see that people will continue to talk at

human frailty, brought about by mankind's inhabitation in "flesh," can resist falling into sin (I.vii.41.8). Arthur, who has agreed to all her other demands, may agree to this, as well; but he adds "Flesh may empaire (quoth he) but reason can repaire" (I.vii.41.9). And *that* is the point of using reason, not animal violence or holy silence, in the postlapsarian world of time.[6]

Only now does her education progress to level of rational discourse, as she listens to "His goodly reason, and well guided speech" (I.vii.42.1) that

> So deepe did settle in her gratious thought,
> That her perswaded to disclose the breach,
> Which loue and fortune in her heart had wrought.... (I.vii.42.2-4)

The Princess of Eden, keeper of unified thought in a world of change, changes her mind after hearing what he has to say and hopes that Arthur's greater "wisedome will direct [her] thought" (I.vii.42.7).

The power of reason over Una is unexpected to those who believe she is a model of behavior to be followed by others on account of her possession of heavenly wisdom. In the traditional view of the poem, Una's unified and heavenly thought should triumph over Arthur's worldly thought, derived from Aristotle's definition of man as the rational animal, but it does not. Instead, Una submits to him, not just because she is a weak woman submitting to a man (although this does not appear to be out of the question as *part* of Spenser's argument), but because Arthur possesses a better argument for navigating the world of time than Una possesses. Arthur's argument requires that men and women divide their experience into parts and weigh each part on its own to judge its moral weight in the radically unequal moral universe of nature.

After disclosing the breach in her heart, Una then tells Arthur her story: how she found an unproved knight whose hands had never been touched by guilty blood, but whose "auenging blade" (I.vii.47.9) she has since seen dismay the "groning ghosts of many" (I.vii.47.8). Along the way, Una continues to speak in terms of the "faire beginnings" (I.vii.49.1) with which she started her journey with Redcrosse. Even after he has disappointed her, she continues to hope that Redcrosse will be able her "captiue languor [to] redeeme" (I.vii.49.2).

---

cross-purposes as long as Arthur is present in this book. That is simply yet another argument for making "triall" of others' words and not taking them for granted.

[6] Although just how much Una, who is not a creature of "flesh," believes that this applies to her I leave as an open question.

But, like Una's dwarf before him, Arthur is more focused on the passage of time *between* the fair beginning in which Una believed that Redcrosse could "well could rule" (I.vii.48.5) and the present moment in which Redcrosse has "left you heare" (I.vii.48.5) as one of the "forlorne reliques of his powre" (I.vii.48.1). He concludes the stanza by asking "Where haue yee left your Lord, that could so well you tosse?" (I.vii.48.9).

This echoes the previously cited line at stanza 27, in which she hears the sorrowful tale told by her dwarf and has her heart nearly torn in two:

> Then she did loue the knight of the *Redcrosse*;
> For whose deare sake so many troubles her did tosse. (I.vii.27.8-9)

In that stanza, Redcrosse seemed to have been the focus of Una's complete attention, but with the appearance of Arthur, the focus changes. In the stream of time, Redcrosse has made some mistakes. He has been deceived by the master of artifice; he has left Una, who loves him; he has fallen in love with another woman; he has dragged Una across the wasteland into this desolate place; and Arthur asks the reasonable question of why he has tossed her away. He asks, however, in a manner that suggests that he thinks she is complicit in having driven him away, a thing that never occurs to her lowly dwarf to suggest.

The Rescue of Redcrosse

Canto viii opens with these lines:

> Ay me, how many perils doe enfold
> The righteous man, to make him daily fall?
> Were not, that heauenly grace doth him vphold,
> And stedfast truth acquite him out of all:
> Her loue is firme, her care continuall,
> So oft as he through his owne foolish pride,
> Or weaknesse is to sinfull bands made thrall:
> Else should this *Redcrosse* knight in bands haue dyde,
> For whose deliuerance she this Prince doth thither guide. (I.viii.1)

It is not Una's love but "heauenly grace," whose love is firm and continual, that upholds her hero, even as *Una* wavers.

The first step on the way to the rescue of Redcrose is for Arthur's squire to blow his magical horn, of which we are told

> No false enchauntment, nor deceiptfull traine

> Might once abide the terror of that blast,
> But presently was void and wholly vaine:
> No gate so strong, no locke so firme and fast,
> But with that percing noise flew open quite, or brast. (I.viii.4.5-9)

Arthur's magic is deeper than the giant's, who was created by Redcrosse's own pride and so is "void and wholly vaine." When approached from the proper perspective of the deeper power derived from the worldly science of alchemy, the doors of Redcrosse's self-made prison fly open.

Deconstructionists often assume that this is enough to dissipate the power of error that comes from false artistic constructions raised up illegitimately over nature by showing that they lack ontology. This act of destruction of artifice suffices to restore balance to the natural universe, but it does not get rid of the division of art from nature, which persist through the destructive act.[7] That is not sufficient in an Augustinian universe, where the negative action of destruction is not enough to eliminate the artistic act, because the human mind has no access to God's created ontology. Acts of destruction merely suppress artistic ideas by purging them from one's limited mind; but, as Derrida notes, elimination of an object from one's own view is not the same as eliminating it entirely.

Destruction of bad artistic ideas in the Augustinian universe requires a positive action after the negative destructive act. Otherwise, those artistic ideas, which the ontologically-oriented critic has eliminated from *their* view, will travel to the margins, where they will launch an equally terrible assault from without. For this reason, *after* Arthur's squire blows his deconstructing horn, Orgoglio uses his remaining power—which the negative act of destruction has not robbed him of—to race forth to meet his foe "as one astownd" (I.viii.5.7). He has been thrown back on his heels by something he cannot understand with his wholly void and wind-filled mind, but he still appears.

Redcrosse has been seen to be eager for battle, sometimes too eager. This indiscriminate readiness for battle has gotten him into trouble more than once, as he will not withdraw his forward foot. This is why Redcrosse

---

[7] This division appears to be undeconstructable, but why that should be remains a mystery unless deconstructionists believe that they have access to nature without an intermediary act of imagination. If this is the case, I would ask them to show me how this is possible (a thing I don't believe they can do without acknowledging their acceptance of Descartes' Enlightenment premises in which ontology meets epistemology in the human mind). Failing that, I would request that they deconstruct the remaining non-yet-deconstructed superstructures on which their beliefs rest.

is God's choice to fight the Dragon: he is unbelievably brave. Arthur, on the other hand, has no problem avoiding danger:

> But wise and wary was that noble Pere,
> And lightly leaping from so monstrous maine,
> Did fayre auoide the violence him nere;
> It booted nought, to thinke, such thunderbolts to beare.
> (I.viii.7.6-9)

Nor is Arthur ashamed of his behavior: "Ne shame he thought to shonne so hideous might" (I.viii.8.1). He realizes, as Redcrosse never does, that's the giant's "furious" (I.viii.8.2) blow is an "ydle stroke" (I.viii.8.2) that needs not be encountered any more than the blows of Errour needed to be encountered by a too-eager Redcrosse. But once engaged in battle, Orgoglio's blows have the power to do real harm to Arthur in spite of their not being built on the principle reason. This is why Arthur dodges Orgoglio's blow, which misses "the marke of his misaymed sight" (I.viii.8.3). Had Redcrosse not been so intent on proving himself, he could have avoided the blows of negatively defined Errour and Orgoglio, as well.

Arthur defeats Orgoglio and Duessa, not by using his sword, but because the cover falls off his magical shield purely by chance, therby allowing the light of heaven to shine through it:

> And in his fall his shield, that couered was,
> Did loose his vele by chaunce, and open flew:
> The light whereof, that heauens light did pas,
> Such blazing brightnesse through the ayer threw,
> That eye mote not the same endure to vew. (I.viii.19.1-5)

In the fight that follows, Arthur lands a blow that levels him, and Duessa cries out, "O helpe Orgoglio, helpe, or else we perish all" (I.viii.20.9). Orgoglio is "much amoou'd" (I.viii.21.1) by her "so pitteous cry" (I.viii.21.1) and thinks to get up and fight again "to ayde his frend" (I.viii.21.2); but any effort he makes is now "all in vaine" (I.viii.21.4),

> for he has read his end
> In that bright shield, and all their forces spend
> Themselues in vaine: for since that glauncing sight,
> He hath no powre to hurt, nor to defend. (I.viii.21.4-7)

The poet ascribes this to the power of "th'Almighties lightning brond" (I.viii.21.8), which dims the eyes and daunt the senses (I.viii.21.9) of vain, void, external creatures like Orgolgio.[8]

The poet indicates that the monster's body must be *physically* destroyed after it has been *intellectually* destroyed, and he gives us a picture of Arthur's brutally hacking off one of Orgoglio's legs (I.viii.22.4). He then gives us two epic similes to spread his poetic vision out from an individual example of defeat in battle to make of the Orgoglio's defeat a general example for all mankind. The first is of an ancient tree that being hacked at falls from its high and ancient perch "on the top of rocky clift" (I.viii.22.6) to its final resting place on the ground.

The second epic simile is of a castle

> reared high and round,
> By subtile engins and malitious slight
> Is vndermined from the lowest ground
> And her foundation forst, and feebled quight,
> At last downe falles, and with her heaped hight
> Her hastie ruine does more heauie make,
> And yields it selfe vnto the victours might. (I.viii.23.1-7)

It is only *after* the giant has been laid flat that Arthur "him smot againe" (I.viii.24.2), striking off the giant's head (I.viii.24.3) and thereby killing the *body* of the monster that otherwise might have revived again:

> That huge great body, which the Gyaunt bore,
> Was vanisht quite, and of that monstrous mas
> Was nothing left, but like an emptie bladder was. (I.viii.24.7-9)

It is interesting that Duessa, who had just told Orgoglio that *she* would perish if he does not get up and fight for her (I.viii.20.9), survives Orgoglio's destruction. The reader is in a position once again to realize that either she was lying or that she cannot predict her fate on the basis of her limited knowledge of her own construction in Spenser's larger fiction. But whatever the cause, she drops her golden cup (I.viii.25.2) and attempts to fly away (I.viii.25.6). But she is stopped by Arthur's "light-foot Squire," who

> her quickly turnd around,
> And by hard meanes enforcing her to stay,
> So brought vnto his Lord, as his deserued pray. (I.viii.25.7-9)[9]

---

[8] Of course, Redcrosse also has eyes dim enough not to have seen his own role in creating the monster who has imprisoned him.

[9] This is so much like the behavior of Redcrosse with fleeing Errour that the similarities

Una's Expression of Gratitude

Una, who stands afar looking on the action of Arthur (I.viii.26.1), expresses her gratitude for Arthur's victory in the following speech:

> But sith the heauens, and your faire handeling
> Haue made you maister of the field this day,
> Your fortune maister eke with gouerning,
> And well begun end all so well, I pray,
> Ne let that wicked woman scape away;
> For she it is, that did my Lord bethrall,
> My dearest Lord, and deepe in dongeon lay,
> Where he his better dayes hath wasted all.
> O heare, how piteous he to you for ayd does call. (I.viii.28)

This is an interesting moment, because Una ascribes Redcrosse's captivity *only* to Duessa's interference and not to anything that Redcrosse has done in *constructing* his fate. At the same that she ignores the role of Redcrosse in constructing his fate, she ascribes Arthur's victory not only to "the heauens," but also his "faire handeling" of his situation. She recognizes that he has mastered his fortune through the process of "gouerning" his behavoir, a process that is within the control of human reason.

The contrast with Redcrosse should be now obvious to the careful reader. Redcrosse does not govern himself well, and as a result does not master his own fortune, being led into danger by his willed manly force, and being led out of his dilemmas by another who has mastered his individual mind through an education that turns him away from his individual mind (a=a) *towards* society and God (a=b) to make up for his lack of "wholeness" within his individually-created body or mind.[10]

Ignaro

After Arthur has defeated Orgoglio, the poet introduces his readers to the character of Ignaro who still stands in the way of Redcrosse's release. He

---

deserve note. It seems to me that the pun on pray/prey indicates Spenser's awareness of the difference between Lord Arthur and the Lord God.

10 This is different from the modern existential construction of the universe, which involves turning away from nature, society, and God towards the self-created individual on the basis of Sartre's contention that existence precedes essence. Spenser also believes that individual existence precedes formal essence in the mind of God but does not believe, as the moderns do, that the created individual can be substituted for the God that made him, as literal existence is not whole. This is the mistake of Redcrosse, who relies on his own animal being and thus engages in the sin of pride, from which the educated Arthur rescues him.

appears to be a wise old man, just like Corceca was a wise old woman; but he faces in two directions:

> For as he forward mooud his footing old,
> So backward still was turnd his wrincled face,
> Vnlike to men, who euer as they trace,
> Both feet and face one way are wont to lead. (I.viii.31.3-6)[11]

This should lead the careful reader to question the difference between Arthur, who has armor that collapses day and night into one pretextual but still scientific unity, and Ignaro, who also appears to be able to face both ways in the universe without making a decision on which way will lead him forward.

The difference becomes even clearer when the poet begins punning on Ignaro's "nature." On the one hand, "His name *Ignaro* did his nature right aread" (I.viii.31.9), but it soon becomes apparent that, though his outward appearance has been formed "with natures pen" (I.viii.33.8), beneath nature's appearance Ignaro is not wise at all. When it falls to Arthur to ask him to tell him where bodies are hidden, he can only answer "He could not tell" (I.viii.31.5). This negative definition undermines his claim to knowledge in the same way that Socrates undermines his claim to knowledge by positing only negative knowledge to himself. Augustine objected to Socrates' attribution of his wisdom *only* to negative knowledge, because it ultimately led to the denial of the real substantial consciousness of the ontologically existing individual and the substitution of a potentially fictional λόγος in its place. This in turn led to the skepticism that closed the philosopher off from the existence of a larger prior world that Augustine was attempting to reconnect the limited human mind to in his own philosophical work.

---

11 The notion of trace is found in Derrida as one of the keys to reading what has been suppressed by acts of power. In Spenser's work, the raising of one dimensional direction perspective over two directional meaning means the reduction of aesthetic knowledge (read metaphysical) to mere scientific knowledge, a debasement of aesthetics itself. The availability of two dimensional knowledge to elite thinkers becomes the keystone to "true" thought that is simply unavailable to one dimensional bourgeois thinkers in Herbert Marcuse's *One-Dimensional Man: Studies in the Ideology of Advanced Industrial Society* (Boston: Beacon Press, 1991). As such, the notion of two dimensional thought becomes an undeconstructable avenue to the only thought that matters to elite members of industrial society, who nevertheless stand outside and above the necessity of direction in human action in the industrial world, as Ignaro and Redcrosse do in Reformation culture. While the attainment of two-dimensional thought is enough to escape deconstruction in Marcuse's modern world, it does not appear to be sufficient in Spenser's Reformation universe.

The positive nature of Arthur's mind gives him positive powers that Redcrosse does not possess. As a result, when Arthur looks at Ignaro's face, he is able to guess the content of his "nature" in a way that Redcrosse, faced with a choice between Una's true beauty and Fidessa's false beauty, never can:

> When as the noble Prince had marked well,
> He ghest his nature by his countenance,
> And calmd his wrath with goodly temperance. (I.viii.34.3-5)

This calming of his mind by temperance is exactly what Redcrosse fails to do every time he gets in trouble.[12]

This new temperance causes Arthur to change his behavior based on changing circumstances:

> Then to him stepping, from his arme did reach
> Those keyes, and made himselfe free enterance.
> Each dore he opened without any breach;
> There was no barre to stop, nor foe him to empeach (I.viii.34.6-9)

After metaphysics is closed off as an avenue of approach to God's created ontology by Augustine's intrusion into classical philosophy, all that is left is the scientific extension of one's arm to take the keys from others who have no idea which way to go. This is why the rational temperance of the individual, not the inaccessible metaphysical wholeness of the pagan gods, is the key to exercising one's free will and to healing the breaches left in the limited individual as well as the social order in Spenser's Christian universe.

The Enlargement of Una

Rather than having Arthur go around looking for people to "free," he knows that all men have the potential within them to be free. So Arthur searches the dungeons for those "whom he *enlargen* might" (I.viii.37.9 italics mine). His amplification of people stems from his Aristotelian definition of man as the rational animal. As a rational man, Arthur extends men outward from the initial premise of their being by activating what is only in each of us in potential through the process of education.

Redcrosse welcomes the bringer of "happy choyce"—something that for all his negatively-defined power he conspicuously lacks—but at the same time Redcrosse is still wishing in his new choice for death:

---

12 This is why the Book of Temperance comes after the Book of Holinesse.

> O who is that, which brings me happy choyce
> Of death, that here lye dying euery stound,
> Yet liue perforce in balefull darkenesse bound? (I.viii.38.3-5)

Una races towards her beloved knight and rebukes him for his wishing to exercise his free will in this manner. Of course, she absolves him of blame as she does so:

> Ah dearest Lord, what euill starre
> On you hath frownd, and pourd his influence bad,
> That of your selfe ye thus berobbed arre,
> And this misseeming hew your manly looks doth marre?
> (I.viii.42.6-9)

By thinking that Redcrosse has fallen under an evil star which has robbed him "of your selfe," she has completely missed the point. As Shakespeare had more famously said, the fault is not in our stars, but in ourselves. Redcrosse's victories may come from Heaven alone, but he lacks inner fortitude to wield his strength properly within the scientific world, where he must be stopped from committing sin by Archimago, Duessa, and Lucifera.

Inarticulate Redcrosse is no match for such philosophical argument, so it is up to the better educated Arthur to correct her:

> Faire Lady, then said that victorious knight,
> The things, that grieuous were to do, or beare,
> Them to renew, I wote, breeds no delight;
> Best musicke breeds delight in loathing eare. (I.viii.44.1-4)

Arthur seems to be saying that Redcrosse should turn away from his past sins, as they are past and will not help him move forward. His past behavior of looking only to himself ($a=a$) got him into the dungeon in the first place. Instead, Arthur believes that Redcrosse should turn himself outwards towards the wider (decentered, in the postmodern vocabulary) music that comes from listening to others ($a=b$).

Arthur seems to accept that a young knight will make such mistakes. The cure is to learn from one's mistakes and not to make them twice:

> But th'onely good, that growes of passed feare,
> Is to be wise, and ware of like agein. (I.viii.44.5-6)

His use of a metaphor of growth adds to the reader's sense that Arthur believes in the process of experiencing things; making the occasional mistake; correcting his mistakes by remembering them, holding on to what works and discarding that which does not; and resolving never to make the same mistakes again. This is the process by which a man amplifies himself in the scientific world of time.

This is a lesson that Arthur follows, as he writes the day's example onto his heart with an iron pen:

> This daies ensample hath this lesson deare
> Deepe written in my heart with yron pen,
> That blisse may not abide in state of mortall men. (I.viii.44.7-9)

Unfortunately, Arthur's resolution can be read in more than one way, as all rational language can be. Not being one to think much about philosophical arguments with any subtlety, Redcrosse is content to hear wise Arthur place blame out of his hands, thus relieving his own conscience; and he thinks no more about it. This is the essence of a=a behavior, and it shows the limitations of Arthur as a rational man without a God to guide the human response of those to which the rational man is speaking.[13]

The Golden Chain

Canto ix begins with a stanza which has as its predecessor one of the chief passages in all of literary criticism, the theme of the golden chain derived from Homer and passed to the reader through Plato's *Ion*:

> O Goodly golden chaine, wherewith yfere
> The vertues linked are in louely wize:
> And noble minds of yore allyed were,
> In braue poursuit of cheualrous emprize,
> That none did others safety despize,
> Nor aid enuy to him, in need that stands,
> But friendly each did others prayse deuize
> How to aduaunce with fauourable hands,
> As this good Prince redeemd the *Redcrosse* knight from bands.
> (I.ix.1)

The discerning reader will immediately recognize that this is not the golden

---

[13] Redcrosse will learn to orient himself towards God only after he has passed through the House of Holinesse in canto x. As a result, Redcrosse learns nothing in this canto, whose purpose is to get Una to subordinate herself to the arguments of rational Arthur. Unfortunately, she still needs Redcrosse to act on her behalf, so the victory, though impressive, is Pyrrhic.

chain of Homer to which Socrates alludes in discussion with Ion. Socrates uses reason to reflect the heavens in a way that Ion could not through a perfect "poetic metaphor" drawn from Homer. This gives Socrates a control that Ion lacks. Aristotle's criticism of Plato's Theory of Forms caused Plato himself to change his theory to one in which the Forms only existed in the mind of wise men like Socrates. This eventually led to a situation in which the best educated in society believed that social coherence depended on *others* believing in things that the *educated* knew to be false.[14] According to Augustine, the resulting academic system was inherently unstable and was held in place, not by any contact with the truth of the matter, but by a veil that was drawn between ordinary common men and the academic elites that kept the rabble in line.

Augustine switched things around by ridding the golden chain of its classical vertical orientation in which its truth is tied to the seat of a potentially fictional other, putting in its place a more appropriate horizontal orientation that links larger groups of existing-but-limited minds together, while leaving God in his place as the creator of the Λόγος.[15] The goal of Augustine's system was not to make claims that would supplant God, as had been Socrates' goal in his philosophy.[16] The human mind could never approach the Λόγος as it was created, but it it could use its own version of λόγος, the image of God in man, to recreate the moral work of God in their own imperfect imagination.

This switch does not rid the notion of the golden chain of its meta-

---

[14] Socrates himself is quite careful to say that he does not know that his beliefs in the otherworld reflect the truth of whether they are fictions or not. Like Pascal much later, he is willing to wager that they are in order to preserve the institutions that make *this* life worthy of living.

[15] I have divided God's perfect, created, *a priori* (capital letter) Λόγος from the (small captial) λόγος of the human mind's reconstruction of creation in their imperfect *a posteriori* minds.

[16] For a picture of the failings of Greek religion to which philosophers like Socrates came to the rescue, see section VII, "Philosophical Religion" in Walter Burkert, *Greek Religion* (Cambridge, MA: Harvard University Press, 1985), 305ff. According to Burkert the success of philosophers over time was the result of the fact that philosophers were marketing themselves, telling anyone who could pay how to divide good arguments from bad in the public domain. This was very different from Greek religion, which remained wedded to rituals of believing in a closed circle from which most were excluded and whose secrets were closely guarded in silence.

Public philosophy survived this encounter with private religion. By Augustine's day, when Homer's mythology had become a religion itself, Augustine used the publication of the private foibles of believers in the Homeric worldview to build his own public religion that appealed to all the people, not just a select few.

phorical characteristics (all human language is metaphorical in any language system, whether pagan or Christian). The mind's role in Augustine's system was always to adhere as closely as possible to God's prior truth, while recognizing the possibility that not only the external world but we ourselves could be false. The demotion of reason from a metaphysical to a scientific process took a lot of the previous certainty away from philosophers who had attained their status as knowers of "the truth" in a sea of seekers, just as the public display of learning had taken a lot of the fire out of private classical mystery religion when it was first proposed. But in exchange for a now lost certainty, it placed control of the unknowable "truth" of metaphor in the hands of educated men like Socrates and Arthur, taking it out of the control of Ion and Redcrosse, who suffer from an inflated sin of pride *and* a corresponding lack of education.

The Tale of Arthur and Gloriana

Arthur stays with Una and the now-freed Redcrosse until "that weake captiue wight now wexed strong" (I.ix.2.3), and they are able once again to "forward fare, as their aduentures fell" (I.ix.2.6). Una asks

> That straunger knight his name and nation tell;
> Least so great good, as he for her had wrought,
> Should die vnknown, & buried be in thankles thought. (I.ix.2.7-9)

In contrasting "thankles thought" to her new power of speech, she seems to be following the horizontal golden chain by linking herself to Arthur in friendship (a=b) through the positive power of limited words rather than remaining in metaphysical silence. Once again, this is something she has only recently learned from the rational man Arthur.

At this point, Arthur takes off his helmet and begins to speak as a man who has a duty to Redcrosse. But he speaks to Una, urging her to "Ensample make of him your haplesse ioy" (I.ix.12.1), and he turns to his own experience of love to make an example for her. He had once been a "proud auenging boy" (I.viii.12.3) whose "prouder vaunt" was "soone pluck[ed] downe, and curbd my libertie" (I.ix.12.3-4).

> For on a day prickt forth with iollitie
> Of looser life, and heat of hardiment,
> Raunging the forest wide on courser free,
> The fields, the floods, the heauens with one consent
> Did seeme to laugh on me, and fauour mine intent. (I.ix.12.5-9)

Each of the phrases that Arthur applies to himself the reader could and should apply to their experience with Redcrosse.

Arthur relates his tale of how he fell in love:

> For-wearied with my sportes, I did alight
> From loftie steed, and downe to sleepe me layd;
> The verdant gras my couch did goodly dight,
> And pillow was my helmet faire displayd:
> Whiles euery sence the humour sweet embayd,
> And slombring soft my hart did steale away,
> Me seemed, by my side a royall Mayd
> Her daintie limbes full softly down did lay:
> So faire a creature yet saw neuer sunny day. (I.ix.13)

He means to recall Redcrosse to his true love, Una, but there are two problems with this strategy. The first is that Arthur had laid down and found Gloriana in a dream, whose figure he then attempted to find in an ontological form. In that process, he never loses the sense that he must make "triall" of his experiences. As such, Arthur had not given himself over to the love of a malicious woman, as the clownish Redcrosse has. Redcrosse, on the other hand, had laid down with the ontologically existing Fidessa who was not telling the truth about herself but who was using the power of words to mask the truth from him. He, being a "clownishe younge man," had accepted her as she presented herself to him.

The second problem proceeds from the fact that Redcrosse has never given any positive indication that he loves Una. At the beginning of the book, he tells her only that he holds himself *bound* to her at I.i.54.2-3 before running away from her entirely. On the other hand, when he meets Fidessa, he takes up with her on account of her showing him a bit of skin and goes so far as to bare parts of his own body that should remain hidden. He is fully prepared to engage in coitus with his *chosen* love. His intention is only interrupted by the appearance of Orgoglio with his giant body and wind-blown mind.

Redcrosse listens intently as Arthur relates his meeting of the Faerie Queene in his dreams. From that day forth Arthur resolves to find her in body. Una agrees that this is a noble story, but she notes a catch:

> O happy Queene of Faeries, that hast fownd
> Mongst many, one that with his prowesse may
> Defend thine honour, and thy foes confound:
> True Loues are often sown, but seldom grow on grownd. (I.ix.16.6-

9)

Once again, Una, who has just reconnected with her (in so many ways) errant beloved, feels that dreams are worth pursuing, but that having a dream is not having it realized. It is not only a question of the Queene of Faery having found one knight among many but also having of having him sticking around long enough to defend her honor. Una has had the experience of having found a love and having him disappoint her. This is perhaps why she qualifies her expression with her noting that true loves "seldom grow on grownd." But it could be that her own raising up of George to the status of Redcrosse hides her part in the cause of her distress in a world in which the same words can have different meanings to different people.

Before Arthur can respond to Una with congratulations or condolences by which we can measure his response to what the ambiguous words she has just spoken, Redcrosse interrupts the flow of dialog, addressing only Arthur:

> Thine, O then, said the gentle *Redcrosse* knight,
> Next to that Ladies loue, shalbe the place, (I.ix.17.1-2)

There is ambiguity in response here, and ambiguity is an invitation by the poet and his readers to explore (make "triall" of) the minds of the participants in the conversation more deeply. In his footnote to this passage, Hamilton notes that

> Ambiguity of precedence is required by the allegory, as Upton 1758 suggests: the knight declares he will place his love for Una before—or more likely—next after his love for the Faerie Queene. Levin 1991:16 infers that he declares 'that his love for Una shall henceforth match Arthur's love for the Faerie Queene.' [17]

Hamilton's inability to set precedence in this passage is testament to the difficulty of using modern techniques without recourse to Spenser's vision of the universe in which God exists as the ground on which we can resolve our questions about which way we should turn in times of doubt. Hamilton himself turns to his modern aesthetic. But in fact, it is equally likely (and perhaps more so) that Redcrosse does not love Una at all; or if he does so, that he loves her lightly. If this is the case, then the one position of three—

---

[17] Spenser, *Faerie Queene (2001)*, p. 116. The internal reference is, of course, to Levin's previously mentioned "The Legende of the Redcrosse Night."

before, equal to, or behind—that Hamilton (despite his declaration in his 2001 edition that he wishes to allow for all sorts of readings) leaves out is the position that the poet intends. It is in the as-yet-unexperienced *future* that Redcrosse will learn to love Una.

The poet continues:

> O fairest virgin, full of heauenly light,
> Whose wondrous faith, exceeding earthly race,
> Was firmest fixt in mine extremest case, (I.ix.17.3-5)

Hamilton feels that Arthur has turned Redcrosse's attention to his own love, Una, at this point. In his reading, it is only after praising his own love, Una, who exists outside the bounds of humanity at the extreme of Heaven, that Redcrosse turns back to Arthur's pursuit of his love:

> And you, my Lord, the Patrone of my life,
> Of that great Queene may well gaine worthy grace:
> For onely worthy you through prowes priefe
> Yf liuing man mote worthy be, to be her liefe. (I.ix.17.6-9)

But there is another way of reading the stanza, and this does not involve Redcrosse changing the subject of his attention from Gloriana to Una and then back again. When Redcrosse talks about Arthur having his place next to "that Ladies loue," he may still be talking about Gloriana. *Gloriana* is the fairest virgin queen. *She* is filled with heavenly light whose wondrous faith exceeds the earthly race (to which Redcrosse does not yet know he belongs), and it is *she* who represents the "fixt" point in Redcrosse's otherwise endless wandering. Gloriana is the creature who can guarantee the only thing Redcrosse has ever sought: his integration into the court through his prowess as a knight.

These things are not the products of Una's granting him an *a priori* armor that guarantees success in every battle he will ever engage in. However helpful such armor may be in achieving victory, it does nothing to contribute to his integration into the world of court, which governs a society built *against* nature, on Aristotelian social principles of *a posteriori* reason, and *against* the immediate animal nature sported by Redcrosse. Una, who wanders like Redcrosse at random in search of her beloved after he abandons her, is not a good candidate for such fixity as Gloriana provides.

These factors make it possible that both men are discussing the *same woman*, and that in this passage Redcrosse is yielding precedence to the

Faerie Queene, the woman who had captured his own imagination, to Arthur, "Lord, the Patrone of my life," on account of his greater "prowes," which Redcrosse, who has God as his "frend" but who has nevertheless been languishing in a dungeon helpless without the means to escape on his own, clearly lacks.

The problem is that Redcrosse has not gone through the experience of learning for himself. *Arthur* has had the example written in his heart with an iron pen. But, rather than making Redcrosse learn for himself, Arthur has charged *Una* with making an example of his experience for him. This vicarious learning is not enough to guarantee Redcrosse's experience. What is more, Arthur has addressed Redcrosse only after taking his own helmet off. This may be why Arthur does not discover that he and Redcrosse are talking at cross purposes. At the moment this conversation takes place, Arthur is not guarded as well as he should be, either.

Spenser is being deliberate in his obfuscation here, but as always he leaves some not-so-subtle clues for the reader to follow. The first comes in the following stanza in which the narrator speaks of their "diuersly discoursing of their loues" (I.ix.18.1). Obviously one way of taking this is that they are simply ranging over their separate and distinct loves. This is clearly how the rational Arthur takes their conversation. But another way of reading the episode is that both are discussing their individual private loves "diuersly" without actually connecting the diverse objects they are talking about in the public space. It is not enough to return to one's initial premises to resolve such a conflict. After an exchange of gifts, they depart as friends. And yet, it is very telling that Arthur goes on his way "To seeke his loue," while Redcrosse simply goes "for to fight / With Vnaes foe" (I.ix.20.2-3).

Unfortunately, Redcrosse does not learn the lessons about the necessity of friendship that Arthur had impressed not upon him but upon Una. Thus they part not having completed the circle of friendship as completely as the reader might have hoped.

The Failure of Will in the House of Despair

If Redcrosse was learning the lessons he should be learning, after his rescue by Arthur he would change his behavior from his purposeless wandering and grab instead onto the forward purpose that Una has been offering him from the beginning of his journey. And it seems that Redcrosse is so resolved when at last they leave Arthur "to fight / With *Vnaes* foe" (I.ix.20.2-3). But is it *Una* who stops him on "*her* forward course" (I.ix.20.6 italics mine) on account of her "weighing the decayed plight, / And shrunken synewes of her chosen knight" (I.ix.20.4-5).

Una's weighing unequal things in the balance is new to her, and it comes as a function of her travel in the domain of time. She fell in love with another (a=b) in this alien land, and, having been separated from her beloved knight soon after, she been gradually drawn out of her own mind (a=a) to listen to the echoes of her own her presence in the world that are reflected back at her.

Redcrosse, by contrast, acts more like Talus in Book V. He is a machine that may be counted on to attack whatever immoral thing is placed in front of him indifferently. But when it comes to "weighing" things in the balance, he continues to treat all things in strict terms of good and evil without weighing the necessity of his interaction with them. This has a cost in the world of time. His sinews have been weakened over time, as he has been wasting more and more of his energy in fights that are not worth having, and it is Una (not "clownishe" Redcrosse) who recognizes this.

Another Distraction

We can measure the extent of Redcrosse's failure to grasp the necessity of making fine-grained judgments in the time-bound world in what happens when Una decides to stop moving forward. Redcrosse becomes distracted by the first shiny object that meets his eye. This time it is Trevisan, a man whose "eye was backward cast, / As if his feare still followed him behynd" (I.ix.21.5-6). Redcrosse tries to speak with him, but he finds him so "sencelesse and aghast / That of him selfe he seemd to be afrayd" (I.ix.23.3-4) that he "answerd nought at all" (I.ix.24.1), standing in mute in astonishment

> as one that had aspyde
> Infernall furies, with their chaines vntide…. (I.ix.24.4-5)

Following so quickly after the previous speech about golden chains being wrought by the mutual help of others, the notion that Trevisan is alone as he faces internal furies with their chains untied is a sign that something is wrong with him.

Eventually, Redcrosse manages to get an answer out of Trevisan, who is fleeing "A man of hell, that calls himselfe *Despayre*" (I.ix.28.5). With that, Redcrosse manages to wrest control of his situation from Una, who (silently) acquiesces in what the reader must now recognize as another in a series of very poor choices that Redcrosse has been making all along the way:

> Certes (sayd he) hence shall I neuer rest,
> Till I that treachours art haue heard and tryde. (I.ix.32.1-2)

In short order Redcrosse finds the Cave of Despair with the help of Trevisan as his guide. Una, still in silence, follows Redcrosse's lead.

Meeting Despair

The cave is exactly as Trevisan promised it would be; it is a picture of stale lifelessness where "carcases were scattered on the greene, / And throwne about the cliffs" (I.ix.34.5-6). On the basis of his poor performance in the House of Pride, one wonders whether Redcrosse has noticed this; but the poet deftly changes the reader's perspective to the fear of Trevisan. Just like Errour, who would have flown from him if he had not forced her to stay, Trevisan would have fled had not the Knight of Holinesse "forst him stay" (I.ix.34.9). It may be no help to the reader that Redcrosse "comforted [Trevisan] in feare" (I.ix.34.9), as this is the same sort of reassurance that he had comforted Fidessa with at I.ii.21.7-8. She was outwardly dressed as the Whore of Babylon, and Redcrosse seems not to have noticed. It is only after

The Failure Of Will In The House Of Despair

he experiences the Cave of Despair for himself that he acknowledge that Trevisan's description is "trew" (I.ix.37.1). But Redcrosse's acknowledgement of the truth of Trevisan's words does not actually answer the question of whether he has seen the whole of the Cave of Despair or whether he is experiencing only that which he wishes to see, ignoring the carcasses that are strewn through the landscape.

The reader does not get an immediate answer to this question. Instead, Redcrosse encounters Despair, who sits

> on the ground,
> Musing full sadly in his sullein mind;
> His griesie lockes, long growen, and vnbound,
> Disordred hong about his shoulders round,
> And hid his face; through which his hollow eyne
> Lookt deadly dull, and stared as astound. (I.ix.35.2-7)

Despair's clothes, even more than Philosophy's in Boethius' *Consolation of Philosophy*, have no substantial existence. Instead, his garment is woven together out of many separate pieces of clothing:

> nought but many ragged clouts,
> With thornes together pind and patched was,
> The which his naked sides he wrapt abouts. (I.ix.36.1-3)[1]

Redcrosse, seeing another knight lying half-dead nearby, focuses on his hand "In which a rustie knife fast fixed stood" (I.ix.36.8).

A Discourse on Justice

In response, Redcrosse speaks of the need for justice:

---

1 In Boethius' *Consolation of Philosophy*, Philosophy declares that she has woven her robe out of indestructible threads, but at the same time she has come to Boethius asking him to sacrifice his life to repair a tear in her garment. Boethius' translator, Joel C. Relihan, pointed this paradox out to me. I conclude that, although Philosophy has woven her robe out of threads that are indestructible, having been woven by God, Philosophy has woven her robe after the fact of its *a posteriori* creation, and her work is not up to the task she sets for herself as an imitator of God's *a priori* work. Spenser has the same sort of scholastic distinction in mind here, as he asks the reader to decide whether Redcrosse is focusing on Despair's substantial body here—a body that has not been well fed—or on the superficial "many ragged clouts" that hang about Despair and make him look larger than he actually is. The correct answer in both Boethius and Spenser is to look past accidental "clouts" and to focus on the essential things God has made. The problem in Spenser is that this strategy focuses the reader on the body of Despair, a thing that still has no substantial existence.

> Thou damned wight,
> The authour of this fact, we here behold,
> What iustice can but iudge against thee right,
> With thine owne bloud to price his bloud, here shed in sight.
> (I.ix.37.6-9)

There is no question of Redcrosse's having noted the "fact" of injustice of Despair's work here, but the careful reader should note that the questions that the poet is raising are arrived at by focusing Redcrosse's attention on what is apparent to his "sight." Is he still looking at the surface of justice, as he had when he encountered Fidessa's pleasing body? His declaration of a *lex talionis*, Old Testament "an eye for an eye" justice is an indication that he has not in a position to see the root of justice. Because the Old Testament doctrines of harsh legal judgment had been supplanted by the New Testament doctrines of love and forgiveness that the assessment of all the facts before rendering a judgment is necessary. The assessment of the whole of the matter includes the fact that it is not Redcrosse's job to exact revenge for injustice. Instead, it is his job to make sure he does not fall into injustice himself. That would involve Redcrosse in reflecting, not only on moral evil in the world, but on his own participation in the creation of the moral world which is being reflected back at him in the distributed allegory.

While such problems never occur to Redcrosse, they are quick to spill from the tongue of Despair, who speaks of the consequences of his participation in the world:

> What franticke fit (quoth he) hath thus distraught
> Thee, foolish man, so rash a doome to giue?
> What iustice euer other iudgement taught,
> But he should die, who merites not to liue? (I.ix.38.1-4)

Despair refocuses Redcrosse on the ends of life; but Redcrosse, though wondering at Despair's "suddeine wit" (I.ix.41.1)—in suddenness we find a parallel with his wanting to win or lose every fight at once—answers that

> The terme of life is limited,
> Ne may a man prolong, nor shorten it;
> The souldier may not moue from watchfull sted,
> Nor leaue his stand, vntill his Captaine bed.
> Who life did limit by almightie doome,
> (Quoth he) knowes best the termes established;
> And he, that points the Centonell his roome,
> Doth license him depart at sound of morning droome. (I.ix.41.2-9)

The Failure Of Will In The House Of Despair

There is nothing wrong with Redcrosse's logic here, but it does not tell the whole story. Redcrosse is in the perhaps unique position of having been fit with the armor of Ephesians at the beginning of his adventure, and he relies on his friendship of God to tip the balance of his fights in his favor every time. But these things are out of his control. Redcrosse has not yet turned his mind away from ends that are out of his control to the middle terms that could be (but are not yet) under his purview. Middle terms can be amplified through the twin processes of a) a continual education that extends oneself beyond the limits of the animal being that one is born with and b) through friendship with others to make up for one's own inevitable failings of an ultimately elusive individual wholeness.

Despair on the Ends of Experience

Despair is clever enough to oppose the imperfect experience and memory of a man in time with the timeless perspective of God. His argument begins

> Is not his deed, what euer thing is donne,
> In heauen and earth? did not he all create
> To die againe? all ends that was begonne.
> Their times in his eternall booke of fate
> Are written sure, and haue their certaine date. (I.ix.42.1-5)

From this position on the ends of experience, Despair weaves another argument about necessity:

> Who then can striue with strong necessitie,
> That holds the world in his still chaunging state,
> Or shunne the death ordaynd by destinie? (I.ix.42.6-8)

His picture of the "still chaunging state" of the world plays on the dual meaning of words. On the one hand, it is "still," a non-moving state out of the realm of time. One the other hand, it is "chaunging." Redcrosse makes a choice when he chooses to see the changing world only from the timeless perspective of God in its state of stillness. This is not, however, the proper perspective of time-bound human beings, who must adapt themselves to changes that come serially through time and are not always in reality as limited human minds expect them to be.

Despair's answer that "When houre of death is come, let none ask whence, nor why" (I.ix.42.9) is an attempt to play on the vanity of Redcrosse's belief in his godlike perception of events. His arguments are designed to stop Redcrosse from acting as he should. He points out that his great battles, for which he will be praised, will be won through "strife, and bloud-shed, and auengement" (I.ix.43.4). They will have to be paid for in the afterlife, and they will have to be paid for by the individual George, not by God.[2] Despair is arguing that Redcrosse should put an end to his life before he does any more harm in his already tainted life.

The Balance of Argument Shifts In Favor of Despair

Rather than causing Redcrosse to rethink his own argument, which Despair is throwing back at him, Redcrosse remains in a stunned silence, as Despair asks him

> For what hath life, that may it loued make,
> And giues not rather cause it to forsake? (I.ix.44.4-5)

The answer that should immediately occur to the careful reader is that the love of a good woman like Una makes life worth living, but it is significant that Redcrosse remains silent still.

Despair continues, turning his attention to Una, who has apparently followed Redcrosse into the cave:

> Is not enough, that to this Ladie mild
> Thou falsed hast thy faith with periuree,
> And sold thy selfe to serue *Duessa* vild,
> With whom in al abuse thou hast thy selfe defild? (I.ix.46.6-9)

It seems that everyone knows that Redcrosse has sinned against Una; but apart from adding insult to Una's injury, Despair's charge that he has sinned against her is serious. And Redcrosse does not answer Despair, for there is no answer available to him; he is guilty as charged. Despair is counting on Redcrosse's own memory of events and his (Despair's) more subtle psychology of man to drive this man into inaction.

Thus, Despair uses Redcrosse's skewed sense of justice against him, as he says,

> Thou wretched man, of death hast greatest need,
> If in true ballaunce thou wilt weigh thy state. (I.ix.45.1-2)

---

2 Of course, the careful reader knows that none of this matters, because God will save him on account of his fitting into the armor of Ephesians; but George is not aware, as his readers may be, that he is so blessed.

Redcrosse's belief that he has the power to put things in the world of time back into balance comes from his substitution of his own errant will for the "goodwill" of God. The fact is that justice from God's perspective is not in fact "balanced." The positive value that comes from being chosen by God is that Redcrosse can be assured of victory, even here with Despair. But events continue to be shaped by God's "goodwill" and not by anything consciously willed on the part of a demonstrably inferior Redcrosse. The superior knowledge of Despair on this point means that his words act "as a swords poynt" that "through his hart did perse" (I.ix.48.2), and this "in his conscience made a secret breach" (I.ix.48.3).

It is here, for the first time since we have met him, that Redcrosse

> did reherse,
> And to his fresh remembrance did reuerse,
> The vgly vew of his deformed crimes…. (I.ix.48.4-6)

That is a good thing in spite of its coming so late in his adventure and despite the fact that it comes during his encounter with Despair. The Redcrosse Knight *should* have been using his memory to "reuerse" his experience back to its origin in himself all along. It is precisely because he has not been doing that that he keeps making the same mistakes on his "forward" way, and as a consequence he keeps getting into the same trouble.

This is a good first step; but having the experience of memory alone is not enough, as it causes him to lose precisely those manly powers that he should be using to fight off Despair:

> That all his manly powres it did disperse,
> As he were charmed with inchaunted rimes,
> That oftentimes he quakt, and fainted oftentimes. (I.ix.48.7-9)

Despair, finding his opponent "weake and fraile" (I.ix.49.2), begins an assault on Redcrosse's conscience "To driue him to despaire" (I.ix.49.5). He does so by showing Redcrosse a tableaux of souls

> painted in a table plaine,
> The damned ghosts, that doe in torments waile,
> And thousand feends that doe them endlesse paine
> With fire and brimstone, which for euer shall remaine. (I.ix.49.6-9)

Despair's ekphrastic work of art freezes the world at its worst point in its ever-dying, ever-renewing cycle; and it is at this point that Despair hands

Redcrosse a rusty knife.

This is an important moment. It is in Despair's power to use words to pierce the soul of Redcrosse's conscience; but in Spenser's Aristotelian universe, words only plant the potential for action in the mind of man. Action is reserved to the individual actor. Redcrosse is not the sort of man to travel through the world with any purpose, and he is reduced to trembling "like a leafe of Aspin greene" (I.ix.51.4)—a tree that we last saw in the catalog of trees in canto i, where it stood for "staues," another word for "spere," exactly the thing Redcrosse had handed to Una's dwarf as "needlesse" before he descends into the Cave of Errour—at the words and images of Despair.

Una Finally Speaks Up

In spite of his having met with the well-intentioned Arthur, Redcrosse has still not learned how to translate his God-given potential into purposeful action; and once again it is up to Una to step in and rescue Redcrosse after he has taken the proffered knife and is preparing "to worke his finall smart" (I.ix.51.8). She has been there listening as Despair has told Redcrosse the extent of his sin in specific terms of his treatment of Una with Duessa. She almost faints once again before recovering herself and snatching the rusty knife out of his hand (I.ix.52.4).

Only now does she speak:

> Fie, fie, faint hearted knight,
> What meanest thou by this reprochfull strife?
> Is this the battaile, which thou vauntst to fight
> With that fire-mouthed Dragon, horrible and bright? (I.ix.52.6-9)

She offers the same advice that he has been given since the beginning of his experience: fly from error. As she does, she acknowledges what apparently Redcrosse still has not realized, that he is a "fraile" human being with a weak "manly hart":

> Come, come away, fraile, seely, fleshly wight,
> Ne let vaine words bewitch thy manly hart,
> Ne diuelish thoughts dismay thy constant spright. (I.ix.53.1-3)

Despair's words are vain because Redcrosse has been guaranteed a part of "heauenly mercies" (I.ix.53.5) from the beginning of his adventure, and his constant diversion into error bewilders her: "Why shouldst thou then despeire, that chosen art?" (I.ix.53.5) she asks him. Redcrosse, not having much ability in the ways of speech—he's more of a 'use-force-now-ask-questions-later' sort of guy—does not answer. Una steps in to answer her question for him:

> Where iustice growes, there grows eke greater grace,
> The which doth quench the brond of hellish smart,
> And that accurst hand-writing doth deface.... (I.ix.53.7-8)

In her argument, she uses a metaphor of growing something on top of justice that continues on after "that accurst hand-writing," which she likens to a "hellish smart," deconstructs. She wins her argument, which is far more compact than Redcrosse's 3 stanza argument about justice, or Despair's argument, which goes on for nine (41-49). Una's argument takes up a single stanza (as is appropriate for a character named Una).

In Despair's reduction of Redcrosse's actions to adventitious products of "luckless" chance (I.ix.45.4), we need to remember that Despair's arguments are projections of Redcrosse's own outward projection of inward phenomenon. But Redcrosse has not connected the Despair he meets in the external world back to his own mind, continuing to believe that he is exempt from participation in despair on account of his undoubtedly manly "forse," which no one but Una has ever called into question. Likewise, even at this late stage in the poem, Redcrosse has yet not connected his election back to its true source in Heaven, instead relying on his own will.

Una knows that his will has no such power; it is directed by a God whose purpose neither Despair (who she also sees as a separate entity) nor Redcrosse knows. Though she is a woman, she is also pictured in this episode as stronger than Redcrosse, who actually "fainted oftentimes" (I.ix.48.9) during Despair's speeches. Una's state is *likened* to a swoon, but in fact she does not faint in fact, as

> through euery vaine
> The crudled cold ran to her well of life,
> *As in a swowne*: but soone reliu'd againe.... (I.ix.52.1-3 italics mine)

Una then reminds Redcrosse of his promise to fight "that fire-mouthed Dragon, horrible and bright" (I.ix.53.9).

Despair's arguments fail in the light of Una's speech. Redcrosse, who has committed another error based on his "clownishe" belief in the power of his own will to put the universe in balance on its own without education in the ways of God or man, does not say anything but follows sheepishly after Una, as she leads him out of the Cave of Despair.

Redcrosse in the Extremity of Heaven

Una has expressed her frustration with the knight who forgets his obligation to her so soon after his rescue from the dungeon of Orgoglio. Instead of following her to Eden and defeating the Dragon, he had run straight to Despair despite her knowledge that he is assured of salvation and has no reason to despair. By expressing herself, she manages to gain control over the situation for a short time; but, as so frequently happens in *The Faerie Queene*, her resolution brings with it as many problems as it solves.

Una feels a cultural obligation to maintain the propriety of the status quo in which women remain passive and follow active men. Una is learning some things about the manners that obtain in the world of time, which diverge in significant ways from those she has been raised with in Eden. In spite of these new facts, some things are the same in the world of time as they were in Eden. Her inclination is maintain the active, vigorous, and male order on which society operates rather than overturning it for a feminine society. But in alienating her power to a male society, she subjects herself to warrior males like Redcrosse, who do not learn but fight.

Spenser's problem is that were he to continue to follow the status quo, the current Queen of England, who stands outside Spenser's Faery as the model for all that happens within, would be disqualified from holding office. More importantly (at least from Una's point of view) Una would never be able to get to the end of her adventure, which is not to follow Redcrosse on his random and increasingly dangerous adventures in the wilderness, but to face the Dragon who stands oppressive outside the walls of Eden. It is only when Una speaks up that the reader begins to see Redcrosse fulfilling his purpose (τέλος). When he takes control from her and follows Trevisan into the Cave of Despair, her initial purpose of maintaining the status quo is fulfilled, but the reader begins to see other purposes slip away.

In spite of her having gained insight into the brave new world of time that makes her a better leader than Redcrosse—though not yet as good a leader as Arthur—the situation that stands by her having overturned the domination of male over female leaves Una facing a paradox for which she can see no clear way out.[1]

To Blame the Woman...

Spenser seems to agree that the patriarchal order should remain in place, even though it means leaving the weak and frail Redcrosse in charge. The poet even opens the next stanza with what appears to be an attack on Una for taking control of the situation by getting Redrosse to yield:

> What man is he, that boasts of fleshly might,
> And vaine assuraunce of mortality,
> Which all so soone, as it doth come to fight,
> Against spirituall foes, yeelds by and by,
> Or from the fielde most cowardly doth fly? (I.x.1.1-5)

The poet also seems to relieve the general set of mankind of blame for their lack of purposeful action, as he continues:

> Ne let the man ascribe it to his skill,
> That thorough grace hath gained victory.
> If any strength we haue, it is to ill,
> But all the good is Gods, both power and eke will. (I.x.1.6-9)

In this citation, one can hear the work of John Calvin, as the poet is explicitly making the case that I have been making throughout this entire book: that mankind's ascription of his victories to his own skill, and not to their proper location in the power and the will of God, is itself a sin.

The question then becomes whether we should include Redcrosse

---

[1] The path in Elizabethan England was much more straightforward for a man than a woman. Elizabeth may have been to the manor born, but in aristocratic society, a man could rise in the world of court by his superior education. This is the process that allowed Spenser, the son of a non-aristocratic cloth maker, to go the Merchant Taylors' School and on that account to be admitted to court. There were few women who achieved power in this manner. All of Elizabeth's advisors were men, and I believe that Spenser was conservative enough that he felt that the status quo needed to be tweaked by educated men who saw deeper than Redcrosse (men like Arthur, for instance), but he shied away from the wholesale revolution of replacing male leadership altogether.

within the class of men described by the stanza, or whether he should be excluded on account of his unique position in the (albeit fictional) world on account of having his actions guaranteed by the grace of God Himself.

Redcrosse has flown from his spiritual foe, and someone must be blamed for his "cowardly" retreat from danger. The most likely candidate is Una, who took him away from his encounter with Despair by speaking up. And lest the reader think that Una's reaction to Redcrosse's imminent suicide was in anyway necessary, she actually interrupts him, not in the process of plunging the rusty knife into his breast, but in the process of drawing his hand "back againe" (I.ix.51.9). It would have been fascinating to see how Redcrosse would have worked his way through the problem of his conflicting interests in the scene. Una's premature dragging of Redcrosse out of the Cave of Despair robs him and the reader of the chance to find out.

This would seem to indicate that Una's cautioning of Redcrosse to make "triall" of his experience before rashly rushing into the Cave of Errour, or her advice that he add faith unto his force when he fails to conquer his opponent instantly, or her dragging him away from Redcrosse's encounter with Despair are themselves obstacles to the achievement of her own purpose in having Redcrosse defeat the Dragon that oppresses her parents and holds them within the brazen walls of Eden. Redcrosse's ultimate victory in that battle has been guaranteed by virtue of the fact that he fits into the armor in the first place. The conclusion the reader is being forced into is that Una is too timid when it comes to facing danger—she has more power than she realizes to compel events—while she is too optimistic when it comes to her own love life.[2] She should remain passive and silent and let men do the work of bringing her potential to action.

...Or Not

On the other hand, Una has recognized what Redcrosse has not: that he was not prepared to fight with Despair; and perhaps the poet has found a way out of his own (and the reader's) dilemma of having made his hero an engine of war who never retreats. Through Una's cautious intervention,

---

[2] I noticed this first in Paul J. Alpers, *The Poetry of the Faerie Queene* (Princeton, NJ: Princeton University Press, 1967), 357-359. In Alpers' reading, the two lovers minds are in sympathetic accord. Alpers argues that Redcrosse feels revulsion at the prospect of his own suicide. Una feels his revulsion and drags him away from danger. While I acknowledge my debt to Alpers, my reading of the initial status of the lovers as being equal in their regard for one another is obviously quite different. In my reading, Redcrosse does not recognize the fact that Una is in love with him on account of his being in love with Gloriana and of Una's not speaking up and letting him know her feelings for him.

she has managed to save her hero from another of the mistakes that he is so prone to making on account of his not having pursued the education that would allow him to integrate himself into the court of Gloriana, a goal that he earnestly seeks. As it is, Redcrosse seeks entry to the court of Gloriana solely through his possession animal force combined with a belief—neither perfectly naïve nor perfectly wise—in his own power to overcome any obstacle placed in his way.

If this is the case, Una is not to blame, for she has rescued him and has made the way forward, a way that Redcrosse could not see in the Cave of Despair. That does not render Una's experience any more whole than Redcrosse's experience. Rather, she suffers under the partial view of herself, as Redcrosse does, on account of both of them concentrating on their *a priori* being, given to them by God the Creator, at the expense of the *a posteriori* experience of learning from their mistakes and moving forward with a fuller memory of mistakes made along the way to a still imperfect recreation of their experience in their limited rational minds.

Redcrosse's problem is that he has no positive knowledge that would get him any closer to his end. Passive Una is no help here, as she urges a negative caution that, if fulfilled, would defeat her purpose in having taken an active man with her to fulfill the potential that she, on account of her womanhood, as well as her fictional and so deconstructable status, can never achieve on her own.

The House of Holinesse

Realizing now (but not before this moment) that she does not have the power within herself to cure her knight, who is "feeble, and too faint" (I.x.2.2) and who does not seem to realize himself that "he was vnfit for bloody fight" (I.x.2.6), Una takes him to the House of Holinesse to rest. Unlike the home of Archimago that they had to travel a long way to find (I.i.29.9), the House of Holinesse is "not farre away" (I.x.3.1). It is a place "Renowmd throughout the world for sacred lore, / And pure vnspotted life" (I.x.3.2-3); but it is also another fiction that, like Errour, Corceca, Lucifera, and Despair, has no ontological foundation in literal reality.

By traveling back to the House of Holinesse, the careful reader may sense that once again Una is traveling and away from her goal, which is the engagement with and defeat of the Dragon in the literal world, and not reversion to comfort in a merely potential heaven; but she detours to find resources in others (a=b) that have become necessary on account of the lack of wholeness that neither Una nor Redcrosse have been able to find within themselves (a=a). It is fitting that it is *here*, as they enter the House of Holinesse (and not at the beginning of the poem where one might have expected it), that the poet announces that "Each goodly thing is hardest to begin" (I.x.6.1).[3]

The difference between Redcrosse and Una on the one hand and the House of Holinesse on the other may be seen in the guardian of the gate. Unlike Redcrosse, who continually takes his armor off and so gets into trouble as a result of his not learning from his experience, they find the door to the House of Holinesse "fast lockt" and "watched night and day" (I.x.5.1) by Humiltá, a man who is described as

> an aged syre, all hory gray,
> With lookes full lowly cast, and gate full slow,
> Wont on a staffe his feeble steps to stay....(I.x.5.5-7)

In the description of Humiltá the careful reader notes his resemblance to Archimago, and this should cause the reader to ask why he opens the gate rather than making "triall" of the pair. The answer appears to be that he knows Una. Redcrosse and Una meeting Archimago made no similar "triall" of his truth; they simply accepted that he was what he said he was. In a world of deceivers, it is never enough to accept things at their face value, even at—especially at—the gate of the House of Holinesse.

First Guides to the House of Holinesse

Once they have entered the House of Holinesse, they meet the franklin, Zele. He exemplifies the lessons that Una has begun and Redcrosse has yet to learn:

> right well [he] *became*,
> For in his speeches and behaueour hee
> Did labour liuely to *expresse* the same, (I.x.6.6-8 italics mine)

In other words, he brings forth his potential being through actions, speeches, and behaviors in the Platonic world of becoming, that is of time. On these he will be judged and not through his bare existence. Having internalized this lesson in a way that neither Redcrosse nor Una have, Zele leads the pair to Reverence, who likewise shows "great modestie" in "word and deed" so that he "knew his good to all of each degree" (I.x.7.4-5).

---

[3] This, of course, makes me wonder what Una and Redcrosse have been doing up to this point in the poem.

Zele and Reverence exemplify abstract principles in a fictional allegory, but they they are nevertheless capable of expressing themselves in the action of words and deeds. This makes them superior to both of the young characters who are encountering such things for the first time.

Cælia

Reverence leads the pair to Cælia, who "was busy at her beades" (I.x.8.3). This characterization poses a challenge to readers who are reading linearly through the narrative without a text to tell them that everything is okay in the House of Holinesse. Careful readers with stout memories will recall that Una had encountered Corceca, who was also busy at her beads (I.iii.13.6-9), and she had less than heavenly intentions towards the stranger. As with Archimago, Una had trusted that Corceca was exactly what her outward appearance told her she was. If Una is not to be fooled, she must make sure she has learned to make "triall" of her experience, even here.

The fact that Una remains silent here turns out to be okay, because Cælia is who she represents herself to be. But Cælia's origins are opaque to Una; she is "*thought* / From heauen to come, or thether to arise" (I.x.4.1-2 italics mine), but whether or not this is in fact true cannot be determined with any more certainty than can the false distinctions with which Corceca had already fooled her. Cælia, on the other hand, "well *knew* [Una] to spring from heuenly race" (I.x.8.7 italics mine). But *how* she knows is not given to the reader. It could be that they were previously acquainted, but it is easily as likely that they had never met and that it is the power of the poet that puts this knowledge in Cælia's mind.

The question becomes one of how the reader is to secure their knowledge of good and evil *in the absence of fiction?* The move to a textbook, by which modern readers secure the lack of a threat from Cælia and so passes over the danger Una *could* be in, is obviously not available to Una herself.[4]

---

4 This is not a small point. Textbooks are great, but they can be wrong. What makes this problem important is the fact that most modern scholars do not believe in God as the ground of existence. This does not leave them without weapons, as they do tend to believe in themselves as guarantors of experience. As a result, they tend to place less authority in books. Derrida had challenged the authority of individual books as being capable of fixing authority with his attack on the λόγος, but he leaves the distributed authority of books in place as the center of decentered view of language, as words in books lead to other words in other books but not to a stable λόγος. The material ground of individuality that readers are left standing on after the ontologically non-existent λόγος has been deconstructed is not questioned with equal vigor by Derrida. This leads postmodern critics to assume that the body that contains the mind is more accessible to the mind than are the intellectual contents

Spenser appears to be attempting to locate the authority of both the λόγος and the individual in the experience of discourse with others (a=b), not in the experience of one's animal being alone (a=a). By repeating the questions that arose from their experience on earth—experiences with Archimago, Corceca, and others—here in a purely imaginary heaven, the poet means for his careful readers to make those connections and to deal with them in a non-trivial manner and not to simply accept the status quo as the product of a fiction that modern man has learned is only that. Rather, the poet is asserting the inviolability of the a=b principle even as the book deconstructs after it is put down. This is what allows the message of the book to survive the deconstruction of its imaginatively created individual characters.

That being said, coming upon Cælia Una's heart swells inwardly "feeling wondrous comfort in her weaker eld" (I.x.8.9). Though Una is *physically* stronger than Cælia, the example set by the franklin Zele would suggest that Una needs to learn to overcome her propensity for silence and learn to *express* herself before she can be Cælia's equal. Until that time, she will have to rely on another older but weaker vessel, just as she relies on the morally weak Redcrosse to do the bloody work of fulfilling her quest to kill the Dragon that she is unable to accomplish on her own.

It is Cælia who speaks first, noting the fact that Una was born in Eden, though she has been traveling in the "happy earth":

> O happy earth,
> Whereon thy innocent feet doe euer tread,
> Most vertuous virgin borne of heauenly berth, (I.x.9.1-3)

Cælia recognizes that the reason that she trods the earth now is "to redeeme thy woefull parents head, / From tyrans rage, and euer-dying dread" (I.x.9.4-5). She then asks a question that could be paraphrased as "What are you doing here if your quest is in the Platonic world of becoming?":

> Hast wandred through the world now long a day;
> Yett ceasest not thy weary soles to lead,
> What grace hath thee now hither brought this way?
> Or doen thy feeble feet vnweeting hither stray? (I.x.9.6-9)

Cælia seems to believe that Una is right to be on earth, and she asks her about the grace that Una has brought back with her to heaven. This does

---

of the mind. If anyone believes this, they should be able to prove it rather than leaving it as an *a priori* assumption held in place by their unquestionable authority as critics.

not make sense unless her imaginary heaven is in some way incomplete. The answer to Cælia's question is that Una has brought the "straunge" presence of an "errant knight" to Cælia's heaven (I.x.10.1), and Cælia does not like it. She scolds mankind with being "partakers of their euill plight" (I.x.10.7) and warns them against hastening their own decay (I.x.10.9). She clearly feels that Redcrosse's errancy is at odds with the holy life.

What Una says next must be parsed carefully. She says that she has come "Thy selfe to see, and tyred limbes to rest" (I.x.11.1).While Una is surely glad to be back on familiar ground, Redcrosse has never shown the slightest interest in or knowledge of Cælia before this moment, and he has never recognized any need for rest. It is likely that in speaking for Redcrosse's eagerness to meet her, uncareful readers may be translating their desire to see the matter in line with their *a priori* assumptions about what is going on in the poem rather than making "triall" of the direct truth of Redcrosse's experience. But when the careful reader looks more carefully at the experience of Redcrosse, they will recognize that Una got him to come to the House of Holinesse with promises that his "prayses and broad-blazed fame" have been "vp to heuen…blowne" (I.x.11.4-5).

Insofar as he partakes of offered rest on his exhausting journey through the world, it is a good thing; but at the same time, Redcrosse's vertical ascent to an imaginary heaven in a distributed allegory must be recognized as a fictional construct that cannot be imitated in the literal lives of readers. That still may still be a good thing as long as it does not turn into a permanent end of Redcrosse's experience or of Spenser's readers.[5]

Alciati's *Emblemata*

This reading is consistent with one of Spenser's chief source for the images of Redcrosse and Una: Andrea Alciati's *Emblemata*.[6] Una is drawn

---

5 This, again, is one of the chief differences in the description of experience between Spenser and critics in the modern world. The Moderns are willing to lay aside questions about the propriety of this experience on account of Coleridge's "suspension of disbelief" as a way around looking to deeply into the rational experience of poetry being described as "objective correlatives" to experience. The postmoderns, too, are so literal in their experience of life, as well as being so focused on art as the end of experience, that they cannot accommodate a non-literal middle experience that is in any way temporary. By positing the middle world of reason as a temporary stop on the way to a much more stable, prelinguistic truth, Spenser is much more flexible in this regard. By denying the power to know things as they are in themselves (a=a), and by focusing instead on the reader's less metaphysically certain but more controllable rational response (a=b), Spenser's system can survive even Nietzsche's declaration that "God is dead."

6 Andrea Alciati, *A Book of Emblems: The Emblematum Liber in Latin and English*,

from Emblem VII, entitled "Non tibi, sed religioni" ("Not for you, but for religion"). The accompanying caption reads as follows:

> A doltish little ass carried a figure of Isis, bearing the revered mysteries upon its curved back. And so everyone in the street adored the goddess reverently, and on bended knee said prayers of worship. But the ass believed such honour was being shown to him, and swelled up, filling entirely with his pride—until the driver, who restrained him with whips, said, 'You are not a god, little ass; rather, you bear a god.'

The caption is a warning about the pride of the ass, who foolishly believes that the acclaim of the crowd is for him and not the god he bears on his back. This is surely the source not only for the backward-bent knees of the satyrs who turn to her ass when she attempts to instruct them, but also of Redcrosse, who is acting with the pride of an ass as well. The lesson that Spenser draws from Alciati's emblem book is that Una, not Redcrosse, is the true object of the people's adoration.

The problem with turning human attention to her is that she is a creature who can only be worshipped within the confines of a Platonic fiction. When the fiction is put down, she, and the values she represents, may deconstruct. Alciati, like Spenser, did not believe that religion could be practiced without action,[7] and this means that Spenser does not mean to eliminate Redcrosse from the universe of religion. It is still up to a limited Redcrosse to carry Una's potential into action.

It is in the preceding emblem in Alciati's book, entitled "Ficta religio" ("False Religion"), that we find the role played by false Fidessa, who comes to Redcrosse dressed as the Whore of Babylon and who unchastely allows Redcrosse to "view" her body:

> A most beautiful whore seated upon a royal throne wears the robe of state distinguished by honorific purple. She delivers wine to all from her flowing bowl. Used to their reclining, the drunken crowd sprawls all about. Thus they look to Babylon: which, with alluring form and false religion, possesses the stupid heathens.

The role of Redcrosse in the Book of Holinesse is to be educated out of his

---

trans. John F. Moffitt (Jefferson, N.C.: McFarland & Co., 2004).

[7] The motto in Alciati's library at Pavia was a quotation from Alexander the Great intended as an example of the care that he had taken in his work: "by never procrastinating." Henry Green, *Andrea Alciati and His Books of Emblems; a Biographical and Bibliographical Study*, (New York,: B. Franklin, 1965), v-vi.

tendency to be deceived by Archimago's magical science and Duessa's seductions, which are motivated by the desire to work the by-nature-unbalanced world to further evil. That desire for evil will be replaced in Redcrosse's mind, not with good—he already is unquestionably good—and not with an education that will make him equal to Archimago in power—he already is in a position to win every battle he engages in—but with a recognition that the power that he wields comes from God and not from his will. He has not learned this lesson as he is still following an errant journey in the wilderness that has him embracing the typological Whore of Babylon.

Fiction in the House of Holinesse

It is important to picture Una's desire to "see" Cælia (I.x.11.1) within the "fiction" created by an allegorical poet. Cælia and the entertainments (I.x.11.7) that "shew her bounteous or wise" (I.x.11.9) cannot actually be seen outside the veil of fiction, as they are the products of an imaginative "poetic metaphor." Unlike Derrida, for whom the presence of metaphor is something that interferes with a Cartesian agreement of epistemology and ontology in the human mind and so must be eliminated as far as possible in order to get the two to reconcile, Spenser believes that there is no point in talking about the metaphysical identity of things as they were created by God (a=a). The human mind recreates *a priori* ontological things in *a posteriori* epistemology using poetic metaphors that necessarily interfere with the direct apprehension of nature as it is. Rather than fleeing our immediate minds for a more distant (and often hostile) nature, Spenser means for each of his readers to make "triall" of their own imperfect minds. In this way, Hayden White's ironic perspective[8] can be arrived at without losing one's humanity in one's desire to master what is from Augustine's point of view a more perfect but ultimately inaccessible nature.[9]

---

8 White, *Metahistory*, 36-38.

9 This is my reading of White's essay on Michel Foucault in his "Foucault's Discourse: The Historiography of Anti-Humanism," in *The Content of the Form: Narrative Discourse and Historical Representation* (Baltimore: Johns Hopkins University Press, 1987). White appears to admire Foucault's willingness to face the "crisis in Western culture" caused by the failure of Kant's Enlightenment identification of philosophy with "transcendental reflection" (106). White points out that Foucault's writings consist of a "series of negations" (107) of Enlightenment ideas, one of which is the denial of "ends" as the last word on philosophy and a renewed emphasis on "middles" (107). But Foucault's philosophy still adheres to nature as the touchstone of true philosophy, and he approaches philosophical discourse from the point of view of existential distrust of any authority external to himself. Therefore, he dispenses with the "illusion of humanism" (138) of limited individuals, whom he has decentered from their central place in the philosophical order, in order to save the more

Fidelia and Speranza

Spenser's point in the deconstructatble fiction of the House of Holinesse is to have Una and Redcrosse meet examples of holy characters who are involved in interlinked relationships with one another before they go back to perform discrete actions in the world of time. Thus, the reader is led along with Una and "straunge" Redcrosse to meet two of Cælia's three daughters, Fidelia and Speranza, "two most goodly virgins" (I.x.12.2), both of whom are described as sporting a "demure countenance, and modest grace" (I.x.12.4). Cælia's third daughter, Charissa, is introduced as being "lincked" with a "louely fere" through "many pledges dere" (I.x.4.8-9), but she does not appear at once.

Fidelia is described as having a "constant mood" (I.x.13.6)[10] that does not change despite her ability to put fear into others on account of her holding a cup with a serpent in it: "That horrour made to all, that did behold" (I.x.13.5). Speranza is described as holding "siluer anchor" (I.x.14.6); she prays and looks "euer vp to heuen" (I.x.14.8);[11] but what was in her heart, "whether dread did dwell, / Or anguish," the poet tells his readers, "is hard to tell" (I.x.14.5). It is not the interior being or intention of these characters that gives them significance to men, but their relationship with one another, which can be seen in their coming "Ylinked arme in arme in louely wise" (I.x.12.3).

The pair, seeing Una, "towardes her gan wend" (I.x.15.1), and "Many kind speeches they *betweene* them spend" (I.x.15.3 italics mine). But it is significant that they ignore Redcrosse until "at *Vnaes* meeke request" (I.x.15.6) they turn themselves toward him and "salute" the stranger with "well beseeming glee" (I.x.15.7). His requiting of their greeting leaves

---

complete philosophical project in which he can make and umake things according to his now liberated will.

This it is obviously different from the philosophy of Augustine, who approaches "middles" in philosophy from the point of view of limited individuals who are defined away from access to metaphysical completeness altogether. Instead, the limited individuals acknowledge breaks in the smooth perception of God's *a priori* creative work and their always imperfect recreation of it in their limited, scientific, and *a posteriori* imaginations.

10 Compare this with Una's errant estimation of Redcrosse as a "constant spright" at I.ix.53.3.

11 If she is looking towards Heaven, it makes me wonder where they are now. My answer is that they are in an imaginatively created heaven that stands midway between the earth and the true Heaven. This intermediary heaven is only available in fiction, and is masked by modern criticism's emphasis on ontology, rather than epistemology, as the basis of truth in fiction.

something to be desired. He "quites, as him beseemed best" (I.x.15.8), but by this point the careful reader should have learned to make "triall" of what seems best to Redcrosse. He does not enter into the middle ground of conversation *between* the sisters. Instead, he changes the conversation to what interests him, hijacking the conversation, as he "gan discourse of many a noble gest" (I.x.15.9).[12]

The Correction of Redcrosse

After the weary pair have rested, Una asks Fidelia

> To haue her knight into her schoolehous plaste,
> That of her heauenly learning he might taste,
> And heare the wisedom of her words diuine. (I.x.18.4-6)

Fidelia agrees to teach

> that knight so much agraste,
> That she him taught celestiall discipline,
> And opened his dull eyes, that light mote in them shine. (I.x.18.7-9)[13]

---

12 Spenser does not make this point explicitly, so it could be otherwise. Here are my reasons for reading the passage in this manner. This is characteristic of Redcrosse's personality in the House of Holinesse, where he has lured by Una's promise that his fame has been "blown" up to "heuen" (I.x.11.4-5) and not by the promise that he will see any of the benefits of heaven itself. Given the reaction of Cælia to the "straunge" errant knight, it seems unlikely that her daughters were discussing noble gests before they were introduced to Redcrosse. His behavior appears to be that of a boor who turns conversation towards things that interest him and then dominates the conversation rather than entering into a preexisting conversation between the three.

Spenser's failure to make explicit the reaction of the sisters should not be met with the reader's response that what is not said is not there and so move on with the critic's *a priori* assumptions intact. The poet's response to the experience of Redcrosse has been to engender caution in the reader even where Redcrosse is not cautious (and need not be on account of his having been chosen by God). It appears likely to me that Spenser's silence on the inappropriateness of Redcrosse's hijacking of the conversation should be regarded as an act of occultatio on the part of the author. Redcrosse's perfection in holy ways will not be announced until I.x.45, and even then he will have to enact his perfection on earth.

13 The pun on might/mote reflects Spenser's thought on the complex relationship between "might" and the Bible's citation of the words of Christ as He is asking sinners not to judge the "mote" in their brother's eye without first having taken into account the beam that is in their own (Matthew 7:3–5; Luke 6:41–42). Redcrosse believes that the might for which God has chosen him confers powers on the reasoning by which he renders judgment on the actions of others. Redcrosse's reason is clearly lacking in the episode in the Cave of Despair. While Spenser's point is to disassociate the unified equation between might and

This makes no sense in the standard reading of the poem. If Redcrosse is already "agraste"—a newly coined word by Spenser which Hamilton tells us means "favoured with grace"—then why should he need an *education* in holy ways unless there is something missing in his makeup. It is only possible if God's granting of grace does not confer any *knowledge* of the ways of the holy on the conferee of grace. Such things must still be learned. Redcrosse's mind has been prepared by God's granting of His grace, and in that way Fidelia teaches the man things "Of God, of grace, of iustice, of free will" (I.x.19.6) that "weaker witt of man could neuer reach" (I.x.19.5) out of her book, "Wherein darke things were writ, hard to be vnderstood" (I.x.13.8-9).[14] In that way, "she was able, with her wordes to kill, / And raise againe to life the hart" (I.x.19.8-9), bringing Redcrosse to his second birth *through her words* (not through silence) as the new man of *Romans* 6.[15]

In the following stanza, the poet treats the intrusion of the miraculous into the natural order:

> And when she list poure out her larger spright,
> She would commaund the hasty Sunne to stay,
> Or backward turne his course from heuens hight,
> Sometimes great hostes of men she could dismay,
> Dry-shod to passe, she parts the flouds in tway;
> And eke huge mountaines from their natiue seat
> She would commaund, themselues to beare away,
> And throw in raging sea with roaring threat.
> Almightie God her gaue such powre, and puissance great. (I.x.20)

This reflects the power that *only* comes from fiction in Plato's *Parmenides*, where things not possible in this life (like the fiction that Aristotle is not now and never was younger than Socrates) can be seen as long as the viewer does not confuse fiction with fact and make a permanent end of what Plato views as a temporary expedient on the way to a deeper, non-empirical truth.

This was something that Augustine understood better than many pagans did. In *The City of God*, he writes of the pagan understanding of a miracle of Venus, which had "changed its colour, size, form, course, which never appeared before nor since."[16] Citing the pagan sage Varro, Augustine

---

reason in the mind of Redcrosse, this is a painfully slow process.

14 I cannot help but wonder what sort of justice Redcrosse was preaching to Despair when he confronted him in the previous canto.

15 And there we have our answer to the question raised in the last footnote. Redcrosse was preaching Old Testament justice there. His spirit is only raised to a New Testament sense of justice after he has received instruction in the House of Holinesse.

16 Augustine, *The City of God*, Modern Library Giants 74 (New York: Modern Li-

declares that "So great an author as Varro would certainly not have called this a portent had it not seemed to be contrary to nature."[17] Augustine denies that there is a break in the natural order. Instead, he believes that the operation of God in the world is more comprehensive than the weaker wit of the pagan mind could understand:

> For we say that all portents are contrary to nature; but they are not so. For how is that contrary to nature which happens by the will of God, since the will of so mighty a Creator is certainly the nature of each created thing? A portent, therefore, happens not contrary to nature, but contrary to what we know as nature.[18]

This is not an invitation to Redcrosse to perform miracles. The poet merely means to have Redcrosse increase his knowledge of the natural universe beyond what is available to a character like Archimago, who uses his education to create sprites who can travel down to the extreme ends of the universe and rouse Morpheus from his slumber, or Duessa, who can rouse Night into amoral action. Neither of these characters knows as much as is available to the heart of a "clownishe" but good character like Redcrosse. In Redcrosse's response to Fidelia's teaching, we are not told of a revolution in his thought that shifts his perspective from one extreme to another, as we find in the modern Marxist reversal of the poles of Hegel, nor do we find Nietzsche's heroic response to Socrates' attempt to reduce humanity to a bundle of sheepish last men by traveling from the center of experience to

---

brary, 1950), XXI.8, p. 776. In my opinion, Augustine takes advantage of the late Roman penchant for mistaking Roman might for the Roman power of reason. It is not as clear to me as it appears to be to Augustine that Plato had not understood the ultimately temporary nature of λόγος in his work. However, the appeal only to the originary power of Plato would discount all the misreadings that took place between Plato's proposal of such ideas in the *Parmenides* (and elsewhere) and his reception in Augustine's day. These misreadings include the philosophy of Plotinus, as well as the official Roman philosophy inscribed in the works of Cicero and Seneca, all of whom operated on the idealistic belief that the body was nothing more than an impermanent vehicle for a more permanent soul embodied in a more permanent λόγος.

In the murder of Cicero, Augustine saw only the willingness of Romans to dispense the body of one of their wisest men for mere political ends. In the suicide of Seneca, Augustine saw only a fool who followed Socrates into death on the basis of his true belief in a false fiction. The power of false pagan ideas to cause action in the world was real, as both wise men had suffered real, permanent, and irreversible damage to their souls by submitting to Roman bloodlust and not having cared enough for their created bodies.

17 Ibid.
18 Ibid.

Redcrosse's Disdain For Life

In spite of his growth, the education of Redcrosse is not finished yet. The poet tells us that he grew

> To such perfection of all heuenly grace,
> That wretched world he gan for to abhore,
> And mortall life gan loath, as thing forlore,
> Greeud with remembrance of his wicked wayes,
> And prickt with anguish of his sinnes so sore,
> That he desirde to end his wretched dayes:
> So much the dart of sinfull guilt the soule dismayes. (I.x.21.3-9)

Having learned something new, Redcrosse once again (and rather predictably) renews his wish for death. Were he focus exclusively on his new remembrance of his "deformed crimes" (I.ix.48.6), he would not be able to fulfill his saintly mission, which is to put his best foot forward, as he has been doing since his first adventure, when he had said

>   shame were to reuoke
> The forward footing for an hidden shade:
> Vertue giues her selfe light, through darkenesse for to wade.
> (I.i.12.7-9).

His problem now, as then, is not that he should turn back or hesitate but that he should be humble in ascribing his "vertue" to God and not to his will as man.

The emotional interference of sympathetic Una takes our eye off the ball of Redcrosse's as yet incomplete education. She feels sorry for him, but his continued dismay *even in the House of Holinesse* bewilders her:

> When him his dearest *Vna* did behold,
> Disdeining life, desiring leaue to die,
> She found her selfe assayld with great perplexity. (I.x.22.7-9)

The poet is reminding his readers to have compassion for sinners—as he

---

19 Both of these dialectical responses would introduce more instability into the fragile social system by catering to the lower classes only in the case of Marx or by catering to only to those aristocrats "heroic" enough not to participate in base democratic social structures at all in the case of Nietzsche.

has shown for Una and that Redcrosse had not—but they should not forget that compassion without reason is not enough in Spenser's grand design.

In a poem in which the poet hopes to create in Arthur "the image of a braue knight, perfected in the twelue morall vertues," the "clownishe" Redcrosse cannot even support himself on his own (a=a), needing others (a=b) to rescue him at every turn. And even now, Speranza comes to his rescue:

> But wise *Speranza* gaue him comfort sweet,
> And taught him how to take assured hold
> Vpon her siluer anchor, as was meet. (I.x.22.1-3)

This turns Redcrosse's focus away from dwelling on his past crimes and his present circumstances and braces him for his previously unthought-of future.

Compassion and Torment as Cures for What Ails Redcrosse

Una's vision of the whole of her circumstance and of his, though limited by a lack of attention to reason, has its own rewards, as she displays compassion towards her beloved knight. She asks Cælia for some relief for Redcrosse, and Cælia complies, sending for the leach Patience (I.x.23.6-9), who administers his medicine, which consists of drawing the "sowle-diseased knight" (I.x.24.1) out of his silence and having him "*tell* his griefe" (I.x.24.2 italics mine). This act of confession eases his "heauie spright" (I.x.24.3) of the burden of "the passion of his plight" (I.x.24.8) and he is able to bear his pain "as seeming now more light" (I.x.24.9). But Spenser is very clear that

> the cause and root of all his ill,
> Inward corruption, and infected sin,
> Not purg'd nor heald, behind remained still.... (I.x.25.1-3)

This is an important point in Spenser's Augustinian poem. Original sin is not to be avoided, but endured. That is why mankind needs education and cannot simply travel through life at one's will, feeding one's desire for instant and immediate pleasure or victory at once. Human beings must learn to be patient in Spenser's universe, extending ourselves beyond ourselves (a=b) to take the comfort that others can offer in the absence of our own strength.

Amendment next plucks out the cause of his errors "with pincers fyrie whott" (I.x.26.8) until there was no more error (except the original) in him.

Penance flogs him "with an yron whip" (I.x.27.1). Remorse "pricke[s]" his heart—and the reader is invited to remember how he had been introduced as "pricking on the plaine" (I.i.1.1)—and Repentance dips his wounded body in salt water (I.x.27.5), "The filthy blottes of sin to wash away" (I.x.27.7). These are harsh but necessary measures, and

> in short space they did to health restore
> The man that would not liue, but earst lay at deathes dore.
> (I.x.27.8-9)

The poet returns to the simile of the lion once again in the following stanza:

> In which his torment often was so great,
> That like a Lyon he would cry and rore,
> And rend his flesh, and his owne synewes eat. (I.x.28.1-3)

This is in contrast to the first appearance of the lion simile in I.i.17, where Redcrosse focused his energy on unreal forces outside himself when he had forced fleeing Errour to stay and fight. Here in the House of Holinesse Redcrosse has been corrected and now turns his mind back in on himself in order to sort truth from falsehood, as Augustine had urged in his *De Trinitate*, rather than fighting all outward forces with equal vigor. Some of those are unreal forces that can be ignored because they represent only privative evil. Others, however, have the power to do real damage to uncareful men.

The reader has probably guessed by now that Redcrosse resembles the lion as Christ resembles the lion, and this is why the poet puts the analogy in front of them. But, rather than pressing the analogy into an identity, the reader should keep in their minds the remaining differences between Christ and Redcrosse. Pressing the analogy between Redcrosse and Christ (a=b) into an identity (a=a) occludes the power that saves the individual: his God-created individual substance.

Una's Role in the House of Holinesse

The point of the scene of the purging of Redcrosse is that Redcrosse has to go through his purge alone. Una, though she loves him, must once again look on helplessly, though she does so with "pitty of his paine and anguish sore" (I.x.28.7).

When the poet tells his readers that Una "well she wist, his crime could else be neuer cleare" (I.x.28.9), we cannot take it for granted that the poet is merely citing a platitude of Augustinian belief that everybody including Una knows. One of the implications of this statement is that either Una has always known that the original sin of man interferes with perfection of Eden that she hopes to restore through the action of Redcrosse, or that she is just learning this at this late point in her adventure. Either way, Una, who grew up in a prelapsarian state of Eden and who wears "guiltlesse garments" (I.x.28.6), stands at cross purposes with the knowledge that Spenser and his readers have. They have always known that the metaphysical source of sin cannot be rolled back to a state of perfection *except through an inimitable fiction.*

When Una speaks once again to Redcrosse, who has been inflated with pride for the first nine cantos and whose pride has been the cause of his demise, she is still advising him

> Himselfe to chearish, and consuming thought
> To put away out of his carefull brest. (I.x.29.5-6)

This, like most of the advice she gives him throughout the book, is based on Una's misunderstanding of the obligations of Redcrosse *as a man*, an area where she has no expertise whatsoever. There can be now no question that Una has been externalizing the blame for the sins of Redcrosse by placing it onto others. Her practice has allowed him to continue with his overly inflated ego intact. But the poet has now given a contradictory simile in which Redcrosse is likened to a lion who has turned his mind inward and has learned to eat away at his prideful sinews. This is a paradox that can only be resolved by deciding that someone, fictional Una or the human poet, is wrong.

Despite Una's Edenic origin, the careful reader should side with the substantially real but imperfect poet rather than the completely fictional Una in resolving this paradox. Redcrosse should redirect his mind away from his prideful quest for worldly glory that does not extend beyond his will (a=a) and acknowledge that his victories are products of the power of God (a=b) to which is will is subordinate. Una's advice here can then be seen as one of classic codependency.

Taking one's obligations seriously is a long process that takes place over time *in time*. This makes Redcrosse's joy at the recovery of "his cured conscience" at I.x.29.3 suspect. The poet does not necessarily mean for us to take the bait here and believe that Redcrosse has finally and fully understood his enormous complicity in his sin. This is another instance of Redcrosse thinking he has reached the end of his long journey before it is over in fact. The careful reader will not make any such rash judgments, as they will recognize that the poet is still referring to him as "the Elfin knight" at I.x.44.1. Redcrosse will not be reminded of his literal name, for which his journey will be remembered, until I.x.61; and he will not be told of his human legacy until I.x.65. Until that time, the reader must hold all this information in their minds, building up a rational picture of Redcrosse from a distance that Redcrosse himself still seems unaware of within the poem.

The Appearance of Charissa

It is at this point that Una takes the "*vnacquainted* guest" (I.x.29.9 italics mine) Redcrosse to meet Cælia's third daughter Charissa, who was too weak to meet them when they first arrived, but who has now "woxen strong" (I.x.29.8). She is likened to an image of the changing moon combines with the image of womanhood in childbirth,[20] and is described as

> a woman in her freshest age,
> Of wondrous beauty, and of bounty rare,
> With goodly grace and comely personage,
> That was on earth not easie to compare. (I.x.30.1-4)

The difficulties in comparison become apparent when Charissa thinks about Cupid, the god that binds one person to another (a=b) on earth. Cupid's love appears to the heavenly daughter of Cælia, who has been absent due to her impending childbirth, as a "wanton snare," which "As hell she hated" (I.x.30.6). She can afford to be so cavalier, as she is performing the act of generation without a father (a=a). But *exactly* how anyone can imitate such behavior on the earth without the interference of a "poetic metaphor" is radically unclear.

This puts Charissa at odds with Una, who has translated herself out of unified Eden into the "extremitie of time," where Cupid rules. She has fallen in love with Redcrosse, who she hopes will be able to redress the wrongs done to her parents by the Dragon that they and she cannot redress themselves. Perhaps she is right to do so. Were she to remain within the brazen walls of Eden, Eden would be forever barred from restoration.

Unfortunately, Una does not immediately understand the processes

---

20 I would add that the birth of Charissa's child comes before the actual cure of Redcrosse of his sin. This indicates that Redcrosse is predestined to go through this part of his training and is destined to emerge on the other side before he actually undergoes it. The reader's misconstrual of the effect of her cure does not have any effect on its cause.

that operate in the "extremitie of time" after she crosses out of Eden. The Fall has corrupted mankind more than perhaps she is aware, but it has also changed her status in respect to the objects she meets in the world of time by dividing Una's mind from immediate contact with object of her affection. As a result of her misunderstanding, she continues to remain silent. The man she loves leaves her, because it gradually becomes apparent that his judgment is superficial, and he cannot see into her heart. She is gradually learning the lessons of the Augustinian world of time, in which one's words can be misunderstood by others and one must master the relative processes that come through an *a posteriori* education in order to align one's spoken meaning with what another hears *after the fact of one having spoken*. And even then, Una's words will have no certainty of success, as the communication process is never guaranteed to be complete in the public sphere.

But the fact is that Una has her existence only within the protected conclaves of the author's imaginatively constructed fiction, and she will disappear when the book is put down. Were it true that fictional realm made possible by "poetic metaphor" was in itself enough to complete the hermeneutic circle—as it was for Socrates—Una would never have felt the need to translate herself out of Eden into the world of time; but Una comes from a kingdom in which power passes to the husband of the Princess of Eden. Therefore, she leaves Eden in order to find a man that can activate what exists in Una only in potential. Therefore, her return to a potential heaven must be seen *by Una* as a detour from her ultimate end, which stands *outside* Eden.

The same thing is true of Charissa. Her ability to reproduce without a father is only possible through the "poetic metaphor" of fiction. In order to emphasize the inadequacy of Charissa as an end unto herself, the poet places her likeness with likenesses of another character his readers have met before. Charissa's "necke and breasts were euer open bare, / That ay thereof her babes might sucke their fill" (I.x.30.7-8). The reader has seen another who bared her breasts in Fidessa. Charissa's wardrobe is also described in similar terms to Fidessa's:

> on her head she wore a tyre of gold,
> Adornd with gemmes and owches wondrous faire,
> Whose passing price vneath was to be told. (I.x.31.5-7)

The careful reader will remember that Fidessa's body was also garnished with "crownes and owches" (I.ii.13.4). The question that should be immediately raised in the mind of careful readers is how they are to distinguish good Charissa from bad Fidessa if each is described in similar terms.

The answer is not that because the poet likes the moral rectitude of Charissa that it is okay that she bares her breasts and wears nice tiaras of "gemmes and owches," while the poet is inclined to hate Fidessa's "crownes and owches" (I.ii.13.4). Such a reading relies on the poet's being able to count on his control of the sympathetic reaction of his readers. This leaves too much power in the hands of the individual, for any reader could decide that they like looking at boobies and owches, which the easy virtue of Fidessa can more easily provide, and that they hate the restrictions that submitting to Charissa entails.[21]

The difference between the two comes from their relationship to the world of time. Charissa exists only in an a-sexual paradise "That on earth was not easie to compare" (I.x.30.4), because in her poetically-constructed Heaven, all that is required of a woman is to identify herself as a woman as clearly as possible, and this includes baring her breasts, not once but "euer" (I.x.30.7). Charissa's values are secure in themselves (a=a), but they can only be realized through the power of fiction to create a "poetic metaphor." Fidessa's imitation of Charissas behavior involves placing Charissa's values in the service of the interdependent relations (a=b) appropriate to the world of time. This introduces a wrinkle that takes away some of the nobility of the everlasting baring of breasts that goes on in Spenser's fictionally-constructed heaven, as we can see if we apply Fidessa's behavior toward Redcrosse to Una. Had *she* bared her breasts to the libidinous Redcrosse, one suspects that she would have had no problem with keeping Redcrosse around, as this is apparently the fastest way into the warrior's heart. Una's problem is that she is attempting to keep her virtue intact, while at the same time being subject to the interdependence of Cupid's love that governs the world of time to which she has traveled as she looks to enact through Redcrosse

---

21 This is how I see many modern critics' reaction to this distinction. The modern reading is based in an existentialism in which will is at the center of all experience. From the modern perspective, Spenser and his model Augustine are blind thinkers who have not yet realized the limitations that attend their reading, nor the vastly superior modern way of reading in which things that didn't make sense in the past make sense to moderns. Such a reading does not consider any lack of clarity as purposeful. In my opinion, Spenser's reading makes more sense that the modern reading precisely because it does not take for granted the superiority of its position in its *a priori* premises but instead argues for it in the *a posteriori* manner that the moderns have elsewhere taken so much pride in for themselves. Spenser simply does not believe the will to be as complete as the existentialists do. Modern readers may disagree with Spenser's position, but the misrepresentation of Spenser's position in order to make it agree with existentialist premises does the modern critic no favors.

what exists in her only in potential.

If it were only a matter of a one-sided authorial decision to hold a strict Augustinian faith as primary in one's mind, then a modern reader would be able to deconstruct Spenser's Augustinian faith on the basis of their having the better sense not to believe in it. But it was exactly for this reason that Spenser overturned the ending of Ariosto's poem. Ariosto's ending had led to the resurrection of Virgilian tyranny at the hands of Christians at the moment that Ruggiero has killed the individual Rodomonte. Ariosto had relied on Christians' absolute connection with the *a priori* truth of the universe in order to force heretics to submit to the truth or be killed. In its place, Spenser put a cooperative effort between the wise author Spenser and his most careful readers, on whom the enactment of his deconstructing fictional world of Faery world depends. This is being done on the basis of his Augustinian background in which no one could know the world as God had created it in his ontology. Therefore, the poet acknowledges his role as a creator of a *temporary* means of entertainment and instruction that can reconstruct in the epistemological minds of readers things that are impossible to encounter in the world of ontology to which the reader will be returned when the book is put down.[22]

---

22 This is the problem with reader response criticism as an approach to this particular poem. Reader response critics decide that the poem and the poet have not got complete control of the reader's mind. Spenser would admit this, as would I. But rather than submitting their reading to an author who can never complete the hermeneutic circle, reader response critics take the power of metaphysical judgment upon themselves, opening up their response to anything that occurs to them or their readers without reference to authorial intention.

In my reading of *The Faerie Queene*, Spenser acknowledges the reader's participation in the creation of meaning in the poem, but the poet's attempt is to subordinate the reader's response to an ordered but limited human reason based in memory of events that both the author and the careful reader can remember. This is a scientific process that relies on limited human memory, but it has several advantages. First, it brings rational discussion out of one's own metaphysically secure private language into a public space. Secondly, it limits the responses of readers to only those branches of thought that occur to them that both the reader and the writer can remember reading. This would make it less likely that Redcrosse is Santa Claus and more likely that he is aligned with Christ, but the complete identification of Redrosse with Christ leaves out the great differences between the two.

The defense of reader response criticism is surer in the scientific aesthetic than it is in the metaphysical aesthetic. In the public space, the better reader is he who can make sense of more of the evidence they have been presented with in the poem, and this is not necessarily the author in all cases. No one has all the information, and thus the process of reading can go on indefinitely by opening the floor to all comers. But some readings are much better than others, and it is the job of scientific criticism to sort good readings from bad.

Even though I would defend reader response as a proper province of the critic, what

Within the protected boundaries of Spenser's artificially-constructed fiction, Charissa does manage to give Redcrosse some useful information that can be imitated by the careful reader. After instructing him in "in euery good behest, / Of loue, and righteousnesse, and well to donne" (I.x.33.3-4), Charissa tells Redcrosse to shun "wrath, and hatred," for individual wrath draws "on men Gods hatred, and his wrath" (I.x.33.5). Only after she has made this clear can Charissa "From thence to heauen...[teach] him the ready path" (I.x.33.9).

Mercie

Charissa calls Mercie "his weaker wandring steps to guyde" (I.x.34.1) and

> To leade aright, that he should neuer fall
> In all his wayes through this wide worldes waue,
> That Mercy in the end his righteous soule might saue. (I.x.34.7-9)

The immediate gratification of victory that Redcrosse has been looking for throughout his adventures is postponed to an indefinite future in "the end." Mankind can only *hope* for salvation from God, a thing that Spenser is able to fix by his ability to create metaphysical truth in his fiction.

A paradox arises from the subsequent behavior of Mercie that calls for the reader's attention. In the Cave of Despair, Una ignored the "ragged clouts" and "thornes" (I.ix.36.1-2) that hung about Despair, because she does not feel that they are merely accidents. This is why Una's only advice to Redcrosse is to urge him not to get distracted by such accidents, which have no bearing on God's choice of him as His hero, and to get on with his preordained mission already. It appears by the subsequent action of Mercie that Una has been wrong. Mercie does not ignore the "bushy thornes, and ragged breares" (I.x.35.3) that hang about Redcrosse as Una had. Instead, she "remou'd [them] away" (I.x.35.3-4); and again, unlike Una, who expects Redcrosse to be able to support himself on his own, Mercie "held him fast, and firmely did vpbeare, / As carefull Nourse her child from falling oft does reare" (I.x.35.8-9).

Mercie then leads Redcrosse to a hospital where seven bead-men had dedicated themselves to the needy. The first of them is the eldest and the

---

is true of literary critics is certainly not true of characters within Spenser's poem, who are dealing with definite circumstances in which making a good or bad decision will have a long tail of consequences.

best (I.x.37.1). His job is to stand as "Guardian and Steward of the rest" (I.x.37.3). His office is "to giue entertainement / And lodging, vnto all that came, and went" (I.x.37.4-5). After meeting all seven beadmen, Redcrosse is returned to greet the first, and there he rests the "more hable he might bee" (I.x.45.2). This is a comment of his restless activity of the previous nine cantos in which Redcrosse had traveled through the world in search of adventure. He had done so with a seriousness of purpose, so much so that among his adventures is one with Sansjoy, whom he pointedly defeats without any joy within himself. Spenser's point seems to be that both instruction *and* entertainment are required in the educative process, as Horace held in his work. These were staples of a Renaissance education.

While Redcrosse is too serious in his pursuit of his ends, the poet, who has derived his hero from the comical genre of the provincial morality play, has a wider perspective on the events he is narrating. Spenser has given up sermonizing for a more entertaining tale to make the same point. Therefore the poet populates his entertaining poem with a knight who *seems* "Full jolly" (I.i.1.8) but who "of his cheere did seeme too solemne sad" (I.i.2.8).

Mercie puts his time at rest to profitable use, instructing him "in euery good behest / And godly worke of Almes and charitee" (I.x.45.3-4). He now becomes "perfect" (I.x.45.6)

> from the first vnto the last degree,
> His mortall life he learned had to frame
> In holy righteousnesse, without rebuke or blame. (I.x.45.7-9)

While the reader has no reason to doubt that this is true, they have previously heard the claim of Fidelia that Redcrosse is perfect at I.x.21.3. The question is whether his perfection is really complete now, or whether it is only complete in terms of Mercie's perspective.

As Redcrosse will continue to make mistakes in judgment in his meeting with Contemplation, it appears that Mercie has amplified Redcrosse's mind even beyond Fidelia's perfection, but to make a metaphysical end of a relative experience would be a mistake. The Book of Holinesse ends only after Redcrosse defeats that Dragon who is oppressing Una's parents. Therefore, the careful reader may be grateful that Redcrosse has finally started learning the lessons that will get him through to his ultimate end, but that end comes elsewhere than here. But before he travels back to the literal world where he will enact the potential that he has encountered here, he is led to meet Contemplation, who will adapt Redcrosse to his situation in important ways.

Reorienting Redcrosse

Spenser derives the character of Contemplation from Aristotle, who featured contemplation as the cardinal intellectual virtue in his *Nichomachean Ethics*.[1] Rather than finding the end of life in individual self-sufficiency, as existentialists in the modern day do, Aristotle returned the energy of the contemplators outwards again to the building up a society that could take the gifts of a hostile nature and *improve* them through art. For this reason, he found the end of individual human experience in those few rich men who had the leisure to devote to the activity of contemplation. While this might seem a perfect system for feudal monarchies to build upon, as it gave the wealthy few a reason to maintain rigid class distinctions, it led to the disenfranchisement of large swaths of the citizenry as lesser others in an ordered society, and this included bourgeois poets like Chaucer and Spenser himself.

It was into the breach of Aristotle's alienation of power from the many to a few wealthy contemplators that Augustine asserted a substantial consciousness as a popular remedy that could extend intellectual activity and political control beyond a few increasingly decadent Roman oligarchs and teachers. *Each* human being had the potential to be Aeneas, and *each* human being could enact their own heroic role without the interference of a tradition that lay outside the control of individuals *and moreover was fictional*, relying on philosophically problematic notion of escape to a stable world of λόγος, while leaving the world of individual mankind behind. The pagan configuration of the universe fed the lower appetites of indi-

---

1 See my discussion of Aristotle's *Nichomachean Ethics* in the chapter "Reading Allegory from New Margins."

vidual epicurean pleasure at the expense of the larger concerns of society and instead placed men on a socially destructive path.

Spenser's Introduction of Contemplation

Like many of the characters the reader meets in the House of Holinesse, Contemplation may be compared with characters that we have already met. His location is comparable to the location of Archimago, as Contemplation occupies a sacred chapel on top of a steep hill (I.x.46.2), whereas the hermitage of Archimago lies in a "dale." Both are off-center in the universe. Spenser also likens Contemplation to Corceca, as he has "earthly eien both blunt and bad" (I.x.47.3) as a result of his contemplative activity.

In spite of such similarities, differences are also important in Spenser's poem. Corceca is completely blind, not only to physical world available to the sight, but also to the immoral reality of her own behavior. Archimago is in many ways worse. He is a man who is using his clearer sight to manipulate the world for advantage over others. But at the same time, Archimago is also a man who reacts to non-existent things (like his creation of the False Una's beauty or his rousal of Morpheus from his moral neutrality) as though they were ontologically real but without reference to God's *a priori* creation.

Contemplation, by contrast, is looking inward towards things that he cannot see in the empirical world (the realm of ontology) but which do exist to the properly-trained mind's eye (the realm of epistemology). And unlike Corceca's blind eyes, Contemplation's intellectual eye is "wondrous quick and persaunt" (I.x.47.5), and the poet likens his eyes to an "Eagles eye, that can behold the Sunne" (I.x.47.6). Unlike Corceca and Archimago, Contemplation has his intellectual eyes set on Heaven, rather than on the lower matter of gaining an advantage over others in the world, and he "Ne other worldly busines did apply" (I.x.46.7). This more correct orientation of his sight gives him a decided advantage over either of these two characters.

Spenser's message seems to be that, if Redcrosse wants to join the court of Gloriana, he should use his trained intellect, rather than viewing the superficial open body of Fidessa that is available to his impatient eye. As soon as he does so, Una will become an object of his contemplative desire. But Redcrosse is not there yet.

Contemplation Snubs the Man of Action

Spenser's reliance on Augustine explains the element of snobbishness in his portrait of Contemplation, who accepts Una on account of his knowledge that she belongs here (as Humiltá had) but is dismissive of Redcrosse (as Cælia had been). Redcrosse's end is elsewhere, and Contemplation seems to know it. When he sees Una and Redcrosse approaching, he is "agrieued sore" (I.x.49.2), for they "forst him lay his heauenly thoughts aside" (I.x.49.3). It is only out of respect for Una, whom we are told "highly he did reuerence and adore" (I.x.49.5), that he deigns to speak with either of them. The clear implication is that he would "not once have moued" (I.x.49.6) if the worldly knight had approached him alone.

The old hermit asks them "what end they clomb that tedious height" (I.x.49.9). The careful reader must once again be suspicious when Una answers

> What end (quoth she) should cause vs take such paine,
> But that same end, which euery liuing wight
> Should make his marke, high heauen to attaine? (I.x.50.1-3)

She thinks it obvious that every living person should point themselves towards "high heaven,"[2] but in her focus on the "end" of "heaven" she misses the way that Redcrosse must attain it. She must stand aside, as he is the actor who must fulfill her potential in what she still thinks of as the "extremitie of time," where things have a tendency to get detoured, lengthened, and amplified rather than closing in on an immediate end.

Contemplation responds, still not speaking to Redcrosse but to Una,

> Thrise happy man, said then the father graue,
> Whose staggering steps thy steady hand doth lead,
> And shewes the way, his sinfull soule to saue.
> Who better can the way to heauen aread,
> Then thou thy selfe, that was both borne and bred
> In heauenly throne, where thousand Angels shine?
> Thou doest the prayers of the righteous sead
> Present before the maiestie diuine,
> And his auenging wrath to clemencie incline. (I.x.51)

---

[2] In my reading, there are two heavens, an ontologically real Heaven and an epistemologically available but temporary heaven. Una's usage of "heaven" is not fully differentiated by her application of "high" to heaven, and the reader must remain aware of potential differences in her words here.

Contemplation clearly believes that Redcrosse is lucky to have Una as his guide, because she can turn God's avenging wrath to clemency. But Redcrosse will take another message from his adventure, and this will limit the scope of Contemplation's words here. First, he will not be the "Thrise happy man" that Contemplation, who is still talking to Una, assumes, until he has defeated the Dragon outside the walls of Eden. And even after that, he will meet the Palmer, who will congratulate him on having achieved sainthood. At that time, Redcrosse will defer the crown of triple happiness to the Palmer, who he tells that he (the Palmer) "may report thrise happie newes" (II.i.33.8), because "For all I did, I did but as I ought" (II.i.33.5), but the Palmer "can wish [his] thought" (II.i.33.7). The process of deferring action to others (a=b) and so lengthening his experience is not a step that the "clownishe younge man" is prepared to take at this point, however, as he is still a character tempted by his own penchant for extremity. He falls back into despair here, even after the reader has been told (and more than once) that he is perfect.

More Correction of Errant Redcrosse

Just as he had taken the rusty knife from Despair upon hearing his life put in God-like perspective, when Contemplation shows him the vertical path that angels tread between the holy city of Jerusalem and the earth, he once again overextends himself through his pride:

> Till now, said then the knight, I weened well,
> That great *Cleopolis*, where I haue beene,
> In which that fairest *Fary Queene* doth dwell,
> The fairest Citiee was, that might be *seene*. (I.x.58.1-4 italics mine)

But on seeing the city of Jerusalem presented to his sight, he has been disabused of this notion:

> But now by proofe all otherwise I weene;
> For this great Citty that does far surpas,
> And this bright Angels towre quite dims that towre of glas.
> (I.x.58.7-9)

It falls to blunt-eyed Contemplation to correct him. It is not for him to tread such a direct path to Heaven; that path is reserved exclusively for Una and the angels. The best he can do is to hope for glory in the world itself:

> Most trew, then said the holy aged man;

> Yet is *Cleopolis* for earthly frame,
> The fairest peece, that eie beholden can:[3]
> And well beseemes all knights of noble name,
> That couet in th'immortall booke of fame
> To be eternized, that same to haunt,
> And doen their seruice to that soueraigne Dame,
> That glorie does to them for guerdon graunt:
> For she is heauenly borne, and heauen may iustly vaunt. (I.x.59)

He acknowledges that Redcrosse must go back to the world to do

>   thy seruice for her grace,
> To aide a virgin desolate foredonne.
> But when thou famous victorie hast wonne,
> And high emongst all knights hast hong thy shield,
> Thenceforth the suitt of earthly conquest shonne,
> And wash thy hands from guilt of bloody field:
> For bloud can nought but sin, and wars but sorrowes yield.
> (I.x.60.3-9)

Only after his adventures in the world are completed should he come back to this place to gain his reward:

> Then seeke this path, that I to thee presage,
> Which after all to heauen shall thee send;
> Then peaceably thy painefull pilgrimage
> To yonder same *Hierusalem* do bend,
> Where is for thee ordaind a blessed end. (I.x.61.1-5)

The meaning of these passages is radically unclear. Contemplation seems to mean that the "desolate virgin" Una is born in heaven and that he should serve her before bending his mind towards his "blessed end" in Jerusalem. But this would decenter the self-centered Redcrosse (not in itself a bad thing) in favor of an end that can only be had in fiction. That would thwart *the poet's goal* and the *careful reader's expectation* of having Redcrosse enact the potential contained in Una.

---

3 This line makes me wonder what Redcrosse is looking at with his eyes if he cannot see what he is clearly seeing. The answer seems to be that Contemplation knows that his universe is a fictional one that will not survive deconstruction as well as the "earthly frame" of the literal Redcrosse will. Redcrosse himself will not survive the deconstruction of Spenser's fictional world. But before he deconstructs, he will learn that he is the key to opening up heaven through the process of his literal humanness. The poet will then defer the process of accomplishment from Redcrosse's inimitable life to the as-yet-unaccomplished future of the reader, lengthening the process of reading his poem indefinitely.

On the other hand, as happened when he and Arthur were talking at cross purposes in their diverse discourse, it appears that Redcrosse hears Contemplation say that he should return to *Gloriana*. So sure is Contemplation of that fact that he should be in charge of mankind that he does not check that his pronoun-laden speech has been taken as he meant it to be taken. But careful readers should consider the implication that Contemplation, who would have ignored the warrior altogether if it were not for the presence of an also fictional Una, may not know of Una's attachment to Redcrosse. If he is a creature like Charissa, who does not give any thought to the role of Cupid in binding Una to Redcrosse in what he, too, thinks of only as the "extremitie of time," it would be up to Una to tell him of her feelings for her beloved. As it is, Una has remained silent on that point.

Despite that fact that Contemplation's chapel is as off-center as Archimago's hermitage is from the point of view of the literal human being who occupies the center of Spenser's poem, the upward and vertical orientation of his thought should not be overturned for the Godless freedom of Archimago to do with the scientific world whatever he wishes.[4] Contemplation still has a lot to recommend him over Archimago. But in spite of the poet's favoring of Contemplation over Archimago, Contemplation is not an end unto himself; and the deferral of the end of experience away from Contemplation to the still ignorant Redcrosse comes with problems of its own.

The Naming Scene

Spenser deflects his readers from Contemplation's inability to resolve the reader's doubts about Redcrosse's "blessed end" by introducing one of the most interesting details about the knight's existence, when he says:

---

[4] This is my reading of modern culture's take on the death of God, which has given mankind a sense of existential freedom. Existentialism relies on some questionable premises, including the notion that the universe is balanced, that the microscopic mind (epistemology) contains a perfect representation of the macrocosmic universe (ontology), that all choices we make are equal, and all we have to do to regain our heroic status is to find suppressed values in what others have written and raise them back to a position of dominance.

I have been attempting to demonstrate that this is not the case with Spenser's poem, where there has been no death of God, but where there is also no way of verifying His existence except by faith. This causes mankind to switch from relying on *a priori* principles of identity (a=a) to principles of likeness built up through an *a posteriori* education (a=b relations). In Spenser's universe, the inequalities of the world are so glaringly obvious that only a "clownishe" simpleton like Redcrosse could ignore them. This is the lesson that self-centered and overly confident Redcrosse will learn before his adventure is over, but he has not learned at this point of his journey.

> And thou faire ymp, sprong out from English race,
> How euer now accompted Elfins sonne,
> Well worthy doest thy service for her grace,
> To aide a virgin desolate fordonne. (I.x.60.1-4)

It turns out that Redcrosse is a member of the human race, and this is why he is especially worthy of doing service to "her grace." This bit of news must come as a shock to Redcrosse, who has been thinking, not just since the reader met him but for his whole life, that he was an elf.

Contemplation goes on to say that he will be remembered as a saint, but his sainthood will not remembered by his figural name of Redcrosse but by his literal name of George:

> For thou emongst those Saints, whom thou doest see,
> Shalt be a Saint, and thine owne nations frend
> And Patrone: thou Saint George shalt called bee,
> Saint George of mery England, the signe of victoree. (I.x.61.6-9)

The late naming of Redcrosse as the human George, who the poet has referred to as recently as I.x.44.1 as an "Elfin knight," brings up one of the most vexing points in the modern reading of *The Faerie Queene*: why has Spenser, who has always known the human origin of Redcrosse, gone to such lengths to hide this fact from his readers?

Rereading the Naming Scene

In *The Spenser Encyclopedia*, Herbert Marks and Kenneth Gross[5] note the sources of the naming conventions in the medieval quest-romance:

> Perhaps the most striking feature of Spenser's name poetry, one he inherits from the tradition of chivalric quest-romance, is the carefully delayed revelation of a name. Beyond producing a common sort of narrative suspense, such delay opens a space of speculative trial for the reader, a studied uncertainty which enlarges the range of the allegorical figures.[6]

---

[5] Gross has written to my mind the best and most original work on Spenser in his *Spenserian Poetics: Idolatry, Iconoclasm, and Magic* (Ithaca, N.Y.: Cornell University Press, 1985). Though I disagree with him on some key points, it is my favorite work of criticism on Spenser's poem, not only for its very insightful readings, but also for its ability to throw whole boxes of wrenches into the standard reading of the poem.

[6] "Names, naming," in Hamilton, *The Spenser Encyclopedia*, 494b.

This is a standard feature of postmodern reading, as it allows the reader to delay the closure of the creation of poets until the critic has reached the poet's end in λόγος. Since the postmoderns do not *recognize* the reality of the λόγος, they turn from the delay of the end to a never-ending openness to new meanings that can never be closed on account of their fundamental belief that there is nothing more beneath experience than a "primal chaos beneath linguistic flux."[7]

Marks and Gross continue beyond the traditional noting of sources to point out some oddities about Spenserian naming conventions. For instance, they note that very often, and not just in this one instance of Redcrosse being renamed George, naming comes only *after* the poet has drawn the reader into a web of artificially-created meaning:

> In Book i, for example, the 'wandring wood' is not so identified until questers and readers have succumbed to its dangers (i 13); the name Una is not revealed until the creation of a false double puts its meaning at risk (i 45); the giant Orgoglio, first defined by his genealogy, is not actually named until after his battle with Redcrosse (vii 14); and Redcrosse himself learns his own name George, identifying him as both warrior saint and fallen man (from Gr *gēorgos* 'plowman, worker of the earth'), only following the successful completion of his preliminary trials and purification at the house of Holiness (x 66). The force of these delays usually depends on some image (semantic or phonic) planted in the preceding narrative, which seems in retrospect to determine the name.[8]

This reversal of the normal rules that obtain in ordinary life, which was papered over or ignored by Modern critics, puzzles these postmodern critics, as well.

Before we get to the explanation of what is going on in Spenser's unusual narrative, I feel is necessary to insert a delay of my own in order to note an instance where these postmodern critics overlook something obvious because it fits in with their own *a priori* disposition towards poetry but which is not in fact motivated by anything in the text itself. This is their noting that "Redcrosse himself learns his own name George" in the House

---

7 Ibid., 495a. Marks and Gross draw their insights by citing parallels from Ovid, of whom this delaying tactic is undoubtedly true. I believe that Spenser is following Augustine's correction to the ambiguity and imprecision within the pagan world, where it was left up to a completely arbitrary individual decision whether someone would posit a possibly non-existent λόγος, a life of decadent epicurean pleasure, or an academic skepticism as the philosophic "end" of their own life.

8 Ibid., 494b.

of Holinesse. This is certainly not true, as George must have always known himself by the name that his parents raised him with. It is also true that this bit of information is not new to the reader, who has been informed of the identity of the "true Saint George" as long ago as I.ii.12.2.

In pointing Redcrosse back to his given name of George, Contemplation means to redirect Redcrosse back to his literal name, out of which he is capable of acting from his presence in the world, and away from a figural name that conceals as much as it reveals to him about his potential for action in that same literal world. Una's rechristening of George with a figural name that makes the lowly "clownishe" man into the exalted figure of Redcrosse is so tempting that he takes hold of it; but it is important to remember that Una's action in renaming him suppresses, but does not eliminate, knowledge of his "clownishe" nature, not only from George, who has no education that would tell him otherwise, but also from Una's experience with him. The same thing holds true of literary critics who attempt to read *The Faerie Queene* from a metaphysical perspective, rather from the limited, literal perspective of science. They are masking from themselves the relative values that Spenser is trying to point them towards.

Freudian Dream Work

Marks and Gross go on to locate what they believe is the source for this major shift, which had eluded previous critics, in the imposition of names that underlies all naming in the poem:

> Within the phantasmagoric world of the text, names come to resemble the 'switch-words' of the 'verbal bridges' of the Freudian dream work. Determined by a process of condescension, they are the poem's 'nodal points,' specific sites of intersection for an indefinite number of associative paths, some of which are motivated by phonetic, others by semantic echoes. And because they point backward and forward simultaneously, they exercise a continually unsettling effect on the progressive or teleological movement of the narrative.[9]

In their identification of "nodal points," where names sport an ability to point "backward and forward" and so to have an "unsettling effect on the progressive or teleological movement of the narrative," they have hit on something real. But like DeNeef, who stops at the borders of modern criticism in his exploration of the poem without identifying a whole reading of the poem, Marks and Gross stop their inquiry into Spenser's poem as soon

---

9 Ibid., 495b.

as they have found what their *a priori* assumptions say *The Faerie Queene* should be telling them. Since they apparently believe in Freud's intellectual construction of the universe, they stop at their identification of "switch-words" that act as "verbal bridges" in "the Freudian dream work" where they are finally resolved.

In other words, Marks and Grosse are resolving the problem of reference, not in the rational consciousness of humanity, but in the malleable human capacity to dream. This dream capacity had allowed Freud to continue the Enlightenment configuration of the universe by pushing the "wholeness" of the Enlightenment underground into a suppressed consciousness or an suppressed id, while configuring reason as nothing more than a repressive ego. Freud wanted to release the suppressed id from the repressive rational ego in order to recover the "whole" person. In Spenser's poem, this same system would release the socially destructive animal behavior of Redcrosse and suppress the very reason that Spenser is pointing to as the solution to the problems he has raised. As a result, Augustine's picture of the limitations of reason that had caused him to invent the substantial consciousness (in opposition to the λόγος) as the locus of human behavior remains suppressed in Marks and Gross' Freudian reading of the poem.[10]

The Purge of Figural Meaning in the Naming Scene

Precision in the face of pagan and Christian doubt is what Spenser is after in his poem, but he does not allow George to participate in such precision. Instead, George asks another question of Contemplation, and once again the object he is referring to is not perfectly clear:

> Vnworthy wretch (quoth he) of so great grace,
> How dare I thinke such glory to attaine? (I.x.62.1-2)

This should be taken as an indication that he has never understood the meaning of the armor that Una granted him at the beginning of the poem, which symbolizes the fact that he has been saved from his birth. Una's

---

10 Careful readers of Spenser's work will want to take a look at Stephen Greenblatt's chapter on Spenser in his *Renaissance Self-Fashioning*, 157-192, for a differing view of what is going on in Spenser's poem. Greenblatt makes the case that he (Greenblatt) has raised sexuality to the fore on account of Spenser's prudish repression of sex in a largely arbitrary and so reversible act of power. While this reading also follows from Freud's post-Enlightenment modernism, it is, in my opinion, a misreading of Spenser's poem, which I obviously see as a scientific and relative Augustinian reaction against exactly such a metaphysical position that had been taken long before Greenblatt or modernism by Ariosto and Tasso.

magical armor merely externalizes that fact for the sake of the reader.

George's lack of knowledge about his true condition might explain why he reacts with a blitheness of spirit that shows him to be happy, even after his painful correction in the House of Holinesse, as he differentiates himself from

> These that haue it attaind, were in like cace
> (Quoth he) as wretched, and liu'd in like paine. (I.x.62.3-4)[11]

And he is still happily focused on arms, which up to this point he has been thinking were the key to his end. He now considers with some incredulity the prospect of giving them up, as if for the first time:

> But deeds of armes must I at last be faine,
> And Ladies loue to leaue so dearely bought? (I.x.62.5-6)

One must wonder once again about Una's reaction to this bit of news, as George considers the prospect of giving up "Ladies loue"; but, of course, he probably means giving up Fidessa's love, which he has "dearely bought," and not Una's love, which he has not worked for and has given no indication that he returns. As Una remains silent, the reader, as always, is left guessing at her reaction.

Contemplation responds to Redcrosse's lingering attachment to arms:

> What need of armes, where peace doth ay remaine,
> (Said he) and battailes none are to be fought?
> As for loose loues they are vaine, and vanish into nought. (I.x.62.7-9)

Arms, as "loose loues," in Contemplation's mind are but instruments of worldly glory. George immediately (and still rather predictably) follows his lead and turns away from the temptations of the world, resolving to end his journey here:

> O let me not (quoth he) then turne againe
> Backe to the world, whose ioyes so fruitlesse are;
> But let me heare for aye in peace remaine,

---

11 The fact that he was shown to be "too solemne sad" at I.i.2.8 must either indicate a change of mind on his part or (as I am inclined to believe) a poor job of hiding his feelings in the face of his knowing how inappropriate his joy at having been given such a great adventure by Gloriana would appear to others.

> Or streight way on that last long voyage fare,
> That nothing may my present hope empare. (I.x.63.1-5)

This is a mistake that even Contemplation recognizes, as it substitutes the immediate access to his end—the same thing that made him take up the rusty knife from the hand of Despair and turn it on himself—for the *lengthening* of his life which puts the end of his life as far into the future as possible. Should he substitute such an immediate end for an end put off into a still uncertain future, he would not go back to kill the Dragon, nor would his marriage to Una ever take place. All would be lost.

This is why Contemplation instantly responds to George's plan to stop here in no uncertain terms:

> That may not be (said he) ne maist thou yitt
> Forgoe that royall maides bequeathed care,
> Who did her cause into thy hand committ,
> Till from her cursed foe thou haue her freely quit. (I.x.63.6-9)

And once again, the careful reader will have noted that Contemplation is inviting him back here after he has been quit of his obligation to "that royall maide." But who George understands to be the referent of "that," and why Contemplation invites him to settle with him and not with *Una*, remains a mystery.

Changelings and Kings in Spenser's World of "Faery Theft"

Spenser, who has repeatedly referred to George as Redcrosse and his race as elfin, is complicit in the deception that has been foisted on the reader. What the reader might have thought was a metaphysical description of their hero turns out to be the relative and scientific perspective of Redcrosse's imperfect view of his own experience. This robs Spenser's entire narrative, whether he is speaking of the literal name of George or the figural name of Redcrosse, of any secure metaphysical foundation in ontology. Contemplation does not feed into that narrative deception, telling George that he is not alone in thinking he is something he is not: "Such men," he tells him, "do Chaungelings call, so chaungd by Faeries theft" (I.x.65.9).

We begin to find clues to Spenser's purpose in robbing both the figural and the literal from any foundation in ontological reality in what follows:

> Thence she thee brought into this Faery lond,
> And in an heaped furrow did thee hyde,

> Where thee a Ploughman all vnweeting fond,
> As he his toylesome teme that way did guyde,
> And brought thee vp in ploughmans state to byde,
> Whereof *Georgos* he thee gave to name. (I.x.66.1-5)

It is he (Spenser) who has hidden George's identity "in an heaped furrow" (his allegory of *The Faerie Queene*). He has only at this late date fully revealed Redcrosse's identity to his readers, and only to the careful ones who have followed the poet's ability to gather up a series of separate experiences into their memories and sort out exactly what is going in the poem rather than following Redcrosse into a situation where they judge things at once before all the possible information has become available to them.

As he does so, Spenser has Contemplation offer a new prize to George, one that the poet designs to make worldly-focused George want to go back to earth. This is the notion that he is descended from a long line of "*Saxon kinges*" (I.x.65.2). This raises George above his lineage as a mere plowman and sets him alongside other worthy men who have been allowed membership in Gloriana's court, not through education, but by birth.

Of course, this completely obviates the possibility that he could ever join himself to Gloriana physically. It also alienates manly George from the heaven-born Una, who nevertheless will later remind him of his obligation to return to the world to fight for her greater glory. And as he distances his hero from Una, Spenser alienates George from any reader who would wish to imitate him by tying him to the royal house, which would bring them before a royal court for treason on charges of pretending.

Contemplation Mistakes George's New Purpose for Pride

Even after he has been named George and his status in the world has been reversed from elf to human and from low shepherd to descendant of the ancient house of British royalty through the process of an intermediary fiction, George still shows too much pride for Contemplation's taste. Contemplation has always known that it was George's courage, and not out of any respect for contemplative activity (that Aristotle had elevated to the "end" of human experience), that George had come to court:

> prickt with courage, and thy forces pryde,
> To Fary court thou cam'st to seeke for fame,
> And proue thy puissaunt armes, as seemes thee best became.
> (I.x.66.7-9)

Contemplation had hoped that George's visit to his chapel would reorient him away from his socially destructive behavior to a more contemplative existence. In many ways, it has. But Contemplation does not pay enough attention to needs for constant vigilance and positive action in the world to which he is sending his charge.

As such, George's vision on the Mount of Contemplation is another step towards his realization that his earlier motivations that "seemed" so real were in fact false:

> O holy Sire (quoth he) how shall I quight
> The many fauours I with thee haue found,
> That hast my name and nation redd aright,
> And taught the way that does to heauen bownd? (I.x.67.1-4)

George will use Contemplation's correct reading of his "name and nation" to go back to Gloriana, for there he thinks is the way to Heaven. This is not how Contemplation imagines George's journey ending, as in his mind George is meant to contribute to the joining of potential to action in his contemplative being. Instead, the poet's focus turns to Redcrosse as the human being who will activate the potential of Una on the literal plane of existence, and Contemplation is no longer central to George's experience.

And yet, it is only now, *for the first time in the book*, that he

> adowne…looked to the ground,
> To haue returnd, but dazed were his eyne,
> Through passing brightnes, which did quite confound
> His feeble sence, and too exceeding shyne.
> So darke are earthly things compard to things diuine. (I.x.67.5-9)

At last, he has learned the lesson of Saint Paul that human beings can glimpse the truth through a glass, if only darkly.

George Returns to Una

George goes back to Una, "who him ioyd to see" (I.x.68.6)—I note that there is still no sign of his returning her affection—and there is still no indication that he has received any inner motivation to guide his wandering steps. *Una* still has to remind him of his obligation to perform his worldly deeds:

> And after litle rest, gan him desire,
> Of her aduenture myndfull for to bee. (I.x.68.7-8)

George's ability to use on his memory is still not his strong suit, and he must rely on Una to guide him to the location where he will fulfil his place in sacred history. But at last, after having been guaranteed a place in Gloriana's court without any of the education that Arthur has been impressing on him as necessary to be a functioning member of court, he submits to her will, once again following Una out of another detour on the way to his final goal on the literal plane of allegory.

Science Outside the Walls of Eden

Una Gets Her Way at Last

Una has been itching for her Redcrosse Knight to take up the fight with the Dragon that placed her parents behind the brazen walls of Eden since she met him. Here at last, she gets her way:

> High time now gan it wex for *Vna* fayre,
> To thinke of those her captiue Parents deare,
> And their forwasted kingdome to repayre. (I.xi.1.1)

The poet's phrasing here deserves note. "High time" is a phrase that has the meaning of "high purpose" but also may contain the colloquial meaning of "about time." Nevertheless, Una gives voice to a direct expression of love for her beloved, a thing which she has failed to do even once until now:

> Deare knight, as deare, as euer knight was deare,
> That all these sorrowes suffer for my sake,
> High heuen behold the tedious toyle, ye for me take. (I.xi.1.7-9)

It may not surprise the reader that that, even after having passed through the House of Holinesse, George does not return her expression of affection for him.

The Return to Una's Native Soil

Una expresses her relief that they have finally arrived on her "natiue soyle / And to the place, where all our perilles dwell" (I.xi.2.1-2). There is, once again, a hidden warning here about the limit of Una's understanding.

She had been forced to leave Eden on account of the fact that her "natiue soyle" has not been enough to guarantee its own safety, and neither she nor her parents have the ability to defeat the Dragon on their own. She does not consider the fact that while all *her* perils dwell in the fictionally-constructed Eden, not all of "*our* perilles" (italics mine) dwell there after the Fall. The possibility that George and Una are not even now on the same page apparently does not occur to Una. Behind these verses is an implicit recognition on the part of the poet of a distinction between Una's native condition and her need to extend herself beyond Eden to find a literal individual to do her fighting for her. I take this is an indication that whatever Una thinks, her troubles will not end after George defeats the Dragon.

Whatever her weaknesses, Una urges George to excel himself:

> The sparke of noble corage now awake,
> And striue your excellent selfe to excel. (I.xi.2.6-7)[1]

The careful reader is well aware that George's human "selfe" alone is not adequate to the task of defeating the Dragon any more than Una and her parents are all by themselves; and, as she invites him to fight, she shows herself conscious of George's true motivations, which still, despite his education in the House of Holinesse, may have nothing to do with his having been pointed towards the truth, but has everything to do with his continuing quest for fame:

> That shall ye euermore renowmed make,
> Aboue all knights on earth, that batteill vndertake. (I.xi.3.8-9)

Whether or not the two are on the same page, the time has come for the battle to begin.

Invoking Clio

Una is decentered from the action of the poem, as George asks her to stand upon a hill "a litle wide" (I.xi.5.5); and once again, we shift from the perspective of Una to the poet, who invokes the principles of space and time in invoking Clio as his muse. Clio is the muse of history, daughter of Apollo, the god of the daylight sun, and Mnemosyne, the nurse of time and

---

[1] These lines are interesting. Line 6 leaves open the possibility that Una thinks that his previous adventures lacked "noble corage." Line 7 leaves open the possibility that even now, after the reader has been told repeatedly that he is "perfect," he could excel his already "excellent selfe."

everlasting fame:

> Now O thou sacred Muse, most learned Dame,
> Faire ympe of *Phoebus*, and his aged bride,
> The Nourse of time, and euerlasting fame,
> That warlike hands ennobles with immortal name. (I.xi.5.6-8)

But the poet adds that he wants Clio to leave her furious fits aside, and here Spenser seems to address what the careful reader has seen as George's worst aspect, his martial fury:

> O gently come into my feeble brest,
> Come gently, but not with that mighty rage,
> Wherewith the martiall troupes thou doest infest,
> And harts of great Heroes doest enrage
> That nought their kindled courage may aswage,
> Soone as thy dreadfull trompe begins to sownd;
> The God of warre with his fiers equipage
> Thou doest awake, sleepe neuer he so sownd,
> And scared nations doest with horrour sterne astownd. (I.xi.6)

In doing so the poet hopes to pass over in himself the fault of rage that the reader has seen manifested again and again in George, but whether Spenser's invoking of Clio without rage will quell *George's* rage or only the *poet's rage* in his telling of his tale remains to be seen.

In sounding the notes of war, the poet uses a reference to polyphonic music, asking that Clio raise the poet's song to her "second tenor":

> But now a while let downe that haughtie string,
> And to my tunes thy second tenor rayse,
> That I this man of God his godly armes may blaze. (I.xi.7.7-9)

The poet's request to raise his voice to the "second tenor" of a polyphonic chorus is related to the poet's recognition that Clio has control of events and that is the poet's role to play his part in the larger whole, and that the second part.

The Description of the Dragon

A lot of the Dragon fight is given over to what might be termed a scientific description of the monster's dimensions. Having said that, the poet is rather cagey about giving away the exact size of the ultimately fictional Dragon, whose "wast" is measured in terms of his shadow, which is "vast," and made more so by his "wrath, and poison, and with bloody gore" (I.xi.8.9). The Dragon is covered in "brazen scales" (I.xi.9.1), but they are only "*like* plated coats of steele" (I.xi.9.2 italics mine). Ovid's *Metamorphoses* is a major source of this idea. In Ovid's four historical periods, the golden age gives way to silver, silver gives way to bronze, and bronze gives way to iron.[2] In Ovid's universe the age of iron brings forth "evil." Modesty, truth and faith fled the earth, and in their place came tricks, plots, snares, violence and the love of gain. As a result, mankind was dispersed, and "[Men] spread sails to the winds," though the direction the winds would take them and their source remained "still a mystery / To sailors."[3]

The pagan Ovid hoped for a return to the golden age in which mankind and nature could be restored to their initial state of equity.[4] In the Christian age, Spenser knows that even *wishing* for such a thing is a sin. In Spenser's *Faerie Queene*, however, there are compensating advantages for the fall from grace. Sacred history has moved on from Ovid's original story, and mankind now lives in an age in which iron has been tempered into an even harder steel. George actually has on steel armor, not the weaker metal bronze that the Dragon's scales are made of and are merely *likened* to steel.

Furthermore, the Dragon's "wast" has grown fat by feeding on others. Since he feasts on the easy pickings of humanity, he does not have to fly too often. As a result, his wings find "vnwonted passage" when he beats them "by force" (I.xi.10.7). The "clowdes before him fled for terror great / And all the heuens stood still amazed with his threat" (I.xi.10.8-9), which is to say that he does not have to *act* in order to strike terror into the hearts of men. Much, if not all, of the Dragon's threat comes from his mere presence, and it is *that* which causes Heaven to stand "still," men to be "amazed," and the clouds to disperse. As a result of his laziness, his tail is "wound vp in hundred foldes" (I.xi.11.1). The poet's fear of the Dragon's iron teeth is real, but the Dragon's breath, which seems "still," is acting on the "cold congealed feare" it breeds in the heart of mankind and not on the basis of anyone's having tested it.

The Dragon's scales are like armor (I.xi.9.1-4), to which the poet adds a simile to indicate the vertical nature of the Dragon's strength: they are likened to the wings of an eagle (I.xi. 9.5). The reference points us back to Contemplation, whose eyes are "blunt and bad" (I.x.47.3) but are nevertheless likened to an "Eagles eye, that can behold the Sunne" (I.x.47.6). The

---

2 Ovid, *Metamorphoses*, I.89-151.
3 Ibid., 1.132-133, p. 8.
4 I remind my readers of my opinion that Rousseau was of like mind.

poet also provides the reader the horizontal nature of the Dragon's wings: they are likened to sails (I.xi.10.1), but they are sails with only a negative reference: they merely catch "the hollow wynd" (I.xi.10.2).[5]

When the Dragon's tail is spread, it "sweepeth all the land behind him farre" (I.xi.11.6). His head

>   my tongue to tell
> Does tremble: for his deepe deuouring iawes
> Wyde gaped, like the griesly mouth of hell,
> Through which into his darke abysse all rauin fell. (I.xi.12.6-9)

The Dragon's iron teeth, likewise, strike fear into the hearts of men of the instant death they bring with them. But George has been educated in patience in the House of Holinesse, and thus his former behavior of wishing to defeat his enemy at once has now been transferred to the Dragon:

> That sight thereof bred cold congealed feare:
> Which to increase, and as atonce to kill,
> A cloud of smoothering smoke and sulphur seare
> Out of his stinking gorge forth steemed still,
> That all the ayre about with smoke and stench did fill. (I.xi.13.5-9).

"Wrath" is another thing that things George had learned to control in the House of Holinesse. Before Una had brought him there, his wrath had caused him to misinterpret the ethical dimension of the world around him, causing him to engage Errour, to flee truth (Una), and embrace falseness (Duessa). Here, George's wrath is tamed.

In the following stanza, the poet likens the Dragon's eyes to "two broad Beacons, set in open fieldes" (I.xi.14.3) that

---

[5] In this example, I find one of the main reasons that deconstruction fails in an Augustinian universe. Such negative attributes may not be reversed to make positive somethings out of things that have not been suppressed but never existed in the first place. This is why it is a mistake to take Errour, Lucifera, Orgoglio, and Despair as seriously as Redcrosse does. One of these characters (Errour) is running away from Redcrosse, and it is he who chases her. He should have ignored her rather than attacking her. The others are reflections of Redcrosse's experience, which he mistakes as independent actors. All one has to do is to ignore those characters who are fleeing, to make a scientific estimate of the true power of one's positive enemies, and to correct oneself if, as is the case with Orgoglio, one finds that they are reflections of the fact that one has taken off one's armor. This is a matter of education that Spenser has been pushing from the beginning of his poem.

> Send forth their flames far off to euery shyre,
> And warning giue, that enemies conspyre,
> With fire and sword the region to inuade;
> So flam'd his eyne with rage and rancorous yre. (I.xi.14.4-7)

But the poet tells us that the real source of their power is not the broadcast of their power. Instead, it, lies "farre within, as in a hollow glade" (I.xi.14.8). Seen from within the perspective of the concavity of the valley—to which George had been contrasted with the mountainous shadow of the Dragon only 9 stanzas before (I.xi.8.5)—they are not "two bright shining shields" at all. They only represent "a dreadfull shade" (I.xi.14.9).

The poet's point here is not that the Dragon's eyes, teeth, and sting are not dangerous. The point is that George must make "triall" of the scientific universe that surrounds him and not to be intimidated by the possibility of the potential extension of the Dragon that is bred in the hearts of passive men. Sometimes things are not what they appear to be on first glance. The lessons for George are clear. He must learn to conquer his very real fear, but he must test his fear in the sphere of action rather than relying on the fear of potential harm that might come to him from an untested reality to avoid taking positive action. This will switch him out of the vertical axis of the Dragon, who operates through the extension of his vertically-oriented potential power, to the horizontal axis of man as actor in the world. This perspective revolves around a more rational view of the world as it is, and not as we fear it might be. This means that George must get an accurate picture of the Dragon's size before he acts without getting caught up in an interfering wrath and rage, as readers have seen him wont to do in the past.

Day One: The Fight Begins

When the fight begins, Spenser returns to his sense of spatial geometry in order to monitor the ethical dimension of the combatants. The Dragon hovers above the "subiect plaine" (I.xi.19.1), much as Orgoglio had inflated himself above the ground. Unlike his behavior with Orgoglio before he had been dragged by Una to her deconstructable heaven, George continues to fight, and "struggling strong did him at last constraine, / To let them downe before his flightes *end*" (I.xi.19.3-4 italics mine). By inviting the reader to notice that the Dragon is focused on his end, and that George brings him back to earth "before his flightes end," the poet continues to focus on lengthening rather than eliminating the middle space between the metaphysical poles of birth and death, for it is there that relief from the Dragon's power is needed.

Once again, the poet is reconfiguring the expectations of his readers. When George is lifted from the ground, he is lifted from what we now know is the source of his strength: the earth. However, the poet likens the attempts of the Dragon to fly away with George in his claw to an eagle who has gripped his prey but who cannot take off because his too-heavy prey is weighing him down: "Which comming down to ground, does free it selfe by fight" (I.xi.19.9). The poet's focus on his ethico-scientific metaphor brings up a legitimate question: is it really possible that the powerful Dragon, whose frame is so "vast" (I.xi.8.7) that it rivals a mountain to George's valley (I.xi.8.5), cannot even lift the armor-laden body of a man? The answer is clearly yes, if the Dragon has grown lazy and fat by feeding off the easy pickings of weak men.

As George attacks the Dragon, the poet tells his readers that his blows are equal to "three mens strength" (I.xi.20.4). That triune sense of strength carries the spiritual meaning to the reader; but it is not clear that George knows that his strength has been compared to the strength of 3 men and not, say, 2 or 3½ or 4 or 6 men. That does not mean that Spenser is engaging in a bit of meaningless poetic language in the passage. It means that Spenser and the reader are in on the metaphysics of the piece, but that George is not. This is because having faith is a given in an Augustinian universe. You either have it, or you do not. However, whether from the inside or the outside, it is impossible to tell whether a person has it or not.

In a universe in which people must build a community with others (a=b), it is still not enough to rely solely on other people's faith.[6] Una's concern to have Redcrosse "Add faith vnto [his] force" (I.i.19.3) in his battle with Errour is meaningless by itself. He already has faith. Redcrosse needs to realize that his fate is not in the hands of his will but in the hands of God before he can truly defeat Errour and her children. He does not learn this until after he has failed to defeat, not only Errour, but Lucifera, Orgoglio, and Despair. After his sojourn in the House of Holinesse, George is able to add, not an already present faith, but the learned value of *a posteriori* patience, to his force. It is by fighting with a properly constructed mind,

---

6 My argument works by having the spiritual meaning of existence not be part of the essence of who we are but an aspect of the relative properties of man (size, strength, stamina, etc.). The poet-creator can make such connections in his poem, but the man inside the poem cannot. The same holds true of readers who have substantial consciousness outside of fiction in a universe of others who do not have access to what in modern philosophy would be considered a "private language." The best recipe in a truly relative universe is to make your private language public through imperfect language and see how one's imperfect expression stands up to public scrutiny when it is received by others.

Science Outside The Walls Of Eden 255

and not on the basis of faith or force alone, that he begins to overcome the Dragon.

George wounds the Dragon, not by his direct blow, which is aimed at the Dragon's throat, but by accident:

> glauncing from his scaly necke, did glyde
> Close vnder his left wing, then broad displayd.
> The percing steele there wrought a wound full wyde,
> That with the vncouth smart the Monster lowdly cryde. (I.xi.20.6-9)

The reader may cheer for the accidental wounding of the Dragon, but the episode testifies to the notion that God's will guides the weapon independently of the purpose of George's will.

The scientific orientation of the poem continues in stanza 21, as the poet expands on the monster's cry at being wounded through simile:

> He cryde, as raging seas are wont to rore,
> When wintry storme his wrathfull wreck does threat,
> The rolling billowes beat the ragged shore.... (I.xi.21.1-3)

This is not the gentle billowing of waves against the summer shore; this is a winter storm; and it is no ordinary winter storm; it is a storm that threatens the very existence of creation:

> As they the earth would shoulder from her seat,
> And greedy gulfe does gape, as he would eat
> His neighbour element in his reuenge:
> Then gin the blustring brethren boldly threat,
> To moue the world from off his stedfast henge,
> And boisterous battaile make, each other to auenge. (I.xi.21.4-9)

Spenser's Reworking of Du Bartas

In this passage, Spenser is deliberately echoing a source in Du Bartas' *Divine Weekes*,[7] but he is changing the terms of victory in significant ways. In his poem, Du Bartas decentered man and his substantial consciousness for a fictional λόγος, as he attempted to imitate God by becoming an eagle

---

[7] Guillaume de Salluste Du Bartas, *Bartas: His Devine Weekes and Works (1605)*, ed. Francis C. Haber, trans. Josuah Sylvester (Gainesville, FL: Scholars' Facsimiles & Reprints, 1965).

"that soaring neere the skie, / Among our Authors Egle-like I flie"[8] in much the same way that Contemplation represents an eagle that can look directly at the sun. As a result, Du Bartas attempted to fly midway between heaven and earth:

> My heedful Muse, trayned in true Religion,
> Devinely-humane keepes the middle Region:
> Least, if she should too-high a pitch presume,
> Heav'ns glowing flame should melt her waxen plume;
> Or, if too-low (neare Earth or Sea) she flagge,
> Laden with mists her moistened wings do lagge.[9]

Spenser corrects Du Bartas' faulty model on the basis of his Augustinian learning. His hero learns to stand firm with his substantial consciousness in the face of what the poet knows is an unreal threat of the universe to "discreate all" back to a "self-jarring masse."[10] Spenser's Augustinian change leaves the state of the universe, which *permanently* tends towards good over evil and daylight over night, in the hands of a God Whose Word cannot be deconstructed, because ist lies outside the limited reason of mankind.[11]

The Amplification of Simile

As the fight continues, blood pours out of the Dragon's wound. The poet extends the description through simile:

> Forth flowed fresh
> A gushing riuer of blacke goarie blood,
> That drowned all the land, whereon he stood;
> The streame thereof would driue a water-mill. (I.xi.22.3-6)

The simile opposes the water born black blood that would "driue a water-mill" to the fire that belches forth

> With bitter sense of his deepe rooted ill,
> That flames of fire he threw forth from his large nosethrill.
> (I.xi.22.8-9)

The difference does not fall out along the lines of ontological reality versus

---

8 Ibid., II.ii.31-32.
9 Ibid., I.i.135-40.
10 Ibid., I.ii.308.
11 This is, in my opinion, the same reason that Spenser had corrected the metaphysical aesthetic of Ariosto and Tasso.

epistemological fiction: both take place within the realm of Faery. The difference is one of time. The Dragon is not dead at once as a result of his being wounded. Instead, his "furious mood" is "Trebly augmented" (I.xi.22.7). George, who the poet had once likened to a "Lyon fierce" (I.i.17) and a ram fighting for control of the flock with Sansfoy (I.ii.16), continues with the patience he has *learned* after the fact (*a posteriori*) of his *a priori* faith.

Nevertheless, in his fury the Dragon manages to unseat George from his horse. This puts him back on the ground which is the source of his strength.[12] But his best position is not to stay on the ground: it is as a man who stands midway between Heaven and earth against his base, socially destructive, animal instincts on the one hand and the temptation to become a god on the other. Thus, he quickly rises (I.xi.23.7) because "that reprochfull fall right fowly he disdaynd" (I.xi.23.9).

Though George has been educated into potential perfection in the extremity of heaven, he must *enact* what he knows in the world of time; and this means that God makes allowance for some backsliding on the part of His created individuals with their limited minds on the way to His end. George is no exception, and he falls back into his old habit of fury, as he

> fercely tooke his trenchand blade in hand,
> With which he stroke so furious and so fell,
> That nothing seemd the puissance could withstand. (I.xi.24.1-3)

Yet, appearance is not reality, and his fury gets him nothing once again against armor that is harder than he thinks:

> Vpon his crest the hardned yron fell,
> But his more hardned crest was armd so well,
> That deeper dint therein it would not make. (I.xi.24.4-6)

So his direct blow fails, but George has struck fear into his opponent by the extreme fury of his blow:

> Yet so extremely did the buffe him quell,
> That from thenceforth he shund the like to take,

---

12 This may be why Spenser has changed the traditional iconography, which has George seated on horseback as he kills the Dragon. See Hamilton's note to I.xi.24: "Unlike the traditional St. George who slays the Dragon on while on horseback, the Red Cross Knight fights on foot, as the Archangel Michael is usually seen in medieval art when he slays the Dragon."

But when he saw them come, he did them still forsake. (I.xi.24.7-9)

George continues his *visibly* unprofitable course, returning to his "outrageous might" (I.xi.25.2) to deal a blow; and while he finds the Dragon's armor still hard as "Adamant rocke" (I.xi.25.5), when the Dragon tries to fly, he finds his wing "vnseruiceable" (I.xi.25.9). The Dragon has been wounded, not by the directed fury of George's blows, but by the accident of his having missed the object he was aiming for and instead having his hand guided by the hand of God, on whose friendship George is still relying, to the place where the blow could do the most good.

George's victory in striking fear into his opponent does not exhaust the Dragon's arsenal of weapons, nor does it put George on a forward course at last. Being made to fight on the ground, the Dragon bellows fire, and the scorching flames causes George to consider retreating from battle for the first time in the entire canto:

> The scorching flame sore swinged all his face,
> And through his armour all his bodie seard,
> That he could not endure so cruell cace,
> But thought his armes to leaue, and helmet to vnlace. (I.xi.26.6-9)

But whatever his first instincts, he does not follow them.

The Poet's Comparison of George to Hercules

Spenser supposes that his reader will remember the bad effects of his having taken off his armor when we knew him as Redcrosse. The poet expands on this, spreading his larger poetic memory to the memory of Hercules, who was poisoned within his armor:

> Not that great Champion of the antique world,
> Whom famous Poetes verse so much doth vaunt,
> And hath for twelue huge labours high extold,
> So many furies and sharpe fits did haunt,
> When him the poysoned garment did enchaunt
> With *Centaures* bloud, and bloudie verses charm'd,
> As did this knight twelue thousand dolours daunt,
> Whom fyrie steele now burnt, that earst him arm'd,
> That erst him goodly arm'd, now most of all him harmd. (I.xi.27)

Hamilton's note to line 1-6 says "the comparison is apt, because the knight's armor is also charmed (cf. iv 50.5-6), but chiefly because Hercules' death was interpreted as a punishment for concupiscence. e.g. by Comes (1616)

VII i." But George has been *justly accused of concupiscence*. The question is what makes George able to *survive* the trial that the greatest hero of antiquity could not. Once again, the distinction is not arbitrary. It is based on Spenser's reading of Augustinian improvements made by a more fluid Christian faith to static pagan idealism when it came to integrating the matter of time into his stories.

In Ovid's *Metamorphoses*,[13] Hercules is killed after Rumor, "Who loves to add the false to the true,"[14] plants a rumor with his wife Deianira that Hercules was burning with passion for another. Deianira sends a tunic laden with poison drawn from a hydra. He throws it over his shoulder as he goes to pray, "offering incense and prayers amidst the kindling flames and pouring wine from a libation bowl upon the marble altar."[15] It is not the fact that he put on tunic that kills Hercules. It is his *nearness to the flames of the pagan altar* that activates the poison that then starts to burn him.

Ovid makes it clear that Hercules feels that Deianira is innocent of having caused his death. Instead, Hercules blames Juno, who is on high ("*ab alto*"). He had invited her to "Feast on my destruction."[16] In other words, Hercules had tempted a goddess, and the goddess was only doing what came naturally to her. After he has been poisoned by his wife, he wonders at the fruitlessness of his having murdered Busiris, who had defiled pagan temples, or of his having killed Antaeus, the man who derived his strength from his contact with the ground.[17]

Hercules' problem is that he never realizes his own role in his destruction. Had he not been pouring wine on marble altars to idolatrous gods or asking them to feast on his destruction, he might have lived. Instead, he is flinging blame out to imaginary gods for deeds that have more immediate human agents. This is an indication of why pagan religion was considered so dangerous in the Christian universe: it revolved around principles of revenge and mutually assured destruction while flinging blame for human acts off to imaginary gods rather than placing blame where it belongs on the substantial consciousness of individual human beings. Those who decide to compete with fictional gods for precedence in fame, as Hercules

---

13 Ovid, *Metamorphoses*, IX.134-272.

14 Ibid,, IX.138-139, p. 241.

15 Ibid., IX.159-160. I use the translation from the Loeb edition in this case because it makes it clear that Hercules is offering his prayers amidst the "kindling flames" (*precantia flammis*), which Lombardo's translation of these lines leaves out: "He had just lit incense and was pouring wine / From a shallow bowl onto the marble altar" (p. 242).

16 Ibid., IX.176, p. 242.

17 Ibid., IX.184.

does, are forever doomed to lose their substantial consciousness.[18]

The difference between Hercules and George is played out in a metaphor of armor. Hercules had attempted to tear his armor off his body when Deianira's tunic started to burn him. As a result, he hastened his own inevitable destruction. This is like the behavior the reader has seen in the adventures of George before he was in the House of Holinesse. He was seen attempting to defeat his enemies with only the power of his human will, and this had led him into the arms of Fidessa. He was saved from moral destruction by the will of God, who interfered with George's human purpose by presenting him with an image of his own pride in Orgoglio. He was saved once again, not by his own will, but by Arthur.

Since his time in the House of Holinesse, George has learned to correctly assess the role his armor in protecting him. He keeps it on to save his body from the heat of the Dragon that would otherwise have killed him sure. This is the difference between the armor of faith, which is based in one's own substantial consciousness, and the values of heroes, who seek fame elsewhere to make up for their lack of individual substance.

George's Judgment and His Actions

George hears the beckoning of death once again in his battle with the Dragon even after he has been perfected in the House of Holinesse:

> Faynt, wearie, sore, emboyled, grieued, brent
> With heat, toyle, wounds, armes, smart, and inward fire
> That neuer man such mischiefes did torment;

---

[18] It is interesting that Spenser takes this tale from a series of Ovidian tales told in the House of Acheloüs, which is modeled on Homer's House of Alcinous. Thus words spoken there are thus not as stable as they purport to be. This ultimate lack of stability is acknowledged in the story by Pirithoüs,

> "You're making all this up, Acheloüs," he said,
> "And you're giving too much power to the gods
> If you think they can give and take away forms." (IX.614-615; p. 225)

Lelex, the mythological founder of Sparta, attempts to put the justified skepticism of Pirithoüs into a firm perspective with his note on the power of heaven:

> "Immense is the power of heaven
> And knows no end. Whatever the gods want
> Is done...." (IX.618-619, p. 255)

Despite the fact that Lelex goes on to tell the story of Philemon and Baucis (one of the few tales with a happy ending in the *Metamorphoses*), Lelex's tale is original to Ovid and could well be a fiction. Spenser seems to be taking the whole complex of Ovid's narrative framework, including the setting of the tale of Hercules in the House of Acheloüs, into account.

Death better were, death did he oft desire.... (I.xi.28.1-4)

The careful reader will not ascribe anymore power to Geoge's will to overcome his despair than they did when he was before his visit to the House of Holinesse. The poet manages to have him overcome his desire for death, not by exercising any positive judgment, but simply because "But death will neuer come, when needes require" (I.xi.28.5). The disjunction between George's judgment and his action continues to be highlighted here, as he is still a passive participant in his newly-trained spiritual life who does not yet have the positive power to "wish" his "will."

When the Dragon sees his foe is still a passive man weary of life, he becomes active himself. Lifting up his "sturdy sterne" (I.xi.28.8), he knocks his foe to the ground. In a note to line 4 in his 1st edition of the poem, Hamilton notes the continuation with earlier episodes of his interaction with Orgoglio, Despair, Penance, and Contemplation. Hamilton notes Carole Kaske's argument that "the Knight's spiritual death comes with his consent."[19] Kaske's reading is unlikely. In all the previous cases, Redcrosse is corrected from his misimpression that his destiny is represented by the end of his life. He is constantly being forced off his focus on ends back to the life that comes between birth and death.

A better explanation than Kaske's assertion of will on the part of George would be that sojourn in the House of Holinesse perfects the mind of man in potential, but the active man must expend his limited resources in a real fight with his enemy in the literal world. Though George's exhaustion here is only physical, it is nevertheless real and must be accounted for in the economy of the body. In spite of his having learned to place limits on his limited body, that fact says nothing about his having gained control of his will. Fortune (I.xi.29.1), not the will of George, is in charge as he falls into "*The well of life*" that is "Behynd his backe vnweeting" (I.xi.29.2).

The well of life "ne yet his vertues had forgot" (I.xi.29.9), and this seems to indicate that George himself has forgotten them. The careful reader will be able to use their memory to compare this episode with the episode in the Cave of Errour in canto i. As a result of his insistence on never withdrawing his forward foot once he had extended it, he had defeated Errour, but only after she had vomited forth all the books and papers that had made her a formidable foe in the first place. After his defeat of Errour, Una congratulated him, but the pair turned "backward" (I.i.28.2); and it was then that

---

19 Carol V. Kaske, "The Dragon's Spark and Sting and the Structure of Red Cross's Dragon Fight: The Faerie Queene I Xi-Xii'," *Studies in Philology* 66(1969): 625.

they found their way to a path that "beaten was most plaine" (I.i.28.3), which they followed to the end (I.i.28.5). In that episode, it was God—not Una or Redcrosse—that fulfilled George's purpose and brought him to his end. In the well of life episode, George has still not learned to fulfill his own end without God's help. The lesson he has learned is to concentrate the purposeful power of his limited body in order to defeat a strong but also limited Dragon whose power he is learning to measure with his rational mind, rather than either living in fear of it or of attacking it unnecessarily on the basis of the substitution of his human will for the goodwill of God. The exercise of will without the acknowledgement of God remains a sin.

As proof that *God* has been providing things throughout his adventures that George knows not of, the careful reader should consider that this is the Well of Life that could restore Fradubio to his human form *if George knew its position in the sacred history he is enacting.* Unfortunately, George never appears to come to terms with his own role as an actor in the sacred drama that is larger than he is. He never fully realizes the whole possibility entailed by his actions in the world of time. Thus, he leaves Fradubio as a tree.

George's Baptism

Having fallen into the Well of Life, he is now baptized. Douglas Brooks-Davies has written that

> The Redcrosse we meet at the beginning is a novice. He has, we are to assume, been baptized; he knows his catechism; he has not (because he is young) undergone the full test of faith.[20]

Brooks-Davies has to "assume" the fact that he has been previously baptized and that he knows his catechism, because there is no evidence to support this contention in the poem itself. In fact, there is some positive counter evidence to his position. George has been raised as an elf by plowmen parents, unreal creatures of Faeryland who have no need of baptism, a *human* sacrament that bridges the gulf between this world and the next and so protects human beings from the realities of a harsh world.

What is even more damaging to Brook-Davies' assumptions is that the first question asked and answered by the Heidelberg Catechism, the catechism used in the Reformed Churches at the time that Spenser was writing,

---

20 Brooks-Davies, Douglas, "*The Faerie Queene*, Book I" in Hamilton, *The Spenser Encyclopedia*, 261b.

is "What is your only comfort / in life and death?"[21] The answer flies in the face of George's behavior that the reader has observed up until this point:

> That I am not my own,
>   but belong—
>   body and soul,
> in life and death—
> to my faithful Savior Jesus Christ.
>
> He has fully paid for all my sins with his precious blood,
> and has set me free from the tyranny of the devil.
> He also watches over me in such a way
> that not a hair can fall from my head
> without the will of my Father in heaven:
> in fact, all things must work together for mutual salvation.[22]

Had he already learned this lesson at the beginning of his adventure, he would have never substituted *his* human force for his faith in his encounter with Errour, nor later would he have given lessons to Despair out of *his* injured sense of injustice. Although George has been given *salvation* at the beginning of his adventure and is helped along his way with "God to frend," even at this late date in his adventure George has not learned the proper orientation of his epistemological reconstruction of things created in ontology by God. That orientation requires a subordination of the human will to the will of God, a lesson that the reader will be able to see that George has learned in the future when he meets with the Palmer at the beginning of Book II.

The situation of George's permanent subordination to a greater power introduces an element of permanent and so undeconstructable inequality into the natural universe. Light is permanently better than dark; day is permanently better than night; and good permanently triumphs over evil. The rite of baptism tips the scales in George's favor once more. George's will cannot alter that unalterable fact; nor can the Dragon affect God's friendship with George. Despite the fact of the Dragon's having "Defyld those sacred waues" (I.xi.29.8), the destruction wrought by the Dragon is not real: the Well of Life has not forgotten *its* own virtues, nor George's. This may be contrasted to the Dragon, who raises himself up "Aboue his wonted pitch" (I.xi.31.8). As he does so Spenser represents the Dragon's "countenance

---

21 *The Heidelberg Catechism with Scripture Texts*, (Grand Rapids, MI: CRC Publications, 1989), 9.
22 Ibid.

fell" (I.xi.31.8) as he claps his iron wings in a sign of victory (I.xi.31.9). Spenser deconstructs the image of raising with a perfectly balanced image of falling, even as the Dragon announces his victory.

It should be apparent to the careful reader that the balance of elements against each other in equal shares is itself a perversion of God's order and that the Dragon has made a mistake in his estimation of his situation. However, it is not apparent to any of the actors *within* Spenser's poem that the Dragon has not indeed won the day. Even Una, who is viewing the day's events "from farre" (I.xi.32.2) and fearing that chance will turn away from her, starts to pray to God to aid her fallen hero (I.xi.32.4-5). The reader knows (or should know) that there is no need to pray, as God has already helped George by having him fall backwards into the Well of Life.

George's revival has nothing to do with his own "will," as it is God who raises George from the Well of Life as a new man. It falls to the *poet* to make the connection between George's individual condition and the state of nature, as he likens the raising of George to an eagle "fresh out of the Ocean waue" (I.xi.34.3), where he has cleansed himself. The reader has seen Contemplation blind eyes compared to an eagle's sight, but in that episode George had been turned away from following contemplative activity for his role as active man. Once again, George "marueiles at himselfe, still as he flies" (I.xi.34.8), indicating that he is as completely surprised at his revived condition as Una is.

Day Two of the Dragon Fight

The Dragon is surprised, as well, and doubts his victory for the first time:

> Whom when the damned feend so fresh did spy,
> No wonder, if he wondred at the sight,
> And doubted, whether his late enemy
> It were, or other new supplied knight. (I.xi.35.1-4)

In spite of neither side having complete knowledge of what is going on, the fight continues. George accepts the gift of new-and-unlooked-for strength and reapplies himself to battle, but not without his (by now familiar) emphasis on proving "his late renewed might" (I.xi.35.5).

> High brandishing his bright deaw-burning blade,
> Vpon his crested scalpe so sore did smite,
> That to the scull a yawning wound it made:

The deadly dint his dulled senses all dismaid. (I.xi.35.6-9)

This time, George's blow to the Dragon's head makes a "yawning wound," and the poet turns to the question of weighing the difference between the first blow and the second. The poet centers his concern on the uncertain prospect of weighing in a scientific manner the exact role of baptism versus hardened steel in the difference:

> I wote not, whether the reuenging steele
> Were hardned with that holy water dew,
> Wherein he fell, or sharper edge did feele,
> Or his baptized hands now greater grew;
> Or other secret vertue did ensew. (I.xi.36.1-5)

All he can say with any certainty is that "the force of fleshly arme" (I.xi.36.6) could never be enough on its own. Nor, for that matter, would the "subtilty, nor slight" nor the "mighty charme" (I.xi.36.9) (presumably of Archimago and Duessa) be enough. George has tapped into something much deeper, something beyond anyone's individual mind to understand, even his.

In response, the Dragon raises his tail and smites him with a blow that would have killed a lesser man:

> The same aduauncing high aboue his head,
> With sharpe intended sting so rude him smott,
> That to the earth him droue, as stricken dead,
> Ne liuing wight would haue him life behott. (I.xi.38.1-4)

George is no ordinary man: not only is he is assured of salvation after death, he is destined to survive his encounter with a Dragon that strikes fear into the hearts of not only ordinary men but Una herself. But here, as before, he cannot rest on his *a priori* assurance of faith in those facts.

The Dragon grips his shield, and the poet employs his ability to pun on talons and talents, as George thinks how he can "unfold" his "talaunts" from the Dragon's grip:

> Much was the man encombred with his hold,
> In feare to lose his weapon in his paw,
> Ne wist yett, how his talaunts to vnfold. (I.xi.41.1-3)

The talent refers to the parable of talents in Matthew 25:14-30, where the master leaves his talents unevenly divided between three servants. When he returns, he finds that two his servants had put their money to work and thereby doubled the value of the property entrusted to them. But a third servant places his talent under a bushel, and when the master returns the third servant returns his original talent to him with the excuse that what the master had given him he had feared to lose. In the biblical parable, the returning master banishes his servant who had not put his money to work but had rest content with it alone. In the same manner, God expects human beings to take His *a priori* gifts and put them to work within the world, building an *a posteriori* scientific and rational view of the universe on top of His *a priori* gifts and not simply to rely on an uncertain connection to God alone.

More immediately here it refers to the necessity of opening up the closed grip of the Dragon's talons. This process of extending the Dragon's talons from their folded position and measuring their true breadth rather than allowing the Dragon's true bulk to remain hidden, and hidden feared, is the key to understanding George's journey in the Book of Holinesse.

After smiting the Dragon "with all his might and maine" (I.xi.43.4), he manages to wound the Dragon, but George fails to free his shield. Instead, he ends up losing his defensive weapon to save his life. If the reader thinks back to Arthur's battle with Orgoglio, they will remember that their battle was even until, by chance, the covering had fallen off of Arthur's shield. Arthur had used the defensive shield to defeat Orgoglio. George, by contrast, though seeming defenseless and vulnerable, must use his *offensive* weapon to defeat the Dragon.

He prepares to fight as he has always done, but the Dragon continues to belch forth fire,

> The heate whereof, and harmefull pestilence
> So sore him noyd, that forst him to retire
> A little backward for his best defence,
> To saue his bodie from the scorching fire,
> Which he from hellish entrailes did expire. (I.xi.45.1-5)

So George retreats once again, and he is ashamed of his backsliding. But the reader is reassured that God is directing his action, even as George falters:

> It chaunst (eternall God that chaunce did guide)
> As he recoyled backeward, in the mire
> His nigh forweraried feeble feet did slide,
> And downe he fell, with dread of shame sore terrifide. (I.xi.45.6-9)

George's mind has not been infected with the fear of the Dragon, nor even of the possibility of his imminent death. He is concerned that the backward motion that saves his body is shameful. But although George is ashamed of his backsliding, his backward motion takes him out of danger and delivers him even more unwilled salvation, for he falls by the Tree of Life.

The Tree of Life

The Tree of Life grows in the Garden of Eden. It was put there by God when nature and mankind were still in accord:

> In all the world like was not to be fownd,
> Saue in that soile, where all good things did grow,
> And freely sprong out of the fruitfull grownd,
> As incorrupted Nature did them sow…. (I.xi.47.1-4)

But that was before "that dreadd Dragon all did ouerthrow" (I.xi.47.5) that perfect balance between mankind and nature. By guiding George into the Well of Life that stands under the Tree of Life against his will, the poet continues to focus on life rather than the death that George has been pursuing at each stage on his journey on account of his having mistaken his human being, which *comes* from God, to mean that he is *equivalent* to God.

There is another "like faire tree" (I.xi.47.6) just outside the brazen walls of Eden: the Tree of Knowledge, "Whereof who so did eat, eftsoones did know / Both good and ill" (I.xi.47.7-8). It is perhaps telling that the still "clownishe" George does not eat from this tree. This may be seen as his having been born pure and unspotted with the friendship of God; but that does not obviate him from participation in the original sin of Adam and Eve that is signified by that tree that "through one mans fault hath doen vs all to dy" (I.xi.47.9). Rather than exercising his "mournfull memory" of "Both good and ill" (I.xi.47.8), George continues to feel shame at the exact moment that God has dragged him out of harm's way to position of safety. He (George) may be correct in doing so, but it means that he still has only partial knowledge of his position in the world. Insofar as he proceeds without rational knowledge, George is still relying on his sword and his will. That means that George continues to rely on his now-calmed but still socially destructive animal genus[23] as a means of entering into the court

---

[23] George's animal genus was calmed by Patience in the House of Holinesse, but the point of that episode was not to substitute a rational framework for George's continuing reliance on his now-calmed animal nature.

of Gloriana[24] instead of raising himself up by the specific difference of his reason, as the poet has done.

Despite the fact that George has not come to the end of his adventure here, the poet makes it clear that these trees represent *life*, and the poet portrays the Dragon as staying away from both, as he detests "al that life preserued" (I.xi.49.3):

> For nigh thereto the euer damned Beast
> Durst not approch, for he was deadly made,
> And all that life preserued, did detest:
> Yet he it oft aduentur'd to inuade. (I.xi.49.1-4)

It is the work of "the euer damned Beast" to make incursions into the realm of life, but the obligation of living beings is not to hasten their end but to expand and amplify their limited lives as much as possible to keep death at bay as long as possible and to extend their works as far as possible through the relative scientific space that falls under mankind's power of control, as the poet has.

Within this limited life, some things happen to human characters that are out of human control, as here, where

> From that first tree forth flowd, as from a well,
> A trickling streame of Balme, most soueraine
> And daintie deare, which on the ground still fell,
> And ouerflowed all the fertill plaine,
> As it had deawed bene with timely raine:
> Life and long health that gracious ointment gaue,
> And deadly woundes could heale, and reare againe
> The senselesse corse appointed for the graue.
> Into that same he fell: which did from death him saue. (I.xi.48)

It would not be wise to count on this aspect of George's experience in our actual lives, however. George has not been given the power to elevate himself to the status of God, nor the power to rollback his own death. He is stuck in the temporal world, which requires purpose and direction; and while there he continues to neglect his memory and the knowledge of good and evil, relying instead on his *a priori* salvation at key moments in which God has to step in and save him.

---

24 I remind the reader that this did not work. Instead, George gained entry into the court of Gloriana by his birth. This was yet another fact that was unknown to him before it was revealed to him by Contemplation.

This is why Spenser keeps the worldly perspective separate from the heavenly perspective throughout the whole of the Book of Holinesse. George's defeat of the Dragon, though admirable in itself, is not a model for human imitation. The power that George wields resides ultimately with God, who exercises his power through his vehicle in much the same way that divine Homer exercises his power through the passive rhapsode Ion in Plato's dialog.

Victory on Day Three of the Dragon Fight

When night falls again, Una fears "for his safetie" (I.xi.50.8) and

> gan deuoutly pray;
> And watch the noyous night, and wait for ioyous day. (I.xi.50.8-9)

Here again, Spenser has divided the whole of metaphysical reality into night and day, as the poet lowers his vision from metaphysical equality of God to participation in the scientific world of values in which day is *permanently* better than night. Daylight comes again to the diurnal earth; and when daylight comes again, George does rise, and the Dragon begins to fear that he, who has never been defeated and who thought that he had eliminated the threat of George, might actually be on the brink of losing the battle (I.xi.52.8).

Spenser, who had asked Clio to leave out all of George's sins from her presentation, suddenly has them appear in his description of the Dragon. He "with wonted rage he him aduaunced neare" (I.xi.52.9), and the poet notes his pride as he thought "attonce" to have swallowed him whole:

> And in his first encounter, gaping wyde,
> He thought attonce him to haue swallowd quight,
> And rusht vpon him with outragious pride. (I.xi.53.1-3)

George takes advantage of the impulsive decision of the Dragon and thrusts his sword into his "darksome hollow maw" (I.xi.53.8), a negative image indicating the hollowness of the Dragon's mouth, before retreating once again.

With this act, in which the conscious will of George coincides with the will of God *for the first time in the Book of Holinesse*, George has killed the Dragon. As a result, Spenser sets up a series of hierarchical structures on which he places the victory. Fire is quenched by the water of the Well of Life. It dissipates first into smoke and then into clouds in the air before at last disappearing altogether:

> So downe he fell, and forth his life did breath,
> That vanisht into smoke and cloudes swift. (I.xi.54.1-2)

Earth, on the other hand, supports the weight of the Dragon's body:

> So downe he fell, that th'earth him vnderneath
> Did grone, as feeble so great load to lift. (I.xi.54.3-4)

The Dragon had been built on a false foundation, and with the coming of George, who has the power of God on his side, the Dragon's fire is extinguished, as he slips into water:

> So downe he fell, as an huge rockie clift,
> Whose false foundation waues haue washt away,
> With dreadfull poyse is from the mayneland rift,
> And rolling downe, great *Neptune* doth dismay. (I.xi.54.5-8)

Now it may be that from God's perspective, Who weighs all things equally in balance, there may be a broader perspective in which night is equal or better than day and fire is equal to or better that water, but in the Reformation thought of Edmund Spenser that perspective is unavailable to a mere human being, who must choose and choose correctly between the unequal choices before him.

After the Fall

Spenser wants to keep his narrative grounded on the plane of bodily existence, despite his own creation of a typological fiction that may tempt lesser minds away from a deeper truth. As a result, he gives the Dragon a real existence in his imaginative poetry that he does not have in actuality. The reader knows this; but George, whose present existence is also the product of Spenser's imaginative fiction, does not have the reader's extra-textual perspective on events. He shudders at the fall of so great a monster:

> The knight himselfe euen trembled at his fall,
> So huge and horrible a masse it seem'd. (I.xi.55.1-2)

Una, who is also a product of imaginative fiction[25] and who has also

---

25 The difference between George and Una is that there is no question that Una's existence is a pure product of the poet's imagination, whereas George is supposed to once

been kept far away in Spenser's geometric organization of the scene, at last approaches:

> But yet at last, when as the direfull feend
> She saw not stirre, off-shaking vaine affright,
> She nigher drew, and saw that ioyous end. (I.xi.55.5-7)

She, who had been focusing since the beginning on the now fulfilled "ioyous end" (I.xi.55.7), gives both God and the conquering might of George their due:

> Then God she praysd, and thankt her faithfull knight,
> That had atchieude so great a conquest by his might. (I.xi.55.5-9)

But the death of the Dragon is not the end of George's adventure. It is important to note that he has not been entirely cleansed of his past sins, some of which originated in the intermediate time since his adventure began; and the reader will find that his sins are merely suppressed, not eliminated, in the next and final canto.

---

have had a substantial existence that Spenser is reviving for the purpose of his moral example. But between that historical existence of George and Spenser's revival of him come imaginative layers of belief that have built up over time. Rather than peeling those layers back for a historical portrait of George as he was in his time, which modern critics from Fletcher to Derrida hold as their obligation in treating a historical text, Spenser has latches onto the baldly comical traditions that had built up over time as a way of highlighting the uncertainty of George's existence as part of his imaginative poetic program. This means that not only is it impossible to tell fact from fiction in Spenser's text, but those modern critics like Fletcher who attempt to bridge the historical gap, or even those like Derrida, de Man, and Quilligan, who believe that this is part of Spenser's point that they can deconstruct, are adding an unwarranted push to a historical certainty to radically uncertain imaginative things that do not proceed from the text but from their untested *a priori* assumptions about what the text means.

Loose Ends in the Restored Kingdom

The Restless Ship of Poetry

After George has delivered Una's kingdom from the Dragon, the poet uses a sailing metaphor to announce that he sees "the hauen nigh at hand, / To which I meane my wearie course to bend" (I.xii.1.1-2). In doing so, he makes it clear that Una's journey is now at an end:

> There this fayre virgin wearie of her way
> Must landed bee, now at her iourneyes end. (I.xii.1.6-7)

At the same time that he announces the end of Una's journey, the poet makes it clear that this is only a "hauen" "safe from storms, that may offend" (I.xii.1.5), for he has other as-yet-uncompleted plans:

> There eke my feeble barke a while may stay,
> Till merry wind and weather call her thence away. (I.xii.1.8-9)

The reason the poet needs to leave should be plain: to stay here in a fictionally-constructed Eden would be to reify an epistemological construction into an ontologically-existing reality, and that would be a sin.

The Caution of the Distant People of Eden

There are some important questions raised by the poet's continuation of the division between the perspectives of heavenly Una and time-bound George after he has defeated the Dragon. The first question is whether the Dragon is in fact dead. This question is raised because George, the human being that Una has brought back with her from her sojourn into the world of time, has a different experience of the death of the Dragon than do those who stand far away, as Una does. From George's perspective, there seems to be no question that he has killed the Dragon, as he has seen the its breath "vanisht into smoke and cloudes swift" (I.xi.54.1-2). But seen from far away, where Una stands, the absolute death of the Dragon is less sure. Una approaches hesitantly, shaking off her "vaine affright" (I.xi.55.6) before acknowledging his death. The same thing is true of the watchmen who stand on the brazen walls that divide Eden from the rest of the world: "That signe of last outbreathed life did *seeme*" (I.xii.2.5 italics mine). They cannot discount the possibility that the Dragon is still alive until they have made "triall" of their experience. For a moment, only the human George is sure that the Dragon is dead.

When the careful reader remembers that the Dragon's "wast" has grown so large on account of the broadcast of his power through the fear that his vast size generates in the minds of men, one is led to wonder whether the people of Eden have always been a little too cowardly. Rather allowing his readers to let their guards down now that the *external* Dragon has been killed, the poet turns his attention to the still hidden dangers that lurk within the Kingdom of Eden itself. These are many.

Walking Through the Brazen Gates of Eden

Once the Dragon is known to be dead, the King asks his followers to open up the "brazen gate" (I.xii.3.6). This is not necessarily wise unless the King is sure the the death of the Dragon has erased any need for having boundaries in the first place. If the Dragon was responsible for the construction of the gates in the first place, then the opening the "brazen gate" would allow free access between the interior world of Eden and the external world of time, as things stood before the Fall. But the same decision would be disastrous if George's slaying of the Dragon does not deliver Eden back to the pristine state that it was in before the Dragon showed up and started terrifying everyone within Eden's scientifically circumscribed walls.[1]

This places an enormous burden on the King to look at the world and to act *correctly* on what he sees, as not all decisions will have equal results in a still postlapsarian world. In particular, if the King opens the "brazen gate" and the world has not been restored, then he may have behaved just

---

[1] Humiltá, the guard in charge of the gates of the House of Holinesse, does not open his gates unless he has reason to trust the person he is admitting within *his* walls. Whether this is because George has not yet killed the Dragon or whether it is because the best holy people are always on guard is not clear at this point in the poem.

like Redcrosse and Arthur, both of whom made the mistake of removing their armor and both of whom suffered consequences for their mistake. The King of Eden could be infecting his united kingdom with something that a warier man could have kept out if he was inspecting his walls more carefully.

The King's perspective is not the only response available to the reader. Una had managed to escape the boundaries of Eden to come into the world of time before she has ever met Redcrosse. That means that it was possible to escape the Dragon's grip on the people of Eden even before she had found George in the court of Gloriana. This brings up the question of whether it was the ontological presence of the Dragon or the fear of the Dragon engendered in the epistemological minds of cowardly men that was responsible for the construction of the "brazen gate" in the first place. Before the reader chooses from various *a priori* premises from within their own experience, they should make "triall" of the whole of their experience.

As part of their judgment, the reader should consider the importance of the welcome that George receives as he walks through the now open gates:

> Vnto that doughtie Conquerour they came,
> And him before themselues prostrating low,
> Their Lord and Patrone loud did him proclame,
> And at his feet their lawrell boughes did throw. (I.xii.6.1-4)

There are serious consequences to raising a "clownishe younge man" over the legitimate ruler of the Kingdom of Eden as their "Lord and Patron" if we take the people at their word. If the reader decides that they are not to be taken seriously, then the reader must decide that that the people of Eden are overly enthusiastic, or that Spenser does not mean it, or that he was unaware of what he is saying. Any such decision could in fact be valid, but all are made on the basis of the *a priori* premise that the reader already knows what Spenser is thinking about the restoration of Eden and not on the basis of their having made "triall" of their *a posteriori* experience with the poem itself, where the lesson appears consistently to have been to distrust one's first impressions. As much as readers may be happy to have had the aesthetic tension of the oppressing Dragon released, the release of aesthetic tension does not release the reader from his obligation to watch carefully for signs that the poet is even now telling them only part of the truth.

The Uncertain Location of Eden

Another tricky question is the exact location of Eden. To the binary system of the Enlightenment, which defines things negatively, Una is a "virgin borne of heauenly brood" (I.iii.8.7), so her kingdom must be in Heaven. This appears to be the case if the reader is not paying too much attention to what is going on when a flurry of maidens come to Una,

> sounding tymbrels song
> In well attuned notes, a ioyous lay,
> And made delightfull musicke all the way,
> Vntill they came, where that faire virgin stood. (I.xii.7.3-6)

Not only do they sing her praises, they "her ador'd by honorable name" (I.xii.8.4). But the careful reader will not forget that names have been a contentious issue in the poem, so the reader should be concerned with which *exact* name they use when they address her. Is it by the name of Una, the name that the poet himself addresses her by,[2] or is it something deeper that lies at the level of Augustine's unified language on the level of God's ontological creation that lies beneath the languages of Greek and Latin?

The question is given more urgency by the fact that the maidens' praise of her "euerlasting fame" to an even higher heaven (I.xii.8.6). This places Eden outside of Heaven. On the other hand, she has clearly left timeless Eden for a temporal domain, so Eden cannot be held to be on earth.

In the modern day, Coleridge's "suspension of disbelief" is useful tool, as it allows fiction to exist without the reader questioning the mechanism by which fiction operates. But it goes without saying that Spenser predates Coleridge by two centuries and that he is operating in a universe in which it is important for human beings to make "triall" of their experience and not to simply give into their *a priori* assumptions about what is going on in this world or in any poem without considering all the evidence being presented to them. In this case, Eden appears in between Heaven and earth, an Erewhon of the poetic imagination that on that account *has no definite location!* As such, it falls outside a Coleridgean, binarily-divided universe. What is more, this appears to be deliberate on Spenser's part. The poet is using Augustine to transform the world from the sure access to metaphysics sported by Socrates and Aristotle, as well as by Enlightenment philosophers and Goethe and Herder, to a scientifically-oriented universe which all hu-

---

2 As Marks and Gross note in their article on "names" in the *Spenser Encyclopedia*, 494b, Una is named only after "the creation of a false double puts [her] meaning at risk."

man beings can imagine in their God-given minds but few have the power to enact in their substantial consciousness without getting sidetracked by a lust for power (as we have seen as the byproduct of the action of Archimago and Duessa) when the guarantees of fiction are withdrawn.

Paradoxes in the Rascal Kingdom

Another bit of confusion about the exact location of these events comes when the "rascal" (I.xii.9.5), who are "Heaped together in rude rablement" (I.xii.9.2), come to gaze on George. They gaze on him "with gaping wonderment" (I.xii.9.5) and admire him as one "from heauen sent" (I.xii.9.4). This is clearly an error from the perspective of the reader, who has followed George through all his poor choices on the way to his ultimate victory. Middles matter in *The Faerie Queene*, and the poet's point is that it is bad to lose sight of the middle terms of argument if everything turns out well in the end.

And this is not a lesson that is reserved to the "rascal" crowd, as even the King of Eden grants to George "princely gifts of yuory and gold" (I.xii.12.6). This should raise the eyebrows of careful reader, as they will be able remember when Duessa cast her magical spell over the body of Sansloy and traveled to the ends of the earth through the gates of ivory and *silver*, both false gates, while Redcrosse merely stood amazed, as the rabble does now. The substitution of gold for silver would seem to indicate the presence of some truth in the gifts of the king, but the continuing presence of ivory in the king's gifts would indicate that there is something not correct here, as well.

There is another paradox that lies at the heart of Eden that preexists the flinging open of the "brazen gate." Spenser appears to assure his readers that the state of affairs in Eden are pure and plain:

> Yet was their manner then but bare and playne:
> For th'antique world excesse and pride did hate;
> Such proud luxurious pompe is swollen vp but late. (I.xii.14.7-9)

But in the previous canto, he had noted that their feast takes place with a scarlet carpet beneath their feet:

> Of all, that royall Princes court became,
> And all the floore was vnderneath their feet
> Bespredd with costly scarlott of great name,

On which they lowly sitt, and fitting purpose frame. (I.xii.13.6-9)

Scarlet is the color that Fidessa was covered in when Redcrosse first saw her, but he had translated "ritch weedes and seeming glorious show" (I.ii.21.5) to "her humblesse low" (I.ii.21.4). The careful reader knew then that Redcrosse was making a mistake. Here in the Kingdom of Eden, how is the reader to be assured that similar mistakes are not being made except by their desire that it should not be so?

Spenser is not ignorant of what he is doing when he glosses over the presence of "daintie dishes," "comely seruices" and "courtly trayne" (I.xii.14.3-4) before admitting

> My narrow leaues cannot in them contayne
> The large discourse of roiall Princes state. (I.xii.5-6)

It seems that Spenser has not been able to get away from the divisions of science back to the unified metaphysical universe which (according to many modern critics) is the goal of all art. Instead, he is applying to Eden itself the question of perspective on events. The careful reader will hold questions of perspective in their memories until a satisfactory solution can be found to the problem of whose perspective can be said to be ultimately correct.

George's Interaction with the King of Eden

During the course of the plain scarlet feast, the King asks George to tell the court

> Of straunge aduentures, and of perils sad,
> Which in his trauell him befallen had.... (I.xii.15.4-5)

George does so carefully, "From poynt to poynt" (I.xii.15.8), a figure that indicates he is drawing on his serial experience of chronological events. But he is neglecting the larger patterns of history, which are not drawn from chronological relationships but are instead drawn from a person's ability to draw generic similarities from a world of discrete differences. George lacks the power to draw such similarities out his experience even after his defeat of the Dragon, as the ability to draw similarities result from the training of the rational mind through education.

This makes it important to note that the King and Queen of Eden react to his story, not with reason, but with passion:

> Great pleasure mixt with pittifull regard,
> That godly King and Queene did passionate,
> Whyles they his pittifull aduentures heard…. (I.xii.16.1-3)

In their passionate response, they

> oft they did lament his *lucklesse state*,
> And often blame the too importune fate,
> That heapd on him so many wrathfull wreakes:
> For neuer gentle knight, as he of late,
> So tossed was in fortunes cruell freakes;
> And all the while salt teares bedeawd the hearers cheaks.
> (I.xii.16.4-9 italics mine)

Their response is eerily close to the dwarf's response to the imprisonment of Redcrosse by Orgoglio. The dwarf had reacted to the dilemma of Redcrosse by laying blame exclusively on others. But the lesson the careful reader learned there was that events are *not* guided by "luck," that luck is guided by God if we look deeper into matters, *and* that at this deeper level Redcrosse bears a lot of the responsibility for his actions, even though others seem willing to lay blame for his actions elsewhere. This was the question that Arthur had presented Una with when he asked her his question about why she had let her "tosse" her away, a word that also appears in the previous quote, as well.

The crowd also responds to George as Duessa had reacted to the magic of Redcrosse's arms:

> O But I feare the fickle freakes (quoth shee)
> Of fortune false, and oddes of armes in field. (I.iv.50.1-2)

Although Duessa had studied magic, this led her only up to a certain point in her knowledge. She had tried to keep everything in balance, because balance remains the only way that she could keep herself on a level playing field with a man like Redcrosse who, however naïve and "clownishe" he might appear, has God's grace on his side. Such *a priori* grace stands above reason's, and so Duessa's, ability to grasp.

The King of Eden ignores such concerns as the careful reader should have been learning to attend to, as he devises an "euerlasting rest" on account of his belief that George's journey is at an end:

> But since now safe ye seised haue the shore,

> And well arriued are, (high God be blest)
> Let vs deuize of ease and euerlasting rest. (I.xii.17.7-9)[3]

But George immediately corrects the King, recalling further obligations:

> Ah dearest Lord, said then that doughty knight,
> Of ease or rest I may not yet deuize;
> For by the faith, which I to armes haue plight,
> I bounden am streight after this emprize,
> As that your daughter can ye well aduize,
> Backe to returne to that great Faerie Queene,
> And her to serue six yeares in warlike wize,
> Gainst that proud Paynim king, that workes her teene:
> Therefore I ought craue pardon, till I there haue beene. (I.xii.18)

The King agrees that George's oaths made may not be broken:

> But since that band ye cannot now release,
> Nor doen vndo; (for vowes may not be vayne).... (I.xii.19.5-6)

This puts emphasis on the permanence of spoken words, which, like the forward footing of Redcrosse at the Cave of Errour, may not be withdrawn once put forward. The problem there was, as Una noted at the time, that one should make "triall" of one's future experience before deciding to put one's foot forward in the first place.

The King of Eden's Vow

The king makes a vow of his own:

> Soone as the terme of those six yeares shall cease,
> Ye then shall hither backe returne agayne,
> The marriage to accomplish vowd betwixt you twayn. (I.xii.19.7-9)

This fulfills a promise made earlier when the King had proclaimed "through the world" that whosoever shall kill "monster most deforme" (I.xii.20.2-3) that he would bestow his only daughter in marriage. He now fulfills his promise:

> Therefore since now to thee perteynes the same,

---

[3] This is another opportunity for the careful reader to compare the words of the King of Eden with the words of the poet, as the poet has specifically spoken only of the end of Una's journey on this shore.

> By dew desert of noble cheualree,
> Both daughter and eke kingdome, lo I yield to thee. (I.xii.20.7-9).

The careful reader will note that it is out of obligation to his previous oath, and not out of any experience with the knight himself, that the King makes George his "heyre apparaunt" (I.xii.20.6).

There are two important things that a careful reader will note in this interchange. The first is the fact that neither George nor Una are consulted in this arrangement. The King simply assumes that George has taken up the quest on account of his having heard the King's proclamation, but we have no direct evidence that he has done so. On the contrary, we have seen, the "clownishe" George takes up the quest in order

> To winne him worship, and [Gloriana's] grace to haue,
> Which of all earthly things he most did craue (I.i.3.4-5)

What is more, George has shown himself almost criminally indifferent to Una all along the path that he has beaten to this moment, abandoning her at one point, taking her dwarf with him in the process, and showing more interest in that which he can "view" in the body of Fidessa.

The second important thing that the careful reader will note in the King's offering is the question of exactly when the King, who lives in an apparently timeless world of Eden in which he still acknowledges the six year service that George owes to Gloriana, is going to die. To answer that question we need to understand more about the *exact* relationship between Eden and the world time than we can glean by looking at the poem through a binary Enlightenment "either/or" lens.[4] The careful reader will have to store this question away in their memory before making a firm decision on this point, as they have learned to do after so many false starts.

The Appearance of Una

Nevertheless, the confident King of Eden calls "His onely daughter, and his only hayre" (I.xii.21.3), whose heritage he has nevertheless just given to George. She appears

> with sad sober cheare,

---

[4] The "either/or" Enlightenment model will give readers an earthly Eden if they look at it from the perspective of its not being Heaven, but will give readers a Heavenly perspective on Eden if they approach it from the point of view of its not being earth. Both perspectives are partial in relation to the more whole Augustinian perspective.

> As bright as doth the morning starre appeare[5]
> Out of the East, with flaming lockes bedight,
> To tell that dawning day is drawing neare,
> And to the world does bring long wished light;
> So faire and fresh that Lady shewd her selfe in sight. (I.xii.21.4-9)

It is only now, in the comfort of Eden, presented within the imaginative and deconstructable universe of Faery, that she brings her "long wished light" into "the world," as she "shewd her selfe in sight."

The distinctions being made are between Una on the one hand and Fidessa and Charissa on the other. Unlike Fidessa and Charissa, Una maintains her chastity, exchanging her mottled clothes of black and white, appropriate for her sojourn in the changeable world, for a gown of pure white that still shows no more than her face:

> For she had layd her mournefull stole aside,
> And widow-like sad wimple throwne away,
> Wherewith her heauenly beautie she did hide,
> Whiles on her wearie iourney she did ride;
> And on her now a garment she did weare,
> All lilly white, withoutten spot, or pride…. (I.xii.22.2-7)

Una's interior body remains the same, still covered, and this is how the poet wishes his readers to approach her: not with the eyes of flesh but with the eyes of the mind.

The most intriguing lines in her description may be these:

> That seemd like silke and siluer wouen neare,
> But neither silke nor siluer therein did appeare. (I.xii.22.8-9)

These lines, like the "many ragged clouts" (I.ix.36.1) that hung about Despair, reflect Spenser's reading of Boethius' *Consolation of Philosophy*. Here there are no thorns holding separate pieces together, and this brings up the question of how much validity the reader can give to such a seamless vision of beauty in the poet's imaginative vision? Only by relaxing the hold on *reality* that Spenser has been pushing for the entire poem can the reader settle on Una's vision of beauty as the end of their experience. In Una's appearance in silk and silver in which "neither silke nor siluer therein did ap-

---

[5] It is interesting that though the poet likens her to Phosphorus, Phosphorus was the morning star that Redcrosse followed when he abandoned her. I note that, although she is likened to the morning star, it is the sun that actually brings "long wished light."

peare," Spenser believes that he can maintain distinctions in epistemology that could never be maintained in the ontological world. So, despite the appearance of "silke and siluer" in the reference—a=b in Frege's terms—the underlying identity of silk and silver (a=a) sports no difference. This meeting of ontology and epistemology that Descartes had placed in ontological reality is only possible in the Reformation in an Augustinian act of epistemological imagination.

It is for this reason that Una shows herself as "faire and fresh, as freshest flowre in May" (I.xii.22.1), an image of perpetual, never-fading beauty that can only exist *out of time*. This may be appropriate for her as the Princess of Eden, but it does not accord with the lesson of the importance of time in this life that *her* friends, from Arthur to Contemplation, have been attempting to get George to respect. Spenser is using the power of imagination to create a reader's experience with Una that can afterwards be deconstructed without having to *actually* the stop the clock and step out of time into a fictional logocentric sphere. George will return to his substantial consciousness within the literal world of time as soon as the Book of Holinesse is put down.

George does not react to Una's appearance as a lover who had been captivated by Una from the beginning of his experience with her would, but as though he was seeing her only now for the first time:

> Ne wonder; for her owne deare loued knight,
> All were she daily with himselfe in place,
> Did wonder much at her celestiall sight:
> Oft had he seene her faire, but neuer so faire dight. (I.xii.23.6-9)

The change here is brought about, not by any change in Una's inward beauty, but by a change of her outer garment. And once again, George's experience is not ordered by reason in any way. He merely "Did wonder much at her celestiall sight."

Aristotle on Goodwill, Friendship, and Love

Despite the lack of rational clarity on George's part, there is a method to Spenser's madness. Consider that in Book IX of the *Nichomachean Ethics*, Aristotle distinguishes goodwill—which the reader will later be assured from George's own mouth that he has—from broader friendship, which sadly thus far poor George has shown he lacks:

> Goodwill is a friendly sort of relation, but is not *identical* with friend-

ship; for one may have goodwill both towards people whom one does not know, and without their knowing it, but not friendship.[6]

Aristotle makes much of this distinction:

> But goodwill is not even friendly feeling. For it does not involve intensity or desire, whereas these accompany friendly feeling; and friendly feeling implies intimacy while goodwill may arise of a sudden, as it does towards competitors in a contest; we come to feel goodwill for them and to share in their wishes, but we would not do anything with them; for, as we said, we feel goodwill suddenly and love them only superficially.[7]

The fact that George ascribes only "goodwill" to himself in the opening of the following book (II.i.33.4) must make the careful reader question whether his "goodwill" has been extended to friendship. It could be that he is only now, at the end of the adventures that have filled the Book of Holinesse, coming to appreciate the gift that he has been given in Una.

Reading a little further in Aristotle's work can help us to secure the important distinction in the reader's mind:

> Goodwill seems, then, to be a beginning of friendship, as the pleasure of the eye is the beginning of love. For no one loves if he has not first been delighted by the form of the beloved, but he who delights in the form of another does not, for all that, love him, but only does so when he also longs for him when absent and craves for his presence....[8]

Aristotle has more to say on the subject:

> ...so too it is not possible for people to be friends if they have not come to feel goodwill for each other, but those who feel goodwill are not for all that friends; for they only *wish* well to those for whom they feel goodwill, and would not do anything with them nor take trouble for them. And so one might by an extension of the term say that goodwill is inactive friendship, though when it is prolonged and reaches the point of intimacy it becomes friendship—not the friendship based on utility nor that based on pleasure; for goodwill too does not arise on those terms.[9]

---

6 Aristotle, *Nichomachean Ethics*, IX.5.1166b30-32.
7 Ibid., IX.5.1166b32-1167a3.
8 Ibid., IX.6.1167a4-7.
9 Ibid., IX.61167a7-13.

Una displays herself in the best possible light in her behavior at the court of Eden, whose King has nevertheless given her kingdom to a man whom the careful reader has been given reasons to believe does not love her for herself alone:

> So fairely dight, when she in presence came,
> She to her Sire made humble reuerence,
> And bowed low, that her right well became,
> And added grace vnto her excellence. (I.xii.24.1-4)

But, though the poet can describe her behavior towards others in the court of Eden, he retreats before the task of describing her beauty in and of itself:

> The blazing brightnesse of her beauties beame,
> And glorious light of her sunshyny face
> To tell, were as to striue against the streame.
> My ragged rimes are all too rude and bace,
> Her heauenly lineaments for to enchace. (I.xii.23.1-5)

The King of Eden's Interrupted Speech

In response to her perfect appearance, the King of Eden is about to speak "with great wisedome, and graue eloquence" (I.xii.24.5). The careful reader may be wishing to hear at last what the King of Eden has to say; but after he has already pledged his kingdom to George, effectively disinheriting his perfect daughter from her inheritance, he is interrupted by a messenger bearing troubling news:

> But eare he thus had said,
> With flying speede, and seeming great pretence,
> Came running in, much like a man dismaid,
> A Messenger with letters, which his message sayd. (I.xii.24.6-9)

The King of Eden falls silent, his potentially unifying thought remaining unexpressed; but the messenger gets to speak. What he has to say will put the King's celebration of George in doubt.

All are "amazed" (I.xii.25.1), and they listen as the messenger speaks word prepared by Duessa that he reads as "writt" (I.xii.25.8). Duessa begins her message by noting the already accomplished disenfranchisement of Una from the line of succession by the rules of patrimony:

> The wofull daughter, and forsaken heire
> Of that great Emperour of all the West. (I.xii.26.3-4)

This description of the King of Eden as the emperor of the *west* calls to mind the division of the Roman Empire into two halves, neither of which held the whole of empire. Moreover, the Western half of the Roman Empire was the part that Fidessa had laid claim to as "the sole daughter of an Emperour, / He that the wide West vnder his rule has" (I.ii.22.7-8). By not speaking, the King of Eden does not lose his right to rule in Eden, but it remains clear that Duessa is attempting to introduce a philosophical division into the unified Kingdom of Eden in the same way that Archimago had introduced philosophical division into the love of Una for Redcrosse.

But the worst is yet to come, as Duessa begins discussing the fact that they really do not know "that new vnknowen guest" as well as they have been led to believe:

> Ere thou thy daughter linck in holy band
> Of wedlocke to that new vnknowen guest:
> For he already plighted his right hand
> Vnto another loue, and to another land. (I.xii.26.6-9)

She then tells the story of Redcrosse at "the burning Altars" at which "he swore" (I.xii.27.5). This information is intended to reflects the burning of heroic Hercules by his own pride in believing in false gods, which according to Christian tradition were not reflections of any underlying reality but were reflections of a myth created by imaginative fiction. This is why it remains so important to have kept watch over the "brazen gate" that the King had flung open as soon as the Dragon had been defeated. After all, this is how the messenger of Duessa gets in to Eden in the first place. That mistake may be laid at the feet of the King of Eden himself.

Duessa, through her messenger, draws the King of Eden, who only moments before was going to offer a grand speech on the ultimate end of the universe in unitary values, out of his comfortable realm by asking him to decide between two poles of argument to render a "iudgement iuste" (I.xii.27.8) based on her fuller knowledge of events, to which she *flies* (I.xii.27.8):

> Therefore since mine he is, or free or bond,
> Or false or trew, or liuing or else dead,
> Withhold, O souerayne Prince, your hasty hond
> From knitting league with him, I you aread. (I.xii.28.1-4)

Duessa is counting on the King to act as a justice of the peace, an action that involves rendering a decision based in binary reason in order to decide between opposing defendants before the law and thereby raising one position over another. It will not do for the King of Eden to "fly" from this choice back to a metaphysical perspective in which unity and balance can be maintained.

Duessa blocks the King's ability to render an advantageous verdict to himself by reminding him that to do so would be to raise force over justice, and so render the King a tyrant:

> Ne weene my right with strength adowne to tread,
> Through weakenesse of my widowhed, or woe. (I.xii.28.5-6)

Duessa appeals to *truth* in matters of justice:

> For truth is strong, her rightfull cause to plead,
> And shall find friends, if need requireth soe,
> So bids thee well to fare, Thy neither friend, nor foe, Fidessa.
> (I.xii.28.7-9)

Duessa's appeal to the King's duty to decide cases impartially is why she declares herself "neither friend, nor foe." Though she is lying when she says this, there is nothing wrong with her argument *as a matter of law*; Duessa, disguised as Fidessa in the written word that the male messenger carries through the unwatched gates of Eden, has temporal priority in the case.

The King's Response to New Information

The King, who has been astonished by the messenger's words, fixes a sterner eye on George; and, seeming to now believe that he has not been told the whole truth after all, asks him to tell him more: "Let nought be hid from me, that ought to be exprest" (I.xii.28.9).

At first, this sounds correct. The proper thing to do in this circumstance is to make "triall" of all the evidence before one, weighing it, not with equal measure, but rightly. So the King asks for an amplification of the meaning of these

> bloudy vowes, and idle threats
> Throwne out from womanish impatient mind. (I.xii.30.1-2)

The problem is that the King is already making assumptions in his question that may not be founded in truth. He has not yet made "triall" of all the evidence before him. One wonders once again how his perpetually silent daughter, who he has already disenfranchised, reacts to the implication of the King's words that *she*, as a woman, has no inherent value.

The King suspects nothing of his own complicity in the current state of affairs, and he announces that his conscience is clear, but he now sees reason to doubt George:

> High God be witnesse, that I guiltlesse ame.
> But if your selfe, Sir knight, ye faulty fynd,
> Or wrapped be in loues of former Dame,
> With crime do not it couer, but disclose the same. (I.xii.30.6-9)

To his credit, George admits all:

> My Lord, my King, be nought hereat dismayd,
> Till well ye wote by graue intendiment,
> What woman, and wherefore doth me vpbrayd
> With breach of loue, and loyalty betrayd.
> It was in my mishaps, as hitherward
> I lately traueild, that vnwares I strayd
> Out of my way, through perils straunge and hard;
> That day should faile me, ere I had them all declard. (I.xii.31.2-9)

Despite the appeal of his argument to hopeful readers, George's indication that he had traveled "Out of my way" is the first indication that George thought he *had* a direction in the book.

The reader, who has been there to witness events first hand and not visiting only from "farre" at the end of his successful completion of his adventure, should more properly ascribe his victory to the will of God and not to George's pursuit of random adventure without weighing the need to engage his enemies through the intermediary lens of reason. Moreover, it is interesting that his confession of his error relies on putting the blame for his "breach of loue" and "loyalty betrayd" on the "intendiment" of another woman's bad faith and not, as readers who have actually seen George in action, on his actions. Those readers are in a position to judge George independently of any authority.

So George does not lie, but he says it was not his fault, because no one could have known. He claims that it was "easie was t'inuegle weaker sight" (I.xii.32.5), because Duessa had exercised her "wicked arts, and wylie skill" (I.xii.32.6) and that her charms were "Too false and strong for earthly skill or might" (I.xii.32.7). This is patently not true, as reason could have been used all along to peer beneath the surface of bodies to their underlying rational cause. George's problem is that he has been relying throughout his adventures on might, not reason. The reader has learned over the course of George's adventures that might is not all. It appears, even at the end of his adventure *after he has killed the Dragon* and has been admitted into Eden, that Geoge has not penetrated to the heart of his problem, as he says he had been betrayed when he least feared ill (I.xii.32.9). This rhetorical flourish does not change the underlying ontological fact. In spite of everyone's having been willing to lay blame elsewhere, George has *actually* been fooled into lying with Duessa after he left Una, the image of perfect unity and beauty, on account of his lack of education in rational ways of thought.

Una's Resolution

Una, who has recently been dismissed by the King's arguments as having no inherent value except as a prize for others, steps forth and apologizes for George. She says she knew of the "secret treasons" that she claims "haue bene wroght by that false sorceresse" (I.xii.33.5-6):

> Shee onely she it is, that earst did throw
> This gentle knight into so great distresse,
> That death him did awaite in daily wretchednesse. (I.xii.33.7-9)

Her repetition of "she" gives us the feel that it is she and only she (an image born nevertheless of Duessa's power of doubling) who is to blame for George's fall into error. Una herself has been led to believe this by her own dwarf, but careful readers have also seen that Una takes from the dwarf's picture of the events he relates dispassionately in order to save her from error something less than the whole truth. She absolves George of responsibility for his past mistakes, placing them all on Archimago (interestingly not on the woman Duessa), who she correctly identifies as the messenger.

The passionate King is "greatly moued" (I.xii.35.1), not by the reason of the case, but by the argument of his only daughter, who is not really in a position to judge fairly. Satisfied with his daughter's experience with George, the King turns his attention to directing his "Gard, which on his state did wait" (I.xii.35.4) to bind Archimago like a chained bear. The reader, perhaps, is willing to go along with this, because it accords with their notion that good should triumph over evil, but this is not really justice. In deciding the case, the King throws out reason, which would have had him decide the case in favor of Fidessa. Instead, he suborns true justice, not to a deeper sense of justice based in Augustine's knowledge of the Creator's pre-linguistic ontology that we have seen deployed in Spenser's allegory of silence and speech, but to his arbitrary whim. His decision brings up the question of whether the King has become a tyrant in order to save his kingdom, and it is not at all clear that he has not.

The Marriage of Heaven and Earth

After the tyrant King's dismissal of the case that has come before his bench, everyone goes on in their former way, as though nothing has changed in the Kingdom of Eden. But things have changed. Whereas the King had been willing to wait six years to conclude the marriage, he now rushes to complete the full service:

> His owne two hands the holy knots did knit,
> That none but death for euer can deuide.... (I.xii.37.1-2)

Once again, he does so without consulting Una or George.

Maidens appear, sprinkling posts with wine, while houses are likewise sprinkled with "frankincense diuine, / And precious odours" (I.xii.38.3-4). The adjective "diuine" might make us think that there has been no division here between Heaven and earth in the marriage which is taking place, but these things are not fetched from the native ground to which Una has returned, but were "fetcht from far away" (I.xii.38.4). This leaves the question of the location of Eden still in doubt. The maidens

> sweete Musicke did apply
> Her curious skill, the warbling notes to play,
> To driue away the dull Melancholy;
> The whiles one sung a song of loue and iollity. (I.xii.38.6-9)[10]

But happiness replaces the melancholy only temporarily.

The reader does not have to wait long for its return. Having seen Una for the first time, George enjoys her presence for a little while:

> Her ioyous presence and sweet company
> In full content he there did long enioy,
> Ne wicked enuy, ne vile gealosy
> His deare delights were hable to annoy. (I.xii.41.1-4)

---

10 The assertion that there is a "dull melancholy" that needs to be driven out of Eden strikes me as an odd thing for Spenser to note.

However, *this* George cannot forget,

> how he whilome had sworne,
> In case he could that monstrous beast destroy,
> Vnto his Faery Queene backe to retourne:
> The which he shortly did…. (I.xii.41.5-9)

Therefore, against the unwary reader's expectations, Una is "left to mourn" (I.xii.41.9) in the extremity of a fictional Eden that can hold time at bay in ekphrasistic images of ever-blooming flowers but which needs a person like George, who has a substantial consciousness, to activate what exists in Eden only in potential.

The Narrator's Final Words

The narrator, has only stopped sailing only until he can repair his ship's "tackles spent" (I.xii.42.6) and get her "wants supplied" (I.xii.42.7). The process of stopping in the "quiet rode" (I.xii.42.2) of Eden means letting of some of the cargo that he has been taking with him, while at the same time rebalancing the load for further adventures:

> And then againe abroad
> On the long voyage whereto she is bent:
> Well may she speede and fairely finish her intent. (I.xii.42.7-9)

To mistake Eden as anything more than a "quiet" stopping place on a much longer "rode," would be to make the same mistake that has prevented George from realizing his destiny, which, like the poet's restless ship, lies elsewhere.

Una will be left behind in her native kingdom, stripped by her naïve father of her inheritance. After a brief sojourn into the terrifying world of time in which she meets people who are happy to make their living raping churches; satyrs who do not listen to her instructions as to how she should be worshipped; men without law who would rape her in order to satisfy their animal desire; a sun that does not responds to her pleas for help but hides its face in shame; and a lover who flees her, taking her dwarf with him, and who falls in love with the first unchaste woman who shows him her body; Una falls silent once more and is never heard from again. The poet's ship passes from the ruins of Eden, taking George with him to continue his six years of promised service to Gloriana.

Conclusion

Spenser's Correction of Modern Aesthetic Assumptions

The premise of my book is derived from my reading of Plato's *Parmenides*, where the process of history is reversed and Socrates lectures an even younger Aristotle. Such things are impossible in the real world, but human beings have no problem imagining them. In this case, I hoped to show that Spenser has something to teach the moderns about their certainty about ends. The Moderns were certain that they were about to close the hermeneutic circle. The postmoderns believed that mankind's inability to close hermeneutic circles meant that they could continue along a skeptical path to the same ends. Both positions take Plato's metaphor of the cyclical return of nature for granted in their aesthetics. This only makes sense if Augustine's contribution to classical philosophy, which changed Plato's cyclical return to one of a progressive building up of science over time in opposition to nature, is ignored. This is what happened in the enthusiasm of the Enlightenment for a new coordinate geometry that rendered Augustine a philosopher that had nothing to teach modern critics.

Book I is not the fall of a Protestant saint away from holiness and his subsequent return to a state of perfection, as Robert Kellogg asserts. Redcrosse's journey is built out of Spenser's Augustinian perception that reason will always sport a breach in its ability to close any hermeneutic circle it proposes. That does not mean, as it meant for Herder and Goethe, that reason is incapable of closing what can be closed by other symbolic means. It means that the human capacity for reason is important, but it must be subordinated to a larger reality on account of its imperfection.

When such imperfections as those that Augustine encountered in the late 5th century were revived at the beginning of the 20th by Kurt Gödel in the face of the perfect rationalist claims of Russell and Whitehead, the moderns did not give up their aesthetic assumptions. Instead, Wittgenstein doubled down, proposing an experiment known as the beetle in the box. That experiment completely undermined the notion of Descartes' private language by making meaning a function of the public expression of private language. This does not deconstruct the Enlightenment principle that everything that used to be thought to come simply and clearly from God or nature. Now meaning comes just as simply and clearly from the interaction of human minds. Wittgenstein introduces a paradox into modern philosophy but he was unable to provide a satisfactory answer to it. This makes resolution of philosophical problems a matter of picking from incompatible premises for resolution. As a result, the Enlightenment forces thinkers to make choices that discount the claim of philosophy to wholeness.[1]

Augustine's view is much more like Plato's statistical estimation of the universe that readers encounter in the *Timaeus* than it is like Descartes' universe of clear and distinct ideas. Carneades had founded the school of academic skepticism on the basis of Socrates' knowledge that the only thing he knew was that he knew nothing, and Augustine followed Carneades in this. But there is a difference between Carneades and Augustine when dealing with the resulting skepticism. Carneades followed Socrates' foundation of a school that defined all values negatively. Augustine's model also required a negative definition of values, but positive action was required in realizing those values, as well. As a result, Augustine overturned the mind's priority

---

[1] Both of these premises are clearer from afar than they are up close. While one can pick through medieval philosophy looking for instances of thinkers who believed that universals were compatible with the mind of God, other thinkers can be found who gainsaid such discoveries in the era itself. Most of the gainsayers were Aristotelian philosophers, who were the keepers of doubt in an era marked in the modern mind by a too willing belief in things that had no foundation in ontological reality. This is particularly true in the case of the School of Chartres, where modern thinkers have found a Platonic philosophy that accords with modern thought. But they have no idea what to do about the Aristotelian component of Chartrian thought, which they simply ignore in favor of the mystical aspects of medieval thought. In this way, the modern have managed not to look into the tricky character of medieval reason, which they do not think matters in literary matters in the first place.

The same thing holds true of modern literary theorists, whose clarity of vision for their own thought is based in either Descartes' premises, as it was for the Moderns, or in the postmodern obfuscation of thought by thinkers like Wittgenstein and Gödel. This leads me to believe that such beliefs in clarity are the product of literary thinkers reading introductory textbooks on philosophy rather than giving themselves up to a detailed study of either period in which the clarity sported by both schools of thought fall apart under the weight of evidence provided by the study of the whole range of beliefs available in the period.

over nature, which had been a feature of Carneades' skepticism, making classical reason scan the larger universe for scientific meanings that were not apparent on first sight. This was in large part due to Augustine's incorporation of Aristotle's relative science into a larger Platonic metaphysical system. This meant that *a posteriori* education played a more central role in Augustine's universe than it does in the classical or modern worlds, where that role can be attained by a human's bare *a priori* being. It is this emphasis on education, which the careful reader can see that the "clownishe" George lacks, that is the most important aspect of Spenser's Book of Holinesse.

By the 16th century, Augustine's approach to skepticism had been incorporated into the most powerful and radical movement of that turbulent century: the Reformation. By incorporating an Augustinian approach to skeptical problems into the reading of Spenser's allegorical masterpiece, the modern critic should be able to see that their presumption of Spenser's innocence about skeptical problems masks the very different approach to the same universe.

A Note on Frank Kermode

The modern approach to literature can be represented by Frank Kermode's *The Sense of an Ending*,[2] in which the ends of literature allows the critic a sense of control of the metaphysical content of the literary universe they are describing. Kermode gives into a mystical account of that universe to tie up loose ends in his avowed end of closing the hermeneutic circle around itself.[3] Augustine would deny to any critic who stands outside the text access to the wholeness of *metaphysical* truth of the text. According to Augustine, Kermode's access to the ends of literature is access to the scientific, relative, and incomplete ends of literature *masking* as metaphysical ends in the same way that Socrates' thought that he expressed in Plato's *Ion* was vastly superior to the thought of the non-thinking Ion but did not close the hermeneutic circle as well as Socrates or Plato thought it did.

That does not mark Kermode as a critic whose thought needs to be thrown out in a revolution that will be led by forward thinking academics. In Spenser's mind, this would be an extreme position that rests on the academic sense that they have a more perfect sense of how the world works

---

2 Frank Kermode, *The Sense of an Ending: Studies in the Theory of Fiction: With a New Epilogue* (New York: Oxford University Press, 2000).

3 This sense may be found in Kermode's *The Genesis of Secrecy: On the Interpretation of Narrative*, The Charles Eliot Norton Lectures (Cambridge, MA: Harvard University Press, 1979).

that others lack. The academic call for call for revolution is given with the understanding that academics will remain in charge after the revolution they are calling for is over. Such a position vastly underrates the probability that revolutions will be taken over by the most ruthless Machiavellian men in the revolutionary circle, men who are more interested in gathering power for themselves than they are in providing justice for all. Spenser, having lived in century of brutal religious wars, takes possibility that his class will be overthrown far more seriously than modern academics do.

Instead of throwing out Kermode's position as incomplete and starting over on the basis of modern and by definition more perfect vision, as many moderns have on the basis of their belief in the security of the metaphysical aesthetic, Spenser would discount Kermode's access to the metaphysics of the text, turning back to the relative scientific thoughts that are available to the incomplete human mind and building his aesthetic from that more secure humanistic position. This what he had done with Homer and Virgil as well as with Ariosto and Tasso. This move would leave Kermode's thought (as well as Fletcher's, Derrida's, de Man's, Quilligan's, and Greenblatt's) intact as partial building blocks for future research on the way to an unrealizable endpoint that moved into the future as a goal rather than being discounted by academics who have realized their ends in the present.

Redcrosse in Later Books

The distribution of the end his adventure into an as-yet-unrealized future affects George. In later books, Una is gone; but George moves back to Gloriana's court for six more years of service. This makes sense to the careful reader, since it now appears that George's motivation throughout the Book of Holinesse appears to always to have been

> To winne him worship, and her [Gloriana's] grace to haue,
> Which of all earthly things he most did craue (I.i.3.4-5).

Since the reader will have been thrown for a loop if they have judged the end of the poet's fiction to be resolved in Una's deconstructing unity and not in the literal and open-ended action of George, it is fair to consider whether George reflects the ultimate end of the poet's work anymore than Una does.

The reasons for thinking that he does not are these. First, George has not learned the ways of expression by which the bread of society is leavened by the bourgeois education of men like Edmund Spenser. He has been informed by Contemplation of his right to take his place at court by his having been to the manor born. This adventitious bounty, like his choice of friendship by God, makes him a poor candidate for the *poet's* end, which is to educate the very best men in the kingdom into service at the court through reason.

Secondly, the Kingdom of Eden, where no one has any reason not to trust the words of another, has been sidelined by the Fall, a fact that neither Una nor her father seem to have come to terms with fully at the end of Book I. Along the way to the poet's recentering of experience away from typological experience to a humankind that exists on the literal level of allegory, the reader has been treated to an absolute separation of God's motivations in reenacting the sacred pageant from the motivations of the literal man who actually accomplishes God's goals through the power of his arms. Those motivations are apparent to the poet from the very beginning of his narration, and they are revealed to the careful reader over time, but they are not apparent to George at any time during his adventure. This makes it unlikely that George has ever fully grasped God's purpose, even at the end of his adventure.

That fact leads to the third major indication that George is not the end of the poet's aim in writing *The Faerie Queene:* others continue to call him Redcrosse for the rest of the book. The meaning of Spenser's reversion is that readers who have seen him up close and who have learned his real name have seen him making mistake after mistake as he bumbles towards the goal on which his fame depends. Those mistakes are redeemed, not by anything having to do with his own will, but by God's willingness to confer on the "clownishe younge man" something that he does not understand even at the end of his journey on account of his still limited perspective on life. The fact that others, being "farre" away from the action that the poet has delivered his readers an up-close view of, mistake his accomplishment for an act of will on Redcrosse's part says more about their partial perspective of the subject than any wholeness that lies within George.

After the Book of Holinesse is complete, it is no longer possible to deal with whole individuals within the poem. The reader's grasp of the fact that they live in a postlapsarian world makes it possible for even a good but uneducated man like George to do his limited part in the joint effort of society, in linked effort with others ($a=b$), to bring the potential world of Heaven to life in collective action after he has realized that no man is an island unto himself ($a=a$).

Redcrosse in Book II

After God's purposes have been fulfilled at the end of the Book of Holinesse, the literal actor George confesses to the Palmer at the beginning of Book II that he was only an acting out God's "goodwill" (I.i.33.4) and that He used him as "the organ of his might" (II.i.33.3) without giving him the power to enact his own will. What George wants is what the unsanctified Palmer already has: control over his destiny through his limited reason. For this reason, he confers on the Palmer what Contemplation had mistakenly conferred on him: the "thrise happie newes" (II.i.33.8) of being able to "wish [his] thought" (II.i.33.7) through medium of Guyon's action.

George's response to the Palmer has to do with the perspectival angle taken on all human experience after Spenser has blocked access of the human mind to things as they exist in themselves.[4] The thing that drove George to accomplish his defeat of the Dragon was never his knowledge of his participation in the sacred pageant, but his hope that on account of his fearlessness (that even Arthur lacks) that he could be accepted into the court of the "royal maid" Gloriana, where Heaven and earth meet. Despite his defeat of the Dragon, his use of socially destructive animal violence to achieve his ends stands in the way of seeing him as a moral leader.

---

4 The term "perspectival" has a definite philosophical meaning as I use it here. It is used in Friedrich Nietzsche's *Will to Power* trans. Walter Arnold Kaufmann and R. J. Hollingdale (New York, NY: Random House, 1967), §481, where Nietzsche drives his readers away from a direct perception of factual essences by redefining the "subject" as "something added and invented and projected behind what there is." Nietzsche does not feel that he can get back to anything "original" behind our individual experience, but he does not doubt, as Spenser does, the mind's own integrity, being still a follower of Descartes' Enlightenment. Therefore, in Nietzsche this lack of ability to secure an external source of meaning drives each of us back to own monadically secure minds, which we use as a lever to impose our meaning of events on other, weaker members of society through the exercise of the will to power: "It is our needs that interpret the world; our drives and their For and Against. Every drive is a kind of lust to rule; each one has its perspective that it would like to compel all the other drives to accept as a norm."

In my reading, Spenser is making a deliberate attempt to protect against Nietzsche's conclusions that leave humanity with an binary "us" or "them" choice by introducing a third choice of a necessary fiction that stands between an inaccessible ontological reality and the mind's reconstruction of facts after the their (*a posteriori*) apprehension through the mind's limited reason. In Spenser's opinion, Nietzsche's existential attempt to ignore the third *fictional* domain of imagination that lies between our epistemological reconstructive minds and ontological reality is unfounded in anything other than his own authority. In Spenser's mind, the boundary of imagination can never be wholly deconstructed in such a way that epistemology and ontology can be perfectly joined, as they were in Descartes' post-Reformation thought.

Redcrosse in Book V

When the reader meets him for the last time in Book V, they see a man that has learned the lessons of the first book, as he is now helping others to achieve their goals rather than looking out only for himself. He has knighted Sir Burbon and given him a defensive shield which gives him the power through the red cross embossed on it to defeat all enemies he encounters:

> True is, that I was at first dubbed knight
> By a good knight, the knight of the Redcrosse;
> Who when he gaue me armes, in field to fight,
> Gaue me a shield, in which he did endosse
> His deare Redeemers badge vpon the bosse:
> The same longwhile I bore, and therewithall
> Fought many battels without wound or losse. (V.xi.53.1-7)

But for some reason, Sir Burbon has thrown this very useful shield away, as it has not gotten him the thing he most desires, which is not victory but the woman Flourdelis.

Artegall scolds him for it, but Burbon responds as follows:

> Not so; (quoth he) for yet when time doth serue,
> My former shield I may resume againe:
> To temporize is not from truth to swerue,
> Ne for aduantage terme to entertaine,
> When as necessitie doth it constraine. (V.xi.56.1-5)

Now the careful reader can be sure that to temporize *is* to swerve from truth, and Artegall responds:

> Fie on such forgerie (said Artegall)
> Vnder one hood to shadow faces twaine.
> Knights ought be true, and truth is one in all:
> Of all things to dissemble fouly may befall. (V.xi.56.6-9)

This means that Burbon should not swerve from the inner truth that Redcrosse confers on him by his external gift and return to it later, because without it he will never achieve victory. Truth is constant, and it is one.

But that does not mean that it is the within the power of Redcrosse's shield to give Burbon the love he craves anymore that it was within the power of Una's magical shield to make sure that Redcrosse stuck around and did not run off with her dwarf to fall in love with Duessa, who was "looser" with her body than Una was willing to be with hers. Something more is needed than one's own belief in oneself (a=a) when it comes to interacting with others in social situations (a=b). Sir Burbon lacks reason that could effect his dreams, and Redcrosse is not contributing to that end.

Last Words

In the end, Spenser denies to the literal Redcrosse the sense of an ending that he bestows on the epistemologically-constructed Una at the end of the Book of Holinesse. The focus on the extremity of ends without middles that Redcrosse displays in the Book of Holinesse will destroy the royal court from within according to Aristotle; and this is why Spenser rewrites Ariosto's Catholic ending to the Virgilian myth that leaves Virgil's act of violence in place. Spenser's rewrite places Redcrosse's violent act at the *beginning* of his adventure; and it is shown to accomplish nothing, as Errour's defeat comes only after she has vomited up all the errors that made her a formidable enemy in the first place. Spenser undermines Redcrosse's use of his formidable strength to defeat her. Although he chops her head off, she is eaten by her cannibalistic children, who though gnat-sized when Redcrosse encounters them, will grow into adult errors of equally monstrous size unless Redcrosse does more to permanently defeat them than he does.

Spenser's portrait of Redcrosse is intended to show a man cut off from direct access to God's created ontology, even as he is benefitting from His friendship to help him through every crisis he encounters. George plays a critical role in warning individual members of the species of mankind not to liken themselves to God (a=a). Instead, Spenser hopes that men will forgo their identification with God and forge friendships with one another (a=b) by listening carefully to the echo of their own experience and to the lessons already learned by others' experience within the world. That practice will not only extend their reach horizontally through a building up of the best men in the world at the royal court but will also graft them back to God by a similarly indirect a=b structure.

Only at the end of the Book of Holinesse has George learned to appreciate the gift of Una, who he had been taking for granted for the entire book. Only at the end of the Book of Holinesse has he learned the important lesson that he is not identical to God but that his effort was dependent on the "goodwill" of God. That is much, but he still has a long way to go before he learns how to behave as an educated man who uses reason in the world of time. That process is left for other men and women to discover for themselves in later books.

Works Cited

Abrams, M. H. *Natural Supernaturalism: Tradition and Revolution in Romantic Literature*. New York: W. W. Norton, 1973.

Adorno, Theodor W. *Adorno: The Stars Down to Earth and Other Essays on the Irrational in Culture*. Edited by Stephen Crook. New York, NY: Routledge, 1994.

Alciati, Andrea. *A Book of Emblems: The Emblematum Liber in Latin and English*. Translated by John F. Moffitt. Jefferson, N.C.: McFarland & Co., 2004.

Alpers, Paul J. *The Poetry of the Faerie Queene*. Princeton, NJ: Princeton University Press, 1967.

Appleyard, Bryan. "A One-Man Market." *The Economist: Intelligent Life Supplement*, October 29, 2011, 14-19.

Ariosto, Lodovico. *Orlando Furioso (The Frenzy of Orlando): A Romantic Epic*. Translated by Barbara Reynolds, The Penguin Classics. New York, NY: Penguin, 1975.

Aristotle. *The Complete Works of Aristotle: The Revised Oxford Translation*. Edited by Jonathan Barnes, Bollingen Series. Princeton, NJ: Princeton University Press, 1984.

———. *The Politics*. Edited by Carnes Lord. Chicago, IL: University of Chicago Press, 1984.

Arnold, Matthew. *Culture and Anarchy*. Edited by Jane Garnett. New ed, Oxford World's Classics. Oxford: Oxford University Press, 2009.

Auerbach, Erich. *Mimesis: The Representation of Reality in Western Literature*.

Princeton: Princeton University Press, 1953.

Augustine. *The City of God*, Modern Library Giants 74. New York, NY: Modern Library, 1950.

———. *Confessions*. Translated by Henry Chadwick, Oxford World's Classics. Oxford: Oxford University Press, 1998.

———. "On the Holy Trinity." In *A Select Library of the Nicene and Post-Nicene Fathers of the Christian Church*, edited by Philip Schaff. New York, NY: The Christian Literature Co., 1886.

Barrett, William. *Irrational Man: A Study in Existential Philosophy*, Doubleday Anchor Books. Garden City, NY: Doubleday, 1958.

Baumgarten, Alexander Gottlieb. *Aesthetica*. Hildesheim: G. Olms, 1961.

Bertens, Johannes Willem. *The Idea of the Postmodern: A History*. New York, NY: Routledge, 1995.

Boethius. *Consolation of Philosophy*. Translated by Joel C. Relihan. Indianapolis, IN: Hackett Pub. Co., 2001.

Bradbury, Malcolm, and James Walter McFarlane. *Modernism, 1890-1930: A Guide to European Literature*. New York, NY: Penguin Books, 1991.

Burkert, Walter. *Greek Religion*. Cambridge, MA: Harvard University Press, 1985.

Bush, Douglas. *Mythology and the Renaissance Tradition in English Poetry*. Minneapolis, MN: The University of Minneapolis Press, 1932.

Calvin, John. *Institutes of the Christian Religion*. Translated by Henry Beveridge. Peabody, MA: Hendrickson Publishers, Inc., 1989.

Campbell, Joseph. *The Masks of God*. 4 vols. New York, NY: Viking Press, 1959.

Canfora, Luciano. *The Vanished Library*, Hellenistic Culture and Society 7. Berkeley, CA: University of California Press, 1989.

Cassirer, Ernst. *The Philosophy of the Enlightenment*. Princeton, NJ: Princeton University Press, 1951.

Cicero, Marcus Tullius. *De Oratore*. Edited by Edward William Sutton and Harris Rackham. 2 vols, Loeb Classics. Cambridge, MA: Harvard University Press, 1942.

Cochrane, Charles Norris. *Christianity and Classical Culture: A Study of Thought and Action from Augustus to Augustine*. Oxford: The Clarendon Press, 1940.

Cohn, Dorrit. *Transparent Minds: Narrative Modes for Presenting Consciousness in Fiction*. Princeton, NJ: Princeton University Press, 1978.

Connor, Steven. *The Cambridge Companion to Postmodernism*. New York, NY: Cambridge University Press, 2004.

Cummings, Brian. "Protestant Allegory." In *The Cambridge Companion to Allegory*, edited by Rita Copeland and Peter T. Struck, 177-190. New York, NY: Cambridge University Press, 2010.

Curtius, Ernst Robert. *European Literature and the Latin Middle Ages*. Translated by Willard R. Trask. Vol. 36, Bollingen Series. Princeton, NJ: Princeton University Press, 1953.

De Man, Paul. "Pascal's Allegory of Persuasion." In *Allegory and Representation*, edited by Stephen Greenblatt, 1-25. Baltimore, MD: Johns Hopkins University Press, 1981.

Derrida, Jacques. "Living On." In *Deconstruction and Criticism*, edited by Harold Bloom, 62-141. New York, NY: Seabury Press, 1979.

———. *Of Grammatology*. Translated by Gayatri Chakravorty Spivak. Corrected ed. Baltimore: Johns Hopkins University Press, 1997.

Descartes, René. *Discourse on Method of Rightly Conducting the Reason and Seeking Truth in the Sciences*. In *The Rationalists*, 37-96. Garden City, N.Y.: Doubleday & Company, 1974.

———. "Geometry." In *Discourse on Method, Optics, Geometry, and Meteorology*, 177-262. Indianapolis, IN: Hackett, 2001.

———. *Meditations on First Philosophy: With Selections from the Objections and Replies*. Edited by Michael Moriarty. Oxford: Oxford University Press, 2008.

Dodds, E. R. *The Greeks and the Irrational*, Sather Classical Lectures. Berkeley: University of California Press, 1951.

Du Bartas, Guillaume de Salluste. *Bartas: His Devine Weekes and Works (1605)*. Translated by Josuah Sylvester. Edited by Francis C. Haber. Gainesville, FL: Scholars Facsimiles & Reprints, 1965.

Eschenbach, Wolfram Von. *Parzival*. Translated by A. T. Hatto, Penguin Classics. New York, NY: Penguin Books, 1980.

Evans, Gareth. "Can There Be Vague Objects?" *Analysis* 38, no. 4 (1978): 208.

Fenik, Bernard. *Studies in the Odyssey*, Hermes: Zeitschrift Für Klassische Philologie. Einzelschriften. Wiesbaden: F. Steiner, 1974.

Fleming, John V. *Reason and the Lover*. Princeton, NJ: Princeton University Press, 1984.

Fletcher, Angus John Stewart. *Allegory: The Theory of a Symbolic Mode*. Ithaca, NY: Cornell University Press, 1964.

Force, James E., and Richard Henry Popkin. *Newton and Religion: Context, Nature, and Influence*. Boston, MA: Kluwer Academic Publishers, 2010.

Frege, Gottlob. "On Sense and Meaning." In *Translations from the Philosophical Writings of Gottlob Frege*, edited by Peter Geach and Max Black, 56-78. Totowa, NJ: Rowman & Littlefield, 1980.

Frye, Northrop. *Anatomy of Criticism: Four Essays*. Princeton: Princeton University Press, 1957.

———. *The Secular Scripture: A Study of the Structure of Romance*, Charles Eliot Norton Lectures 1974-1975. Cambridge, MA: Harvard University Press, 1976.

Gadamer, Hans-Georg. "Idea and Reality in Plato's *Timeaus*." In *Dialogue and Dialectic: Eight Hermeneutical Studies on Plato*, 156-192. New Haven, CT: Yale University Press, 1980.

Gay, Peter. *The Enlightenment, An Interpretation: The Science of Freedom*. New York: W.W. Norton, 1977.

Gilson, Etienne. *History of Christian Philosophy in the Middle Ages*. New York, NY: Random House, 1955.

Gödel, Kurt. *On Formally Undecidable Propositions of Principia Mathematica and Related Systems*. New York: Basic Books, 1962.

Green, Henry. *Andrea Alciati and His Books of Emblems; a Biographical and Bibliographical Study*, Burt Franklin Bibliography & Reference Series, #131. New York, NY: B. Franklin, 1965.

Greenblatt, Stephen. *Renaissance Self-Fashioning: From More to Shakespeare*. Chicago, IL: University of Chicago Press, 1980.

Greenblatt, Stephen, and The Institute of English. *Allegory and Representation*. Edited by Stephen Greenblatt, Selected Papers from the English Institute. Baltimore: Johns Hopkins University Press, 1981.

Gross, Kenneth. *Spenserian Poetics: Idolatry, Iconoclasm, and Magic*. Ithaca, NY: Cornell University Press, 1985.

Hamilton, A. C. *The Spenser Encyclopedia*. Toronto: University of Toronto Press, 1990.

———. *The Structure of Allegory in the Faerie Queene*. Oxford: Clarendon Press, 1961.

Hans, James S. *Socrates and the Irrational*. Charlottesville, VA: University of Virginia Press, 2006.

The Heidelberg Catechism with Scripture Texts. Grand Rapids, MI: CRC Publications, 1989.

Homer. *The Iliad*. Translated by Richmond Alexander Lattimore. Chicago, IL: University of Chicago Press, 1951.

———. *The Odyssey of Homer*. Translated by Richmond Alexander Lattimore. New York, NY: Harper Perennial, 1999.

Horace. *Satires, Epistles, and Ars Poetica, with an English Translation*. Translated by H. R. Fairclough. Rev. ed, Loeb Classical Library. Cambridge: Harvard University Press, 1961.

Hume, David. *A Treatise of Human Nature: A Critical Edition*. Edited by David Fate Norton and Mary J. Norton. 2 vols, The Clarendon Edition of the Works of David Hume. Oxford: Clarendon Press, 2007.

Jauss, Hans Robert. *Toward an Aesthetic of Reception*. Vol. 2, Theory and History of Literature. Minneapolis, MN: University of Minnesota Press, 1982.

Johnson, Paul. *A History of Christianity*. New York, NY: Atheneum, 1976.

Jones, Richard Foster. *Ancients and Moderns: A Study of the Background of the Battle of the Books*. St. Louis, MO: Washington University Press, 1936.

Kaske, Carol V. "The Dragon's Spark and Sting and the Structure of Red Cross's Dragon Fight: The Faerie Queene I Xi-Xii'." *Studies in Philology* 66 (1969): 609-638.

———. *Spenser and Biblical Poetics*. Ithaca NY: Cornell University Press, 1999.

Kermode, Frank. *The Genesis of Secrecy: On the Interpretation of Narrative*, The Charles Eliot Norton Lectures. Cambridge, MA: Harvard University Press, 1979.

———. *The Sense of an Ending: Studies in the Theory of Fiction: With a New Epilogue*. New York: Oxford University Press, 2000.

Kneale, W. C., and Martha Kneale. *The Development of Logic.* New York, NY: Clarendon Press, 1984.

Kretzmann, Norman, Anthony Kenny, and Jan Pinborg. *The Cambridge History of Later Medieval Philosophy: From the Rediscovery of Aristotle to the Disintegration of Scholasticism, 1100-1600.* New York, NY: Cambridge University Press, 1982.

Kripke, Saul A. *Naming and Necessity.* Cambridge, MA: Blackwell Publishing, 1980.

Levenson, Michael H. *The Cambridge Companion to Modernism.* New York, NY: Cambridge University Press, 1999.

Levin, Richard A. "The Legende of the Redcrosse Night and Una: Or, of the Love of a Good Woman." *Studies in English Literature: 1500-1900* 31, no. 1 (1991): 1-24.

Lewis, C. S. *The Allegory of Love: A Study in Medieval Tradition.* Oxford: The Clarendon Press, 1936.

Longinus. *On the Sublime.* In *Poetics*, 143-308. Loeb Classical Library. Cambridge, MA: Harvard University Press, 1995.

Lorris, Guillaume de, and Jean de Meun. *The Romance of the Rose.* Translated by Charles Dahlberg. Princeton, NJ: Princeton University Press, 1971.

———. *Le Roman de la Rose.* Edited by Ernest Langlois. 5 vols. Paris: Firmin-Didot, 1914.

Lucian. *Chattering Courtesans and Other Sardonic Sketches.* Translated by Keith C. Sidwell. New York, NY: Penguin Books, 2004.

Lucretius Carus, Titus. *Lucretius, De Rerum Natura.* Edited by Ettore Paratore and W. H. D. Rouse. 2nd edition. ed, The Loeb Classical Library. Cambridge, MA: Harvard University Press, 1982.

Macrobius, Ambrosius Aurelius Theodosius, and Marcus Tullius Cicero. *Commentary on the Dream of Scipio.* Translated by William Harris Stahl, Records of Civilization, Sources and Studies No. 48. New York: Columbia University Press, 1952.

Manuel, Frank Edward. *The Eighteenth Century Confronts the Gods.* New York, NY: Atheneum, 1967.

———. *Isaac Newton, Historian.* Cambridge, MA: Belknap Press of Harvard University Press, 1963.

Marcuse, Herbert. *One-Dimensional Man: Studies in the Ideology of Ad-*

vanced Industrial Society. Boston: Beacon Press, 1991.

Natoli, Joseph P., and Linda Hutcheon. *A Postmodern Reader*. Albany: State University of New York Press, 1993.

Nelson, William. *The Poetry of Edmund Spenser: A Study*. New York, NY: Columbia University Press, 1963.

Nietzsche, Friedrich Wilhelm. *The Will to Power*. Translated by Walter Arnold Kaufmann and R. J. Hollingdale. New York, NY: Random House, 1967.

Nohrnberg, James. *The Analogy of the Faerie Queene*. Princeton, NJ: Princeton University Press, 1976.

Ovid. *Metamorphoses*. Translated by Frank Justus Miller. Edited by G. P. Goold. 2nd ed. 2 vols, Loeb Classical Library. Cambridge, MA: Harvard University Press, 1984.

———. *Metamorphoses*. Translated by Stanley Lombardo. Indianapolis, IN: Hackett Pub. Co., 2010.

Petrarca, Francesco. *The Triumphs of Petrarch*. Chicago, IL: Chicago University Press, 1962.

Plato. *The Collected Dialogues of Plato, Including the Letters*. Edited by Huntington Cairns and Edith Hamilton, Bollingen Series 71. Princeton, NJ: Princeton University Press, 1993.

Pope, Alexander, and Pat Rogers. *The Major Works*, Oxford World's Classics. New York: Oxford University Press, 2006.

Popkin, Richard H. *The History of Scepticism: From Savonarola to Bayle*. Rev. and expanded ed. Oxford: Oxford University Press, 2003.

Ptolemy, and G. J. Toomer. *Ptolemy's Almagest*, Duckworth Classical, Medieval, and Renaissance Editions. London: Duckworth, 1984.

Quilligan, Maureen. *The Language of Allegory: Defining the Genre*. Ithaca, NY: Cornell University Press, 1979.

Relihan, Joel C. *The Prisoner's Philosophy: Life and Death in Boethius's Consolation*. Notre Dame, IN: University of Notre Dame Press, 2007.

Rousseau, Jean-Jacques. "A Discourse on the Arts and Sciences." In *The Social Contract and the Discourses*, edited by G. D. H. Cole, 1-29. New York, NY: J. M. Dent, 1993.

———. *Emile: Or, On Education*. New York: Basic Books, 1979.

Russell, Bertrand, and Alfred North Whitehead. *Principia Mathematica*.

Cambridge, MA: Cambridge University Press, 1910.

Ryle, Gilbert. "Plato's *Parmenides*." *Mind* 48 (1939): 129-51; 302-25.

Salles, Ricardo. *God and Cosmos in Stoicism*. New York: Oxford University Press, 2009.

Saussure, Ferdinand de. *Course in General Linguistics*. New York, NY: Philosophical Library, 1959.

Scruton, Roger. *From Descartes to Wittgenstein: A Short History of Modern Philosophy*. London: Routledge & Kegan Paul, 1981.

Seneca, Lucius Annaeus. *Letters from a Stoic: Epistulae Morales Ad Lucilium*. Translated by Robin Campbell. Harmondsworth: Penguin, 1969.

Seuren, Pieter A. M. *Western Linguistics: An Historical Introduction*. Oxford: Blackwell Publishers, 1998.

Sextus. *Sextus Empiricus, with an English Translation*. Translated by Robert Gregg Bury. 4 vols, Loeb Classical Library. Cambridge, MA: Harvard University Press, 1961.

Shumaker, Wayne. *Literature and the Irrational: A Study in Anthropological Backgrounds*. Englewood Cliffs, NJ: Prentice-Hall, 1960.

Spenser, Edmund. *The Faerie Queene*. Edited by A. C. Hamilton. 1st ed, Longman Annotated English Poets. New York, NY: Longman, 1977.

———. *The Faerie Queene*. Edited by A. C. Hamilton, Hiroshi Yamashita and Toshiyuki Suzuki. 2nd ed. Harlow: Pearson Education, 2001.

Strabo. *Geography*. Edited by Horace Leonard Jones. 8 vols, Loeb Classical Library. Cambridge, MA: Harvard University Press, 1930.

Tasso, Torquato. *Jerusalem Delivered (Gerusalemme Liberata)*. Translated by Anthony M. Esolen. Baltimore: Johns Hopkins University Press, 2000.

Troyes, Chrétien de. *Perceval : The Story of the Grail*. Translated by Burton Raffel. New Haven, CT: Yale University Press, 1999.

Valla, Lorenzo. *On Pleasure = De Voluptate*. Translated by A. Kent Hieatt. Edited by Maristella De Panizza Lorch. New York, NY: Abaris Books, 1977.

———. *The Treatise of Lorenzo Valla on the Donation of Constantine*. New Haven: Yale University Press, 1922.

Virgil. *Virgil*. Translated by H. Rushton Fairclough. Rev. ed. 2 vols, The Loeb Classical Library. Cambridge, MA: Harvard University Press,

1986.

White, Hayden V. "Foucault's Discourse: The Historiography of Anti-Humanism." In *The Content of the Form: Narrative Discourse and Historical Representation*, 104-143. Baltimore, MD: Johns Hopkins University Press, 1987.

———. *Metahistory: The Historical Imagination in Nineteenth-Century Europe*. Baltimore, MD: Johns Hopkins University Press, 1973.

Wittgenstein, Ludwig. *Philosophical Investigations*. Translated by G. E. M. Anscombe. 3rd ed. Upper Salle River, NJ: Prentice Hall, 1958.

———. *Tractatus Logico-Philosophicus*. New York, NY: Harcourt, Brace & Company, 1922.

Zammito, John H. *The Genesis of Kant's Critique of Judgment*. Chicago, IL: University of Chicago Press, 1992.

Index

A

a=a 89, 91, 93-96, 124, 125, 126, 137, 139, 170, 179, 180, 181, 188, 191, 199, 213, 215, 218, 224, 225, 226, 227, 229, 238, 282, 295, 298
   as description of identity 117, 126
   as superficial identity structure 131
   available in fiction 131
   equivalence to a=b structure 86
   identity of Redcrosse and Jesus as 95
   in Frege 85–87
   Lucifera's orientation towards herself as 144

a=b 87, 89, 91, 93, 96, 121, 124, 125, 128, 139, 170, 179, 180, 181, 188, 191, 194, 199, 212, 215, 224, 225, 226, 227, 229, 236, 238, 254, 282, 295, 298
   appropriate to the world of time 174
   as love 138
   attraction to another as 130
   constructions survive deconstruction
      in the mind of the reader 181
   equivalence to a=a 86
   False Una's love for another as 101
   good ruler's orientation 144
   in Frege 85–87
   seeking identity with another 126
   structure of knowledge as 131
   structure of love as 130
   Una's realization that she must join herself with another as 138

abandonment
   of God
      in Augustine 38
   of natural family
      by lion 121
   of Una 175
      by Redcrosse 84, 102, 125, 130, 197, 280

abatement
   of lion's force 120
Abessa 122–124
abhoration
   Una's fear of 124
abhorred
   bloodshed 148
abhorrence
   of Una
      by Redcrosse 120
   of wretched world 223
abiding
   of bliss
      in mortal men 192
ability
   of reason 278
   of Redcrosse
      to wear the armor of God 95
      to listen to echoes of experience developing in Una 174
      to overcome obstacles
         by Redcrosse 150
      to see what is in front
         of Redcrosse 154
Abrams, M. H. 20
abroad 290
absence
   longing for 283
   of Charissa 227
   of fiction 214
absolute 8, 31
   death 273
   division
      between good and evil 157
      of bodies 162–163
   in Spenser 94
   metaphysical perspective 173
   separation
      from God's purpose 295
   tendencies

of Redcrosse and Una 95
truth 145
absolution
of responsibility 288
absolving
from blame
of Redcrosse 191
abstract
personification 53
principles
in allegory 214
abstraction
mental 15
typological 45
absurd 72
absurdity 18
abuse
of fantasy 77
of Una
by Redcrosse 204
abyss
dark 252
academic 98, 294
elite 193
pagan 170
skepticism 240
school of 292
system
inherent instability of 193
acceptance
of George 45
of Jove 160
of Redcrosse
by Una 124
access
sure
to metaphysics 275
to dark forces
by Archimago 70
to moral information 69
to native virtue
of mankind 142
to relative terms of moral landscape
by Redcrosse 61
to something more permanent than physical being
by Una 138
to truth
by Stoics and Epicureans 76
to world of Eden 175
accessibilty
of *a posteriori* methods of inquiry
in Frege 86
accident 7, 31, 32, 77, 231, 255, 258
of birth 166
accidental
products
of fiction 66
accomplishment
of nothing 62
accord 288

of nature and mankind
in Garden of Eden 267
with expectations 142
accounting 261
accursed
hand writing
defacement of 207
usury 147
accusation
of concupiscence 259
of dishonesty
by Abessa and Corceca 123
of hidden fate 78
accusative 75
Acheloüs
House of 260
Acheron 64
achievement
of greatest honor
by Redcrosse 151
of purpose
obstacles to 211
of victory 297
acknowledgement 226
acorn 97
act 140
obligation to 55
of generation 227
of pagan metamorphosis 115
of translation 2
of violence
by Virgil 298
of will 295
passive 135
violent
of Redcrosse 298
wide distinction in
in Calvin 26
acting
by George 241
monads 80
action 15, 42, 46, 96–99, 100, 123, 211, 217, 246
amoral 222
appropriate 64
call to
of Lucifera 146
of Night by Duessa 156
collective 41, 43, 295
consequences of 66
played out externally 162–163
cooperative 181
course of 180
critical observer of 128
deferring of 236
dictated to Redcrosse
by Fradubio 143
directing of
by God 266
discrete

Index

in the world of time 219
disjunction of 126
driven forward
   by Archimago's intention 77
God's priority over 116
guarantee of success in 46
human 259
immediate
   of Redcrosse 106
impulsive 54, 60, 61
incorrect course of 82
in the world 158
lack of
   in Dragon 251
man of 55
   Redcrosse as 77
necessity of 160
of Æsculapius 160
of Arthur 188
of character 84
of good men 158
of George 262
of Guyon 296
of King of Eden 273
of Kirkrapine 122
of poem 249
of Redcrosse 163, 226, 278
   after seeing False Una in love with another 101
   Archimago's intention has no bearing on 77
   in leaving Una 84
   in the battle with Errour 65
of solitary man 40
of Una 126
   in separation from Redcrosse 117
of violence
   implications for the social order of 151
open-ended
   of George 294
proceeding from God-given potential 106
philosophical 76
political 41
positive 81, 246, 253, 292
   defines Redcrosse 82
potential for
   in Redcrosse 74
   words provide only 206
principle of 42
purposeful 206
reserved to the actor 206
restraint before 54
Spenser's stand on 127
sphere of 253
takes away possibilities 55
Una's need of others for 55
underworld 77
untested 91
virtuous 142
woman in 94
world of 55, 117
activation
   of poison 259
   of potential 132, 177, 228
   by George 246, 290
   by joining with another 138
   of human being 190
   of Una's conception 67
   of what only lies within Una as potential
   by Redcrosse 138
active 261
   assertion
      of Una's will 137
   character
      Archimago as 119
      Una as 118
   control 135
   intellect 15
      uses *a posteriori* reason 166
   knight 118
   man 81, 209, 261
   nature
      of Archimago 77
   posture towards experience 143
   Redcrosse 117
   role 155, 172
activity
   contemplative 245, 264
      of Contemplation 234
   intellectual
      extension of 233
   restless
      of Redcrosse 232
actor
   individual
      action is reserved to the 206
      man as 253
   Redcrosse as an 55, 61, 81
   separation of
      from act of writing 8
   within the poem 264
actual
   death 168
   violence 128
actuality 42, 270
   of knowledge 87
actualization
   of potential
      in Redcrosse 74
Adam
   fall of 162
   orignal sin of 267
adamant
   rock 258
addition
   of faith to force 56, 254
   of grace
      to excellence 284
adjectives
   of relative space 69
administration
   of justice 99
admiration
   of Una

by Satyrane 136
adoption
　of George
　　by plowman parents 83
　　of name of Redcrosse 83
adoration
　by the Queen of Pride 154
　of Redcrosse
　　by Una 120
　of the people 217
　of Una
　　by Contemplation 235
　　by honorable name 275
　　by Redcrosse 117
　passive object of
　　Una as 118
adorned
　with gems and owches
　　Charissa as 228
　with crowns and owches
　　Fidessa as 108-109
advance
　in law 135
　of action 60
　of Archimago
　　towards Una 123
advancement
　vain
　　of Redcrosse 165
　　with favorable hands 192
advantage 234
　compensating
　　for the fall from grace 251
　gaining
　　over others 234
　of satyrs
　　of functioning on the ground of literal earth 133
advantageous
　verdict 286
adventure 43, 81, 83, 84, 167, 205, 226, 237
　beginning of
　　of George 263
　　of Redcrosse 298
　beginning of Una's 118
　dangerous
　　of Redcrosse 209
　end of
　　of George 268, 283
　　of Una 135, 209
　forward nature of 194
　further 290
　　Archimago's promise of 81
　mindful of Una's 246
　of George 288
　　in the world 271
　of Redcrosse 28, 46, 68
　pitiful
　　of George 278
　random 67, 287
　　of Una 131
　　of Redcrosse 209

search for
　by Redcrosse 232
strange 277
successful completion of 287
adversity
　in Calvin 26
advice 111
　discrete 180
　of Una 226
　　to Redcrosse 231
　rightness of 69
advise 78
advisement
　strong 144
Aegisthus 35
Aeneas 36, 47, 63–67, 233 See also Virgil
　fictional 147
　son of Anchises 75
　travel to the underworld 170
Aeneid, The See Virgil
Aeolus
　father of Orgoglio 163
aesthetic
　criticism 93
　distance
　　in Derrida's work 6
　distinctions 11
　knowledge 189
　methods 12
　modern
　　of A. C. Hamilton 196
　position 11
　relative 95
　Romantic 5
　scientific 95
　tension 274
　terms 2
aesthetics 291
　debasement of 189
　Enlightenment 10
　modern 61, 98, 167
　science of 4
Æsculapius 159–160
afar 292
　wonder from 134
affairs
　control over 182
affection 66
　deeper 121
　for Fidessa
　　by Redcrosse 111
　object of 125
　of Una 137, 228
　returning of
　　by George 246
afterlife
　paying the price for action in this life in the 204
Agamemnon 34–37, 169
age
　Christian 251

freshest 227
golden 37, 251
modern 40, 93
of Descartes 181
of heroes 169
of science 88
aged
  bride 250
  man 236
  sire 68
    Humiltá as 213
  Tithonus 95
agents
  human 259
  of change 3
aghast
  shepherd 110
agony
  of poet
    when confronted by the abandonment of Una by Redcrosse 118
agraste 221
agreement
  expression of
    with Night by Duessa 156
  of epistemology and ontology
    in the human mind 218
aid 176, 182
  calling for
    by Redcrosse 188
  of friendship 110
  secret
    assistance by 151
  sure 79
aiding
  friend
    of Orgoglio 186
aim
  missing the object of 258
  of action
    in Aristotle 16
aimless 62
air 186, 252, 270
  dewy 95
  empty 112
  filling of the 154
  liquid 101
  subtle 101
alchemical
  arms
    of Arthur 178
alchemy 178–179
  perspective of 185
Alciati, Andreas 216–217
Alcinous 260
  house of 35, 169
Alexander the Great 217
algebra 34
  variables 5

alien
  land
    of time 199
  terms 57
  tradition
    of allegory 42
  world of time
    Una's relationship to the 117
alienation
  of George
    from reader 245
    from Una 245
  of power 209
    by Redcrosse's reliance on the armor of God 102
    in Aristotle 233
alighting
  from lofty steed
    by Arthur 195
alignment
  of mind
    with scientific information 171
    with truth 78
  of one's spoken meaning with what another hears 228
  of Spenser's poetry with Augustine 83
alive 159
  Dragon as 273
  Una considers the consequences of Redcrosse's being 172
all
  discreation of 256
allegiance 118
ἀλληγορία 5
allegorical
  figures 239
  levels 93
  meaning 10
  poet 218
allegory 2, 12, 14, 43, 176
  abstract principles in 214
  as a dream 25
  as alien tradition 42
  as dark conceit 30
  as empty speculation 24
  as enigma
    in Augustine 71
  as fiction 163, 214
  as trope 7
  Augustine's thought on 71–74
  basis of Romantic rejection of 22
  cicumlocution
    by Latin translators 71
  definition of 6
    as genre 8
    as saying one thing while meaning another 5, 103
    in modern criticism 33
    postmodern 8
  distinction between critics and characters in 53
  distributed 161–162

enigmatic 104
etymology 5
every enigma is an 72
figuring in 95
form of allegory
   Augustine's discovery of the 71
fragmentation of sense in 27
genre of 8
historical 33
image 27
in Augustine 71
in modern world 5–7
levels
   dismissed by Quilligan 8
   treated in Carol Kaske's work 27
literal level of 295
literal plane of 247
literature of 179
modern perceptions 33
nature of 6
of divided consciousness 83
of silence and speech 71–74, 289
   Spenser's 74–76
of Spenser 84, 137
of *The Faerie Queene* 245
particular accidents of 31
proscribed by Luther 24
requires ambiguity of precedence 196
saying one thing while meaning another 5
several species of 71
signification of one thing by another 71
traditional definition 5
translation of 2
typological 61
waning in Spenser's day 30
writing 8
Allegory of the Cave *See* Plato
Allegory of the Poem, The (postscript to Tasso's *Jerusalem Delivered*) 40
allowance
   for backsliding 257
allowing
   entrance to everyone by Malvenu 143
alluring
   form
      of Babylon 217
Almighty
   God 221
   lightning brand of the 186
alms 232
Alpers, Paul J. 211
altar
   burning 285
   marble 259
alternation
   diurnal
      of day and night 155
alternative
   incompatible 53

altruism
   defined by Stoics 180
amazed 251
   deer 123
   Una stands 129
   vulgar 152, 162
amazement
   at Archimago's presence beneath the armor of Redcrosse 129
   of Redcrosse 276
   of satyrs
      at uncouth beauty of Una 133
   of sight
      in lion 120
ambiguity 57, 240
   of precedence
      required by allegory 196
ambiguous
   meaning 121
   words
      measuring reponse to 196
ambition
   as characteristic of pride 106
ambivalence 42
amenable
   conclusions 173
Amendment 224
amoral
   action 222
Amoret 27
amplification 59, 82, 190, 235
   of limited life 268
   of mankind
      over time 192
   of meaning 286
   of middle terms 203
anagogy 27
analogy 19, 225
   between Redcrosse and Christ 225
analysis
   point-to-point 173
analytic
   meaning 85
   philosophy 85
   value
      of a=a 85
analytical philosophy 88–92
Anchises 75
anchor
   silver 219, 224
ancient
   allegory 8
   grandmother 155
   perch 187
   philosophers 3
ancients
   confusion of
      over defintion of allegory 5

Index

angel 4, 95
  face
    of Una 119
angels
  thousand 235
  vertical path of 236
anger
  cooling of 123
angle
  perspectival 296
Anglo Saxon 94
anguish 219, 225
  pricked with
    Redcrosse as 223
  secret 80
animal
  a priori sense of being of 104
  behavior
    of Redcrosse 148, 242
  being 203, 215
    of Redcrosse 188
  desire
    satisfaction of 290
  destructive violence of 149
  force
    of Redcrosse 212
  genus 105, 267
  instincts 123
    socially destructive 257
  nature 15
  powers 105
  protector 130
  rational 15, 73, 183
  state of being 104
  violence 149, 183
    socially destructive 168
  war 176
  wrath
    destructive 159
animals 99
  king of 121, 132
  mankind as the best of 99
  savagery of 47, 99
announcement
  of victory 264
annoy 289
another 79, 188
  attraction to 130
  binding one person to 227
  burning with passion for 259
  care of 155
  hearing of 228
  land 285
  love of 137, 199, 285
  raising one position over 286
  realization that Una must join herself with 138
  rousing of the heart of Redcrosse for 176
  woman 184
  words of 295
answer 84, 129

definite 174
difficulty of arriving at
  in Frege 85
immediate 201
obvious 130
of night
  to question raised by Æsculapius 159
of Redcrosse
  to Despair 204
of Trevisan 200
to question of the location of the truth 84
Antaeus
  killing of
    by Hercules 259
antique
  poets 34
  world
    champion of 258
    hatred of excess in 276
antiquity
  hero of 259
anti-rational
  position
    of Augustine 97
Apellicon of Teos 20
Apollo
  daughter of
    Clio as 249
apology
  by Una
    for George 288
  for enraged fight 149
  for error
    by pagan 149
aporia 11 *See also* paradox
a posteriori 75, 77, 99, 155, 174, 193, 229, 257, 266, 274, 296
  created thing 105
  education 67, 124, 167, 228, 238, 293
  evidence 54, 145
  experience
    of learning 212
  imagination 219
  in Augustine 23
  knowledge available to the human mind 104
  method
    of inquiry 86
  reason 167, 174, 197
    of Una's dwarf 166
  reconstruction of the scientific universe 170
  reference
    in Frege 88
  scientific reason 76
  sense 87
  source of teleological direction 62
  value
    of patience 254
apostle 71
apparent
  heir 280

appeal
　of Arthur
　　to might 182
appearance 158
　false
　　of Archimago 129
　mistaken for reality
　　in Plato's Allegory of the Cave 14
　not reality 257
　of Arthur 184
　of chains of necessity 158
　of death 168
　of Fradubio
　　as unrecognized reflection of Redcrosse's
　　　behavior 147
　of Ignaro
　　as wise old man 189
　of Orgoglio 195
　　after blowing of horn by Arthur's squire 185
　of silk and silver 281
　of things 125
　of Una 282
　　Sansloy's reaction to 132
　outward 73
　　of Corceca 214
　　of Ignaro 189
　perfect
　　of Una 284
　plain 114
　rude 133
　superficial 124, 145
　surface 141
appetite
　lower 109
　　of individual epicurean pleasure 233
applause
　of others 154-155
application
　of reason 170
apprehension 296
approach
　of human mind
　　to the Λόγος 193
　to experience 4, 142, 160
appropriateness
　of manner 65
approximation
　statistical 155
a priori 23, 44, 52, 62, 75, 93, 155, 193, 219,
　　220, 229, 271, 274, 293
　armor
　　of Una 197
　assumptions 96, 242, 275
　　by uncareful readers 216
　　in modern criticism 54
　　potentially faulty 145
　assurance of faith 265
　being 212
　　of Una 136
　　Redcrosse is secure in his 80

belief 100
binding force of love 174
chance 124
condition of being human 166
creation 167
　of God 152, 234
　of saints 105
disposition
　towards poetry 240
experience
　processed by passive intellect 166
faith 57, 257
gifts 266
God's choice of Redcrosse as 158
goodness 67
grace 164, 278
grant of armor of *Ephesians* 177
grant of faith 62
grant of grace 47
holiness 167
identity proposition (a=a) 87
　in Augustine 23
inner glory 152
knowledge of ontological things 170
meaning
　in Frege 85
premises 274
principles of identity 238
salvation 268
sense
　in Frege 88
　of animal being 104
similarity 88
statement 85
state
　of self-sufficiency 80
things created by God 104
virtue 99
apt
　comparison 258
arbiter 50
　impartial 11
arbitrariness
　of claims
　　in Frege 86
arbitrary
　whim 289
arbor
　shady 133
arc
　of narrative
　　lack of in Brooke-Davies' argument 117
Arcesilaus 155
archaism 30
arch-deceiver 69, 70, 119 See also Archimago.
archetypal
　patterns 169
archetype
　of the evil artificer
　　Archimago as 129

Index

Archimago 28, 67–71, 74–82, 84, 90, 99, 102, 180, 182, 213, 215, 265, 276, 285
  active nature of 119
  archetype of the evil artificer 129
  as arch-deceiver 70
  as arch-magician 163
  as master of worldly science 102
  as messenger 288
  as villain 118
  as weak man 129
  comparison of
    to Contemplation 234
  cowardice of 128
  cowardly 129
  deception by 218
  description of 123
  educated 124, 222
  effectiveness of lies 125
  equality of power in 218
  failure of
    in respect to Redcrosse's motivation 80
  false appearance of 129
  Godless freedom of 238
  has never taken the field to fight 129
  helmet of 129
  hermitage of 91, 234, 238
  home of 212
  hope of
    unfounded 129
  immediate threat of 119
  in accounting for Una's sadness 95
  intention 77, 125
  intent of 77
  intercession of
    before Redcrosse kills Una 149
  knowledge of
    greater than Una's 125
  likeness of
    to Humiltá 213
  magic of 104
  meets Corceca and Abessa 123
  misformed thought of 100–102
  misguided magical art of 178
  on ends 102–106
  perfomance of the work of God 101
  playing at being Redcrosse 128
  power of 105
  presentation of
    to Una 124
  role of 119
  science of 179
  stops Redcrosse from committing sin 191
  tells Una the truth 125
  Una's exercise of power over 131
  Una's flight from 96
  wearing feigned armor of Redcrosse 124
  white hair of 129
architecture
  mind's multi-tier 74
  of classical education 38
arch-magician
  Archimago as 163
arduous
  desire
    of Redcrosse to prove himself in battle 146
Argive
  fleet 7
argument 286
  better 183
  middle terms of 276
  of Despair 203
    are projections of mind of Redcrosse 207
  of George 287
  of philosophy 192
    Redcrosse no match for 191
  of Redcrosse 204
  of Spenser 126, 183
  of the King of Eden 288
  of Una 207
  on necessity
    woven by Despair 203
  poles of 285
Ariosto, Ludovico 83, 95, 230, 242, 294, 298
  works
    Orlando Furioso 40, 63–68
arising
  of Una 136
Aristotle 14, 31, 45, 98, 156, 221, 245, 275, 282, 298
  action and potential in 96–99
  animal nature 15
  as limited source 31
  as rational thinker 14
  as author of the twelve moral virtues 30
  criticism by
    of Plato's Theory of Forms 14, 193
  definition of mankind 15, 183
  direct impact
    denial of on Spenser's poem 31
  division of the mind 15
  end
    in itself 16
    in politics 16
    outside of itself 15
  ethics 15
  extreme
    beasts and gods at the 17
  fate of his works 19
  in Plato's *Parmenides* 17
  intelligence combined with virtue in 102
  logic of 15
  natural state in 16
  on goodwill 282–284
  perfection in 16
  philosophical thought of 126
  priority in 16
  Problem of Fiction in 14, 15
  psychology of 15
  reading of 81
  reason
    as a tool of relative science 23
  relative knowledge of 133
  relative science of 293

scientific ideas of 17
smooth transition between language and nature 75
social instinct in 16
source of contemplation 233
state
    as the goal of human life 16
system of 91
the good
    as the aim of all human action 15
universals 15
universe of
    in Spenser's poem 206
works
    De Anima 15
    Metaphysics 14
    Nichomachean Ethics 15, 31, 233, 282
    On interpretation 73
    Politics 47, 98
    Posterior Analytics 72
arm
    extension of 190
    fleshly 265
    right 64
armed
    goodly 258
    injustice 99
armor 49, 121, 251
    a priori
        of Una 197
    charmed
        of the knight 258
    exterior 45, 57–58
    fictional 57, 102
    holy 110
    light of Redcrosse's 56
    magical 45, 102, 107
        of Una 243
    mighty
        of Redcrosse 168
    of Dragon 257, 258
    of *Ephesians* 45, 58, 96, 105, 152, 177, 204
    of faith 260
    of God 49, 95
    of Hercules 260
        poison within 258
    of others 121
    of Redcrosse 48, 65, 67, 74, 80, 163, 168
        as a burden to him 147
        feigned by Archimago 124
        gets him out of trouble 60
    of Sansfoy 148
    Redcrosse lays aside his 119
    removing
        mistake of 274
    role of
        in defeat of enemies 152
    source of armor 105
    steel
        George wears 251
    superficial 124
    taking off 127, 213
        bad effects of 258
        by Redcrosse 167
    wearing
        by Redcrosse 147
armor-laden
    body
        of a man 254
arms 48, 162, 260, 279, 297
    alchemical
        of Arthur 178
    deeds of 243
    enchanted
        of Redcrosse 151
    feats of 130
    focus on 243
    godly
        blaze of 250
    in field
        odds of 278
    linked 219
    magic in the
        of Redcrosse 151
    mankind equipped at birth with 99
    of Arthur 178, 179
    of Redcrosse 178, 278
    of Sansfoy 149
    origin of 178
    power of 295
    profession of
        by Redcrosse 140
    puissant 245
    sacred 58
    sacred law of 152
    won by conquest 149
    worn by others 83
arousal
    of heart of Redcrosse
        for another 176
    Una's heart
        for Redcrosse 176
array
    royal 146
arrogance 65
arrow
    iron 180
art 15, 51, 147
    assumptions about 12
    deconstructable 61
    dedicated to achieving the whole of experience 167
    ekphrastic work of 205
    false construction of 185
    goal of 277
    human 98
    lessons provided by 147
    magical
        of Archimago 178
    of Æsculapius 159
    of Despair 200
    on the side of unity
        in the modern world 134
    role of

        in Aristotle 233
Artegall 297
Arthur 30, 114, 178-198, 206, 238, 247, 260,
        274, 282
    action of 188
    alchemical arms of 178
    appeal of
        to might 182
    appearance of 184
    arms of 179
    as image of knightly perfection 224
    as leader 210
    as rational man 192, 194
    at cross purposes
        with Redcrosse 198
    battle of
        with Orgoglio 266
    change of
        behavior in 190
    consort of Gloriana 177
    defeat
        of Duessa 186
        of Orgoglio 186
    difference
        with Ignaro 189
        with Redcrosse 180
    duty of
        towards Redcrosse 194
    educated 188, 191
    enlargement
        of people 190
    heart of 192
    helmet of 194, 198
    lack of fearlessness in 296
    linked to Una 194
    listens to Una's story 183
    looking at Ignaro's face 190
    mind of
        positive nature of 190
    rational 198
    relates his dream 195
    rescue of Redcrosse 199
    resolution of 180, 192
    resolve of
        to find the body of the Faerie Queene 195
    shield of 266
    socially-constructed world of 181
    squire of 184
    subordination to
        by Una 192
    tale of
        and Gloriana 194–198
    victory of 188
    worldly thought of 183
artifacts
    of philosophy 90
artifice 75, 231
    human 66
    master of 184
artificer
    evil 129

artificial
    barriers
        created by Duessa 158
    creation
        of meaning 240
        of sprite 100
    judgment 90
artist 98
    Virgil's role as 75
artistic
    power 97
arts 70
    devilish 102
    hidden 100
    liberal 107
    medical 16
    mischievous 113
    wicked 287
ascent
    vertical
        to an imaginary heaven 216
ascription
    to skill 210
a-sexual
    paradise
        House of Holinesse as 229
ashamed. *See also* shame.
    of backsliding 266
aside
    laying stole 119, 122
asking
    of the sprite 77
aspect 44
    truth in its philosophical and religious 117
    worst
        of George 250
aspen
    green 206
ass 217
    of Una 140, 160
    pride of an 217
    worship
        of Una's 135
assault
    on conscience
        of Redcrosse 205
assertion
    active
        of Una's will 137
    of will 261
assessment
    of all the facts 202
    of the whole 202
    poor
        by reader of Redcrosse 143
assistance
    by secret aid
        by Duessa 151

associative
   paths 241
assumption 8, 35, 220
   about art 12
   about Cupid's cruel dart
      by Una 96
   a priori 242, 275
      by uncareful readers 216
      of Una about Cupid's cruel dart 96
   Enlightenment 155
   of balanced perspective
      by Una 140
   of closure
      by the reader 174
   of equal love
      by Una 172
   of King of Eden 286–287
   of original balance of nature
      modern world's 142
   of Una 96
   postmodern 56
   potentially faulty *a priori* 145
   Stoic 180
   that Redcrosse is dead
      by Una 136
   that things are what they represent themselves to
      be 180
   untested 271
assurance 110
   of faith 265
   of morality 210
   of victory
      of Redcrosse 205
   that love fell not of the ground 81
astonishment
   of satyrs 133
   in epic simile of rams 106
   mute
      of Trevisan 200
   of Redcrosse 162
astounded
   Redcrosse is 162
   stare
      of the eyes of Despair 201
astounding
   of nations
      with stern horror 250
astray 166
   led 148
   men whose lives had gone 147
astronomy
   discoveries of 86
asymmetry
   between reading and acting 55
atom
   individual 80
at once 67, 166, 173, 224, 245, 252
   to kill 252
atonement 63

atrophy
   of metaphysics
      in romance literature 169–170
attachment
   of Duessa
      to Sansfoy 109
   social 66
   to Redcrosse
      by Una 238
attack
   of Errour 60
   on friend
      by Sansloy 129
attacks
   general 141
attempt
   to fly away
      by Duessa 187
   to teach satyrs
      by Una 135
attention
   focus of 177, 184
      of Redcrosse 202
      of Contemplation 246
      of Despair 204
   of Redcrosse
      in conversation with Arthur 197
   to reason
      lack of 224
attributes 77
   negative 150, 189
attuned
   notes 275
augmention
   treble
      of furious mood of the Dragon 257
Augustine 26, 40, 50, 66, 86, 94, 98, 105, 133,
      156, 164, 171, 175, 228, 229, 275, 291
   Aeneas in 37–39, 47
   allegory
      as enigma in 104
      of silence and speech in 71–74
      as a moral man 104
      as a rational man 104
      as philosopher 83
   autobiography of 182
   belief that individual cannot imitate God 59
   borrowing from Plato 23
   claim that pagan knowledge has a false bottom
      170
   definition of ends
      out of philosophy 181
   definition of evil
      as priviative 157
   denial of access through one's will to holiness 46
   Enligtenment perception of 76
   fallible reason in 104
   flipping of ends for middles 181
   Homer as liar in 76
   improvements in
      to pagan idealism 259

Index 323

individual in 72
intrusion of
   into classical philosophy 190
knowledge in
   of Creator's prelinguistic ontology 289
limits of reason in 242
no man is is innocent in the world of time 115
objection to Socrates 189
philosophical work of 189
point of view of 218
position gells with Ovid 37
power of 170
radicalism of 23
rejection
   of pleasure as a human end 52
reliance on
   by Spenser 235
role of reason in 181
skeptical position of 104
solution to the problem of power 66
substantial consciousness in 233
systematic problems that reason cannot solve 88
system of
   goal of 193
theory of language 71–74
universe of 155
   chain of necessity in 158
works
   City of God 92, 109, 221–222
   Confessions 37–39, 175
   On the Trinity 22, 71, 225

Augustinian
act
   of imagination 282
change
   in Spenser 256
faith
   deconstruction of 230
learning 256
poem
   of Spenser 224
reaction 242
universe 48, 118, 252
   role of doubling in 134

Augustus 36
authenticity 16, 41
author 220
as eagle
   in Du Bartas 256
constuction of grace by 164
Duessa as 113
imaginatively constructed fiction of 228
of fact 202
pagan
   belief of 161–162
wise
   Spenser as 230

authority 11, 287

distributed
   of books 214

external 218
location of
   in discourse with others 215
metaphysical 51
of Augustine 28
of books 214
of the Church weakened by skepticism 13

autonomy 16, 33, 42
autotelic
λόγος 9

availability
of good
   to the mind of mankind 138

available
facts 177

Ave Maria 70
avengement 255
victory through 204

avenging
blade 183
boy 194
of the pains of Night 157
wrath
   of God 235

Avernus 158
Aveugle (father of Sans brothers) 156
avoidance
of evil 143

avoiding
danger
   by Arthur 186
of violence
   by Arthur 186
positive action 253

awakening
of Morpheus 74
of noble courage 249
of Pluto's grisly dame 70
of Redcrosse 78
the god of war 250

away
bearing
   of Una 131
far
   House of Holinesse not 212
   satyrs and fawns 133
putting
   of Una's fear 134
running
   by Sansloy 133
turning
   from words towards swords 150

awful
behavior
   with Fidessa 172

axiom 22. *See also* premise.

axis
horizontal

of man as actor 253
vertical
  of the Dragon 253

B

babes
  of Charissa 228
Babylon 217
back 59
  behind
    well of life as 261
  true love has no power to look 126
backsliding
  allowance for 257
  of George 266
backward 130, 221, 241, 262, 266
  bent knees
    of satyrs 134, 217
  face
    of Ignaro 189
  motion 267
  travel after Redcrosse's defeat of Errour 62
bad 176
  behavior
    of Redcrosse 125
  counsel 144
  effects
    of taking off armor 258
  escheat 157
  eyes
    of Contemplation 234, 251
  influence
    of evil stars 191
  man 70
  witchcraft 74
badge 48
  of the Redeemer 297
badness 68
  of death
    Una assesses 171
  of Redcrosse 84
balance 81, 278, 286
  between light and dark
    in armor 56
  doubtful 114
  equal 81, 106, 150
    in argument of Despair 204
    of God 270
    of Lucifera 150
  in Hamilton's criticism 50
  lack of
    in Spenser's poem 142
  natural 96
  of elements 264
  original
    of nature 142
  perfect
    between mankind and nature 267

power of reason to 177
scales put out of 114
temperate 94
tipping 95, 151
  in fights 203
  towards good 152
universe in
  through the will of Redcrose 207
weighing unequal things in the
  by Una 199
balanced
  perspective of Eden 140
  universe 238
    equality in 158
bale
  bitter 180
baleful
  darkness 191
  stound 171, 172
balm
  trickling stream of 268
band 279
  holy 285
bands 192
  of Errour 56
  sinful 184
banks
  swelling of Nile beyond its 59
baptism
  of George 262–263
  role of 265
baptized
  hands 265
bare 276
  feet 68
baring
  of breasts
    by Charissa 228
    by Fidessa 229
    by Una 229
  parts of body
    of Redcrosse 195
bark
  feeble 272
barriers
  artificial
    created by Duessa 158
  to entry 39
base
  of experience 163
bath
  in a living well 115
bathing
  in applause of others 155
  in pleasance of joyous shade 161
  in wanton bliss 77
  in wicked joy 77

battle 66, 67, 95, 206, 218, 249, 264, 269 *See*

Index   325

also fight.
boisterous 255
conclusion of 173
defeat in 187
end of 142
equal
   deciding the outcome of 152
   even 152
for control
   of Una's physical body 138
for Una's heart 137
fought without loss
   by Sir Burbon 297
furious 148
guarantee
   of success in 58, 197
   of victory in 110
indiscriminate readiness for
   of Redcrosse 185
mental 115
of physical violence 138
proof in 146
Redcrosse's strategy in 106
ritualized
   with Sansjoy 151–153
tipping the balance of every 147
unritualized
   with Sansjoy 148–151
violent
   with Sansjoy 151
with couched sprear 128
with Dragon 260
with Orgoglio 266
within mind 116
battlefield
   flight from the 136
   prowess
      externalized by Redcrosse's possession of the arms of Sansfoy 149
Battle of the Books 2–3
battles
   of Redcrosse 204
Baucis. *See* Philemon and Baucis.
Baumgarten, Alexander Gottlieb 4–5, 61, 167
beacon
   broad 252
   of Dragon' power
   of good behavior
      Una as 172
bead-men 231
beads
   busy at her
      Cælia as 214
      Corceca as 214
beam 220
bear
   chained 288
beard
   gray 68
bearing

a charmed shield
   by Redcrosse 151
away
   of Una 131
each part 171
of a god
   by an ass 217
thunderbolts
   by Arthur 186
beast 4
   ever-damned 268
   lion as lord of every 120
   monstrous 290
   of the field 120
   unhasty 119
beastly 47
   heart
      of Sansloy 132
beasts
   half
      satyrs as 137
   king of
      lion as 137
   master of
      Satyrane as 136
beaten
   mariner 126
beating
   wings
      by force 251
beautiful
   ladies 145
beauty 114, 288
   borrowed 114
   bright
      astonishment by satyrs at Una's 133
   deformed
      of Frælissa 114
   description of 284
   equal 114
   false
      of Fidessa 190
   heavenly 281
   ideal
      determination by culture 133
   indescribable
      of Una 119
   inner
      expression of 120
   inward
      of Una 282
   never-fading 282
   of False Una 77, 234
   of Una 132
      causes lion to forget his appetite 121
   perfect prelapsarian 120
   perpetual 282
   perspective on 133
   precedence in 114
   principle of 91
   revelation of Una's physical

  by Sansloy 130
 shining
  of Una 132
 true
  of Una 190
 vision of
  of Una 281
 wondrous 227
becoming 15, 19
 in time 163
 world of 215
bed 202
 of Tithonus 95
bedewing
 of cheeks
  with salt tears 278
bees 77
beetle
 in a box
  argument proposed by Wittgenstein 50, 292
before 196
 eyes of true love fixed 126
 the Fall 273
 Una
  stands her knight 126
  veil hanging 132
begging
 for mercy
  by Una 129
begin 171
 bitter baleful stound 172
beginning 18, 47, 142, 173, 188, 262
 fair 183, 184
 of action
  of Redcrosse 158
 of adventure
  of George 263
  of Redcrosse 298
  of Una 118
 of education
  of Una 135
 of experience 177
 of friendship
  in goodwill 283
 of journey
  of Redcrosse 199
 of love 283
 of pity
  by satyrs 133
 of poem 65, 105, 138, 213
 of whole discourse 174
beginnings
 come to an end 203
behavior
 animal
  descent of Redcrosse to lowest form of 148
  of Redcrosse 242
 awful 95
  of Redcrosse with Fidessa 172
 bad

  of Redcrosse 125
 braying 123
 change of
  from purposeless wandering to forward purpose 199
  in Arthur 190
 cultivated 123
 destructive 246
  of Redcrosse 149, 242
 expression of disapproval of Redcrosse's
  by Spenser 161
 good
  Redcrosse not a model of 110
  Una as a beacon of 172
 governing
  of Arthur 188
 imitation of 227
 immoral
  of Corceca 234
 model of 183
 natural
  of birds 52
 of George 260
 of Mercie
  paradox in 231
 of Odysseus 83
 of Redcrosse 140
  Fradubio as unrecognized reflection of 147
  negative condemnation of 141
  with Orgoglio 253
 of Una 171
 of Zele 213
 past
  of Redcrosse 191
 reflection of
  of Redcrosse 162
 respectable 123
 troublesome 174
 wanton
  of Redcrosse 168
behind 197
 back of George
  well of life as 261
 fear followed 200
 troubles of Una are not 128
beholding
 of Una's visage
  by Sansloy 130
being 19, 35
 and Becoming 15
 animal 203, 215
  as an *a priori* sense 104
  of Redcrosse 188
 a priori 212
  of Una 136
  Redcrosse's security in his 80
 chain of 4
 form of 14
 human *See* human being
 in Augustine 22
 infinite 98
 interior 219

Index

in world of time 138
living 180, 268
material 98
morally unequal 152
of pagan gods 3
of Una 81
order of 52
physical 138
taking control of
   by Una 138
true seat of 95
world of 141
belching
  of fire 256
belief 13, 19
  a priori 100
  Christian 38
  Manichaean
    by Duessa 157
  in equal power
    by Duessa 150
  of Fradubio 113
  of Hercules
    in false gods 285
  of Lucifera's six counselors 145
  of others 193
  of poet 175
  of Redcrosse
    that he has nothing to learn from the triumph passing before him 147
  of Spenser
    in the temporality of desire 137
  of Una 175
    if false Redcrosse 128
    that she has found her own knigh 127
  philosophical
    Homer as touchstone of 20
  Redcrosse's
    in the effects of Archimago's magic 104
believing
  one's eyes 114
  too lightly
    in dear loved dame 141
bellowing
  of fire 258
  sound 162
bells
  golden 109
beloved
  division of Una from her 118
  errant
    of Una 196
  form of the 283
  knight 191, 224
  of Redcrosse 111
  of Una 117, 125
    not dead 173
  sundering
    of Una from her 138
Belphoebe 27, 94
belt

book hanging from Archimago's 68
bend 62
bended
  knee 217
bending
  of Archimago's spear 129
  of course 272
  of eyes towards the ground 68
  of wit
    of Redcrosse 111, 147
  towards Jerusalem 237
beneath
  appearance 124
    Ignaro is not wise 189
  the surface 154
    of the heart 141
bent
  backward knees
    of satyrs 134
bequeathed
  care 244
best 220
  educated 193
  men 295
  music 191
  position 257
betokening
  of signs 168
betrayal 109
  of truth
    by Archimago 70
  of Una 118
    by Redcrosse 127
betrayed
  loyalty 287
better 137
  argument 183
  countenance 145
  days
    of Redcrosse 188
  information 145
between
  beginning and end 59, 142, 173
  heaven and earth 256
  speeches b. sisters 219
beware
  of fickleness and fraud
    in choice 141
bewitching
  all men's sight 114
  of manly heart
    by vain words 206
beyond
  comprehension
    of Duessa 151
  the state of Lucifera 144
bias
  towards good 58

Bible 27, 220
  immediate experience of reading 24
  Protestant belief in direct access to the word of
      God through 13
biblical
  parable 266
bidding
  of Despair 118
biding
  the blustering breath of heaven 127
billowing
  of waves 255
billows
  rolling 255
binary
  system
    of the Enlightenment 275
  universe 275
  values 285
binding
  force
    love as 174
  of fate
    of Una and Redcrosse 172
  of one person to another 181, 227
  of Una
    by love 138
    to Redcrosse 195, 238
birds 4, 52
  cheerful 160
  song of 62
birth 245, 261
  accident of 166
  equipped at 99
    with arms 47
  heavenly
    of Una 215
    Una's 121
  in Eden 172
  metaphysical pole of 253
  of Una 275
  salvation at
    of Redcrosse 242
  second 221
bitter
  bale 180
  despite 148
  sense
    of deep-rooted ill 256
  stound 171, 172
black 281
  blood 256
  ink
    of squid 60
  Pluto's grisly dame 70
  weeds 68
black and white
  terms 66
bladder
  empty
    Orgoglio as 187
blade 59
  avenging 183
  burning 264
  trenchant 257
blame 259, 278
  absolving from 191
  assigning
    for Redcrosse's flight from despair 211
  externalizing
    for the sins of Redcrosse 226
  for Una's predicament 136
  laying 278, 288
  of dear loved dame 141
  of Redcrosse 119
  of Una 84, 125
  placed onto an evil star 192
  placed at the feet of God 58
  question of
    asked by Sansloy 129
blast
  dull 114
  of terror
    from the horn blow by Arthur's squire 185
blaze
  of godly arms 250
blazing
  brightness 186
bleeding
  caused by Redcrosse's spear 168
  smart 171
blessed
  end 237, 238
  state of being
    of George 204
blessing
  of God 279
  of heart with grace 110
  of Neptune
    by a merchant who sees his ship come in 127
  of Redcrosse 163
blind
  brightness 118
  Cupid 139
  devotion 121
  eyes 12
    of Contemplation 264
    of Corceca 234
  god (Cupid) 79
  love
    of Cupid 138
  metaphorically 141
  purpose 79
  sitting 124
  woman 121
blindness 12
  moral 70
  of Redcrosse 60
    in fight with Errour 57
  of Una 182

Index

bliss
  may not abide in state of mortal men 192
  shining lamp of 124
  wanton 77
blitheness 243
blocking
  of King of Eden
    by Duessa 286
  of the reader
    from imitation of Redcrosse 47
blood 48, 237
  black gory 256
  for blood
    justice as conceived of as 202
  fresh 256
  guilty 183
    in Virgil's *Aeneid* 63
  of Centaurs 258
  of Errour 60
  of vanquished pagan 173
  pouring of
    out of the Dragon's wound 256
  precious
    of Jesus 263
  purple 106
bloodshed
  abhorred 148
  horror of 152
  victory through 204
bloody
  field 150
    guilt of 237
  gore 251
  verses 258
  vows 286
  work 215
blot
  of sin 225
blow 258, 265
  direct 255, 257
  fury of 257
  of giant
    as idle stroke 186
blowing
  magical horn
    by Arthur's squire 184
blown
  up to heaven 216
blows
  of Errour 186
  of George
    directed fury of 258
  of Orgoglio 186
blunt
  eyes
    of Contemplation 234, 236, 251
blushing
  face
    of Una 132

blustering
  breath
    of heaven 127
Boccaccio, Giovanni 24–25
bodies 165
  hidden 189
  surface of 288
bodily
  existence 270
  integrity 161–162
body 18, 57, 162, 188, 222, 260, 263
  armor-laden
    of a man 254
  Arthur's resolution to find
    of the Faerie Queene 195
  desire for
    by Sansloy 140
  economy of 261
  external 66
  freedom from 64
  giant
    of Orgoglio 195
  great
    of Orgoglio 187
  in work of Stephen Greenblatt 78
  integrity of
    breached in Redcrosse 161
  knowledge of the 72
  limits of 261
  literal
    Rinaldo as 41
  looser with
    Duessa as 298
  of Dragon 270
  of Errour 60
  of Fidessa 143
  of Kirkrapine
    ripped into a thousand pieces 122
  of monster 187
  of Sansloy 276
  of Una 140
  of woman 147, 290
  open 109
    of Fidessa 234
  parts of 195
  physical
    battle for control of Una's 138
  saving
    from scorching fire 266
  searing 258
  seeming 101
  signs 73
  subordinated to soul 41
  viewing 217
    of Fidessa 280
  virginal
    integrity of 120
  wounded 225
Boethius, Anicius Manlius Severinus
  Consolation of Philosophy 201, 281
  liberal arts curriculum 107

Boileau-Despréaux, Nicolas 3
boisterous
   battle 255
bold
   bad man 70
   pagan 129, 149, 173
bond 285
bondslave
   eternal 163
bones 166
   of men 147
book 83, 217, 230
   deconstruction of the 215
   eternal
      of fate 203
   hanging from Archimago's belt 68
   of fame 237
   of Fidelia 221
Book of Holinesse, The 11, 43, 47, 217, 266,
      269, 282, 283, 293, 294, 295, 296, 298
books 60, 261
   of Archimago
      returns to 80
      searching of 100
   authority of 214
   distributed authority of 214
   Errour's disgorging of 66
   magic 70
Boötes
   as constellation 82
   as plowman 82
   echoed in "bootelesse paines" 101
bootless
   pains 101
born 156
   in time 138
   of God 73
   with animal being 203
borrowed
   beauty 114
bosom
   of false faith 148
boss (raised area used in ornamentation) 109
bottom
   false
      of knowledge 170
bough
   laurel 274
   plucking of 111, 147
bound
   in baleful darkness 191
   Redcrosse holds Una to be b. to him 81
boundaries
   erasure of 273
   in House of Pride 143–146
   protected
      of Spenser's artificially-constructed fiction 231
boundary

between timeless Eden and earth 67
   metaphysical 169
bounds
   of humanity 197
bounteous
   Cælia as 218
bounty 227
bourgeois 167
   men 294
bow
   ebony 176
bowed
   low 284
bower 150
Bower of Bliss
   destruction of 143
bowl
   libation 259
box
   beetle in a
      argument proposed by Wittgenstein 50, 292
   poor man's 122
boy
   proud avenging 194
braced 158
Bradamante 63
branch
   earthly 101
branches
   green 111, 147
   thrusting into ground 115
brand
   lightning
      of the Almighty 186
   of hellish smart 207
brass
   paved
      way to heaven 146
brave *See also* brazen.
   knight
      Arthur as 224
   pursuit
      of chivilrous emprise 192
bravery
   unbelievable
      of Redcrosse 186
braying 123
   behavior 123
   of Una's screams 133
brazen
   castle 80
   gate 273, 276, 285
      construction of 274
      opening of 273
   scales 251
   walls 68, 122
      of Eden 100, 138, 211, 248, 267

breach 183

Arthur in the 177
  in bodily integrity
    of Redcrosse 161
  in logic 72
  in modern "rule" that character and narrative function interdependently 161–162
  in Una's personality 95
  of love 287
  of power
    in Aristotle 233
  secret
    in conscience 205
  within nature 51
break
  in continuity 97
  in reason 86
breaking
  of circle
    by satyrs 133
  of oaths 279
  of the chains of necessity 158
breast 113
  careful
    of Redcrosse 226
  feeble
    of poet 250
  knocking of
    by Archimago 68
  of Redcrosse 211
  of Una 171
breasts
  baring of
    by Fidessa 229
    by Charissa 228
    by Una 229
breath
  blustering
    of heaven 127
  of Dragon 251
breathing
  wind 160
breeding
  of children
    by Errour 66
  of delight 191
briars
  ragged 231
bride
  aged 250
bridge
  verbal
    of Freudian dream work 241
bridle 109
bright
  as the morning star 281
  beauty
    astonishment by satyrs at Una's 133
    Dragon 206
  eye of heaven
    seen in Una's face 119
  heavens 154
  mirror 144
  shield 253
    of Arthur 186
  sunny
    Duessa as 155
brightest
  sky 132
brightness 246
  blazing 186
  blind 118
  heavenly 93
brimstone 205
British
  royaly
    George as descendant of 245
Britomart 27, 94
broad
  beacons 252
  day 122
  seven-mouthed Nile 154
broad-blazed
  fame 216
broadcast
  of power 253
    through fear 273
broken
  tower 108
bronze 251
brood
  eternal 151
  heavenly 275
Brooks-Davies, Douglas 117
brother
  of Sansloy (Sansfoy) 129
brutality
  of nature 96, 105
buff 257
building
  up of an intermediate temperance 149
bulk 266
Burbon, Sir 297–298
burden
  enormous 273
buried
  in thankless thought 194
Burkert, Walter 193
burning
  altars 285
  blade 264
  in fire 128
  in fiery steel 258
  of Hercules 259, 285
  of Troy 38
  shields 106
  with passion 259
burnt 260
Bush, Douglas 42

bushel
  talent placed under a 266
bushy
  thorns 231
business
  worldly 234
Busiris
  murdering of
    by Hercules 259
buying
  literary education 38
  of death
    by Fradubio's mistake 112
  with the blood of vanquished pagan 173
byway 62

C

Cælia 214–216, 224, 235
  heavenly daughter of 227
  opaque origins of 214
  seeing 218
  third daughter of
    Charissa as 227
  thought to come from heaven 214
caitiff
  thralls 165
calculus
  infinitesimal 2
call
  by name
    Archimago's daring 70
  for aid
    by Redcrosse 188
  loud
    of Duessa for Sansjoy 153
  to action
    of Lucifera 146
    of Night by Duessa 156
    pagan skepticism as 76
  to rest
    by chamberlain Sloth 150
callousness
  indifference
    of Redcrosse towards Una 120
calm 64
  Christian 63, 65
calming
  effects of reason 105
  wrath 190
Calvin, John 2, 25–27, 28, 66, 94, 164, 170, 210
  denial of access through one's will to holiness 46
  doctrine of effectual perseverance 25
  on grace 25
  various states of the will 26
  works
    Institutes of the Christian Religion 25
cannibalistic

children
  of Errour 298
capacity
  human
    to dream 242
captain 202
captive
  langour 183
  weak 194
captivity
  hidden cause of 166
capture
  of Redcrosse
    by Orgoglio 173
    by the applause of the crowd 154
  of Una
    by Sansloy 140
carcasses
  scattered
    on the green 200
care
  bequeathed 244
  continual
    of truth for the righteous man 184
  of Sansfoy
  for God or man 105
careful
  breast
    of Redcrosse 226
  inspecting of walls 274
careful reader 2, 35, 52, 61, 62, 69, 70, 80, 83, 95, 100, 107, 109, 110, 116, 133, 145, 146, 152, 172, 175, 178, 188, 189, 202, 204, 212, 213, 215, 216, 220, 226, 227, 228, 230, 231, 235, 237, 242, 244, 249, 250, 261, 262, 264, 275, 276, 277, 278, 279, 280, 283, 284, 288, 293, 295, 297
  See also reader.
  given insight into the mind of Redcrosse 148
  graditude of 232
  knowledge of the
    of difference between perception and reality 127
  lesson of Spenser for the 138
  mind of
    survives deconstruction 181
  notes the perversion of true intents to false ones 122
  noting of the role of Redcrosse in the betrayal of Una 118
  problem of the 175
  remembering of
    of Redcrosse's abandonment of Una 130
  Renaissance-educated 69
  stout memory of 214
careless
  of fame 161
  of health 161
  sleep 80
carelessness

Index

unkind 161
cares
  another's 155
cargo 290
Carneades 76, 155
carpet
  scarlet 276
Cartesian. *See also* Descartes, René.
  system 91
Carthage 39
case
  accusative 75
  cruel
    endurance of 258
  extremest
    of Arthur 197
  like 243
  nominative 75
cases
  impartial decisions in resolutions of 286
cast
  lowly looks
    of Humiltá 213
casting
  of eye
    of Sansjoy 153
castle 68
  brazen 80
  epic simile of 187
catalog
  epic 53, 62
  of kings and princes 166
  of trees 206
catechism 262
  of George 262
Catholic 42, 95
  ending 298
Catholicism
  in the eyes of Luther 24
  of Ariosto 66
causal
  dwarf 173
  framework 172
cause 65
  for worry 119
  hidden 78, 166
  new
    for invoking the wrath of Jove 159
  of concern
    for the reader 152
  of confusion of reference
    in the reader 175
  of Corceca's tears 123
  of death
    of Hercules 259
  of Duessa's flight 187
  of enmity 154
  of Redcrosse's flight from Una 116
  of Redcrosse's return to Fidessa 116
  of royal maid 244
  present 108
  rational 288
  rightful 286
  Una's dwarf as bearer of 165–167
  wrought in heaven above 78
cause and effect 94
caution
  necessity of
    in the world of time 140
  negative
    urged by Una 212
  of Una
    at the entrance to the Cave of Errour 53
    sounds a note of in the hermitage of Archimago 69
cautious
  intervention
    of Una 211
cave 204
  allegory of the 14
  darksome 150
  of Night 155
Cave of Despair 174, 182, 208, 211, 212, 220
    See also Despair.
Cave of Errour 53–66, 67, 69, 81, 90, 104, 105, 106, 110, 111, 121, 163, 164, 206, 211, 261, 279 *See also* Errour.
celebration
  of the King of Eden 284
celestial
  discipline
    taught by Fidelia 220
  sight
    of Una 282
Centaur
  blood of 258
center
  Archimago's hermitage off 69
  of experience 222
  off
    of Archimago's chapel 69
  of Spenser's poem 238
  of universe 4
central
  question
    whether Una has heard the dwarf's whole discourse 177
  stone
    in Arthur's arms 179
  to George's experience
    Contemplation not 246
ceremony 111
certain
  date 203
  hate 79
certainty 21
  of knowledge 21
  of names 85
  of peril 58, 65
  of success 228

chaff 6
  separation of
    from wheat 143
chafing
  of the chin
    of Una 169
chain
  endless
    of horizontal reference 6
  golden 192–193, 194
  of being 4
  of necessity 156, 158
    broken for the Furies 158
  of reason 4
  Venus' shameful 101
chained
  bear 288
chains
  of necessity
    apparant, not real 158
  untied
    of infernal furies 200
chair
  golden
    of Juno 146
Chaldeans 26
challenge
  of false distinctions
    failure of Redcrosse to 143
  of Redcrosse
    by Sansjoy 148
  to readers 214
chamberlain
  Sloth as 150
champion 54, 108, 182
  of the antique world 258
chance 58, 178, 186, 264, 266
  a priori 124
  encounter
    of Fradubio with knight 114
  guide of
    God as 266
  hapless 123
    Archimago's ability to overcome 123
  of meeting with Archimago 68
change
  agents of 3
  Augustinian
    in Spenser 256
  between day and night 96
  diurnal 96
  in behavior
    from purposeless wandering to forward purpose 199
  in love
    of Redcrosse 147
  in Night 156
    from moral indifference to partisanship for evil 156
  in perception

    of Una 45
  in position
    of Una 126
  into idolaters 137
  in scientific powers of the universe 155
  lack of
    in the constant mood of Fidelia 219
  of behavior
    in Arthur 190
  of circumstance 190
  of Duessa's countenance towards Redcrosse 109
  of faith 63
  of focus 184
  of loved dame 141
  of mind
    bu Una 183
  of outer garment
    of Una 282
  of satyrs's looks 134
  of state
    of Fradubio 115
  of the look of lion
    towards Una 134
  of Una
    from passive to an active character 118
  to Theory of Forms
    by Plato 193
  to Virgil's ending by Ariosto 65
  world of 183
changeable
  world 281
changeling 244
changing
  course 142
  moon 227
  state
    of world 203
  terms of victory 255
chaos
  primal
    beneath linguistic flux 240
chapel
  of Contemplation 238, 246
  off center 69
  sacred
    of Contemplation 234
character 28, 43, 57, 80, 135, 161–162, 222, 228
  action of 84
  active
    of Archimago 119
    Una as 118
  DeNeef, A. Leigh's treatment of 32–34
  flaws in Una's 121
  in allegory 53
  incomplete of
    of Una 95
  individual
    imaginatively created 215
  moral

Index

of Duessa 108
narrative as the extension of 161
of Contemplation 233
of Redcrosse 48
phantom
    Malvenu as 143
true 114
within Spenser's fiction 128
characteristics
    metaphorical
        of the golden chain 194
characters 234
    fictional 94
    imaginatively created
        deconstruction of 215
    that react to Una's essential unity 117
charge
    of pride
        Redcrosse's indictment of the 146
    of the world of science
        in the hands of Duessa 159
    serious
        against Redcrosse 204
charges
    of pretending 245
chariot
    of Lucifera 146
Charissa 103, 219, 231, 238, 281
    as an end unto herself
        inadequacy of 228
    breasts of
        baring of 228
    Cælia's third daughter 227
    gems and owches of 229
    her hatred of Cupid 227
    neck of
        baring of 228
    teaches the path to heaven
        to Redcrosse 231
    wardrobe of 228
charity 232
charm
    exterior magical 106
    mighty 265
charmed
    armor
        of the knight 258
    shield
        of Redcrosse 151
    with bloody verses 258
    with enchanted rhymes 205
charms 100, 129
    Archimago's search for 70
    of Duessa 287
    of wealth 145
chaste
    maid 116
chastity 94, 281
    flower of 123
    of Una

    threatened by Sansloy 132
Chaucer, Geoffrey 167, 233
checking
    diverse sense impressions against God-given
        potential 106
    of senses 112
cheeks
    of hearers 278
cheer 49
    sad 280
    sober 280
    trembling 116
cheereful
    whistle 127
cheerful
    birds 160
    day 124
cheering
    of Archimago
        by Una 128
cheerless
    night 124
cherishing 226
child 231
    of Charissa 227
    of glorious great intent 151
childbirth
    impending 227
    womanhood in 227
children
    cannibalistic
        of Errour 298
    famous
        of Night 156
    of Errour 60, 254
    of Night 156
chin
    chafing of
        of Una 169
chivalric
    quest-romance 239
chivalrous
    emprise 192
chivalry 42, 115
    joy of 113
    noble 280
    Redcrosse plays at 109
choice 58, 93, 98, 148, 286
    between suppression and elimination 44
    between two equal loves 114
    by God 84
    by Una 84
    correct 55, 149
    equal 160, 238
    for adventure 84
    freedom of 50
    happy 190–191
    in use of language
        Virgil's 75
    of actors 55

of Archimago
    when faced with actual violence of battle 128
of God 57, 231
of human beings 79
of love
    of Redcrosse 147
    of Redcrosse for Duessa 153
of Redcrosse
    as friend of God 105
    between Una's true beauty and Fidessa's false beauty 190
    by God 186
of Redcrosse's will 111
of will 50
of women 141
poor 61
    made by Reddcrosse 115, 141, 200, 276
    positive 141
    unequal 270
choosing
    of own free will
        in the Augustinian universe 134
chosen
    knight
        of Una 199
    love
        Fidessa as Redcrosse's 195
        Redcrosse as 206
Chretien de Troyes 44
Christ 25, 48, 76, 95, 220, 225, 263
    death and resurrection 40
    difference from Redcrosse 96
    identification of 95
    identity with Redcrosse 95
    likeness of lion to 225
    rendering of the veil 39
Christian 38, 170, 194
    age 251
    doctrine of confession 182
    doubts 242
    experience 143
    faith 259
    hero 63, 66
    message 40
    poet 133, 161–162
    poetry 83
    tradition 285
    tyranny 230
    universe 76, 259
        Homer as substitute for the divine in 76
        pagan skepticism as a powerful call to action in 76
    values
        raised over pagan values 63
Christianity 1, 63, 96
    three-dimensional world of 97
Christians 170
    suppression of 181
chronological
    events 277
    relationships 277

church
    holy 1
    the one true 70
    universal 13
Church
    authority weakened by skepticism 13
    Reformed 262
    reputation of 24
churches 95
    rape of 122, 290
    robbery of 122
Cicero, Marcus Tullius
    De oratore 7
    murder of 222
    source for temporality of allegory 7
circle
    Boötes' team of oxen driven in 82
    breaking of closed and relative 133
    breaking of
        by satyrs and fawns 133
    hermeneutic 76, 291, 293
        completion of 228
    of friendship 198
circularity
    of Redcrosse's journey 46
circumlocution
    of Latin translators
        in talking about allegory 71
circumscribed
    walls
        of Eden 273
circumstance
    change of 190
    whole
        of Una 224
circumstances
    present
        of Redcrosse 224
    Una's control of her 129
citizens 41
city 236
    holy
        of Jerusalem 236
    of man 109
civilization 47
civil war 36
clad
    fully
        Una 147
    in green leaves
        Gluttony 146
cladding 68
claim
    of Fidessa
        to empire 285
    medieval
        to knowledge 2
    rightful
        lack of 144
    that would supplant God 193

to be called a word 73
  to knowledge 170
    by Ignaro 189
    by Socrates 189
clapping
  of the people 154 *See also* applause.
clarification
  of the logic of enigma 72
clarity 30, 31, 38, 84, 229
  rational
    lack of 282
class
  distinction 233
  of humanity 113
  of men 211
classical
  models 4
  philosophers 292
  philosophy 96, 170, 190
    metaphysical role of 98
  religion
    private nature of 194
  world 24, 170
classicism
  two dimensional world of 97
claws
  of lion
    rescue of Una likened to being snatched from the 132
clean
  hold
    of Una's garment 130
cleansing
  of George 264
  of past sins 271
clear
  conscience
    of the King of Eden 287
  ideas
    of Desartes 292
  points 4
clearer
  sight
    of Archimago 234
clemency
  of God 235, 236
Cleopolis 236
cleverness
  of Despair 203
cliff
  rocky 187, 270
cliffs
  scattered carcasses on the 200
climbing
  into chariot
    by Lucifera 146
Clio 249–251, 269

clock
    stopping the 282
closed 266
  circle 133
  posture of self-reflection 180
closing
  metaphysics
    as an avenue of approach to God 190
  of possibility
    of seeing Redcrosse again 173
    the philosopher to the existence of a larger prior world
  by skepticism 189
closure
  delaying 240
  illicit
    of gulf of reference 94
cloth
  of state 144
clothes 146, 160
  mottled 281
  of Despair 201
clothing
  pieces of
    Despair's garment woven out of 201
cloud
  foggy 132
  of gnats 77
  of smothering smoke 252
  of sulphur 252
clouding
  of the mind
    of Redcrosse 153
clouds 270
  dispersal of 251
  swift 270
clouts
  ragged 201, 231, 281
clown
  Redcrosse as a 105
clownish 44, 60, 62, 70, 90, 102, 108, 121, 152, 155, 158, 159, 171, 195, 199, 207, 222, 224, 238, 241, 278, 293
  hands 60
  mind 143
"clownishe younge man" 43–47, 83, 95, 99, 105, 137, 138, 167, 195, 236, 274, 295
  citation in *Letter to Raleigh* 43
clownishness 44
clues
  subtle 198
  to truth and falseness 81
Clytemnestra 35
coals
  fresh 173
Cochrane, Charles Norris 22, 181
  the claim of reason to transcend itself 21
Cocytus 70
codependent
  Una as 226

cognitive
  procedure 90
  values 91
coherence
  Gloriana's presence causes of law 131
  social 193
Cohn, Dorrit 35
coincidence
  between ontology and epistemology
    in Cartesian system 91
  between the will of God and the will of George
    269
coitus
  of Redcrosse
    with Fidessa 195
cold 64
  congealed fear 251, 252
  curdled
    runs through Una's veins 207
Coleridge, Samuel Taylor 275
  suspension of disbelief 112
collapse
  of day and night
    into unity 189
collective
  action 43, 295
  good
    according to Romans 181
  sense 15
collective action 23
colloquial
  meaning 248
color 221
  as accident 32
  of Fidessa 277
combat 152
  with Sansjoy 173
combatant 106
combination
  of images 227
  of words and letters 87
comedy 18, 32
  genre
    of the provincial morality play 232
  in Spenser's modeling of Redcrosse 43
comely
  personage 227
  services 277
Comes, Natalis 258
comfort
  in expression 180
  in life and death 263
  of Fidessa
    by Redcrosse 200
  of Una 134
  of weeping and wailing 180

  reversion to
    by Una 212

  shown for Una
    by dwarf 168
  sweet 224
  wondrous 215
comforting
  of Trevisan
    by Redcrosse 200
coming
  of death 261
command
  by Sir Walter Raleigh 30
commandment 109
  of queen Lucifera to refrain from combat 149
  of the sun to stay 221
  taking
    from Una's eyes 120
commanding
committing
  sin 191
common
  man 193
communication
  of inner virtue 136
  process 228
community 254
  human 105
    detours from 176
companion
  of false faith 148
company
  sweet
    of Una 289
comparison 110
  apt 258
  as a fuction of memory 121
  between Contemplation
    and Archimago 234
    and Corceca 234
  difficulty of 227
  of earthly things to things divine 246
  of George and Hercules 258–260
  of the strength of George to the strength of three
    men 254
  of the wealth of Lucifera to the wealth of Persia
    144
  of Una and Odysseus 122
  on earth
    not easy 227, 229
compassion 224–225
  of lion 120
  for sinners 223
  for Una 119
  lack of
    shown by Redcrosse for Fradubio 115
  location of 119
  melting of Una's heart in 120
  of mind 118
  of Night 156
  of Redcrosse
    for Fradubio 115

of Una 224
of Spenser
  for Una's plight 118
  overwhelmed by 120
  without reason 224
compel
  events
    power to 134, 211
compensating
  advantages
    for the fall from grace 251
competing
  for power
    with the gods 146
competition 50
competitors
  in a contest 283
complaint
  of Una 132
complete
  knowledge 97
  lack of 264
completeness 228
completion
  of being in the world of time 138
  of oneself 175
  of Redcrosse's battle 59
  of reference 86
  of the hermeneutic circle 228
  of Una
    by other 160
  successful
    of adventure 287
complication
  of easy relationship between language and nature
    in Plato 75
    in Spenser 75
complicity
  in sin
    of Redcrosse 226
  of Redcrosse
    in fleeing his literal name 83
    of the reader 150
  of Una 84
    in driving away Redcrosse 184
composite
  creatures
    satyrs as 135
comprehension
  of love
    Una's lack of 138
  of the power of Redcrosse's arms
    beyond Duessa 151
comprehensiveness
  of God 222
compromising
  position 134

concavity
  of the valley 253

conceiving
  Una's intent
    by lion 120
conception
  of intent 121
  of love
    superficial 121
concern
  cause of
    for reader 152
  for individual 66
  lack of
    for destruction wrought by violence on the social order 151
  of Una 254
conclusion
  of battle
    at once 173
  of marriage 289
conclusions
  amenable 173
concupiscence
  accusation of 259
  punishment for
    of Hercules 258
condemnation
  negative 141
  by poet
    of Redcrosse 142
condescension
  process of 241
condition
  individual
    of George 264
  native
    of Una 249
  of being human 166
  revived 264
  true
    of George 243
condolences 196
conferee
  of grace 221
confession
  doctrine of 182
confidence
  in Una's unspoken identity with herself 137
configuration
  Enlightenment
    of universe 242
  pagan
    of universe 233
confinement
  of magic within fiction 103
conflict
  grows
    in Una's mind 172

  luckless
    with Orgoglio 173

Spenser pictured as ignorant of 42
conflicting
  interests
    problem of 211
confounding
  foes 195
  of feeble sense
    of George 246
  of Sansloy 129
confrontation
  of paradox 172
  of the Dragon 104
confusion
  logical
    at the mouth of Errour's Cave 53
  of ancients
    over definition of allegory 5
  of fiction and fact 221
  of reference
    in the reader 175
  of Una
    on account of love 173
congealed
  fear 251, 252
congratulations 67, 83, 196
  by Una 262
connection 215
  between fiction and reality 39
  between individual condition and state of nature
    poet's role in making 264
  between nature and man 36
  between objects and names 86
  loose
    between Plato and Homer 76
  necessary
    betwen words and things 76
  of discrete facts in the mind of Redcrosse 112
  of dots 143
  of language to nature
    in Virgil 75
  of moments in the poem
    through the use of memory 145
  of outward phenomena with inner life
    lack of 207
  of the will of Redcrosse to its source of Heaven 207
  uncertain
    to God 266
connections 12
conquering
  fear 253
  might
    of George 271
conqueror 64
  doughty 274
conquest 153
  arms won by 149
  by might 271
  earthly 237
conqureor

sign of the 108
conscience
  clear
    of the King of Eden 287
  cured
    of Redcrosse 226
  of Redcrosse
    assault on 205
  relieving of
    of Redcrosse 192
  secret breach in
    of Redcrosse 205
conscious
  control
    over events by Una 129
  will 205
consciousness 2, 42
  division of 83
  growth of Una's 118
  knowledge as bringing forth unconscious things to 74
  lack of
    in Archimago 28
    in Duessa 28
    on Spenser's part 42
  of humanity 242
  of poetic creation 53
  of true motivation
    of George 249
  of understanding
    of Una's power 134
  substantial 37, 40, 84, 97, 180, 189, 242, 254, 255, 259, 260, 282, 290
    Augustine's discovery of 21–23
    confusion over location in naming 175
    defined 22
    direction of thought of 138
    embrace of 147
    enacting potential in 276
    in Augustine 233
    of Elizabeth 93
    of Redcrosse 175
    of Spenser's hero 256
    rationality of 179
    reality of 175
consecration
  of Redcrosse's relationship with Fidessa through physical intercourse 116
consent
  one 194
  to spiritual death
    by George 261
  to will
    of Sansloy 131
consequence
  of action
    played out externally 162–163
consequences 274
  of one's own actions 66
  of other's actions 66
  of Redcrosse's sins 164

Index 341

serious 274
weighing 60
conservative 14
consideration
  of enigmatic allegory
    in Augustine 104
consistency
  lack of in the *Timaeus* 19
  of mind 90
  of nature 90
Consolation of Philosophy. See **Boethius, Anicius Manlius Severinus.**
consort 77
  of Gloriana 177
conspiring
  enemies 253
constancy
  of motion 37
  of Una 131
constant
  heart
    of Una 131
  mood
    of Fidelia 219
  truth as 297
  vigilance 246
constellation
  fixity of 83
  of Boötes 82
constituent
  parts
    division of whole into 118
constraint 56, 80
  of Dragon
    through struggle 253
  of Errour 56
  of necessity 297
constructed
  fiction 228
  framework 164
construction 231
  epistemological 272
  existential 188
  fictional 45
    of satyrs 135
  genitive 175
  intellectual 242
  of brazen gate 274
  of Duessa
    in Spenser's fiction 187
  of false art 185
  of gates 273
  of meaning 54
  of metaphysical universes
    in Plato 161–162
  of mind 254
  of nature 142
  of Redcrosse's universe 115
  of situation
    by Redcrosse 110

  of things 155
  of universe 159
  rhetorical 6
constructive
  reason 168
consultation
  lack of 280
consuming
  thought 226
consummation
  of relationship of Duessa and Redrcrosse 162–163
contact
  immediate
    with object 228
  lack of
    with the truth of matters 193
  with ground
    as source of Antaeus' strength 259
containment
  in language 134
  in narrow leaves
    of poet 277
contemplation 40
  as the cardinal intellectual virtue in Aristotle's Nichochean Ethics 233
  in Aristotle 233
  knowledge of
    as wisdom 72
Contemplation 84, 232, 233–248, 261, 268, 282, 295, 296
  attention of 246
  blunt-eyed 236
  chapel of 238, 246
  correct reading of 246
  eagle eyes of 256
  element of snobbishness in 235
  imagination of 246
  mind of 243
  moral 12
  notes that Redcrosse was raised in a house of a plowman 82
contemplative
  activity 245, 264
    of Contemplation 234
  desire 234
  existence 246
content 39
  full 289
  guessing the
    of nature 190
  negative
    of Redcrosse's mind 101
  of mind 172
  rational 104
contention
  in mind
    of Una 172
contentment
  of Redcrosse

only after male hermit speaks 69
contest
  between Redcrosse and Sansjoy
    governed by the "the sacred lawes of armes" 152
  competitors in a 283
  Fradubio's victory in 114
  political 63
context 89
  historical 32
  philosophical 45, 113
continual
  care
    of truth for the righteous man 184
  education 203
continuation 272
  in the mind
    of the prior language of the heart 73
  of education 59
  of error after Errour's death 60
continuity
  break in 97
contradictory
  desires 110
contrary
  evidence 12
  opinions 116
  to nature
    of portents 222
contrast 253
  in portrait of the Dragon 263
  of Redcrosse
    with Arthur 188
control 39, 157, 210
  active 135
  conscious
    oever events by Una 129
  fight for
    between two evenly-matched opponents 138
  gain
    Archimago's attempt to 77
  given to man by *a posteriori* education 124
  human 66, 268
  individual 138
  lack of
    by Una in the world of time 174
    in character of Ion 193
  losing
    of individual mind 79
  of contrary opinions 116
  of events 135
    by Clio 250
  of human reason 188
  of flock 257
  of individuals 233
  of love
    rests with Cupid 138
  of man
    reason as being under 4
  of metaphor 194
  of middle terms

    of experience 203
  of situation
    by Redcrosse 209
    by Una 209
    wrested by Redcrosse from Una 200
  of Socrates 193
  of Una over her environment 118
  of Una's physical body 138
  of will 261
  of wrath 252
  out of
    Redcrosse as 203
  over affairs 182
  over destiny
    through limited reason 296
  over individual fate 79
  political
    extension of 233
  power of 268
  sense of
    given to the reader 131
  taking
    of Una's being 138
  Una's lack of
    over her circumstances 129
convention 39
  naming
    in Spenser 240
conversation 220
  between Arthur and Redcrosse 198
  of Duessa
    with Sansjoy 151
  of Morpheus with Archimago's sprite 71
  participants in 196
  with Fradubio 143
conversion 63
  of Ruggiero 64
conveyance
  of knowledge 73
conviction
  of Redcrosse 142
  religious 6
cooling
  of anger 123
  shade 160
cooperation
  between individuals
    as basis for social compact 181
  social 66
cooperative
  effort
    between wise author and careful reader 230
  social action 181
coordinate geometry 2, 34, 291
coordination
  between human epistemology and natural ontology
    in Descartes 3

  lack of
    between the heart of Redcrosse and God or

Una 152
copulation 111
Corceca 212, 214, 215
   a creature who lives in perpetual darkness 122
   as wise old woman 189
   busy at her beads 214
   comparison of
      with Contemplation 234
   House of 121–124
   roused into a into a whirlwind of passion
      by Archimago 123
   sitting blind 124
   story of 123
cornea 75 *See also* eye
corpse
   senseless 268
   Una's tender 119
correct 277
   behavior of Una 122
   choice 149
   judgment 135
   reading
      by Contemplation 246
   sorting of Redcrosse's experience 116
correction
   in Calvin 26
   of Du Bartas 256
   of King of Eden 279
   of mistakes 192
   of Redcrosse 146, 261
   of Una
      by Arthur 191
   painful
      in House of Holinesse 243
correctly
   weighing
      things of unequal measure 150
correlative
   objective 216
correspondence 87
   1:1 18
   probaility of 18
   with work of God 94
corrupt
   woman
      Duessa as 175
corruption
   of intermediaries 24
   of mankind 228
   of nature 26
cosmology
   mythical 18
cosmos 18
   in *Timaeus* 18
   pictured in terms of nature 18
   role of fiction in the reconstruction of the 19
cost
   of George's flight from his name 83

weighing
   in world of time 199
couch
   of verdant grass 195
couched
   spear 128
counsel
   bad 144
counselors
   of Lucifera 145
      led by Idleness 146
counsels
   spent
      by Una 135
countenance
   better 145
   change of Duessa's 109
   demure 219
   fell 263
   no better 145
   of Ignaro 190
   sad 134
Counter-Reformation 25
country 68
courage 106, 245
   flaming 151
   hot 113
   noble
      awakening of 249
   of George 245
   of Redcrosse 163
course 221
   changing 142
   detour off 115
   forward 258
      of Una 199
   of action 180
   of the sun 221
   unprofitable
      of George 258
   weary
      of poet 272
courser 54
   free
      of Arthur 194
   light 131
court 47, 96, 105, 168, 245, 277
   faery 245
   goodly
      made by Redcrosse 161
   integration into
      through prowess 197
   of Eden 284
   of Gloriana 55, 91, 96, 105, 138, 166, 167, 176,
      182, 212, 234, 245, 247, 267, 274
      law of 131
   of Lucifera 145
   of Prince of Eden 276
   of reason 46
   ordered world of 44

royal 245, 298
  service at 295
courteous
  deeds 136
courtesy
  of Lucifera's counselors
    to Duessa 146
courtiers
  educated 105
courting 150
  of Una
    with fawning words 131
courtly 44
  train 277
cover
  falls off magical shield 186
  of dress
    as a distinguishing characteristic of the difference between Una and Duessa 109
covered
  in gold foil 143
covering
  of crime 287
  of shield
    of Arthur 266
  of Una's body 281
  of virgin's face 130
cowardice 210
  of Archimago 129
    as False Redcrosse 128
  of people
    of Eden 273
cowardly
  men 274
  retreat
    from danger 211
crafty
  crocodile 154
craving
  for a foothold on the Ladder of Ambition
    by Redcrosse 149
  for Gloriana
    by Redcrosse 177
  of earthly things 280, 294
  of love
    by Sir Burbon 297
  of pardon 279
  of Redcrosse for earthly things 105
  presence 283
created
  by God 94
  individuals 257
  in myth
    satyrs 135
  ontology 190
    of God 298
  universe
    of God 158
creation 155
  a priori

    of God 152, 167
  artificial 75, 100
    of meaning 240
  by God 178, 218, 234
    implanting of good in the mind of man at 138
    without intermediary reason 41
  by poet
    of Faery 162
  by power of imagination 282
  existence of 255
  in fiction
    of Una 67
  inimitable 76
  in posteriori world 105
  of a false double 240, 275
  of Archimago 102
  of fiction 76
    by an allegorical poet 218
    in imagination 178
  of God 23, 38, 61, 93, 137, 155
    compromised in pre-linguistic language 111
  of imaginative fiction
    myth as 285
  of life
    for death 203
  of ontology
    by God 263
  of saints 105
  of Spenserian fiction 84
  of the moral world 202
  of the poet 62
  of typological fiction
    by Spenser 270
  of universe
    by God 133
  ontological
    of God 66, 275
  ontology of
    perception of by Archimago 100
creator 40
  God as
    of Λόγος 193
  poet as
    of temporary means 230
Creator 22, 104, 222 *See also* creation and God.
  prelinguistic ontology of 289
creature 158, 181, 238
  born in time 138
  cursed 69
  deceitful 182
  fair 195
  human beings as 22
  of Faery
    Redcrosse as 162
  of light 122
creatures 96
  created in myth
    satyrs as 135
  external 187
  fictional

Index

satyrs as 133
in God's creation 137
mythical 3
naïve 121
credit
  for victory 67
crest
  hardened 257
crested
  scalp
    of Dragon 264
Creusa
  ghost of 38
crew
  increasing of Lucifera's 145
cries
  of Una 133
crime
  covering of 287
  deformed 223
    of Redcrosse 205
  disclosing of 287
  past
    of Redcrosse 224
criminal
  indifference
    of George towards Una 280
critic
  A. C. Hamilton's posture as 53
  insightful
    recreation of metaphysics by 169
  modern 56, 277
  role of
    in the work of Northrop Frye 170
critical
  modern c. method 161
  objectivity 54
  observer 128
criticism
  aesthetic 93
  bias
    towards history 31
  distance of 54
  literary
    golden chain in 192
  maintenance of balance in 50
  modern
    problem of reference in 33
  modern method of 31
  of Plato's Theory of Forms
    by aristotle 193
critics 10, 11, 51, 98
  baffled by *Letter to Raleigh* 30
  literary 31, 241
  modern 2, 28, 32
    move away from Tasso's disseverance of good from politics 43
  Modern 240
  postmodern 240
crocodile
  cruel and crafty 154
cross 107
  red 297
  Sansfoy's curse of the 106
cross-purpose 182, 198, 226, 238
  of Una
    with dwarf 172
crowd 276
  applause of the 154
  drunken 217
  middest 144
  of amazed vulgar 152
crown
  of triple happiness 236
crowning
  of Fidessa 111, 116
crowns
  on Duessa's head 108
cruel
  case
    endurance of 258
  crocodile 154
  dart 96, 176
  fate 78
  freaks
    of fortune 278
  heart
    of Redcrosse 120
  spies 106
cruelty
  of Cupid's darts 138
  of sky 52
crutch
  of the poet 141
cry
  lamenting
    of Abessa and Corceca 123
  loud
    of the Dragon 255
  of Corceca 123
  of the monster 255
  of trader 59
  of Una 132
  piteous
    of Duessa 186
crying
  of a lion 225
  of Una 56
    to distant sun and stars 133
cult
  mystery 38
cultivated
  behavior 123
cultural
  taste 133
culture
  clash of 63
  relative nature of 133
  Western
    crisis of 218

cunning
   hand
      of Æsculapius 159
      of Cupid 176
      of darts of Cupid 138
cup
   golden 187
   with a serpent in it
      held by Fidlelia 219
Cupid 96, 176, 238
   as governor
      of the extremity of time 138
   as the blind god 79
   blind 139
   blind love of 138
   Charissa's thoughts on 227
   darts of 138
   love of 12, 227, 229
   rule of 227
curbing
   of liberty 194
curdled
   cold
      runs through Una's veins 207
cure 191
cured
   conscience
      of Redcrosse 226
curious
   skill 289
curse
   of Corceca 123
   of God's cross 107
   put on Una
      by Abessa and Corceca 123
cursed
   creature 69
   foe 244
cursing 64
   heaven 70
Curtius, Ernst Robert 167
custom 3
cycle
   ever-dying, ever-renewing 205
cyclical
   return 133
      of nature 291
cyclops
   defeat of 35

D

dagger 64
   in Ariosto 64
daily 282
   fall
      of the righteous man 184
dainty
   dishes 277

forehead 147
limbs
   of Gloriana 195
dale 69, 234
damage 225
dame 151
   dearest
      Lucifera addressed as 149
   former
      love of 287
   loved
      beware of change of 141
   of Pluto (Proserpina) 70
damnation 47
damned
   fiend 264
   ghost 112, 205
   sprites 158
   wight 202
dancing
   in a round 133
danger 110, 130, 188, 267
   avoiding
      by Arthur 186
   dwelling of 68
   external 162
   hidden 54
   hiding 111
   in Wandering Wood 52
   moral 166
   of armed injustice 99
   of pagan religion 259
   of Una's virtue 130
   retreat from 211
   security against 111
dangerous 253
   adventures
      of Redcrosse 209
dangers 240
   hidden 273
daring 70
dark 263
   abyss 252
   conceit 31, 43
   Corceca sitting blind in the 124
   glass 246
   praying
      in the dark 121
   sitting in the 121
   things
      written in the book of Fidelia 221
   through a dark glass 149
darkness 54, 101
   baleful 191
   of earthly things 246
   of ignorance 72
   of Redcrosse's armor 56
   perpetual 122
   virtue gives light to wade through 223
darksome

cave 150
  hollow maw 269
dart
  cruel 96, 176
darts
  of Cupid 138
    cruel and unbalanced 139
date
  certain 203
daughter 122, 156, 279, 280
  heavenly
    of Cælia 227
  of Apollo
    Clio as 249
  of Cælia
    Charissa as third 227
  of Eden 131
  of the Roman Emperor 109
  of Western Empire
    Fidessa's claim as 285
  only
    argument of 288
  perfect 284
  woeful 285
  yielding of 280
daughters
  of Cælia 219
  linked in holy band 285
daunting
  the senses 186
David
  descendant of 95
dawning
  day 71, 281
day 152, 165, 178, 213, 263, 269, 270
  broad 122
  cheerful 124
  collapse of
    with night 189
  dawning 71, 281
  example of the
    written on Arthur's heart with an iron pen 192
  in diurnal alternation with night 155
  joyous 269
  mist in 114
  rule of
    by Jove 159
daylight 256
  sun 249
days
  better
    of Redcrosse 188
  wretched
    desire to end 223
dazed
  eyes
    of George 246
dead 136, 172, 285
  half 201
  revival of
    by wondrous science of Æsculapius 159
  skulls 147
  to the reflections of things 165
  Una's beloved not 173
  within
    in the description of the dwarf's heart 168
deadly
  dint 265
  Dragon 268
  dullness
    of eyes of Despair 201
  ebony bow 176
  tidings
    signs of 168
  wounds 268
dear
  delights
    of George 289
  knight 248
  loved dame 141
  slight heart
    of Una 124
dearest
  dame
    Lucifera addressed as 149
dearth 125
  eternal 125
death 18, 64, 79, 109, 171, 173, 260, 261, 268, 288
  absolute 273
  actual 168
  appearance of 168
  as the due of False Una 79
  badness of
    Una assesses 171
  buying
    by Fradubio's misake 112
  cause of
    of Hercules 259
  comfort in 263
  coming of 261
  desire for 261
  door of 225
  focus on
    by George 267
  hour of 203
  imminent 267
  in battle 59
  metaphysical pole of 253
  mock 168
  need of 204
  of Christ 37, 40
  of Dragon 272, 273
  of Errour 60
  of God 238
  of Hercules 258
  of Jesus Christ 76–75
  of King of Eden 280
  of lion 130
  of Redcrosse 136
    prevented by the intervention of truth 184

of Sansfoy 129
of Socrates 222
of Una's light heart 124
pronouncement of
   of Redcrosse 173
rollback of 268
shunning
   ordained by destiny 203
spiritual
   of George 261
the shadow of 124
thought of 63
wishing for
   by Redcrosse 190, 223
debate
   endless 51
decadence
   of Romans 233
decadent
   goal 171
decay 216
decayed
   plight
      weighing the 199
deceit 19, 41, 42, 64
   in Eden
      lack of 67
   necessary 83
deceitful
   creatures 182
   train 184
deceivers 36
   world of 213
deceiving
   of the mind 142
decentering 191, 237
   in Foucault 218
   of man
      in Du Bartas' poem 255
   of Una 249
deception 35, 64, 244
   by master of artifice 184
   of Archimago 218
   of Fradubio 114
   of world 104
   Una's lack of experience with 96
decision 54, 189, 280
   disastrous 273
   firm 177
   immediate 92
   impartial
      in matters of law 286
   impulsive
      of Dragon 269
   individual 240
   rendering a
      based in reason 286
   terrible 116
   willful
      by Æsculapius 160

declaration
   by George 287
   of definite preference
      for Sansjoy by Duessa 153
   of love
      by Una 175
   of meaning 31
deconstruct
   inability to
      the Word of God 256
deconstructable
   art 61
   fiction 58, 181
      of the House of Holinesse 219
   heaven
      of the House of Holinesse 253
   names 155
   status
      of Una 212
   universe
      of Faery 281
deconstructing
   fiction 133
   unity
      of Una 294
deconstruction 6, 46, 237, 271, 296
   assumption of 185
   failure of
      in an Augustinian universe 252
   of Augustinian faith 230
   of Derrida 155
   of Errour 61
   of fiction 112, 131, 164
   of imaginatively created characters 215
   of magic
      question of the 104
   of things 155
   of Una 282
   of weak handwriting
      in the presence of grace 207
   surviving 215
      in the mind of the reader 181
dedication
   to God 38
deed 48, 118, 203, 213
   courteous 136
   of arms 243
deep 78, 82
   affection 66, 121
   devouring jaws 252
   sorrow 180
deeper 133, 154
   dint 257
   level 278
      of existence 152
   moral duty 154
   purpose 79, 152
   rational process as looking 166
   reason 5
   sublime 5
   substance

of God 178
sympathy 134
truth 166, 270
deep-rooted
  ill 256
deer
  amazed 123
defacing
  of accursed hand writing 207
defeat 68
  all enemies 297
  in battle 187
  of Archimago 102
  of cyclops 35
  of Dragon 104, 209, 212, 266, 269, 277, 285, 296
  of Duessa
    by Arthur 186
  of enemies 260
    at once 252
  of Errour 60, 261, 298
  of God 136
  of Orgoglio 188
    as a general example 187
    by Arthur 186
  of purpose
    of Una 212
  of Redcrosse
    by Orgoglio 162–163
  of Sansfoy 105
  of Sansjoy 152
defend
  power to 186
defendants
  opposing 286
defending
  honor 195
defense 266
  of Duessa
    to the charges leveled at her by Sansjoy 150
  of faith 14
defenselessness
  of George 266
defensive
  posture
    of Errour 60
  shield 266, 297
deferring
  action 236
defiance 64
defiling
  of mankind 72
  of sacred waves 263
  of self 204
  of Una
    by Sansloy 131
definite
  answer 174

  location
    lack of 275

preference
  declared by Duessa 153
definition 5, 10, 51
  in modern criticism 31
  logic of
    in Augustine 71
  negative 275, 292
    of Errour 186
    of Ignaro 189
    of Orgoglio 186
    of Socrates 189
  of allegory 6, 33
    by Paul de Man 7
  of man
    as the rational animal 183
  of Redcrosse
    by positive action 82
  of value
    in classical philosophy 292
  traditional
    of allegory 5
deflection
  of reference 113
deflowering
  of Una 131
deformed
  crimes 223
  of Redcrosse 205
  monster 279
  wight 114
deformity
  of Frælissa's beauty 114
degree 232
  knowledge of
    of good 213
Deianira (wife of Hercules) 259
  innocence of 259
deity
  refusal of
    by Odysseus 122
delay 59
  force of 240
delayed
  revelation
    of a name 239
delaying
  closure 240
delays 127
deliberate
  obfuscation
    by Spenser 198
delight 37, 53, 62
  best music breeds 191
  in self love
    by Lucifera 144
  in the defeat of Archimago 102
  in the world 180

  of mind
    of Redrosse 160

delighted
  by the form of the beloved 283
delightful
  music 275
delights
  dear
    of George 289
deliverance
  of Redcrosse
    by Arthur 184
delivery
  of Eden
    to pristine state 273
delusion 100
  of knowers 142
demands
  of Lucifera 149
de Man, Paul 7, 32, 271, 294
demonic
  detour
    from the truth 170
demons
  non-spatial 34
demonstration 18, 22
demotion
  of reason
    from a metaphysical to a scientific process 194
demure
  countenance 219
DeNeef, A. Leigh 31–35, 241
denial
  of access to holiness through one's will 46
  of access to truth
    by Stoics and Epicureans 76
  of credit for victory to Redcrosse 67
  of faith 56
  of being a ghost of guileful sprite
    by Fradubio 113
  of nature 36
  of substantial consciousness 189
denoted
  objects 141
departing
  at sound of morning drum 202
deployment
  of *a posteriori* reason 174
  of logic 175
  of reason
    in Spenser's work 173
depth
  in the scientific world 179
Derrida, Jacques 6, 10, 174, 185, 271, 294
  choice between suppression and elimination 44
  deconstruction of 155
  use of whole logic in 89
Descartes, René 2–5, 11, 12, 13, 22, 50, 88, 93, 142, 218, 282, 292
  age of 181
  as founder of modern philosophy 6, 34

  inventor of coordinate geometry 34
descendant
  of British royalty
    George as 245
descent 40
  from Saxon kings
    by George 245
  of David 95
  of Una 57
description 256
  in Plato 18
  in terms drawn from the science of alchemy 178
  metaphysical 244
  of Archimago 123
  of beauty 284
  of Cupid's darts 138
  of Dragon 250–253, 269–270
  of Gluttony 160
  of situation 110
  of the King of Eden
    as Emperor of the West 285
  ontological 90
  scientific
    of the Dragon's dimensions 250
  true
    of the Cave of Despair 201
descriptor
  rigid 89-90
desert
  due
    of noble chivalry 280
design 80
  grand
    of Spenser 224
designation
  in Frege 87
  mode of 86
desirability
  of merchant's patience 59
desirable
  step 166
desire 44, 68
  animal 15
    satisfaction of 290
  arduous
    of Redcrosse to prove himself in battle 146
  bodily
    of Sansloy 140
  contemplative 234
  end of 137
  fades
    of Sansloy for Una 136
  for death 261
  for glory 121
  for immediate pleasure 224
  for love
    by Sir Burbon 297
  for the end of knowledge 56

  frustration of
    of Redcrosse 158

Index   351

George importuning his 44
immediate 149
lack of
   in goodwill 283
mastery of
   by will 137
negotiating the world of contrary 110
of limited material being 98
of the reader
   for a perfect Redcrosse 61
of Una 246
physical proximity of the object of 137
satisfaction of
   of another 140
thwarting of
   of Una 173
to achieve maximum freedom 55
to end his days
   by Redcrosse 223
desolate
   place 184
   virgin 237, 239
despair 182
   bred by grief 182
   divorce in 118
   driving to 205
   in Calvin 26
   of Redcrosse 206, 236
   pagan 64
   reason to
      lack of 209
Despair 118, 199–208, 209, 212, 244, 252, 254, 261, 263
   arguments of
      as projections of mind of Redcrosse 207
   attention of 204
   description of 201
   rusty knife of 236
   sudden wit of 202
   tongue of 202
   Una listens to speeches of 206
despite
   bitter 148
destiny 79, 261
   avenging 79
   control over
      through limited reason 296
   of George 290
   of Redcrosse 84
   ordained by
      death as 203
   steam of 156
destroying
   royal court 298
destruction 37
   feast on 259
   intellectual
      precedes physical destruction 187
   moral 260
   mutually assured 259
   of Bower of Bliss 143

   of Errour 121
   of false distinctions 143
   of Hercules 259
   of Orgoglio
      survival by Duessa 187
   of social order
      wrought by violence 151
   physical
      follows intellectual destruction 187
   social
      of animal violence 168
      of animal war 176
      of the Thirty Years War 3
   unreality of
      wrought by Dragon 263
destructive
   animal violence 149
   animal wrath 159
   behavior 246
      of Redcrosse 149, 242
   socially 234
      animal genus 267
      animal instincts 257
details
   indifferent treatment of
      by Redcrosse 147
determination 50
   by God 78
   of beauty
      by cultural ideals 133
determined
   rapist 133
detour 84, 115, 212, 235
   demonic
      from the truth 170
   from end
      House of Holinesse as 228
   from the human community 176
development
   of Una's mind 174
devil
   tyranny of 263
devilish
   arts 102
devise 132
devising
   of a plan for Una to arise
      by Satyrane 136
   of rest 279
devoid
   of good will
      Archimago as 119
devotion
   blind 121
      of Una and Corceca 122
   to God 39, 121
devouring
   jaws 252
   Una by lion 119
devout

prayer
  of Una 269
dew 268
  burning blade 264
  of holy water 265
dewy
  air 95
dialectic 45, 54
dialectical
  framework 137
dialog
  flow of 196
  of Plato 293
diamond
  resistance of rock to 131
Diana 27, 94
didacticism 42
Dido 38
die 267
  judgment of justice is to
    says Despair 202
difference 11, 101, 234, 256
  between *a priori* sense and *a posteriori* reference 87
  between Arthur
    and Ignaro 189
    and Redcrosse 180
  between blows 265
  between George
    and Hercules 260
  between lion
    and Christ 225
  between pagan and Christian experience 143
  between reality and fiction
    in Augustine 38
  between Redcrosse
    and Christ 96
    and Una 55
  between signs 87
  between Spenser;s and modern aproach to experience 142
  between thought and speech 180
  between Una
    and Duessa 109
    and Redcrosse 55
  discrete
    between objects 277
  ignoring 95
  of meaning 50
  in moral judgment
    of Redcrorsse's actions 142
  in perspective
    on character 128
  in terms of science 265
  in the mode of presentation 87
  lack of 282
  moral 108

  of obligations
    between actors and critics 55

of sense
  in Frege 88
of time 257
questions of 86
specific 97, 268
  of reason in mankind 105
different
  meanings
    of words 196
  people 196
differentiation
  between truth and falsehood 35
  process of 87
differing
  values 147
difficulty
  in comparison 227
  sign of 177
digression 71
dilemma 188, 211
  of reader 84
  of Redcrosse 278
diligence
  of lion's waiting 120
dim
  eyes
    of Redcrosse 187
dimension
  ethical
    of combatants 253
    of the world 252
  social 180
dimming
  of the eyes 186
dint
  deadly 265
  deeper 257
  of untried deadly steel 128
direct 139
  application
    of reason 170
  blow 255, 257
  evidence 280
  expression
    of love 248
  imitation
    of nature 76
  means of imitating God's creation
    Archimago's 102
  naming 77
  parallels 116
  path 84
  reason
    in pagan authors 161–162
  truth
    of Redcrosse's experience 216
  warning of fraud 113

directed
  fury

Index 353

of George's blows 258
directing
  of action
    by God 266
  thought
    of Una 183
direction 98, 268
  given *a posteriori* to *a priori* faith 62
  imparting 81
  lack of 67
  losing of
    by Redcrosse 148
  of errant knight 116
  of George 287
  of wandering Odysseus
    given by constellation Boötes 82
  of winds 251
  sense of 79
directionality of time
  in Aristotle 17
  reversal of
    in Plato 17
directionless
  life
    of Redcrosse 148
directions
  two
    Ignaro facing in 189
directly
  looking
    at the sun 256
directness
  of representation
    in human mind 58
direful
  fiend 271
disappearance 46
  in exchange 57
  of Una 228
disapproval
  of the behavior of Redcrosse
    by Spenser 161
  Spenser's
    of Duessa 108
disarray
  of universe 142
disassociation
  of unity
    between might and reason 220
disastrous
  course of action 180
  decision 273
disavowal 64
disbelief
  of poet 101
  suspension of 45, 112, 216, 275
discarding 192
discipline 34
  celestial
    taught by Fidelia 220

of faith and verity
  taught by Una to Satyrane 136
disclosing
  of a breach
    in Una's thought 183
  of crime 287
  of intent
    by Una to Satyrane 135
disclosure
  of Una's love for Redcrosse 96
discord
  note of rage 66
discourse
  diverse 238
    on loves 198
  of royal prince's state 277
  of Una
    with Archimago 128
  on noble gests
    by Redcrosse 220
  rational 183
  whole 171, 173–175, 177
    told by dwarf 168
  with others 215
discovery 86, 122
  ancient 87
  of teleological purpose 62
discreation
  of all 256
discrete
  action
    in the world of time 219
  advice 180
  differences
    between objects 277
  experiences 112
disdain 80
  high 56
  of reprochfull fall
    of George 257
  for earth
    by Lucifera 144
disdainful
  spite 131
disease
  soul 224
disenfranchisement 233
  of Una 284
disgorging 60
disgrace
  to knighthood 69
disguise 103
  imperfect and superficial 124
  of Archimago 128
  of truth
    by Odysseus 83
dishes
  dainty 277
dishonesty
  accusation of

aimed at Una 123
dishonor 109
disinheriting
  of perfect daughter 284
disjunction 48
  disjunction between action and the mind's opera-
      tion on its object 126
dismal
  performance 68
dismay 108, 183, 287
  of dulled senses 265
  of Redcrosse 223
    on seeing False Una 78
dismayal
  of hosts of men
    by Fidelia 221
dismayed 131
  description of Una 130
  man 284
dismissal
  of false dreams 75
dismounting
  of Una 119
disordered
  hair
    of Despair 201
dispassion
  of dwarf 288
dispensing
  in one loving hour many years of pain 125
dispersal
  of clouds 251
  of mankind 251
  of manly power
    of Redcrosse 205
display
  helmet
    of Arthur 195
  of body
    ofFidessa 143
  of left wing
    of Dragon 255
  ostentatious
    of entertainment 146
  public
    of learning 194
displaying
  active posture 143
displeasure 124
  high
    of queen Lucifera 149
disposition
  a priori
    towards poetry 240
disqualification
  of membership at court 105

disruption
  of order

    of Lucifera 149
dissembling 297
disseverance 91
  of sense and reference
    in Frege 88
  of unified meaning
    in Tasso 40
  of whole into parts 40
dissipating
  the power of error 185
dissipation
  of fire 269
  of loss
    over time 172
distance
  between Redcrosse's ends 102
  between Spenser and Redcrosse 151
  critical 50, 54
  from immediate desire 149
  ironic
    of Redcrosse from the Triumph of Pride 148
  of reader 227
  placid
    from action 127
distancing
  by the poet
    of his hero from the reader 47
distant
  stars 133
  sun 133
distaste 37
distinct
  ideas
    of Descartes 292
  loves 198
distinction
  between Creator and creature
    in Augustine 22
  between goodwill and friendship
    in Aristotle 283
  between Spenser and Redcrosse 59
  between Una's native condition and the need to
      extend herself beyond Eden 249
  class 233
  in act 26
  in poet's logic 175
distinctions
  aesthetic 11
  false 143
    of Corceca 214
  resolution of
    in epistemology 282
distinguishing
  true love from false love 126
  Una and Corceca 124
distraction
  of Redcrosse 200
distress 69
  dreadful 128
  expression of 142

Index

of Una 196
throwing into 288
distributed
  allegory 161–162
  authority
    of books 214
distributive
  allegory 162
distrust
  of Archimago 68
  of one's first impression 274
disturbance
  of calm 65
  of Redcrosse
    by his dreams 78
diurnal
  alternation
    of day and night 155
  earth 269
  progress
    of life 179
  turning of day into night 71
diverse
  discourse 238
  guile 131
diversely
  discoursing
    of loves 198
diversion
  into error
    by Redcrosse 206
diversity
  of doubt 53
  of the mouths of man 73
divided
  subject 94
divine
  frankincense 289
  Homer 76, 269
  majesty 93, 235
  things 246
  words
    of Fidessa 220
divinely
  human 256
divinity 6
division 31
  absolute
    between good and evil 157
    of bodies 162–163
  between Heaven and earth
    in the marriage 289
  between the wisdom of the heart and the knowl-
    edge of the body
    in Augustine 72
  by Tasso
    of collective political action from individual
      good 43–44
  experience of 161–162
  into different levels 83

into double parts 102
of experience 183
of good from bad 176
of mind 78
of modern philosophy
  into two camps after Frege 88
of One True Church 70
of perspective 272
of philosophy
  in the ancient world 20
of Redcrosse and Una 102
of science 43, 118
of sense from reference 92
of rational contentl available to the *a posteriori*
  mind 104
of Roman Empire 285
of thought
  as an image of God 74
of Una
  from her beloved knight 118
  from Redcrosse 96
of whole experience
  into parts 118
philosophical 285
progressive 43
through logic 90
time of
  ushered in by Jove 157
uneven
  of talents 265
divisiveness
  evil on the side of
    in the modern world 134
divorce
  in despair 118
doctrine
  of confession 182
  of forgiveness 202
  of harsh legal judgment 202
  of love 202
  of λόγος 181
doleful
  fate 137
dolors
  of George 258
domain
  fictional
    of imagination 296
  of God's pre-linguistic creation 111
  of time
    Una's travel in the 199
dominance 238
domination
  of male over female 210
dominion
  of Philosophy over the world 107
Donation of Constantine
  shown to be a forgery 24
doom 260
  rash 202

door
  ivory 75
  of Corceca's House 121
  of death 225
  of the House of Corceca 122
doors
  of prison
    of Redcrosse 185
doorstep
  of the House of Pride 145
double
  echo 134
  false 240, 275
  gates 76
  parts 102
doubling 77
  in Augustine universe 134
  of Fradubio's love 114
  of perspective 134
    a necessary step 135
  of True Una and False Una 114
  power of
    of Duessa 288
  production of 134
  value of property 266
doubt 284
  about the location of Eden 289
  Christian 242
  diverse 53
  dreadful 54
  in allegorical interpretation 31
  in classical philosophy 170
  of reader 238
  of senses
    by Redcrosse 112
  of victory 264
  of wits 53
  pagan 170, 242
  reason for 287
  standing in
    Redcrosse's fate 173
doubtful
  balance 114
  words
    of False Una 80
doughty
  conqueror 274
  knight 279
  tournament 151
down 69, 270, 286
  fall of castle 187
  fell 266
  letting
    the haughty string 250
  looking
    by George 246
  to ground 254
downfall 104
dragon 103
  dreadful
    Lucifera's defeat of 144

Dragon 44, 68, 84, 104, 122, 186, 209, 227, 232, 236, 244, 254, 255, 261, 263, 265, 266, 268, 272
  armor of 258
  as alive 273
  battle with 260
  bellowing fire by 258
  body of 270
  brazen scales of 251
  breath of the 251
  bright 206
  death of 273
  defeat of 84, 209, 212, 248-271, 272, 277, 285, 296
  description of 250–253
  dread 267
  engagement with 212
  exact size of 250, 253
  external 273
  eyes of the 252
  fear of 267, 274
  fictional 250
  fire-mouthed 206, 207
  fury of 257
  head of 265
  heat of 260
  horrible 206
  impulsive decision of 269
  iron teeth of 251
  killed
    by George 269
  killing of 215, 288
  limited 262
  mistake of 264
  mountainous shadow of 253
  mouth of
    hollowness of 269
  ontological presence of 274
  oppressing 274
  potential extension of 253
  power of 253-254
  slaying of 273
  strength of the
    vertical nature of 251
  strong 262
  talons of 266
  threat of the 251
  throat of 255
  transfer of sins to 252
  vertical axis of 253
  waist of 273
  wings of the
    horizontal nature of 252
  wounding of 255, 258
  wound of
    blood pours from 256
drama 42
dread 49, 52, 219
  at prospect of transformation 115
  darkness 101
  Dragon 267

Index   357

ever-dying 215
of shame 266
misplaced 108
dreadful
  distress 128
  dragon
    Lucifera's defeat of 144
  passion 111
  poise 270
  shade 253
  sound 49
  trompe 250
  wound 162
dream
  feigning 101
  human capacity to 242
  idle 74
  of Arthur 195
  of Redcrosse 77
  swooning
    of Redcrosse 153
  work 241–243
dreamer 42
  prudish 78
dreams 171
  false 75, 178
  gate
    of false 77
    of true 75, 77
  gates of 143
  in Luther's definition of allegory 25
  of Arthur
    of meeting the Faerie Queene 195
  pagan 77
  pursuit of 196
  sent by spirits to the world above 75
  sex 78
dress
  of Archimago 68
  outward
    by Fidessa as the Whore of Babylon 200
dressing
  hasty 84
drifting 52
driving
  a water mill 256
  to despair 205
dropping
  of the weeping eyes of stars 132
drowning 80
  of the land 256
drum
  sound of morning 202
drunken
  crowd 217

dual
  meaning
    of words 203

Du Bartas, Guillaume de Salluste 255–256
due
  desert
    of noble chivalry 280
  of George 271
  of God 271
Duessa 28, 49, 112, 116, 150, 151, 157, 167,
    204, 222, 265, 276, 288
  action of 155
  as author 113
  as corrupt woman 175
  as cruel crafty crocodile 155
  as falseness 252
  as false sorceress 113
  as loose with body 297
  as sunny bright 155
  as villain 118
  blocks the King of Eden 286
  charms of 287
  consummation
    of relationship with Redcrosse 162–163
  continues to live after the destruction of Orgoglio 187
  conversation of
    with Sansjoy 151
  creation of artificial barriers to immediate action 158
  cries out
    in love for Sansjoy 153
  declares definite preference
    for Sansjoy 153
  defeat of
    by Arthur 186
  difference from Una
    in dress 109
  exercise by
    of wicked arts 287
  false 141, 153
  flips her position 153
  Fradubio takes D. for his dame 115
  gives herself the name of Fidessa 112
  hidden nature of 114
  in charge of the world of science 159
  intention of 158
  limitations of 157
  lying with 288
  magic of 112, 276
    turns Fradubio into a tree 112
  message
    to the court of Eden 284–286
  misunderstanding of
    of the source of Redcrosse's power to overcome obstacles 150
  power of doubling of 288
  reaction of
    to arms of Redcrosse 278
  reign
    over Night 158
  seductions of 218
  stops Redcrosse from committing sin 191
  study of magic by 278
  success of 158

turning to
  by Lucifera's counselors 145
unlikely intercession of 163
use of reason by 167
weary of the toilsome way 143
dull
  blast 114
  eyes
    of Despair 201
    of Redcrosse 220
  melancholy 289
dulled
  senses 265
dullness
  of Redcrosse's ears 110
dungeon 165, 188, 190, 191
  languishing in a 198
  of Orgoglio 118, 163, 209
dust 38, 178
duty
  deeper moral 154
  of Arthur
    towards Redcrosse 194
  of the King of Eden 286
dwarf 52, 53, 54, 84, 91, 96, 104, 111, 148, 160, 163, 171, 172, 179, 184, 197, 206, 280, 288, 290
  as bearer of causal reason 165–167
  as keepr of relative scientific perspective 173
  causal 173
  heart of
    described as being dead within 168
  picks up Sansfoy's shield 108
  Redcrosse takes Una's 102
  response of 278
  speech of the 174
  whole discourse of 168, 177
  words of 69
dwelling
  in misformed house 115
  in passion
    of Redcrosse 110
  of evil 68
  of peril 249
dying 48, 118, 191, 203
  unknown 194
dynamic
  nature
    of time 37

E

eager
  Redcrosse 186
eagle 264
  author as
    in Du Bartas 256
  eye of 234, 251
  eyes

    of Contemplation 256
  gripping prey 254
  sight of an 264
  wings of an
    Dragon's scales likened to 251
ear
  loathing 191
  of a poet 110
ears 73
  dullnes of Redcrosse's 110
  hearing with
    what Fidessa is saying 121
earth 171, 227, 236, 255, 256, 270, 289, 296
  as source of strength
    of George 254
  comparison on
    not easy 227, 229
  deeds done on 203
  disdain of
    by Lucifera 144
  diurnal 269
  Eden on 275
  ends of 276
  fleeing the 251
  happy 215
  in terror 162
  knights on 249
  literal 133
  plentiful 125
  rules of identity on 96
  skill of
    to bring forth fruit 125
  the mother of Orgoglio 163
  worker of the 240
earthly
  branch 101
  conquest 237
  frame 237
  race 197
  skill 287
  things 105, 177, 280, 294
    darkness of 246
ease 279
east 281
easy
  comparison
    on earth 227, 229
  pickings
    of weak men 254
  virtue
    of Fidessa 229
eat
  of sinews
    by lion 225
eating
  neighbor elements 255
  of Errour 298
ebony
  bow 176
echo 165

Index 359

double 134
not writer's but allegory's according to Quilligan 8
of experience 298
   of Una 174
of the woods 134
   with the cries of Una 133
echoes
   in Spenser's poem 142
   listening to 142, 199
   of epic simile 82
   phonetic 241
   semantic 241
echoing
   of Du Bartas 255
economy
   of the body 261
ecstasy
   sexual 161
Eden 51, 57, 66, 96, 100, 141, 155, 209, 215, 227, 288
   as holder of potential 290
   balanced perspective of 140
   birth in 172
   brazen walls of 138, 248, 267
   court of 284
   daughter of 131
   delivery of
      to pristine state 273
   extension beyond 249
   fictional 290
   fictionally-constructed 249, 272
   following Una to 209
   garden of 267
   heart of
      paradox at 276
   King and Queen of 122
   kingdom of. *See* Kingdom of Eden.
   leaving 249
      by Una 182
   location of
      in doubt 289
   on earth 275
   origin in 226
   outside of heaven 275
   people of 273, 274
   perfect 55
   perfect intelligence in 174
   prelapsarian state of 226
   Princess of 183, 228
   principle of identity in 96
   quiet road of 290
   restoration of 274
   ruins of 290
   rule in 285
   rules of identity in 96
   timeless 67, 275, 280
   translation out of 126, 228
   Una's flight from 96
   uncertain location of 274
   unified 227
   unwatched gates of 286
   voice of 160
   walls of 209, 227, 236, 273
   world of time outside 115
edge
   of the universe 89
   sharper 265
educated 39, 44, 46
   Archimago 124
   Arthur 188, 191
   best 193
   knowledge of the 193
   man 194
      in the world of time 298
education 131, 188, 190, 207, 212, 245, 247, 252, 277, 294, 295
   action without 67
   allows Archimago to overcome hapless chance 123
   allows reader to look backward and forward 130
   a posteriori 67, 124, 167, 228, 238, 293
   beginning of Una's 135
   buying and selling literary 38
   classical 38
   continual 203
   effort of 116
   incomplete
      of Redcrosse 223
   in harsh realities
      by Una 140
   in holy ways 221
   in patience 252
   in Spenser's world 158
   in the House of Holinesse 249
   into potential perfection 257
   lack of 194
      of George 241
   lifetime of continuing 59
   literary 38
   neverending 177
   of Archimago 100, 222
   of Edmund Spenser 67
   of intellect 119
   of knights 167
   of mankind 224
   of Redcrosse 99, 217, 223
      in science 218
      into knowledge of royal connection 121
      lack of 67
   of reader 61
   of will 176
   of Una 126, 129, 183
      by the poet 176
   power of 67, 98
   Renaissance 69
      Horace as a staple of 232
educative
   process 232

   value
      Redcrosse's indifference to differences in 147
educators

pagan 39
effect
    calming of human reason 105
    of Una's will
        by Redcrosse 70
    Redcrosse's belief in the e. of Archimago's magic 104
    unsettling
        on teleological progress 241
effecting
    Una's will 136
effectiveness
    of Archimago's lie 125
effects
    bad
        of taking off armor 258
effort
    cooperative
        between the wise author Spenser and the careful reader 230
    educational 116
    joint
        of society 295
    linked 295
    of will 62
    redoubled
        of Sansjoy 153
    vain
        of Orgoglio 186
ego
    of Redcrosse 226
    rational 242
    repressive 242
egoist
    interests 180
either
    side 153
either/or 280
ekphrastic
    images
        of ever-blooming flowers 290
    work of art 205
elaboration
    of harsh judgment of Redcrosse 141
elder
    weaker 215
eldest
    bead-man 231
election 25
    of Redcrosse 207
element
    neighbor 255
    of pride
        in Redcrosse 148
elements
    balance of 264
elephant 75
elevated
    social position
        lack of 132
elevation
    to figural status
        of George 83
elf 162, 245
    George raised as 262
    Redcrosse as 62, 162
    Redcrosse portrayed as an 112
    son of 239
elfin
    knight 115, 227, 239
        element of pride in 148
    race 244
eliminating
    the middle space 253
elimination 217
    lack of
        of sins 271
    of clownish nature 241
    of comic elements 44
    of metaphor
        in Derrida 218
    of threat 269
elite
    academic 193
Elizabeth I, Queene of England
    on literal level 93
    dissipation of her ontology in fiction 27
    representatives of 94
    substantial consciousness of 93
eloquence
    grave 284
elusive
    individual wholeness 203
embellishment 32
Emblemata
    Alciati, Andreas Alciatus
        as source 216–217
embodiment
    of human community
        in Gloriana's court 176
    of the greatest shame a knight can suffer
        Redcrosse as 141
emboiled 260
embossing
    of red cross 297
embrace
    of substantial consciousness
        by Redcrosse 147
emergence
    of meaning 55
emotion
    dissipation of
        over time when not immediately present 172
emotional
    interference
        by sympathetic Una 223

Index

emotions
  powerful 4
emperor
  of Rome 109
    worshipped as a god 181
  of the west 285
empire
  whole of 285
empirical
  experience 172
  world 234
empty
  air 112
  bladder
    Orgoglio as 187
enacting *See also* action.
  potential 232
    by human being 276
    in the world of time 257
enchanted
  arms
    of Redcrosse 151
  rhymes 205
enchantment
  false 184
  of garment
    of Hercules 258
enclave 52
encoding
  speech 5, 7
encounter 114
  of satyrs
    with something deeper than they knew before 133
  with Despair
    by Redcrosse 205
encumbrance 60
end 12, 19, 53, 84, 98, 142, 171, 173, 188, 210, 231, 237, 243, 262, 276, 287
  absolute 23
  as preference
    of Redcrosse 173
    of Una 173
  blessed 237, 238
  Charissa as
    inadequacy of 228
  concentration on
    by Una 125
  desire for
    by Una 172
  failure of Redcrosse in his 46
  furthest from 53
  God's rescue of Redcrosse in the 143
  guarantee of
    of Redcrosse 142
  hastening of 268
  Heaven as 235
  immediate 235, 244
  in relation to mode of acting 26
  in *Timaeus* 18

journey of
  of George 278
joyous 271
metaphysical 232
of adventure
  of George 268, 283, 287
  of Una 135, 209
of Archimago
  in Una's wandering 102
of Ariosto's poem 65
of book 70, 83
of Dido in death 38
of every battle 142
of experience 177, 281
  deferral of 238
  reason not the 166
of fiction 294
  in ontological reality 58
of flight
  of Dragon 253
of God 257
of human experience 245
  in Aristotle 233
of inquiry 94
  in classical philosophy 104
of journey
  of George 295
  of Redcrosse 243
  of Una 272, 279
of knowledge 56
of life 204, 240, 244
  in individual self-sufficiency 233
of narrative 58, 177
of Orgoglio 186
of path
  that beaten was most plaine 62
of poet 295
of Redcrosse 62, 104, 158, 212, 235
  battle with Errour 62
of Sansloy's desire 137
of story
  told by dwarf 173
of strife 64
of troubles
  of Una 249
of Una's journey 117
of Virgil's *Aeneid* 65
of whole discourse 174
of work
  of poet 294
permanent 221
  of experience 216
pleasure as
  Augustine's rejection of 52
power of heaven knows no 260
predetermination of 78
ultimate
  detour from 228

worst 47
  of mankind 105
ending

happy 260
  in bitter balefull stound 172
  of Ariosto's *Orlando Furioso* 230
endless
  chain
    of horizontal reference 6
  debate 51
  error
    Corceca's prayer for Una to fall into 123
  life
    Jove's prevention of 159
  pain 205
ends 291
  Archimago on 102–106
  extreme
    of the universe 222
  extremity of 298
  focus on 261
  in Foucault 218
  of all that is begun 203
  of Archimago 119
  of Duessa 148
  of earth 276
  of experience 181, 203
  of life
    Despair on 202
  of literature 293
  of theoretical response to texts 84
  out of control 203
  Redcrosse on 102–106
  tempation of 58
  worst 99
endurance
  of cruel case 258
  of false distinctions
    in the House of Pride 143
  of the whole 171
  of woeful stours by Una 126
enemies 152
  conspiring 253
  defeat of 260, 297
  equally matched 138
enemy 61, 64, 66, 261, 264
  defeat of
    at once 252
  far from 71
  formidable 298
  launching at
    of Redcrosse 152
  of life
    fretting grief the 148
  other 65
  strong 67
energy
  unfocused chivalric 115
  waste of
    by Redcrosse 199

engagement 50
  with Dragon 212
  with monster vile 60

  with text 44
engaging
  Errour 252
engendering
  of Una
    in the poet's imagination 175
engine
  of war
    Redcrosse as 211
engines
  subtle 187
England 13
  merry 239
  Protestant 70
English
  race 239
enigma 74
  allegory as 104
    in Augustine 71
  every allegory is not an 72
enjoy 289
enlarging
  range
    of allegorical figures 239
Enlightenment 3–4, 14, 97, 142, 218, 291, 292, 296
  aesthetics 10, 11
  assumption 155
  binary system of 275
  configuration
    of universe 242
  French 4
  lens 280
  philosophers 275
  post 86
  post-Enlightenment 12
  pre-Enlightenment 10, 14
    reliance on Augustine 26
  reason 76
  wholeness of 242
enmity
  cause of 154
enormous
  burden 273
enrage
  the hearts
    of heroes 250
enraged
  fight
    apology for 149
  half 78
  wight 149
ensuring
  recognition by others
    of Una's true nature 136
entertain 297
entertaining
  spectacle 147
  tale 232

Index

Triumph of Pride 148
entertainment 230, 232
  in House of Pride 166
  of Cælia 218
  of Redcrosse
    by Lucifera 145
  ostentatious display of 146
  perspective of 146
  vile 131
enthusiasm
  of the people 274
entity
  separate
    Despair as 207
entrails
  hellish
    of Dragon 266
entry
  allowed to everone
    by Malvenu 143
  into mouth
    does nor defile a man 72
  into the mystery of things 39
enumerated
  powers
    of Archimago 119
envious
  eyes 166
environment
  assessment of 55
  growth of Una's control over her 118
  natural 52
  reflected in character 53
  scanning
    for clues to truth and falseness 81
envy 106
  lack of
    in giving aid to others 192
  of specialists for the positions of others 59
  snare of 118
  wicked 289
Envy 147
Ephesians, Book of 45, 45–48, 96
  armor of 105, 108, 152, 177, 203, 204
epic 53, 83
  seriousness of 60
  simile 59, 60, 82, 187
    meeting of opposites in 106
    of lion in the Cave of Errour 121
epicurean 23
  pleasure 233, 240
epicureanism 21, 52, 76, 97
epicureans 20, 22
epistemological
  construction 272
  fiction 257
  imagination 282
  mind 274
  orientation

    towards God's prior ontology 263
  problems 2
  reconstruction 263
epistemology 15, 19, 46, 60, 88, 91, 98, 142, 167, 170, 219, 234, 238, 282, 296 *See also* mind.
  agreement with ontology in human mind 218
  as human trait 3
  joined to ontology 93
  reconstruction of ontology in 230
  recreation of God's ontology in 58
equal 159, 196
  balance 150
    of God 270
    of Lucifera 150
    weighing right and wrong in 147
  battle
    deciding the outcome of 152
  beauty 114
  choice 160, 238
  fight
    between Satyrane and Sansloy 174
  lists 149
  matching
    of opponents 138
  measure
    in law 286
  outcome
    in world of time 172
  results 273
  sides
    in fight 152
  to Archimago
    in power 218
equality 264
  as a relation between names 86
  in battle
    with Errour 65
  in love
    lack of 140
  metaphysical
    of God 269
  of balance 81, 106
  of combatants
    in the epic simile of rams 106
  of force 225
  of indifferent treatment of details
    by Redcrosse 147
  of nature of things 155
  of perspective
    from a safe ironic distance 148
  of Redcrosse
    in the fight with Errour 57
  of reference
    in Frege 87
  of Una with Cælia
    lack of 215

equally
  matched
    enemies 138

equation 220
equipage
  fierce
    of war 250
equitable
  justice 138
  universe 37
equity
  gives rise to questions
    in Frege 85
  of position 59
  state of 251
equivalence
  of morally unequal beings 152
  to God 267
era
  premodern 13
erasure
  lack of
    in ontology 282
  of balance towards good
    by Lucifera 152
  of boundaries 273
Erewhon 275
errancy
  in Una's way of looking at things 126
  of Redcrosse 216
errant
  beloved
    of Una 196
  intention
    joined to errant knight 116
  journey
    in the wilderness 218
  knight 113, 216
    forward motion of 116
  perception
    of Redcrosse 62
  Redcrosse 62
  will
    of Redcrosse 205
error 68, 224, 276
  after the death of Errour 60
  apology for
    by pagan 149
  as a permanent feature of imaginative landscape 61
  covering up of 38
  draws men away fron their devotion to God 39
  endless
    Corceca's prayer for Una to fall into 123
  fall into 288
  fly from 206
  ignorance of 66
  of enraged wight 149
  of Redcrosse 181
  of satyrs 160
  of Una 128
  power of 185
errors

adult 298
  vomiting up of 298
Errour 53, 65, 68, 83, 104, 108, 121, 150, 155, 176, 212, 252, 254, 263
  battle with 254
    active posture of Redcrosse in 143
  blows of 186
  defeat of 262, 298
  engaging 252
  flight of 200, 225
  likened to Sansfoy 150
  permanent evil 142
  read too literally
    by Redcrosse 66
  Redcrosse's encounter with 56–67
escape 188
  from dungeon 198
  from satyrs
    by Una 135
  from the brazen walls of Eden 138
escheat 157
essence
  follows existence 188
  general 32
  of Redcrosse 231
essential
  unity
    of Una 117
established
  terms 202
establishment
  of equitable justice 138
estate
  sad
    of Una 120
estimation
  statistical
    of universe 292
eternal 19
  bondslave 163
  book of fate 203
  brood 151
  dearth 125
  God 266
  Night 160
  pain 149
  providence 132
ethical
  dimension
    of combatants 253
    of the world 252
ethico-scientific
  metaphor
    of the poet 254
ethics 40, 43
  Aristotelian 15

etymological
  sense 56
Evans, Gareth 90

Index

Eve
  orignal sin of 267
even
  battle 152
evening
  star 85, 88, 179
evenly-matched
  opponents 138
event 76
  arbitrarily producible 86
  historically conditioned 87
  miraculous 48
events 145, 166
  chronological 277
  compel
    power to 134, 211
  control of 135
    by Clio 250
  godlike perception of
    by Redcrosse 203
  in poem 130
  memory of 204
  picture of 288
  power over
    Una's 129
  reality of 112
  that fall between the beginning and the end 173
  true significance of 162
ever-blooming
  flowers 290
ever-damned
  beast 268
ever-dying
  cycle of renewal 205
  dread 215
everlasting
  fame 275
    Mnemosyne as nurse of 250
  Night 159
  rest 278, 279
evermore 131
ever-renewing
  cycle 205
every
  sense 195
everyone
  allowed entrance
    by Malvenu 143
evidence 55, 57, 93, 275, 287
  a posteriori 54, 145
  contrary 12
  direct 280
  of skepticism
    in Spenser's work 10
  Redcrosse's confrontation with 109
  weighing of
    in law 286
evil 101, 102, 150, 157, 199, 214, 263
  artificer 129
  avoidance of 143
  brought into being
    by the active nature of Archimago 77
  defined as privation of good
    in Augustine 106
  dwelling of 68
  good is permanently better than 138
  hearing of 156
  in age of iron
    of Ovid 251
  led by 148
  moral 12, 202
  nature of
    as privative 158
  of pagan life 64
  on side of divisiveness
    in the modern world 134
  partisan of 156
  permanent 143
  plight 115
    mankind as partakers of 216
  principle of 156
  priority of good over 138
  privative 157, 225
  reader's knowledge
    of Archimago's 70
  side of 157
  star 191
  temptation to 118
  triumph of good over 288
evocation
  of pity 132
exact
  name 275
  size
    of fictional Dragon 250
exacting
  revenge
    for injustice 202
examination
  of parts 180
example 3, 141, 194
  general 187
  individual
    of defeat in battle 187
  mistake to follow
    of Redcrosse 143
  of experience 198
  of hapless joy 194
  of idleness
    Redcrosse not an 146
  proof
    by plain 141
  rational stages in the process of making an 166
  specific 141
  written in Arthur's heart
    with an iron pen 192
examples
  moral 110
exceeding
  earthly race 197
  pride 144

thought
  eternal providence as 132
excellence
  addition to
    of grace 284
excellent
  glory 151
  self
    excelling George's 249
excelling
  excellent self 249
exception 257
  from inclusion in the set of denoted objects
    of Redcrosse 141
excess
  hatred of
    in the antique world 276
excessive
  Gluttony 150
exchange
  of Ariosto's Catholicism for Spenser's Protestantism 66
  of certainty
    for control 194
  of gifts 198
  of individual for figural meaning
    in Una's translation 57
  of literal for typological expression of mankind
    by Una 124
  of "natural" pride for an "unnatural" social standing as king among men 121
  of true friend for new foe 110
  of true heart for a false one 111
  of Una for Fidessa 110
  superficial 113
excitement
  dramatic 42
  of reading 42
exclamation
  Fradubio's 114
exclusion
  of accidents
    in *Letter to Raleigh* 45
  of Æsculapius
    from hope of heaven 159
  of pagans
    form ordered society 64
  of Redcrosse
    from the class of men 211
exclusionary
  social priorities 165
exempting
  of Redcrosse
    from making a choice 148
exercise 97
  manly
    shunned by Idleness 146
  of direct reason 161–162
  of free will 191
  of power 269

by Una 131
of wicked arts
  by Duessa 287
exhaustion
  physical
    of George 261
exile 36, 46
existence 47
  bodily 270
  contemplative 246
  deeper level of 152
  in fiction
    of Una 96
  mere 132
  of creation 255
  of George 271
  of God 238
  of larger prior world 189
  of Una 228
    outside the bounds of humanity 197
  of underlying ontology 86
  of Zele 213
  ontological 88
    lack of 143
    of Fidessa 195
  precedes essence 188
  present
    of George 270
  questioning Una's ontological 46
  real 270
  separate 98
  substantial 175
    lack of 201
  unreal 37
existential
  construction 188
  freedom 238
  individual 182
existentialism 16, 41, 218, 229
existentialists
  find end of life in individual self-sufficiency 233
  perfect freedom desired by 135
existing
  minds 193
ex machina
  solution 132
expansion
  of knowledge 88
  of limited life 268
  of the definition of allegory 6
  through simile 255
expectation 5
  not always in line with reality 203
  of careful reader 237
  of human beings
    by God 266
  of modern criticism 31
  of reader
    reconfiguring 254
    by poet 145

of Una
    thwarted by Redcrosse's actions 140
expectations
    of experience 142
    of unwary readers 290
expense
    of pagan configuration of universe 234
experience 2, 192, 211, 273, 274
    a posteriori
        of learning 212
    approach to
        learned and rational 160
    as a young knight 113
    base of 163
    beginning of 177
    center of 222
    changing course based on 142
    Christian 143
    correct reading of 57
    deeper
        of memory 110
    discrete 112
    division of 183
    echo of 174, 298
        beyond ourselves 142
    empirical 172
    end of 166, 177, 181, 203, 281
        deferral of 238
    epicurean approach to 52
    example of 198
    external 143
    factual 39
    guide to
        love as 126
    human 92, 233, 245
        end of 52
        perspectival angle on 296
        univocal τέλος of 159
    immediate 25, 110, 172
        processed by passive intellect 166
    imperfect
        of man 203
    imperfect view of
        of Redcrosse 244
    individual 233
    learning from 213
    lengthening of 236
    limited
        of Redcrosse with deadly steel 128
    literal 27
    margins of 222
    metaphysical point of view on 66
    modern approach to 142
    of animal being 215
    of discourse with others 215
    of division 161–162
    of Fradubio 116, 143
        parallels between Redcrosse and 112

    of George 246
        absence of reason in 282
    of knowing

        reversal of normal poles in the 175
    of love
        of Arthur 194
    of memory 205
    of reader 274
        of Redcrosse 145
        with Redcrosse 145
        with Una 282
    of Redcrosse 216
        in the House of Pride 144
        permanent end of 216
        with time 134
    of the Cave of Despair
        by Redcrosse 201
    of Una
        of advance toward lawfulness 135
    ontological
        of sinning 47
    pagan 143
    rational approach to 4
    raw data of 15
    recreaction of
        in imperfect mind 212
    relative 232
    separate 245
    sorting of Redcrosse's 116
    surface of 125
    trial of 214
    truth of one's own 39
    typological 295
    unified
        of Una 124
    whole
        listening to 153
expiration
    of scorching fire
        from Dragon's entrails 266
expired
    fates
        renewed by wondrous science 159
explanation 86
exposure
    of cowardice of Archimago 128
expression 18, 33, 38, 48, 111, 215, 286
    comfort in 180
    direct
        of love 248
    external 152
        of Redcrosse 152
    horrified 133
    imperfect 254
    of affection
        for Fidessa 111
    of agreement
        by Night with Duessa 156
    of difference between thought and speech 180
    of disapproval
        by Spenser 161
    of difference between thought and speech 180
    of distress 142
    of frustration

with Redcrosse 209
of general meaning 31
of gratitude
  by Una 188
of inner beauty 120
of inner intention
  weaknesses of Redcrosse in 151
of joy
  at Una's meeting with false Redcrosse 127
of love 182
of natural object in human language 76
of a particular language 73
of puzzlement
  by Una 136
of Redcrosse's passion for Fidessa 111
of Una 209
  of fear 56
  of her plight in screams 133
of wisdom
  of the heart 73
of Zele 213
struggle for
  by Una 152
ways of 294
extending
  talons
    of the Dragon 266
extension 32, 89
  beyond
    Eden 249
    limits of one's being 203
  of character
    narrative as the 161
  of Fradubio's plight to Redcrosse's plight 115
  of goodwill
    to friendship 283
  of human being
    beyond itself 224
    through activation of potential 190
  of intellectual activity 233
  of knowledge 87
    in a=b propositions 85
  of one's arm 190
  of political control 233
  of potential
    of Dragon 253
  of vertically-oriented potential power
    of Dragon 253
  of works 268
  social 33
  temporal 33
exterior
  image
    of Una 135
  magical charm 106
  perfection 57
external 48
  armor 45
  authority 218
  creatures 187
  danger 162

Dragon 273
experience 143
expression 152
  of Redcrosse 152
location 118
protection 131
secret magic
  in Redcrosse's shield and arms 151
to mind 98
warrior's glory 148
world 177, 207
  of time 273
externality 65
  of armor of God
    to Redcrosse 95
  of body 66
externalization
  for sake
    of reader 243
  of Redcrosse's battlefield prowess 149
externalizing
  blame
    for sins of Redcrosse 226
extinction 44
extreme 16
  ends
    of the universe 222
  Heaven 197
extremes
  temperate balance between 94
extremest
  case
    of Arthur 197
extremity 5
  drive to
    in Ariosto 65
  of ends 298
  of fictional Eden 290
  of heaven 257
  of time 136, 137, 138, 152, 227, 235, 238
    cited at I.vi.13.2 134
    Una in 117–138
  temptation to
    by Redcrosse 236
extrinsic
  identity
    of Redcrosse 83
eye 165, 237
  casting of
    of Sansjoy 153
  enduring the blazing brightness
    of Arthur's uncovered shield 186
  fiery
    of lust 132
  for an eye
    justice as conceived of as 202
  impatient
    of Redcrosse 234
  inner 36
  intellectual
    of Contemplation 234

lustful
  of Sansloy 132
 mortal 119
 of eagle 234, 251
 offered 137
 of heaven
  seen in Una's face 119
 of mind 234
 of reason 101
 of Una 124
 pleasure of 283
 sudden
  of Sansjoy 153
 superficial 127
eyes 64, 73, 138, 166, 234
 bad
  of Contemplation 251
 believing one's 114
 bent to the ground 68
 blind 12
  of Contemplation 264
  of Corceca 234
 blunt
  of Contemplation 251
 carnal 71
 dazed
  of George 246
 dim
  of Redcrosse 187
 dimming of the 186
 dull
  of Redcrosse 220
 envious 166
 feeble
  of Redcrosse 165
  of satyrs 135
 hollow
  of Despair 201
 lack of 60
 of Dragon 252, 253
 of flesh 281
 of mind 281
 of true love
  fixed before 126
 of Una 171
 open
  can deceive one's mind 142
 opening of 141
 rude
  of satyrs 133
 superficial 110, 116
 taking commandment from 120
 trust in 121
 viewing with 138
 weeping 132

F

fables 3
fabulousness 39
face
 angel's
  of Una 119
 blushing
  of Una 132
 covering of virgin's 130
 hidden
  in shame 290
  of Despair 201
 naked 134
 of great mother Night 156
 of Ignaro 190
 of Lucifera 144
 of Una 109
  veil snatched from the 131
 open
  of Fidessa 110
 singeing of
  of George 258
 value 125, 178, 213
 viewing of
  of Fidessa 110, 121
 wrinkled
  of Ignaro 189
faces
 shadow of two 297
face to face 71, 74
facing
 in two directions 189
fact
 author of 202
 confusion of fiction and 221
 of injustice
  of Despair 202
 ontological 288
 sorting of
  on a logical level 172
facticity 35
facts 3
 available 177
 reconstruction of 296
factuality
 of Christ's death and resurrction 40
factualness 39
faculty
 of intellect 41
 of soul 41
 of thought
  lower 74
 solitary 40
fading
 of desire
  of Sansloy for Una 137
Faerie Queene, The 2, 8, 9, 10, 11, 12, 26, 28,
  33, 34, 42, 93, 127, 141, 144, 145, 166,
  168, 195, 209, 239, 241, 242, 251, 276,
  295
 allegory of 245

Book II 1
Book III
  Garden of Adonis 8–9
Book V 199
Mutabilitie Cantos, The 28
faery
  court 245
  fiction 152
  knight 151
  son of 137
  stout
    Redcrosse as 144-145
  theft 244
Faery 61, 181, 257, 262
  creature of
    Redcrosse as 162
  deconstrction of 164
  depiction of
    in Spenser's fiction 164
  fiction of 175
  poet-created 162
  Realm of 127
  world of 142
Faery Queen 198, 236, 279, 290 *See also* Gloriana.
failing
  strategy
    of Sansloy 131
failings
  inevitable 203
  of Redcrosse 146
failure
  lack of
    on the part of God 139
  of deconstruction
    in an Augustinian universe 252
  of direct blow 257
  of God 46, 164
  of reason
    to achieve the whole 168
  of Redcrosse 46, 164, 190
    to grasp the necessity of making fine-grained judgments 199
  of Redcrosse's force 60
  of Virgil 36
  of will
    in the House of Despair 199
  to bring potential into action 100
  to connect mankind and nature
    in Augustine's assessment of Virgil 39
  to follow fixed star 84
faint 260
  Redcrosse as 212
  through fear 128
faint-hearted
  knight 206
fainting
  of Redcrosse 205, 207
  of Una 168, 206
faintness 56

fair 281
  beginning 183, 184
  creature 195
  Fidessa 168, 173, 174
  handling
    by Arthur 188
  morning 95
  tree 267
  Una
    abanonment of 141
  virgin 275
  Una as 272
fairest
  piece 237
  virgin 197
faith 23, 41, 56, 62, 72, 79, 155, 182, 238, 251, 263
  adding
    to force 211, 254
  addition of 56
  a priori 62, 257
  armor of 260
  assurance of 265
  Augustinian
    deconstruction of 230
  basis of victory in 255
  change of 63
  Christian 259
  defense of 14
  discipline of
    taught by Una to Satyrane 136
  distance of 76
  false 148
  falsing of
    by Redcrosse 204
  flower of 123
  in Augustine 25
  lack of
    denoted in the name of Sansfoy 106
    of Redcrosse towards Una 127
  leap of 76
  of arms 279
  of others 254
  of Redcrosse 254
  present 254
  test of 262
  wondrous
    of fairest virgin 197
faithful
  guard
    removal of Una's 130
  knight 223, 271
  mariner 127
faithfulness 48
fall 231
  daily
    of the righteous man 184
  from grace 251
  into error 288
  into sin 1
  of Adam 162

of castle 187
of Dragon 270
of Night's famous children 156
reprochful
  of George 257
fallen
  hero 264
fallible
  self 177
falliblity
  of reason 104
falling
  before Lucifera 154
  image of 264
  in love 138
    with Duessa 151
  into silence
    by Una 290
  of love
    on the ground 81
Fall, The 46, 51, 142, 155, 228, 249, 295
  before the 273
  implications for human mind 155
  Redcrosse's lack of knowledge of the 115
false 170, 246, 259, 285, 287
  appearance 158
    of Archimago 129
  artistic construction 185
  beauty
    of Fidessa 190
  bottom
    of knowledge 170
  distinctions 143
    of Corceca 214
  double 240, 275
  dreams 76, 178
  Duessa 141, 153
  enchantment 184
  faith 148
  fancy 111
  fiction 222
  Fidessa 168, 173, 174, 217
  fortune 109, 278
  foundation 270
  gates 276
  gods
    belief of Hercules in 285
    of pagans 176
  grief
    of crocodile 154
  heart 111
  imagination 101
  intent 122
  love 126
  Lucifera 154
  position 70
  reality 163
  Redcrosse 128
  religion 217
    of Babylon 217
  shows 77

sorceress 288
  Duessa as 113
falsehood 76, 78, 225
  in language of Odysseus 169
  in tale of Aeneas 39
falseness 81
  of educated men 193
  embrace of 252
False Seeming (character in the *Roman de la Rose*) 179
False Una 77–81, 101, 103, 114
  beauty of 234
  created by charms and hidden arts 100
  her love for another 101
  profession of love for Redcrosse 82
falsification
  of the truth 171
falsifying
  genius 143
  Lucifera 154
falsing
  of faith
    by Redcrosse 204
faltering
  of George 266
fame 162, 260, 295
  book of 237
  broad-blazed 216
  careless of 161
  everlasting 275
    Mnemosyne as nurse of 250
  hunting 140
  precedence in 260
  quest for 162, 163, 249
  seeking 245
familiarization 180
family
  moral well-being of 122
  natural
    abandonment of by Una's lion 121
  of the King of Eden 45
famous
  children
    of Night 156
  poets 258
  victory 237
fancy
  falsed 111
fangs 63
fantastic
  world
    of fiction 175
fantasy 78
  abuse of 77
  epistemologically created
    in Luther 24
  inexorability of 78

far 68, 69, 252, 253, 287, 295

away
  House of Holinesse not 212
  royal maid flees 138
fetching from 289
from enemies
  Morpheus' position 71
from Una's thought 125
light from 82
Redcrosse not
  from Una 167
spying port from 127
standing
  Una as 188, 273
Una's position
  in battle with Dragon 264
  in battle with Errour 61
wandering
  of Saint George 104
far and near 68
farness 83
  in place 114
  of Una
    from the battle with the Dragon 271
fast 185, 231
  locked 213
fastness
  of faith 182
fat
  Abessa grows
    with feast of offerings 122
  waist
    of Dragon 251
fate 163
  binding of
    of Una and Redcrosse 172
  cruel 78
  doleful 137
  eternal book of 203
  expired
    renewed by the wondrous science 159
  giving one's
    to another 79
  importune 278
  individual 79
  of Night 156
  of Redcrosse 81
  of sons of Night 156
  prediction of 187
father
  generation without a 227
  grave 235
  in heaven 263
  of Duessa 109
  of Orgoglio
    Aeolus as 163
  of Una 295
  reproduction without 228
fatness
  of Dragon 254
fault 287
  of rage 250

one man's 267
potential
  in assumptions 145
faults
  ignorance of
    of Redcrosse by Una 130
faulty 287
  hierarchy of knowledge 109
  model
    of Du Bartas 256
favor 147, 151, 171
  of Arthur
    by field, flood, and heavens 194
  of God 95
  of Redcrosse 203
  of Sansjoy
    in fight with Redcrosse 153
  of Una
    bestowed on Satyrane 136
    permanent switch of balance
      in mankind's 81
favorable
  hands
    advancement with 192
favored
  with grace 221
fawning
  words 131
fawns 133
fealty 118
fear 74, 103, 171, 200, 253, 265, 266, 269, 273
  congealed 251, 252
  conquering 253
  faint through 128
  Fidessa's feigning of 116
  flying from 104
  followed
    behind Trevisan 200
  good that grows out of past 191
  jealous 104
  of abhoration
    by Una 124
  of Corceca 123
  of Dragon 267, 274
  of ill 288
  of loss 265
  of potential harm 253
  of satyrs
    by Una 134
  of self
    by Trevisan 200
  of the Dragon's teeth
    by the poet 251
  of Trevisan 200
  of Una
    as she considers the consequences of Redcrosse's being alive 172
    over pagan's presence 138
  putting away
    of Una's 134

real 251
    shown by Redcrosse after his meeting with Fradubio 116
Redcrosse urges Duessa to put f. apart 108
sign of 63
striking
    into enemies 66
    into opponent 257, 258
testing
    in sphere of action 253
wrought by Fidelia 219
fearful
    shepherd 110
fearfulness
    of shame 58
fearless
    Fidessa 116
fearlessness
    of George 296
    of Redcrosse 128
fears 79
    worst 131
fearsomeness
    of Errour 60
feast 276, 277
    of offerings 122
    on destruction 259
feasting 150
feats
    of arms 130
feeble 270
    bark 272
    breast
        of poet 250
    eyes
        of Redcrosse 165
        of satyrs 135
    feet 215, 266
    Redcrosse as 212
    sense
        of George 246
    steps
        of Humiltá 213
feebleness
    of castle 187
feeding
    his fiery lustful eye 132
    on others 251
feel
    in heart
        of Una 171
feeling 118
    friendly 283
    of Archimago
        of the hope of new good hap 129
    of sharper edge 265
    speeches 156
feelings 33
feet 166
    bare 68

feeble 215, 266
    horned 134
    innocent
        of Una 215
    of George 274
    scarlet carpet beneath 276
    weary
        of Una 120
feigning
    dream 101
    of fear
        by Fidessa 116
    of the armor of Redcrosse
        by Archimago 124
fell 268, 270
    countenance 264
    down 266
    into the dark abyss 252
    stroke 257
female 210
    form 100
feminine
    society 209
fere (archaic: spouse or companion)
    lovely
        Charissa linked to 219
ferocity 63
    of Orion's hound 127
    of Redcrosse 152
        on seeing False Una 78
fertile
    plain 268
fetching
    from far away 289
feudal
    monarchy 233
fickle
    freaks
        of fortune 278
fickleness 141
    of choice
        in Redcrosse 147
Ficta religio (Emblem VI in Alciati's *Emblemata*) 217
fiction 18, 32, 37, 91, 94, 103, 233, 237, 254
    a=a only available in 131
    absence of 214
    Aeneid as a work of 40
    artificially-constructed
        of Spenser 231
    as creator of Una 67
    as domain of metaphysical truth 231
    as the way to access Eden 176
    confusion of fact with 221
    construction 45
    creation of
        by an allegorical poet 218
        in poet's imagination 178
    deconstructable 58, 181
        House of Holinesse as 219

deconstructing 112, 133
end of 294
epistemological 257
existence in
  of Una 96
faerie 152
false 222
guarantee of 276
historical 31
Homeric 39
imaginative 112, 285
  nebulousness of 161–162
  of Spenser 270
imaginatively constructed 228
inequality in 27
inimitable 226
interference of 181
intermediary 245
in *Timaeus* 19
intrusion of 91
mechanism of 275
necessary 19
  in the ancient world 20
  in the work of Plato 161–162
of Aristotle being younger than Socrates 221
of Faery 175
of Spenser 128, 187
of Una's armor 102
of worshipping Roman emperors
  as gods 181
ontology of
  of Spenser's *Faerie Queene* 127
opens up the world to questions 46
outside of
  the possibility of otherworldly journeys 170
pagan 40
perfect metaphysical 175
poetic metaphor of 228
power of 93
  in Plato's *Parmenides* 221
  to create poetic metaphor 229
product of 143
  Una as 95
realistic 112
reality in 94
reintroduces intermediate things 26
Spenserian 84, 152
Spenser's 66, 132
substitution of
  for reality 175
truth in 219
typological 270
universe of 178
veil of 218
work of 31, 179
world of
  as universal, figural, but ultimately fantastic 175
fictional
  Aeneas 147
  allegory 214
  armor 57
  characters 94

construction
  of Eden 249, 272
  of satyrs 135
creation 76
creatures
  satyrs as 133
domain
  of imagination 296
Dragon
  exact size of 250
Eden 290
gods 260
logocentric sphere 282
object
  λόγος as 6
other 193
poem
  depiction of Faery in Spenser's 164
religion 217
status
  of Una 212
Una 238
universe 127, 169
  of allegory 163
world 211, 237
λόγος 180, 189, 255
Fidelia 56, 219–221, 220
book of 221
perfection of Redcrosse by 232
teaching of 221-222
Fidessa 110, 116, 119, 141, 150, 153, 195, 260, 281, 286, 288
as the Whore of Babylon 95
awful behavior
  of Redcrosse with 172
breasts of
  baring of 228
claim to empire by 285
color of 277
comfort of
  by Redcrosse 200
crowning of 116
  as Redcrosse's beloved 111
Duessa gives her name as 113
easy virtue of 229
exchange of Una for 110
expression of body by 182
failure to make trial of
  by Redcrosse 143
fair 168, 173, 174
false 168, 173, 174, 217
fearless 116
gems and ouches of 229
intercourse with Redcrosse 111
lies of 195
nakedness of 171
ontologically existence of 195
open body of 234
physical looseness of 130
pleasing body of 202
profession of love to 163

Redcrosse's affection for 111
Redcrosse's superficial perception of 121
resting with 160–163
viewing body of 280
wanton loves of 174
field 48, 120, 129
  Archimago has never taken the 129
  arms in
    odds of 278
  beast of the 120
  bloody 150, 237
  Lord of the 131
  master of the
    Arthur as 188
  of battle 136, 210
  playing
    leveling of 278
  semantic 27, 89
fields 194
  open 252
  verdant 106
fiend
  damned 264
  direful 271
fiends
  thousand 205
fierce
  equipage
    of war 250
  lion 59, 257
fier (Fr. pride) 106 *See also* pride.
fiery
  lustful eye 132
  pincers 224
  steel 258
fight 57, 69, 148, 187, 206, 209, 225, 258, 261,
       264, 266, 297 *See also* battle.
  between Sansloy and Archimago 129
  enraged
    apology for 149
  equal 65
    between Satyrane and Sansloy 174
  for control
    between two evenly-matched opponents 138
  for fame and honor
    by Redcrosse 162
  freedom by 254
  furious
    Lucifera's interference in the 149
  George continues to 253
  mortal 152
  not every f. is worth having 61
  of rams
    in epic simile 106
  power of Errour's ideas 66
  Redcrosse's inability to 60
  with Errour 65
fighting 42
  alike 151
  Archimago's lack of experience in 129
  for control

of the flock 257
for praise and honor 152
for right 152
for the shield of Sansfoy
  by Redcrosse 150
for Una 249
of Satyrane and Sansloy 136
outward forces
  with equal vigor 225
Una's foe 198
with a properly constructed mind 254
with spiritual foes 210
fights
  furious
    of Redcrosse 166
  tiping the balance of 203
figura 27
figural
  name 84, 241
    of Redcrosse 239, 244
  state of Redcrosse 105
  world
    of fiction 175
figuration
  in poetry 95
figurative
  name 241
figure 32, 41
  allegorical 239
  figural and literal 6
  in relation to unity 57
  of Gloriana 195
  of Redcrosse 57
filled
  air
    with smoke and stench 252
filling
  of the air 154
  the pride
    of the Lord of the field 131
final
  resting place 187
  smart 206
finding
  of knight
    by Una 127
fine-grained
  judgments 200
finishing
  of intent 290
fire 205, 253, 266, 269, 270
  belching 256
  bellowing 258
  burning in 128
  double entendre (fier) 106
  flames 256
  glorious 176
  inward 260
  kindling 96
  of love 113, 173

scorching 266
without smoke 54
wrathful 153
fire-mouthed
  Dragon 207
firm 185
  decision 177
  fixity 82
    in extreme case of Arthur 197
  standing
    by Spenser's hero 256
first
  episode 65
  impression 274
  wound 171
1st person perspective 50
fish 4, 103
fit
  frantic 202
fits 258
  furious 250
fitting
  purpose
    framing of 277
fixed
  before
    eyes of true love 126
  point
    in Redcrosse's errant wanderings 197
  rusty knife
    in body 201
  star 82
fixing
  of Una's perception of her situation 128
fixity
  firm
    in extreme case of Arthur 197
  of norther star 83
flame
  glowing
    of Heaven 256
flames 253
  kindling 259
  nearness to 259
  of fire 256
  scorching 258
    of Orion's hound 127
flaming
  courage 151
  eyes 253
  locks 281
flattering 80
flattery
  Duessa's of Redcrose 109
flaw
  of Redcrosse's lack of knowledge of untruth 105

flaws 95
  in Una's character 121

fleeing
  Errour 225
  forcing f. things to stay
    as a behavioral attribute of Redcrosse 122
  the earth 251
fleet
  Argive 7
flesh 183, 225
  eyes of 281
  frail 108
  impairment of 183
  living 144
  mouth of the 73
fleshly
  arm 265
  might 210
  wight 206
Fletcher, Angus 5, 32, 42, 271, 294
  definition of allegory 6
flies *See also* gnats.
  little 77
flight
  end of 253
  of Dragon 253
  from chaste maid 116
  from field of battle 210
  from reason
    in modern aesthetics 167
  from Una
    defines Redcrosse 82
  of Archimago
    after he is unmasked by Sansloy 129
  of Duessa
    from Arthur 187
    from the battle of Redcrosse and Sansfoy 108
  of Errour
    from Redcrosse's armor 65
  of evil 143
  of fire from the forge 106
  of George
    to protection offered by Una's bestowal of a
      sacred name 83
  of passive Una
    back to her true love 140
  of Phoebus
    from Una in her hour of need 132
  of Redcrosse
    from Archimago's hermitage 84
    from his own thought 104
    from Una 104, 127
  of Styx 70
  of the souls of men that live amis 108
  of Una 119
  stillness in 264
  to faith 79
  to heavens bright
    of the glee of the crowd 154
  Una booteth not to fly 130

flipping
  of position

Index 377

by Duessa 153
flitted
  life 169
flock
  control of the 257
  fight for rule of the 106
flood
  divided
    by Fidelia 221
  of weakness in the poet's catalog of Redcrosse 62
floods 194
floor 276
Flourdelis 297
flourish
  rhetorical 288
flow 37
  of dialog 196
flower
  in May 282
  of chasity 123
  of faith 123
  thin as a 163
flowers
  ever-blooming 290
flurry
  of maidens 275
flute 97
flux
  linguistic
    primal chaos beneath 240
fly
  Errour attempts to 59
  from error 206
    urged by Una's dwarf 53, 111
flying 103
  far away
    by Una 138
  from the Cave of Errour 163
  of Duessa 285
  speed 284
focus
  change of 184
  of attention 177
  of Redcrosse 224
  of Una 184
    on the essence of Redcrosse 231
  on arms 243
  on death
    by George 267
  on ends 261
  on life
    by poet 267
focusing
  attention
    of Redcrosse 202
foe 58, 61, 110, 156, 286
  cursed 244
  irreligious 63
  of Una 198

rage of 63
revenge on
  by Redcrosse 153
yielding no foot to 106
foes
  confounding 195
  spiritual 210
foggy
  cloud 132
  mist 114
foil
  gold
    House of Pride covered in 143
folded
  position 266
folds
  hunderd
    of the Dragon's tail 251
following
  fear 200
  fixed northern star 84
  of Redcrosse
    by Una 200
  the northern star 82–83
  Una 123
  Wrath
    by mischiefs 148
folly
  of action
    dictated to Redcrosse by Fradubio 143
fooling
  of Redcrosse
    by Archimago 103
  of Sansloy
    by False Redcrosse 128
  of Una
    by Archimago 103
foolish
  faery's son 137
  man
    Redcrosse as 202
    swallowed by crocodile 154
  pride 184
foot
  forward 223
    of Redcrosse 185
  of Redcrosse 163
  yielding no f. to foe 106
footing
  forward 54, 62, 223
    of Redcrosse 279
  of people 121
  of the Ladder of Ambition
    by Redcrosse 149
footsteps 121
  in trodden grass 121
force 38, 64, 69, 163
  adding faith to 56, 211, 254
  animal
    of Redcrosse 212

basis of victory in 255
beating wings by
  of Dragon 251
binding
  love as 174
driving Redcrosse 140
failure of Redcrosse's 60
furious 121
  forgetting of by lion 120
hasty 163
human 263
is not one's own 56
manly 57, 188
of delay 240
of fleshly arm 265
of nature 176
of Redcrosse 99
of Spenser's imagination 60
outward 225
over justice 286
pride of 245
Redcrosse's use of 59
spending of 186

forces
dark 70
unreal 225

forcing
Errour to stay 121
fleeing Errour
  to stay 200, 225
fleeing things to stay
  as a behavioral attribute of Redcrosse 122
fleeing Trevisan
  to stay 200
King and Queen of Eden to live behind brazen
    walls 122
retirement
  of George 266
Una's chastity
  by Sansloy 132

forehead
framing garland
  for Fidessa 147
of Fidessa 111
sweaty
  of Redcrosse 160

foreheads
frowning 134

foreordained
will
  of God 106, 135

forest 52, 69, 102
ranging the
  by Arthur 194

forestalling 44

forests
resound with Una's cries 133

forever
prolongation of battle 153

forge
flight of fire from 106

forgery 24, 297
of sprights by Archimago 101

forgetful
of his own 155

forgetfulness
of victory 106

forgetting 23
by poet 119
fabulous fictions 39
how to read and write 39
hungry rage
  by lion 120
in the epic simile of rams 106
obligation
  to Una 209
of element of pride in Redcrosse
  by reader 148
of furious force
  by lion 120
of virtues 261
  by the well of life 263
the reins
  of reason's rule 149
what Una previously knew 125

forgiveness
New Testament doctrine of 202

forgiving
of Redcrosse 150
for his unkindness 161

forlorn
maid 130
relics of Redcrosse's power
  Una as 184
weed 168

form 40, 97, 100, 221
alluring
  of Babylon 217
attenuated
  of once powerful literary motif 169
female 100
hylomorphic 101
intellectual
  of pure reason 87
lack of 115
lowest
  of animal behavior 148
of a=b knowledge 131
of a "perfect" shape 87
of a triangle 87
of being 14
of judgment 114
of the beloved 283
of thought
  of Archimago 100–102
ontological
  of Gloriana 195
thought f.'d by the thing which we know
  in Augustine 73
vagrancy of 37

formal logic 88

former

Index

dame
  love of 287
shield
  of Sir Burbon 297
formidable
  enemy 298
  strength
    of Redcrosse 298
forms 103, 260
Forms 193
  Theory of
    dismissed by Aristotle 14
formula
  rational 97
forsaken
  heir 285
forsaking
  of blows
    by Dragon 258
forth
  bringing
    of excellent glory 151
fortune 79
  blamed for Una's troubles
    by Satyrane 136
  breach of 183
  cruel freaks of 278
  false 109, 278
  lack of
    of Corceca and Abessa 123
  mastery of
    by Arthur 188
    lack of 188
  of Arthur
    in battle 188
  tempestuous 171, 174
  unkndness of 118
forward 54, 130, 194, 212, 241
  advancement
    by Archimago towards Una 123
  Archimago's intention in driving action 77
  best foot 223
  course 258
  of Una 199
  drive
    not the love of Una, Eden, or heaven but arms
      by Redcrosse 141
  foot
    of Redcrosse 185
  footing 54, 62, 223
    of Redcrosse 279
  journey 122
  movement
    of Ignaro 189
  pressing 78
  progress 167
  purpose
    offered by Una 199
  Una's dwarf's role in moving the pair 165
  way
    of Redcrosse 205
  with Fidessa 116
forwardness 52, 53
  of action
    driven by Archimago's intention 77
forwasted
  kingdom 248
Foucault, Michel 218
foul
  Duessa 114
  reproach 131
foulness
  of disgrace to knighthood 69
  of dishonor in death 109
foundation 33, 35, 98
  false 270
  illegitimate
    of Lucifera 144
  in God's ontological work
    lack of 66
  in history 33
  in truth 287
  metaphysical 244
  of castle
    in epic simile 187
  of Odysseus' thought
    in reality or in his own imagination 169
  ontological
    in literal reality 212
  solid
    of language 50
  true
    of literature 169
foundational
  work of modern philosophy of language 85
founder
  of modern philosophy 34
fountain
  resting by a 136
fowl 103
fox 103
Fradubio 111–115
  appearance of
    as unrecognized reflection of Redcrosse's
      behavior 147
  as a tree 262
  compassion of Redcrosse for 115
  conversation with 143
  exclamation of 114
  experience of 112, 113, 143
  intrusion of 116
  not in a house 115
  plight of 115
  poor choice of 114
  responds plainly 113
  turned into a tree 143
  unawareness of 112
Frælissa (consort of Fradubio) 113
  transformation of 114
fragile
  social order 151

fragmentation
  of sense in allegory 27
frail 205
  class of humanity 113
  flesh 108
  humanity
    of Redcrosse 206
  Redcrosse 210
frailty
  human 183
  of man 112
frame
  earthly 237
framework
  casual 172
  constructed and rational 164
  dialectical 54, 137
  metaphysical
    Una sets her problems in a 172
  moral 149
  narrative
    of Ovid 260
  rational 15, 172
  scientific 172
framing
  of garland
    for Fidessa's forhead 147
    of green branches 111
  of goodwill
    by Redcrosse 163
  of mortal life 232
  of the ivory gate of sleep 76
frankincense
  divine 289
franklin
  Zele as 213
frantic
  fit 202
fraud 113, 141
freaks
  cruel and fickle
    of fortune 278
free 285
  courser
    of Arthur 194
  will 221
    exercise of 191
    in the Augustinian universe 134
    problem of 157
freedom
  by fight 254
  existential 238
  from body 64
  from tyranny
    of the devil 263
  Godless
    of Archimago 238
  maximum 55
  of choice 50
  of linguistic usage 89

of one hand
  in Redcrosse's fight with Errour 56
of right arm 64
of will 79
perfect
  desired by existentialists 135
  potential for 190
freely
  sprung
    out of fruitful ground 267
freezing
  of the world
    in ekphrasis 205
Frege, Friedrich Ludwig Gottlob 85, 88, 91, 282
Frege's Puzzle 85–96
French
  Enlightenment 4
fresh 264, 281
  blood 256
  coals 173
  remembrance
    of deformed crimes 205
freshest
  age 227
Freud, Sigmund 241–243
  ego consciousness 74
  unconscious 74
friend 110, 116, 286
  affection for 66
  attack of
    by Sansloy 129
  of God 105, 198, 263
  of Orgoglio 186
  of the nation 239
  praise of 192
friendly
  feeling 283
friends 286
  of Una 282
friendship 282, 298
  Aristotle on 282
  beginning of
    in goodwill 283
  Calvin on 25
  circle of 198
  extension of goodwill to 283
  inactive
    goodwill as 283
  of God 62, 203, 258, 263, 267, 295
  of Una
    with Arthur 194
  to goodwill 282
  with others 203
fright 111
  vain 273
    of Una 271
frivolity 52
frogs 60
front

Index 381

horned 106
frowning
  foreheads 134
fruit
  product of the skill of earth 125
fruitful
  ground 267
fruitless
  joy
    of the world 243
fruitlessness
  of engagament
    with Errour 60
frustration
  expression of
    by Una 209
  of desire
    of Redcrosse 158
  of Una 68
Frye, Northrop 169–170
  translation of romance 171
fulfillment
  of purpose 209
  of Sansloy's desire 137
  purpose
    of George 262
full
  content 289
  of unfocused chivalric energy 115
fuller
  knowledge 145
  of events 285
fully
  clad
    Una as 147
  loyal
    Una as 147
functioning
  member
    of court 247
funeral 108
furies 258
  chain of necessity broken for 158
  infernal
    with chains untied 200
furious 186
  animal war 176
  battle 148
  fight
    Lucifera's interference in the 149
    of Redcrosse 166
  fits 250
  force 121
    forgetting of by lion 120
  ire 101
  mood
    of the Dragon 257
  stroke 257
furiousness
  half 58, 65

furniture
  dewe 45
furrow
  heaped 244
further
  adventure 290
    hermit's promise of 81
furtiveness 64
fury 65
  directed
    of George's blows 258
  habit of 257
  mad 137
  martial 250
  of blow
    of George 257
  of Dragon 257
  refraining from
    by Redcrosse and Sansjoy 149
  temporary
    of Redcrosse 154
future 126, 263
  indefinite 231
  perfection 51
  predicted in *Isaiah* 2:4 in which swords are beaten into plowshares 150
  uncertain 244
  unexperienced 197

G

gain
  love of 251
  unlawful 26
gaining
  active control 135
  advantage
    of others 234
gainsaying
  of George
    by Una 44, 80, 166
gait
  slow
    of Humiltá 213
gales
  southern 59
gall 56
gaping
  of greedy gulf 255
  wonderment 276
Garden of Adonis 8
Garden of Delights (in the *Roman de la Rose*) 146
garland
  of green branches 111
  for Fidessa 147

garment
  guiltless

worn by Una 226
of Despair 201
outer
  change in 282
poisoned
  of Hercules 258
Una's 130
white 281
gate 185
  brazen 273, 285
    construction of 274
    opening of 273
  double 70, 76
  guarding of the
    of the House of Holinesse 213
  of false dreams
    in Virgil's *Aeneid* 75–78
  of ivory 100
  of silver 100
  of Bower of Bliss 143
  of House of Holinesse 213
  open
    of Maluenu 151
    of Humiltá 213
gates
  brazen 276
  construction of 273
  false 276
  of dreams 143
  of the House of Holinesse 273
  unwatched
    of Eden 286
gathering
  separate experiences
    into memory 245
gazing
  of the gods
    on Juno's golden chair 146
gems
  Charissa adorned with 228
general
  attacks 141
  example 187
  man 178
  name
    of Redcrosse 45, 113
  sense 113
generation
  act of 227
  of fear
    in the minds of men 273
generations
  of scholars
    ignorance of 169
generic
  similarity
    between objects 277
  term
    of allegory 71
genitive
  construction 175

genius
  falsifying 143
  guarding the Bower of Bliss 143
genre
  allegory defined as a 8
  comical
    of the provincial morality play 232
  of allegory 8
gentle
  greening 134
  knight 278, 288
  play 160
  wit 135
    bending of 147
gentleman 34
gentleness 48
  of Una 101
genus 15, 97
  animal 267
  Redcrosse's reliance on his animal 105
geometric
  organization 271
geometry
  spatial 253
George 82, 83, 196, 240, 245, 252, 254, 263,
    264, 265, 269, 270, 276, 278, 280, 282,
    284, 287, 293, 295. *See also* Redcrosse
  adventure of 288
    in the world 271
  alienation of
    from reader 245
    from Una 245
  as individual name 45
  as Redcrosse 244
  as son of a plowman 245
  as uneducated man 295
  baptism of 262–263
  behavior of 260
  blows of
    directed fury of 258
  catechism of 262–263
  conquering might of 271
  continues to fight 253
  courage of 245
  destiny of 290
  direction of 287
  experience of 246
  faltering of 266
  focus of
    on death 267
  human purpose of 260
  human will of 158
  imperfection of 105
  individual 57, 105, 204
  journey of 246, 266
    end of 278
  killing of Dragon by 269
  lifted from the ground 254
  lineage of 245
  literal 175
  literal name of 239

memory of
  not his strong suit 247
  not clued in to metaphysical aspects of his experience 254
  perspective of 273
  physical exhaustion of 261
  rage of 250
  rechristening of
    by Una 241
  rejection of literal 124
  revival of 264
  Saint 84, 104
  sainthood of 105
  shield of 266
  sins of 269
  status of 245
  time-bound 272
  unawareness of
    of his state of blessedness 204
  unseating of
    from his horse 257
  victory of 258
  visit of
    to Contemplation's chapel 246
  welcome of 274
  wholeness of 295
  will of 261, 269
gēorgos 240
Germany 13
gest
  noble 220
ghost 108, 113
  from lake of limbo 112
  grieved 169
  of Creusa 38
ghosts
  damned 205
  groaning 183
giant
  blow of
    as idle stroke 186
  body
    of Orgoglio 195
  head of 187
  Orgoglio as 162
  stout 173
gift
  of grace 164
  of Una
    to George 283
gifts
  a priori 266
  exchange of 198
  natural 97
  of nature 233
  of the king 276
  princely 276
Gilbert of Poitiers 107–108
glade
  hollow 253

glad
  look
    on lion's face after seeing Una 134
gladness
  to gain the favor of Una
    by Satyrane 136
glancing
  sight 186
glass
  as an image
    in Augustine 71
  dark 246
  of allegory 74
  through a g. darkly 71, 149
  tower of 236
glee 219
  great 154
glimpse
  of truth 246
Gloriana 27, 44, 46, 245, 246, 290, 296
  cohering presence of 131
  comparison of
    with Una 197
  consort of 177
  court of 55, 91, 96, 105, 138, 166, 167, 176, 182, 212, 234, 245, 247, 268, 274
    law in the 131
  grace of 280, 294
  guarantee of 197
  kindling fire for
    in the heart of Redcrosse 176
  return to 238
  story of her yearly feast 43
  tale of
    Arthur and 194–198
  wonder of
    at George 44
glorious
  fire 176
  intent 151
  seeming show 109, 145
  show 277
glory 48, 61, 67, 153, 236, 237, 242
  desire for 121
  excellent 151
  external warrior's 148
  inner
    a priori 152
  of Gloriana 245
  vain 144
    of Redcrosse 165
  worldly 104, 226, 243
glowing
  flame
    of Heaven 256
gluttony 47, 99

Gluttony
  as steward 166
  description of 160

excessive 150
in the Triumph of Pride 146
gnats 60, 298 *See also* files.
cloud of 77
goal 55, 295
decadent 171
in Spenser's poetry 78
of art 277
of Augustine's system 193
of Socrates 193
of the poet 237
of Una 212
god 180
ass not a 217
blind 78, 79
of the daylight sun
Apollo as 249
of war 250
temptation to become a 257
that binds one person to another 227
God 2, 4, 16, 26, 152, 154, 188, 221, 255, 262, 264, 271
affection for 66
Almighty 221
a priori choice
of Redcrosse by 158
Archimago speaks reproachful shame of 70
armor of 49, 95
as *a priori* creator 166
as creator 104
of ontology 152, 158, 263
of the universe 133
of Λόγος 193
as director
of action 266
as friend 62, 67, 116, 198, 263
as good 210
as guide 192
of chance 266
of luck 278
as source
of good will 210
of power 210
blessing of 279
born of 73
choice of 231
of Redcrosse 84, 105, 186
created by 94
creation
Archimago's attempt to imitate 102
creation by 218
of individual substance 225
creation of 23, 61, 93, 137, 155, 234
death of 238
dedication to
in Augustine 38
deeper purpose of 79
defeat of 136
determination by 78
devotion to 121
divided thought

as an image of 74
equivalent to 267
eternal 266
expectation of
of human beings 266
favor of 95
foreordained will of 106
friendship of 203, 267, 295
gift of potential to man by 106
goodwill of 99, 163, 205, 296
lacking in Orgoglio 163
grace of 81, 211, 278
granting of grace 221
gratitude to
in Augustine 38
guarantee of animal being by 104
guarantor of Redcrosse's success 2
guiding hand of 132
hand of 254, 256, 258
hatred of 231
higher purpose of 138
hope of salvation from 231
identical to
Redcrosse not 298
image of 73
knowledge is not the 74
Λόγος as 193
implants good in the mind of man at his creation 138
inaccessible 181
in Eden 96
in heaven 132
knowledge of
through a leap of faith 76
likeness to 74
love of 12
man of 250
man's imitation of
through reason 149
metaphysical equality of 269
mind of 188
moral work of 193
naked before 122
ontological creation 66
ontology of 155
operation of
more comprehensive than pagan mind could understand 222
order of 264
perfection of 2
perspective of 236, 270
power of 134, 226
praying to
by Una 264
prior ontology of 181
pure direction given to Redcrosse by 116
purpose of 295
reasoning of 99

Redcrosse as
instrument of 2
of Una's life 120

Index

reliance on
  by Redcrosse 179
relationship with
  of George 158
rescue of Redcrosse 143
return to
  blocked by the poet 47
sacred ontology of 58
Sansfoy's lack of care for 105
sees all 79
service to 154
status of 268
subordination to
  by Redcrosse 218
supplanting of 193
supplies victory
  to Redcrosse 158
timeless perspective of 203
uncertain connection to 266
victory ascribed to 108
virtue of 223
will of 222, 260, 262, 263, 269, 287
  instrument of 135
Word of 256
work of 94, 163
  performed by Archimago 101
wrath of 231
τέλος provided by 176

goddess 217
  Gloriana as 93
  of hunt 94
  of love 94
  temptation of
    by Herclues 259

Gödel, Kurt 292
  on problems with Frege's legacy 88–90

Godfrey of Bouillon 40–41, 179
  as intellect 41

God-given
  mind 276
  potential 206

godless
  freedom
    of Archimago 238

godlike
  perception
    by Redcrosse 203

godly
  arms
    blaze of 250

God of Sleep 77. *See also* Morpheus.

gods 36
  competing for power with the 146
  deception of 19
  false
    belief of Hercules in 285
    of pagans 176
  fictional 260
  gazing of
    on Juno's golden chair 146
  hostile 40, 83

hostility of 35, 36
idolatrous 259
imaginary 259
imitation of 19
power of 260
worship as
  of Roman emperors 181
worship of false 181

Goethe, Johann Wolfgang von 5, 167, 181, 275

gold 122, 276
  foil
    House of Pride covered in 143
  in the clothes of Duessa 108
  tire of 228

golden
  age 251
    in Ovid 37
    Ovid's hope of return to 251
  bells 109
  chain 192–193, 194
  chair
    of Juno 146
  cup 187

good 15, 150, 157, 176, 199, 214, 258, 263, 267
  balance towards 152
  behavior 110
    Una as a beacon of 172
  collective
    according to Romans 181
  government 99
  great 194
  grows out of past fear 191
  hap 129
  higher 45
  intent 122
  in the heart 138
  is permanently better than evil 138
  knight 176
  knowledge of
    degrees of 213
  man is
    by access to "native virtue" 142
  men
    action of 158
  of subjects 43
  permanent 142
  priority of
    over evil 138
  privation of
    definition of evil in Augustine 106
  rests with God 210
  separation of
    from reason 41
  side of the 81
  things 267

  triumph of
    over evil 288
  unified 157
  will

Archimago as devoid of 119
of God 134
woman
Una as 204
good and evil
absolute division between 157
knowledge of 268
goodly
armed 258
court
made by Redcrosse 161
grace 227
reason 183
temperance 190
thing
hardest to begin 213
virgins 219
goodness 103
a priori 67
in mind
of Redcrosse 218
of Redcrosse 222
orientation to 67
goodwill 25–26, 70, 282, 298
as inactive friendship 283
extension of
to friendship 283
framing of
by Redcrosse 163
in Aristotle 283
of God 99, 163, 205, 296
lacking in Orgoglio 163
Redcrosse's ascription to himself of no more than 28
related to friendship 282
superficiality of
in Aristotle 283
gore
bloody 251
gorge
stinking 252
Gorgon
Prince of Darkness 70
gory
blood 256
governance
of society 105
of the contest between Redcrosse and Sansjot
by the "sacred lawes of armes" 152
of the world
by love 174
governing
behavoir
of Arthur 188
fortune mastered by
of Arthur 188
government
administration of
by educated men 105
good 99

of the world of time
by Cupid's love 229
by the impe of Jove 96
principle of 125
governor
Cupid as
in the extremity of time 138
gown
of pure white 281
grace 51, 215, 221, 237, 239
addition of
to excellence 284
a priori 105, 164, 278
conferee of 221
constructed
by the author 164
fall from 251
favored with 221
gift of 164
God's 81
goodly 227
granting of
by God 47, 221
great 242
greater
grows on top of justice 207
heart blessed with 110
heavenly 158, 163
in Una's face 119
upholding of the righteous man by 184
in Calvin 25–27
mirror of 93
modest 219
of Gloriana 177, 280, 294
of God 211, 278
of great queen of Faery 197
perfection of
Redcrosse grows into 223
restoration through 1
true-seeming
of Duessa 158
victory through 210
gracious
ointment 268
thought
of Una 183
gradual
revelation of evidence
to the the reader 145
graft 298
grammar 33
imperfect 88
irrational 88
raised above fiction 39
subject to logic 89
grammarians 37, 39

grand
design
of Spenser 224

Index

grandmother
  Night as ancient 155
granting
  of grace 221
    by God 221
  of Una's armor 177
grass
  trodden 121
  verdant 195
grassy
  ground 161–162
gratification
  immediate 231
gratitude
  expression of
    by Una 188
  of careful reader 232
grave 108
  eloquence 284
  father 235
  intention 287
gravity
  theory of 2
gray
  beard
    of Archimago 68
  hoary
    Humiltá as 213
great
  battles
    of Redcrosse 204
  body
    of Orgoglio 187
  glee 154
  good 194
  grace 242
  intent 151
  name
    of scarlet carpet 276
  queen
    of Faery 197
greater
  grace
    grows on top of justice 207
  loss 173
  love 173
  no g. shame to knight 141
greatest
  honor 151
greatness
  achieved by the loss of another 157
greed
  unbalance of 37
greedy
  gulf 255
Greek 73, 275
  word 5
green
  aspen 206
  branches 111, 147
  leaves 160
  scattered carcasses on the 200
  vine leaves 146
Greenblatt, Stephen 9, 78, 242, 294
greening
  gentle 134
greeting
  of Archimago (disguised as Recrosse)
    by Una 124
grief 56, 104, 149, 180
  breeds depair 182
  false
    of crocodile 154
  growth of
    on False Una 80
  telling of 224
grieved 260
  ghost 169
grip 266
  of Dragon 265
gripping
  of prey
    by an eagle 254
grisly
  locks
    of Despar 201
  mouth of hell 252
groaning
  ghosts 183
  of earth 270
Gross, Kenneth 239–242, 275
ground 63, 187, 258, 261, 268
  as source of his strength
    of George 257
  assurance that love did not fall on the 81
  branches thrust into 115
  contact with
    source of Antaeus' strength 259
  down to 254
  eyes bent to the ground 68
  fruitful 267
  grassy 161–162
  growth of true love of 195
  inflation above
    by Orgoglio 253
  in nature 87
  lifting from the
    of George 254
  looking at
    by George 246
  lowest
    castles undermined from the 187
  metaphysical 112
  native 289
  of a stable shore 127
  of metaphysics 18
  of the literal earth 133
  seed spilled on 167
  shift in the
    of philosophy 170

sitting of the
    by Despair 201
unlucky 110
wearing the
    with satyrs' horned feet 134
grounded
    in False Una's swollen heart 80
grounding
    of action in God-given potential 106
grove
    shady 110
growth
    metaphor of
        by Arthur 191
    of baptized hands 265
    of conflict
        in Una's mind 172
    of good
        out of past fear 191
    of good things 267
    of grief 80
    of justice 207
    of Redcrosse
        in the House of Holinesse 223
    of true love
        on ground 195
    of Una's conscious mind 118
guarantee
    metaphysical 67
    of animal being 104
    of end
        of Redcrosse 142
    of fiction 46, 276
    of Gloriana 197
    of goodness 67
    of heavenly mercy
        given to Redcrosse 206
    of place
        in Gloriana's court 247
    of Redcrosse's 62
    of safety
        of Eden 249
    of success 2, 62, 67, 68, 126, 211
        in battle 197
        of the communication process 228
    of victory 58, 152
        by Redcrosse's armor 163
guard 111
    faithful
        removal of Una's 130
guardian 232
guarding
    of the gate
        of the House of Holinesse 213
    the Bower of Bliss 143
guerdon 237
    of Archimago's guile 129

guessing
    contents of nature 190
guest
    unacquainted
        Redcrosse as 227
    unknown 285
guidance
    by God 258
guide
    for life 84
    God as 62
        to the listener ro rational men 192
    of chance
        God as 266
    of wandering steps 246
    to experience 126
    to truth
        by the sun in Plato's Allegory of the Cave 137
    Trevisan as
        of Redcrosse 200
    Una as a 84
    weaker wandering steps as
        of Redcrosse 231
guided
    by deeper power than human will 79
    by God
        luck as 278
    by team of oxen 245
guiding
    hand of God 132
    of one's way 148
    of weapons
        by God 255
guile 114
    diverse 131
    guerdon of Archimago's 129
    harmful
        of crocodile 154
    of sprite 112
guileful
    handling 118
guilt
    of bloody field 237
    of others 157
    of Redcrosse
        to charges leveled by Despair 204
guiltless
    garments
        worn by Una 226
guiltlessness
    of the King of Eden 287
guilty
    blood 183
        in Virgil's *Aeneid* 63
guise
    shameless 78
gulf
    between this world and the next 262
    greedy 255
    of reference 25, 94
    yawning
        of Avernus 158

gushing
  river
    of blood 256
Guyon 2
  action of 296
  destruction of the Bower of Bliss 143

H

habit
  of fury 257
habits
  man-made 3
hair 263
  rending of Corceca's 123
  white
    of Archimago 129
half
  beasts
    satyrs as 137
  dead 201
  enraged 78
  furious 58
  fury 65
  mad 123
  of divided mind 78
  shame
    of Sansloy at having attacked Archimago 129
half-furious
  Redcrosse 65
hall 150
halves 285
Hamilton, A. C. 8–10, 51, 196–197, 261
  1977 text 8–9, 51
  2001 text 9, 51
  as a reader 55
  maintenance of critical balance 50
  sides with Una 54
  Wandering Wood as emblematic of the reader's dilemma 10
hand 2, 56, 244, 258, 272
  cunning
    of Æsculapius 159
  guiding
    of God 132
  hasty 285
  of God 258
  of knight
    holds knife in Cave of Despair 201
  of Lucifera 144
  of Redcrosse 206, 211
  right 285
  steady
    of Una 235
  Una left in the h. of Sansloy 129
handling
  fair
    by Arthur 188
    guileful 118
hands

baptized 265
clownish 60
extended in height 154
favorable
  advancement with 192
lily 120
of God 254, 256
of Redcrosse
  never touched by guilty blood 183
warlike 250
washing
  of guilt 237
handwriting
  accursed
    defacement of 207
hanging
  book
    from Archimago's belt 68
hap 178
  hope of new good 129
hapless
  chance
    Archimago's ability to overcome 123
  joy
    example of 194
happiness 289
  location of
    in Horace's *Satires* 59
  of Redcrosse 83, 84
    after the Triumph of Pride 148
  perfection of 59
  triple
    crown of 236
happy 243, 274
  choice 190–191
  earth 215
  ending 260
  news 236, 296
  star 61, 67
  thrice 235
harbor
  in the heart
    of Una 171
harboring
  virtuous thought 151
hard 287
  means
    forcing Duessa to stay by 187
  to tell
    the contents of Speranza's heart 219
  work 165
hardened
  crest 257
  iron 257
  steel 265
hardiment
  heat of 194

hardness
  of metals 251

of the Dragon's armor 257
   of understanding 221
harlot 123
harm 96, 204, 258
   helpless 180
   of gnats 77
   potential
      fear of 253
   real 186
   satyrs mean Una no 135
   way of 80
harmful
   guile
      of crocodile 154
   pestilence 266
harmony 52
harsh
   judgment
      of Redcrosse 140, 141
   measures 225
   realities
      of the world of time 140
hastening
   of end 268
hastiness
   of heat 78
hasty
   dressing of Redcrosse 84
   force 163
   hand 285
   ruin
      of castle 187
hate 229
   certain 79
hatred
   as a hissing snake
      of Una by Archimago 103, 119
   as hell
      by Charissa for the love of Cupid 227
   in heart of Night 156
   in Redcrosse's heart
      for Una 120
   of God 231
   of pride
      in the antique world 276
   of self
      by senseless man 137
   of the lowly
      by Lucifera 144
   shunning of 231
haughty
   string 250
haunting
   of Hercules
      by furies and fits 258
haven 272

head 263
   cleaving the

   of Sansfoy 107
   of a lady 179
   of Charissa 228
   of Duessa
      covered with Persian mitre 108
   of Errour 60
   of giant 187
   of Orgoglio
      filled with wind 163
   of Redcrosse 77
   of woeful parents
      of Una 215
health 16
   careless of 161
   long 268
   restoration of 225
heaped
   furrow 244
height
   of castle 187
heaping
   of rude rable 276
heaps
   of wealth 145
hear 184
hearers
   cheeks of 278
hearing 68, 110, 162
   of another 228
   of evil 156
   of Una 171
   the art of Despair
      by Redcrosse 200
   wisdom of divine words
      by Redcrosse 220
   with ears
      what Fidessa is telling 121
   words
      of Fradubio 116
heart 25, 49
   arousing of
      for Redcrosse 176
   beastly
      of Sansloy 132
   beneath the surface appearance 141
   blessed with grace 110
   breach in
      of Una 183
   change of
      in Augustine 38
      in Night 156
   constant
      of Una 131
   coordination of
      of Redcrosse with God or Una 152
   cruel
      of Redcrosse 120
   feelings in the
      of Una 171
   good 138
   heroic 145

Index

inner
  failure to percieve i. h. of Redcrosse 124
interior 57
iron arrow in 180
language of
  in Augustine 50
light
  of Una 124
  linking two h. together 96
love as dear to Redcrosse's h. as as life 81
manly
  bewitching of 206
  of Redcrosse 206
melting of manly 77
noble 151
of Arthur 192
of dwarf
  described as being dead within 168
of Eden
  paradox at 276
of Kirkrapine 122
of mankind 251
of Night 156
of problem 288
of Redcrosse 222
  kindling fire in 176
of Speranza 219
of Una 137, 182
  melting of in compassion 120
  swelling of 215
piercing of
  by words of Despair 205
plunged in deep sorrows 180
precedence in
  of Una 174
pricking the
  of Redcrosse 225
purity of 44
raising
  by words of Fidelia 221
Redcrosse's 96
  his attempt to plunge a knife into his own 118
removal of
  from dear loved dame 141
revival of
  of Una's dwarf 168
rousing the
  for another 176
slumbering
  stolen by sweet humors 195
speeches of the 72
stabbing the
  of Una's lion 130
stout heroic 109
surrender of 79
swollen 79, 80
true
  compromised in expression 111
wisdom of the 72
word we speak in the 73
writing on
  with an iron pen 198

hearts 265
  of heroes 250
  of men
    terror wrought in the 251
  of passive men 253
  of weak women 147
heat 111, 146, 160, 260
  hasty 78
  of Dragon 260
  of fire
    of Dragon 266
  of hardiment 194
heathens
  stupid
    of Babylon 217
heaven 78, 141, 171, 216, 234, 237, 256, 275, 276, 289, 295, 296
  blown up to
    fame of Redcrosse 216
  brass-paved way to 146
  bright 154
  brightness of 93
  Cælia thought to come from 214
  Charissa teaches the ready path to 231
  cursing 70
  deconstructable
    of the House of Holinesse 253
  deeds done in 203
  extremity of 257
    Una at the 197
  eye of
    in Una's face 119
  father in 263
  God in 132
  high 235, 248
  higher 275
  hope of 159
  imaginary 215
    vertical ascent to an 216
  kingdom of 144
  light of 186
  looking to
    by Lucifera 144
  looking up to 219
  outside of
    Eden as 275
  potential 228
  power of 260
  Redcrosse's victories from 191
  reflection of 193
  spheres of Jove's 146
  standing will of 251
  way to 235, 246
  wide hollowness under 118
heavenly
  beauty 281
  birth
    of Una 121, 215
  brood 275
  daughter
    of Cælia 227

grace 158, 163
  in Una's face 119
  perfection of 223
  upholding of the righteous man by 184
intentions
  less than 214
learning 220
light
  of fairest virgin 197
mercy
  given to Redcrosse 206
perspective 269
race 214
thought
  of Contemplation 235
throne 235
Una 272
wisdom 136, 183
heavens 188, 194
heavy
  lifting 165
  memory 145
  plight 171
  sprite 224
Hecate 74, 77, 81
heedful
  muse 256
heel
  iron 129
Hegel, Georg Wilhelm Friedrich 222
Heidelberg Catechism 262–263
height
  hands extended in 154
  heaped
    of castle 187
  tedious 235
heir
  apparent 280
  forsaken 285
  of Eden
    Una 280
hell 159
  hatred as
    by Charissa for love of Cupid 227
  man of 200
  messengers of 100, 101
  mouth of 252
hellish
  entrails
    of Dragon 266
  science 114
  smart
    brand of 207
helmet 107
  of Archimago 129
  of Arthur 194, 198
    as pillow 195
  Redcrosse's 124
  unlacing of 258
help 182

cry for
  by Duessa 186
helpless
  harm 180
  Redcrosse 114
helplessness
  of Night
    in light of the triumph of Jove 156
  of Redcrosse 198
  of Una 179
    in the purge of sin from Redcrosse 225
heralds 154
herbs
  hidden power of 103
Hercules 258–259
  burning of 285
Herder, Johann Gottfried 5, 167, 181, 275
heritage
  of Una 280
hermeneutic
  circle 76, 291, 293
    completion of 228
  gulf of reference 94
hermit
  lack of truth in the 69
  male 69
  promise of further adventure 81
hermitage
  lowly 69
  of Archimago 84, 91, 234, 238
hero 45, 61, 147, 151, 231, 245
  Aeneas as 37
  fallen 264
  journey to the other world 169
  knowledge available to 169
  of antiquity 259
  of popular epic 60
  Redcrosse as 99
  skill of 63
  Spenser's Christian 66
  traveling to the underworld 169
heroes
  hearts of 250
  values of 260
heroic
  heart 145
  response 222
  role 233
  status 47, 238
hesitation
  reasons for
    by Sansloy 131
Hesperus 84, 87, 88, 91, 92
  = Hesperus 85
  = Phosphorus 85
  as the evening star 85
  likening of the central stone in Arthur's sheild
    to 179
hidden 195, 266, 286
  arts 100

Index

bodies 189
cause 78, 166
danger 54
dangers 273
face
   of Despair 201
keeping
   the sorrows of Una's heart 180
nature of Duessa 114
power 103
shade 223
warning 248
hide
   tawny 127
hideous
   horror 152
   might
      shunned by Arthur 186
   train
      of the dragon that Lucifera has defeated 144
hiding 145, 175
   ever present danger 111
   face
      in shame 290
   for shame
      Phoebus 132
   heavenly beauty 281
   in a heaped furrow 244
   in Homer 35
   light of heaven 53
   motivations 64
   the humanity of Redcrosse from himself 84
hierarchical
   order 63
   structures 269
hierarchies
   normal
      reversal of 175
hierarchy
   Church
      seen as intermediate in Calvin 25
   normal
      reversal of 121
   of knowledge 109
   of values 64
   social
      of Elizabethan England 167
hierocrat 13
high
   displeasure
      of queen Lucifera 149
   heaven 235, 248
   house
      of Jove 146
   perch 187
   purpose 248
   sitting on
      by Lucifera 144
   time 248
higher
   language of the heart 73

purpose
   of God 138
highest
   Jove 96, 176
   sky 84, 91
highlight
   the magic of poetry 112
highness
   of Redcrosse's disdain 56
hill 249
   steep 234
hills 95
hinge
   steadfast 255
hint
   subtle 69
hissing
   snake
      hatred of Una by Archimago as 103, 119
historical
   periods
      of Ovid 251
   poets 34
   texts 127
history 31, 32
   conditioned event 87
   human 76
   muse of
      Clio as 249
   perception of 34
   progressive role of 150
   sacred 251
      George's place in 247
   solid foundation of 33
hoary
   gray
      Humiltá as 213
hold 265
   taking
      of silver anchor 224
holding
   of scepter
      by Lucifera 144
   onto Una's garment
      by Sansloy 130
hole
   of Avernus 158
holiness 46, 48
   a priori 167
   guaranteed
      Redcrosse's lack of interest in his 69
   houses of 141
   of Redcrosse
      not a model for others to follow 164
   socially destructive 168
hollow
   eyes
      of Despair 201
   glade 253
   howling

of Abessa and Corceca 123
man 53
maw 269
wind 252
hollowness 62
  of mouth
    of Dragon 269
  wide
    under heaven 118
holy
  armor 65, 110
  band 285
  church 1
  city
    of Jerusalem 236
  knots 289
  lady 120
  life 216
  man 68, 236
  righteousness 232
  saints
    robbed of their vestments 122
  scripture 24
  water 265
  ways
    education in 221
home
  marching 154
  of Odysseus 127
  of Redcrosse 83
homebred
  evil 68
Homer 20, 39, 43, 82, 83, 192, 193, 260, 294
  as academic skeptic 21
  as Epicurean 21
  as Stoic 21
  as substitute for the divine 76
  as touchstone of philosophical belief
    in Seneca the Younger 21
  Boötes in 82
  divine 269
  overreliance on
    by pagan thinkers 170
  works
    Iliad, The 19, 34, 156
    Odyssey, The 19, 34, 83, 127, 169
  worldview of 193
honor 162
  defending 195
  fighting for 152
  greatest 151
  worldly 152
honorable
  name 275
honorific
  purple 217
hope 155
  dismayed 130
  of Archimago 77
  unfounded 129
  of heaven 159
  of new good hap 129
  of Redcrosse
    to gain entry into Gloriana's court 105
  of salvation 231
  of the reader 198
  of Una 95, 132
  present 244
hopeful
  readers 287
Horace (Quintus Horatius Flaccus) 232
  Satires 58–59
horizontal 47
  axis
    of man as actor 253
  golden chain 194
  nature
    of the Dragon's wings 252
  orientation
    of golden chain 193
    of ruler 144
  plane
    woods as 142
  reading 12
  reference
    endless chain of 6
  world of time 48
horn
  gate of 75
  magical
    blown by Arthur's squire 184
horned
  feet 134
  fronts 106
horns
  rough 134
horrible
  Dragon 206
  mass 270
  words 77
horrified
  expression 133
horror
  hideous 152
  of bloodshed 152
  of serpent 219
  rustic 134
  stern
    of scared nations 250
horse 129
  of George 257
  spurring of 129
  wooden 37
hospital 231
hostile
  gods 40, 83
  nature 83, 98, 218, 233
    law stands as bulwark against 131
hostility
  of nature 52, 104

of world 83
hosts
  of men
    dismayed by Fidelia 221
hot
  courage 113
  pincers 224
hound 63
  of Orion 127
hour 37
  of death 203
  one loving 125
  unhappy 109
house
  Fradubio not in a 115
  high
    of Jove 146
  misformed 115
  of Acheloüs 260
  of Alcinous 169
  of Corceca 121–124
  of pride 143
  royal 245
    Redcrosse's connection to 121
household
  of a plowman 82
  royal
    of Una 171
House of Despair
  failure of will in the 199–208
House of Holinesse, The 103, 192, 225, 234, 240, 248, 249, 252, 254, 260, 267
  deconstructatble fiction of 219
  gates of 273
  painful correction in 243
  Redcrosse's meeting with Patience in 149
House of Morpheus 71
House of Pride 143, 145, 151, 165, 173
  boundaries in 143–146
  poor performance in the 200
hovering
  above the subject plane 253
howling
  hollow
    of Abessa and Corceca 123
hue
  misseeming 191
huge
  mass 270
  mountains
    moved from their native seat 221
hugeness
  of misfortune 180
human 4, 52, 245
  acts 259
  agents 259
  art 98
  attempt to reach the end of inquiry 58
  being *See human being*
  capacity

to dream 242
community 105
  detours from 176
control 268
divinely 256
epistemology 3
experience 92, 233, 245
  perspectival angle on 296
  univocal τέλος of 159
force 263
frailty 183
imagination 27, 91
imitation 269
inheritance 157
legacy
  of Redcrosse 227
limitations 84
memory 164
mind 98, 167, 193, 218, 296
  statistical approximation in the 155
minds 203
names
  imposition of 87
nature 155
purpose
  of George 260
race 239
rationality
  limits of 155
reason
  calming effects of 105
  control of 188
  Redcrosse as 84
response 192
sacrament
  baptism as 262
shelter 115
will 152, 262, 263
  weakness of 158
human being 62, 67, 76, 84, 181, 233, 246, 262, 266, 267, 270, 272, 275, 276, 293
  at center of the universe 15
  imposition of names as an attribute of 104
  individual mind of a 126
  levels of memory in 72
  literal 238
  potential of 177
  Redcrosse as 145
  role of 104
  sight of a 138
  teleological purpose of 62
  time-bound 203
humanism
  birth of 24
  illusion of 218
  Renaissance 44
humanity 36, 83, 157, 222
  activation of potential of 177
  as concieved by Stoics 20
  as creator of an emergent artifice 66
  bounds of 197

consciousness of 242
location of in Plato 15
loss of 218
of Redcrosse 120, 206
Redcrosse's membership in the class of 113
humankind 295
humble
  obedience
    of satyrs 134
  reverence 284
  service 120
humbleness
  low 109, 145, 277
humility 28, 70
  of Spenser's thoughts 93
Humiltá 213, 235, 273
  description of 213
humors (doctrine of) 195
hundred
  folds
    of the Dragon's tail 251
hunger
  of lion 119
hungry
  rage
    of lion 120
hunt
  goddess of 94
hunting
  fame 140
hurt 60
  power to 186
hurtless
  Una as 136
husband
  power passes to the 228
hydra
  poison of 259
hylomorphism 101

I

ice 64
iconography 30
id
  suppressed 242
idea
  source of
    in Ovid's *Metamorphoses* 251
    the power of Errour's 66
ideal 6
  of beauty
    determination by culture 133
idealism 98
  pagan 259
  Platonic 8
ideas 103
  clear and distinct
    of Descartes 292
identical
  with God
    Redcrosse not 298
identification 31
  of cause and effect 94
  of Redcrosse and Jesus 95
  of things 126
  with God 298
identity 2, 91, 155, 225
  as an *a priori* (a=a) proposition 87
  fixing of 83
  individual
    trumped by love 138
  lack of
    between goodwill and friendship 282
  logic of 176
  metaphysical 218
  of certain names 85
  of nature and language
    in Virgil 75
  of objects 124
  of Redcrosse and Jesus 95
  of silk and silver 282
  of true Saint George 241
  prelapsarian sense of 131
  principle of 17, 238
    in Eden 96
    in Revelations 95
  problem of 92
  proposition of 179
  question of 85, 86
  rules of 96
  seeking
    with oneself (a=a) 126
  sense of
    of Una with herself 139
  statement of 89
  superficial 131
  Una's unified principle of 125
  unspoken
    of Una with herself 137
idiom
  scientific 12
idle
  pomp 166
  stroke 186
  threats 286
idleness
  example of
    Redcrosse not an 146
Idleness
  leader of the Triumph of Pride 146
  shuns manly excerise 146
idolaters
  change into 137
  teaching the truth to 135
  woodland 135

idolatrous
  gods 259

idolatry
  of Una's exterior image 135
Ignaro 188
  face of 190
  nature of 189
ignorance 47, 72
  darkness of 72
  moral 166
  of error 66
  of Spenser 42
  of strewn carcasses
    around the Cave of Despair 201
  of the role of armor
    by Redcrosse 152
  of Una 57
  of Redcrosse's faults 130
ignorant
  of true seat of being
    Redcrosse as 95
  Redcrosse 238
ignoring
  dissimilarity 95
  Errour 61
  of Redcrosse
    by Contemplation 235
    in House of Holinesse 219
Iliad, The. See Homer: works.
ill 267
  deep-rooted 256
  fear of 288
  men 158
  strength to 210
illegitimacy
  in deconstruction 185
  in naming
    of George 175
illegitimate
  manner 146
  position
    of Lucifera 144
illicit
  closure
    of gulf of reference 94
illumination 56
illusion
  of humanism 218
image 24, 240
  exterior
    of Una 135
  glass as
    in Augustine's definition of allegory 71
  integration
    in drama 30
  maker 70
  negative 269
  of a brave knight 30
  of beauty 288
  of Christ 1
  of Despair 206
  of falling 264
  of God 73
    in the divided faculties of mind of mankind 72
  λόγος as 193
  of mankind 105
  of perfect unity 288
  of pride
    Orgoglio as 260
  of raising 264
  of the changing moon 227
  of unity 128
  of womanhood
    in childbirth 227
  renewal of i. to perfection 73
  worshipping of
    of Una 135
images 11
  ekphrasistic
    of ever-blooming flowers 290
imaginary
  gods 259
  heaven 215
    vertical ascent to an 216
  λόγος 179
imagination 10, 42, 169, 172, 175
  a posteriori 219
  as the source of fiction 178
  Augustinian act of 282
  conceived in terms of monstrous shapes 60
  construction through
    of fiction 228
  engendering of Una in
    of the poet 175
  false 101
  fictional domain of 296
  human 27, 91
  imperfect 175, 193
  landscape 61
  of Contemplation 246
  of human being 276
  of poet 270
  of Redcrosse 198
  of Una 171
  poetic 275
  power of 282
imaginative
  fiction 112, 285
    nebulousness of 161–162
    of Spenser 270
  poetic program 271
  poetry 270
  things
    uncertainty of 271
  universe
    of Faery 281
  vision
    of poet 281
imagining
  mind
    alignment of with scientific information 171
imbalance
  in fiction 27

in Redcrosse 48
of human greed 37
of nature 143
permanent 138
imitability
of native virtue 107
imitation 19, 35, 179
by the careful reader 231
direct
of nature 76
human 269
in Augustine 59
of classical models 4
of George
by reader 245
of God
by mankind's reason 149
of heavenly behavior
on earth 227
of lying behavior
of Odysseus' 83
of Redcrosse
discouraged 47
of the Knight of Holinesse 164
of Virgil
by Spenser 75, 76
past as a model for 76
immateriality
of sprites 100
immediacy
Redcrosse's interest in 158
immediate
answer 201
contact
with object 228
decision 92
desire 149
end 235, 244
experience 110, 172
processed by passive intellect 166
gratification 231
human agents 259
mind 218
pleasure 224
present 172
problem
of rescue of Una 132
threat
of Archimago 119
victory 224
imminent
death 267
suicide
or Redcrosse 211
immoral
reality
of Corceca's behavior 234
immorality 199

immortal
book of fame 237
name 250
immortality 21
immunity
of Redcrosse
to the charms of Lucifera 145
imp
of English race 239
of Jove (Cupid) 96, 176 *See also* Cupid.
of Phoebus
Clio as 250
impact
of Frege
on modern philosophy 88
impartial
arbiter 11
decisions
in matters of law 286
imparting
direction 81
impatience
of Sansfoy 106
impatient
eye
of Redcrosse 234
mind
of woman 286
impending
childbirth 227
imperfect
experience
of man 203
expression 254
imagination 175, 193
language 254
memory
of man 203
mind 218
of the substantial individual 181
poet 226
view
of experience 244
imperfection
of George 105
of grammar 88
of information 105
of Redcrosse 175
of superficial disguise 124
implanting
of good
in the mind of man 138
implication 132
moral 84
of words
of the King of Eden 287
importance
of metaphysical struggle 65
of time 282

importune
fate 278

Index

imposition
  of names 87, 104, 155, 178, 241
  of the name of Redcrosse 46
impossibility
  of ontological distintions
    in Plato's work 46
  of recreating fiction 230
  of Una's having access to armor of *Ephesians* 45
imprecision 240 *See also* precision.
impression
  first 274
  of God's good will 134
impressions
  sense 106
imprisonment
  of Redcrosse
    by Orgoglio 278
improvement
  of hostile nature
    in Aristotle 233
improvements
  Augustinian
    to pagan idealism 259
impulse 54
impulsive
  action 60, 61
  decision
    of Dragon 269
inaccessible
  God 181
  metaphysical wholeness
    of the pagan gods 190
  nature 218
  ontological reality 296
  thought
    of God 99
inaccuracy
  of Fradubio's belief 114
inactive
  friendship
    goodwill as 283
inadequacy
  of true love 126
  of Una's mind 126
  of Virgilian position on the static nature of time 37
inappropriateness
  of showing body
    by innocent virgin Una 120
inarticulate
  Redcrosse 191
inborn
  nobility 121
incense 259
incidents
  individual
    joined in memory 121

inclusion
  in set of denoted objects 141

of Redcrosse
  in the class of men 210
incompatibility 92
  of alternatives 53
  of philosophical doctrines 21
incompatible
  positions 93
incomplete
  education
    of Redcrosse 223
  truth 145
incompleteness
  of Una's character 95
inconclusive
  clash of two proud rams 106
inconsistency
  systematic
    in Gödel 88
inconstancy
  in love
    no greater shame to knight than 141
incorporeal
  substance 71
incorrupted
  nature 267
increase 252
increasing
  knowledge
    of the natural universe 222
  Lucifera's crew 145
  tension
    in Una's mind 173
incursion
  into the realm of life 268
indefinite
  future 231
  number
    of associative paths 241
indescribable
  beauty
    of Una 119
index 12
indifference
  callous
    of Redcrosse towards Una 120
  criminal
    of George towards Una 280
  moral 108
    of Night 156
  of judgment
    of life and death matters 79
  of nature
    to the choices human beings make 79
  of Redcrosse
    to moral gradations 199
  passive
    of Redcrosse 147

to fate
  of False Una 79

indifferent
  treatment of details
    by Redcrosse 147
indirection
  by Spenser 168
individual 16, 40, 97, 180, 215, 230
  actor
    action is reserved to the 206
  as location of immediate pleasure 22
  Augustine does not abandon the i. for the realm of
      λόγος 72
  character
    imaginatively created 215
  concern for 66
  condition
    of George 264
  control 138
  control of 233
  decision 240
  epicurean pleasure of 233
  example
    of defeat in battle 187
  existential 182
  experience 233
  fate 79
  George 57, 105, 204
  human being 62, 84
    mind of 126
  identity
    trumped by love 138
  images 28
  incidents
    joined in memory 121
  in relationship with God
    in Tasso 41
  language 73
  limited 190
    bodily integrity of 161–162
  literal 249
  man 21, 95
  mankind 233
  members
    of the species of mankind 298
  men 14
  microscopic 162–163
  mind 79, 188
    understanding of 265
  name
    of George 175
  nature
    of Errour 65
  obligation of the 143
  ontologically existing
    denial of 189
    Elizabeth as 93
  rational temperance of the 190
  reference 113
  salvation of 225
  self 93
  self-sufficiency of the 233
  sense 113
  specific 178
  stability 36
  substance 260
    God-created 225
  substantial 100, 181
  substantial consciousness of 72
  wholeness
    elusiveness of 203
  will 79, 125
  wrath 231
individuals
  cooperation between
    as basis for social compact 181
  created 257
indivisibility
  principle of 117, 126
indivisible
  material 178
  statement of identity 89
indulgences 24
inequality
  in fiction 27
  between man and gods
    in Homer 19
  in reference 94
inevitable
  failings 203
inexorability
  of fantasy life 78
infamy
  act of 108
infecting
  united kingdom
    of Eden 274
infection
  of mind
    with fear 267
inferior
  social position
    of Una's dwarf 168
infernal
  furies
    with chains untied 200
infestation
  by martial troops 250
infinite 98
  being 98
infinitesimal
  calculus 2
inflated
  sin
    of pride 194
inflation
  of Orgoglio
    above the ground 253
influence
  bad
    of evil stars 191
information 54, 55, 58, 70, 227, 241
  better 145

Index

imperfect 105
  in relation to memory 68
  moral 69
  scientific
    alignment of with imagining mind 171
  waiting for 54
  whole 169
inherence 15
inherent
  instability
    of academic system 193
  value 287
    lack of 288
inheritance
  human 157
  of Eden 284
  of Una 290
inimitabilty
  of fiction 76
inimitable
  falsehood 76
  fiction 226
  life
    of Redcrosse 237
initial
  premise
    of being 190
initiation
  of Redcrosse's action 59
injury
  adding insult to
    of Una 204
injustice
  armed 99
  of Despair's work 202
  sense of 263
ink
  black
    of squid 60
inner 6
  beauty
    expression of 120
  eye 36
  glory
    a priori 152
  heart
    failure to percieve 124
  life 136
  meaning
    of allegory 53
    of signs 168
  motivation 246
  puropse 78
  thought 182
  virtue
    communication of 136
innocence
  limits of Redcrosse's 102
  of Deianira 259
  of man

  in the world of time 115
  of Spenser 293
  unitary
    of Redcrosse 102
innocent 99
  feet
    of Una 215
  Redcrosse as 102
  virgin
    Una as 120
inquiry
  end of 94
  in classical philosophy 104
  into nature 91
  rational 179
  scientific 179
  stopping 6
insect 4
insight 36
  into the mind of Redcrosse 148
  lack of
    by Redcrosse 163
    of dwarf 165
insightful
  critic
    recreation of metaphysics by 169
insolence 65
inspecting
  of walls 274
inspection
  of signs 69
instability
  inherent
    of academic system 193
instant 107
  victory 105
instinct 60
  animal 123
    socially destructive 257
  moral
    of Redcrosse 154
  of George 258
  social 16
  warrior
    of Redcrosse 154
Institutes of the Christian Religion. See Calvin, John.
instruction 30, 146, 230, 232
  of readers 127
  of Redcrosse 232
  of satyrs 217
  of sprites 100
  of worship
    fiven by Una 290
instructive
  value 147
    of the Triumph of Pride 151

instrument
  of God's will 135

instrumentality
  of God 2
instruments
  of will 135
  of worldly glory 243
insufficiency
  of Una's mind
    to the task of reforming the opinion of men 135
  of unified knowledge
    on earth 96
insult
  adding to injury
    of Una 204
integration
  into court
    of Gloriana 212
    through prowess 197
  of time
    into the picture of philosophy 259
integrity
  bodily 161–162
    breached in Redcrosse 161
  of virginal body 120
intellect
  active
    uses *a posteriori* reason 166
  as judge of mutable (as opposed to necessary)
    things 41
  comes from God 41
  passive 15, 166
  power of 43
  speculative 40
  trained 234
  well-educated 119
intellectual 46
  activity
    extension of 233
    construction 242
  destruction
    precedes physical destruction 187
  eye
    of Contemplation 234
  form
    of pure reason 87
  universe 89
  virtue
    contemplation as an 233
intelligence 47, 99, 102
  natural 3
  perfect
    in Eden 174
  rational 100
intelligible 19
intension 90
intensity
  lack of
    in goodwill 283

intent 151, 290
  conceiving

below surface 121
  of Una by lion 120
disclosing of
  by Una to Satyrane 136
glorious great 151
good 122
  of Archimago 77
  of Arthur 194
intention 18, 33, 50, 96, 219
  expression of
    weaknesses of Redcrosse in 151
  general 31
    focus of *Letter to Raleigh* 45
  grave 287
  hidden
    of Spenser 168
  interruption of
    of Redcrosse 195
  less than heavenly 214
  of Archimago 77, 125
    not issue when it comes to Redcrosse's action
      77
  of Duessa 158
  of errant knight with errant 116
  of Spenser 130
    on supsension of disbelief 112
  of Virgil 36
  whole 30
interaction
  interpersonal 134
intercession
  by Archimago
    before Redcrosse kills Una 149
  by Fradubio 116
  by Lucifera
    in unritualized battle between Redcrosse and
      Sansjoy 149
  unlikely
    of Duessa 163
intercourse
  of Redcrosse and Fidessa 111
  physical 116
interdependence
  of Cupid's love 229
interdependent
  relations 229
interest
  in Una or her the mission
    of Redcrosse 148
  lack of
    in deeper purpose by Redcrosse 152
    in learning by Redcrosse 158
    of Cælia in Redcrosse 216
  of Archimago
    in fomenting rebellion 124
  of Redcrosse 57
    in adventure 68
  of the egoist 180
  short term 28
interests
  conflicting

Index

problem of 211
interference
  emotional
    by sympathetic Una 223
  in furious fight
    by Lucifera 149
  of fiction 181
  of poetic metaphor 75, 227
  of tradition 233
interfering
  rage 253
  wrath 253
interior 48
  being 219
  heart 57
  of Una 281
  virtue 48
  world
    of Eden 273
interlinked
  relationships
    in the House of Holinesse 219
intermediary
  fiction 245
  lens of reason 287
  logical
    between mind and object 90
intermediate
  period 84
  steps 173
  temperance
    building up of an 149
  time 271
internal
  lesson
    by Zele 213
  location 118
interpersonal
  interaction 134
interpretation 10
  lack of
    in wilderness 165
  moral priority in
    comes from reason 165
  needs drive
    in Friedrich Nietzsche 296
  of meaning 84
  of the death of Hercules 258
  of things available to the sight 166
  of Una 83
interpreter 24
interrupting
  the flow of dialog
    by Redcrosse 196
interruption
  of action
    by Una 211
  of intention
    of Redcrosse 195
  of speech

    of the King of Eden 284–286
intersection
  points of 87
intervention
  cautious
    of Una 211
intimacy
  implied by friendly feeling 283
introspection
  power of 78
intrusion 37–36, 44
  of Augustine
    into classical philosophy 190
  of fiction 91
  of Fradubio 116
  of men
    into balanced nature 142
  of the miraculous
    into the natural order 221
  of vertical truth 48
intuition
  of the reader 145
invasion
  of region 253
inveigling
  of weaker sight 287
invention
  of fiction
    by Spenser 127
  of logic
    by Aristotle 15
inviolability
  of the a=b principle 215
invisible 6
invitation
  to perform miracles 222
invocation 79
  of Hecate 74
  of Homer's Odyssey
    by Senser 127
inward 53
  beauty
    of Una 282
  fire 260
  light 73
  phenomenon
    projected outward by Redcrosse 207
  to the true source 72
  turn 72
    of mind 226
  turn of self
    by Una 136
  view
    of Contemplation 234
Ion (character) 193, 194, 293. *See also* Plato.
  as passive rhapsode 269
ire
  furious 101
  raging
    of Sansjoy 153

rancorous 253
iron 106, 251
  age of
    in Ovid 251
  arrow 180
  hardened 257
  heel 129
  pen 192, 198
  teeth
    of Dragon 251
  whip 225
  wings
    clapping of 264
ironic
  distance
    of Redcrosse from the Triumph of Pride 148
  perspective 218
irony 5, 150
  perspective of 128
  Spenserian 101, 125
  stance of
    offered by Hayden White 127
irreducible
  mind 50
irrefutablity 19
irreligion 63
irrevocability
  of decision in action 55
Isaiah, Book of
  2:4 ("swords into plowshares") 150
Isis 217
Islam 63
iudge
  of life and death 79
ivory 75, 76, 100, 276
  door 75
  gate of 100
  presence of 276

J

jaws
  deep devouring 252
jealousy
  vile 289
Jerusalem 237
  holy city of 236
Jerusalem Delivered. See Tasso, Torquato.
Jerusalem, Temple of 39
Jesus. *See* Christ.
Job, Book of 26
joining
  in memory
    of individual incidents 121
  of errant knight to errant intention 116
  of potential to action 246

  of Una
    with another 138

ontology with epistemology 93
joint
  effort
    of society 295
jollity
  of Arthur 194
  passing the night in 150
  song of 289
Jonson, Ben 30, 167
journey 128, 267
  beginning of
    of Redcrosse 199
  end of
    of George 243, 278, 295
    of Una 117, 272, 279
  errant
    in the wilderness 218
  fair beginnings of
    of Una 183
  forward 122
  of George 246, 266
  of self-realization 246
  of the soul
    in Stoicism 180
  otherworldly
    outside of fiction 170
  to the other world
    by a hero 169
  to the realm of Night
    by Duessa 154–156
  to the underworld
    in Homer 35
  weary
    of Una 281
Jove
  heaven of
    spheres of 146
  highest 96, 176
  high house of 146
  imp of (Cupid) 96 *See also* Cupid.
  lawful 144
  Night is older than 155
  overthrow of Saturn by 157
  rein of 155
  triumph of 156
  wrath of 159
joy 52
  hapless
    example of 194
  in victory 59
  of chivalry 113
  of living speech 180
  of Una 246
  passing the night in 150
  Una's expression of
    at meeting false Redcrosse 127
  wicked 77
joying
  of weak women's hearts 147
joyous
  day 269

Index 405

end 271
lay 275
presence
  of Una 289
shade
  bathe in pleasaunce of 161
sight 124
joys
  fruitless
    of the world 243
judgment 58, 92, 165, 287, 288
  against Despair
    rendered by Redcrosse 202
  artificiality in 90
  correct 135
  harsh
    of Redcrosse 140, 141
  just 285
  legal 202
  moral
    of characters who lack ontological existence 143
    of Redcrosse's actions 142
  negative
    of the soothsayer 152
  new form of 114
  of Redcrosse 150
  other 202
  positive 261
  rendering 202
  reversal of
    in Augustine 39
  superficial
    of Redcrosse 228
judgments
  fine-grained 200
Julius Caesar 36
Juno 259
  golden chair of 146
just
  accusation
    of concupiscence 259
  judgment 285
justice 47, 66, 221, 288, 294
  administration of 99
  as bond of men in states
    according to Aristotle 99
  equitable 138
  force over 286
  growth of 207
  in Redcrosse's defeat of Sansfoy 105–107
  matters of 286
  need for
    speech of Redcrosse on the 201
  of the peace 286
  principle of order in political society
    according to Aristotle 99
  root of 202
  separation of mankind from 99
  skewed sense of
    of Redcrosse 204

Stoic social 180
surface of 202
teaching of 202
the bond of men in states 47
true
  subornation of 288
justification
  of violence
    in Virgil's *Aeneid* 63
just, the 40

K

Kant, Immanuel 5, 85, 86, 218
Kaske, Carol 261
  on levels of allegory 27–29
keeping
  hidden
    the sorrows of Una's heart 180
Kellogg, Robert 1, 46, 291
Kermode, Frank 293–294
kernel 6
key
  to exercising free will 190
  to healing breaches in the limited individual 190
  to understanding 266
keys 190
kids
  wanton 134
kill
  at once 252
killed 56
killing 63
  of Dragon 273, 288
    by George 269
  of Errour 66, 298
  of Redcrosse
    Sansloy's denial of his 136
  ofRedcrosse's dreadful passion 111
  of Rodomonte 230
  the body
    of the monster 187
  with words
    by Fidelia 221
kind
  speech 219
  sundry 160
kindling
  fire 96
    in Redcrosse's heart 176
  of love 113
  flames 259
kindness
  of Lucifera's counselors
    to Duessa 146
  of strangers 174

kinds 70
  of literature 6

king 30
  of animals 121
    lion as 132
  of beasts
    lion as 137
  of men 121
  pagan 279
King
  of Eden 44, 45, 122
kingdom 284, 289, 295
  forwasted 248
  Lucifera's
    upheld by bad counsel 144
  native 290
  of Eden 67, 79, 228
  of God 109
  of heaven 144
  of Una 272, 275, 284
  repairing the
    of Una's parents 248
  rightful 144
    of Lucifera 149
  united
    of Eden 274
  yielding of 280
Kingdom of Eden 57, 92, 138, 273, 277, 295
  as unified 285
  legitimate ruler of 274
kingdoms
  rulership of 144
King of Eden 273, 276, 277, 280, 284
  arguments of 288
  celebration by 284
  description of
    as Emperor of the West 285
  duty of 286
  speech of 284
  throws out reason 288
  words of 279
kings 166
  Saxon 245
Kirkrapine 122–123
  heart of 122
kissing 78
  of Fidessa 116
  Una's weary feet 120
knee
  backward bent
    of satyrs 134, 217
  bended 217
  lowly 154
knife 118
  pagan 136
  proffered
    by Despair 206
  rusty 206, 244
    in the Cave of Despair 201
  of Despair 236
  of rancor 148
  Una snatchers away the 206

knight 56, 61, 104, 109, 120, 128, 153, 154, 220, 270, 297
  active 118
  adventerous 68
  beloved
    of Una 117, 191, 224
  brave
    Arthur as 224
  charmed armor of 258
  chosen
    of Una 199
  dear 248
  divorce from
    by Una 118
  doughty 279
  elfin 115, 227, 239
    element of pride in 148
  encountered by Fradubio 114
  errant 216
    forward motion of 116
  faery 151
  faint hearted 206
  faithful 223, 271
  gentle 48, 278, 288
  good 176
  hand of
    holds knife in Cave of Despair 201
  loved
    of Una 282
  love of
    by Una 125
  misfeigning of Una's true 129
  new 264
  no greater shame to 141
  of the Redcrosse 174
  protector 140
  Redcrosse 196
  redoubted 80
  soul-diseased 224
  stoutest 136
  strange
    Redcrosse as 145
  stranger 194
  unproved 183
  victorious 191
  wandering 122
  worldly 235
  young 140
    Fradubio as 113
    mistakes of 191
knighthood 69
  shame of 125
  unearned
    Redcrosse's interest in his 69
knightly
  view 144
Knight of Holinesse 44, 69, 116, 140, 150, 164, 200

knights 44, 136, 237
  errant 113

of noble name 237
on earth
  renown above 249
knitting 285
knocking
  of breast
    by Archimago 68
knots
  holy 289
knowers
  delusion of 142
  of the truth
    in a sea of seekers 194
knowledge 23, 33, 54, 89, 158, 226
  active intellect as 72
  aesthetic 189
  ancient 2
  as bringing forth unconscious things to consciousness 74
  as product of relational proposition a = b 87
  certainty of 21
  claim to
    by Ignaro 189
    by Socrates 189
  complete 97
    lack of 264
  contained in a=b statements 87
  contemplative 72
  conveyance of 73
  expansion of 88
  extension of 86, 87
    in a=b propositions 85
  forgetting previous
    by Una 125
  fuller
    of events 285
  hierarchy of 109
  higher
    obtained through fiction 18
  in Augustine 22
    thought formed by the thing we have k. of 73
  inwardly spoken 73
  lack of 172, 243
    by Redcrosse and Una 67
    of deeper purpose by Redcrosse 152
    of law 131
    of wisdom in women's wit by Satyrane 136
  limited
    of Duessa 187
  medieval 2
  metaphysical 55, 104, 170
  new 169
  not image of God 74
  of Archimago
    greater than Una's 125
  of Augustine
    of the Creator's prelinguistic ontology 289
  of Cælia 214
    Redcrosse's lack of 216
  of degrees
    of good 213
  of Duessa
    in Lucifera's court 145
    limits of 278
  of George 262
  of good and evil 267, 268
  of heroes 169
  of insufficiency
    of unity on earth 96
  of nature 222
  of ontology 170
  of participation
    in the sacred pageant 296
  of reader 277
  of rightness 148
  of rude shepherd poets 111
  of salvation
    of Redcrosse 209
  of Sansloy
    of Archimago 129
  of Socrates 292
  of the body 72
  of the careful reader
    of difference between Una's perception and reality 127
  of the educated 193
  of the reader 143
  of the ways of the holy 221
  of things 72
    in Augustine 73
  of truth 69
  of Una
    by Humiltá 213
  of universe 159
    increasing 222
  pagan 150
  partial 267
  positive
    lack of 212
  proper 86
  rational 22, 267
  reversal of
    poles of normal 175
  separateness in 98
  strucutured in terms of a=b 131
  superior 170
    of Despair 205
  that things are not what they appear to be 125
  true 87
  unified
    of Una 129
  withholding
    by Spenser 145
Kripke, Saul 89–90, 94
  symmetry of 94

L

labor
  long 140
  of Archimago 101
  to expression

by Zele 213
labors
   of Hercules 258
labyrinth 53
lack
   of balance
      in Spenser's poem 142
   of control
      by Ion 193
   of education 194
   of eyes 60
   of faith
      denoted in the name of Sansfoy 106
   of form 115
   of fortune
      of Corceca and Abessa 123
   of individual substance 260
   of insight
      by Redcrosse 163
   of knowledge 172, 243
   of ontology
      in deconstruction 185
   of threat
      from Cælia 214
   of wholeness 188, 212
lacked
   Lord 124
lacking
   of ontological reality
      of Errour 66
   of rightful claim 144
ladder
   social
      of Gloriana's court 166
Ladder of Ambition 149, 155
ladies
   beautiful 145
lady 137, 175
   fairness of 114
   head of a 179
   holy 120
   mild
      Una as 204
   sake of 153
lagging
   of moistened wings 256
lair
   of Archimago 81
lake 103
   of limbo 112
lament 169
   of fate
      by Una 180
lamenting
   cry
      of Abessa and Corceca lamenting 123
   luckless state
      of George 278
lamp 84, 91
   of Phoebus 93

shining
   of bliss 124
land 252
   alien
      of time 199
   another 285
   drowning of the 256
landing
   of Una 272
landscape
   imaginative 61
   moral 61
   of the Cave of Despair 201
language 75
   Augustine's thought on 71
   changing the pagan relationship between ontology and
      in Spenser 76
   choice in use of language
      Virgil's 75
   expectation that our words mean what they say 5
   expression of natural object in 76
   imperfect 254
   in Aristotle 73
   individual 73
   interpersonal interaction not contained in 134
   metaphorical nature of
      of human 194
   modern philosophy of 85
   natural 90
   of heart
      in Augustine 50
   of Odysseus 169
   of perfection
      in Virgil 75
   perspectives on 50
   private 50, 51, 254, 292
      Wittgenstein's critique of 50
   rational 192
   Redcrosse knight's naïveté about 56
   solid foundation of 50
   stability 8
   subversion of 5
   system 194
   unified
      of God's ontology 275
languages
   of Greek and Latin 275
languishing
   in dungeon 198
languor 79
   captive 183
larger
   spright
      of Fidelia 221
   whole 250
world
   in the thought of Augustine 189

last 165

men 222
late
  classical world 170
  swelling of luxurious pomp 276
lateness
  of Una's troubles 128
Latin 73, 275
laughter
  of nature
    at Arthur 194
  suppression of 18
launching
  at enemies
    of Redcrosse 152
laurel
  boughs 274
lavishness
  of lovers 109
law 47, 133, 286
  advance in 135
  lack of
    in Lucifera's government of her realm 144
  lack of knowledge of 131
  matter of 286
  men without 290
  natural 155
  of Gloriana's court 131
  respect for
    Sansloy's lack of 135
  sacred
    of arms 152
  separation of mankind from 99
lawful
  Jove 144
lawlessness
  of victor's (Sasnloy) will 130
lay 195
  joyous 275
laying
  aside
    horror 134
  of blame 278, 288
  stole aside 119, 122
lazy
  Dragon 251, 254
  masters 165, 166
  Una's dwarf seems 165
leach
  Patience as 224
leader
  of Triumph of Pride 146
leadership 210
  of Jove 160
leaf
  of aspen
    trembling like a 206
league 285
leap
  of faith 76

leaping
  lightly 186
  like wanton kids 134
learned
  approach to experience 160
  leech 159
  men and women 158
  value
    of patience 254
learning 38, 72, 97
  Augustinian 256
  from experience 213
  from mistakes 191, 212
  heavenly 220
  interest in
    lack of by Redcrosse 158
  lack of
    in Redcrosse 67
  lessons 199
    by Redcrosse 232
  of George 263
  of poet 62
  of Redcrosse 198
  public display of 194
  Redcrosse not 142
  that not all choices are equal
    by Una 160
  that people do not always hear words as they are spoken
    by Una 137
  the truth 145
  things we already know
    by bringing them into consciousness 74
  to frame mortal life 232
  to read Duessa
    by Fradubio 112
  vicarious 198
  way of Patience, the 149
leaves
  green vine 146, 160
  narrow 277
  spreading of 110
  trembling 160
leaving 125
  Eden 249
  of arms 258
  of Una
    by Redcrosse 152, 172
Lechery 147
led
  by Duessa
    into the House of Pride 151
  by evil 148
leech
  learned 159
left
  wing
    of Dragon 255

leg
  of Orgoglio

brutally chopped off 187
legacy
　human
　　of Redcrosse 227
　partial 157
legal
　judgment 202
legion
　of sprites 100
legitimate
　ruler
　　of the Kingdom of Eden 274
Leibniz, Gottfried 2, 26, 89
Lelex 260
lengthening 235
　of distance between Redcrosse's end and Redcrosse himself
　　as the goal of Archimago 102
　of experience 236
　of middle space 253
　of time
　　between beginning and end of Redcrosse's actions 158
　　in narrative 173
lens
　distorting 43
　of Enlightenment 280
　of reason 12, 287
lessening
　the role of the individual 67
lesser
　lights 179
　man 265
　minds 270
　others 233
lesson 67, 238
　internalizing
　　by Zele 213
　in logic of definition 71
　of the day's example 192
　of the extermity of time 136
　that not every creature Una meets can protect her 137
　the reader's learning of 68
lessons 147
　learning 199
　　by Redcrosse 232
　of outward nature 162
　poet's learning 62
　provided by art 147
letter 40, 87
　of Paul 45
letters
　of Aeneas' name 39
　message of Duessa written in 284
Letter to Raleigh 30–47, 57, 80, 83, 166

letting

down
　of haughty string 250
level
　beyond comprehension
　　of Duessa 151
　deeper 278
　　of existence 152
　literal 93
　　of allegory 10, 11, 295
　logical 172
　of consciousness 74
　of rational discourse 183
　playing field 278
　typological 93
levels 83
　allegorical 8, 93
　of human memory 72
　of spiritual existence 28
Levin, Richard A. 153
lewd
　lust 137
lex talionis 202–204
libation
　bowl 259
liberal
　arts 107
liberated
　will
　　of Foucault 219
liberty
　curbing of 194
libidinous
　Redcrosse 229
library 217
license 202
lie 76, 124
　of Archimago
　　effectiveness of 125
　of False Una 79
lies 83
　Odysseus as a forger of 36, 127
life 18, 64, 79, 173, 221, 268 *See also* living.
　breathing forth
　　of Dragon 270
　comes between birth and death 261
　comfort in 263
　diurnal progress of 179
　endless
　　Jove's prevention of 159
　end of 204, 240, 244
　　Despair on 202
　　in individual self-sufficiency 233
　enemy of
　　fretting grief the 148
　fantasy 78
　flitted 169
　focus on
　　by poet 267
　God of Una's 120
　holy 216

Index

inimitable
  of Redcrosse 237
inner
  in silence 136
limited 268
  amplification of 268
  by the Almighty 202
  expansion of 268
looser
  of Arthur 194
lord of 70
mortal 232
  loathing of 223
of men 147
  that had gone astray 166
of mind 172
of soldier 59
ontological 179
ordinary 240
pagan
  as evil 64
patron of
  of Redcrosse 197
preservation of 268
realm of 268
spiritual 261
subordinated 63
tainted 204
teleological purpose of human 62
this 171
time-bound 171
unspotted 212
weary of 261
well of
  of Una 207
whole of 107
lifelessness
  stale
    of Cave of Despair 200
lifelike 77
lifetime
  of continuing education 59
lifting
  from the ground
    of George 254
  heavy 165
  of load 270
light 54, 124, 224, 263
  armor 56
  courser 131
  creature of 122
  from far 82
  heart
    of Una 124
  heavenly
    of fairest virgin 197
  inward 73
  Lord of 70
love
  of Redcrosse for Una 196
of heaven 53, 186

of reason 72
of the morning star 281
of virtue 223
of wisdom 71
light-foot
  squire 187
lightly
  blame
    of dear loved dame 141
  leaping 186
lightness
  in love
    no greater shame to knight than 141
  of gentle dame 101
lightning
  brand
    of the Almighty 186
lights
  lesser 179
like
  case 243
likeness 36, 101
  in *Timaeus* 19
  of bronze
    to steel 251
  of Charissa
    to Fidessa 228
  of Dragon's scales
    to wings of an eagle 251
  of Dragon's wings
    to sails 252
  of Duessa
    to a fair lady 114
  of George
    to an eagle 264
  of Humiltá
    to Archimago 213
    to Malvenu 143
  of light to darkness
    in Redcrosse's armor 56
  of Lucifera
    to Mutabilitie 146
  of poet
    to lion's reaction to Una's beauty 120
  of Redcrosse
    to a trembling aspen leaf 206
  of right to wrong 147
  of Sansfoy and Errour 150
  of sound 73
  of wisdom
    in women's wit 136
  ontological
    of Una 78
  principle of 238
  to eagle's eye
    of Contemplation's eye 234
  to God 74
lily
  hands 120

  white

garment of Una 281
limbo
  lake of 112
limbs
  dainty
    of Gloriana 195
  tired 216
limit 98
  of bodily integrity
    of individual 161–162
  of life
    by the Almighty 202
  of logical perfection 89
  of poet 62
  of reason 22
  of Redcrosse's innocence 102
  of understanding
    of Una 248
limitation 102
  human 84
  of knowledge
    of the sources of moral truth 157
  of rational power 67
  of reason
    in Augustine 242
  of the perspective of science 241
  of vision
    of Redcrosse 154
limited
  body 262
  Dragon 262
  experience
    of Redcrosse with deadly steel 128
  individual 190
  life
    amplification of 268
  mind 94, 97, 98, 193, 203, 212
    of created individuals 257
  part 295
  perspective
    of George 295
  reason 97, 167, 256, 296
  resources
    of active man 261
  term
    of life 202
  words 194
limits
  of animal being 203
  of body 261
  of human rationality 155
  of modern critical methods 161
  of power
    Una's realization of 135
line
  of succession 284
lineage
  of George 245

linear
  readers
    of *The Faerie Queene* 145
  reading 8
    of narrative 214
lingering
  of logical paradox 172
linguistic
  flux
    primal chaos beneath 240
linguistics 89
link
  of love
    between Una and Redcrosse 138
linked
  arms 219
  effort 295
  in holy band 285
  virtues 192
linking
  of Charissa
    with lovely fere 219
  of two hearts together 96
  of Una
    and Redcrosse 160
    to Arthur 194
    with Archimago 128
lion
  as king of beasts 137
  claws of
    rescue of Una likened to being snatched from the 132
  fierce 257
  likeness of Christ to 225
  Redcrosse as Una's 120
  simile of 225
    in canto i 59, 62
  strength of 130
lion (attendant to Una) 119–120, 121, 122, 128, 130
  changes his look 134
  forgets his furious force when he sees Una's beauty 121
  hungry 119
  meaning of Una's
    Archimago questions Una about the 128
  reliance on pity of
    for Una 132
  response of
    to Una's beauty 132
  tears open the door to the House of Corceca 122
lips 78
liquid
  air 101
listening 143, 174
  for echoes 142, 199
    of experience 174
  of Una
    to the speeches of Despair 206
  required as part of speech act 71

Index

to others 191
to reason 3
to the whole
   of experience 153
lists
  equal 149
  round 129
literal
  as domain of substantial conscious 175
  body
    Rinaldo as 41
  earth 133
  events
    fragmented in allegory 27
  George 175
    Una's rejection of 124
  human being 84, 238
  individual 249
  level
    of allegory 10, 11, 295
    of Elizabeth 93
  man 295
  meaning 6
  name 83, 175, 227
    of George 241, 244
  narrative 33
  perspective of science 241
  picture
    of Corceca 121
  plane
    of allegory 247
    of existence 246
  reading
    of Errour by Redcrosse 66
  reality 61
    ontological foundation in 212
  self 83
  world 212, 241, 261
    orientation of the reader towards the 175
  world of time 282
literary
  criticism
    golden chain in 192
  critics 31, 241
  motif 170
literature 3, 31
  modern approach to 293
  of allegory 179
  of romance 169–170
  secular 27
  true foundations of 169
little
  space 223
  wide
    Una stands on a hill a 249
live
  meriting to 202
living 136, 172, 285 *See also* life.
  being 180, 268
  flesh 144
  in baleful darkness 191

love of a good woman makes life worth 204
man 69, 197
men 53
speech 180
well 115
wight 235
load
  lifting of 270
  rebalancing of 290
loath
  was the other 128
loathing
  ear 191
  of mortal life
    by Redcrosse 223
loathsomeness
  of frogs and toads 60
location
  definite
    lack of 275
  external 119
  internal 119
  of armor 46
  of authority
    in discourse with others 215
  of compassion 119
  of Eden
    in doubt 289
  of Forms in the universe 15
  of reasons 118
  of truth 84
    relative 66
  of Una
    by dwarf 167
  of virtue 99
  stories without 43
  uncertain
    of Eden 274
lock 185
locked
  fast 213
locking
  of double gates of sleep 76
locks
  flaming 281
  grisely
    of Despair 201
lodging 232
lofty
  steed
    alighting from by Arthur 195
logic 45, 72, 88
  a posteriori 174
  as partial
    in modern criticism 31
  breach in 72
  cause and effect 33
  consistency 9
  deployment of 175
  formal 88

invention of
  by Aristotle 15
limited perfection of 89
of definition
  in Augustine 71
of enigma 72
of identity 176
of poet 175
of Redcrosse 203
of Saussure's irrational grammar 89
ontological 18
paradoxes in 172
perfect 89
  breaks down 88
premises 22
purpose of 174
specific difference 15
terms 77
logical
  intermediary
    between mind and object 90
  level 172
logocentric
  sphere
    of fiction 282
logocentrism 170
  unified 71
λόγος 21, 22, 23, 43, 79, 97, 214, 215, 222, 233, 240, 242, 255
  as fiction 180
  as source of referential stability 89
  as the image of God in man 193
  autotelic 9
  doctrine of 181
  imaginary 179
  in Augustine 72
  in Derrida 6
  mythical 89
  non-existence of 240
  potentially fictional 189
  required for cooperative social action 181
  stability of 92
Λόγος
  inaccessible
    of God 193
long
  health 268
  labor 140
  process 226
  voyage 244, 290
longing
  for in absence 283
Longinus 4
look
  change in the
    of lion 134
looking
  around 141
  at herself
    by Lucifera 144
  at Ignaro's face 190
  at the ground
    by George 246
  backwards
    true love has no power to 126
  beneath the surface 126
  deeper 154
  directly
    as the sun 256
  for purpose 178
  for Redcrosse 167
  for wisdom 147
  lovely
    by Sansloy 131
  on the action of Arthur
    Una's position of 188
  to heaven
    by Lucifera 144
  up to heaven
    to heaven 219
looks
  change of
    by satyrs 134
  lowly cast
    of Humiltá 213
  manly
    of Redcrosse 191
  resistance to Sansloy's
    by Una 131
loose
  loves 243
looseness
  on grassy ground 161–162
  physical
    of Fidessa 130
loosening
  of bands of Errour 56
  of social attachments 66
looser
  life
    of Arthur 194
  make 162
  with body
    Duessa as 298
lord 274
  lacked 124
  lion as 120
  noble 120
  of the field 131
Lord 48
  Archimago speaks reproachful shame of 70
lore
  sacred 212
Lorris, Guillaume de 146. *See also* Roman de la Rose.
lose 58
losing
  control
    of individual mind 79

direction
  by Redcrosse 148
  fights at once 202
  of old foe 110
loss 157, 297
  greater 173
  of humanity 218
  of Redcrosse
    Una considers the 172
lost 53
lot
  of human beings 58
loud 162, 274
  call
    of Duessa for Sansjoy 153
  cry
    of the Dragon 255
love 35, 78, 80, 96, 101, 112, 138, 147, 177, 283, 290
  as a quest for satisfaction of physical desire 140
  as dear as life 81
  assumption of
    by Una 172
  as binding force
    in the world of time 174
  beginning of 283
  blind
    of Cupid 138
  breach of 183, 287
  choice of
    of Redcrosse 147, 153
  chosen
    Fidessa as Redcrosse's 195
  conception of
    superficial by Redcrosse for Fidessa 121
  confusion by having fallen in
    of Una 173
  control of 138
  craving of
    by Sir Burbon 297
  declaration of
    by Una 175
  Dido dies for 38
  equality in
    lack of 140
  experience of
    of Arthur 194
  expression of 182
  falling in 79, 138
    with Duessa 151
  false 126
  fawning 80
  fire of 113, 173
  for another 285, 199
  goddess of 94
  greater 173
  hoped for 79
  in Aristotle 282–284
  inconstancy in
    no greater shame to knight than 141

lack of
  in the heart of Night 156
  of Redcrosse for Una 196
lightness in
  no greater shame to knight than 141
link of
  between Una and Redcrosse 138
loose 243
New Testament doctrine of 202
not enough to guarantee success in endeavor 126
of a good woman makes life worth living 204
of Cupid 12, 227, 229
of False Una
  for another 101
of fellow human beings
  according to universal reason 180
of Fradubio
  for Frælissa 113
of gain 251
of God 12
of lady 196
of Redcrosse
  for Fidessa 184
  for Una spoken of by Archimago 125
of self 80
  by Lucifera 144
of steadfast truth
  for the righteous man 184
of Una 80, 127, 285
  for Redcrosse 125, 174, 184
  making trial of 140
one another 137
origins of
  of False Una for Redcrosse 79
overwhelmed by
  Una's mind as 125
power of
  assuaging 174
problem of
  as a guide to experience 126
profession of
  by False Una 78, 82
  to Fidessa 163
pursuit of 197
question of Redcrosse's 197
refusal of deity for
  by Odysseus 122
return of
  by Redcrosse to Una 176
seeking
  of Arthur 198
separation from 137
song of 289
true 125, 126, 174
  has no power to look backward 126
  inadequacy of 126
  often sown but seldom grows of ground 195
  of Una fror Redcrosse 168
  Una's 125
Una in 96, 126, 130, 227
  profession of 120
unhappy 177

unredeemed 177
violent 121
wanton
  of false Fidessa 168
  world governed by 174
loved
  dame
    beware of change of 141
  knight
    of Una 282
lovely
  fere
    Charissa linked to 219
  looking 131
  wise
    virtues linked in 192
  words
    as recompense for long suffering 125
lover 282, 290
lovers
  lavishness of Duessa's 109
  pair of 111
loves
  distinct 198
  diversly discoursing of 198
  separate 198
  wanton
    of Fidessa 173, 174
loving
  hour 125
low
  bowed 284
  humbleness 145, 277
  humbless 109
  prostration 274
  shepherd 245
lower
  appetite 109
    of individual epicurean pleasure 233
  faculty of thought 74
lowering
  of vision 269
lowest
  form
    of animal behavior 148
  ground
    castles undermined from the 187
  things 38
lowly 68
  hatred of the
    by Lucifera 144
  hermitage 69
  knee 154
  looks
    of Humiltá 213
  sitting 277
loyal
  love
    of weak women 147

loyalty
  betrayed 287
  making seen of
    of Redcrosse 154
  of Una 147
    light misdeeming of 141
Lucian 170
Lucifer 92, 179
  as Phosphorus
    in Vives' *Commentary on De trinitate* 92
Lucifera 148, 155, 165, 212, 252, 254
  called to action 146
  counselors of 145
  demands of 149
  equal balance of 150
  erasure by
    of balance towards good 152
  false 154
  falsifying 154
  intercession of
    in unritualized battle between Redcrosse and Sansjoy 149
  interference in furious fight 149
  likeness of Mutabilitie to 146
  palace
    described 144
    Redcrosse's rejection of 146
  stops Redcrosse from committing sin 191
  submission to
    by Redcrosse 152, 163
luck 278
  guided by God 278
luckless
  conflict
    with Orgoglio 173
  maid 135
  state 278
lucky
  maid 135
Lucretius, Titus Lucretius Carus 20
Luke, Book of
  6:41-42 220
lust 47, 77, 99
  for power 276
  lewd 137
  overwhelmed by 131
  Sansloy's reaction to Una's beauty characterized by 132
  sense of 130
  to rule
    in Friedrich Nietzsche 296
lustful
  eye
    of Sansloy 132
Luther, Martin 2, 24–25, 28, 94, 170
  allegory proscribed by 24
luxurious
  pomp 276

Index 417

lying 62, 187, 286
  by Duessa
    to Sansjoy 150
  Odysseus 83
  of Duessa 153
  under a shady tree
    by Redcrosse 160
  with Duessa 288

M

Machiavelli, Niccolò 294
  rule based on rage and force in 64
  separation of good from political will in 43
machine
  indifferent
    Redcrosse as 199
macrocosmic
  universe 238
  world 162–163
mad
  fury 137
made
  by God 73
  secrets of the world
    seen by Night 155
madness 38
  half 123
Maecenas (Gaius Cilnius Maecenas) 58
magic 129, 157
  armor 45–48, 107
  books 70
  making trial of Archimago's 104
  of Duessa 112
    turns Fradubio into a tree 112
  of the poet 112
  science as 103
  secret external magic
    in Redcrosse's shield and arms 151
  spell 103
  study of
    by Duessa 278
magical
  armor 102
    of Una 243
  art
    of Archimago 178
  charm 106
  horn
    blown by Arthur's squire 184
  science
    of Archimago 218
  shield
    of Arthur 186
    of Una 297
  spell
    of Duessa 276
magician
  Archimago as 101, 163
  Protean 67

maid
  chaste 116
  forlorn 130
  luckless lucky 135
  pensive
    Una as 136
  royal 138, 195, 244
    Gloriana as 296
  silly 150
maidens
  flurry of 275
main
  monstrous 186
mainland
  rift 270
majesty
  divine 235
make
  looser 162
maker 101
male 210
  hermit 69
  messenger 286
  order
    of society 209
  society 209
males
  warrior 209
malice 123
  void of
    Archimago's appearance as 68
malicious
  slight 187
  woman 195
Maluenu 143
  erection of false distinctions by 143
  open gate of 151
man 4, 181, 228, 261, 265 *See also* men.
  active 81, 261
  aged 236
  bold 70
  control of
    reason as being under 4
  decentering of
    in Du Bartas' poem 255
  definition of
    as the rational animal 183
  dismayed 284
  educated
    in the world of time 298
  fault of one 267
  foolish
    Redcrosse as 202
    swallowed by crocodile 154
  general 178
  good 113
    by access to native virtue 142
  goodliest 45
  holy 68, 236
  individual 21, 95

innocence of no 115
in time 203
lesser 265
literal 295
living 197
λόγος as the image of God in 193
mind of 138, 142
   impact of words on 206
new 221, 264
of action
   Redcrosse as 77
of God 250
of hell 200
old 129
   Ignaro as 189
passive
   Geoege as 261
powerful 150
rational 192
   Arthur as 194
Redcrosse as 112, 148, 226
righteous 184
Sansfoy's lack of care for 105
senseless 137
skill of 210
soul of 108
teaching of
   by Fidelia 221
thrice happy 235
uneducated
   George as 295
virtuous 35
   Redcrosse as 99
warier 274
weak 129
wise
   Ignaro as 189
   Socrates as 193
word of 73
wounding of the
   who wields the arms of Redcrosse 151
wretched
   Redcrosse as 204
manhood
   awakening
     of Redcrosse 111
   Redcrosse's lack of knowledge of his 115
Manichean 157
mankind 46, 52, 155, 238, 251, 267
   beats swords into plowshares 150
   behavior of 298
   dispersal of 251
   education of 224
   general example for all
     defeat of Orgoglio as 187
   heart of 251
   hope of salvation of 231
   identity of
     trumped by love 138
   individual 233
   lack of access by
     to Eden by 175

limited reason of 256
mind of 97
permanent access to good
   in nature 142
prupose of 91
redefinition of 105
science of 4
scolding of
   by Cælia 216
steps of
   guided backward and forward by God 62
whole of 97
worst ends of 105
manly
   excerise
     shunned by Idleness 146
   force 188
   heart
     bewitching of 206
   look
     of Redcrosse 191
   powers
     loss of 205
man-made
   habits 3
manner
   appropriateness of 65
   illegitimate 146
   random 67
   scientific 265
manners
   of knights 167
man-tree 113
maple 53
marble
   altar 259
marching
   home 154
Marcuse, Herbert 189
margins 44
   of experience 223
mariner
   faithful 127
   simile of the 126–127
mark 1, 48, 107
   making one's 235
   of misaimed sight
     of Orgoglio 186
Marks, Herbert 239–242, 275
marriage 120, 167
   conclusion of 289
   of George
     to Una 244
   of Heaven and earth 289
   vowed 279
marring
   of manly looks
     of Redcrosse 191
martial
   fury 250

Index 419

troops 250
marveling 264
Marx, Karl 222
mask 35
masking 241, 293
  the truth 195
  truth
    from modern readers 2
mass
  horrible 270
  huge 270
  monstrous 187
  self-jarring 256
master 166, 171, 265
  of artifice 184
  of beast
    Satyrane as 136
  of the field
    Arthur as 188
  of worldly science
    Archimago as 102
masterless
  armor
    of Redcrosse 168
masters
  lazy 165, 166
  social 165
mastery
  by men
    of scientific principles 179
  of desire
    by will 137
  of fortune
    by Arthur 188
    lack of 188
  of mishaps
    by discrete advice 180
mastiff 63
matched
  equally
    enemies 138
    opponents 138
matching
  in royal rich array 146
material
  being 98
  indivisible 178
mathematics 37
matter 97
  of law 286
  of time
    integration of into philosophy 259
  subject 86
matters
  of justice 286
Matthew, Book of
  7:3–5 220
  25:14-30 265

maw
  darksome 269
  hollow 269
maximum
  freedom 55
May
  flower in 282
meaning 8, 11
  allegorical 10
  ambiguous 121
  amplification of 286
  artificially-created 240
  at risk 240
  colloquial 248
  definite 31
  differences of 50
  different
    of words 196
  disseverance of unified
    by Tasso 40
  dual
    of words 203
  emergent 55
  epistemological 46
  figural 6
  general 31–32
  given by sun
    in Plato 92
  hermeneutic circle of 76
  hidden 35
  in Frege 85
  inner 6
    of signs 168
  interpreted 84
  in the world of time 96
  literal 6, 10
  more than one 96, 105
  of reading
    attendant on temporal process 175
  of Una's lion 128
  of words 67, 113
  one dimensional 189
  openness of
    reader's awareness of 55
  other 121
  outer 6
  saying one thing while m. another 103
  scientific 5
  self-contained 27
  spiritual 254
  spoken 228
  switch
    from ontological to epistemological reading 46–47
  two dimensional 189
  whole 5
  worldly 6
meaningless 254
  poetic ornament 12

means
- hard
  - forcing Duessa to stay by 187
  - of Archimago 119
  - of blind Cupid's darts
    - God's operation through 139
- of reason
  - to explain itself to itself 86

measure
- equal
  - in law 286
- unequal
  - reason as a matter of weighing things of 150

measurement
- by shadow 250

measures
- harsh but necessary 225

measuring 266
- response
  - to ambiguous words 196

mechanism
- of fiction 275

mediated
- view
  - of nature 76

mediation
- between object and name 86

medical
- arts 16

medicine
- of Patience 224

medieval
- allegory 8
- claims
  - to knowledge 2
- philosophers 3
- scholasticism 24
- world 97
- writers
  - ignorant of skepticism 8

meditating
- by Redcrosse 152
- on the lessons of the Triumph of Pride
  - by Redcrosse 148

medium
- of Guyon's action 296
- of human imagination 27
- of speech 96

meekness
- of Una 68

meeting
- of Heaven and earth 296
- of ontology and epistemology 282
- of the Faerie Queene
  - in Arthur's dream 195
- of Una
  - with Sansloy 128–133

melancholy 289
- dull 289

melting
- in compassion 120
- of manly heart 77
- of waxen plume 256

member
- functioning
  - of court 247
- of the human race
  - Redcrosse as 239

members
- individual
  - of the species of mankind 298

membership
- at court 105
- in the class of humanity 113

memory 12, 23, 79, 83, 110, 177, 230, 277, 280
- as forgetting and remembering 23
- experience of 205
- gathering separate experiences into 245
- heavy 145
- human 164
- imperfect
  - of man 203
- in relation to information 68
- levels of human 72
- mournful 267
- neglect of 268
- of careful reader 261
- of events 204
- of George
  - not his strong suit 247
- of mistakes 212
- of reader 70, 121, 174
- operation of 121
- stout 179
  - of careful readers 214
  - of the reader 145
- training of 79

men 132, 178 *See also* man.
- active 209
- best 295
- bones of 147
- bourgeois 294
- class of 211
- cowardly 274
- educated 194
- frail 112
- good
  - action of 158
- hosts of
  - dismayed by Fidelia 221
- ill 158
- individual 14
- intrusion of
  - into balanced nature 142
- king of 121
- last 222
- learned 158
- living 53

mastery by

of scientific principles 179
minds of 273
modern 169
mortal
   state of 192
opinion of
   reformation of 135
ordinary 193, 265
passive
   hearts of 253
rich
   in Aristotle 233
ruthless 294
skulls and bones of dead 166
three
   strength of 254
uncareful 225
unlikeness to
   of Ignaro 189
weak
   the easy pickings of 254
without law 290
mental
   battle 115
merchant
   envy of soldier's position 59
   patience 59
   view from the firm ground of a stable shore 127
Merchant Taylors' School 167, 210
Mercie 231–233
   paradox in behavior of 231
mercy
   heavenly
      given to Redcrosse 206
   Una begs for 129
merit
   as the basis of social promotion 167
   of Una for the ills that have been visited on her 118
meriting
   to live 202
Merlin 178
merry
   pipes 134
   wind 272
message
   Christian 40
messenger
   Archimago as 288
   male 286
   of hell 100
   speech of 284–286
messengers
   of hell 101
metals
   hardness of 251
Metamorphoses. See Ovid (Publius Ovidius Naso).

metamorphosis
   pagan 115
metaphor 7, 15, 18, 33, 75, 272
   control of 194
   ethico-scientific
      of the poet 254
   of cyclical return
      in Plato 291
   of growth
      used by Arthur 191
   poetic 57
   presence of 218
metaphorical
   blindness 141
   characteristics
      of the golden chain 193
   nature
      of human language 194
metaphysical
   authority 51
   boundaries 169
   description 244
   end 232
   equality
      of God 269
   fiction 175
   foundation 244
   framework
      Una sets her problems in a 172
   guarantee 67
   identity 218
   knowledge 170
   ontology 94
   permanence
      of desire 137
   perspective 241, 286
   point of view 66
   poles
      of birth and death 253
   process 194
   reality 269
   role
      of classical philosophy 98
   silence
      of Una 194
   source
      of sin 226
   system 293
   truth 231
      of text 293
   universe 277
      construction in Plato 161–162
   wholeness
      of the pagan gods 190
metaphysics 254
   absolute 31, 173
   closing off of
      by Augustine 190
   ground of 18, 112
   knowledge of things as they are 104
   of God's creation 93
   pagan 133

position of identity in 125
problem built into 21
struggle 65
value in 55
method
 aesthetic 12
 a posteriori
  of inquiry 86
 modern critical 161
 scientific 12
Meun, Jean de 107, 179. *See also Roman de la Rose.*
microscopic
 individual 162–163
 mind 238
middle 23, 276, 298
 in Foucault 218
 in Spenser 173
 of narrative 177
 region 256
 space 142
  lengthening the 253
 terms 203
  amplification of 203
  of argument 276
Middle Ages 17, 179
midway
 between heaven and earth 256
might 69, 220, 264, 266, 288
 appeal to 109
 conquering
  of George 271
 conquest by 271
 fleshly 210
 hideous
  shunned by Arthur 186
 of magic spells 103
 of victor 187
 organ of
  of God 296
 outrageous
  of George 258
 rage of Sansloy more of 131
 skillful 100
 will to 182
 wondrous 129, 179
mighty
 armor
  of Redcrosse 168
 charm 265
 in the world of politics 182
 rage 250
mild
 lady
  Una as 204
 mother 176
mill
 water
  stream would drive a 256
mimesis 42

between nature and language 75
mind 15, 23, 26, 35, 36, 90, 162, 166, 188 *See also* epistemology.
 a posteriori 104
 a switch in Una's 45
 battle in 116
 change of
  by Una 183
 compassion of 118
 consistency of 90
 construction of 254
 content of 172
 continuation of the prior language of the heart in the 73
 contrary opinions held in one 116
 deception of 142
 delight of
  of Redcrosse 160
 divided 78
 division of
  according to Augustine 72
 epistemological
  reconstruction of ontology in 230
 external to 98
 eye of the 234, 281
 God-given 276
 growth of Una's 118
 human 98, 167, 193, 218, 296
  statistical approximation in the 155
 imagining
  alignment of with scientific information 171
 immediate 218
 impatient
  of woman 286
 imperfect 218
  of the substantial individual 181
 imperfection of 58
 increasing tension in
  of Una 173
 individual 188
  understanding of 265
 infection of
  with fear 267
 intentional
  strengthening of 131
 inward
  turn of 226
 irreducible 50
 life of 172
 limited 94, 193, 212
 losing control of 79
 microscopic 238
 monadic 50
 multi-tier architecture of 74
 negative content of 101
 of Arthur
  positive nature of 190
 of careful reader
  survives deconstruction 181
 of Contemplation 243
 of God 188
 of man 138, 142

perfection of 261
words give potential for action in the 206
of mankind 97
of participants
   in conversation 196
of reader 60, 145, 227
of Redcrosse 109, 142, 148
   dissociation of might and reason in the 221
of Una 67, 125, 126, 228
   gradually drawn out of 199
   question of the similarity between things in 120
of wise men 193
operation of
   on its object 126
pagan
   weaker wit of 222
presence of nature in 91
properly constructed 254
rage affecting the 123
rational 212
   training of 277
reconstruction of 46
reconstructive 296
redirection of
   of Redcrosse 226
relationship of
   with God's *a priori* ontological creation 152
resolution in 58
sullen
   of Despair 201
tension in the
   of Una 172
uneducated 143
unified
   assumption of 180
   of Una 126
untroubled 80
wholly void 185
wind-blown
   of Orgoglio 195
wind-filled
   of Orgoglio 185
word which we bear in our 73
mindful
   of adventure 246
minding
   another's cares 155
minds 88
   of cowardly men 274
   existing 193
   human 203
   lesser 270
   limited 98, 203
   of created individuals 257
   noble
      linked in lovely wise 192
   of men 273
   presence of 91
   rational
      individual's control of 135
   sleepy 70

miracle
   of Christ's death and resurrection 37
   of Venus 221
miracles 222
miraculous
   event 48
   intrusion of
      into the natural order 221
mire 266
mirror
   bright 144
   of divine majesty 93
   of grace 93
misaimed
   sight 186
misappellation
   of Redcrosse as an elf 62
misapprehension
   by Una 128
mischief 54, 123, 261
mischiefs
   follow Wrath 148
mischievous
   arts 113
miscreation 100
misdeeming
   light
      of the loyalty of Una 141
misery 123
misfeigning
   of Una's true knight 129
misformed
   house 115
   thought
      of Archimago 100-102
misfortune 180
mishaps
   are mastered by discrete advice 180
   of George 287
misimpression
   of Redcrosse 261
misinterpretation
   by Una 171
   of the ethical dimension
      of the world around George 252
misplacement
   of Una's mind in distant sun and stars 133
misseeming
   hue 191
misshaping
   of Fradubio 113
missing 168, 221
   object of aim 258
   the joyous sight of Redcrosse
      by Una's eye 124
mission
   lack of interest in Una's
      displayed by Redcrosse 148

preordained
    of Redcrosse 231
saintly
    of Redcrosse 223
mist
    foggy 114
mistake 112, 165, 267, 285
    occasional 192
    of appearance for reality
        in Plato's Allegory of the Cave 14
    of Dragon 264
    of individual and general sense 113
    of making a metaphysical end out of relative
        experience 232
    of naïve reader 141
    of Redcrosse 277
        in lunging forward 54
    of removing armor 274
    of Una 96
        in believing that she has found her knight 127
    to follow the example
        of Redcrosse 143
mistakes 47, 277, 288
    correction of 192
    learning from 191, 212
    memory of 212
    of Redcrosse 28, 184, 205, 212, 295
    of young knight 191
    Redcrosse's 61
    serious 163
mistress
    of dwarf 168
mists 256
misunderstanding
    of the source of Redcrosse's power to overcome
        obstacles
            by Duessa 150
    of Una 226
    of words
        by naïve creatures 121
        in the world of time 228
    possibility of
        in the world of time 96
misweening 141
mitre
    Persian
        on head of Duessa 108
mixture
    of pleasure and pitiful regard 278
Mnemosyne 249
mock
    death 168
mockery
    of Una
        by Archimago's deception 129
mode 5
    of acting
        in relation to ends 26
    of designation 86
    of encoding speech 7
    of presentation 87
model
    Chretien de Troyes as 44
    faulty
        of Du Bartas 256
    for *Letter to Raleigh* 40
    for the reader 47
    holiness as a
        of Redcrosse 164
    life of St. George as a comic model 44
    of behavior 183
    of outside world by perfect logic
        in Russell and Whitehead 88
    past as a
        for passive imitation 76
    philosophical
        of Virgil 76
    role
        Redcrosse as a positive 101
    Wolfram Von Eschenbach as 44
models
    classical 4
modern 26, 233, 291
    aesthetic
        of A. C. Hamilton 196
    aesthetics 61, 98, 167
    age 40, 93
    approach
        to experience 142
        to problem of making trial 141
    critic 2, 56, 277
    critical method 161
    discovery of problem of reference 8
    existential construction 188
    men 169
    philosophy 2–6, 88, 254, 292
        of language 85
    reader 2, 51, 167, 214
    reading 27
        of allegory 10
        of *The Faerie Queene* 239
    reason 171
    solution 95
    technique
        of reading 169
    terms 169
    world 102
        allegory in 5–7
        of science 169
Modern
    critic 45, 240
Modernism 6–7, 11, 26
modest
    grace 219
modesty 251
    in word and deed
        of Reverence 213
moistened
    wings
        lagging of 256
molestation 110

Index

molten
  stars 132
moment
  present 184
monad 26, 80, 161, 296
monadic
  mind 50
monarchy
  feudal 233
money
  put to work 266
Monica (mother of Augustine) 38
monster 57, 255, 270
  body of 187
  cry of the 255
  deformed 279
  killing the body of the 187
  vile 60
monstrosity 60, 66
monstrous
  beast 290
  main 186
  mass 187
mood
  constant
    of Fidelia 219
  furious
    of the Dragon 257
moon 178
  changing 227
moral
  beings 152
  blindness 70
  Contemplation 12
  danger 166
  destruction 260
  difference 108
  duty 154
  evil 12, 202
  examples 110
  framework 149
  ignorance 166
  implications 84
  indifference
    of Night 156
  information 69
  instinct
    of Redcrosse 154
  judgment
    of characters who lack ontological existence 143
    of Redcrosse 142
  neutrality 234
  priority
    of Una's rational dwarf 165
  truth
    sources of 157
  universe 183
  virtue 70

virtues
  perfection in twelve 224
weakness
  of Redcrosse 215
well-being 122
work
  of God 193
  world 202
morality
  of Augustine 104
  play 232
morning 86, 95, 122
  sound
    of drum 202
  star 85, 88, 95
    Una as 92, 95, 281
Morpheus 71–72, 77, 78, 222
  attitude of 101
  awakening of 74
  rousal of 234
  waking 81
morrow 149
mortal
  eye 119
  fight 152
  life 232
    loathing of 223
  men
    state of 192
  sin 101
  wight 132
mortality
  of mankind 19
  vain assurance of 210
mote 220
mother 38, 122
  mild 176
  Night 156
  of Orgoglio
    was the earth 162
motif
  literary 170
motion
  backward 267
  constancy of 37
  forward 116
  of compassion of mind 118
motivation 33
  by wrath 103
  hiding 64
  inner 246
  of George 246, 294
  true
    of George 249
mottled
  clothes
    of black and white 281
motto
  of Andrea Alciati 217
mountain 254

mountainous
    shadow
        of the Dragon 253
mountains
    huge
        moved from their native seat 221
mounting
    of steed
        by Sansloy 133
Mount of Contemplation 246 *See also* Contemplation.
mourn 169
    Una left to 290
mournful
    memory 267
    plight 155
    sight 166
    stole 281
mouth 72
    hollowness of
        of Dragon 269
    of the body 73
    of the flesh 73
    of the heart 73
    of hell 252
    what proceeds out of the mouth defiles a man 72
mouths
    seven
        of the Nile 154
moved 109
    Orgoglio is 186
movement
    forward
        of Ignaro 189
    lack of in Calvin's act of belief 25
    of lion
        by Una's sight 120
    of loyal love 147
    of narrative 241
    of Redcrosse's heart
        rich weeds and seeming glorious show 145
    of the world 255
    to wrath
        by Redcrosse 153
muddy
    shore
        of seven-mouthed Nile 154
murder
    of Busiris
        by Hercules 259
    of Cicero 222
    unmanly 148
murmuring
    wind 77
muscle
    Redcrosse as
        to effect Una's will 70
muse
    Clio as 249
    heedful 256

sacred 250
music 21
    breeds delight 191
    delightful 275
    polyphonic 250
    sweet 160, 289
    wider 191
Mutabilitie 144
    Cantos. *See Faerie Queene, The.*
    likeness of Lucifera to 146
    rise of 146
mute
    astonishment
        of Trevisan 200
mutual
    salvation 263
mutually-assured
    destruction
        principle of 259
mysteries
    revered 217
mystery 20, 42
    acceptance of 38
    access to metaphysical
        granted to philosopher kings 23
    authority over 51
    in Augustine 22
    to sailors 251
    unapproachable 104
    veils of 39
myth
    as creation of imaginative fiction 285
    pagan
        satyrs as composite creatures created by 135
    Virgilian 298
mythical
    creatures 3
    λόγος 89
    worlds
        ontological stability of 89

N

naïve
    creatures 121
    perfectly 212
    reader 141
    Redcrosse as 102, 278
    Spenser as 11
        in the work of Northrop Frye 169
naïveté
    of Redcrosse 56, 102
naked
    before God
        after the robbery of Kirkrapine 122
    face 134
    sides
        of Despair 201
nakedness
    of Fidessa 171

Index

name 194, 241, 246–247
  as sign of object 85
  exact 275
  figural 84, 241
    of Redcrosse 239, 244
  general
    of Redcrosse 113
  great
    of scarlet carpet 276
  honorable 275
  immortal 250
  imposition of 87
  individual
    of George 175
  literal 83, 84, 175, 227
    of George 241, 244
  meaning of
    of Kirkrapine 122
  noble
    of knights 237
  of Aeneas 39
  of George 295
  of Redcrosse 46
  of Sansfoy
    reveals his lack of faith 106
  of Una 275
  poetry
    of Spenser 239
  proper
    of Duessa 153
  relationship between object and 85
  sacred 83
  switch in
    by Una 45
  to call by
    Archimago's daring 70
names 78, 85, 90, 275
  certain 85
  deconstructable 155
  equality as a relation between
    in Frege 86
  imposition of 104, 155, 178, 241
  proper
    in Kripke 90
  relation between 86
naming 241
  by figural status 83
  conventions
    if Spenser 240
  of Boötes
    implications for Redcrosse 82
  of gate of true dreams
    by its *a posteriori* attributes in Spenser 77
  of George 238-244, 245
    by plowman 82
  of Odysscus 35
  of substantial consciousness
    confusion over 175
narration 295
  by the poet 152

narrative 44, 46, 84, 161–162, 174, 175, 214, 240
  arc
    lack of in Brooke-Davies' argument 117
  as logical expression 32
  coloring of 32
  DeNeef's treatment of 32–34
  end of 58, 177
  framework
    of Ovid 260
  intrusion of Fradubio in 116
  journey of George defined 105
  middle of 177
  movement of 241
  of Spenser 270
  of Una 119
  suspense 239
  time in 171
  within the 69
narrator 130
narrow
  leaves 277
nation 194, 246–247
  friend of the 239
  savage 134
nations
  scared 250
native
  condition
    of Una 249
  ground 289
  kingdom 290
  prison
    returning Una to her 169
  seat
    mountains moved from their 221
  soil
    of Una 248–249
  sovereignty
    lack of 144
  virtue 105–107, 108, 132, 142
    Fradubio does not rely on 114
natural
  animal instincts 123
  behavior
    of birds 52
  family
    abandoned by Una's lion 121
  gifts 97
  intelligence 3
  language 90
  law 155
  object 75
  ontology 3
  order
    intrusion of the miraculous into the 221
  philosophy 4
  pride 121
  reason 3
  universe 222

nature 11, 14, 15, 16, 18, 36, 46, 75, 91, 185, 188, 251, 267 *See also* ontology.
  active
    of Archimago 77
  alignment of mind with 78
  artist in relation to 75
  balance of 96
    modern assumption of 142
  brutality of 96, 105
  consistency of 90
  construction of 142
  contrary to
    portents as 222
  cyclical return of 291
  domain of 15
  dynamic
    of time 37
  forces of 176
  gifts of 233
  ground in 87
  guessing the content of 190
  horizontal
    of the Dragon's wings 252
  hostile 83, 98, 218, 233
    law stands as bulwark against 131
  hostility of 52, 104
  human 155
  imbalance of 143, 177
  imperfect 107
  inaccessible 218
  incorrupted 267
  individual 65
  of allegory 6
  of evil
    as privative 158
  of Ignaro 189
  of prize 135
  of things
    equality in Night's perception of the 155
  ontological problems of 170
  opposition to 291
  outward 162
  pen of 189
  positive
    of Arthur's mind 190
  presence of 91
  rational 4
  reading 189
  relative
    of culture 133
  society built against 105, 123, 197
  state of 49, 75, 264
  true 83
    of Una 136
  unbalanced 218
  underlying
    Virgil's connection between poetry and 76
  unequal moral universe of 183
  vertical
    of the Dragon's strength 251
  view of
    mediated 76
navigating
  the world of time 183
near 68, 69
nearness 53
  to flames 259
nebulous
  imaginative fiction 161–162
necessary
  element of deciet 83
  fiction
    in the work of Plato 161–162
  measures 225
  step 112, 135
necessity
  argument of
    woven by Despair 203
  chain of 156, 158
    apparent, not real 158
    broken for the Furies 158
  constraint of 297
  for caution
    in the world of time 140
  lack of
    in Redcrosse's attack on Errour 121
  of action 160
    in the face of imminent suicide of Redcrosse 211
  of collecting all the facts 202
  of connection
    between words and things 76
  of embracing all species
    in generic defintion of allegory 71
  of making fine-grained judgments 199
  of scouting environment
    for clues to truth and falsehood 81
  problem of 157
  strong
    striving with 203
neck
  of Charissa
    baring of 228
  scaly 255
need 168, 286
  drives interpretation
    in Friedrich Nietzsche 296
  for justice
    speech of Redcrosse on the 201
  for rest 216
  of death 204
  of relief
    from the Dragon's power 253
  standing in 192
needfulness 73
needless
  spear 206
needments 165
needy 231
negation
  in Foucault 218

Index

negative
  attributes 189
    definition of Sansfoy by 150
  caution
    urged by Una 212
  condemnation 141
  content
    of Redcrosse's mind 101
  definition 275, 292
    of Errour 186
    of Ignaro 189
    of Orgoglio 186
    of Socrates 189
    of value 292
  image 269
  judgment
    of the soothsayer 152
  reference
    of sails 252
neglect
  of memory 268
  of moral well-being 122
negotiating
  contrary desires 110
  historical texts 127
negotiation
  between external world and one's fallible self 177
  of world 164
neighbor
  element 255
Neleus of Scepsis 19
Nelson, William 43
neoplatonism 20, 42
nephew 156
Neptune 270
  blessing of 127
neutral
  stance 157
neutrality 101
  moral 234
never 71
  failing God 139
neverending
  education 177
never-fading
  beauty 282
new
  cause
    for invoking the wrath of Jove 159
  death
    of purple bloud on the verdant fields 106
  experience
    of weighing unequal things in the balance 199
  form of judgment 114
  hap 129
  knight 264
  knowledge 169
  man 221, 264
New Academy 155
New Jerusalem 28

news
  happy 236, 296
  troubling 284
newspeak
  Orwellian 5
New Testament 202
Newton, Isaac 2
next
  life 171
  to lady's love 196
Nietzsche, Friedrich 98, 222
  works
    The Will to Power 296
night 151, 152, 165, 178, 256, 263, 269, 270
  as the shadow of death 124
  cheerless 124
  collapse of
    with day 189
  dead 70
  drawing near of 69
  ill succeeding 101
  in diurnal alternation 155
  passing the
    in jollity 150
    in joy 150
  rule of
    by Jove 159
  weary 80
Night 155, 157, 158, 222
  children of 156
  Duessa's reign over 158
  eternal 160
  everlasting 159
  limitations of 157
  province of 178
  realm of
    Duessa's journey to 154–156
  rousal of 234
night and day
  watching 213
Nile
  seven mouthed 154
  simile of 59, 154
  swelling of 80
nill 131
nobility 34
  inborn 121
  lack of
    of Redcrosse 137
noble
  chivalry 280
  courage
    awakening of 249
  gest 220
  heart 151
  minds
    linked in lovely wise 192
  name
    of knights 237
  peer 186

story 195
thought 151
nodal
  points 241–243
noise
  piercing 185
  white 77
nominative 75
non-empirical
  truth
    in Plato 221
non-existent
  λογός 240
non-moving
  state 203
Non tibi, sed religioni (Emblem VII of Alciati's *Emblemata*) 217
normal
  hierarchy
    of experience reversed 121, 175
northern
  star 82
  wagonner 82
nosethrill 256
notes
  attuned 275
  warbling 289
nothing 49, 62, 147, 257, 298
  wrong with mind of Redcrosse 142
notion
  problematic
    of escape 233
nought 28, 178
  hid that ought to be expressed 286
  prayers of Una n. prevail 131
  under heaven's wide hollowness 118
noun
  transparency of
    in Virgil 75
novel 33
novice 262
number
  indefinite
    of associative paths 241
nurse
  Mercie as 231
  of pompous pride 144
  of time
    Mnemosyne as 249

O

oak
  tree 97
    foot of Redcrosse gets stuck in an 163
oaten
  pipe 110

oaths
  breaking of 279
obedience
  teaching Una
    by satyrs 134
obfuscation
  deliberate
    by Spenser 198
object 90, 242
  arbitrarily producible 86
  fictional
    λόγος as 6
  identity of 124
  name of 85
  natural 75
    expression of in language 76
  of adoration
    Una as passive 118
  of affection 125
  of aim
    missing of 258
  of desire
    back into physical proximity 137
    Una as 234
  of reference 90
  operation of mind on 126
  passive
    worship of Una as 137
  status of 86
objection
  raised by Augustine
    to Virgil's easy philosophical models 76
objective
  correlative
    in Coleridge 216
objectivity
  critical 54
objects
  denoted 141
  of pure reason 87
obligation 280
  differing
    between actors and critics 55
  of human beings
    to open themselves to others 180
  of individual 143
  of living beings 268
  of reader 178
  of Redcrosse
    to Una 209
  of the heart
    of Una 174
  to action 55
obligations
  of George 279
  of Redcrosse 226
oblique 75
obscuring
  perception
    of Una 177

observation
  by others 135
observer
  critical 128
obstacle
  power to overcome 212
obstacles
  overcoming
    by Redcrosse 150
  to achievement
    of goals 211
obvious
  answer 130
  sign 109
  of weakness 150
occasional
  mistake 192
occultatio 220
ocean
  wave 264
  wide 127
odds 124, 151
  of arms 278
odors
  precious 289
Odysseus 19, 34–37, 35, 83, 169
  as teller of lies 127
  in Virgil 36
  language of 169
  refusal of deity by 122
  travel to the underworld 170
  Una compared to 122
  wandering 82
Odyssey, The. See Homer: works.
off-center 234
  Archimago's hermitage as 238
  Contemplation's chapel as 238
offending
  storms 272
offensive
  weapon 266
offered
  eye 137
offering
  of purpose
    by Una 199
offerings
  feast of 122
office 209
οἰκείωσις. *See familarization*
ointment
  gracious 268
old
  man 129
    Ignaro as 189
    wizards 144
  woman
    Corceca as 189

older
  vessel 215
Old Testament
  justice 202
oligarchs
  Roman 233
Olympus 156
onanism 162–163
once
  at 166
one
  consent 194
  loving hour 125
  man's fault 267
  meaning
    more than one in the world of time 96
  truth as 297
one and the many, the 40
oneself
  completion of 175
only
  daughter
    argument of 288
ontological
  creation
    by God 152, 263, 275
  description 90
  existence
    of Fidessa 195
  fact 288
  form
    of Gloriana 195
  foundation
    in literal reality 212
  individual
    denial of 189
  life 179
  logic 18
  presence
    of the Dragon 274
  problems of nature 170
  reader 104, 164
  reality 98, 157, 234, 256, 272, 282
    as inaccessible 296
  stability
    of mythical worlds 89
  terms 27, 102
  things 170
  universe
    created by God 158
  world 88, 282
ontology 2, 15, 43, 45, 46, 78, 88, 90, 91, 142, 167, 180, 219, 234, 238, 244, 282, 296
  See also nature.
  agreement with epistemology
    in the human mind 218
  belief in
    by Archimago 100
  created 190
    of God 298

fictional 127
in Luther 24
joined to epistemology 93
lack of
   in Archimago's magic 104
   in deconstruction 185
   in evil 157
   of Una and Errour 143
metaphysical 94
natural 3
of creation 66
of God 155
of object 75
of universe 101
of Venus 87
of λόγος
   Derrida's denial of 6
pre-linguistic state of 104
   of the Creator 289
prior
   of God 181
reality 57, 96
reference to 87
relationship between language and 76
sacred
   of God 58
underlying 124
   of the planet Venus 86
world of 230
opaque
   origins
      of Cælia 214
open 186
   body
      of Fidessa 234
   eyes
      can deceive one's mind 142
   face
      of Fidessa 110
   fields 252
   gate
      of Maluenu 151
   posture
      of Duessa 151
open-ended
   action
      of George 294
opening 46, 266
   dull eyes
      of Redcrosse 220
   of eyes 141
   of gate 185, 273
      by Humiltá 213
   of possibility
      of seeing Redcrosse again 173
   of self
      to others 180
openness
   of body 109
   perpetuity of 55

operation
   of God
      by comprehensive mind 222
   of mind on its object 126
opinion
   of men
      reformation of 135
opinions
   contrary 116
opponent
   of Despair 205
   striking fear into 257
opponents
   equally-matched 138
   evenly-matched 138
opportunity 115, 127
opposing
   defendants 286
opposite
   ontologically real 105
opposites
   meet
      in epic simile 106
opposition
   of imperfect human memory and the perfect
      memory of God 203
   to nature 291
oppressing
   Dragon 274
   of Una's parents 232
oppression
   outside the walls of Eden 209
ordained
   by destiny
      death as 203
order 172
   according to godly righteousness 64
   disruption of
      of Lucifera 149
   hierarchical 63
   male
      of society 209
   natural
      intrusion of the miraculous into the 221
   of being 52
   of God 264
   of hierarchical values 64
   of society 64, 209
   patriarchal 210
   principle of 47
      in political society 99
   rational 90
   social 190
      fragility of 151
ordering
   the kingdom of the heavens
      by Jove 144
ordinary
   life 240
   man 193, 265

Index 433

reason 4
organ
  of might
    of God 296
organization
  geometric 271
Orgoglio 49, 162–163, 187, 252, 254, 260, 261
  appearance of 195
  battle with 266
  behavior with
    of Redcrosse 253
  blows of 186
  conflict with 173
  defeat of 188
    as a general example 187
    by Arthur 186
  dungeon of 118, 209
  imprisonment by
    of Redcrosse 278
  leg of
    brutally chopped off 187
  misses the mark
    of his misaimd sight 186
  naming of 240
orientation
  horizontal
    of golden chain 193
  of a ruler
    towards people 144
  of epistemology
    towards God's prior ontology 263
  of self
    towards the external universe 143
  of sight 234
  scientific
    of the poem 255
  to good 67
  to literal world
    by the reader 175
  typological 93
  vertical
    of golden chain 193
origin
  in Eden 226
  of arms 178
  of love
    of False Una 79
  of power
    in God 67
    of Redcrosse 67, 83
  opaque
    of Cælia 214
  story
    of Ovid 251
original
  balance
    of nature 142
  sin 224
    of Adam and Eve 267
Orion

hound of 127
Orlando Furioso. See Ariosto, Ludovico: works.
ornament
  poetic 12
ornaments
  robbery of the ornaments of churches 122
Orwell, George
  newspeak 5, 7
ostentatious
  display of entertainment 146
other 162
  clothes 146
  enemy 65
  external 65
  inadequacy of Redcrosse's mind to deal with the 102
  in love 138
  judgment 202
  loath was the 128
  meaning 121
  members of the species 180
  pleasure given to the 111
  potentially fictional 193
  Una's inability to appreciate 124
  who completes Una 160
  women
    Satyrane's comparison of courteous deeds of 136
  works 69
others 45, 57, 111, 190, 226
  action of
    in Una's separation from Redcrosse 117
  arms worn by 83
  bathing in the applause of 155
  belief of
    in things that the educated knew to be false 193
  binding oneself to 181
  discourse with 215
  envious eys of 166
  faith of 254
  feeding on 251
  friendship with 203
  gaining advantage over 234
  guilt of 157
  laying blame on 278
  lesser 233
  listening to 191
  lying to 83
  misunderstanding of words by 228
  need of
    by Una 55
  observation by 135
  opening oneself to 180
  prize for
    Una as 288
  protection of 131
  recognition by
    of Una's true nature 136
  safety of 192
  see Redcrosse's battlefield prowess 149

thoughts of
    untroubled by 80
    universe of 254
otherworldly
    journey
        outside of fiction 170
ouches (settings for precious stones)
    adorned with
        Charissa as 228
        Fidessa as 108–109
ought 68
out
    of control
        of Redcrosse 203
    of sight 124
    of the way 287
    of time
        existence 282
outcome
    deciding the
        of equal battle 152
    equal
        in the world of time 172
outcry
    of Una 133
outer 6
    garment
        change in 282
outrageous
    might
        of George 258
    pride 269
outside 254
    bounds of humanity
        Una's existence lies 197
    control of individuals 233
    God's good will impressed upon you from the 134
    limited reason 256
    of diurnal turning of day into night 71
    of fiction 31
        the possibility of otherworldly journeys 170
    of heaven
        Eden as 275
    of human shelter 115
    of will 130
    of world 71
    walls of Eden 236
        science 248-271
    world 86
outward
    appearance 73
        of Corceca 214
        of dwarf 168
        of Ignaro 189
    dress
        of Fidessa 200
    force 225
    nature 162
    projection
        of inward phenomenon 207
    signs 168

word 73
overcast 114
    with silver
        in description of the gate of sleep 76
overcoming
    obstacles
        by Redcrosse 150
    of skepticism
        in Augustine's work 189
    power of
        of obstacles 212
overextension
    of Redcrosse 236
overflowing
    fertile plain 268
overlooking
    of facts
        by Una 125
    the role of doubling
        in the Augustine universe 134
overreliance
    on Homer
        by pagan thinkers 170
overthrow
    of Saturn
        by Jove 157
overthrowing
    of perfect balance 267
overturned
    world
        trope of the 167
overwhelmed
    by compassion 120
    by love
        Una's mind as 125
overwhelming
    of lust 131
Ovid (Publius Ovidius Naso) 36, 142, 170, 179, 251
    and Augustine 37
    imitation of Pythagoras' speech in 46
    original story of
        of the fall of ages 251
    works
        Metamorphoses 49, 142, 177, 251, 259, 259–261
own
    forgetful of one's 155
ownership
    of Una's heart 137
oxen
    team of 82

P

pagan 42, 153, 171, 194
    academics 170
    apology for error 149
    author

Index 435

belief of 161–162
bold 129, 149, 173
configuration
   of the universe 233
doubt 170, 242
experience 143
idealism 259
ill-behavior of 64
king 279
knife 136
knowledge 150
metamorphosis 115
metaphysics 133
mind
   weaker wit of 222
myth
   satyrs as composite creatures created by 135
premises 133
proud 138, 152
rage 63
religion
   danger of 259
sage
   Varro as 221
skepticism
   in a Christian universe 76
temples
   defiling of 259
understanding
   of miracles 221
values
   subordinated to Christian values 63
world 76
pagans 40
   false gods of 176
pageant 147
   sacred 28, 295, 296
pain 56, 81, 225, 243
   bootless 101
   endless 205
   eternal 149
   of Lucifera's counselors
      to be kind to Duessa 146
   of Night 157
   of Redcrosse 224
painful
   correction
      in the House of Holinesse 243
   pilgrimage 237
pains 125
painted
   table 205
pair
   of lovers 111
   weary 220
   wretched
      transformed into a tree 173
palace
   of Lucifera
      description of 144
      rejection of Lucifera's
         by Redcrosse 144
palfery
   plucking Una off of her 130
palfrey
   wanton of Duessa 109
Pallas (character in Virgil's *Aeneid*) 63
Palmer 1, 70, 236, 263, 296
   unsanctified 296
panegyrist 42
panic
   of Una 56
papers 60, 261
   Errour's disgorging of 66
parable
   biblical 266
parade 146
paradise
   a-sexual
      House of Holieness as 229
paradox 84, 90, 136, 292
   confrontation of 172
   in behavior
      of Mercie 231
   logical
      solving 172
   of a living-dead Redcrosse 136
   of Eden 276
   puzzlement over
      in Una's mind 136
   resolution of 226
parallels
   between discrete experiences 112
   direct 116
paralysis 152
paraphrase 215
   of Una's response 120
pardon
   craving of 279
   error of enraged wight 149
parents
   of George 83, 241
   of Una 55, 232, 248
   plowmen 262
   woeful
      of Una 215
Parmenides (character) 17. *See also* Plato:
      works.
parsing
   the expression
      of Una 216
part 16
   endurance
      of each 171
   limited 295
   of created individuals 257
   of the human inheritance 157
   of truth 274
   tender 169
partial 28, 31

knowledge 267
legacy 157
perspective 295
vision
  of the whole truth 95

participant
  passive 261
  in conversation 196

participation
  in creation
    of the moral world 202
  in precision
    by George 242
  in sin 147
  in society 64
  in the sacred pageant 296
  unconscious 147

particular 116

partisan
  of evil 156

partisanship 70

partners
  willing 125

parts 101, 183
  constituent
    division of "whole" perspective into 118
  discrete 43
  division into
    in Tasso 42
  double 102
  examination of 180
  of body 195

Pascal, Blaise 193

pass 69
  with great distresse 69

passage
  of time
    between beginning and end 184
  unwonted 251

passing
  night
    in joy and jollity 150
  of heaven's light 186
  price 228

passion 6, 110
  burning with 259
  dreadful 111
  in the King and Queen of Eden 277-278
  of plight
    Redcrosse relieved of the 224
  of Redcrosse
    for Fidessa 111
  renewal of
    in Corceca 123
  restless 151
  whirlwind of 123

passive 42, 54
  act 135

  indifference

    of Redcrosse 147
  intellect 15, 166
  man
    George as 261
  men
    hearts of 253
  object
    worship of Una as 118, 137
  participant 261
  Redcrosse 159
  rhapsode
    Ion as 269
  stance
    of Redcrosse 155
  Una 117, 140, 172, 212
  women 209

passivity
  of A. C. Hamiltion 55
  of participants in Jove's order 160
  of Redcrosse 81, 82, 119
  of Una 55, 68, 132, 138, 160

past 126, 168, 253
  as a model for passive imitation 76
  behavior
    of Redcrosse 191
  crimes
    of Redcrosse 224
  pains 125
  sins 271
  Una speaks no more of the 126
  unkindness 161

pastoral 42

patching
  of ragged clouts
    into the garment of Despair 201

path 53, 79
  beaten most plain 62
  direct 84
  praise for those who follow other 58
  ready
    to heaven 231
  socially destructive 234
  vertical
    of angels 236

paths
  associative 241

patience 257
  in Calvin 26
  learned value of 254
  need for 224
  of Una 171, 174

Patience 149, 224, 267

patriarchal
  order 210

patron 274
  of life
    of Redcrosse 197
  of nation 239

patterns

archetypal 169
Paul, Saint 45, 71, 74, 246
paved
   brass way to heaven 146
paw 265
paying
   price
      for action 204
      of other's guilt 157
peace 37, 243
   in a world of hierarchical values 64
   justice of the 286
pearl
   in the clothes of Duessa 108
peer
   noble 186
peering
   beneath the surface 154
Pelagian doctrine 25
pen
   iron 192, 198
   of nature 189
Penance 225, 261
Penelope
   the circumspection of 35
penetration
   lack of 154
pensive
   maid
      Una as 136
people 103, 154
   adoration of the
      Una as object of 217
   different 196
   of Eden 274
   tract of 121
perception 34, 104
   direct 34
   godlike
      of Redcrosse 203
   of Fradubio's thought 115
   of Redcrosse
      as an elf 62
      as type 124
   of the reader 143
   of the way the world actually is 177
   of Una 57
      of George 45
   of Una's dwarf
      by both Una and Redcrosse 165
perch 187
perfect 105
   appearance
      of Una 284
   balance
      between mankind and nature 267
   daughter 284
   Eden 55
   freedom

      desired by existentialists 135
   intelligence
      in Eden 174
   logic 89
   nature 218
   person 57
   reason 14
   system
      of Northrop Frye 169
   Una 175
   unity 288
   vision
      of Descartes 11
perfection 16, 55
   exterior 57
   Fidelia's claim of
      of Redcrosse 232
   future 51
   in Aristotle's *Politics* 47
   in *Timaeus*' description of nature 18
   in twelve moral virtues 30
      by Arthur 224
   language of
      in Virgil 75
   limited logical 89
   of differentiation between truth and falsehood 35
   of heavenly grace
      Redcrosse grows into 223
   of logic
      in analytical philosophy 88
   of metaphysical fiction 175
   of mind
      of man 261
   of nature
      as the role of Virgilian artist 75
   of prelapsarian beauty 120
   of Redcrosse 220, 232, 236
      by Fidelia 232
   potential
      of George 257
   reader's desire for
      of Redcrosse 61
   renewal of image to 73
   state of 226
perfectly
   naïve 212
   wise 212
performance
   dismal 68
   poor
      in the House of Pride 200
peril 248–249
   certain 58, 65
   dwelling of 249
   of Una 137
   surrounding the House of Pride 173
   without show 54
perilous
   way 154

perils

enfolding the righteous man 184
　sad 277
　strange 287
period 84
　intermediate 84
periods
　historical
　　in Ovid's *Metamorphoses* 251
perish 186, 187
perjury
　of Redcrosse 204
permanence 19
　metaphysical
　　of desire 137
　of day over night 263
　of error 61
　of God's bias towards good 58
　of good over evil 138, 263
　of light over dark 263
　of non-physical things 138
　of reality 175
　of switch in mankind's favor 81
　of unequal values 269
permanent
　end 221
　　of experience 216
　evil 143
　good 142
　imbalance 138
perpetual
　beauty 282
　darkness 122
　silence
　　of Una 136
　state of passivity 132
perpetuity
　of openness
　　for the reader 55
perplexity 56
　of Una
　　at misfeigning her true knight 129
　　at Redcrossse's despair 223
Persia
　the nurse of pompous pride 144
　wealth of 144
Persian
　mitre 108
person 5, 35, 227
　bad 84
　disseverance of unified
　　by Tasso 40
　perfect 57
　whole
　　in Freud 242
personage
　comely 227
personality
　of Una
　　breach opened up in 95
　　unified 95

personification 33, 53
perspectival
　angle 296
perspective 55
　absolute metaphysical 173
　balanced
　　of Eden 140
　division of 272
　doubling of 134
　　a necessary step 135
　extra-textual 270
　heavenly 269
　ironic 128, 218
　limited
　　of George 295
　metaphysical 241, 286
　of alchemy 185
　of concavity 253
　of entertainment 146
　of George 273
　of God 236, 270
　of Medcie 232
　of poet 249
　of reader 26, 200, 276
　of reason 253
　of science 241
　of Spenser
　　from the stable shore 127
　of time 134
　of time-bound human beings 203
　of Una 249
　　change in 83
　partial 295
　prelasparian 117
　question of 277
　relative 244
　　on experience 66
　scientific 173, 244
　　on experience 66
　sufficient 135
　timeless
　　of God 203
　unified
　　of Una 134
　whole
　　division into constituent parts of 118
　　of Redcrosse 146
　　of Una 117
　wider
　　of poet 232
　worldly 269
perspectives
　on language 50
perversion
　of true intents 122
pestilence
　harmful 266
petitio principii 133
Petrarch, Francesco 24–25, 146

phantasmagoric

Index 439

world of the text 241
phantom
  character
    Malvenu as 143
phenomenon
  inward
    projected outward by Redcrosse 207
Philemon and Baucis 260
philosopher 42, 189
philosopher king 23
philosophers
  ancient 3
  classical 292
  Enlightenment 275
  medieval 3
philosophical
  argument 192
    Redcrosse no match for 191
  division 285
  terms 92
philosophy 9, 32, 40, 51, 76, 171, 233, 292
  ancient 12
  artifacts of 90
  classical 22, 96, 104, 170, 190
    metaphysical role of 98
    reliance on ends 19
  context of 45, 113
  epicurean 36
  in Augustine
    definition of 181
  medieval 12
  modern 2–6, 12, 34, 254, 292
    impact of Frege on 88
  natural 4
  of Aristotle 126
  of Augustine 83
  of language 85
  of Socrates' 193
  Platonic 292
  public 193
  Roman 20
  truth in 39, 117
  work of
    of Augustine 189
Philosophy (character in Boethius' *Consolation of Philosophy*) 107, 201
Phoebus 93, 132
  imp of 250
  pure 160
phonetic
  echoes 241
phonic 240
Phosphorus 87, 88, 92
  as Lucifer
  in Vives' *Commentary on De trinitate* 92
  as morning star 85
physical
  being 138
  body

battle for control of Una's 138
  destruction
    follows intellectual destruction 187
  exhaustion
    of George 261
  intercourse 116
  looseness
    of Fidessa 130
  power
    of lion 123
  proximity 123, 137
  salvation 137
  strength
    of Una 215
  violence
    battle of 138
  world 234
physics
  quantum 51
pickings
  easy
    of weak men 254
picture
  of an unfallen universe
    in fiction 57
  of Corceca 121
  of events 288
  rational
    of Redcrosse 227
piece
  fairest 237
pieces 104
  1,000
    Kirkrapine's body ripped into a 122
  of clothing
    Despair's garment woven out of 201
  separate 281
piercing
  arms of Redcrosse 151
  noise 185
  of heart
    by words of Despair 205
  of poet 118
  steel 255
piles
  of truth and falsehood 78
pilgrim 136
pilgrimage
  painful 237
pillow
  helmet of
    Arthur as 195
pincers
  fiery hot 224
pinning
  of ragged clouts
    to the garment of Despair 201
pipe
  oaten 110
pipes

merry 134
Pirithoüs 260
pitch
  too-high 256
  too-low 256
  wonted 263
piteous 188
  cry
    of Duessa 186
pitiful
  adventures
    of George 278
  regard 278
pity 225
  born of untroubled mind 80
  evocation of 132
  for Una's sad estate
    by lion 120
  in the heart of Night 156
  lack of
    in Archimago's rescuing of False Una 101
  of foolish man
    for crocodile tears 154
  of poet
    for Una after she has been abandoned by Redcrosse 118
  of Una's unhappy state 133
  overrides cultural taste 133
  without the guiding hand of God 132
place 282
  desolate 184
  fairness in 114
  in Gloriana's court 43
  next to that lady's love 196
  of peril 248–249
  on the Ladder of Ambition 155
  pride of 166
  shady
    sunshine in a 119
  stately 146
placid
  distance
    from action 127
placing
  of Redcrosse
    in a schoolhouse 220
plagues 123
plain 161–162, 277
  appearance 114
  example
    proof by 141
  fertile 268
  painted table 205
  path that was beaten most 62
  pricking on the 48, 225
  response
    of Fradubio 113
  sense 31

plainness

  of Eden 276
plains
  of Eden 68
plaint
  unpitied 80
plane
  horizontal
    woods as 142
  literal
    of allegory 247
    of existence 246
  of bodily existence 270
  subject
    hovering above the 253
planet 87
  Venus as 85, 92
  reference to 86
Plato 14, 15, 16, 31, 45, 85, 86, 91, 92, 221, 269, 293
  Allegory of the Cave 14, 91, 92, 137
  as guide to truth 20–21
  as rational thinker 14
  idealism of 8
  influence of
    in modern criticism 31
  metaphor in 18
  metaphor of cyclical return 291
  reason in
    as tool of metaphysics 23
  Spenser's following of 75
  statistical estimation in
    of the universe 292
  the One in 17
  Theory of Forms 14, 15, 17, 193
  victory over Aristotle 20
  works
    Crito 23
    Ion 156, 192, 293. See also Ion (character).
    Parmenides 17, 17–19, 46, 85, 161–162, 175, 221, 291. See also Parmenides (character).
    Republic 14
    Timaeus 18–20, 161–162, 292 See also Timaeus (character).
Platonic
  fiction 18
  philosophy 292
  system 293
  world of becoming 213, 215
play
  gentle 160
  morality 232
  of love 77
  of lust 77
  wanton 166
playing
  Archimago
    at being Redcrosse 128
  field
    leveling of 278
  of warbling notes 289
plays

Index

St George 44
plea
  for mercy
    by Una 129
pleading
  for right
    not with words but with swords 150
  of rightful cause 286
pleas
  for help 290
pleasance 111
  bathing in
    of joyous shade 161
pleasant
  spring 134
pleasantness 77
pleasure 21, 23, 30, 278, 283
  as an end
    Augustine's rejection of 52
  epicurean 52, 234, 240
  immediacy of 22
  immediate 224
  in discoursing with another 128
  in troubles
    taken by Archimago 119
  led forward with 52
  of Duessa 150
  of eye 283
  principle 21
  sexual 150
  vassal of 131
pledges 219
pledging
  of kingdom
    by the King of Eden 284
plentiful
  earth 125
plenty
  of Gluttony 150
plight
  decayed
    weighing 199
  evil 115
    mankind as partakers of 216
  expression of 133
  heavy 171
  mournful 155
  of Fradubio 115
  of Una 118, 168
    with Sansloy 132
  passion of
    Redcrosse relieved of the 224
  woeful
    of Una 133
plighting
  of right hand 285
Plotinus 20, 222
plots 251
plowman 83, 240, 245
  Boötes as 82

George as a 245
  origins 83
  state 245
plowmen
  parents 262
plowshares
  swords beaten into 150
plucking
  of bough 147
  of proud vaunt
    of Arthur 194
  of Una
    from claws of a lion 132
    off of her palfrey 130
plume
  waxen 256
plunder 26
Pluto
  black 70
  grisly dame of (Proserpnia) 70
poem 30, 84, 121, 128, 130, 221, 227, 242,
    245, 264, 274, 275
  action of the 249
  Augustinian
    of Spenser 224
  beginning of 105, 138, 213
  fictional
    depiction of Faery in Spenser's 164
  of Spenser
    beginning of 65
    center of 238
poet 11, 40, 59, 70, 82, 93, 99, 112, 119, 127,
    141, 176, 178, 188, 197, 213, 215, 219,
    221, 223, 226, 234, 249, 252, 255, 264,
    265, 268, 269, 272, 273, 274, 281, 295
  allegorical 218
  as creator
    of temporary means 230
  asks his readers to weigh differeing values 147
  belief of the 175
  change in reader's perspective by 200
  Christian 63, 133, 161–162
  condemnation by
    of Redcrosse 142
  construction of fiction 45
  creation of 62
  crutch of the 141
  disbelief of the 101
  ear of the 110
  end of 295
  expectation of the
    for the reader 145
  Faery as creation of 162
  fear of
    of Dragon's teeth 251
  focus on life by 267
  goal of 237
  imagination of the 175
  imaginative vision of 281
  imperfect 226

indulgence in delays, suspense, and retardation 127
likened to birds in the Wandering Wood 53
logic of 175
love of 290
moral judgment of 142
narration by 152
perspective of 249
places blame
   on Redcrosse 119
point of 253
power of 214
reason of 178
reliance on pity of
   for Una 132
role of
   in larger whole 250
specificity of 141
words of 178, 279
work of
   end of 294
poetic
   imagination 275
   ornament 12
   program 271
poetic metaphor 14, 57, 75, 156, 193, 218, 227, 228, 229
poetics
   of Virgil 75
poetry 240
   Christian 83
   epic 53, 83
   imaginative 270
   name
     of Spenser 239
     of Virgil 38
       guides him back to underlying nature 76
   pagan 58
   Reformation 161
   restless ship of 272
poets
   antique 34
   famous 258
   historical 34
   rude 111
poignant
   spear 168
point 2, 105
   fixed
     in Redcrosse's errant wanderings 197
   of a sword 205
   of intersection 87
   of the poet 253
   of view
     of Augustine 218
points
   clear 4
   nodal 241–243
   turning 144
point-to-point 277
   analysis 173

poise
   dreadful 270
poison 251
   activation of 259
   of hydra 259
   within armor
     of Hercules 258
poisoned
   garment
     of Hercules 258
poles
   metaphysical
     of birth and death 253
   of argument 285
policy
   rule of realm of
     by Lucifera 144
political
   control
     extension of 233
   position
     subordination of one to the other by 157
   society 99
politics 16, 40, 182
   contest 63
polyphonic
   music 250
pomp
   idle 166
   luxurious 276
pompous
   pride
     Persia as the nurse of 144
poor
   assessment
     by reader of Redcrosse 143
   choices
     by Reddcrosse 141
     of George 276
   man's boxes 122
   performance
     in the House of Pride 200
   reader 93
pope 13
Pope, Alexander 4, 5, 16
   works
     Essay on Man 4
popes 70
Popkin, Richard H. 3, 14
popular
   remedy 233
port 127
portent
   contrariness to nature of 222
   definition in Augustine 222
position
   aesthetic 11
   best 257
   elevated social

Index

Sansloy's lack of 132
false 70
flipping of
   by Duessa 153
folded 266
illegitimate
   of Lucifera 144
inferior social
   of Una's dwarf 168
in fiction
   of Arthur 178
metaphysical 125
of power
   of Duessa 150
of reader 187
of safety 267
of Una 126
on ends
   of experience 203
political
   subordination of one to the other by 157
potentially compromising 134
raising one
   over another 286
social 166
   of lion 132
superiority of 50
uncomfortable 125
whole 157

positioning
   of things in relative space
      in the reader's mind 69

positions
   incompatible 93

positive 116, 150
   action 81, 246, 253, 292
      defines Redcrosse 82
   choice 141
   judgment 261
   knowledge
      lack of 212
   nature
      of Arthur's mind 190
   power 261
   role model 101

possession
   of a foothold on the Ladder of Ambition
      Redcrosse's lack of 149
   of postive power 190

possibility
   of action 55
   of imminent death 267
   of the Dragon being alive 273
   opening of the
      of seeing Redcrosse again 173
   whole
      realization of 262

possible
   reaction 153
   recipients
      of Una's affection 137

postern 166
postive
   power
      of Arthur 190
postlapsarian
   world 183, 273, 295
postmodern 26
   assumptions 56
   critic 45
   critics 240
   λόγος in 240
   reading 240
   skepticism 9
   vocabulary 191
postmodernism 6–7, 8
posture
   active
      of Redcrosse 143
      towards experience 143
   defensive 60
   of reflection 180
   open
      of Duessa 151
potential 96–99, 100, 211, 230, 232, 246
   activation of 132, 228
      by George 290
      by Redcrosse 138
      by Una 138
      of human being 190
   extension
      of the Dragon 253
   fiction
      of the other 193
   for action
      Redcrosse's 74
      words provide only 206
   for fault
      in assumptions 145
   for freedom 190
   God-given 106, 206
   harm
      fear of 253
   heaven 228
   of human being 177, 233
   of Una 217, 246
   perfection
      of George 257
      of the mind of man 261
   power 253
   sacred 96
   world
      of Heaven 295
potentially
   compromising position 134
   fictional λόγος 189
pouring
   forth of the plenty
      of Gluttony 150

   of blood
      out of the Dragon's wound 256

wine 259
power 24, 109, 171, 294, 297
  alienation of 209
    in Aristotle 233
  artistic 97
  as equally balanced 150
  bestowed on Redcrosse with his arms 58
  broadcast of 253
    through fear 273
  civil 41
  competing for
    with the gods 146
  conscious understanding of
    by Una 134
  differences in
    in Homer 19
  equality in 218
  exercise of 269
    by Una 131
  hidden
    of herbs 103
  kingly 41
  lack of
    in pagan world 133
    of true love to look backwards 126
    to look backwards 130
    to stop the flight of Una 119
  limited 67
  limits of
    Una's realization of 135
  lust for 276
  of a purely imaginary λόγος 179
  of Archimago
    to defeat Redcrosse 105
  of arms 295
    of God 95
  of Augustine 170
  of control
    of mankind 268
  of doubling
    of Duessa 288
  of Dragon 253
  of education 67, 98
  of equally matched rams 106
  of error 185
  of everlasting Night 159
  of fiction 93
    in Plato's *Parmenides* 221
    to create poetic metaphor 229
  of Fidelia
    granted by God 221
  of God 134, 210, 226
    as friend 116
  of gods 260
  of heaven 260
  of Hecate 81
  of ideas
    of Errour 66
  of imagination 282
  of individual will 79
  of intellect 43
  of introspection 78
  of love
    assuaging 174
  of magic
    of Archimago 104
  of moon 178
  of moral instinct 154
  of natural body 57
  of overcoming
    of obstacles 212
  of poet 214
  of reason 97, 183
    to put balance into unequal nature 177
  of Redcrosse's will
    in the Cave of Errour 81
  of shield
    of Redcrosse 297
  of speech 194
  of sun 178
  of transmutation 178
  of warrior instinct 154
  of will 260
    of George 261
  of words 195
  origin
    of Redcrosse 67
  over Errour 67
  over events
    of Una 129
  physical
    of lion 123
  position of
    of Duessa 150
  positive 261
    of Arthur 190
  potential 253
  problem of 66
  purposeful
    of limited body 262
  relics of
    of Redcrosse 184
  rightful claim to
    lack of 144
  scientific 155
  source of 253
    in Redcrosse's will 109
    of Errour 66
    of Redcrosse 102, 158
    of Redcrosse's arms 179
  subordination of
    to God 218
  to compel events
    Una's 134
  to defend 186
  to do damage 225
  to do harm 186
  to hurt 186
  to overcome obstacles
    of Redcrosse 150
  to wish will 261
  translating 67
  true
    depends on moral framework 149

use of
   by Redcrosse 60
usurpation of
   by Lucifera 149
vertically-oriented
   of the Dragon 253
warlike assupmtion of 47
will to
   in Friedrich Nietzsche 296
yielding
   to Redcrosse 163
powerful
   Dragon 254
   emotions 4
   man 150
   woman 150
powers
   animal 105
   enumerated
     of Archimago 119
   limited
     of reason 167
   manly
     loss of 205
practice
   in Aristotle 97
   of war
     Redcrosse's engagement in 148
praise
   fighting for 152
   for those who follow other paths 58
   for victory
     in great battles 204
   of friend 192
   of God 271
praises 216
   singing
     of Una 275
pray 119, 188
prayer
   of Archimago 68
   of Corceca
     for plagues, mischiefs, and long misery 123
   of Hercules 259
prayers
   of the righteous seed 235
   of Una
     do not prevail 131
     of worship 217
praying
   in the dark 121
   to God
     by Una 264
preacher 42
precedence 17
   ambiguity of
     required by the allegory 196

   in beauty
     Fradudio fights for 114

   in fame 260
   in heart
     of Una 174
   priority of 137
   yielding
     in love 197
precious
   blood
     of Jesus 263
   odors 289
   stone 179
precision 5, 35, 242
   Cartesian 34
   participation in
     by George 242
   rational 118
predicament
   of Una 136
predicate 5, 15, 16, 45, 175
   emphasis on in Plato 15
prediction
   of fate 187
predilection
   of modern aesthetic 167
preference
   definite
     declared by Duessa 153
   of careful reader
     for Redcrosse's course of action 128
   of swords to words 151
prelapsarian
   perfect beauty 120
   perspective
     of Una 117
   sense of identity 131
   state
     of Eden 45, 226
preliminary
   trials 240
pre-linguistic
   creation 111
   ontology 104
     of the Creator 289
premise 274. *See also axiom*
   initial
     of being 190
premises
   a priori 274
   fictional 181
   modern 32, 94
   pagan 133
premodern
   era 13
preordained
   mission
     of Redcrosse 231
   victory 84

preparation
   of Redcrosse 57

    of Sansloy 128
        for fight with False Redcrosse 128
pre-Romantic
    Spenser's p. universe 132
presence 238, 284
    craving 283
    echoes of 199
    Gloriana's cohering 131
    in the world 241
    joyous
        of Una 289
    of evil
        in the universe 143
    of ivory 276
    of metaphor 218
    of minds 91
    of nature
        in mind 91
    of Redcrosse 109
    of the Dragon 251
    of truth 276
    of Una 129, 289
    ontological
        of the Dragon 274
present 126
    cause 108
    circumstances
        of Redcrosse 224
    danger 111
    existence
        of George 270
    faith 254
    hope 244
    immediate 172
    moment 184
presentation
    mode of 87
    of Archimago
        to Una 124
    of things 126
preservation
    of life 268
pressing
    forward 78
prestige 170
pretence 284
pretending 245
pretextual
    unity 189
prevail
    prayers of Una do not 131
prevailing
    of words
        of Night 159
prevention
    of endless life
        by Jove 159

preverbal
    nature of mind's alignment 78

truth
    of God's ontologically created universe 158
preview
    of the rise of Mutabilitie 146
prey 59, 119, 187
    gripping of
        by an eagle 254
    of lion 132
    yielded 130
price
    of blood 202
    passing 228
    paying the
        of others' guilt 157
pricked
    with anguish
        Redcrosse as 223
    with courage
        George as 245
    with pride
        characteristic of Sansfoy 106
pricking
    of Arthur 194
    of lion
        with hungry rage 120
    of the heart
        of Redcrosse by Remorse 225
    on the plain 48, 225
    Sansloy as 128
pride 46, 65, 106, 120, 131, 245
    ambitious 106
    charge of
        Redcrosse's indictment of the 146
    element of
        in Redcrosse 148
    excessive 144
    foolish 184
    hatred of
        in the antique world 276
    image of
        Orgoglio as 260
    natural 121
    of an ass 217
    of Dragon 269
    of force 245
    of Hercules 285
    of place 166
    of Redcrosse 236
    outrageous 269
    pompous
        Persia as the nurse of 144
    pricked with
        characteristic of Sanfoy 106
    queen of
        adoration by 154
    sin of 47, 60, 188, 194
    submission 120
    trees "yclad with sommers" 52
    yielded 120, 121
pride (of lions) 121
primal

Index

chaos
  beneath linguistic flux 240
prince
  Arthur as 184
  royal
    state of 277
princely
  gifts 276
  puissance
    abatement of 120
prince of darkness
  Gorgon as 70
princes 166
princess 144
  too exceeding proud
    Lucifera as 144
Princess
  of Eden 183, 228
principle 215
  of beauty 91
  of evil 156
  of government 125
  of identity 17, 96, 238
    in the world of time 96
  of indivisibility 117, 126
  of likeness 238
  of mutually assured destruction 259
  of order
    in political society 99
  of reason
    lack of 186
  of revenge 259
  of space 249
  of time 249
  of truth 91, 126
    Una as 125
  of unity 84, 92, 95, 104
    Una as 95
  pleasure 21
  scientific 179
principles 34
  abstract
    in allegory 214
  sacred 96
  social
    of Aristotle 197
  Stoic 180
prior
  ontology
    of God 181
  world 161–162
priorities
  social
    exclusive and exclusionary 165
prioritizing
  of things
    according to reason 165
priority
  moral

    of Una's ratinal dwarf 165
  of divine over the worldly 6
  of faith
    over reason 23
  of figural over the literal meaning 6
  of God's creation 76
  of good over evil 138
  of history over fiction 32
  of ideal over the real 6
  of inner over the outer 6
  of invisible over the visible 6
  of kernel over the chaff 6
  of language of the heart
    to signs 73
  of precedence 137
  of wisdom of the heart 73
  of world
    in the thought of Augustine 189
  temporal 286
prison
  doors
    of Redcrosse 185
  native
    returning Una to her 169
pristine
  state 273
private
  language 50, 51, 254, 292
    Wittgenstein's critique of 50
  nature
    of classical religion 194
  religion 193
privation
  of good
    definition of evil in Augustine 106
privative
  evil 225
  nature
    of evil 157
privy
  wise 136
prize 245
  for others
    Una as 288
  true nature of the 135
probability 18, 21, 294
  in *Timaeus* 19
problem
  for the careful reader 175
  heart of 288
  immediate
    of rescue of Una 132
  lack of
    of Archimago with Sansloy 128
  long term
    of rescue of Una 132
  of Archimago 103
  of Augustine 88
  of conflicting interests 211
  of continuing to follow the status quo 209
  of Frege's Puzzle 85

of how Una can express her inner beauty while
    maintaining the integrity of her virginal
    body 120
of identity 92
of love as a guide to experience 126
of making "triall" of one's experiences 141
of methodology 21
of ontology and epistemology 88
of power 66
of precedence of beauty 114
of Redcrosse's naïveté about language 56
of reference 33
of sense and reference 92
of Una
  in keeping her virtue in tact 229
with placing words in a dialectical framework 137
with Redcrosse 151
with the strategy employed by Arthur in addressing
    himself to Redcrosse 195
with words 96

problematic
  notion
    of escape 233

Problem of Fiction 15, 34, 40, 91
  Aristotle's invention of 14–16

problems
  epistemological 2
  ontological
    of nature 170
  scientific 11

procedure
  cognitive 90

process 188
  communication 228
  educative 232
  long 226
  metaphysical 194
  of a neverending education 177
  of condescension 241
  of differentiation 87
  of doubling 77
  of intermediary fiction 245
  of love 138
  of mankind's amplification of himself 192
  operating in the world of time 227
  rational 166
  scientific 194
  temporal 175

proclaim 274
proclamation 280
procrastinating 217
product
  of fiction 143
    Una as 95
production
  of doubling 134

products
  accidental

of fiction 66
profession
  of arms
    by Redcrosse 140
  of love
    by False Una 78, 82
    to Fidessa 163
proffered
  knife
    by Despair 206
progress 33, 40
  diurnal
    of life 179
  forward 167
progressive
  movement of the narrative 241
  role of history 150
projection
  outward
    of inward phenomenon 207
prolongation
  of battle 153
prolonging
  of life
    by man 202
promise
  of Trevisan 200
promotion
  social 167, 168
pronouncement
  of Redcrosse's death 173
pronoun-laden
  speech
    of Contemplation 238
proof 236, 262
proper
  knowledge 86
  name
    of Duessa 153
  names
    in Kripke 90
property
  emergent 66
  value of 266
proposition
  identity 87, 179
  perfect logical
    in Russell and Whitehead 88
  relational 87
prostration 274
  before Lucifera
    by Redcrosse 154
protagonist 65
protected
  boundaries
    of fiction 231
protection 52
  external 131
  of others 131

of sacred name
  of Una 83
  of Una 140
    by lion 120
    lack of by Redcrosse 130
protector
  animal 130
  knight 140
  need for
    by Una 120
Protestant 1
  England 70
Protestantism
  of Edmund Spenser 66
protestation
  of False Una
    of love for Recrosse 80
Proteus 67, 103
proud
  avenging boy 194
  luxurious pomp 276
  pagan 138, 152
prouder
  vaunt 194
providence
  eternal 132
  of God 28
province
  of Night 178
proving 60
  by plain example 141
  in battle 146
  of Redcrosse's force
    on a strong enemy 61
  of strength 67
  pity
    in the heart of Night 156
  Redcrosse as a warrior 148
  sense 78
  worthiness
    for adventure 84
prowess
  as way to integrate oneself into court 197
  battlefield
    externalized by Redcrosse's possession of the arms of Sansfoy 149
  of Arthur 198
    in defending the honor of the Faerie Queene 195
  worthiness through 197
proximity
  physical 123, 137
proxy
  Archimago as
    for underworld action 77
prudishness
  of dreamers 78

psychology
  in Aristotle 15

subtle
  of Despair 204
psychomachia 116
Ptolemy, Claudius
  Almagest 86
public
  display
    of learning 194
  philosophy 193
  rule of the p. state
    in Aristotle 102
  scrutiny 254
  space 50, 174
  sphere 50
puissance 120, 221, 257
puissant
  arms 245
punishment 40
  for concupiscence
  of Hercules 258
punning
  on Ignaro's nature 189
pure 267
  direction
    given by God 116
  Phoebus 160
  reason 76, 87, 161–162
  white
    gown of 281
  woman
    Una as 175
purification 240
puritan 42
purity
  of Eden 276
  of Una 84
puropse
  of reader 93
purple
  blood 106
  honorific 217
  robe 95
purpose 52, 53, 174, 210, 268
  deeper 61, 78, 152
    of God 79
    of poet 178
  defeat of
    of Una 212
  fitting
    framing of 277
  forward
    offered by Una 199
  fulfillment of 209
    by George 262
  goodly
    intercourse of Redcrosse and Fidessa described in terms of 111
  high 248
  higher
    of God 138

human
  of George 260
  inner 78
  in the Wandering Wood 53
  lack of
    in Redcrosse's life 148
    in Redcrosse's travels 206
  looking for 178
  nature's blind 79
  of Archimago 123
  of God 295
  of logic 174
  of mankind 91
  of Spenser 244
  of will 255
  particular 31
  seriousness of 232
  teleological 62
purposeful
  action 206
  power
    of limited body 262
purposeless
  wandering
    of Redcrosse 199
pursuit
  brave
    of chivilrous emprise 192
  of dreams 196
  of love 197
  of random adventure
    by George 287
  of Una
    by everyone but Redcrosse 124
putting
  away
    of Una's fear 134
puzzlement
  over a paradox
    in Una's mind 136
Pyrrhic
  victory 192
Pythagoras
  in Ovid's *Metamorphoses* 36
  speech
    in Ovid 46

Q

quaking
  of Cocytus 70
  of Redcrosse 205
quality 5
quantum
  physics 51
queen
  great
    of Faery 197
  Lucifera as 149
  maiden

  Una as 111
  of pride
    adoration by 154
  sovereign
    Lucifera as 154
Queen of Eden 44, 45, 57, 122
Queen of England 209
quell 257
quelling
  of violence
    in the social world 149
  the rage of George 250
quest 60, 91, 215
  a lack of direction in 67
  for fame 163, 249
  for individual fame
    seen by soothsayer as sad 162
  for the ends of experience
    in Augustine 181
  of Redcrosse 166, 280
  stalling of
    of Una's 135
questers 240
question 69, 70, 84, 120, 132, 280, 286
  central
    whether Una has heard the dwarf's whole
      discourse 177
  of despair in chosen Redcrosse 206
  of difference 86
  of difference between Arthur and Ignaro 189
  of how reader they are to choose between equal
      alternatives when the book is closed 141
  of how the knowers know that they are not deluded
      142
  of identity 85, 86
  of inclusion of Redcrosse within the class of men
      210
  of interpetation of the northern star 83
  of mankind's posture towards natural world 52
  of permanence of fiction and reality 175
  of perspective 277
  of reference
    after Redcrosse has checked his senses 112
  of similarity
    in Una's mind 120
  of Spenser's belief in magic 103–104
  of Spenser's disposition towards his reader's ability to suspend disbelief 112
  of the deconstruction of magic with Spenser's
      fiction 104
  of the existence of Archimago's sprites 101
  of the location of truth 84
  of the wisdom of Redcrosse 60
  of Una's blame 84
  of Una's reaction to Redcrosse's performance in
      the battle with Errour 68
  of what "reasons rule" should be 150
  of what Redcrosse makes of his experience in the
      House of Pride 144
  of when there will be enough information to act 55
  of where Redcrosse is in space

in space 172
of where the home of Redcrosse lies 82
of whether a powerful Dragon can lift the body of a man 254
of whether he has seen the "whole" of the Cave of Despair 201
of whether outward environment is reflected in or distinguished from inward character 53
of whether Redcrosse can build of his native virtue 108
of whether Redcrosse has anything to fear from Duessa 108
of whether Redcrosse should follow the northern star 82
of whether the Dragon is dead 272–273
of whether the King has become a tyrant in order to save his kingdom 289
of why a pagan knows what the Knight of Holinesse does not 150
of why Redcrosse goes into battle with Errour 58
of why Una is so worried about Redcrosse's ultimate victory 58
of why why Redcrose left Una 172
raised by Æsculapius 159
reasonable
  asked by Arthur 184
Sansloy's q. of where to place blame for his attack of Archimago 129
questioning
  of reality 112
  of Una's ontological existence 46
questions
  of equality
    in Frege 85
quest-romance
  chivalric 239
quickness
  of eyes
    of Contemplation 234
quiet
  road
    of Eden 290
Quilligan, Maureen 8, 271, 294
  on adding faith to force 56–57
  Language of Allegory, The 8
quitting 132

R

rabble 193, 276
rablement
  rude 276
race 1
  earthly 197
  elfin 244
  English 239
  heavenly 214
  human 239
  timely 160
rage 64, 65, 253, 269
  affecting the mind 123
  discordant note of 66
  drives Ruggiero to extermity 65
  fault of 250
  hungry
    forgetting by lion 120
  interfering 253
  mighty 250
  of Aeneas 63
  of George 250
  of pagan foe 63
  of Sansloy more of might 131
  of the poet 250
  of tyrant 215
ragged
  briars 231
  clouts 201, 231, 281
  shore 255
raging
  ire
    of Sansjoy 153
  sea 221, 255
  spoil
    of lawless victor's will 130
railing
  of Abessa and Corceca 123
  of Corceca 123
rain 52, 77, 111
  timely 268
raising
  art above nature 98
  by Duessa's hellish science 114
  image of 264
  of heart
    by words of Fidelia 221
  one position over another 286
  over nature 185
  to the second tenor
    of the poet's song 250
  "unnatural" structures over nature
    by society 123
Raleigh, Sir Walter 30. *See also* Letter to Raleigh.
ram 257
  in epic simile 106
rancor
  rusty knife of 148
rancorous
  ire 253
random
  adventure 67, 287
    of Redcrosse 209
    of Una 131
  course of Redcrosse's adventures 115
  walk
    of Una 197
  wandering 83, 167
    by Una 119
randomness 62
  in wilderness 160

of walk 165
range
  of allegorical figures
    enlarging the 239
ranging
  forests
    by Arthur 194
rape
  of the churches 122
  of Una 131, 160, 290
    by Sansloy 131, 140
raping
  churches 290
rapist
  determined 133
rare 227
  heavenly wisdom 136
  speeches 112
rascal 276
rash
  doom 202
rashness 54
rational
  animal 15, 73, 183
  approach
    to experience 4, 160
  cause 288
  clarity
    lack of 282
  consciousness
    of humanity 242
  content 104
  discourse 183
  ego 242
  formula 97
  framework 15, 164, 172
  inquiry 179
  intelligence 100
  knowledge 22
  language 192
  man 192
    Arthur as 194, 198
  mind 97, 212
    individual's control of 135
    training of 277
  nature 4
  order 90
  picture 227
  precision 118
  process 166
  social structures 123
  substantial consciousness 179
  temperance
    of the individual 190
  terms 60, 97
  view 266
    of the world 253

rationality
  human

    limits of 155
  of Augustine 104
ravin (a thing taken as prey) 252
ray
  shining 114
reaction
  Augustinian 242
  lack of
    to Archimago's saying the Ave Maria 70
  of soothsayer 162
  of Una 68
    to sign of deadly tidings 168
  of uneducated crowd 152
  possible 153
  sympathetic
    of readers 229
  to Una's beauty
    by Sansloy 132
  wise 143
reader 5, 43, 46, 48, 50, 62, 69, 75, 93, 94, 99, 104, 110, 114, 115, 127, 142, 147, 148, 150, 151, 155, 160, 163, 164, 168, 174, 188, 198, 201, 211, 225, 227, 234, 239, 241, 243, 244, 260, 263, 264, 266, 274, 288, 295 *See also* careful reader.
  alienation of
    from George 245
  asked by poet to weigh differeing values 147
  assurance of his own salvation 47
  cause for concern for 119, 152
  cause of confusion
    of reference in 175
  clued in to metaphysical aspects of the poem 254
  desire to achieve maximum freedom 55
  dilemma of 84
  doubt of 238
  educated 61
  expectations of
    reconfiguring of 254
  experience of
    with failure of Redcrosse 46
    with Redcrosse 145
    with Una 282
  faced with choice 44
  given alternatives 54
  heavy memory of 145
  hope of the 198
  intuition of 145
  invited to use memory 83
  knowledge of 143
    Archimago's evil 70
  lack of certainty of 131
  learning of lesson 68
  memory of 121, 174
  mind of 60, 145
  modern 2, 84, 167, 214
  naïve 141
  no obligation to act 55

  not meant to forget element of pride in Redcrosse 148

Index 453

obligation of 178
ontological 104, 164
perception of 143
perspective of 200, 276
   on Una's beauty 133
poor 62, 93
position of the 187
questiong of Redcrosse's moral insight 166
reaction to Archimago 68
reassurance of 266
recognition by 145
Reformation 84
Renaissance 43
revulsion of 84
spiritual meaning available to 254
stance outside the text 57
standing outside of fiction 28
stout memory of 179
stout memory of the 145
structure of knowledge in the 131
translation of
   out of substantial consciousness 76
uncareful 12, 150, 168, 216
unwary 290
warning to 148
reader response 9, 10, 50, 84, 220
readers 39, 204, 216, 226, 240, 253, 273, 274, 276, 281
   challenge to 214
   hopeful 287
   linear
      of *The Faerie Queene* 145
   message to 152
   modern 51
   of Spenser 105
   Reformation
      on the question of the suspension of disbelief 112
   sympathetic reaction of 229
   uncareful 57
readiness
   for battle 185
   of Redcrosse
      to face the Dragon 68
reading 34, 38, 52
   beneath the surface 169
   correct 57
      by Contemplation 246
   end
      of Orgoglio 186
   excitement in 42
   horizontal 12
   linear
      ofnarrative 214
   line-by-line method of 12
   literal
      of Errour by Redcrosse 66

   modern 169
      of allegory 10
   of *The Faerie Queene* 239
   of monstrous shapes 60, 66
   of name
      of Ignaro 189
   of name and nation
      of George 246–247
   of ontological reality 26
   other works 69
   postmodern 240
   procees of 8
   process of 175
   sorrow
      in sad countenance by satyrs 134
   standard 221
ready
   path
      to heaven 231
real 6, 180, 246
   existence 270
   fear 251
   harm 186
   ontologically 157
realism
   in fiction 112
realistic
   fiction 112
realities
   harsh
      of the world of time 140
reality 20, 33, 38, 43, 47, 169
   appearance mistaken for
      in Plato's Allegory of the Cave 14
   appearance not 257
   false 163
   grounded in 80
   immoral
      of Corceca's behavior 234
   in fiction 94
   lack of connection between fiction and 39
   literal 61
      ontological foundation in 212
   metaphysical 269
   of chains of necessity 158
   of events 112
   of human expectations 203
   of limited substantial consciousness 175
   ontological 26, 45, 57, 66, 96, 98, 234, 256, 282
      as inaccessible 296
      God's creation of 58
      lack of in Archimago's magic 104
      temptation to reach the ends of fiction in 58
   ontologically-existing 272
   relaxing hold on 281
   substantial
      lack of 66
      of the poet 226
   substitution of fiction for 175
   underlying 285
   untested 253
realization 32
   by dwarf

of how far Redcrosse has actually strayed 168
of dreams 196
of potential
   of Redcrosse 99
of the limits of Una's power 135
of whole possibility 262
on a conscious level 74
that one's force is not one's own 56
that Una must join herself with another 137
realm
   of Faery 127
   of life 268
   of Lucifera 144
   of Night
      Duessa's journey to 154–156
   of time 203
reason 21, 22, 51, 105, 165, 166, 176, 183, 220, 282, 288, 295, 298
   ability of 278
   access to the truth of
      denied to Stoics and Epicureans 76
   a matter of correctly weighing things
      of unequal measure 150
   a posteriori 76, 166, 167, 174, 197
      of Una's dwarf 166
   as end of inquiry 91
   as intermediary 41
   as substitute
      for God's creation 93
   as tool
      of Platonic metaphysics 23
      of relative science 23
   attention to
      lack of 224
   causal
      Una's dwarf as bearer of 165–167
   central role of
      in the Elizabethan social hierarchy 167
   chain of 4
   claim of reason to transcend itself 21
   constructive 168
   decision based in 286
   deeper 5
   demotion of
      of reason from a metaphysical to a scientific process 194
   deployment of
      in Spenser's work 173
   direct
      in pagan authors 161–162
   direct application of 170
   expanded by Augustine 23
   eye of 101
   failure of
      to achieve the whole 168
   fallible 104
   for doubt 287
   for hesitation
      by Sansloy 131
   goodly 183
   governs collective action 41
   human

   calming effects of 105
   control of 188
   imperfect 57
   in Augustine 22–23
   in the relative world of 67
   in Virgil 76
   lack of 224
      in the King and Queen of Eden 277
   lens of 12, 287
   light of 72
   limitation of
      in Augustine 242
   limited 57, 97, 167, 296
      of mankind 256
   limited powers of 167
   listening to 3
   location of 118
   man imitates God through 149
   modern 171
   natural 3
   no obvious 109
   not the binding force in the world of time 174
   not the end of experience 166
   of God 99
   of poet 178
   of Redcrosse 99
   of Socrates 193
   of Una 175
   ordinary 4
   perfect 14
   power of 97, 183
      to put balance into unequal nature 177
   principle of
      lack of 186
   pure 76, 87, 161–162
   relative 97
   role of
      in Augustine 181
   rule of 149
   scholastic
      as intermediary 24
   secular 26
   separated from personal good 41
   solution 66
   specific difference of 105, 268
   system of
      inconsistencies in 88
   throwing out of 288
   to despair
      lack of 209
   universal 180
   use of 86, 133
reasonable
   question
      asked by Arthur 184
Reason (character in the *Roman de la Rose*) 107, 176, 179
reassurance
   of reader 266
rebalancing
   of load 290

Index

rebellion
  in Archimago's interest 124
rebounding
  sound
    through the woods 162
recalling
  the dwarf's words 69
rechristening
  of George
    by Una 241
recipients
  possible
    of Una's affection 137
recklessness
  of Redcrosse 54
  with his life 81
reclining 217
recognition
  by others
    of Una's true nature 136
  by poet
    of his limits 62
  by reader 145
  of Duessa
    by Fradubio 112
  of fraud
    by Redcrosse 113
  of λόγος
    by postmoderns 240
  of membership in the class of humanity
    by Redcrosse 113
recoiling
  of George 266
recompense
  of lovely words
    for long suffering 125
reconfiguration
  of the social world
    of Rome 181
reconfiguring
  expectations
    of readers 254
reconnection
  of the world back to its creator 40
reconstruction
  epistemological 263
  in minds
    of readers 230
  of facts 296
  of universe
    by Duessa 155
    of science 170
reconstructive
  mind 296
recovery
  the whole person 242
recreation
  in mind
    of preexisting ontology 88
  of experience

    in imperfect mind 212
  of ontological reason in the human mind 58
  of prior ontology
    in the imperfect mind of human beings 181
  of the moral work of God
    in human imagination 193
red
  cross 297
  scarlet 108
Redcrosse 1, 12, 28, 43, 47, 52, 64, 65, 67, 68, 74, 77, 78, 83, 90, 92, 96, 99, 100, 101, 104, 105, 110, 116, 117, 119, 124, 125, 129, 136, 154, 157, 158, 166, 172, 190, 194, 209, 217, 222, 225, 231, 235, 238, 240, 248, 254, 258, 262, 274, 277, 278, 285, 295, 297, 298. *See also* George.
  abandonment of Una by 130, 197
  accounting for Una's sadness 95
  action of 226
    in thhe battle with Errour 65
  amazement of 276
  animal being of 188
  Archimago plays at being 128
  arduous desire of 146
  armor of
    as a burden to him 147
  arms of 278
  Arthur's duty towards 194
  as active character 117
  as a superficial thinker 166
  as clown 105, 171
  as elf 112
  as human being 145
  as leader 210
  as man 226
    of action 77
  as member of the human race 239
  as reflection of the worst ends of mankind 105
  as rude man 149
  as serious 44
  as simpleton 238
  as stout faery 145
  as too simple and too true 116
  as wielder of destructive animal violence 149
  attachment to
    by Una 238
  attention of
    in conversation with Arthur 197
  awareness of his participation in God's sacred pageant 28
  bad behavoir of 125
  bathes in applause
    of others 155
  behavior of 140, 242
  belief of
    that he has nothing to learn 147
  blame of 119
  both living and dead 136
  callous indifference
    towards Una 120
  character of 48

clownish 195, 199
compassion for Fradubio 115
construction of his universe 115
construction of the situation he is describing 110
consummation
    of relationship with Duessa 162–163
contrast
    with Arthur 188
conviction of 142
correction of 261
declaration of love for
    by Una 175
defeat of Sansfoy 105–107
description of 48
difference between
    and Arthur 180
    and Christ 96
    and Una 55
dilemma of 278
dim eyes of 187
distraction of 200
distrust of Archimago 68
disturbance of
    by dreams 78
eager 186
education of 223
embodiment of the greatest shame a knight can suffer 141
emphasis on force alone 56
end of 62, 235
endures false distinctions 143
errancy of 216
errant 62
essence of 231
example of 141
experience of 216
    with time 134
expresses his affection for Fidessa 111
failure of 190
    as protector of Una 130
    to follow the "fixt" star 84
    to learn lesson after the battle with Errour 62
faith of 254
False 103, 128
fearlessness of 128
fighting for honor 152, 162
figural name of 84, 239, 244
figural state of 105
flight of
    from Despair 211
following of
    by Una 200
forces Errour to stay 121
forward footing of
    at the Cave of Errour 279
frail 210
freed 194
George referred to as 244
God's choice
    to fight the Dragon 186
goodness of 222
half-furious 65

hands of
    never touched by guilty blood 183
happiness of 83
harsh judgment of 141
heart of 96
    roused for another 176
helmet 124
helpless 114
human 120
identical to Jesus
    to Jesus 95
identification of 95
ignorance
    of the power bestowed on him with his arms 58
    of faults by Una 130
ignorant 238
ignored
    in the House of Holinesse 219
imminent suicide of 211
imperfect view of his experience 244
imprisonment of
    by Orgoglio 278
inarticulate 191
intercourse with Fidessa 111
interrupting
    the flow of dialog 196
in the Wandering Wood 52
introduction of 43–44
job of 202
judgment of 150
Kellogg's summary of adventures 1
killing of Errour 66
knight 196
knighting of Sir Burbon by 297
knight of the 174
knowledge of
    lack of 197
laying armor aside 119
leading a directionless life 148
learns to love Una
    in the as-yet-unexperienced future 197
leaving Una 152, 172
libidinous 229
listens intently
    to Arthur's dream of meeting the Faerie Queene 195
location of
    in space and time 172
logic of 203
looking for 167
looks at naked Fidessa 171
loss of
    Una considers the 171
love of
    lack of 196
manhood of 112
mind 148
    dissociation of might and reason in the 221
    negative content of 101

mistake of 184, 277
    of substituting individual sense for a general

Index

sense 113
moral weakness of 215
not a model of good behavior 110
not an example of idleness 146
not learning to read his experience 142
not meditating on the Triumph of Pride 148
on ends 102–106
passive 159
perception
   of Una's dwarf 165
   superficial p. of Fidessa 121
perfection of 220
pity of
   lack of 132
playing at chivalry 109
poor choice of 114
potential for action 74
power of shield of 297
presence of 109
prevention of death of
   by truth 184
problem with 151
puropse of
   lack of 148
purpose of
   lack of 206
reader's experience with 145
reader's poor assessment of 143
redemption of
   by Arthur 192
redirection of the mind of 226
rejection of Lucifera 146
release of 188
reliance of
   on animal genus 105
   on God 179
reorienting 233–248
rescue of 206
   by God 143
   by others 200
response
   to the leader of the Triumph of Pride 146
returns love of Una
   assumption of modern critics that 176
romance of
   with Una 153
saved from mortal sin
   by Archimago 101
search for danger and evil 68
seduced by Fidessa 120
self-centered 237
selfish 134
shield of 128
sin of
   against Una 204
socially destructive behavior of 234
speech of
   on the need for justice 201
startled by hearing a reflection of his own behavior
   back at him 162
status of 173
   as living or dead 172

strangeness of
   in the House of Holinesse 219
stunned silence of 204
submission of
   to Lucifera 152
substantial consciousness of 175
superficial sight of 176
talking to Arthur
   at cross purposes 198
theft of Una's dwarf 165
treatment of False Una 77–81
triumphant
   on account of his armor 148
typological status of 124
unconscious of the source of his victory in faith 62
understanding of
   lack of 153
unlikeness
   to lion 120
urged to be cautious
   by Una 54
violent act of 298
weak 118, 150, 210
wearing armor 147
wholeness of
   lack of 212
will of 104, 111
   to put the universe in balance through 207
wishing for death 190
without his armor on 163
wounding by
   of Una 171
wrests control of situation
   from Una 200
Redeemer
   badge of the 297
redeemption
   of government 36
redefinition
   of mankind 105
redemption
   of captive langour
      of Una 183
   of Problem of Fiction
      in Augustine 40
   of Redcrosse
      by Arthur 192
   of woeful parents
      of Una 215
redirection
   of mind
      of Redcrosse 226
   of sense 72
redoubled
   effort
      of Sansjoy 153
redoubling
   of raging ire
      of Sansjoy 153
   of wrath of Jove
      Æsculapius fear of 159

redressing
    of wrong
        by Redcrosse 227
reference 88
    a posteriori
        in Frege 87–88
    associated with *a priori* similarity
        in Frege 88
    claims of
        in a=b propositions 86
    completion of 86
    confusion of
        in the reader 175
    deflection of 113
    gulf of 25, 94
    horizontal
        endless chain of 6
    individual 113
    inequality in 94
    negative
        of sails 252
    object of 90
    of evening star 88
    of northern wagoner 82
    of sign 87
    problem of 33
    question of
        after Redcrosse has checked his senses 112
    sense of 57
    stability of 7
    switching terms of 87
    to creation
        of God 234
    to λόγος 89
    to mode of designation 86
    to nominative or accusative case 75
    to ontologically-existing object 85
    to polyphonic music 250
    to subject matter 86
    to the northern star 82
    to underlying ontology 87
    whole of 137
reflection
    in fuller knowledge 145
    of behavior
        of Redcrosse 162
    of echoes 199
    of heavens 193
    of inner life in silence 136
    of moral world 202
    of outward environment
        in inward character 53
    of self 151
    of things 165
    of underlying reality 285
        lack of 66
    of whole experience
        of the dwarf 168
    posture of 180
    transcendental 218
    unrecognized
        Fradubio as 147

reformation
    of opinion 135
Reformation 3, 13, 14, 34, 49, 76, 91, 93, 112,
        189, 282, 293, 296
    followers of Augustine 26
    poetry 161
    readers 84
        on the question of the suspension of disbelief
            112
    thought 270
Reformed
    Church 262
refraining
    from fury
        by Redcrosse and Sansjoy 149
refusal
    of deity
        by Odysseus 122
regard
    pittiful 278
region
    invasion of 253
    middle 256
rehearsal
    of deformed crimes
        in the mind of Redcrosse 205
reification 272
reign
    of Duessa
        over Night 158
    of Jove 155
reins
    of reason's rule
        forgetting 149
rejection
    of George
        as an individual 45
        as literal man 124
    of Lucifera
        by Redcrosse 144, 145, 146
    of pleasure
        as the end of human experience 52
relation
    between a thing and itself 86
    between goodwill and friendship 282
    between language and ontology 76
    between names 85, 86
    between objects 85
    between potential and action 97
    between signs 86
    in Frege 85
    proposition of 87
relations
    interdependent 229
relationship 75, 219
    between individuals and forms
        in Plato 14

    between mankind and nature
        severed after the Fall 46

Index

consecration of
  through physical intercourse 116
  mapped onto an algebraic grid 34
  of the microscopic individual to the macrocosmic world 162–163
  of mind
    with God's *a priori* ontological creation 152
  of Redcrosse and Una 84
relationships
  chronological 277
  interlinked
    in the House of Holinesse 219
relative 98
  aesthetic 95
  circle 133
  culture 133
  experience 232
  perspective 244
    of science 173
    on experience 66
  reason 97
    of Aristotle 133
  science
    of Aristotle 293
  space 69, 268
  truth 145
  values 64, 241
  world of reason 67
relativism
  of science 31
relaxing
  hold of reality 281
release
  from bands
    of oaths 279
  of aesthetic tension 274
  of Redcrosse 188
  of suspense 140
reliance
  on *a priori* armor 62
  on assumption that things are what they represent themselves to be
    by Una 180
  on native virtue 114
  on the kindness of strangers
    by Una 174
relics
  of power
    of Redcrosse 184
relief 122
  from the Dragon's power 253
relieving
  of conscience
    of Redcrosse 192
religion
  aspect of truth in 117
  Christian 26
  classical 194
  contest of 63
  false 217
    of Babylon 217

fictional 217
pagan
  danger of 259
private 193
true 256
universe of 217
religious
  wars 294
Relihan, Joel C. 201
remedy
  popular 233
remembered
  by literal name 239
remembering 23
  by Una
    of Redcrosse's abandonment of her 130
  passed mistakes 192
remembrance 48
  of deformed crimes
    by Redcrosse 205, 223
  of wicked ways 223
remorse
  lack of
    in Orgoglio 163
Remorse 225
removal
  of heart
    from dear loved dame 141
  of thorns and briars
    by Mercie 231
removing
  armor
    mistake of 274
Renaissance 17, 34, 52
  education 69
    Horace as a staple of 232
  skepticism in the 13
  writers
    ignorant of skepticism 8
renaming
  of George 241
  of Redcrosse
    to George 240
rendering 77
  decision
    based in reason 286
  judgment 202
rending
  hair
    of Coceca 123
  of veil 38, 39
renewal
  of expired fates
    by wondrous science of Æsculapius 159
  of image to perfection 73
  of passion
    in Corceca 123
  of past grief 191
  of time 37
renown 212

above all knights 249
reorienting
  of Redcrosse 233–248
repair
  of weakness of the flesh
    through reason 183
repairing
  kingdom
    of Una's parents 248
repentance 68, 137
Repentance 225
representation 33
  of temptation
    in an Augustinian universe 118
  of Una as the One Church 70
representatives
  of Elizabeth 94
repressive
  ego 242
reproach
  foul 131
reproachful
  fall
    of George 257
  strife 206
reproduction
  of *a priori* creation in human epistemology 167
  of Charissa 228
republic 41
reputation
  of Redcrosse
    protected by dwarf 166
  of the Church 24
request
  of Una
    to Fidelia and Speranza 219
requirement
  of purpose 268
  of wholeness 173
rescue
  by lion 130
  from the hands of evil-doers 109
  of Redcrosse 224
    by Arthur 199
    by God 143
    by Una 206
    from the dungeon of Orgoglio 209
  of Una
    by God 132
    by Satyrane 135
    from Sansloy 135
resemblance
  of Humiltá
    to Archimago 213
  of light of Redcrosse's armor to darkness 56

resignation
  of Una
    to the loss of Redcrosse 171
resistance 38
resisting
  words, looks, and sighs
    of Sansloy 131
resolution 242
  in mind 58
  metaphysical 66
  of Ariosto 65
  of Arthur 180, 192
  of distinctions
    in epistemology 282
  of paradox 226
  of placing words in a dialectical framework 137
  of problem 209
resolve
  of Arthur
    to find the body of the Faerie Queene 195
resolving
  not to repeat past mistakes 192
resounding
  of the woods
    with Una's cries 133
resources
  limited
    of active man 261
respect
  for law
    Sansloy's lack of 135
  for Una 235
respectability
  animal violence not the way to 149
respectable
  behavior 123
response 104
  heroic 222
  human 192
  measuring
    to ambiguous words 196
  of dwarf 278
  of Redcrosse
    to False Una's protestation of love for him 80
    to the leader of the Triumph of Pride 146
  of the sky
    to Una's appeal 132
  paraphrase of Una's 120
  plain
    of Fradubio 113
  to Archimago's Catholicism
    lack of 70
  to overreliance on Homer 170
responsibility 28
  absolution of
    of George 288
rest 151, 279
  calling to
    by chamberlain Sloth 150
  everlasting 278, 279
  lack of
    by Archimago 119

Index

need for 216
of George 246
of weary pair
  of Una and Redcrosse 220
Una's urging of Redcrosse to 69
resting 110
  by a fountain 136
  in silence 151
  never
    of Redcrosse 200
  of tired limbs 216
  place 187
  with Fidessa 160
restless
  activity
    of Redcrosse 232
  passion 151
  ship 290
  of poetry 272
restoration 1
  of Eden 227, 274
  of Fradubio's humanity 115
  of health 225
  of power
    of literary motif 170
  of Redcrosse
    by living well 115
    to state of equity
      in the golden age 251
restraint
  before action 54
  of ass 217
  of Redcrosse by Archimago 101
restriction
  of submission
    to Charissa 229
results
  equal 273
  of Redcrosse's use of force 60
resurrection
  of Christ 37, 40, 76–75
retardation 127
retirement
  forcing
    of George 266
retreat
  cowardly
    from danger 211
  of George 266
retreating
  of George 269
return
  back to Faery Queene 290
  cyclical 133
    of nature 291
  of George
    to Eden 279
  of hero 169
  of love
    of Redcrosse for Una 176
  of Redcrosse
    to the unified self of Una 117
  to books
    by Archimago 80
  to holiness 46
returning
  affection
    by George 246
  of Duessa
    to the realm of sunlight 160
  of waste words 71
  Una
    to her native prison 169
revealing
  face of Una 109
revelation
  delayed
    of a name 239
  gradual
    of evidence to the reader 145
  of beauty
    of Una 121, 130
  of true character 114
Revelation, Book of
  22:16 95
revenge 255
  exacting
    for injustice 202
  taken by Redcrosse 153
  vow of
    by Sansloy 129
  will bent on 123
revenging
  steel 265
revered
  mysteries 217
reverence
  for Una
    by Contemplation 235
  humble 284
Reverence 214
reversal
  in Augustine 38
  of classical education 38
  of deformed crimes
    of Redcrosse 205
  of judgment
    in Augustine 39
  of normal hierarchy 121
    of knowledge 175
  of progressive role of history 150
  of status
    of George 245
  of Una's warnings 61
reverse
  life and death 18

reversion
  to comfort

by Una 212
revival
    of dead
        by wondrous science of Æsculapius 159
    of George 264
    of heart
        of Una's dwarf 168
    of learning 24
    of Orgoglio
        ends when Arthur kills body 187
    of Una
        by dwarf 168
revived
    condition 264
revocation 62
    of foward footing is shameful 54
revolution 222, 294
revulsion
    of reader 84
reward 40
    of Una 142
rewards
    of compassion 224
rewriting
    Christian poetry 83
    of Virgil's ending
        by Ariosto 63
    pagan poetry 83
rhapsode 159
    passive
        Ion as 269
rhetoric 6, 25, 32
rhetorical
    flourish 288
rhymes
    charmed with enchanted 205
rich
    array 146
    men
        in Aristotle 233
    weeds 109, 145, 277
ride
    of Juno 146
ridiculousness 44
rift
    mainland 270
right 64, 66, 114, 147, 148, 286
    advice 69
    arm 64
    fighting for 152
    hand 285
    judgement for 202
    pleading for
        not with words but with swords 150
    side 150
    striving for 152

    to possess shield
        of Sansfoy 149

righteous 68
    man 184
    seed 235
    soul 231
righteousness 64
    holy 232
rightful
    cause 286
    claim
        lack of 144
    kingdom 144
        of Lucifera 149
rightly
    weighing
        of evidence 286
rightness
    of Una 174
rigid
    class distinctions 233
    descriptor 89, 90
Rinaldo 40–41, 179
ring
    with double echo 134
rings 122
rising
    of George 257
    of Lucifera
        from her stately place 146
    of Mutabilitie 146
    of sun 152
risk
    meaning at 240
ritualized
    battle with Sansjoy 151–153
rivalry
    between Plato and Aristotle 30
    of Duessa and Frælissa 114
river 37
    gushing
        of blood 256
    Nile 59
road
    quiet
        of Eden 290
roaring
    of a lion 225
    of raging seas 255
    threat 221
robbery
    of churches 122
    of self
        by evil star 191
robe
    of state 217
    purple 95
rock 7
    adamant 258
    diamonds as 131
rocky

Index

cliff 187, 270
Rodomonte 63–68, 230
role
  active 155, 172
  as king of animals 121
  heroic 233
  in destruction
    of Hercules 259
  metaphysical
    of classical philosophy 98
    of Archimago 119
      in imparting direction to action 81
  of artist 75
  of baptism 265
  of intent
    of Archimago 77
  of poet
    in larger whole 250
  of reason
    central in the Elizabethan social hierarchy 167
    in Augustine 181
  of Redcrosse
    in the destruction of Errour 121
  of specialist 59
  progressive
    of history 150
  social 121
rollback
  of death 268
rolling
  billows 255
Roman
  belief in the role of λόγος
    in social compact 181
  embrace of Stoic principles 180
  oligarchs 233
  teachers 233
romance 153
  literature of 169
Roman de la Rose 146, 176, 179
Roman Empire
  division of 285
Romans
  scientific inclination of 20
Romans, Book of 221
Romantic
  aesthetic 5
Romanticism
  flight from reason in 22
Rome
  appropriation of Pythagorean philosophy in 36
  Augustan 58
rooftop 77
room
  of sentinel 202
root
  of justice 202
  of the Tree of Jesse 95
rose (color) 95

rough
  horns 134
round 187
  dancing in a 133
  lists 129
rousal
  of Morpheus 234
  of Night 234
rousing
  of Morpheus 71, 74
  of Redcrosse 101
Rousseau, Jean-Jacques 49, 142, 251
royal
  array 146
  court 245, 298
  house 245
    Redcrosse's connection to 121
  household
    of Una 171
  maid 138, 195, 244
    Gloriana as 296
  prince
    state of 277
  Prince of Eden 276
  throne 217
royalty
  British
    George as descendant from 245
rubbing
  of temples
    of Una 169
rude
  appearance 133
  eyes
    of satyrs 133
  rablement 276
  Redcrosse 149
rudeness
  of shepherd poets 111
rue 80
rueful
  sight 165
Ruggiero 63–67, 230
ruin
  hasty
    of castle 187
  of Night 157
ruins
  of a broken tower 108
  of Eden 290
rule 161–162, 184, 285
  by Cupid 227
  by policy, not laws
    by Lucifera 144
  in Eden 285
  lust to
    in Friedrich Nietzsche 296

  of day and night

    by Arthur's arms 178
    by Jove 159
    of flock 106
    of intellect 43
    of reason 149
    of Rome 109
    of ruthless Machiavellian 43
    of state 102
    pagan 64
    submission to
        of Lucifera 150
    unfitness for
        of Lucifera 144
ruler
    legitimate
        of the Kingdom of Eden 274
    of kingdoms 144
    ruthless 43
    tyrannical 36
rulership
    of the heavens
        by Jove 144
rules
    of patrimony 284
rumor 259
Rumor 259
running
    away
        by Sansloy 133
    away of Archimago
        in the face of violent battle 128
    of timely race 160
rupture 181
Russell, Bertrand 88, 292
rustic
    horror 134
rusticity 43
rusty
    knife 206, 244
        in the Cave of Despair 201
        of Despair 236
        of rancor 148
        Una snatchers away the 206
ruthless
    men 294
    rulers 43

S

sacrament
    human
        baptism as 262
sacred
    arms 58
    chapel
        of Contemplation 234
    history
        George's place in 247
    law

        of arms 152
    lore 212
    muse 250
    name 83
    ontology
        of God 58
    pageant 28, 295, 296
    potential 96
    principles 96
    waves 263
sacrifice 63
sad 232
    cheer 280
    countenance 134
    estate 120
    perils 277
    shores of Acheron 64
    sight 152
    tongue 171
sadness 49
    of Archimago 68
    of Redcrosse's quest for individual fame 162
    of Una 95
    solemn 243
safe
    ironic distance 148
    opportunity 115
safety 269
    guarantee of
        of Eden 249
    in a world of determined rapists 132
    of others 192
    position of 267
saffron
    bed of Tithonus 95
sage
    pagan
        Varro as 221
sageness
    of Archimago's appearance 68
sailing 272
sailors
    mystery to 251
sails
    Dragon's wings likened to 252
    negative reference of 252
    to the winds 251
saint 1, 239
    creation of 105
    George's canonization as 104
Saint George 104–105, 239
    true 241
sainthood 46, 236
    of George 239
        as unalterable 105
saintly
    mission
        of Redcrosse 223

saints 70, 141

Index

vestments of holy 122
sake
  of lady 153
Salles, Ricardo 180–181
salt
  tears 278
  water 225
salty
  tear
    of Tethys 127
salutation 124
saluting
  of Redcrosse
    by Fidelia and Speranza 219
salvation 47, 265
  a priori 268
  at birth
    of Redcrosse 242
  by Una's beauty 119
  hope of 231
  knowledge of
    of Redcrosse 209
  mutual 263
  of George 204, 263
  of individual 225
  of Redcrosse 105
  of righteous soul
    of Redcrosse 231
  physical 137
  status of
    defined by God 46
  unwilled 267
sameness
  in Frege 86
Samos 36
Sansfoy 136, 157, 257
  armor of 148
  arms of 149
  death of 107
  defeat of 105–107
  shield of 148, 150, 153
Sansjoy 232
  combat with 173
  Duessa declares preference for 153
  lack of sense of
    of deeper purpose by 152
  likened to Errour 150
  raging ire of 153
  ritualized battle with 151–153
  unritualized battle with 148–151
Sansloy 140, 174
  amazement of
    at Archimago's presence 129
  Archimago's lack of a problem with 128
  body of 276
  capture of Una 140
  confounding of 129
  confrontation of
    by Una and Satyrane 136
  knowledge of arms of 130
  perspective of
    on Una's beauty 133
  pity for Una
    lack of 132
  rescue of Una from
    by satyrs 135
  social position
    lack of 132
  staying of 129
  tearing of Una's veil by 130
  thought of 131
  Una meeting with 128–133
  unmerciful 129
  vow of revenge by 129
Sartre, Jean Paul 188
Satan 26
satire 42
satisfaction
  of animal desire 290
  of desire
    of Una 173
Saturn
  overthrowing of
    by Jove 157
  overthrow of
    bu Jove 157
Satyrane 136, 174
  admiration
    for Una 136
  as master of beasts 136
  rescue of Una by 135–136
  stopping of Sansloy's desire by
    by a speech from 137
  winning battle for Una's heart 137
satyrs 140, 290
  amazement of
    at uncouth beauty of Una 133
  as fictional creatures 133
  as half-beasts 137
  backward-bent knees of 217
  change their looks 134
  error of the 160
  far away 133
  on horizontal plane 142
  relative culture of 133
  Una among the 133–135
  worship
    of nature 137
    of Una 135, 160
Saussure, Ferdinand 89
savage
  nation 134
savagery
  of animals 99
saving 130
  body
    from scorching fire 266
  helpless Redcrosse
    by Arthur 114
  sinful soul

of Redcrosse 235
Saxon
    kings 245
scales
    brazen 251
        of the Dragon 251
    no longer in balance 114
scalp
    crested
        of Dragon 264
scaly
    neck 255
scared
    nations 250
scarlet 108, 277
    carpet 276
scath (injury)
    unthrifty 148
scattered
    carcasses
        on the green 200
    skulls and bones 166
scattering
    of dead skulls and bones 147
scepter
    of Lucifera 144
scheintod 169
scholars
    ignorance of 169
    scholastic 3
    superficial 169
scholastic
    reason
        as intermediary 24
    scholars 3
scholasticism
    universe of 24
school
    classical 38
    house 220
    of academic skepticism 292
    of Epicureans 76
    of Stoics 76
    pagan 39
School of Chartres 292
Schrödinger, Erwin 51
Schrödinger's cat 51, 98
science 5, 10, 16, 31, 103, 291
    age of 88
    a posteriori 76
    demonstrative 18
    divisions of 118
    divisive
        triumph of 102
    hellish 114
    imperfect 158
    magical 103
        of Archimago 218
    modern world of 169
    of aesthetics 4
    of alchemy 178–179
    of Archimago 179
    of mankind 4
    perspective of 241
    process of
        as relative knowledge 19
    reason as a tool of 23
    relative
        of Aristotle 293
    relative perspective of 173
    triumph of 3
    wondrous 160
        of Æsculapius 159
    worldly
        Archimago as master of 102
        of alchemy 185
    world of 191
        left unattended by Redcrosse 159
scientific
    aesthetic 95
    agents of change
        pagan gods and demons as 3
    description
        of the Dragon's dimensions 249-271
    framework 172
    idiom 12
    information
        alignment of with imagining mind 171
    inquiry 179
    manner 265
    methods 12
    orientation
        of the poem 255
    perspective 244
        on experience 66
    power 155
    principle 179
    problems 11
    process 194
    space 268
    terms 2
    unity 189
    universe 170
        making trial of 253
    view 266
    world 179, 192, 238
    of values 269
scientifically
    circumscribed walls 273
scientifically-oriented
    universe 276
scolding
    of mankind
        by Cælia 216
scorching
    fire 266
    flames 258
        of Orion's hound 127

scorn 52

Index

of the children of Night 156
screams
  expression of Una's plight in 133
scripture
  holy 24
  literal sense of 25
scrutiny
  public 254
Scruton, Roger 2, 50
Scylla and Charybdis 94
sea 256
  of deep sorrow 180
  of seekers 194
  raging 221
seamless
  vision
    of beauty 281
search
  for adventure
    by Redcrosse 232
searing
  of body 258
seas
  raging 255
seat
  native
    mountains moved from their 221
  of being 95
  of earth 255
second
  birth 221
  error 68
  tenor 250
secret
  aid
    assistance by 151
  breach
    in conscience 205
  councils
    wit in 135
  external magic
    in Redcrosse's shield and arms 151
  smart
    of Una 134
  treason 288
  virtue 265
secrets
  of sexual pleasure 150
  of the world made and unmade 155
secular
  throne 109
secure
  knowledge of things as they are 104
  metaphysical foundation 244
security
  against danger 111

seduction
  of Redcrosse
    by Fidessa 120
seductions
  of Duessa 218
see
  Lucifera's followers wish to 144
seed
  activating the
    of human potential 177
  righteous 235
  spilled on ground 167, 168
seeing 53, 160
  and interpretation 171
  by others
    of Redcrosse's battlefield prowess 149
  Cælia 218
  deceit
    in Ariosto 64
  into heart
    by Redcrosse 228
  of Redcrosse's mistakes
    by readers 61
  of Una
    by George 282
  Redcrosse 173
  the abandonment of Una
    by the poet 118
  Una mocked
    by Archimago's deception 129
  with eyes 165
  with wisdom
    rather than with carnal eyes 71
seekers
  sea of 194
seeking
  another 126
  fame 245
  identity with oneself (a=a) 126
seeming 49, 52, 246, 270, 277
  body 101
  glorious show 109, 145
  great pretence 284
  of Archimago 68
  of False Una's speech 79
  of lovely words 125
  of Una's dwarf 165
  pain
    of Redcrosse 224
  to separate the wheat from the chaff 143
  true
    grace of Duessa 158
  wisdom 103
seen
  present service 154
seizing
  of shore 278
self 83, 177
  barriers to action of 132
  defiling of 204
  excellent

excelling George's 249
fallible 177
fear of
  by Trevisan 200
individual 93
inward turn toward 136
literal 83
love of 80
  by Lucifera 144
of Una
  mocked by Archimago's deception of her 129
reflection 151
robbery of
  by evil star 191
selling of
  to Duessa 204
true
  dispute over the location of 57–59
unified
  of Una 117
self-centered
  Redcrosse 237
selfish
  Redcrosse 134
self-jarring
  mass 256
self-realization
  journey of 246
self-sufficiency 17
  a priori state of 80
  in Aristotle 16
  in modern world 16
  of individual 233
selling
  literary education 38
  of self
    to Duessa 204
semantic 240
  echoes 241
  field 27, 89
semblance
  glad 134
  of self love
    delight in 144
semblant 104
Seneca the Younger 21
  suicide of 222
sense 88
  anagogical 27
  a priori
    in Frege 88
  bitter
    of deep-rooted ill 256
  collective 15, 41
  daunting of the 186
  difference of
    in Frege 88
  diverse impressions of 106
  etymological 56
  every 195

exegetical 27
feeble
  of George 246
general 113
God-given 111
individual 113
in Frege 85, 87–88
  as *a priori* identity proposition 87
inward 72
literal 25
metaphorical 33
moral 27
more than one 105
of animal being 104
of control
  given to the reader 131
of deeper purpose
  lack of 152
of direction 79
of goodness
  lack of a 67
of identity
  of Una with herself 139
of injustice 263
of justice 204
of knowing and not knowing
  in Aristotle 72
  in Augustine 72
of lust 130
of manhood 111
of reader
  that Una is not deploying her *a posteriori* reason 174
of reference 57
of spatial geometry 253
of taste 133
of the sign 87
plain 31
prelapsarian
  of identity 131
triune
  of strength 254
tropological 27
unitary 103
weaker 77, 101
senseless
  corpse 268
  man 137
senselessness
  in the epic simile of rams 106
senses 39
  bodily 73
  checking of 112
  doubt of
    by Redcrosse 112
  dulled 265
sensing
  by satyrs 134

sentence 33, 175 *See also* **grammar**.

Index

meaning of
  revealed by temporal process 175
  subject of 175
sentinel 202
separate
  entity
    Despair as 207
  existence 98
  experiences 245
  loves 198
  pieces 281
    of clothing 201
  world
    of being 97
separateness
  in knowledge 98
separation
  absolute
    from God's purpose 295
  from law and justice 99
  of act from actor in Quilligan 8
  of allegory into discrete parts 27
  of Forms in Plato 15
  of mankind from nature
    in Homer 40
  of modes of action from ends 26
  of perspectives 269
  of reason from personal good 41
  of true love from the object of its affection 125
  of Una
    from her beloved knight 137
    from herself 117
    from Redcrosse 102, 117, 121
  of wheat from chaff 143
  of will
    in Calvin 26–27
serial
  nature of human experience 203
series
  of lies
    told by Odysseus 127
  of poor choices
    by Redcrosse 200
serious
  charge
    against Redcrosse 204
  consequences 274
seriousness
  of epic 60
  of purpose 232
sermonizing 232
serpent
  in a cup
    held by Fidlelia 219
servants 265
service 59, 237, 239
  at court 295
  humble 120

  making seen
    of Redcrosse 154
  of interdependent relations 229
  six years of
    to the Faerie Queene 279, 290
  to God 154
  to Lucifera
    by Redcrosse 154
services
  comely 277
serving 166
set
  of denoted objects 141
setting
  postion of northern star 82
settling
  of reason
    in mind of Una 183
Seuren, Pieter 90
seven
  mouths
    of the Nile 154
sevenfold 82
severance
  of mankind and nature
    in the Fall 46
severing
  of will of mankind from will of God
    in Calvin 25
  the connection between nature and man 36
Sextus Empiricus 13, 76
sexual
  ecstasy 161
  pleasure 150
shade 127
  cooling 160
  dreadful 253
  hidden 54, 223
  joyous
    bath in pleasance of 161
  likeness to light 56
shades
  true 75
shadow 14, 34
  measurement by 250
  mountainous
    of the Dragon 253
  of night 124
  of two faces 297
shadows
  of human experience 92
shady
  arbor 133
  grove 110
  place
    sunshine in a 119
  tree 160
Shakespeare, William 30, 167, 191

shaking

of the earth 162
shame 62, 65, 123, 153, 267
   dread of 266
   fear of 58
   half
      of Sansloy at having attacked Archimago 129
   hiding face in
      by sun 290
   hiding for
      by Phoebus 132
   in Redcrosse's leaving Una 125
   lack of
      of Arthur 186
   no greater s. to knight 141
   of knighthood 125
   of Sansloy
      at having attacked Archimago 129
   of subordinated life 63
   of sun 137
   reproachfull 70
   to revoke forward footing 54
shameful
   sight 132
   Venus chain 101
shameless
   guise 78
shape 87
   of events 205
shapes 103
   ugly monstrous 66
sharing 55
   in Plato's Theory of Forms 14
sharper
   edge 265
shedding
   of blood 202
sheen
   of polished ivory 75
shelter
   human 115
shepherd
   fearful 110
   low 245
   simile of 110
   simile of gentle 60
shew
   a semblance glad
      by satyrs 134
shield 48, 153, 154, 237, 265
   bright
      of Arthur 186
   charmed
      of Redcrosse 151
   defensive 266, 297
   former
      of Sir Burbon 297
   magical
      of Arthur 186
      of Una 297
   magic in

      of Redcrosse 151
   of Arthur 178, 186, 266
   of George 266
   of Redcrosse 128, 163
   of Sansfoy 108, 148, 150, 153
   of Sansjoy 153
   of Sir Burbon 297
   power of
      of Redcrosse 297
   right to
      of Sansfoy 149
   silver 168
   worthy
      of Sansfoy 150
shields
   bright 253
   burning 106
   shining 253
shift
   of ground
      of philosophy 170
shining 179
   beauty
      of Una 132
   lamp of bliss 124
   light
      of heaven 186
      of Phoebus 93
   of a thousand angels 235
   ray 114
   shields 253
ship
   in Horace's *Satires* 59
   of poet 290
   restless 290
      of poetry 272
   viewed from stable shore 127
shipbuilder 16
shire 253
shock
   in the epic simile of rams 106
shore
   muddy
      of seven-mouthed Nile 154
   of Acheron 64
   ragged 255
   seizing of 278
   stable 127
   summer 255
short
   space 225
   time 172, 173
shortening
   of distance 102
   of life
      by man 202
shoulder 255
   of Despair 201
   of Hercules 259
shouting

Index 471

of the people 154
show
  glorious 277
    seeming 109, 145
  simplicity of 68
  worldly 145
showing 54
  kindness and courtesy
    to Duessa 146
  of Una
    in sight 281
  the way 235
  what you be
    location of being in 56–59
shows
  false 77
shrieking
  of Una 132, 133
shrunken
  sinews
    of Redcrosse 199
shunning 231
  death
    ordained by destiny 203
  hideous might
    by Arthur 186
  to take another blow
    by Dragon 257
  unlucky ground 110
Sibyl 75
side 69
  either 153
  laying a-
    rustic horror 134
  of evil 157
  of knight
    met by Fradubio 114
sides
  equal
    in fight 152
  naked
    of Despair 201
sighing
  sore 131
sighs
  resistance to Sansloy's
    by Una 131
sight 234, 264
  all men's 114
  amazement of
    in lion 120
  beguiling of 101
  blood shed in 202
  celestial
    of Una 282
  clearer
    of Archimago 234
  glancing 186
  interpretation of 166
  joyous 124

  misaimed 186
  mournful 166
  of eagle 264
  of men 101
  of Redcrosse 113–116, 236
  of Una 281
    moves lion 120
    tames the lion 128
  orientation of 234
  out of 124
  rueful 165
  sad 152
  shameful 132
  superficial
    of Redcrosse 176
  uncouth 78, 133
  weaker 179, 180
    of George 287
  wonder at the
    of Archimago by Sansloy 129
sign 73, 86
  linguistic
    subject to logic 89
  of conqureor 108
  of difficulty 177
  of fear 63
  of heat or rain 111
  of victory 264
    Saint George as 239
  of weakness
    in Redcrosse and the reader 150
  of word
    gives light inwardly 73
  sense of the 87
  that something is wrong
    with Trevisan 200
  vestigia as
    of God's prior creation 76
significance 219
  true
    of events 162
signification 73, 267
  of one thing by another 71
signifier and signified 89
signs 87, 274
  bekotening of 168
  bodily 73
  difference between 87
  obvious 109
  of deadly tidings 168
  outward 168
  poet's 69
  relation between 86
silence 111, 215, 221, 289
  allegory of speech and
    of Augustine 71–74
    of Spenser 74–76
  eternal 71
  falling into
    by Una 290
  metaphysical

of Una 194
of God's pre-linguistic creation
  compromised in expression 111
of Redcrosse 28
of Spenser 68
of the King of Eden 284
of Una 129, 211, 214, 228, 238
perpetual
  of Una 136
reflection of inner virtue in 136
resting in 151
stunned
  of Redcrosse 204
unity of 71
silk 281
silly
  maid 150
Silvanus 133, 134
silver 48, 76, 251, 276, 281
  anchor 219, 224
  gate of 100
  shield 168
similarity 1, 2
  a priori 88
  between Duessa's champion and ruins of a broken tower 108
  between Redcrosse and Gluttony 161
  between Spenser and Tasso 42
  generic
    between objects 277
  question of
    in mind of Una 120
simile 256
  epic 59, 82, 121, 187
    meeting of opposites in 106
    of shepherds 110
  expansion through 255
  in Ariosto 63
  of Christ as lion 225
  of gentle shepherd 60
    of gentle shepherd 60
  of lion 225
  of mariner 126–127
  of Nile 154
  of patience and action 58–61
  of Redcrosse as lion 62
  orientation of 59
simple
  Redcrosse as too 116
simpleton
  Redcrosse as 238
simplicity 44
  of show
    in Archimago's appearance 68
simultaneity
  of knowing and not knowing
    in Aristotle and Augustine 72
simultaneously
  backward and forward 241
sin 46, 183, 210, 237, 251, 272

blots of 225
committing 191
complicity in
  of Redcrosse 226
fall into 1
inflated
  of pride 194
late attempted
  of Sansloy 137
metaphysical source of 226
mortal 101
of pride 47, 188
of Redcrosse
  against Una 204
original 224
  of Adam and Eve 267
pageant of 147
participation in 147
sinews 226
  eaten by lion 225
  shrunken
    of Redcrosse 199
sinful
  bands 184
  soul
    of Redcrosse 235
singeing
  of face
    of George 258
singing
  praises
    of Una 275
sinners 220
  compassion for 223
sins 223
  consequences of
    of Redcrosse 164
  of George 269
  of Redcrosse 226
  past 271
  suppression of
    of George 271
  unequal
    in the Triumph of Pride 161
sire
  aged 68
  Humiltá as 213
sites
  specific
    of intersection 241
sitting
  blind 124
  in dark 121
  lowly 277
  of high
    by Lucifera 144
situation
  control of
    wrested from Una by Redcrosse 200
  misapprehension of 128
  of Una 135

Index

whole
  of past, present, and future 126
six
  old wizards 144
  years of service 279, 290
size 221
  exact
    of fictional Dragon 250
  of Dragon 253
  vast 273
skepticism 3, 10, 11, 23, 89, 94, 189, 293
  academic 20, 21, 240
    school of 292
  available to Renaissance thinkers 13–15
  doubts power of reason 22
  of Augustine 104
  pagan
    as call to action 76
  postmodern 9
skeptics 76
skewed
  sense of justice
    of Redcrosse 204
skill 100
  ascription to 210
  curious 289
  earthly 287
  greater 64
  of Christian hero 63
  of earth
    to bring forth fruit 125
  of man 210
  wily 287
skin 127, 195
skull
  of Dragon 264
skulls 166
  dead 147
sky 52, 179
  brightest 132
  domain of gods 36
  highest 84, 91
  response of
    to Una's appeal 132
  Una's appeal to 132
slaying 129
  of Dragon 273
  of False Una 78
  of Redcrosse 136
sleep 70, 80, 150
  careless 80
  god of. *See* Morpheus
  of Arthur 195
  of Morpheus 77
  passive
    of Redcrosse 77
  sound
    of the god of war 250
sleepiness

physical 70
sleeping 120
  Redcrosse 77
  spark
    of native virtue 107
sleepy
  minds 70
sliding
  of feeble feet 266
slight 265
  malicious 187
slipping
  away
    in mind 115
  of puropse 210
Sloth 150
slow
  gait
    of Humiltá 213
  travel of Una 124
slumber 222
slumbering
  heart 195
smart 119, 260
  bleeding 171
  final 206
  hellish
    brand of 207
  secret
    of Una 134
  uncouth 255
smiting 187, 264
smoke 54, 252, 270
  smothering 252
smothering
  smoke 252
snake
  hissing
    hatred of Una by Archimago as 103, 119
snare
  of envy 118
  wanton 227
snares 251
snobbery
  of Una
    in *Letter to Raleigh* 166
snobbishness 235
sober
  cheer 280
sobriety
  of Archimago 68
social
  coherence 193
  cooperative action 181
  destruction
    of animal violence 168
    of animal war 176
    of Thirty Years War 3
  elevated position

Sansloy's lack of 132
hierarchy
　of Elizabethan England 167
instinct 16
justice
　of the Stoics 180
ladder
　of Gloriana's court 166
masters 165
order of 190
　fragility of 151
position 166
　of lion 132
　of Una's dwarf 168
prinicples
　of Aristotle 197
priorities
　exclusive and exclusionary 165
promotion 167, 168
　based on merit 167
role 121
standing as king among men 121
superior 166, 168
world
　destructive animal violence in the 149
socially
　destructive 234, 246
　　animal genus 267
　　animal instincts 257
socially-constructed
　world
　　of Arthur 181
society 16, 176, 188
　best educated in 193
　built against nature 105–106, 197
　cooperation of 66
　feminine 209
　governance of 105
　in Aristotle 233
　larger concerns of 234
　male 209
　order 209
　ordered 64
　political 47, 99
　rational structures of 123
Socrates 15, 20, 156, 194, 221, 222, 228, 275, 292, 293
　as wise man 193
　death of 222
　in Plato's *Crito* 23
　in Plato's *Parmenides* 17
　use of reason by 193
"Socrates is a man" 16, 45
　predicate emphasis in Plato 15
soft 195
soil 267
　native
　　of Una 248–249
sojourn
　of Una 272
solace

treating of 161
soldier 38
　envy of merchant's position by 59
　may not move from watchful stead 202
solemn
　sadness 243
solemnity 49
soles
　weary
　　of Una 215
solid
　education 130
　foundation
　　of language 50
solitary
　man 40
solution 277
　ex machina 132
　modern 95
　of pity 132
　rational 66
　to Frege's Puzzle
　　lack of 85
　to problem of power 66
　traditional Crusader 63
solving
　paradoxes in logic 172
son
　foolish faery's 137
　of elf 239
　of Venus (Cupid) 96, 176
song
　of birds 52, 62
　of jollity 289
　of love 289
　timbrel 275
sons
　of Night 156
soothsayer
　can see beneath the surface of things 162
　negative judgment of 152
　wise 152
sophists 25
sorceress
　false 288
　　Duessa as 113
sore 260, 266
　afraid 138
　sighing 131
　Una's toil 126
sorrow 237
　deep 180
　in the sad countenance of Una 134
　of Una 171
　years of 125
sorrows
　suffering
　　by George 248
sorting

Index

of facts
  on a logical level 172
of Redcrosse's experience 116
of truth from perception 62
the question of Una's reaction to Redcrosse's performance with Errour 68
soul 18, 40, 263
  disease 224
  of men who live amiss 108
  powers of the 41
  righteous 231
  sinful
    of Redcrosse 235
  Stoic journey of 180
souls
  tableaux of 205
sound 53, 73
  asleep
    Silvanus in shady arbor 133
  dreadful 49, 162
  likeness of 73
  of cheereful whistle 127
  of merry pipes 134
  of morning drum 202
  of oaten pipe 110
  of swarming bees 77
  outward word 73
  sleep
    of the god of war 250
  utterable in 73
sounding
  of dreadful trompe 250
  of timbrel song 275
  of triumph 154
source 9, 31, 240, 241
  animal 75
  for battle with Errour 63
  metaphysical
    of sin 226
  observable 112
  of Errour's power to defeat mankind 66
  of external armor of Redcrosse 105
  of idea
    in Ovid's *Metamorphoses* 251
  of knowledge 14
  of moral truth 157
  of potential
    in Aristotle 97
  of power 253
    of Redcrosse's arms 179
  of Redcrosse's power
    in his own will 109
  of strength
    earth as 254
    ground as 257
  of voice of Fradubio 111
  of winds 251
  true 72
    of power 158
sovereign

queen
  Lucifera as 154
sovereignty
  native
    lack of 144
sowing 150, 267
  of true love 195
space
  little 223
  location in 83
    of Redcrosse 172
  long 69
  middle 142
    lengthening the 253
  of speculative trial 239
  principle of 249
  public 50, 174
  Redcrosse in 172
  relative 268
  scientific 268
  short 225
sparing
  of life 63
spark
  sleeping
    of native virtue 107
Sparta 260
spatial
  geometry 253
speak 68
  signs
    of deadly tidings 168
speaker 50
  required for speech acts 71
speaking 180, 194
  by Redcrosse
    of the need for justice 201
  no more of past 126
  of Una 209
  reproachful shame 70
  words
    at odds with what Archimago thinks 124
speaking up 70
spear
  bending of Archimago's 129
  couched 128
  needless 54, 56, 206
  of Arthur 178
  poignant 168
specialist
  role of 59
species
  allegory as
    in Augustine 71
  necessity of embracing all s. in generic definition of allegory 71
  other members of the 180
specific
  difference 97, 105
  example 141

individual 178
sites
  of intersection 241
terms
  of sin 206
specific difference 15
specificity
  of the poet 141
spectacle 37, 147
  entertaining 147
  of Virgil's poetry 38
  whole
    of the Triumph of Pride 146
speculation 9
  allegory as empty 24
  individual
    based on faith 41
    of intellect 40
speculative
  trial
    space of 239
speech 71, 180, 188, 285, 289
  allegory of silence and
    of Augustine 71–74
    of Spenser 74–76
  conveyance of knowledge in 73
  encoding 5, 7
  interruption of
    of the King of Eden 284–286
  joy of living 180
  kind 219
  medium of 96
  of King of Eden 284
  of Morpheus 74
  of rational man 192
  of Zele 213
  power of 194
  pronoun-laden
    of Contemplation 238
  seeming of False Una's 79
  stopping Sansloy's desire with a 137
  well-guided 183
  witches 156
speeches
  feeling 156
  of the heart 72
  rare 112
speed 290
  flying 284
spell 115
  magical 103
  of Duessa 276
spelling
  the name of Aeneas 39
spending
  counsel
    of Una 135
  of force 186

spite

  of fortune 171
Spenser, Edmund 1, 10, 11, 13, 26, 32, 43, 49,
    51, 52, 53, 66, 76, 77, 78, 84, 90, 91,
    94, 95, 96, 99, 101, 103, 109, 110, 111,
    112, 121, 123, 124, 125, 132, 141, 148,
    151, 154, 156, 157, 160, 165, 169, 171,
    174, 177, 179, 188, 226, 229, 232, 233,
    234, 242, 251, 264, 269, 270, 274, 275,
    276, 281, 289, 293, 294, 296, 298
  allegorical universe of 137
  allegory of of silence and speech 74–76
  approach to experience in 142
  argument of 126, 183
  Aristotelian universe in 206
  as creator of fiction 128
  as reasonable man 77
  as serious poet 44
  as wise author 230
  Augustinian faith of 230
  Augustinian universe of 155
  belief
    in the temporality of desire 137
  breaks the chain of necessity
    for the Furies 158
  clued in to metaphysical aspects of the poem 254
  compassion for Una's plight 118
  correction of Du Bartas 256
  deconstructing fiction of 133
  deployment of logic in 175
  engagement with skeptical arguments 11
  faery fiction of 152
  fiction of 152, 187
  follows Plato 75
  his intention
    stated in *Letter to Raleigh* 30
  humanness of 58
  irony 101, 125
  message
    to reader 152
  middles in 173
  modeling his work on Homer 127
  poem of
    center of 238
  position of 127
  pre-Romantic universe of 132
  problem of 209
  purpose of 244
  raises himself
    from his individual self to a type 93
  reliance on Augustine 235
  silence of 68, 70
  solution to Frege's Puzzle 91–94
  solution to the problem of power 66
  treated by Northrop Frye 169
  universe of 138, 179, 224
  unwillingness to delve into the secrets of sexual
    pleasure 150
  warning to his reader 148
  world of 158

Spenser Encyclopedia, The 1, 31, 117, 239, 275

Index

Speranza 219–220
  comes to the rescue of Redcrosse 224
sphere
  logocentric
    of fiction 282
  of action 253
  public 50
spheres
  of Jove's heaven 146
spies
  cruel 106
spilling 130
spirit 64
  health of 1
  in Calvin 25
  of St Paul 71
spirits 75
spiritual
  death
    of George 261
  foes 210
  life 261
  meaning 254
spite 80
  disdainful 131
  of tempestuous fortune 174
  spending of
    of fortune 171
spoil
  of war 150, 153
  raging
    of lawless victor's will 130
spoken
  meaning 228
sports
  wearying of
    by Arthur 195
spot
  cooling 110
  without 281
spotless 148
spouse 83
sprawling
  crowd 217
spread
  tail
    of the Dragon 252
spreading
  of sun's purple robe 95
spring
  pleasant 134
sprite 74, 77, 101, 222
  as artificial creation 100
  as proxy for underworld action 77
  guileful 112, 113
  heavy 224
  of Archimago 70–71
  substance of 101
sprites 77

  damned 158
  legions of 100
  ungendered 100
sprung
  freely
    out of fruitful ground 267
spurring
  of horse 129
spy 264
spying 171
  port
    from afar 127
squid 60
squire 101
  light-foot 187
  of Arthur 184
    stops flight of Duessa 187
stabbing 64
  of Rodomonte 63
  of Una's lion
    by Sansloy 130
stability 6
  of fictional λόγος 180
  of language 8
  of reference
    in Eden 67
  of λόγος 92
  ontological
    of mythical worlds 89
stable
  shore 127
  world
    of λόγος 233
staff
  of Humiltá 213
staggering
  steps
    of Redcrosse 235
staid
  faith 182
stale
  lifelessness
    of the Cave of Despair 200
stalling
  of Una's quest 135
stance
  ironic 127
  neutral 157
  passive
    of Redcrosse 155
stand
  of soldier 202
standard
  reading 221
standing
  amazed 129

  far
    Una as 273

firm
  by Spenser's hero 256
in doubt
  of Redcrosse fate 173
in need 192
social
  unnatural 121
star 53, 83
  distant 83
  evening 85, 88, 179
  evil 191
  fixed 84
  happy 61, 67
  morning 85, 88, 95
    Una as 92, 95, 281
  northern 82
  of Venus 88
  steadfast 82
  steady northern 82
stare
  astounded
    of the eyes of Despair 201
stars 67, 83, 132
  distant 133
  molten 132
  vertical plane of 142
state 16, 144, 204
  as a creation of nature 16
  changing
    of the world 203
  cloth of 144
  figural
    of Redcrosse 105
  justice is the bond of men in
    according to Aristotle 99
  luckless 278
  non-moving 203
  of animal being 104
  of equity 251
  of mortal men 192
  of nature 49, 75, 264
  of passivity
    of Una 132
  of perfection 226
  of plowman 245
  of royal prince 277
  of yielded pride and proud submission 120
  prelapsarian
    of Eden 226
  pre-linguistic
    of ontology 104
  pristine 273
  robe of 217
  rule of the public
    in Aristotle 102
  still
    of the world 203
  the bond of men is justice in the 47

unhappy
  of Una 133

wretched 79
stately
  place 146
statement
  a priori 85
  of identity 89
  open and direct 5
static 37
statistical
  approximation 155
  estimation
    of the universe 292
statistics 167
status
  deconstructable
    of Una 212
  exterior
    of perfection 57
  fictional
    of Una 212
  figural 83
  heroic 238
  of George 245
  of God 268
  of moral virtue 69
  of Redcrosse 173
  of salvation
    defined by God 46
status quo 209
staves 206
stay
  commanding the sun to 221
  forcing Duessa to 187
  forcing Errour to 121, 225
  Redcrosse bids Duessa to 108
staying 59, 272
  of Sansloy 129
  of steps
    of Humiltá 213
  to protect Una
    by lion 120
stead
  of Una
    born by false Duessa 141
  watchful
    of soldier 202
steadfast
  hinge 255
  star 82
steadfastness
  of diamond to rock 131
steady
  hand
    of Una 235
stealing
  of heart
    of Arthur 195

  Una's dwarf
    by Redcrosse 165

steaming 252
steed 116
  alighting from lofty
    by Arthur 195
  mountiing of
    by Sansloy 133
steel 107
  armor
    George wears 251
  deadly 128
  fiery 258
  hardened 265
  harder than iron 251
  piercing 255
  revenging 265
  untried 128
steep
  hill 234
stench 252
step
  desirable 166
  necessary 135
stepping
  out of time 282
steps
  feeble
    of Humiltá 213
  intermediate 173
  staggering
    of Redcrosse 235
  wandering 231
  of George 246
stern
  horror
    of scared nations 250
  sturdy
    of Dragon 261
steward 150, 232
  Gluttony as 166
St. George, life of
  as comic model 44
still 251, 252
  breath
    of the Dragon 251
  in flight 264
  state
    of the world 203
stillness
  a river's lack of 37
  as a non-moving state 203
sting
  of the Dragon 253
stinking
  forge 252
Stoic 20, 21, 22
  assumption 180
  development of logic 19
  location of humanity 20
  principles 180
  social justice 180

Stoicism 76, 97
stole
  laying aside 122
    by Una 119
  mournful 281
  removal of Una's 120
stone 178
  central
    in Arthur's arms 179
  precious 179
stopping
  copulation 111
  of forward course
    by Una 199
  of Sansloy's desire
    by a speech from Satyrane 137
  of time
    in Virgil 37
  Redcrosse
    from committing sin 191
  the clock 282
storm 53, 62
  winter 255
storming
  of heaven 144
storms
  offending 272
story 27
  end of the
    told by dwarf 173
  noble 195
  of Corceca's fear 123
  of Una 183
  original
    of Ovid 251
stound (archaic: short time) 173, 174, 191
  bitter baleful 171, 172
  definition of 172
stour (tempest, storm)
  woeful 126
stout
  faery
    Redcrosse as 144, 145
  giant 173
  heart 145
  memory 179
    of careful readers 214
    of the reader 145
stoutest
  knight 136
stoutness
  of Kirkrapine 122
  of heroic heart
    of Redcrosse 109
Strabo 19
straight 114
  way 244

strange
  adventures 277

knight
  Redcrosse as 145
  perils 287
  presence
    of an errant knight 216
stranger
  knight 194
  Redcrosse as
    in the House of Holinesse 219
strangers
  kindness of 174
strangle 56
  Errour threatens to s. Redcrosse 56
strategy
  failing
    of Sansloy 131
  of following Una
    by Corceca and Abessa 123
  of taking fallible reason to its end
    employed by Augustine 104
straying
  of George 287
stream 256
  of destiny 156
  of time 184
  trickling
    of balm 268
streets 146
strength 286
  equal 106
  formidable
    of Redcrosse 298
  greater 64
  manly 56
  of enemy 61
  of George 264
  of lion 130
  of man
    to ill 210
  of Redcrosse 163
  of the Dragon
    vertical nature of 251
  of three men 254
  physical
    of Una 215
  proving of 67
  source of
    earth as 254
    ground as 257
  triune sense of 254
  wielding 191
strengthening
  ntentional mind
    of Una 131
strict
  terms
    of good and evil 199

strife
  end of 64

reproachful 206
tumultuous 148
victory through 204
striking
  fear
    into opponent 257, 258
string
  haughty 250
striving 152
  for mastery
    of sorrow 171
  to match in royal rich array
    by Lucifera 146
  with strong necessity 203
stroke 54
  fell 257
  furious 257
  huge
    by which Redcrosse defeats Sansfoy 107
  idle 186
strong 69, 185, 287
  advisement 144
  Dragon 262
  necessity
    chain of 158
    striving with 203
  societal attachments 66
  struggling 253
  truth is 286
  waxing 194
    Charissa as 227
structure
  of reader's knowledge 131
  of scientific universe 155
structures
  hierarchical 269
  rational social 123
struggle 63
  for expression
    by Una 152
  metaphysical 65
  of Redcrosse and Errour 65
struggling
  strong 253
studied
  uncertainty 239
study
  of Archimago 70
  of magic
    by Duessa 278
stunned
  silence
    of Redcrosse 204
stupid
  heathens
    of Babylon 217

sturdy
  stern

Index

of the Dragon 261
Styx 70
subject 16, 45, 296
  divided 94
  matter 86
  plain
    hovering above the 253
subject (semantic) 175
  of sentence 175
sublime
  deeper 5
sublimity 4
submission
  of Redcrosse
    to Lucifera 152
  of Una
    to Arthur 183
  proud 120
  restriction of
    to Charissa 229
  to Lucifera
    by Redcrosse 163
  to rule
    of Lucifera 150
  to satyrs
    of Una 160
subordinate
  will
    of Redcrosse 226
subordination
  of one to another
    after the oeverthrow os Saturn by Jove 157
  of pagan to Christian 63
  of Una
    to Arthur 192
  of will of man
    to will of God 263
subornation
  of true justice 288
subsiding
  of temporary fury
    of Redcrosse 154
substance 24, 34
  beneath hylomorphic nature 101
  deeper
    of God 178
  incorporeal 71
  individual 260
    God-created 225
  of the sprite 101
substantial 47
  consciousness 40, 72, 76, 84, 97, 180, 189, 242, 254, 255, 259, 260, 282, 290
  confusion over location in naming 175
  direction of thought of 138
  embrace of 147
  enacting potential in 276
  in Augustine 233
  of Elizabeth 93
  of Redcrosse 175

of Spenser's hero 256
  rationality of 179
  reality of 175
  existence 175
    lack of 201
  individual 181
  reality
    of the poet 226
substantiality
  lack of 138
  of ontological reality 66
substitute
  Homer as
    for the divine 76
substitution 33, 37
  of fiction
    for reality 175
  of gold for silver 276
  of goodwill of God
    with individual will 205
  of human force
    for faith 263
  of human will
    for the will of God 262
  of man for God
    in existential construction 188
  of potentially fictional λογός 189
  of substantial conscioussness
    in metaphysical fiction 175
subtle
  clues 198
  engines 187
  psychology
    of Despair 204
  trains
    of Archimago 173
subtlety 69
success 156
  certainty of 228
  depends on Ephesian armor 45
  guarantee of 126
    in battle 197
  in fiction 46
  guranteed by God 68
  in expression
    by Una 152
  of Duesss 158
  of Redcrosse 167
successful
  completion
    of adventure 287
succession
  line of 284
succor 79
sudden
  eye
    of Sansjoy 153
  uprising
    by Lucifera 146
  wit
    of Despair 202

suddenness
  of mischief 54
  to win or lose all at once 58
suffering
  pain 157
  sorrows
    by George 248
sufficient
  perspective 135
suicide
  imminent
    of Redcrosse 211
  of Seneca 222
suit
  of earthly conquest 237
Sulla (Lucius Cornelius Sulla Felix) 20, 36
sullen
  mind
    of Despair 201
sulphur 252
summer
  shore 255
sun 92, 132, 178, 251
  as guide to truth
    in Plato's Allegory of the Cave 137
  beheld by eagle's eye 234
  commanding the
    to stay 221
  daylight 249
  distant 133
  hiding face of 132
  in Plato's allegory of the Cave 14, 137
  looking directly at 256
  of being 91
  rising 86, 152
  turning away from Una by 137
  unresponsive 290
  vertical plane of 142
sundering
  of Una
    from her beloved Redcrosse 138
sundry
  kind 160
sunny
  bright
    Duessa as 155
sunshine
  in a shady place 119
superficial
  appearance 124, 145
  armor 124
  eyes 110
  identity 131
  judgment
    of Redcrosse 228
  open body
    of Fidessa 234
  scholars 169
  sight
    of Redcrosse 176

terms 126
things 138
thinker
  Redcrosse as 166
superficiality
  in exchange 113
  of conception
    of Redcrosse for Fidessa 121
  of eyes 116, 127
  of goodwill
    in Aristotle 283
  of imperfect disguise 124
superior
  knowledge 170
    of Despair 205
  social 166, 168
superiority
  of position 50
  of reading and writing
    in Augustine 38
  of Zele and Reverence
    to Una and Redcrosse 214
superstition 14
  Christian 14
  of Augustine 89
supplanting
  of God 193
supplement 105
  of faith 57
  of human limitations
    with education 62
supplying
  of wants 290
supposing
  Duessa to be Fidessa 141
suppressed
  id 242
  values 238
suppression 44
  of Christians 181
  of clownish nature 241
  of sins
    of George 271
supsension
  of disbelief 112
sure
  access
    to metaphysics 275
surface 48, 113
  appearance 141
  looking beneath the 121, 126, 154
  of bodies 288
  of experience 125
  of justice 202
  things 162
  visible 113

surprise
  of Dragon

Index

at George's revived condition 264
of George
at his revived condition 264
surrender
to blind god 79
surrendering
of fallible reason 104
survival 83
human 35
of children of Errour 60
of deconstructed objects
in the mind of the reader 181
of Duessa
after the destruction of Orgoglio 187
of trial 259
surviving
deconstruction 215
suspecting
of truth
of False Una 80
suspense 127
narrative 239
release of 140
suspension
of disbelief 45, 216, 275
swallowing
of foolish man
by crocodile 155
swarming
bees 77
swaying
judgment between two equal poles 114
swearing 285
sweaty
forehead
of Redcrosse 160
sweet
comfort 224
company
of Una 289
humor 195
music 160, 289
sweetness 52
swelling
of ass 217
of heart 80
of Una 215
of luxurious pomp 276
of Nile 59, 80
of Tethys' salty tears 127
swerve
from truth 297
swift
clouds 270
switch
from ontology to epistemology 46–47
in mind of Una 45
of Una
in action 126

switching
things in mankind's favor 81
switch-words 241
swoon 207
likeness to a 207
swooning
dream
of Redcrosse 153
sword 38, 68, 107, 186, 253, 267, 269
point of a 205
swords
beaten into plowshares 150
preference of
to words 151
turning towards
in pleading for right 150
symbol 5, 6, 22, 291
of the universe 61
symmetry
Kripkean 94
sympathetic
reaction
of readers 229
Una 223
sympathy 42
by dwarf
for Una's plight 168
deeper
for Una 134
system
academic
inherent instability of 193
binary
of the Enlightenment 275
Cartesian 91
inconsistencies in
in Gödel 88
language 194
metaphysical 293
of Aristotle 91
of Augustine
goal in 193
perfect
of Northrop Frye 169
rational 88

T

table
painted 205
tableaux
of souls 205
Redcrosse's glimpse of Lucifera in a 144
tackles 290
tail
of Dragon 265
wound up in a hundred folds 251
spread
of the Dragon 252

tainted
  life 204
taking
  armor off 127, 213
    by Redcrosse 147
  hold
    of silver anchor 224
tale
  entertaining 232
  of Arthur and Gloriana 194–198
talents 265
talking
  tree 112
talons 265
  of Dragon 266
Talus 199
taming
  of lion
    by the sight of Una 128
Tasso, Torquato 83, 95, 179, 242, 294
taste
  cultural 133
  sense of 133
tawny
  hide 127
teachers
  Roman 233
teaching
  art
    of Æsculapius 159
  of Archimago 123
  of Charissa 231
  of Fidelia 220, 222
  of justice 202
  of obedience
    to Una by satyrs 134
  prestige of 38
  satyrs
    by Una 135
  truth
    to idolaters 135
team
  of oxen
    of George's father 245
  steadfast
    of Boötes 82
  toilsome 245
tear
  bitter
    of Corceca 123
  salty
    of Tethys 127
tearing
  of the veil from Una's face 130
tears 79
  salt 278

technique
  modern

  of reading 169
tedious
  height 235
  toil 248
teen (archaic: misery, trouble) 279
teeth
  iron
    of Dragon 251
  of Dragon 253
teleological
  movement of the narrative 241
teleology 62
tell
  hard to
    the contents of Speranza's heart 219
telling 68, 110, 121, 252
  by Ignaro 189
  heavy plight 171
  hidden power 103
  name and nation
    by Arthur 194
  of grief 224
τέλος 167, 174 *See also* purpose.
  fulfillment of 209
  provided by God 176
  univocal 159
temperance
  goodly 190
  intermediate
    building up of 149
  rational
    of the individual 190
temperate
  balance 94
tempest 52
tempestuous
  fortune 171, 174
temples
  pagan
    defiling of 259
  rubbing of
    of Una 169
temporal
  priority 286
  process 175
  world 96, 268
temporary
  fury
    of Redcrosse 154
temporize 297
temptation
  of goddess
    by Hercules 259
  of Lechery 147
  of Una's constant heart
    by Sansloy 131
  of weaker sense 77
  to become a god 257
  to evil 118
  to extremity

of Redcrosse 236
temptations
   of the world 243
tempting
   feigned truth 78
tendencies
   absolute
      of Redcrosse and Una 95
tender
   corpse
      of Una 119
   part 169
   tears
      of crocodile 154
tenor
   second 250
tension
   aesthetic 274
   increasing
      in Una's mind 173
term 172
   generic
      of allegory 71
   limited
      of life 202
   long
      problem of rescue of Una 132
      prescribed by spell 115
terms
   aesthetic 2
   alien 57
   black and white 66
   change of
      of philosophical engagement of Virgil in Spenser 76
   drawn from the science of alchemy 178–179
   epistemological 46
   established 202
   Frege's 95
   logical 77
   middle 203
      of argument 276
   modern 43, 169
   of good and evil 199
   of Virgil 76
   ontological 27, 102
   philosophical 92
   post-Enlightenment 12
   rational 60, 97
   relative 61
   scientific 2, 34
   similarity of 228
   specific
      of sin 206
   superficial 126
   translation of 169
terrible
   decision 116

terribleness

of the Dragon 68
terrified 266
terrifying 273
   world of time 290
terror 49
   blast of
      from the horn blow by Arthur's squire 185
   in hearts of men
      caused by Dragon 251
   of earth 162
   of shock
      in simile of rams 106
test
   of faith 262
testimony
   of angel 95
testing
   fear
      in the sphere of action 253
   of experience 251
Tethys (titaness of the sea; daughter of Uranus and Gaia) 127
text 240
   as it is given to the reader 70
   engagement with 44
   lack of a 214
   phantasmagoric world of 241
   reader response 84
   reader's place outside the 57
texts
   classical 24
   historical 127
thanking
   of faithful knight 271
thankless
   thought
      buried in 194
theater 30
theft
   faery 244
theme
   of the golden chain 192
theology 4
theory
   of gravity 2
   of language of heart
      Augustine's 71–74
   of universals 91
Theory of Forms 17, 91
   criticism
      by Aristotle 193
thickness
   of wood 119
thief
   Kirkrapine as 122
thin
   as a flower 163

thing

goodly
    hardest to begin 213
    relation to itself 86
things 76, 166
    dark
        written in the book of Fidelia 221
    divine 246
    earthly 105, 177, 280, 294
        darkness of 246
    good 267
    imposition of names on 104
    nature of
        equality in Night's perception of the 155
    ontological 170
    prioritized according to reason 165
    reflection of 165
    superficial 138
    surface of 162
    unequal
        weighing 199
thinker
    superficial
        Redcrosse as 166
thinking
    priority of
        in action 60
third person 40
3rd person perspective 50
Thirty Years War 3
thorns 231, 281
    bushy 231
    patching garment of Despair 201
thought 78, 180, 214
    consuming 226
    directing
        of Una 183
    divided
        as an image of God 74
    eternal providence exceeding 132
    faculties of 74
    formed by the thing we know
        in Augustine 73
    foundation
        of Odysseus 169
    gracious
        of Una 183
    heavenly
        of Contemplation 235
    inner 182
    misformed
        of Archimago 100–102
    noble
        of future victory in violent battle 151
    of Aristotle 126
    of Sansloy 131
    of Spenser 93
    of Una 125
        on Redcrose 68
    perception of Fradubio's 115
    Redcrosse's flight from his own 104
    Reformation 270

speaking words at odds with Archimago's 124
thankless
    buried in 194
unexpressed 284
unified
    in a world of change 183
unifying 284
unity of Morpheus' 71
virtuous
    of Redcrosse 151
wishing 236, 296
worldly
    of Arthur 183
thousand
    angels 235
    fiends 205
thrall 109, 132
    caitiff 165
    to sinful bands
        through weakness 184
threat 255
    elimination of 269
    idle 286
    immediate
        of Archimao 119
    lack of
        from Cælia 214
    of the Dragon 251
    roaring 221
    unreal 256
threatening 100
    the existence of creation 255
three
    daughters
        of Cælia 219
    men
        strength of 254
    "thrise happie newes" 1
three-dimensional
    world
        of Christianity 97
threshold
    of Errour's Cave 56
thrice
    happy man 235
    happy news 236, 296
throat 56, 63
    of the Dragon 255
throne
    heavenly 235
    royal 217
    secular 109
throwing
    into distress 288
    of laurel boughs 274
throwing out
    of reason 288

thrusting

Index

of Æsculapius
   into hell alive 159
thunderbolts 186
thundering
  Jove 159
thwarting
  of desire
    of Una 173
  of will
    of Redcrosse 167
tiara 229
Tiber River 109
tidings 68
  deadly
    signs of 168
tier
  multiple
    of mind 74
Timaeus (character in Plato's *Timaeus*) 18
timbrel
  song 275
time 3, 17, 34, 48, 67, 68, 92, 226, 248, 295, 297
  becoming in 163
  born in 138
  constant motion of 37
  difference of 257
  dissipation over
    of loss 172
  domain of
    Una's travel in the 199
  experience in 203
  extremity of 152, 227, 235, 238
  Una in 117–138
  held at bay
    in Eden 290
  high 248
  importance of 282
  in narrative 171
  integration of into philosophy of 259
  intermediate 271
  lengthening of
    between beginning and end of Redcrosse's actions 158
  location of
    of Redcrosse in 172
  man in 203
  of division
    ushered in by Jove 157
  out of
    existence 282
  passage of
    between beginning and end 184
  perspective of 134
  principle of 249
  process of amplification takes 192
  realm of 203
  short 172, 173
  stopping of
  in Virgil 37
  stream of 184
  universe of 117
  words in the world of 121
  world of 48, 67, 96, 99, 103, 105, 118, 125, 133, 174, 182, 199, 209, 210, 219, 228, 229, 257, 273, 282, 290, 298
    being in 138
    extra-Edenic 115
    Gloriana as cynosure of the 131
    harsh realities of the 140
    navigating the 183
    prelasparian unified perspective in 117
  written
    in the book of fate 203
time-bound
  George 272
  human beings 203
  life 171
timeless
  Eden 275
  perspective
    of God 203
  world
    of Eden 126, 280
    of eternal Night 160
timelessness
  of Eden 67
timely
  pride 60
  race 160
tinsell
  trappings 109
tip
  balance 151
  of every battle 147
tire
  of gold 228
tired
  limbs 216
Tithonus (pagan lover of Eos and Titan of dawn) 95
toads 60
to and fro 53, 69, 79
toil 126, 260
  tedious 248
toilsome
  team 245
  way 143
token
  of war 148
tongue
  of Despair 202
  sad 171
too-high
  pitch 256
too-low
  pitch 256
torment 151, 225, 261

wailing in 205
toss 169
tossing
  away of Una
    by Redcrosse 184
  of Una
    for love of Redcrosse 174
touching
  the heart 73
tounge
  trembling 252
tournament
  doughty 151
towards
  swords 150
tower
  of glass 236
  ruins of a broken 108
trace
  in Derrida 189
tracing
  of feet
    of men 189
tract
  of peoples 121
trade
  of Envy
    in accursed usury 147
trader 59
tradition 13
  Christian 285
  corrupt 24
  interference of 233
  Virgilian 66
traditional
  Crusader solution 63
  definition
    of allegory 5
tragedy
  of Eden 67
train
  courtly 277
  decietful 184
  hideous
    of the dragon that Lucifera has defeated 144
trained
  intellect 234
  in true religion 256
training
  of the rational mind
    through education 277
trains
  subtile
    of Archimago 173
traitor
  art of 200
transcendental
  reflection 218
transfer

of sins
  of Redcrosse 252
transformation 36
  into a tree 173
  of Frælissa 114
  of image 74
translation 11, 12
  act of 2
  by Una
    of George into Redcrosse 57, 84
  distorting lens of 43
  in Augustine 22
  into alien terms 57
  into a mediated view of nature 76
  into extremity of time
    by Una 227
  into modern terms 34
  of allegory 2
  of Duessa's pomp
    into humbleness low 109
  of imperfect grammatical speech into perfect logi-
    cal propositions
    in Russell and Whitehead 88
  of individuality
    to power of stars 67
  of potential into purposeful action 206
  of reader
    out of his substantial consciousness 76
  of Spenser
    of Ariosto 65, 66
  of terms 169
  of the experience of Redcrosse
    by Una 216
  of wealth into humbleness low
    by Redcrosse 145
  out of direct inimation of nature 76
  out of Eden 126, 228
  to stars 67
translators
  Latin 71
transmutation
  power of 178
trappings
  tinsel 109
travel 67, 69
  in domain of time
    by Una 199
  slow
    by Una 124
  to underworld 170
  without purpose 206
traveling
  away from goal
    of Una 212
travels
  of George 277
treading
  on rights 286
treason 245
  secret 288

Index 489

treating
  of all details indifferently
    by Redcrosse 147
  of solace 161
treatment
  of Una
    by Redcrosse 206
treble
  augmention
    of the furious mood of the Dragon 257
tree 267, 268
  fair 267
  Fradubio as 112, 143, 262
  Frælissa as 113
  maple 53
  oak 97
    foot of Redcrosse gets stuck in an 163
  shady 160
  talking 112
  transformation into a 173
Tree of Knowledge 267
Tree of Life 267–269
trees 110, 268
  catalog of 206
  trembling 162
  "yclad with sommers pride" 52
trembling
  at the fall
    of Dragon 270
  cheer 116
  leaves 160
  like an aspen leaf 206
  tongue 252
  trees 162
trenchant
  blade 257
Trevisan 200–202
trial 61, 68, 78, 96, 102, 104, 113, 116, 126, 136, 140, 141, 142, 145, 151, 163, 180, 183, 195, 196, 211, 213, 216, 218, 220, 253, 273, 274, 275, 279, 286, 287
  citation at I.i.12.1-6 54
  failure to make
    by Redcrosse 143
  of Archimago's magic 104
  of experience 214
  of truth
    in meeting Archimago 213
    of False Una 82
  speculative
    space of 239
trials
  preliminary 240
triangle
  form of a 87
trickling
  stream
    of balm 268
tricks 251

triple
  happiness
    crown of 236
triumph 146, 151
  of good over evil 288
  of Jove 156
  of science 3
  sounding of 154
triumphant
  Redcrosse
    on account of his armor 148
Triumph of Pride 145–148, 151, 161, 165
triune
  sense
    of strength 254
trodden
  grass 121
troop
  of satyrs and fawns 133
troops
  martial 250
trope 5, 8
  of allegory 7
  in Augustine 71
trouble
  of Knight of Holinesse 69
  of Redcrosse 60, 190, 213
  of Una
    pleasure taken by Archimago in 119
  sleepy minds 70
  worldy 68
troubles
  of Una 249
    blamed on fortune 136
    lateness of 128
    on account of love of Redcrosse 174
troublesome
  behavior 174
troubling
  news 284
Troy
  burning of 38
  new 36
  Virgil's lament for the destruction of 36
true 48, 259, 285
  appearances 158
  balance
    in argument of Despair 204
  beauty
    of Una 190
  character 114
  condition
    of George 243
  description
    of the Cave of Despair 201
  dreams 75, 77
  foundations
    of literature 169
  heart 111
    compromised in expression 111

intent 122
justice
   subornation of 288
knight
   misfeigning of Una's 129
knowledge 87
love 125, 126, 174
   has no power to look backward 126
   inadequacy of 126
   often sown but seldom grows of ground 195
   of Una 125, 168
   seldom grows on ground 195
motivation
   of George 249
nature 83
   of prize 135
   of Una 136
obligation of knight to be 297
power
   depends on moral framework 149
   Redcrosse as too 116
religion 256
Saint George 241
seeming grace
   of Duessa 158
self 57
shades 75
significance
   of events 162
source 72
Una as 136
trumpet
   dreadful 250
trumpets
   sounding of 154
trumping
   of makind's individual identity
      by love 138
trust
   in eyes 121
   of the poet's creation 62
truth 19, 64, 66, 78, 81, 184, 195, 225, 249, 251
   absolute 145
   access to
      denial of to Stoics and Epicureans 76
   Archimago's betrayal of the 70
   Archimago's telling of
      to Una 125
   as constant 297
   attempt to teach satyrs 135
   beneath layers of falsehood 154
   deeper 39, 166, 270
      grounded in God-given potential 106
   demonic detour from the 170
   direct
      of Redcrosse's experience 216
   fall from 1
   falsification of
      by Nortrop Frye 171
   feigned 78
   foudation in 287
   glimpsing of 246
   in a sea of seekers 194
   incomplete 145
   in fiction 219
   in its philosophical and religious aspects 117
   in language of Odysseus 169
   in tale of Aeneas 39
   interference with apprehension of
      by fiction 20
   is one 297
   is strong 286
   knowledge of 69
   lack of 69, 193
   learning the 145
   location of 66, 84
      in allegory 83
   masking
      from modern readers 2
   masking the 195
   metaphysical 231
      of text 293
   moral
      sources of 157
   non-empirical
      in Plato 221
   of ontology of God 155
   part of 274
   Plato as a guide to 20–21
   presence of 276
   preverbal
      of God's ontologically created universe 158
   principle of 91, 126
      Una as 125
   relative 145
   sun as guide to
      in Plato's Allegory of the Cave 137
   suspecting of 80
   teaching
      to idolaters 135
   to swerve from 297
   trial of
      in meeting Archimago 213
   Una as 252
   unknowable
      of metaphor 194
   vertical 48
   visibility of 7
   whole 96, 169, 288
truth-telling
   by Archimago 125
tumultuous
   strife 148
tunes
   of the poet 250
tunic 259
turn 169
   back to the world 243
   inward 72

turning

Index

away from Una
  by the sun 137
cheerful day into cheerless night 124
Fradubio into a tree 143
inward
  towards self 136
of attention
  of Despair 204
of mind 188
of Una outward 126
points 144
to Duessa
  by Lucifera's counselors 145
to education of idolaters 135
Turnus 63–67
twelve
  labors
    of Herucles 258
  moral virtues 30, 31
    perfection in 224
twice
  making mistakes 191
twisting
  of God's purpose
    by the backward kneed satyrs 134
two
  broad beacons 252
  dames 114
  directions
    Ignaro facing in 189
  equally matched enemies 138
  goodly trees 110
  halves of empire 285
  hearts together 96
  poles of argument 285
two-tiered
  problem of identity 92
type 93
typological
  allegory 61
  experience 295
  fiction 270
  level
    of Elizabeth 93
    Redcrosse 124
    Whore of Babylon
      Fidessa as 218
typology 27
  abstraction 45
  orientation to 93
Tyrannion 20
tyranny 36, 42
  Christian 230
  of devil 263
  usurpation with
    by Lucifera 144
  Vigilian 230
tyrant 286, 289
  rage of 215

U

ugliness 42, 66
uholding
  of the righteous man
    by heavenly grace 184
ultimate
  end
    detour from 228
    of Redcrosse 232
  victory 276
Una 12, 43, 52, 55, 90, 91, 94, 96, 104, 122, 125, 127, 131, 134, 141, 151, 152, 153, 172, 220, 225, 226, 228, 235, 247, 262, 264, 269, 275, 280, 281, 295, 298
  abandonment of
    by Redcrosse 130, 197
  access to something more permanent than physical being 138
  adventure of
    end of 209
  alienation from George 245
  amazement
    at Archimago's presence beneath the armor of Redcrosse 129
  among the satyrs 133–135
  appearance of 282
  aquires love of Redcrosse
    in the as-yet-unexperienced future 197
  Archimago's pursuit of 123
  armor of 102
  Arthur speaks to 194
  article in *The Spenser Encyclopedia* 117
  as creature of light 122
  as chaste maid 116
  as codependent 226
  as daughter of Eden 45
  as fictional 238
  as flawed character 121
  as fully clad 147
  as fully loyal 147
  as gift 283
  as holder of the end of Redcrosse's adventure 102
  as image of perfect unity and beauty 288
  as keeper of absolute metaphysical perspective 173
  as morning star 95
  as object
    of desire 234
  as passive 81
  as potential 81, 246
  as principle of unity 84, 92, 104
  as pure woman 175
  assumption of
    about Cupid's cruel dart 96
  as truth 252
  attachment of
    to Redcrosse 238
  awareness of her participation in God's sacred pageant 28
  beauty of 132

belief of 175
beloved knight of 191
blame of 84, 125
born in Eden 66
bound to Redcrosse
   by love 138
change in perspective 83
charged with making an example of her experience 198
choice of Redcrosse 84
comparison of
   with Gloriana 197
concern of 254
congratulations by 262
control of her cirumstances 129
creation of 84
cries
   to distant sun and stars 133
decentering of 249
deconstructing unity of 294
difference from Duessa
   in dress 109
difference from Redcrosse 55
disenfranchisement of 284
dwarf of 148
education of 126
   beginning of 135
   lack of 241
encounters her error 128
exchanged for Fidessa 110
existence of
   outside the bounds of humanity 197
eyes of 171
failure to learn lesson
   after battle with Errour 62
faints
   when she sees dwarf carrying Redcrosse's armor 168
fair
   abanonment of 141
farness of
   from the battle with the Dragon 270
fear of 265
flight of
   from Archimago 119
focus of
   on essence of Redcrosse 231
foe of 198
follows Redcrosse 200
gainsaying George 44, 80
grant of arms of *Ephesians* 105
has not been raped 160
heart of 137, 182
   aroused for Redcrosse 176
   swelling of 215
heavenly 272
helpless 179
hope of 132
ignorance
   of the power bestowed on Redcrosse 58
in extremity of time 117–138
in *Letter to Raleigh* 43–44

in love 130
insistence on seeing the whole 180
inward beauty of 282
joy of 246
kingdom of 272
knowledge of
   by Humiltá 213
lack of interest in
   displayed by Redcrosse 148
lament
   of fate 180
learning of 137
left by Redcrosse 152
left to mourn 290
left with less than she came with 84
limit of understanding of 248
listens
   to the speeches of Despair 206
located by dwarf 167
looks on Arthur's actions
   from afar 188
love of 285
   for Redcrosse 225
magical armor of 45–48, 107
marriage of
   to George 244
mind of 228
   as unified and unifying 126
misapprehension by 128
mistake of 96
   in believing that she has found her knight 127
named
   after the creation of a false double 240
name of 275
naming of 240
native condition of 249
native soil of 248–249
need of
   for Redcrosse 122
not loved by Redcrosse 196
offer by
   of purpose 199
of wholeness in
   lack of 212
ontological likeness of 78
overlooked in Redcrosse's expression of love 111
panics 56
parents of 232
passive 140, 172, 212
passivity of 117, 138
perception of
   of her dwarf 165
perfect 175
perpetual silence of 136
personality
   breach opened up in 95
perspective of 249
position of 126
potential of 217
presence of 129
pure 84

Index 493

rape of
  by Sansloy 140
reacts
  to the sign of deadly tidings 168
real 79
reason of 175
request of
  to Fidelia and Speranza 219
rescue
  by Satyrane 135–136
  of Redcrosse 206
respect for 235
romance of
  with Redcrosse 153
sadness 95
separated from Redcrosse 121
sight of
  tames the lion 128
silence of 200, 214
sin against
  by Redcrosse 204
slow travel by 124
sojourn of 272
speaking up of 209
stands far 264
  from battle with Dragon 273
story of 183
subordination of
  to Arthur 192
sympathetic 223
true 114
true love of 125
uncouth sight of 133
unified 134, 135
unlikeness
  to Redcrosse 142
unspotted 84
vision of beauty of 281
wakes to find her knight gone 95
wandering of 102

unacquainted
  guest
    Redcrosse as 227

unalterablity 19

unattended
  world of science 159

unawareness 227
  lack of
    in Una's mind 126
  of foolish man 155
  of Fradubio 112
  of George 287
    of his state of blessedness 204
  of Spenser 274
  of Una
    to Archimago's betrayal of the truth 70

unbalance
  of blind Cupid's darts
    God's operation through 139

unbalanced
  nature 218

unbelievable
  bravery
    of Redcrosse 186
unbound
  hair
    of Despair 201
uncareful 111
  men 225
  reader 12, 57, 168, 216
uncertain
  connection
    to God 266
  future 244
  imaginative things 271
  location
    of Eden 274
uncertainty
  of George's existence 271
  of the poet 265
  studied 239
unchaste
  woman 290
uncomfortable
  position 125
unconscious 28, 74
  participation 147
unconsciousess
  of source of victory 62
uncouth
  sight 78, 133
  smart 255
undeconstructable
  work of God 61
under
  heaven's wide hollowness 118
underlying 75
  nature 76
  ontology 86, 87, 124
  reality 285
undermining
  claim to knowledge
    by Ignaro 189
    by Socrates 189
  metaphysical importance of Ariosto's poem 65
  of castle
    from lowest ground 187
  of the leader
    of the Triumph od Pride 146
underneath
  feet 166
understanding 30, 56
  conscious
    of Una's power 134
  hardness of 221
  key to 266
  lack of
    by Redcrosse 153
  limit of
    of Una 248
  of individual mind 265

of processes of time
    by Una 227
wise
    of arms by Sansloy 130
underworld 77
    House of Morpheus 70
    outside of the world 71
    travel to the 169, 170
unearned
    knighthood
        of Redcrosse 69
uneducated
    man 47, 95
        George as 295
    mind 143
    Redcrosse 149
uneducated, the 39
unequal
    choices 270
    measure
        reason as a matter of weighing things of 150
    moral beings 152
    nature 177
    sins
        in the Triumph of Pride 161
    things
        weighing 199
    universe 183
    weight 147
uneven
    division
        of talents 265
unexperienced
    future 197
unexpressed
    thought 284
unfallenness
    of universe 57
unfitness
    for rule
        by Lucifera 144
unfocused
    chivalric energy 115
unfolding
    of talents 265
unfounded
    Archimago's hope 129
    notion 102
ungendered
    sprite 100
unhappiness 109
unhappy
    love 177
    state
        of Una 133
unhasty
    beast 119
unholiness 47, 99

unified
    Eden 227
    experience
        of Una 124
    good 157
    individual will 125
    Kingdom of Eden 285
    knowledge 129
    language
        of God's ontology 275
    metaphysical universe 277
    mind
        assumption of 180
        of Una 126
    perspective
        of prelasparian experience 117
        of Una 134
    self
        of Una 117
    thought
        in a world of change 183
    truth
        Una as principle of 126
    Una 135
unifying
    mind
        of Una 126
    thought 284
unitary
    virtue 103
united
    kingdom
        of Eden 274
uniting
    the sun and moon
        in Arthur's arms 178
unity 84, 94, 286
    art on the side of
        in the modern world 134
    deconstructing
        of Una 294
    Homeric 43
    image of 128
    in literal events 27
    of logocentrism 71
    of λογός 43
    of Morpheus' thought 71
    of personality 95
    of silence 71
    of Una 117
    perfect 288
    pretextual 189
    principle of 92, 95, 104
        Una as 95
    scientific 189
    through the use of words 46
    unity 92
universal
    reason 180
    world
        of fiction 175

Index

universals 15, 18, 91
universe 2, 11, 91, 142
  allegorical 137
  Augustinian 48, 155, 252
    role of doubling in 134
  balanced 238
    equality in 158
  binary 275
  center of 4
  Christian 76, 259
    Homer as substitute for the divine in 76
  construction of the 159
  deconstructable
    of Faery 281
  disarray of 142
  Enlightenment configuration of 242
  equitable 37
  existential construction of 188
  extreme ends of the 222
  fictional 127, 169, 178
    of allegory 163
  general 59
  God's created 133
  imaginative
    of Faery 281
  in balance
    through the will of Redcrose 207
  intellectual 89
  knowledge of 88
  macrocosmic 238
  Manichean 157
  metaphysical 277
    construction in Plato 161–162
  moral 81
  natural 222
  of Augustine 118
    chain of necessity in 158
  of binary values 285
  of nature 46
  of others 254
  of religion 217
  of Spenser 138, 179, 224
  of time 117
  ontological
    created by God 158
  ontology of the 101
  pagan configuration of 233
  pre-Romantic
    of Spenser 132
  presence
    of evil in the 143
  Redcrosse's construction of his 115
  scientific 170
    making trial of 253
  scientifically-oriented 276
  statistical estimation of
    in Plato 292
  structure of the 155
  symbolic 61
  unequal moral
    of nature 183

univocal
  τέλος 159
unkind
  carelessness 161
unkindness
  forgiving Redcrosse for his 161
  of fortune 118
unknowable
  truth
    of metaphor 194
unknown 54
  dying 194
  guest 285
  ways 53, 122
unlacing
  of helmet 129, 258
unlikely
  intercession
    of Duessa 163
unlikeness
  in glass of allegory 74
  of lion's reaction to Una's beauty
    to Redcrosse's reaction 120
  of love to the priority of good over evil 138
  of Redcrosse
    to Una 142
  to men
    of Ignaro 189
unmade
  secrets of the world
    seen by Night 155
unmanly
  murder 148
unmerciful
  Sansloy 129
unnatural
  social standing 121
unprofitable
  course
    of George 258
unprompted 68
unproved
  knight 183
unreal
  forces 225
  threat 256
unreality
  of destruction
    wrought by Dragon 263
  of existence 37
unreason 98
unrecognized
  reflection
    Fradubio as 147
unredeemed
  love 177
unritualized
  battle
    with Sansjoy 148–151

unsanctified
  Palmer 296
unseating
  of George
    from his horse 257
unserviceable
  wing
    of Dragon 258
unsettling
  effect
    on teleological progress 241
unspoken
  identity
    of Una with herself 137
unspotted 267
  life 212
  Una 84
untested
  action 91
  assumptions 271
  reality 253
unthrifty
  scath 148
untied
  chains
    of infernal furies 200
untold
  magic of Archimago 129
untried
  steel 128
untroubled
  with thoughts of others 80
untruth 80, 101, 109
  as a flaw, not a virtue 105
  lack of of knowledge of 80
  Una knew no 96
unwary
  reader 290
unwatched
  gates
    of Eden 286
unwilled
  salvation 267
unwillingness 28
  to delve into the secrets of sexual pleasure
    by Spenser 150
unwonted
  passage 251
unworthiness 83
  of George 45
  of Redcrosse
    to bear the arms of Sansfoy 150
    of the rude eyes of satyrs
      to behold the sad plight of Una 133
  of Una
    to receive ills 118
unworthy
  wretch 242
  wretchedness 118

upbearing
  of Redcrosse
    by Mercie 231
upbraiding 287
upholding
  of Lucifera's kingdom 144
urgency
  lack of
    in Una's wandering 119
usage
  poetic
    in Virgil 75
use 166
  of reason 86
  of the past
    as a model for passive imitation 76
usurpation
  of power
    by Lucifera 149
  with wrong and tyranny
    by Lucifera 144
usury
  accursed 147
utility 283
utterable
  sound 73

V

vagrancy
  of form 37
vain
  advancement 165
  assurance
    of mortality 210
  creature 186
  effort
    of Orgoglio 186
  fright 273
    of Una 271
  glory 144, 165
  vows 279
  wholly 185
  words
    betwitching of manly heart by 206
  worship of Una
    by satyrs 135
Valla, Lorenzo 52
  on the Donation of Constantine 24
valley 254
  concavity of the 253
value
  Archimago's sense of 103
  educative
    indifference to 147
  face 125, 178, 213
  human determination of 39
  inherent 287
    lack of 288

instructive 147
   of the Triumph of Pride 151
learned
   of patience 254
   of property 266
pagan
   subordinated to Christian values 63
Una's sense of 103
values 292
   binary 285
   Christian
      raised over pagan values 63
   cognitive 91
   defined negatively
      in classical philosophy 292
   differing 147
   of heroes 260
   relative 64, 241
   scientific world of 269
   suppressed 238
vanishing
   of body
      of Orgoglio 187
vanity
   of Archimago's threats 100
   of sprite's use of waste words 71
vanquished
   pagan 173
Varro (Marcus Terentius Varro) 92, 221
vassal
   of pleasure 131
vast
   size 273
vastness
   of body
      of the Dragon 254
   of shadow
      of Dragon 251
vaunt
   prouder 194
veil 130, 186
   of academia 193
   of fiction 218
   of mystery 38
   of Una 130
   snatched
      from the face of Una 131
vein 207
Venus (goddess) 20, 27, 94, 96
   shameful chain of 101
   son of 96, 176
Venus (planet) 85, 88, 89, 92
   miracle of 221
   mode of presentation of 87
   ontology of 87
   reference to 86
verbal
   bridges
      of Freudian dream work 241

verdant
   fields 106
   grass 195
verdict
   advantageous 286
verity
   discipline of
      taught by Una to Satyrane 136
verse
   of famous poets 258
verses
   bloody 258
vertical 8, 47
   ascent
      to an imaginary heaven 216
   axis
      of the Dragon 253
   nature
      of the Dragon's strength 251
   orientation
      of golden chain 193
   path
      of angels 236
   plane
      of sun and stars 142
   truth 48
verticality
   of mythic λογός 89
   of power
      of Dragon 253
Vespasian (Titus Flavius Caesar Vespasianus Augustus) 181
vessel
   of God's choice
      for action in the world 158
   older 215
   weaker 215
vestigia 23, 76, 121
vestments
   of holy saints 122
vicarious
   learning 198
vice
   of wrath 103
victor
   lawless 130
   might of 187
victories 226
victorious
   knight 191
victory 62, 67, 152
   achievement of 297
   announcement of 264
   ascription of
      to the will of God 287
   assurance of
      of Redcrosse 205
   credit for 67

debt of
  owed by Redcrosse to God 108
doubt of 264
famous 237
forgetfulness of 106
guarantee of 58, 67, 152
  assured by Redcrosse's armor 163
immediate 224, 231
in any battle 110
in Horace's *Satires* 59
instant 105
lack of desire for
  by Sir Burbon 297
of Arthur 188
of George 258
of Redcrosse
  against Sansfoy 106
  from Heaven 191
over Dragon 84
over Errour 83
portrayed in rational terms 60
provided by God
  to Redcrosse 158
Pyrrhic 192
sign of 264
  Saint George as 239
terms of 255
through grace 210
ultimate 276
view
  imperfect
    of experience 244
  knightly 144
  mediated
    of nature 76
  of body 217
  point of
    of Augustine 218
  rational 266
    of the world 253
  scientific 266
  with eyes 138
viewing
  body
    of Fidessa 234, 280
  from a safe ironic distance 148
  of blazing brightness
    of Arthur's uncovered shield 186
  of face
    of Fidessa 110, 121
    of Lucifera 144
vigilance
  constant 246
vile
  entertainment 131
  jealousy 289
  monster 60
  witch 118
vileness
  of Spenser's thoughts 93

villain
  Archimago and Duessa as 118
vine
  leaves 146, 160
violence 42, 251
  act of
    of Virgil 298
  actual 128
  animal 149, 183
    socially destructive 168
  avoiding of
    by Arthur 186
  justification of
    in Virgil's *Aeneid* 63
  physical
    battle of 138
  wrongness of
    in the social world 149
violent
  act
    of Redcrosse 298
  battle
    with Sansjoy 151
  love 121
Virgilian
  myth 298
  tyranny 230
Virgil (Publius Vergilius Maro) 36–39, 77, 83, 100, 170, 294
  act of violence 298
  Aenied, The
    as source for the battle with Errour 63–67
    gates of sleep in 75–78, 143
  theory of language of 76
  tradition of 66
virgin 129, 130
  desolate 237, 239
  fair 275
    Una as 272
  fairest 197
  innocent
    Una as 120
  Una as 275
  virtuous
    Una as 215
  widow
    Duessa's representation of herself as 109
virginal
  body
    integrity of 120
virgins
  goodly 219
virtue 34, 47, 99, 102, 105
  a priori 99
  easy
    of Fidessa 229
  enacted in time 34
  gives her self light 54, 56, 223
  innate
    Archimago's lack of 100

inner
  communication of 136
intellectual
  contemplation as an 233
interior 48
lacking 99
location of 99
moral 70
native 105–107, 108, 132, 142
  Fradubio does not rely on 114
Odysseus as model of 34–37
of gleaming armor 60
of Redcrosse 223
of Una 229
  endangered 130
particular 33
private 33
  Rinaldo as an example of 40
secret 265
those who lack
  are savage animals 47
twelve moral 30, 31
unitary
  Una as possessor of 103
virtues
  forgetting of 261
  by the well of life 263
  linked 192
  of Redcrosse 150
  perfection in twelve moral 224
virtuous
  action 142
  man
    Redcrosse as 99
  thought
    of Redcrosse 151
  virgin
    Una as 215
visage
  beholding of Una's
    by Sansloy 130
visible 6
  surface 113
visibly
  unprofitable course
    of George 258
vision
  imaginative
    of poet 281
  inner 36
  limitation of
    of Redcrosse 154
  lowering of 269
  of beauty
    of Una 281
  partial
    of the whole truth 96
  perfect
    of Descartes 11
  seamless
    of beauty 281

visit
  of George
    to Contemplation's chapel 246
Vives, Juan Luis 92
vocabulary
  postmodern 191
voice
  of a ghost from the lake of limbo 112
  of Eden 160
  source of
    of Fradubio 111
void 98, 185
  creature 187
  of malice
    in Archimago's appearance 68
Voltaire 4
  ecrasez l'infame 14
vomit
  of Errour 60, 261
vomiting
  of error 298
Von Eschenbach, Wolfram 44
vow
  of revenge
    by Sansloy 129
  of the King of Eden 279–280
vowed
  marriage 279
vowing
  vengeance
    by Night on Redcrosse 157
vows
  bloody 286
  to Neptune
    by a merchant who sees his ship come in 127
  vain 279
voyage
  long 244, 290
vulgar
  amazed 152, 162
vulnerability
  of Una 140

W

wagon
  weary 160
wagoner
  northern 82
wailing
  in torment 205
  of caitiff wretched thralls 165
  woes 180
waist
  fat
    of Dragon 251
  of Dragon 273
  of the Dragon 250

waiting
  for order
    by someone else 172
    for temporal process 175
  of lion
    on Una 120
  of reader 131
waking
  of Redcrosse 77
  of Una 120
walls
  brazen 122
  of Eden 100, 138, 211, 227, 248, 267
  circumscribed
    of Eden 273
  inspecting of 274
  of Eden 209, 236
wandering 82
  far
    of Saint George 104
  in empty air 112
  in ocean 127
  in wilderness 160, 167
  knight 122
  Odysseus 82
  of Una 102
    in the wilderness 117
    in the world of time 215
  purposeless
    of Redcrosse 199
  random 83
    by Una 119
  steps 231
    of George 246
  way 154
  wood 240
Wandering Wood 52–68, 62, 67
  problem of the reader likened to being lost in 9
wanting
  credit for victory 67
  of might 69
  of rest 69
wanton
  behavior
    of Redcrosse 168
  bliss 77
  kids 134
  love
    of Fidessa 168, 173, 174
  palfrey of Duessa 109
  play 166
  snare 227
wants
  supplying of 290
war 68
  engine of
    Redcrosse as 211
  furious animal 176
  god of 250
  practice of
    Redcrosse's engagement in 148

spoil of 150, 153
token of 148
warbling
  notes 289
ward
  lion keeps
    over Una 120
wardrobe
  of Charissa 228
warier
  man 274
wariness
  of Arthur 186
  of making past mistakes again 191
warlike 47
  hands 250
warning
  giving 253
  hidden 248
  of Fradubio 112
  of Spenser
    to his reader 148
  reversal of Una's 61
warrior 238
  external glory of 148
  instinct
    of Redcrosse 154
  lack of patience in 59
  Machiavellian 43
  males 209
  proving Redcrosse as a 148
wars 152, 237
  religious 294
washing
  away of false foundation 270
  away sin 225
  hands
    of guilt 237
waste 18
  of energy
    by Redcrosse 199
  of the better days
    of Redcrosse 188
  of the weary night 80
wasteland 79, 184
wasting 68
watch 274
  lion keeps 120
watchful
  stead
    of soldier 202
watching
  night and day 213
water 256, 269, 270
  falling 77
  holy 265
  mill 256
  salt 225

Index

watery
  wilderness 127
wave 37, 109
  ocean 264
wavering
  of Una 184
waves 270
  billowing of 255
  sacred 263
  western 160
waxen
  plume 256
waxing
  of Una's time 248
  strong 194
    Charissa as 227
way 53
  brass-paved
    to heaven 146
  forward
    of Redcrose 205
  guiding of one's 148
  make
    none appears who can 132
  of Patience 149
  out of the 287
  perilous 154
  showing the 235
  straight 244
  to heaven 235, 246
  toilsome 143
  wandering 154
  wondrous
    provided by eternal providence 132
ways
  holy
    education in 221
  of expression 294
  wicked
    remembrance of 223
weak 205
  captive 194
  hearts
    of women 147
  man 129
  men
    the easy pickings of 254
  Redcrosse 150, 210
  sense 101
  societal attachments 66
  woman 183
  years 79
weaker
  elder 215
  sight 179, 180
    of George 287
  vessel 215
  wandering steps 231
  wit 221

weakness 182, 184, 286
  flood of
    in Redcrosse 62
  humble 120
  moral
    of Redcrosse 215
  of Charissa 227
  of expression
    of Redcrosse's feelings towards Una 151
  of Redcrosse 116, 118
  of sense 101
  of will 158
  sign of
    if Redcrosse and the reader 150
weak, the 43
wealth 145
  charms of 145
  heaps of 145
  of Corceca's House 122
  of Persia 144
wealthy 233
weapon 265
  offensive 266
weapons
  guiding of
    by God 255
weariness
  of Tithonus' bed 95
  of Una's feet 120
wearing 48
  armor 45, 57, 95
    by Redcrosse 147
  of ground
    by satyrs' horned feet 134
weary 260
  course
    of poet 272
  journey
    of Una 281
  night 80
  of life 261
  of toilsome way 143
  pair 220
  soles
    of Una 215
  virgin
    Una as 272
  wagon 160
wearying
  of sports
    by Arthur 195
weather 272
  bad 52
  in Horace's *Satires* 59
  rain 52, 77
  tempest 52
  wind 77
weaving
  argument on necessity
    by Despair 203

of silk and silver 281
wedding
  of Bradamante and Ruggiero 63
wedlock 285
weed
  forlorn 168
weeds
  black 68
  rich 109, 145, 277
weeping
  eyes 132
  of crocodile 154
  of Una 124
  woes 180
weighing
  correctly
    things of unequal measure 150
  differing values 147
  inequality
    in advance of taking action 60
  in true balance
    in argument of Despair 204
  of decayed plight
    of Redcrosse 199
  of parts 183
  right and wrong
    in equal balance 147
  rightly
    of evidence 286
  unequal things
    in the balance 199
weight
  of body
    of Dragon 270
  unequal 147
welcome
  of George 274
  of Una
    to her light and shining lamp of bliss 124
well 115, 268
  living 115
  of life
    of Una 207
well-being
  moral 122
well-guided
  speech 183
Well of Life 261, 262, 263, 264
west 285
  emperor of the 285
western
  waves 160
Western
  culture
    crisis of 218
West, the 109
wheat
  separation of
    from chaff 143
whereabouts
  of Redcrosse 172
  of Una 123
whim
  arbitrary 289
whip
  iron 225
whips 217
whirlwind
  of passion 123
whistle
  sound of cheereful 127
white 281
  hair
    of Archimago 129
  lily
    garment of Una 281
  noise 77
  pure
    gown of 281
White, Hayden V. 218
  ironic stance in the works of 127
Whitehead, Alfred North 88, 292
whole 1, 16, 40, 64, 97, 105
  Cave of Despair 201
  circumstance
    of Una 224
  discourse 171, 173–175, 177
    told by dwarf 168
  endurance of the 171
  in Augustine 59
  information 169
  intention 30
  larger 250
  meaning 5
  modern critic's identification with the 31
  of divided thought
    as image of God 74
  of empire 285
  of experience
    listening to the 153
  of justice 202
  of life 107
  of mankind 97
  of Redcrosse's adventures 28
  of reference 137
  of *The Faerie Queene* 144
  person
    in Freud 242
  perspective
    division of into constituent parts 118
    of Redcrosse 146
    of Una 117
  poem 10
  position 157
  possibility
    realization of 262
  situation
    of past, present, and future 126
  spectacle
    of the Triumph of Pride 146

truth 96, 169, 288
  Una's insistence on seeing the 180
  world 37, 161–162
wholeness
  elusive 203
  in Derrida 89
  lack of 188, 212
  metaphysical
    of the pagan gods 190
    of Enlightenment 242
  of George
    lack of 295
  requirement of 173
wholly
  vain 185
whoredom
  Kirkrapine's use of Abessa in 122
Whore of Babylon 84, 138, 145, 200, 217
  Fidelia as 95
wicked
  arts 287
  envy 289
  joy 77
  ways
    remembrance of 223
  witch 114
  woman
    Duessa as 188
wicked, the 40
wide 69, 82
  forest 194
  hollowness under heaven 118
  little
    Una stands on a hill a 249
  ocean 127
wider
  music 191
  perspective
    of poet 232
widow 281
  virgin
    Duessa's representation of herself as 109
widowhood 286
wielding
  strength 191
  the arms of Redcrosse
    none can wound the man 151
wife 35
wight
  damned 202
  deformed 114
  enraged 149
  fairest 111
  fleshly 206
  living 235
  mortal 132
wild 54
wilderness 10, 47, 165, 167
  adventures
    of Redcrosse 209
  errant journey in the 218
  wandering in 117, 160
  watery 127
will 43, 50, 131, 207, 224, 267, 296
  access to holiness 46
  act of 295
  against the 131
  appeal to 109
  assertion of 261
  as the part of man
    in Calvin 26
  as source of power 109
  conscious 205
  consent to
    of Sansloy 131
  control of 261
  depraved 26
  determined 137
  effecting of 136
  effort of 62
  errant
    of Redcrosse 205
  failure of
    in the House of Despair 199–208
  free 25, 221
    exercise of 191
    in the Augustinian universe 134
    problem of 157
  good 25–26
    Archimago as devoid of 119
    from God 26
    of God 134
  human 152, 262, 263
    weakness of 158
  ill 26
  in Augustine 22
  individual 79, 125
  instruments of 135
  in the world of time 133
  lack of
    in providing τέλος 176
  liberated
    of Foucault 219
  manly force of 188
  of another 130
  of Archimago 123, 125
  of Augustine 38
  of George 260, 261, 264, 269, 295
  of God 25, 41, 106, 210, 222, 260, 262, 263, 269, 287
    in Calvin 25
    instrument of 135
  of lawless victor's 130
  of mankind 25
  of Redcrosse 81, 104, 152, 218, 223, 254
    faulty expression of 111
    negative verdict on 116
    putting universe in balance through 207
  of Una 70, 120, 247
    ignorance of 130
  power of 260
    of George 261

purpose of 255
revenging 123
subordinate
  of Redcrosse 226
superficial 114
thwarting of
  of Redcrosse 167
to might 182
to power
  in Friedrich Nietzsche 296
various states of 26
wishing of 261
willful
decision
  by Æsculapius 160
willing
partners 125
wily
skill 287
wimple 109, 281
win 58, 151, 153
worship 177
wind
breathing 160
head filled with 163
hollow 252
merry 272
murmering 77
wind-blown
mind
  of Orgoglio 195
wind-filled
mind
  of Orgoglio 185
winds
sails to the 251
wine 217
pouring of 259
wing
left
  of Dragon 255
unserviceable
  of the Dragon 258
wings
iron
  clapping of 264
moistened
  lagging of 256
of Dragon
  horizontal nature of 252
of eagle
  Dragon's scales likened to 251
wining
fights at once 202
winning 61, 79, 136
arms
  by conquest 149
furious fights 166
of worship 280

winter
  storm 255
wisdom 71, 284
  contemplative knowledge as 72
  heavenly 136, 183
  in wariness 191
  looking for 147
  of Arthur 183
  of divine words
    of Fidelia 220
  of heart 72
  of Ignaro 189
  of King of Eden 273
  of Redcrosse 60
wise
  Arthur 186
  author
    Spenser as 230
  Cælia as 218
  knowledge of arms
    by Sansloy 130
  lovely
    virtues linked in 192
  man
    Ignaro as 189
    Socrates as 193
  old woman
    Corceca as 189
  perfectly 212
  privy 136
  reaction 143
  soothsayer 152
wish 152
wishes 283
wishing
  for death
    by Redcrosse 190, 223
  of thought 2, 236, 296
  of will 261
  to do well 137
wit
  bending
    of Redcrosse 111
  doubting 53
  gentle 135
    bending of 147
  in secret 135
  of mortal wight 132
  of women 136
  sudden
    of Despair 202
  weaker 221
  wondrous 101
witch
  derivation of love to 118
  Duessa as wicked 114
  speech of 156
witchcraft 81
  goddess of bad 74
withdrawal
  of forward foot 279

by Redcrosse 185
of Una
from the extremity of time 138
withdrawing
of guarantee of fiction 276
withholding
knowledge
by poet 145
of hasty hand 285
of stroke 54
without
pride 281
Spenser's fiction 132
spot 281
the heart of man 72
withstanding
of puissance 257
witness 287
witnessing
battle with Errour 61
Wittgenstein, Ludwig 50, 292
wizards
old 144
woe 286
woeful
daughter 285
parents
of Una 215
plight
of Una 133
stour 126
woes
wailing 180
weeping 180
woman 116, 127, 144, 147, 227, 287, 288
another 184
blind 121
corrupt
Duessa as 175
good
Una as 204
impatient mind of 286
malicious 195
powerful 150
pure
Una as 175
Una as 120
unchaste 290
weak 183
wicked
Duessa as 188
wise
Corceca as 189
womanhood
in childbirth 227
of Una 212
womankind
fealty to 118
women 123, 132, 153
choice of 141

learned 158
other
Satyrane's comparison of courteous deeds of 136
passive 209
weak hearts of
joying of 147
wit of 136
wonder 264
at celestial sight
of Una 282
at sight
of Archimago by Sansloy 129
of Gloriana 44
of Silvanus 134
wonderment
gaping 276
wondrous
beauty 227
comfort 215
faith
of fairest virgin 197
might 129, 179
science 160
of Æsculapius 159
worth 179
wonted
pitch 263
wood 52, 110, 128
out of the 62
thickest 119
within the 133
woodland
idolaters 135
woods 102
echo of 134
on the horizontal plane 142
resound with Una's cries 133
word 48, 87, 213
empty 14
Greek 5, 71
of God 25, 256
of man 73
of rational animal 73
sign of the
gives light inwardly 73
sounds outwardly 73
which we bear in our mind 73
which we speak in the heart 73
written 286
wordplay
not writer's but allegory's 8
words 6, 76, 96, 118, 182, 295
act as a sword's point 205
akin to the matters we speak of 18
ambiguous 121
measuring reponse to 196
as guides to unity 46
away from
in pleading for right 150
different meanings of 196

divine
  of Fidessa 220
dual meaning of 203
fawning 131
float free 89
horrible 77
hung up on 8
in dialectical framework 137
in world of time 121
killing with
  by Fidelia 221
lack of
  in Redcrosse's pleading for right 150
limited 194
lovely
  as recompense for long suffering 125
making trial of 113
mean other things 121
mean what they say 67–66
of Despair 206
of dwarf 69
of King of Eden 279
of poet 178, 279
of Una 67
power of 195
preference of swords to 151
prevailing of
  of Night 159
problem with 96
reference of
  of Fradubio 113
requirements of using
  a speaker 71
  someone to listen 71
resistance to Sansloy's
  by Una 131
speaking
  at odds with Archimago's thought 124
vain
  betwitching of manly heart by 206
waste 71
work 41
  bloody 215
  dream 241–243
  hard 165
  in world 266
  moral
    of God 193
  of Despair 202
  of ekphrastic art 205
  of evil
    through active nature of Archimago 77
  of fiction 179
  of God 94, 163
    performed by Archimago 101
  of poet
    end of 294
  philosophical
    of Augustine 189
worker
  of the earth 240

works
  extension of 268
world 6, 246, 266, 267, 275, 281
  action in the 158
  adventure in 271
  antique
    champion of 258
    hatred of excess in 276
  changeable 281
  classical 24
  delight in the 180
  empirical 234
  external 177, 207
    of time 273
  fictional 211, 237
  freezing of the
    in ekphrasis 205
  governed by love 174
  hostile 83
  in still changing state 203
  interior
    of Eden 273
  late classical 170
  literal 212, 241, 261
    orientation of reader to 175
  macrocosmic 162–163
  medieval 97
    of scholasticism 24
  modern 102
    allegory in 5–7
  moral 202
  movement of the 255
  next 7
  of action 55, 117
  of becoming 215
  of being 141
  of change 183
  of deceivers 213
  of determined rapists 132
  of Faery 142
  of fiction
    as universal, figural, but ultimately fantastic 175
  of individual mankind 233
  of ontology 230
  of science 191
    left unattended by Redcrosse 159
  of Spenser 158
  of time 48, 96, 99, 103, 105, 118, 125, 133, 172,
    174, 182, 199, 209, 210, 219, 228, 229,
    257, 272, 282, 290, 298
    being in 138
    extra-Edenic 115
    Gloriana as cynosure of 131
    harsh realities of the 140
    navigating the 183
    unified perspective in 117
  ontological 88, 282
  outside 86
  overturned
    trope of the 167
  pagan 76
    use of Homer in 76

perception of
  by King of Eden 273
phantasmagoric
  of the text 241
physical 234
postlapsarian 183, 273, 295
potential
  of Heaven 295
presence in the 241
prior 161–162
priority of
  in the thought of Augustine 189
rational view of 253
scientific 169, 179, 192, 238
  values of 269
separate
  of being 97
social
  destructive animal violence in the 149
socially-constructed
  of Arthur 181
stable
  of λόγος 233
temporal 96, 268
temptations of 243
this 7
three-dimensional
  of Christianity 97
timeless
  of Eden 126
  of eternal Night 160
  of world 280
turning back to 243
two dimensional
  of classicism 97
wasteland of 79
whole 37, 161–162
wretched 223
worldly
  business 234
  glory 104, 226, 243
  honor 152
  knight 235
  perspective 269
  science
    of alchemy 185
  show 145
  thought
    of Arthur 183
worlds
  mythical
    ontological stability of 89
worldview
  of Homer 193
worry
  cause for 119
  Una's 67
worship 294
  by satyrs 135
  instruction on
    given by Una 290

of ass
  of Una 135
of false gods 181
of Roman emperors
  as gods 181
of satyrs
  of nature 137
  of Una 137
  by satyrs 135, 160
prayers of 217
win 177
winning of 280
worshipper 42
worshipping
  of Una's image 135
worst
  aspect
    of George 250
  fears 131
  mankind w. animal of all
    when separated from law and justice 99
worth
  of metaphysical position 55
  wondrous 179
worthiness
  for service 239
  of armor 67
  of Redcrosse 84
  to wear armor 61
  through prowess 197
worthy
  shield
    of Sansfoy 150
  warrior 148
wound 255, 266, 297
  first 171
  of the Dragon
    blood pours from 256
  yawning 264
wounded
  body 225
wounding
  of Archimago
    by Sansloy 129
  of Dragon 255, 258
  of man
    who wields arms of Redcrosse 151
  of Una
    by Redcrosse 171
wounds 159, 260
  deadly 268
woven
  out of pieces of clothing 201
wrapped
  in love
    of former dame 287
wrath 153, 251
  animal
    destructive 159
  Archimago's motivation by 103

avenging
  of God 235
calming of 190
individual 231
interfering 253
of God 231, 236
of Jove 159
shunning of 231
Wrath
  cruel 148
wrathful
  fire 153
  wreaks 278
  wreck 255
wreaks
  wrathful 278
wreck
  wrathful 255
wretch
  unworthy 242
wretched 243
  days
    desire to end 223
  man
    Redcrosse as 204
  pair
    transformed into a tree 173
  thralls 165
  world 223
wretchedness 113, 288
  of state 79
  unworthy 118
wrinkled
  face
    of Ignaro 189
writing 38
  allegory 8
  of heart
    with an iron pen 198
written 284
  dark things
    in the book of Fidelia 221
  time
    in the book of fate 203
  word 286
wrong 143, 147, 200
  striving for 152
  usurpation with
    by Lucifrea 144
wrongness
  of Redcrosse's instincts 60
  of violence
    in the social world 149

X

x 34–35
  algebraic variable 5

Y

y
  algebraic variable 5
yawning
  gulf
    of Avernus 158
  wound 264
years
  of sorrow 125
  six
    of service 279, 290
  weaker 79
  weight of 59
  youthly 113
yield 151
  no foot to foe 106
yielded
  prey 130
  pride 120, 121
yielding
  of castle
    to victor's might 187
  of daughter 280
  of Duessa
    to Sansfoy 150
  of kingdom 280
  of mighty pride to humble weakness 120
  power
    to Redcrosse 163
  precedence
    in love 197
young
  knight 140
    Fradubio as 113
    mistakes of 191
youth 37
  years of 113

Z

Zele 213

www.ingramcontent.com/pod-product-compliance
Lightning Source LLC
Chambersburg PA
CBHW071055230426
43666CB00009B/1723